THE
ORGANIZATION
AND
ORDER OF BATTLE
OF
MILITARIES
IN
WORLD WAR II

VOLUME VII
GERMANY's & IMPERIAL JAPAN's
ALLIES, CO-BELLIGERENT & PUPPET STATES

By the same author in this series

The Organization and Order of Battle of Militaries in World War II

Volume I: Germany	2005	ISBN: 1-4120-7498-3
Volume II: The British Commonwealth	2006	ISBN: 1-4120-8565-5
Volume III: The United States	2006	ISBN: 1-4251-0659-5
Volume IV: Japan	2007	ISBN: 1-4251-2422-4
Volume V - Book A: Union of Soviet Socialist Republics	2009	ISBN: 1-4269-0281-9
Volume V - Book B: Union of Soviet Socialist Republics	2009	ISBN: 1-4269-2251-0
Volume VI: Italy and France	2010	ISBN: 1-4269-4633-2

Next Book in the Series

Volume VIII: China   To Be Published Summer 2012

THE
ORGANIZATION
AND
ORDER OF BATTLE
OF
MILITARIES
IN
WORLD WAR II

VOLUME VII
GERMANY's & IMPERIAL JAPAN's
ALLIES, CO-BELLIGERENT & PUPPET STATES

CHARLES D. PETTIBONE

Order this book online at www.trafford.com
or email orders@trafford.com

Most Trafford titles are also available at major online book retailers.

Printed in the United States of America.

ISBN: 978-1-4669-0350-0 (sc)
ISBN: 978-1-4669-0351-7 (e)

Library of Congress Control Number: 2011919843

Trafford rev. 01/11/2012

North America & international
toll-free: 1 888 232 4444 (USA & Canada)
phone: 250 383 6864 ♦ fax: 812 355 4082

To my family,
who has stood behind me
in this endeavor;
my wife, Peggy,
my son Michael and his wife Marcy,
and to my grandchildren,
Sasha and the triplets,
Collin, Austin, and Owen.

Contents

SECTION B - IMPERIAL JAPAN's ALLY and PUPPET STATES

INTRODUCTION

What started out as five books, is now nine. Book five being split into three books. This book represents the seventh of nine I plan to write. The series will contain: Volume I - Germany; Volume II - The British Commonwealth; Volume III - The United States; Volume IV - Japan; Volume V, Book A - Union of Soviet Socialist Republics; Volume V, Book B - Union of Soviet Socialist Republics; Volume VI - Italy and France; Volume VII - Germany's Allies ; Volume VIII - China; and Volume IX - Other Nations at War (Albania, Belgium, Brazil, China, Czechoslovakia, Denmark, Estonia, Greece, Latvia, Lithuania, Luxembourg, Netherlands, Norway, Poland, Yugoslavia).

After being discharged from the service in January 1970, I developed an interest in World War II. I wanted to know everything I could about the war. As I read, I started to collect names of different military unit leaders. While other people were collecting stamps or baseball cards, I collected names. The careers of Marshal Carl Mannerheim and Gdl Axel Eric Heinricks of Finland, FM Ion Antonescu and LG Petre Dumitrescu of Romania, and Adm. Miklós Horthy de Nagybánya of Hungary, can easily be traced. But, I wanted to know about the generals who commanded the Army Groups and Armies of 1944 and 1945. Who were these men like Romania's LG Nicolae Ciupercă, Hungary's Gen. Jenö Rátz, Bulgaria's MG Konstantin L. Lukash and MG Georgi N. Popov, Croatia's LG Dragutin Rumler, and Finland's LG Karl L. Oesch? What were their careers like? And, only few of us known anything about the generals from southeast Asia. Generals from Burma, Thailand, Free India, Cambodia, to name a few countries. So as I read, I wrote down names and the commands of units.

This series of books is a composite of more than forty years of collecting names. Military leaders of General or Admiral ranks are listed. In a few cases there are leaders listed below the rank of a general officer, such as staff positions within an Army or the Commander of a naval ship. The majority are military commanders from division level on up.

This book is broken down into two sections. Section A contains Germany's Allies (Romania, Hungary, and Bulgaria), Co-belligerent (Finland) and Puppet States (Slovakia, Croatia, and Serbia). Section B contains Imperial Japan's Ally (Thailand) and her Puppet States (Great Empire of Manchukuo [Manchuria], Mengjiang [Inner Mongolia], Republic of China-Nanjing, State of Burma, Second Philippine Republic, Azad Hind [Provisional Government of Free India], Empire of Vietnam, the Kingdom of Cambodia, and the Kingdom of Luang Phra Bang [Laos]). Unlike my other books there are no appendices in this one. Table of Equivalent Ranks, Senior Commanders, Navies, and Selected Military Units are included with each country.

The major difference between this Order of Battle from others that have been written is, one can trace the career of individual commanders as they advanced through the ranks and the commands they held. This will be described in the next few pages.

Over the years, this book has been rewritten numerous times. As new information became available, the book has been updated. I do not claim this to be the book's final form and to be100% accurate. This author would be grateful to anyone who has any information pertaining to any of the United States leaders listed; such as their given name, date of birth, date of death, dates leader commanded unit, etc. If anyone can assist me with any additions or corrections, please write me in care of the publisher.

Charles D. Pettibone
Rochester, New York
June 19, 2011

HOW TO USE THIS BOOK

This book and the others in the series are an excellent resource tool. Each book in the series actually started out as an addendum to another book that I was going to write, "A Directory of Military Leaders". But, each addendum when finally written ended up being between three and five (300-500) hundred pages in length, making each of them no addendum, but a book in their own right. So I decided to put my original idea aside and just concentrate on then five (5), now seven (7) books in this series. I plan on writing and publishing a book a year for the next three (3) years.

There are numerous Order of Battle books on the market. So what makes this series so special? Why should one decide on this particular book?

First, the first part of each book contains the overall command structure of the country's armed forces. Then it gives command structure for the army, navy, and air force, in the case of Germany, the command structure of the Schutzstaffel (SS) is included. For the British Commonwealth, the armed force's command structure of Great Britain, including India, Australia, Canada, New Zealand and South Africa are included. For the United States, the Marine Corps, although part of the Navy, is listed separately. For Japan, only the Army and Navy are listed, with the Air Forces divided between them. And for the Soviet Union, the Soviet Army makes up the majority of the Armed Forces, with the Soviet Navy and Soviet Air Force just beginning to become separate entities from the Army.

Second, a complete Order of Battle is given. Most Order of Battle usually deal with only the armies of the country/countries involved, and then only at the division and sometimes at the corps level. Higher echelons of commands are usually not covered. In this series of books, all of the commanders known are spelled out, and not just for the army, but all the branches of the armed forces; giving a breakdown of all the major echelons of command, from theater level down to division. Under each major component, in the book (Army Group, Armies, Corps, and Divisions), the equivalent commands of the other military branches (navy, air force, marine, etc.) of the country's armed forces are included.

For the Volumes on the British Commonwealth and the United States, there is a third part in the book that contains the overall command structure of each Anglo-American Theater of Operation.

Third, most Order of Battles list the commanders and their dates of tenure. This one includes those, but also lists of their next duty assignment, where the officer went after leaving this post. One can literally trace a general or flag officer's career through the upper echelons of command with these books. Making this series of books completely different from all the others on the market.

Fourth, military unit and/or ship insignia, crest, emblem, or patch is pictured next to the unit/ship, whenever it was found.

Fifth, the Appendix is broken down into several parts. There is an appendix that has the usual table of Equivalent Ranks. An appendix that lists senior officers, Field Marshal, Admiral of the Fleet, Colonel General, full Generals and Admirals. Another appendix lists some Military Units used in different campaigns.

Sixth, there is a unique appendix that lists the Major Naval Warships and their commanders. I know of no other book on the market that offers this. This appendix shows: 1) the silhouette of the major warship whenever found. A major ship is classified as aa aircraft carrier (to include fleet, light, and escort), battleship, battlecruiser, heavy and light cruiser. Two, an Order of Battle for the ship's commanders; and third, in some cases, the ship's crest and emblem when found is also given.

So how does one use this book? Let's look at the entry for the Romanian 1st Infantry Division.

1st Infantry Division (line division; pre-war; Home Station: Timişoara [Timisoara], VII Corps Area; 09/41, Eastern Front; 12/41, Romania; 03/42, Eastern Front; 02/43, Romania; 03/44, Eastern Front; 09/02/44, disbanded): 01/01/40 BG Emanoil Bârzotescu (retired; /45, recalled; /45, in reserve; /45 Commanding General, VI Territorial Corps Area) 05/10/42 BG Constantin Panaitiu (Commanding General, 9th Infantry Division) 08/01/42 BG Ioan Mihaescu (Chief of Staff, Inspectorate-General of the Army) 03/21/43 BG Alexandru Saidac ...

Following the unit's name, it states that the 1st Infantry Division was a line divison; was fromed prior to the war. Its home station was Timişoara [Timisoara] in the VII Corps Area. In September 1941, it fought on the Eastern Front; in December 1941, it was stationed back in Romania for refitting. In March 1942, it was again assigned to the Eastern Front; then back again to Romania in February 1943. The Romanian 1st Infantry Division, did a third tour of duty on the Eastern Front in March 1944; before being disbanded on September 2, 1944.

On January 1, 1940, BG Emanoil Bârzotescu commanded the 1st Infantry Division. He retired on May 10, 1942 when BG Constantin Panaitiu took over command. BG Bârzotescu was also recalled to duty in 1945, placed in reserve the same year, andbecame the Commanding General, VI Territorial Corps Area also in 1945. BG Panaitiu led the 1st Infantry Division until August 1, 1942, when he took over command of the 9th Infantry Division. On that date, August 1, 1942, BG Alexandru Saidac took over command of the 1st.

There will be four different endings following a General officer's name:
1. Officer's name followed by a date.
2. Officer's name followed by (new assignment) then a date.
3. Officer's name followed by [concurrent assignment] then a date.
4. Officer's name followed by [concurrent assignment] (new assignment) then a date.

Ending one (1) will occur if a General officer took a leave of absence but returned to take command of that unit again (see example A below) or if the officer involved has the rank of Colonel (Captain in the Navy) or lower. In the majority of these cases, these officers next assignments have not been tracked (see example B below).

Example A: from **Italian Eleventh Army**:
... Gen. Carlo Geloso /41 LG Sebastiano Visconti Prasca (acting; /43 to /45, German prisoner-of-war) 04/41 Gen. Carlo Geloso ...

Explanation of Example A:
Gen. Carlo Geloso, for whatever reason, medical, leave, rest, etc, left being the Commander-in-Chief of the Eleventh Army in 1941 and returned to command that unit later in April 1941.

Example B: from **Italian "Legnano" Artillery Regiment**:
... /35 Col. Antonio Formisano /37 Col. Giuseppe ...

Explanation of Example B:
Colonel Antonio Formisano assignment ended in 1937. Since his rank was Colonel (Captain in the Navy) or lower, and his name does not appear on any list as a Major General/Rear Admiral or higher, his next assignment or duty is not tracked.

Ending two (2) will occur in the majority of the General/Flag officers listed. This will be their new duty assignment followed by the date their present assignment ended (see Example C).

Example C: from **Italian 7ᵗʰ "Lupi di Toscana" Infantry Division (reduced)**:
... / 41 MG Angelico Carta (Commanding General, 51ˢᵗ "Sienna" Infantry Division) /41 MG Ernesto Cappa ...

Explanation of Example C:
MG Angelico Carta held command of the 7ᵗʰ "Lupi di Toscana" Infantry Division (reduced) from sometime in 1941. In 1941, he was given his new assignment, Commanding General of the 51ˢᵗ "Sienna" Infantry Division.

Ending two (2), may have three (3) different conclusions. The first one, as stated above, the new duty assignment, and shown in Example C. Second, it may contain a question mark (see Example D); or, third, it may state a date, assignment, (see Example E).

Example D: from **Italian 15ᵗʰ "Bergamo" Infantry Division**:
... /39 MG Ugo Gigliarelli Fiumi (?   ) 06/10/40? ...

Explanation of Example D:
MG Ugo Gigliarelli Fiumi left command of the 15ᵗʰ "Bergamo" Infantry Division around June 10, 1940, but his next duty and/or future duty assignment are unknown.

Example E: from **Italian 18ᵗʰ "Messina" Infantry Division**:
... /39 Col. Attilio Amato (acting; /43, Commanding General, 14ᵗʰ Coastal Division) /39 MG Francesco Zani ...

Explanation of Example E:
Col. Attilio Amato was acting commander and gave up command of the 18ᵗʰ "messina" Infantry Division in 1939. What duty he assumed next is unknown, but in 1943, he became the Commanding General, 14ᵗʰ Coastal Division. Since there was a difference of one year between assignments, the date of the next assignment and the future duty will be listed. Anytime a future duty assignment can be listed; it will be used instead of the question mark in example D.

Another ending that does not show a person's new assignment may be:

Example F: also from **18ᵗʰ "Messina" Infantry Division**.
... /39 MG Francesco Zani (attached to General Headquarters, Albania) 06/41? MG Guglielmo ...

Explanation of Example F:
MG Francesco Zani gave up the command of the 18ᵗʰ "Messina" Infantry Division around June 1941. At that time he was attached to the General Headquarters, Albania, with no particular assignment.

Ending three (3) will occur if a General officer is holding a concurrent command. At the date next to the bracket occurs, that officer gave up this command and went back to his other concurrent command (see Example G).

Example G: from **Army Group South [Gruppo Armate Sud]**:
... Mar. [Retired '20] Emilio De Bono [+ Member, Fascists Grand Council] /41 Mar. His Royal ...

Explanation of Example G:
Mar. [Retire '20] Emilio De Bono who was Commander-in-Chief, Army Group South, was concurrently a Member of the Fascists Grand Council.. In 1941 when Army Group South was turned over to Mar. His Royal Highness Crown Prince Umberto Piemonte [di Savoia], Mar. Emilio De Bono did not get a new assignment but continued as a Member of the Fascists Grand Council.

Ending four (4), the General/Flag officer gave up both this command and his concurrent command and was given a new duty assignment; with the old assignment ending on that date (see Example G).

Example H: from **Army Group East (#1)**.
... 12/39 LG Carlo Geloso [+ Commanding General, XXVI Army Corps] (Commander-in-Chief, Third Army) 06/10/40 Gen Camillo Grossi

Explanation of Example H:
LG Carlo Geloso was made Commander-in-Chief of Army Group East (#1), while concurrently serving as Commanding General, XXVI Army Corps. On June 10, 1940, he became Commander-in-Chief of the Third Army, giving up both assignments.

Dates before and/or after an officers name and assignment.

A date may appear in several forms. They are:

Date	Explanation
Date	**Explanation**
09/01/39	This is the true date the assignment began and/or ended.
09/01/39?	When it appears before the name, the officer had his present assignment on this actual date, but it might be earlier. When it appears after the assignment, the officer in question had a new assignment on this actual date, but the assignment might be earlier
09/39	This is the true month and year the assignment began and/or ended. The actual date is unknown.
09/39?	When it appears before the name, the officer had his present assignment n this month and year, but it might be earlier. When it appears after the assignment, the officer in question had a new assignment in this month and year, but the assignment might be earlier
/39	This is the year the assignment began and/or ended. The actual month and date are unknown.
/39?	When it appears before the name, the officer had his present assignment n this year, but it might be earlier. When it appears after the assignment, the officer in question had a new assignment in this year, but the assignment might be earlier
/4?	No date was found to suggest when assignment was made. In this case, /4?, the assignment started/ended in the 40's. Sometimes only a (/) may be found.

Other assistance that will help you with this book are:
There may be a time when two officers appear to hold the same post. When this happens, the officers will be listed one under the other with the date of their assignment before their name and what their next duty assignment is and the date they left their assignment. See example I.

Example I: from **206th Regional Military Tribunal (Judical) Torino [Turin]**:
206th Regional Military Tribunal (Judical) Torino [Turin] (10/43): MG America Cappi or BG Cino Gaggiotti

Explanation of Example I: It appears that in October 1943, two commanders, MG America Cappi and BG Cino Gaggiotti, were both found to be Chief, 206th Regional Military Tribunal (Judical) in Torino [Turin]. But, the problem lies that both have been listed with a starting date of 1941, so they are listed either side by side with an "or" between them or, under one another by order in they left for their next duty assignment. It is possible In some circumstances that there could be more than one officer in a position at the same time.

Sometimes you will come across another strange entry as in Example J.

Example J: from **Army Group South [Gruppo Armate Sud]**:

... (0610/40): Mar. [Retired '20] Emilio De Bono [+ Member, Fascists Grand Council] /41 Mar. His Royal ...

Explanation of Example J: When Army Group South was`formed on June 10, 1940, Mar. [Retired '20] Emilio De Bono was brought out of retirement, placed on active duty, and assigned as Commander-in-Chief, Army Group South. He was retired in 1920, since the subscript [Retired '20] appears after his rank. In a lot of cases, a General or Admiral would retire and then be recalled back to active duty, sometimes the same year they retired, to fill a position permanently or until some other officer could be appointed, and then they would be retired again. Whenever I found a General/Flag Officer who retired and was recalled to active duty, the subscript "[Retired and either the month and year of retirement, if known, will be listed; or, the year of retirement]" as in this case, [Retired '20]. If I could not find a year only Retired appears, [Retired].

Section A - Germany's Allies, Co-Belligerent and Puppet States

Romania
Hungary
Bulgaria
Slovakia
Croatia
Serbia
Finland

Section B - Imperial Japan's Ally and Puppet States

Thailand (Siam)
Great Empire of Manchukuo [Manchuria]
Mengjiang [Inner Mongolia]
Republic of China-Nanjing
State of Burma
Second Philippine Republic
Azad Hind [Provisional Government of Free India]
Empire of Vietnam
Kingdom of Cambodia
Kingdom of Luang Phra Bang [Laos]

SECTION A

GERMANY's ALLIES, CO-BELLIGERENT and PUPPET STATES

Romania
Hungary
Bulgaria
Slovakia
Croatia
Serbia
Finland

ROMANIA

(German Ally)

Romanian Government

Head of State: 06/08/30 King CAROL II (abdicated to his son) 09/06/40 King MIHAI [MICHAEL] I.

A. **Marshal of the Royal Court**: 08/23/44 LG Constantin Sănătescu (Prime Minister) 08/27/44

B. **Adjutant to the King**: /44 BG Elimian Ionescu [RRAF].

C. **Head, Royal Military Household**: /37 LG Gheorghe Mihail (/39, Under-Secretary of State, Ministry of Defense) /38 LG Constantin Ilasievici (Commanding General, Fourth Army) /39 unknown? /41 BG Socrat Mardari (Vice Chief of the General Staff) /42 BG Ion Codreanu (Vice Chief of the General Staff) /43 LG Constantin Sănătescu (Marshal of the Royal Court) 08/23/44 MG Constantin Niculescu (/48, retired; /48, arrested and condemned to 7 years imprisonment; /55, released).

Head of Romanian Government:

Prime Minister: 12/28/37 OCTAVIAN GOGA (dismissed) 02/11/38 Patriarch MIRON CRISTEA (resigned due to ill health) 03/07/39 ARMAND CĂLINESCU (assassinated) 09/21/39 LG Gheorghe Argeşanu (Commanding General, I Army Corps) 09/28/39 CONSTANTIN ARGETOIANU (dismissed; 06/28/40, Foreign Affairs Minister) 11/24/39 GHEORGHE TĂTĂRESCU [+ to 11/30/39, Interior Minister] (resigned; 03/06/45, Foreign Affairs Minister) 07/04/40 ION GIGURTU (dismissed) 09/04/40 FM [Retired '40] Ion Victor Antonescu [+ Commander-in-Chief, Armed Forces; + to 06/41, Minister of National Defense; 12/01/40, Foreign Minister; + 06/41 to 08/01/41, Commander-in-Chief, Army Group Antonescu; + 08/01/41, Minister of National Defense] (dismissed) 08/23/44 IULIU MANIU (acting) 08/27/44 [formation of new government] LG Constantin Sănătescu [+ 10/13/44 to 11/04/44, Finance Minister] (lost confidence, resigned; Interior Minister) 12/02/44 LG [Retired '33] Nicolae Rădescu (resigned; /46, fled to the United States; /53, died in New York) 03/06/45 PETRU GROZA.

[NOTE: in opposition to official Prime Minister; exile in Germany; 08/24/44 HORIA SIMA 04/12/45**]**

1. **Under-Secretary of State for the Prime Minister**: /44 BG Dumitru Dămăceanu (Under-Secretary of State for Land Forces) /45

A. **Vice Premier**: 02/02/38 ARMAND CĂLINESCU [+ Interior Minister; + 03/30/38 to /38, Health & Social Protection Minister; /38, National Education Minister; 02/01/39, National Defense Minister] (Prime Minister) 03/07/39 unknown? 09/40 HORIA SIMA (exiled to Germany; imprisoned in a special, humane, section of the Buchenwald Concentration Camp, one meant for Iron Guard members) 01/41 MIHAI ANTONESCU [+ 01/01/43, Foreign Affairs Minister] (arrested; later found guilty of war crimes and executed by firing squad) 08/24/44

B. **Council of Ministers**
1. **President, Council of Ministers**: /39 LG Gheorghe Argeşanu (Prime Minister) 09/21/39

C. **Minister without Portfolio [Minister of State]**
02/02/39 ALEXANDRU AVERESCU 03/30/38
02/02/39 ARTUR VĂITOIANU 03/30/38
02/02/39 ALEXANDRU VAIDA-VOEVOD 03/30/38
02/02/39 NICOLAE IORGA 03/30/38
02/02/39 CONSTANTIN ANGHELESCU 03/30/38
02/02/39 GHEORGHE TĂTĂRESCU (Interior Minister) 11/21/39

D. **Interior Minister**: 02/02/38 ARMAND CĂLINESCU [+ Vice Premier; + 03/30/38 to /38, Health & Social Protection Minister; /38, National Education Minister; 02/01/39, National Defense Minister] (Prime Minister) 03/07/39 BG Gabriel Marinescu (arrested and executed in prison) 09/28/39 NICOLAE OTTESCU 11/21/39 GHEORGHE TĂTĂRESCU [+ 11/24/39, Prime Minister] 11/30/39 MIHAIL GHELMEGEANU 07/04/40 MG David Popescu [+ Commanding General, 11th Infantry Division] (retired; /50, arrested; /53, released) 09/14/40 MG [Retired '38] Constantin Petrovicescu (condemned to 25 years imprisonment As member of the Iron Guard; /44, released; /4?, arrested; /49, died in prison) 12/15/41 LG Dumitru I. Popescu [+ 03/21/44 to 04/21/43, acting Commanding General, Third Army] (/45, arrested and condemned to 10 years imprisonment; /56, released) 08/23/44 LG Aurel Aldea (Commander-in-Chief, Territorial Command) 11/04/44 NICOLAE PENESCU 12/06/44 LG Constantin Sănătescu [+ 12/11/44, Chief of the General Staff] 12/14/44 LG [Retired '33] Nicolae Rădescu [+Prime Minister] (resigned; /46, fled to the United States; /53, died in New York) 03/06/45

   1. **Secretary of State, Public Wealth Registering**: 02/01/39 TRAIAN POP 09/28/39
   2. **Secretary of State, Minorities**: 02/01/39 SILVIU DRAGOMIR 09/28/39
   3. **Under-Secretary of the Interior**: MG P. Văşiliu.
   4. **Under-Secretary of State, Interior**: /37 BG Gabriel Marinescu (/39, Under-Secretary of State, Ministry of Interior) /37 unknown? 02/01/39 BG Gabriel Marinescu (Interior Minister) 03/07/39 CORIOLAN BĂRAN 09/28/39 unknown? /44 BG Dumitru Dămăceanu (Under-Secretary of State, Prime Minister) /44 MG [Retired '40] Gheorghe Liteanu (/53, arrested; /57, condemned to 25 years imprisonment; /59, died in prison)
   5. **Under-Secretary of State, Government Presidency** (03/30/38): MIHAIL MĂGUREANU 09/28/39
   6. **Under-Secretary of State, Interior for Press and Information** (03/30/38): EUGEN TITEANU (Under-Secretary of State, Propaganda) 02/01/39
       a. **Assistant Chief, Central Information Service, Ministerial Center**: 06/03/41 Col. Ioan D. Popescu (Commandant, Artillery Instruction Center) /41
   7. **Under-Secretary of State, Interior for Police & Security**: /42 MG Constantin Z. Văşiliu [Inspector-General of Gendarmes] (arrested; /46, condemned to death and executed) /44
   8. **Under-Secretary of State, Propaganda**: 02/01/39 EUGEN TITEANU 09/28/39
   9. **Minister of Propaganda**: /40 MIHAI ANTONESCU (Vice Premier) 02/02/38

E.   **Foreign Affairs (External Affairs) Minister**: 12/28/37 ESTRATE MICESCU 02/11/38 GHEORGHE TĂTĂRESCU (removed; 02/02/39, Minister without Portfolio) 03/30/38 NICOLAE PETRESCU-COMNEN 01/31/39 GRIGORE GAFENCU 06/01/40 ION GIGURTU (Prime Minister) 06/28/40 CONSTANTIN ARGETOIANU 07/04/40 MIHAIL MANOILESCU 09/15/40 MIHAIL R. STURDZA 01/17/41 FM [Retired '40] Ion Victor Antonescu [+ Prime Minister; + Commander-in-Chief, Armed Forces; + to 06/41, Minister of National Defense; + 06/41 to 08/01/41, Commander-in-Chief, Army Group Antonescu; + 08/01/41 to /42, Minister of National Defense] 01/01/43 MIHAI ANTONESCU (arrested; later found guilty of war crimes and executed by firing squad) 08/24/44 GRIGORE NICULESCU-BUZEŞTI 11/05/44 CONSTANTIN VISOIANU 03/06/45 GHEORGHE TĂTĂRESCU.

1.   **Under-Secertary of State, External Affairs**: 02/02/38 NICOLAE PETRESCU-COMNEN (Foreign Affairs Minister) 03/30/38

2.   **Under-Secretary of State, Romanization, Colonization, & Education**: /41 BG Eugen Zwiedinek (retired; /50, arrested; /56, released) /42

3.   *Ambassadors*

a.   **Ambassador to Berlin (Germany)**: /43 BG Ion Gheorghe (in reserve?) /44

b.   **Ambassador to Nanking (China)**: /41 MG Gheorghe Bagulescu [+ Military Attaché Tokyo & Ambassador to Tokyo) /43

c.   **Ambassador to Tokyo (Japan)**: /34 Col. Gheorghe Bagulescu [+ Military Attaché Tokyo] (/41, Ambassador to Tokyo and Nanking-China & Military Attaché Tokyo) /39 unknown? /41 MG Gheorghe Bagulescu [+ Military Attaché Tokyo & Ambassador to Nanking-China) /43

F.   **Finance Minister**: 02/02/38 MIRCEA CANCICOV [+ Justice Minister] 02/01/39 MITIŢĂ CONSTANTINESCU (Governor, Romanian National Bank) 07/04/40 GHEORGHE N. LEON 09/14/40 GHEORGHE CRETZIANU 01/27/41 BG Nicolae Scariat Stoenescu (Director, Higher Military Education) 09/25/42 ALEXANDRU NEAGU 04/01/44 GHERON NETTA 08/23/44 Gen. Gheorghe Potopeanu 10/13/44 LG Constantin Sănătescu [+ Prime Minister] 11/04/44 MIHAIL ROMNICEANU 03/01/45 DUMITRU ALIMĂNIŞTEANU.

G.   **Justice Minister**: 02/02/38 MIRCEA CANCICOV [+ Finance Minister] 03/30/38 VICTOR IAMANDI 09/28/39 unknown? /44 LG Ion Boiţeanu [+ Minister of Culture] (Commanding General, IV Army Corps) 12/04/44

H.   **National Education Minister**: 02/02/38 VICTOR IAMANDI [+ Religious Affairs and Arts Minister] (Justice Minister) 03/30/38 NICOLAE COLAN [+ Religious Affairs and Arts Minister] /38 ARMAND CĂLINESCU [+ Vice Premier; + Interior Minister; + Health & Social Protection Minister; 02/01/39, National Defense Minister] /38 PETRE ANDREI 09/28/39 unknown? /41 BG [Retired '24] Radu R. Rosetti (/46, arrested and released; /48, arrested and condemned to 2 years imprisonment; /49, died in prison)

1.   **Under-Secretary of State, National Education**: 03/30/38 DUMITRU ŢONI

09/28/39 unknown? /42 MG [Retired '37] Victor Traian Iliescu (State Youth Organization Leader) /43

I.   **Religious Affairs (Culture) and Arts Minister**: 02/02/38 VICTOR IAMANDI [+ National Education Minister] (Justice Minister) 03/30/38 NICOLAE COLAN [+ to /38, National Education Minister] 02/01/39 NICOLAE ZEGRE 09/28/39 unknown? 07/04/40 HORIA SIMA (resigned) 07/08/40 unknown? /44 LG Ion Boiţeanu [+ Minister of Justice] (Commanding General, IV Army Corps) 12/04/44
   1.   **Under-Secretary of State, Religious Affairs and Arts**: 03/30/38 NAE POPESCU 02/01/39 ION MARIN SADOVEANU 09/28/39

J.   **National Defense Minister**: /37 LG. Constantin Ilasievici (Head, Royal Military Household) /37 FM Ion Victor Antonescu [+ 02/02/38,Air and Marine Minister] 03/3038 LG Gheorghe Argeşanu (/39, President, Council of Ministers) /38 LG Nicolae Ciupercă (Commanding General, Second Army) 02/01/39 ARMAND CĂLINESCU [+ to 03/07/39, Vice Premier; + Interior Minister] (Prime Minister) 03/07/39 LG Ioan Ilcuş (Commanding General, Fourth Army) 09/04/40 FM [Retired '40] Ion Victor Antonescu [+ Commander-in-Chief, Armed Forces; 12/01/40, Foreign Minister] (Commander-in-Chief, Army Group Antonescu) 06/41 LG Isoif Iacobici [+ Commanding General, Fourth Army] 08/01/41 FM [Retired '40] Ion Victor Antonescu [+ Commander-in-Chief, Armed Forces; + Foreign Minister] (dismissed) 08/24/44 LG Mihail Racovita (Inspector-General of Cavalry) 11/05/44 LG Constantin Văşiliu-Rascanu
   1.   **War Minister**: /42 LG Constantin Pantazi (arrested; /46, condemned to death, but communicated to life imprisonment; /58, died in prison)12/16/44 LG Ion Negulescu (retired; /48, arrested; 1949, died in prison).
      a.   **Director, Personnel, War Minister**: /39 BG Nicolae Şova (Commanding General, 1st Guards Division) 06/22/41 unknown? /44 BG Vasile Mainescu (Deputy Commander, Capital Military Command) /45
      b.   **Judge Advocate General, War Minister**: /40 BG Constantin Manoliu (Judge Advocate General, Ministry of War, Romanian Government in Exile) 08/24/44
   2.   **Under-Secretary of State, National Defense**: 02/02/38 Col. Paul Teodorescu [+ Under-Secretary of State, National Defense] (Air and Marine Minister) 03/30/38 ALEXANDRA GLATZ 02/01/39 LG Gheorghe Mihail (Chief of the General Staff) /40 MG Constantin Pantazi (War Minister) /42 unknown? 02/19/43 MG Nicolae Şova (in reserve; 09/21/44, Commanding General, VII Army Corps) 08/23/44
   3.   **Under-Secretary of State, Land Forces**: 11/04/44 BG Ilie Creţulescu (Vice Chief of the General Staff) /44 unknown? /45 BG Dumitru Dămăceanu.
      a.   **Secretary-General for Under-Secretary of State of Land Forces**: /40 BG Corneliu Calotescu (Deputy Governor-General, Bucovina) /41 unknown? /42 BG Petre Camenita (Commanding General, 8th Infantry Division) 09/12/44
   4.   **Under-Secretary of State, Army Supply**: /41 MG Constantin S. Constantin

(in reserve; /44, Deputy Commander, Capital Military Command) /43 MG Ioan Arbore (in reserve; /45, retired; /46 arrested; /48, condemned to 10 years imprisonment as a traitor) /44 unknown? /45 BG Grigore Nicolau (Commanding General, II Army Corps; /47, Commanding General, 2nd Military Region; /48, retired).

5. **Judge Advocate General, Ministry of National Defense**: unknown? /43 MG Stroia

6. **General-Secretary Department, Ministry of National Defense**: unknown? /37 Col. Nicolae Dascalescu [+ Commanding Officer, 12th Artillery Brigade] (Commanding Officer, 1st Anti-Aircraft Artillery Brigade) /38 unknown? /40

   /40 BG Ilie Şteflea (Commanding General, 3rd Infantry Division) 02/20/41

   /40 BG Nicolae Scariat Stoenescu (Commanding General, 1st Armored Division) /41

   /41 MG Ion Boiţeanu (Commanding General, 3rd Infantry Division) 02/10/43

   02/11/42 BG Vintila Davidescu (Commanding General, VII Territorial Corps Area) /44

   a. **Assistant General-Secretary Department, Ministry of National Defense**: /41 Col. Petre Antonescu (Chief of Staff, Fourth Army) /43

7. **Secretary-General of Administration, Ministry of Defense**: /41 BG Constantin S. Constantin (Under-Secretary of Supply) /41

8. **Supreme Council of National Defense**:
   a. **Members, Supreme Council of National Defense**:
      /43 LG Henric Cihoski (.45, in prison; /50, died in prison) /43

K. **Air and Marine Minister**: 02/02/38 FM Ion Victor Antonescu [+ Defense Minister] 03/30/38 Col. Paul Teodorescu [+ Under-Secretary of State, Air and Navy] 09/28/39

   1. **Under-Secretary of State, Air and Navy**: 02/02/38 Col. Paul Teodorescu [+ to 03/30/38, Under-Secretary of State, National Defense; 03/30/38, Air and Marine Minister] (Commanding General, 1st Guards Division) 05/11/40 Col. Achile Diculescu [RRAF] 09/14/40 Col. Gheorghe Jienescu [RRAF]

   2. **Under-Secretary of State, Air Force**:
      a. **Head, Intendance Service, Under-Secretary of State, Air Force**: /41 Col. Constantin Constantiniu (Head, Intendance Service of the Army) /44

L. **Armaments & War Production Minister** (/42, originally formed 03/30/38 as **Armament Endowment Minister** (03/30/38): **Armament Endowment Minister**: 03/30/38 LG Iosif Iacobici (Commanding General, Fourth Army) 02/01/39 VICTOR SLĂVESCU 09/28/39 unknown? /42 redesignated **Armaments & War Production Minister**: /42 MG Gheorghe Dobre (/45, arrested; /46, condemned to life imprisonment; /59, died in prison) /44

   1. **Under-Secretary of State, Armaments**: /40 MG Gheorghe Dobre (Minister of Armaments & War Production) /42
      a. **General-Secretary, Ministry of Armaments**: /40 MG Gheorghe

Dobre (Under-Secretary of State, Ministry of Armaments) /40
      b.   **Director, Munitions Fabrication Department**: /40 BG Gheorghe Dobre (General-Secretary, Ministry of Armaments) /40

M.   **Agriculture and Domains Minister** (02/01/39, originally **Agriculture, Domains and Cooperatives Minister**: <u>Agriculture, Domains and Cooperatives Minister</u>: 02/02/38 CONSTANTIN ARGETOIANU [+ Public Works and Communications Minister] (0928/39, Prime Minister) 03/30/38 GHEORGHE IONESCU-SIŞEŞTI 02/01/39 redesignated <u>Agriculture and Domains Minister</u>: 02/01/39 NICOLAE D. CORNĂŢEANU 09/28/39 unknown? /41 LG _[Retired '37] Ioan Sichitiu (/48, condemned to 10 years imprisonment; /52, died in prison) /42
     1.   **Under-Secretary of State, Agriculture and Domains** (02/01/39): MIHAIL ŞERBAN 09/28/39

N.   **National Economy Minister** (02/01/39, originally **Industry and Commerce [Economic Co-ordination] Minister** (03/30/38): <u>Industry and Commerce [Economic Co-ordination] Minister</u>: 03/30/38 MITIŢĂ CONSTANTINESCU (Finance Minister) 02/01/39 redesignated <u>National Economy Minister</u>: 02/01/39 ION BUJOIU 09/28/39 unknown? /40 Col. Nicolae Dragomir (Liaison Officer for General Headquarters at Third Army) /41 unknown? 08/16/44 MG Gheorghe Potopeanu (arrested; /45, released; /48, arrested; /49, condemned to 5 years imprisonment; /53, released; /57, arrested and condemned to 15 years imprisonment; /63, released) /44
     1.   **Under-Secretary of State, National Economic**: 02/01/39 VICTOR JINGA 09/28/39 unknown? /40? Col. Gheorghe Potopeanu (Commanding General, 1st Frontier Division) 06/22/41? BG Eugen Zwiedinek (Under-Secretary of State, Romanization, Colonization & Education) /41

O.   **Public Works and Communications Minister**: 02/02/38 CONSTANTIN ARGETOIANU [+ Agriculture, Domains and Cooperatives Minister] (09/28/39, Prime Minister) 03/30/38 MIHAIL GHELMEGEANU (11/30/39, Interior Minister) 09/28/39 unknown? 11/39 ION GIGURTU (Foreign Affairs Minister) 06/01/40 unknown? /41 BG Grigore Georgescu (/46, arrested; /48, condemned to 3 years imprisonment; /52, died in prison) /41 unknown? /44 BG Constantin Eftimiu (Vice Chief of the General Staff) /45

P.   **Labor Minister**: 02/02/38 VOICU NIŢESCU 03/30/38 MIHAI RALEA 09/28/39
     1.   **Romanian Working Youth Organization**: /41 Col. Emil Palangeanu (Inspector of Pre-Military Preparation) /44

Q.   **Health and Social Protection Minister** (02/01/39; originally **Labor, Health and Social Protection Minister**): <u>Labor, Health and Social Protection Minister</u>: 02/02/38 ION COSTINESCU 03/30/38 ARMAND CĂLINESCU [+ Vice Premier; + Interior Minister] (National Education Minister) /38 MG Nicolae M. Marinescu (Health and Social Protection Minister) 02/01/39 redesignated <u>Health and Social Protection Minister</u>: 02/01/39 MG Nicolae M. Marinescu (/40, retired; /44, Ministry-

Secretary of State, Department of Works, Sanitary and Social Health) 09/28/39
1. **Under-Secretary of State for Works, Sanitary and Social Health**: /41 BG Constantin Voiculescu (Military-Governor, Bessarabia) /41
2. **Ministry-Secretary of State, Department of Works, Sanitary and Social Health**: /44 MG [Retired'40] Nicolae M. Marinescu (Head, Army Sanitary Service) /45
3. **State Youth Organization Leader**: /43 MG [Retired'37] Victor Traian Iliescu (/46, arrested; /48, condemned to 10 years imprisonment; /56, released)

Romanian Government in Exile [located in Germany]

Prime Minister (08/24/44, exile in Germany): HORIA SIMA 04/12/45
A. **Minister of Defense, Government in Exile**: /45 BG Platon Chirnoagă (Soviet prisoner-of-war) /45
B. **Minister of War**
1. **General-Secretary Department, Ministry of War**:
09/12/44 MG Dumitru Carlaonţ (in reserve; /45, retired; /48 arrested; /50, acquitted and released; /51, condemned to 12 years imprisonment for crimes against humanity; /55 pardoned and released; /59 arrested; /60 condemned to 7 years imprisonment for contra social activities but released later that year) /45
09/12/44 BG Ioan Eftimiu (Commanding General, 8th Cavalry Division) 03/13/45
2. **Judge Advocate General, Ministry of War** (08/24/44): BG Constantin Manoliu.

Allied Occupation

Soviet Military Commander (08/31/44): Rodion Yakovlevich Malinovskiy [Russian] 09/12/44

Chairman, Allied Control Commission (09/12/44): Rodion Yakovlevich Malinovskiy [Russian] 10/28/44 Fyodor Ivanovich Tolbukhin [Russian].
A. **Acting Chairman, Allied Control Commission** (09/12/44): Vladislav Petrovich Vinogradov [Russian]. (acting for Malinovskiy [Russian]) 10/28/44 Sergey Semyonovich Biriuzov [Russian]. (acting for Tolbukhin [Russian]).

Military High Command

Commander-in-Chief, Armed Forces: 09/04/40 FM [Retired '40] Ion Victor Antonescu [+ Prime Minister; + to 06/41, Minister of National Defense; 12/01/40, Foreign Minister; + 06/41 to 08/01/41, Commander-in-Chief, Army Group Antonescu; + 08/01/41, Minister of National Defense] (dismissed) 08/23/44

A.   **Special Information Service**: /44 BG [Retired '41] Gheorghe Savoiu (/45, retired; /49, arrested; /51, condemned to 2 years imprisonment; /54, released).

Chief of the General Staff: /37 MG Gheorghe Ştefan Ionescu (Commanding General, Unknown? Army Corps) /39 MG Florea Ţenescu (retired) /40 LG Gheorghe Mihail (retired; 08/23/44, Chief of the General Staff) 09/06/40 BG Alexabdru Ioaniţiu (killed in an air crash) 09/22/41 LG Iosif Iacobici [+ to 11/08/41, Commanding General, Fourth Army] (retired; /46, arrested, but released later that year; /48, arrested; /49, condemned to life imprisonment as a traitor; /52, dies in prison) 01/20/42 LG Ilie Şteflea (Commanding General, Fourth Army) 08/23/44 LG [Retired '40] Gheorghe Mihail (Inspector-General of Infantry) 10/12/44 vacant 10/15/44 LG [Retired '33] Nicolae Radescu (Prime Minister) 12/06/44 vacant 12/11/44 LG Constantin Sănătescu.

A.   **Vice Chief of the General Staff**:
>   /39 BG Constantin S. Constantin (/41, Secretary-General of Administration, Ministry of Defense) /40
>   /39 BG Ilie Şteflea (Chief of Staff, First Army) /40
>   /40 MG Gheorghe Ştefan Ionescu (/53, arrested; /55, released) /41
>   /40 BG Nicolae Tataranu (Chief of Staff, Fourth Army) /41
>   /41 BG Nicolae Mazarini (Commanding General, 5th Infantry Division) 02/11/42
>   /41 BG Nicolae Tataranu (Commanding General, 20th Infantry Division) 07/04/42

02/11/42 BG Socrat Mardari (Commandant, Higher War School) /43 BG Ion Codreanu (Commandant, Higher War School) /43 BG Ioan Arhip (Commanding General, 15th Infantry Division) 09/03/44 BG Ştefan Bardan (in reserve; /47, retired) /44 BG Ilie Creţulescu (Commanding General, Frontier Troops) /45 BG Constantin Eftimiu (/46, in reserve; /46, arrested and condemned to life imprisonment; /47, retired; /50, died in prison) /45 BG Corneliu Carp (in reserve; /47, retired; /50, arrested; /51, condemned to 12 years imprisonment; /55, released) /46

[NOTE: one source has MG Socrat Mardari returning as Vice Chief of the General Staff from Commandant, Higher War School in 1943; /43 MG Socrat Mardari (in reserve; /47, retired; /48, arrested and condemned to 7 years imprisonment; /54, died in prison) /45]

B.   **Commander-in-Chief, Territorial Command**: /44 LG Aurel Aldea (retired; /46, arrested & condemned to life imprisonment; /46 , in prison; /49, died in Aiud Prison) /45

1.   **Deputy Commander-in-Chief, Territorial Command**: 12/06/44 MG Gheorghe Ionescu-Sinaia (Commanding General, Frontier Guard Corps) 12/16/44 BG Ioan Mihaescu (Chief of Staff, V Territorial Corps Area) /45

C. **Operations, General Staff**: /43 BG Paul Leonida (Commanding General, 10th Artillery Brigade) 04/05/44 BG Ion Codreanu (Inspector of Cavalry) /45

D. **Director, Department of Higher Administration of the Army**: 10/15/44 BG Grigore Nicolau (Under-Secretary of State, Army Supplies) /45

E. **Propaganda Section, General Staff**: /41 Col. Constantin Brătescu (Romanian Liaison Officer to German Military Mission) /41 unknown? 05/11/42 Col. Corneliu Teodorini (Commanding Officer, 6th Cavalry Division) 10/16/44

F. **Adjutant Section, General Staff**: /41 Col. Ioan Beldiceanu (Deputy Commander, 1st Guards Infantry Division) /42

G. **4th Section, Forward Echelons, General Headquarters**: /42 Col. Ilie Antonescu (Chief of Staff, V Territorial Corps Area) /42

H. **6th Transportation Bureau, General Staff**: /39 Col. Olimpiu Stavrat (Commanding General, 7th Infantry Division) 03/10/40 Col. Gheorghe Avramescu (Commanding General 10th Infantry Division) /41 unknown?

I. **Intendance Service of the Army**: /44 BG Constantin Constantiniu (Director, Higher Audition Department) /45.

J. **Instruction Section, General Staff**: /41 Col. Nicolae Vladescu (Commanding Officer, 2nd Security Division) 03/15/42

K. **Judge-Advocate General of the Army**: /41 MG Ioan Topor

L. *Directors of Armed Forces*

  1. **Director of Infantry**: /41 BG Constantin Văşiliu-Rascanu (Commanding General, 1st Mixed Mountain Brigade) 02/10/42 unknown? 10/06/44 MG Ioan Arhip (Deputy Commander, II Army Corps) /33

  2. **Director of Artillery**: /43 BG Ioan Dimulescu (Commandant, Dobrogei) /44

  3. **Director of Cavalry**: 11/44 BG Corneliu Teodorini (/45, retired).

  4. **Director, Mechanization Department**: /41 Col. Gheorghe Niculescu (Infantry Commander, 10th Infantry Division) /43 unknown? 09/14/44 BG Gheorghe Niculescu [+ Commandant, Mechanization Instruction School] (retired) /45.

  5. **Chief of Signals**: /42 BG Nicolae T. Petrescu (in reserve?) /43 BG Constantin Eftimiu (Minister of Public Works & Communications) /44

  6. **Director of Higher Infantry Department**: /41 BG Nicolae Costescu (Commanding General, 18th Infantry Division) 09/01/41 unknown? 01/06/42 BG Nicolae Costescu (retired) 07/04/42 BG Gheorghe B. Georgescu (Deputy Commander, Capital Military Command) /44

  7. **Director, Higher Artillery Department**: /42 MG Gheorghe Rozin (Commanding General, IV Army Corps) 03/20/43

    a. **Deputy Director, Higher Artillery Department**: /42 BG Mihail Lăcătuşcu (Commanding General, 19th Infantry Division) 10/29/43

    b. **Chief of Staff, Higher Artillery Department**: /42 BG Emanoil Leoveanu (Commanding General, II Territorial Corps Area) /42 Col. Hercule Fortunescu (acting Commanding Officer, 1st Cavalry Division) /43

  8. **Director, Higher Cavalry Department**: /41 Col. Ion Codreanu (Commanding Officer, 6th Cavalry Division) 07/25/41 unknown? 03/23/43 BG Vasile Mainescu (Commanding General, 8th Cavalry Division) 04/05/44 unknown?

07/25/44 BG Vasile Mainescu (Director, Personnel, Ministry of War) /44

M. **_Directors of Support Services_**
  1. **Director, Fortification Department**: /36 BG Dumitru Văşiliu (?) /41
  2. **Director, Higher Technical Department**
     a. **Chief of Staff, Higher Technical Department**: /40 Col. Gheorghe Cosma (Commanding Officer, 6th Field Artillery Regiment) /41 unknown? /41 Col. Gheorghe Cosma (Commanding Officer, 9th Artillery Brigade) /42
  3. **Director-General, State Railways**: /43 MG Teodor Constantin Orezeanu
N. **Director of Military Geographic Institute**: /43 BG Bodnarescu
O. **Director, Army Sanitary Service**: /45 MG [Retired '40] Nicolae M. Marinescu (retired).
P. **Historical Service, General Staff**: 02/11/42 BG Ion Codreanu (Head, Royal Military Household) /42
Q. **Director, General Police Department**: 06/21/41 BG Emanoil Leoveanu (Director, Higher Artillery Department) /42
R. **Prisoner-of-War Section, General Staff**: /41 Col. Ioan Stănculescu (Commandant, Artillery Instruction Center) /42 unknown? /44 BG Mihail Camarasu (Commanding General, 10th Infantry Division) 11/14/44
S. **Director, Higher Military (War) Education Department**: /37 Col. Ilie Şteflea (Vice Chief of the General Staff) /39 unknown? 11/09/41 MG Gheorghe Rozin (Director, Higher Artillery Department) 09/25/42 BG Nicolae Scariat Stoenescu (Commanding General, 1st Armored Division) 03/21/43 MG Radu Gherghe (Commanding General, I Army Corps) 04/05/44 BG Dumitru Dumitrescu-Polihron (Commanding General, 21st Infantry Division) 09/02/44 MG Carol Schmidt (Inspector-General of Artillery) 02/13/45

[NOTE: also listed /44 MG Nicolae Vladescu (/47, retired) /45]
  1. **Director, Higher Military School**: /43 BG Ion Codreanu (Chief, Operations, General Staff) 04/05/44 MG Ion Boiţeanu (Minister of Culture & Minister of Justice) /44
  2. **Commandant, Bucharest Military Academy**: /39 BG Alexabdru Ioaniţiu (Chief of the General Staff) 09/06/40
  3. **Commandant, Sibiu Officers School**: /37 Col. Radu Băldescu (Commanding Officer, 16th Infantry Brigade) /40
  4. **Commandant, Infantry Instruction School**: /40 Col. Paul Leonida (/43, Chief of Operations, General Staff) /41 Col. Ştefan Bardan (Chief of Staff, Fourth Army) /43 Col. Ioan Dumitriu (Commanding General, 3rd Infantry Training Division & Commanding General, 3rd Infantry Division) 09/05/44 BG Vasile Pascu (/45, Commanding General, 1st Mountain Division; /45, Director, Department of Higher Administration of the Army; /46, in reserve; /47, retired; /56, arrested and condemned to 5 years imprisonment; /58, sentence changed to 15 years imprisonment; /60, died in prison).
     a. **Deputy Commandant, Infantry Instruction School**: 10/06/44 Col. Enache Juganaru (Deputy Commander, 1st Mountain Division) /45
  5. **Commandant, Cavalry Instruction School**: /40 Col. Gheorghe Munteanu (Commanding Officer, 6th Cavalry Brigade) 06/30/41 Col. Vladimir Constantinescu (Commanding Officer, 8th Rosiori Cavalry Regiment) /42 Col.

Vladimir Constantinescu (Chief of Staff, Mechanized Troops Command) 01/02/43 Col. Corneliu Carp (Commanding General, 5th Cavalry Division) 07/16/43 Col. Ioan Eftimiu (Commanding General, 6th Cavalry Division) 07/25/44

[NOTE: also listed /41 Col. Constantin Talpeş (Prefect of Iasi) /43]

6. **Commandant, Artillery, Instruction Center**: /40? Col. Ioan Mihaescu (Vice Chief of Staff, Third Army) /41 Col. Ioan D. Popescu (Commanding General, 3rd Artillery Brigade) /42 Col. Ioan Stănculescu (Artillery Commander, II Army Corps) /43

7. **Commandant, Mechanization Instruction Center**: /40 Col. Pompeius Demetrescu /41 Col. Ion Constantinescu (Commanding Officer, 35th Infantry Regiment) /42 Col. Pompeius Demetrescu (Commanding General, 2nd Infantry Brigade) 05/27/44 BG Gheorghe Niculescu (Commanding General, 1st Armored Division) /44 unknown? 09/14/44 BG Gheorghe Niculescu [+ Director, Mechanization Department] (retired) /45.

8. **Commandant, Reserve Officer School**: /42 Col. Ioan Iucal (Commanding Officer, 9th Infantry Brigade) /44

9. **Commandant, Arad Reserve Officer School**: /42 Col. Ghedeon Seracin (Commanding General, 1st Infantry Brigade) /44

10. **Commandant, Sarata Instruction Center**: /42 Col. Alexandru Poenaru (Commanding General, 7th Infantry Division) 03/21/43

T. *Military Attachés*

1. **Military Attaché Berlin (Germany)**: /38 Col. Titus Gârbea (Military Attaché Stockholm) /40 Col. Ion Gheorghe (Ambassador to Berlin) /43

2. **Military Attaché Rome (Italy)**: /40 Col. Mihail Corbuleanu (in reserve; 09/01/44, Commanding General, 13th Infantry Training Division) /44

3. **Military Attaché Stockholm (Sweden)**: /40 Col. Titus Gârbea (Head, Liaison Detachment Gârbea, German Army Group South; /43, Commanding General, 18th Artillery Brigade) /43

4. **Military Attaché Tokyo (Japan)**: /34 Col. Gheorghe Bagulescu [+ Ambassador to Tokyo] (/41, Military Attaché Tokyo & Ambassador to Tokyo and Nanking-China) /39 unknown? /41 MG Gheorghe Bagulescu [+ Ambassador to & Ambassador to Nanking-China] (in reserve?) /43

U. *Liaison Officers & Representatives*

1. **Romanian Liaison Officer to the German General Staff**: /40 BG Gheorghe R. Gheorghe (Deputy Commander, 5th Infantry Division) /41 unknown? /44 MG Titus Gârbea (in reserve; /45, Artillery Commander, IV Army Corps) /45.

2. **Romanian Liaison Officer to German Military Mission**: /40 Col. Gheorghe R. Gheorghiu (Deputy Commander, 5th Infantry Division) /41 Col. Constantin Brătescu (Commanding General, 1st Cavalry Division) 07/17/42

3. **Liaison Officer to German Army Group South**: /42 Col. Ilie Antonescu (Chief, 4th Section, Forward Echelons, General Headquarters) /42

4. **Liaison Officer for General Headquarters at Third Army**: /41 Col. Nicolae Dragomir (Romanian Liaison Officer to Italian Expeditionary Corps in Russia) /41

5. **Romanian Liaison Officer to Italian Expeditionary Corps in Russia**: /41

Col. Nicolae Dragomir (Vice Chief of Staff, Fourth Army) /42

6. **Romanian Liaison Officer to XVII German Army Corps**: /44 BG Mihail Camarasu (Chief, Prisoner-of-War Section, General Staff): /44

7. **Government Representative for Evacuation of the Eastern Territories**: /43 Col. Gheorghe Mosiu (Chief of Staff, General Rear Area Command) 08/21/44

8. **Romanian Liaison Officer to the Soviet Command in Moldova**: /44 BG Damian Raşcu (Chief of Staff, First Army) 04/05/44

Inspectorate-General of the Army:

A. **Chief of Staff, Inspectorate-General of the Army**: 03/21/43 BG Ioan Mihaescu (Commanding General, 4th Infantry Division) 04/30/43

B. **Inspector-General of Infantry**: 10/12/44 LG [Retired '40] Gheorghe Mihail (retired; /48, arrested and condemned to 12 years imprisonment; /57, released).

C. **Inspector-General of Artillery**: 03/21/43 LG Vasile Atanasiu (Commanding General, First Army) 02/13/45 MG Carol Schmidt (in reserve; /45, retired).

   1. **Director of Artillery, Inspectorate-General of Artillery**: 12/05/44 MG Costin Ionaşcu (Commanding General, II Army Corps) 03/08/45

D. **Inspector-General of Cavalry**: /40 MG Constantin Atanasescu (retired) /40 unknown? 11/05/44 LG Mihail Racovita (Commandant, 3rd Inspectorate-General; /46, Commanding General, First Army; /47, retired; /50, arrested; /54, died in prison) 05/20/45 MG Ion Codreanu.

   1. **Assistant Inspector-General of Cavalry**: 09/20/44 BG Ilie Antonescu (Commanding General, 9th Cavalry Division) 12/18/44

   2. **Chief of Staff, Inspectorate-General of Cavalry**: 03/13/45 BG Hercule Fortunescu (/47, retired).

E. **Inspector of Motorized Troops**: /44 LG Corneliu Dragalina (retired) /45.

F. **Inspector of Engineers**: /40 BG Grigore Georgescu (Minister of Public Works & Communications) /41 Col. Barbu Alinescu [+ Commanding General, 1st Engineers Brigade] (Commanding General, 4th Infantry Division) 08/02/42 MG Gheorghe Zaharescu

G. **Inspector-General of Gendarmes (Secret Police)**: /38 MG Ioan Bengliu (retired; /40, arrested and executed in prison) /40 BG Ioan Topor (/41, Judge-Advocate General of the Army) /40 MG Constantin Z. Văşiliu [+ /42 to /44, Under-Secretary of State, Police & Security, Ministry of Interior] (arrested; /46, condemned to death and executed) /44 BG Constantin St. Anton (arrested; /59 released) /46

H. **Inspector of Pre-Military Preparation**: /44 BG Emil Palangeanu (/45, retired; /52, arrested and condemned to 5 years imprisonment; /53, died in prison) /44

   1. **Inspectors, Inspectorate-General of Pre-Military Preparation**: 07/13/44 MG Radu Nicolescu-Cociu (Commanding General, VII Army Corps) 04/09/45

I. **Inspector-General of Sanitary**:

   1. **Chief of Staff, Inspector-General of Sanitary**: /41 Col. Ioan Stănculescu (Vice Chief of Staff, Fourth Army) /41

J. **Inspectorate of Industrial Mobilization**: /44 MG Constantin Visarion (Commanding General, 20th Infantry Training Division) 08/23/44

Commander-in-Chief, Royal Romanian Navy [Marinei Militare Române]: 11/02/37 Adm. Petre Bărbuneau [RRN] (in reserve?) 09/06/40 vacant 09/21/40 VA (Eng) Eugeniu Raşca [RRN] (?) 06/16/42 VA (Eng) Ioan Georgescu [RRN] (in reserve?) 03/27/45 Adm. Petre Bărbuneau [RRN].

Air Force Headquarters (1940): LG Constantin Celăreanu [RRAF]
A.   **Chief of Staff, Air Force Headquarters** (1940): Col. Gheorghe Jienescu [RRAF] (Under-Secretary of State, Department of Defense for Air and Navy) 09/14/40

Army Groups

First Army Group: /39 LG Dumitru Moțaş (in reserve?) /39 Gen. Constantin Ilasievici [+ Commanding General, Fourth Army] (retired) 06/02/40

Army Group West (/40; disbanded, /40): Gen. Gheorghe Florescu (retired; /41, Mayor of Bucharest) /40 MG Grigore Cornicioiu (retired; /51, arrested; /52, died in prison) /40 disbanded.

Army Group Antonescu (06/41; 08/01/41, disbanded): FM [Retired '40] Ion Victor Antonescu [+ Commander-in-Chief, Armed Forces; + Foreign Minister] (Minister of National Defense) 08/01/41 disbanded.
A.   *Components* - **Army Group Antonescu** (06/41)
    1.   **Third Army**
    2.   **Fourth Army**
    3.   **II (Independent) Army Corps**
    4.   **11th Infantry Division**

Army Group Dumitrescu (03/26/44; 08/24/44, disbanded): Gen. Petre Dumitrescu [+04/21/43, Commanding General, Third Army] (in reserve; /46, suspected of war crimes) 08/24/44 disbanded.
A.   *Components* - **Army Group Dumitrescu** (06/41)
    1.   **Third Army**
    2.   **German Sixth Army**

Armies

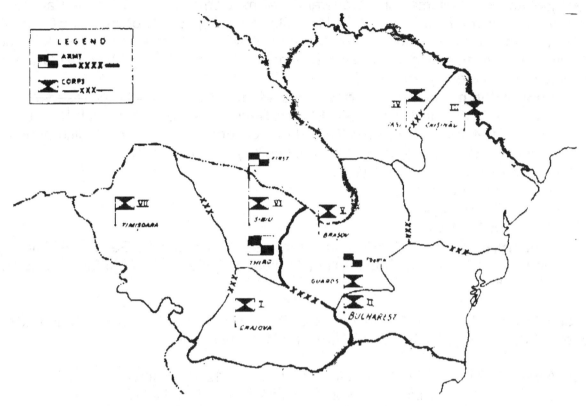

Map of Romania, showing territorial organization.

Bessarabia-Moldavia Inspectorate:
A.   *Components* - **Bessarabia-Moldavia Inspectorate**
   1.   **I Army Corps**
   2.   **V Army Corps**

Dobruja-Walachia Inspectorate:
A.   *Components* - **Bessarabia-Moldavia Inspectorate**
   1.   **III Army Corps**
   2.   **IV Army Corps**

Transylvania Inspectorate:
A.   *Components* - **Bessarabia-Moldavia Inspectorate**
   1.   **VI Army Corps**
   2.   **VII Army Corps**

Central Region Inspectorate:
A.   *Components* - **Bessarabia-Moldavia Inspectorate**
   1.   **II Army Corps**
   2.   **Guards Army Corps**

First Army (HQ: Sibiu): /39 LG Gheorghe Florescu (Commander-in-Chief, Army Group West) 03/04/40 MG Grigore Cornicioiu (Commander-in-Chief, Army Group West) /40 BG Gheorghe Leventi (Commanding General, V Army Corps) /41 MG Dobre Paraschiv (Deputy Commander, First Army) 03/25/41 LG Dumitru I. Popescu (Commanding General, XI Army Corps) 11/09/41 MG Nicolae Macici (relieved and retired; /45, arrested and condemned to life imprisonment as a war criminal; /50, died in prison) 02/13/45 LG Vasile Atanasiu (/48, in reserve) /46

A.   **Deputy Commander, First Army**: 03/25/41 MG Dobre Paraschiv (in reserve?) /41
B.   **Chief of Staff, First Army**: /40 BG Ilie Şteflea (Secretary-General, Ministry of National Defense) /40 unknown? 04/24/42 BG Agricola Filip (Commanding General, 7th Infantry Division) 04/05/44 BG Damian Raşcu (/51, retired).
C.   *Components* - **First Army** (07/43)
      1.   **I Army Corps**
      2.   **VI Army Corps**
      3.   **VII Army Corps**
D.   **Artillery, First Army**: /44 BG Ioan Stănculescu (Commanding General, 9th Infantry Division) 12/31/44 BG Paul Alexiu (Commanding General, 18th Infantry Division) 04/18/45

Second Army (06/20/40; 11/01/40, disbanded): /39 LG Nicolae Ciupercă (Commanding General, Fourth Army) 06/02/40 unknown? 11/01/40 disbanded.

Third Army (06/41, Russia;HQ: Simferopol, Crimea; 12/41, Romania; 11/42, Russia; 12/42, Romania; /43, Russia; 12/43 Romania; 05/44, Russia; 08/44, Romania): 03/25/41 LG Petre Dumitrescu (Commander-in-Chief, Army Group Dumitrescu) 03/21/43 LG Dumitru I. Popescu [acting; + Interior Minister] 04/21/43 Gen. Petre Dumitrescu (in reserve; /46 Suspected of war crimes) 08/29/44
[NOTE: acting Commanding General /43 LG Corneliu Dragalina [+ Commanding General, VI Army Corps] /43; and /44 LG Nicolae Dascalescu [+ Commanding General, II Army Corps] /44**]**

A.   **Chief of Staff, Third Army**: /42 Col. Dumitru Dumitrescu-Polihron (Commanding Officer, #rd Security Division) 03/15/42 BG Iaon Arbore (Under-Secretary of Supply) /43 unknown? 07/16/44 BG Ioan Mihaescu (Chief of Staff, Territorial Command) 12/16/44
B.   **Vice Chief of Staff, Third Army**: /40 Col. Ion Gheorghe (Military Attaché Berlin) /40 unknown? /41 Col. Ioan Mihaescu (Deputy Commander, 1st Frontier Division) /41 Col. Dumitru Dumitrescu-Polihron (Chief of Staff, Third Army) /41 Col. Platon Chirnoagă (Commanding Officer, 7th Artillery Regiment) /42 Col. Constantin Eftimiu (Chief of Signals) 12/42 Col. Platon Chirnoaga (Commanding General, 4th Artillery Brigade) /44
C.   **Operations, Third Army**: /41 Col. Platon Chirnoagă (Vice Chief of Staff, Third Army) /41
D.   *Components* - **Third Army** (on formation)
      1.   **Mountain Corps**
      2.   **10th Infantry Division**
      3.   **19th Infantry Division**

4. **6th Cavalry Brigade**
5. **9th Cavalry Brigade**

E. ***Components* - Third Army** (06/41)
1. **IV Army Corps**
2. **Mountain Corps**
3. **Cavalry Corps**
4. **Third Army Cooperative Command** (Air Force Brigade)

F. ***Components* - Third Army** (06/28/42)
1. **III Army Corps**
2. **VI Army Corps**
3. **VII Army Corps**
4. **Mountain Corps**
5. **Cavalry Corps**
6. **1st Cavalry Division**
7. **7th Cavalry Division**
8. **9th Cavalry Division**
9 **2nd Mountain Division**
10 **3rd Mountain Division**
11 **9th Infantry Division**

G. **Rear Area East**: /42 BG Mircea Dimitriu (Commanding General, 13th Infantry Division) 03/21/43 MG Gheorghe Ionescu-Sinaia (Commanding Genera, Rear Area 1) 10/25/44

Fourth Army (06/41, Russia; HQ: Bucharest /42, Romania; /43, Russia; /43, Romania; 05/44, Russia; 08/44 Romania): /39 LG Iosif Iacobici (in reserve?) /39 Gen. Constantin Ilasievici [+ Commander-in-Chief, First Army Group] (retired) /40 LG Ioan Ilcuş (retired; /50, arrested) 06/02/40 LG Nicolae Ciupercă (relieved/retire; /48, arrested; /50, died in prison) 09/14/41 LG Iosif Iacobici [+ 09/22/41, Chief of the General Staff] (relieved) 11/08/41 MG Constantin Constantinescu-Klaps (relieved & retired; /51, arrested; /54, condemned to 15 years imprisonment; /55, exonerated and released) 02/11/43 LG Constantin Sănătescu (Head of Royal Household) 01/25/44 LG Mihail Racovita (Defense Minister) 08/23/44 LG Ilie Şteflea (arrested; /45, released) 09/04/44 LG Gheorghe Avramescu (resigned) 01/12/45 LG Nicolae Dascalescu (Commanding General, II Army Corps) 02/19/45 LG Gheorghe Avramescu (replaced; /45, arrested by the Soviets as a pro-German) 03/03/45 LG Nicolae Dascalescu (retired; /46, accused of war crimes but acquitted; /51, arrested; /55, released) /45.

A. **Chief of Staff, Fourth Army**: /41 Col. Ioan Stănculescu (Chief, Prisoner-of-War Section, General Staff) /41 BG Nicolae Tataranu (Vice Chief of the General Staff) /41 unknown? /43 BG Ştefan Bardan (Commanding General, 15th Infantry Division) 12/11/43 Col. Ioan Dumitriu (Commandant, Infantry Instruction Center) /44 BG Petre Antonescu (Commanding General, 1st Guards Division) 07/13/44 unknown? /45 BG Nicolae Dragomir (arrested; /46, condemned to 10 years imprisonment; /53, released; /57, arrested) /45.

B. **Vice Chief of Staff, Fourth Army**: /41 LCol. Dumitru Tudosie (Commanding Officer, Unknown? Frontier Sector; /42, Infantry Commander, 5th Infantry Division) /41 unknown? /42 Col. Nicolae Dragomir (Commanding Officer, 8th Field Artillery

Regiment) /43 Col. Enache Juganaru (Chief of Staff, VI Army Corps) /43 unknown? /44 BG Nicolae Dragomir (Chief of Staff, Fourth Army) /45

C.   *Components - Third Army* (on formation)
1.   **II Army Corps**
2.   **III Army Corps**
3.   **IV Army Corps**
4.   **V Army Corps**
5.   **Guards Army Corps**

D.   *Components - Fourth Army* (06/41)
1.   **III Army Corps**
2.   **V Army Corps**
3.   **XI Army Corps**
4.   **Fourth Army Cooperative Command** (Air Force Brigade)

E.   **Operations, Fourth Army**: /41 Col. Constantin Eftimiu (Commanding Officer, Detachment Eftimiu) /41

F.   **Artillery, Fourth Army**: 10/15/44 BG Petre Antonescu (Commanding General, 21st Infantry Division) 12/19/44 BG Gheorghe Cosma (Commanding General, 18th Infantry Division) 05/09/45

Corps

Army Corps

I Army Corps (unknown?; Home Station: Craiova; 01/15/42, in First Army, Romania): /39 MG G. Popescu (in reserve?) /39 LG Gheorghe Argeşanu (retired; /40 arrested & executed in prison) 06/12/40 MG Teodor Ionescu (retired) 03/18/43 vacant 03/20/43 LG Ion Boiţeanu (Director, Higher Military School) 04/05/44 LG Radu Gherghe (Soviet prisoner-of-war;/45, retired) 12/01/44 disbanded.

A. **Artillery Commander, I Army Corps**: /42 Col. Romulus Stănescu (Commanding General, 100th Infantry Division) /43 BG Constantin Rosetti-Balanescu (Artillery Commander, VII Army Corps) /44

B. *Components - I Army Corps*
   1. **2nd Infantry Division**
   2. **3rd Infantry Division**
   3. **11th Infantry Division**
   4. **1st Càlaraşi Cavalry Regiment**
   5. **1st Heavy Artillery Regiment**

C. **At Disposal of I Army Corps**:
   /42 Col. Marin Ceausu (Artillery Commander, IV Army Corps) /43

II Army Corps (unknown?;Home Station: Bucharest; 01/15/42, in Third Army, Soviet Union): /40 MG Vasile Atanasiu (Commanding General, III Army Corps) 03/04/40 unknown? 01/01/41 MG Nicolae Macici (Commanding General, First Army) 11/09/41 MG Nicolae Dascalescu [+ /44, acting Commanding General, Third Army] (Commanding General, Fourth Army) 01/12/45 BG Edgar Rădulescu (acting; Commanding General, 11th Infantry Division) 02/19/45 LG Nicolae Dascalescu (Commanding General, Fourth Army) 03/03/45 BG Edgar Rădulescu [acting/+ Commanding General, 11th Infantry Division] 03/08/45 MG Costin Ionaşcu.
[NOTE: acting Commanding General, II Army Corps 11/14/44 MG Constantin Trestioreanu (arrested; /45, condemned to death as a war criminal but sentence communicated to life imprisonment; /56, released)]

A. **Deputy Commander, II Army Corps**: /44 MG Ioan Arhip (in reserve) /45

B. *Components - II Army Corps*
   1. **9th Infantry Division**
   2. **10th Infantry Division**
   3. **Guards Division**
   4. **4th Càlaraşi Cavalry Regiment**
   5. **2nd Heavy Artillery Regiment**

C. Components - 06/22/41
   1. **9th Infantry Division**
   2. **10th Infantry Division**
   3. **7th Cavalry Brigade**

D. **Artillery, II Army Corps**: /42 Col. Edgar Rădulescu (Commanding General, 11th

Infantry Division) 04/12/43 Col. Ioan Stănculescu (Artillery Commander, First Army) /44 BG Atanasie Petculescu (/45, Director, Geographical Military Institute; /46, in reserve, /47, retired).

III Army Corps (unknown?;Home Station: Chişinău [Chisinau]; 01/15/42, in Fourth Army, Soviet Union): /39 MG Grigore Cornicioiu (Commanding General, First Army) 03/04/40 MG Vasile Atanasiu (Inspector-General of Artillery) 03/21/43 MG Hugo Schwab (Commanding General, Mountain Corps) 10/06/43 LG Gheorghe Avramescu (Commanding General, VI Army Corps) 02/22/44 LG Emanoil Leoveanu (Commanding General, VI Army Corps) 10/13/44

A.   **Deputy Commander, III Army Corps**: 08/02/42 MG Cosma Marin Popescu (Commanding General, IV Army Corps) 01/24/44
B.   *Components - III Army Corps*
    1.   **12ᵗʰ Infantry Division**
    2.   **15ᵗʰ Infantry Division**
    3.   **21ˢᵗ Infantry Division**
    4.   **8ᵗʰ Càlaraşi Cavalry Regiment**
    5.   **3ʳᵈ Heavy Artillery Regiment**
C.   **Components** - 06/22/41
    1.   **Guards Infantry Division**
    2.   **15ᵗʰ Infantry Division**
    3.   **35ᵗʰ Reserve Infantry Division**
    4.   **7ᵗʰ Field Artillery Regiment**
    5.   **2ⁿᵈ Light Armored Regiment**
D.   **Components** - 06/28/42
    1.   **1ˢᵗ Security Division**
    2.   **2ⁿᵈ Security Division**
    3.   **3ʳᵈ Security Division**
    4.   **1ˢᵗ Odessa Fortress Division**

IV Army Corps (unknown?;Home Station: Iaşi [Iasi]; 01/15/42, in Fourth Army, Soviet Union): /41 MG Dumitru Coroama (/44, arrested; /64, released) 02/01/41 MG Constantin Sănătescu (Commanding General, Fourth Army) 02/10/43 vacant 03/20/43 MG Gheorghe Rozin (Commanding General, Motomechanized Corps) 01/24/44 MG Cosma Marin Popescu (in reserve; /44 retired) 04/05/44 MG Nicolae Scariat Stoenescu 09/13/44 BG Dumitru Tudosie [acting/+ Commanding General, 2ⁿᵈ Infantry Division] 09/30/44 MG Nicolae Scariat Stoenescu (in reserve, /45, retired; /45, arrested; /46, condemned to 10 years imprisonment; /52, condemned to a further 10 years imprisonment; /59, died in prison) 12/04/44 LG Ion Boiţeanu (in reserve?) 04/08/45 MG Agricola Filip (Commanding General, VII Army Corps; /47, in reserve then retired; /48 arrested; /49 condemned to 10 years imprisonment for war crimes; /52, condemned to 25 years imprisonment for crimes against humanity; /55, released) /46.

A.   *Components - IV Army Corps*
    1.   **7ᵗʰ Infantry Division**
    2.   **8ᵗʰ Infantry Division**
    3.   **14ᵗʰ Infantry Division**

4. **12th Càlaraşi Cavalry Regiment**
5. **4th Heavy Artillery Regiment**
B. **Components** - 06/22/41
1. **6th Infantry Division**
2. **7th Infantry Division**
3. **4th Artillery Regiment**
C. **Artillery, IV Army Corps**: /41 Col. Ioan A. I. Georgescu (acting Commanding Officer, 2nd Infantry Division or Artillery Commander, VI Army Corps) /42 Col. Grigore Nicolau (Commanding General, 2nd Guards Division) 04/24/42 Col. Mihail Voicu (Commanding General, 14th Infantry Division) 03/21/43 Col. Marin Ceausu (Artillery Commander, V Army Corps) /44

V Army Corps (unknown?;Home Station: Braşov [Brasov]; 01/15/42, in First Army, Soviet Union): /39 MG Ilie Partenie (in reserve?) 03/25/41 LG Gheorghe Leventi (retired) 07/08/41 MG Aurelian Son (retired) 03/18/43 vacant 03/20/43 LG Constantin Niculescu (in reserve; /44, Head, Royal Military Household) 09/18/44 disbanded.
A. **Deputy Commander, V Army Corps**: 01/11/42 BG Iosif Teodorescu (Commanding General, Capital Military Command) 01/25/44
B. *Components - V Army Corps*
1. **5th Infantry Division**
2. **6th Infantry Division**
3. **13th Infantry Division**
4. **6th Càlaraşi Cavalry Regiment**
5. **5th Heavy Artillery Regiment**
C. **Components** - 06/22/41
1. **1st Frontier Guards (Graniceri) Division**
2. **21st Infantry Division**
D. **Artillery, V Army Corps**: 04/28/44 BG Atanasie Petculescu (Artillery Commander, II Army Corps) /44 Col. Marin Ceausu (Commanding General, 21st Infantry Division) 02/17/45 BG Constantin Rosetti-Balanescu (/47, retired).
F. **Reserves, V Army Corps**: /41 Col. Romulus Dimitriu (Deputy Commander, 21st Infantry Division) /41

VI Army Corps (unknown?;Home Station: Sibiu; 01/15/42, in Soviet Union): 01/01/40 LG Corneliu Dragalina [+ /43, acting Commanding General, Third Army] (Governor-General, Bucovina) 03/21/43 LG Flores Mitrănescu (Commanding General, VII Army Corps) 09/16/43 LG Emanoil Leoveanu (Commanding General, III Army Corps) 02/23/44 LG Gheorghia Avramescu (Commanding General, Fourth Army) 08/24/44 MG Nicolae Tataranu (in reserve; /45, retired; arrested; /53, died in prison) 09/28/44 BG Agricola Filip (acting) [+ Commanding General, 7th Infantry Division] 10/13/44 LG Emanoil Leoveanu (retired; /51, arrested; /56, condemned to 10 years imprisonment; /57, sentence changed to 15 years imprisonment; /59, died in prison) 10/29/44 MG Gheorghe R. Gheorghiu 01/04/45 MG Petre Camenita [acting] (Commanding General, 18th Infantry Division) 01/26/45 MG Gheorghe R. Gheorghiu (retired; /53, arrested) 03/31/45 MG Gheorghe Stavrescu (?) 05/12/45
A. **Deputy Commander, VI Army Corps**: /44 MG Radu Bāldescu (Commanding

General, V Territorial Corps Area) /45
B.   **Chief of Staff, VI Army Corps**: /41 Col. Ioan Dumitriu (Infantry Commander, 4th Infantry Division) /42 Col. Damian Raşcu (Commanding General, 20th Infantry Brigade) /43 Col. Enache Juganaru (Commanding Officer, 5th Infantry Brigade) /44
C.   *Components - VI Army Corps*
   1.   **16th Infantry Division**
   2.   **17th Infantry Division**
   3.   **18th Infantry Division**
   4.   **20th Infantry Division**
   5.   **7th Càlaraşi Cavalry Regiment**
   6.   **6th Heavy Artillery Regiment**
D.   **Components** - 06/28/42
   1.   **2nd Infantry Division**
   2.   **4th Infantry Division**
   4.   **Mobile Infantry Regiment**
E.   **Artillery, VI Army Corps**: /42 Col. Ioan A. I. Georgescu (Commanding General, 15th Infantry Division) 03/20/43 BG Ioan D. Popescu (Commanding General, 7th Infantry Training Division) 09/29/44

VII Army Corps (unknown?;Home Station: Timişoara [Timisoara]; 01/15/42, in First Army, Romania): /37 MG Cristea Vasilescu (?   ) /39 LG Ioan Ilcuş (Minister of National Defense) /39 unknown? /40 MG Pion [Pavel Ion] Georgescu (/46, arrested) 03/25/41 MG Florea Mitrănescu (Commanding General, VI Army Corps) 03/21/43 MG Emanoil Leoveanu (Commanding General, VI Army Corps) 09/15/43 LG Florea Mitrănescu (in reserve?) 02/21/44 vacant 04/01/44 MG Gheorghe Potopeanu (Economy Minister) 08/16/44 MG Hugo Schwab (committed suicide) 09/18/44 BG Mihail Lăcătuşcu (acting) 09/21/44 LG Nicolae Şova (in reserve; /45, retired; /46, arrested and condemned to 10 years imprisonment; /56, released) 02/08/45 BG Mihail Lăcătuşcu (acting) 02/17/45 LG [Retired '41] Eugeniu Vartejanu (retired) 02/17/45 unknown? 04/09/45 MG Radu Niculescu-Cociu (Commanding General, V Territorial Corps Area; /47, Commanding General, 1st Military Region; /48, Retired).
A.   **Chief of Staff, VII Army Corps**: /40 Col. Mihail Camarasu (Commanding General, 103rd Mountain Command) /43 unknown? /44 BG Vasile Chiţu (Commanding General, 1st Infantry Training Division) 08/24/44
B.   *Components - VII Army Corps*
   1.   **1st Infantry Division**
   2.   **4th Infantry Division**
   3.   **19th Infantry Division**
   4.   **10th Càlaraşi Cavalry Regiment**
   5.   **7th Heavy Artillery Regiment**
C.   **Components** - 06/28/42
   1.   **8th Cavalry Division**
   2.   **10th Infantry Division**
   3.   **19th Infantry Division**
D.   **Artillery, VII Army Corps**: /43 Col. Alexandru Nasta (in reserve; /43, Deputy Commander, Capital Military Command) /43 Col. Gheorghe Cosma (Soviet

prisoner-of-war) /44 BG Constantin Rosetti-Balanescu (acting Commanding General, 19th Infantry Division) 02/07/45 BG Gheorghe Mosiu (Commanding General, 19th Infantry Division) 03/03/45

VIII Army Corps (pre-war; 11/01/40, disbanded): unknown? 11/01/40 disbanded.

X Army Corps (pre-war; 07/18/41, disbanded): /39 MG Constantin Constantinescu-Klaps (Commanding General, XI Army Corps) 07/18/41 disbanded.

XI Army Corps: /40 MG Aurelian Son (Commanding General, V Army Corps) 07/08/41 MG Constantin Constantinescu-Klaps (Commanding General, Fourth Army) 11/09/41 LG Dumitru I. Popescu (Interior Minister) 12/15/41 disbanded.
A.   **Components** - 06/22/41
    1.   **1st Fortress Brigade**
    2.   **2nd Fortress Brigade**

Guard Army Corps (pre-war; 11/01/40, disbanded): unknown? 11/01/40 disbanded.

Motomechanized Corps (11/01/43): LG Mihail Racovita (Commanding General, Fourth Army) 01/24/44 LG Gheorghe Rozin (in reserve; /45, retired; /48, arrested; /49, condemned to 20 years imprisonment; /61, died in prison) 10/14/44 disbanded.
A.   **Chief of Staff, Mechanized Troops Command**: /43 Col. Vladimir Constantinescu (Commanding Officer, 1st Cavalry Division) 07/07/44
B.   *Components - Mechanized Corps* (08/31/44)
    1.   **Niculescu Armored Detachment**
    2.   **8th (Motorized) Cavalry Division**
    3.   **1st Cavalry Division** (horse mounted)
    4.   **9th Infantry Division**

Mountain Corps (unknown?;Home Station: Bucharest; 01/15/42, in Soviet Union): **Mountain Corps (#1)** 06/03/41 MG Gheorghe Avramescu (Commanding General, III Army Corps) 10/06/43 MG Hugo Schwab (Commanding General, VII Army Corps) 08/15/44 MG Ioan Dumitrache (Deputy Commander, Mountain Corps) 10/15/44 disbanded; reformed **Mountain Corps (#2)** 03/09/45 MG Leonard Mociulschi (/47, retired; /48, arrested; /55, released).
[NOTE: also listed /43 MG Nicolae Tataranu (Commanding General, VI Army Corps) 08/24/44**]**
A.   **Deputy Commander, Mountain Corps**: 10/15/44 MG Ioan Dumitrache (in reserve; /49, arrested and suspected of war crimes) /45 dissolved.
B.   **Components** - 06/22/41
    1.   **1st Mountain Brigade**
    2.   **2nd Mountain Brigade**
    3.   **4th Mountain Brigade**
C.   *Components - Mountain Corps*
    1.   **1st Mountain Division**
    2.   **2nd Mountain Division**

3. **3rd Mountain Division**
4. **4th Mountain Division**
D. **Components** - 06/28/42
1. **1st Mountain Division**
2. **18th Infantry Division**
E. **Artillery, Mountain Corps**: /41 BG Mihail Lăcătuşcu (Deputy Director, Higher Artillery Department) /42 unknown? /44 BG Gheorghe Cosma (Fourth Army) 12/19/44 dissolved.

Cavalry Corps (unknown?; 01/15/42, in Third Army, Soviet Union): 01/10/41 MG Mihail Racovita (in reserve; 03/20/43, Commanding General, Capital Military Command) 03/11/42 BG Marin Manafu (acting/Commanding General, 9th Infantry Division) 03/26/42 BG Traian Cocorascu (retired) 01/02/43 MG Gheorghe Cialâk (arrested; /45, retired; /46, acquitted and released; /51, arrested and charges with crimes against humanity; /55, released) 10/24/44 BG Alexandru Saidac (acting/Deputy Commander, IV Territorial Corps Area) 10/31/44 disbanded.
A. **Chief of Staff, Cavalry Corps**: /41 Col. Gheorghe I. Georgescu (03/11/42, Commanding General, 1st Cavalry Division) /41 Col. Ioan Eftimiu (Commandant, Cavalry Instruction Center) /43
B. *Components* - Cavalry Corps
1. **1st Cavalry Division**
2. **2nd Cavalry Division**
3. **3rd Cavalry Division**
C. **Components** - 06/22/41
1. **5th Cavalry Brigade**
2. **8th Cavalry Brigade**
D. **Components** - 06/28/42
1. **5th Cavalry Brigade**
2. **6th Cavalry Brigade**

Frontier Guards Corps: /37 MG Grigore Cornicioiu (Commanding General, III Army Corps) /39 MG Dumitru I. Popescu (Commanding General, Capital Military Command) /40 MG Teodor Şerb (in reserve?) 08/01/40 MG Ion Negulescu (War Minister) 12/16/44 LG Gheorghe Ionescu-Sinaia (Commanding General, II Territorial Corps Area) /45 BG Mihail Stănescu.

Territorial Corps

Capital Military District (Comandamentul Militar al Capitalei [CMC]): /40 MG Dumitru I. Popescu (03/25/41, Commanding General, First Army) /40 MG Dumitru Coroama (Commanding General, IV Army Corps) /41 LG Constantin Niculescu (Commanding General, V Army Corps) 03/20/43 LG Mihail Racovita (Commanding General, Motomechanized Corps) 01/25/44 LG Iosif Teodorescu (in reserve; /45, Inspector of Infantry; /46, in reserve; /47, retired) /45 MG Ioan Mihaescu (/47, in reserve; /50, condemned to 20 years imprisonment in absentia; /56, arrested and sentence confirmed; /57, died in prison).

A.   **Deputy Commander, Capital Military District**: /43 BG Alexandru Nasta (acting Commanding General, 4th Infantry Division) 01/44 MG Constantin S. Constantin (in reserve; /45, retired; /46, arrested; /48, Condemned to 10 years imprisonment) /44 BG Gheorghe B. Georgescu (/45, Commanding General, VII Territorial Corps Area) 11/28/44 BG Dumitru Dumitrescu-Polihron (/46, in reserve; /47, retired) /45 BG Vasile Mainescu (/46, in reserve; /47, retired; /50, arrested; /53, condemned to 15 years imprisonment as a war criminal; /53, died in prison).

B.   **Chief of Staff, Capital Military District**: Col. Ioan Dimulescu (Artillery Commander, 19th Infantry Division) 12/42 Col. Dumitru Dămăceanu (Under-Secretary of State, Ministry of Interior) /44

Governor-General, Bessarabia:

/41 BG Petre Vasilescu (Commanding General, 2nd Guards Division) 11/23/43
/41 MG Constantin Voiculescu (Commanding General, 1st Guards Division) 02/19/43

/43 MG Olimpiu Stavrat (Commanding General, Rear Area Command) 08/21/44

Governor-General, Bucovina (region of the Ukraine which was taken under Romanian control at the beginning of World War II): /41 BG Corneliu Calotescu (Commanding General, 3rd Infantry Division) 03/21/43 LG Corneliu Dragalina (in reserve; /44, Inspector of Motorized Troops) /44

A.   **Deputy Governor-General, Bucovina**: /41 BG Corneliu Calotescu (Governor-General, Bucovina) /41

Governor-General, Transnistria (Soviet Union): /44 MG Gheorghe Potopeanu (Commanding General, VII Army Corps) 04/01/44

I Territorial Corps Area: 08/02/42 MG Olimpiu Stavrat (Governor-General, Bessarabia) /43 MG Marin Manafu (Commanding General, I Territorial Army Corps) /44 vacant 08/23/44 MG Marin Manafu (Commanding General, V Territorial Corps Area) 09/18/44

II Territorial Corps Area: /42 BG Emanoil Leoveanu (Commanding General, VII Army Corps) 02/21/43 MG Nicolae Palangeanu (in reserve?) 06/43 MG Gheorghe Potopeanu (Governor-General of Transnistrien) 08/23/44 MG Nicolae Patageanu (?) 09/18/44 unknown? 03/03/45 MG Mihail Lăcătuşcu (in reserve; /45, Commanding General, Mountain

Corps) /45 LG Gheorghe Ionescu-Sinaia.

III Territorial Corps Area: /43 BG Radu Fâlfănescu (retired; /52, arrested) 08/23/44 MG Constantin Voiculescu (arrested; /45, retired; /46, condemned to life imprisonment as a war criminal; /55, died in prison) 08/31/44

IV Territorial Corps Area: 01/11/42 MG Hugo Schwab (Commanding General, III Army Corps) 03/21/43 MG Gheorghe Manoliu (/45, retired; /49, condemned to 45 years imprisonment as a war criminal in absentia; /53, arrested; /54, acquitted and released).
A.   **Deputy Commander, IV Territorial Corps Area**: /44 BG Alexandru Saidac (Deputy Commander, VII Territorial Corps Area) /44 BG Simion Coman (/46, in reserve; /47, retired) /45
B.   **Chief of Staff, IV Territorial Corps Area**: /41 Col. Sava Caracas (Infantry Commander, 10th Infantry Division) /41 Col. Ilie Crețulescu (Commanding General, 9th Infantry Brigade) /42

V Territorial Corps Area: 08/23/44 MG Constantin Văşiliu-Rascanu (in reserve?; /45, Minister of Minister of National Defense; /48, retired) 08/31/44 unknown? 09/18/44 MG Marin Manafu.
A.   **Chief of Staff, V Territorial Corps Area**: /42 Col. Ilie Antonescu (Deputy Commander, 5th Cavalry Division) /43 unknown? /45 BG Ioan Mihaescu (Commanding General, Capital Military Command)

VI Territorial Corps Area: 08/02/42 BG Marin Manafu (Commanding General, I Territorial Corps Area) /43 MG Gheorghe Stavrescu (/45, Commanding General, Fourth Army; /45, Inspector of Artillery; /46, in reserve; /47, retired; /47, arrested; /48, condemned to life imprisonment as a war criminal; /51, died in prison).
A.   **Chief of Staff, VI Territorial Corps Area**: /41 Col. Stefan Balaban (Infantry Commander, 1st Fortress Division) /42 Col. Constantin Visarion (Inspector of Examination, VI Army Corps; /44, Inspectorate of Industrial Mobilization) /43

VII Territorial Corps Area: 08/02/42 MG Gheorghe Cialâk (Commanding General, Cavalry Corps) 01/02/43 unknown? 03/21/43 MG Carol Schmidt (in reserve; 09/02/44, Director, Department of Higher Military education) /44 MG Vintila Davidescu (in reserve; /45, retired) /44 unknown? /45 MG Gheorghe B. Georgescu (/46, retired).
A.   **Deputy Commander, VII Territorial Corps Area**: /44 BG Alexandru Saidac (/47, retired; /51, arrested).
B.   **Chief of Staff, VII Territorial Corps Area**: /41 Col. Vasile Chiţu (Chief of Staff, VII Army Corps) /44

Miscellaneous Corps Commands

Oil Field Military Zone: /40 Col. Vintila Davidescu [+ Commanding Officer, 2nd Mixed Guard Brigade] (Commanding General, 31st Reserve Infantry Division) 01/11/41 Col. Corneliu Carp (Deputy Commandant of Odessa) /41
A.   **Detachment 18, Oil Fields Zone**: /43 Col. Grigore Mosteoru (Commanding General, 19th Infantry Brigade) /44

Anti-Aircraft Defense Command: /44 MG Gheorghe D. Marinescu (/46, in reserve; /47, retired; /50, arrested and condemned to 25 years imprisonment).
A.   **Deputy Commander, Anti-Aircraft Defense Command**: /39 Col. Gheorghe D. Marinescu (Commanding Officer, 1st Anti-Aircraft Echelon) /41 unknown? /41 BG Gheorghe D. Marinescu (Commanding General, Stationary Defense) /43
B.   **Chief of Staff, Anti-Aircraft Defense Command**: /41 Col. Dumitru Drajna (Commanding General, 14th Artillery Brigade) /43

Stationary Command: /43 MG Gheorghe D. Marinescu (Commanding General, Anti-Aircraft Artillery) /44

Rear Area East: /42 BG Mircea Dimitriu (Commanding General, 13th Infantry Division) 03/21/43 MG Gheorghe Ionescu-Sinaia (Commanding General, Rear Area 1) 10/25/44
A.   **Chief of Staff, Rear Area East**: /42 Col. Gheorghe Mosiu (Commanding Officer, 3rd Artillery Brigade) /43

General Rear Area Command (Comandamentul general al etapelor) (08/21/44): MG Olimpiu Stavrat (/47, retired; /48, arrested; /49, condemned to life imprisonment as a war criminal; /55, released).
A.   **Chief of Staff, Rear Area Command** (08/21/44): Col. Gheorghe Mosiu (Artillery Commander, VII Army Corps) /45

Rear Area 1 (Comandamentul etapelor nr. 1) (10/25/44): MG Gheorghe Ionescu-Sinaia (Deputy Commander-in-Chief, Territorial Command) 12/06/44 BG Sava Caracas (in reserve?) 03/16/45 Col. Ion Nicolau 04/02/45 MG Constantin Cernatescu (in reserve?) 05/02/45

Rear Area 2 (Comandamentul etapelor nr. 2) (10/10/44): MG Atanasie Trincu (in reserve?; /47, retired) 10/21/44 MG Dumitru Tudosie (retired; /48, condemned to 20 years imprisonment as a war criminal but sentence communicated to 10 years imprisonment; /55, released; /66, rehabilitated).

Special Reparation Corps: 12/02/43 BG Tudorance Ciurea (retired) /44

Transylvania Army Detachment (/44):
A.   *Components* - Transylvania Army Detachment
       1.   **Anti-Aircraft Brigade** (/44)

Royal Romanian Air Corps

Air Corps (Corpul Aerian) (1942)

I Air Corps (Corpul I Aerian) (06/43?): MG Elimian Ionescu [RRAF]
A.   *Components* (06/43)
    1.   **1st Fighter Flotilla**
        a.   **7th Fighter Group**
            i.   **56th Fighter Squadron**
            ii.   **57th Fighter Squadron**
            iii.   **58th Fighter Squadron**
        b.   **9th Fighter Group**
            i.   **43rd Fighter Squadron**
            ii.   **47th Fighter Squadron**
            iii.   **48th Fighter Squadron**
        c.   **8th Assault Group**
            i.   **41st Assault Squadron**
            ii.   **42nd Assault Squadron**
            iii.   **60th Assault Squadron**
    2.   **3rd Bomber Flotilla**
        a.   **3rd Dive Bomber Group**
            i.   **73rd Bomber Squadron**
            ii.   **81st Bomber Squadron**
            iii.   **85th Bomber Squadron**
        b.   **5th Bomber Group**
            i.   **77th Bomber Squadron**
            ii.   **78th Bomber Squadron**
            iii.   **80th Bomber Squadron**
        c.   **6th Bomber Group**
            i.   **74th Bomber Squadron**
            ii.   **86th Bomber Squadron**
            iii.   **87th Bomber Squadron**
    3.   **2nd Long Range Recon Squadron**
    4.   **105th Transport Squadron**
    5.   **115th Liaison Squadron**
    6.   **116th Liaison Squadron**

II Air Corps (Corpul II Aerian) (04/01/44; 07/44 redesignated **III Air Corps**):
A.   *Components* (04/01/44)
    1.   **2nd Fighter Flotilla**
        a.   **1st Fighter Group**
            i.   **43rd Fighter Squadron**
            ii.   **66th Fighter Squadron**
            iii.   **67th Fighter Squadron**
        b.   **45th Fighter Squadron**

2. **2nd Bomber Flotilla**
   a. **1st Bomber Group**
      i. **71st Bomber Squadron**
      ii. **72nd Bomber Squadron**
   b. **2nd Bomber Group**
      i. **82nd Bomber Squadron**
      ii. **83rd Bomber Squadron**
   c. **4th Bomber Group**
      i. **76th Bomber Squadron**
      ii. **78th Bomber Squadron**
   d. **7th Bomber Group**
      i. **17th Light Bomber Squadron**
      ii. **18th Light Bomber Squadron**
3. **11th Observation Squadron**
4. **12th Observation Squadron**
5. **13th Observation Squadron**
6. **14th Observation Squadron**
7. **101st Seaplane Squadron**
8. **102nd Seaplane Squadron**
9. **1st Squadron**
10. **109th Squadron**
11. **114th Liaison Squadron**

III Air Corps (Corpul III Aerian) (07/44, from **II Air Corps**)

2nd Air Region (Regiunii II-A Aeriene)

3rd Air Region (Regiunii III-A Aeriene)

Royal Romanian Naval Commands
[Corps Status]

Sea Naval Force (Black Sea Naval Forces) (Naval Command): RA Horia Marcellariu [RRN]

A. *Components*
  1. **Destroyer Squadron** (4 ships)
  2. **Gunboat Section** (3 ships)
  3. **Corvette Section** (3 ships)
  4. **Mine-laying Section** (5 ships)
  5. **Submarine** (1 sub) **and Torpedo Boats Group** (3 ships)

Divisions

Infantry Divisions

Map of Romania, showing the home stations of divisions.

1st Guards Division (line division; pre-war as **Royal Guards Division**; Home Station: Bucharest; II Corps Area; 07/41, Eastern Front; 10/41, Romania; 03/44, Eastern Front; 08/44, disbanded?): /39 BG Dumitru Coroama (Commanding General, Capital Military Command) 09/14/40 BG Paul Teodorescu (retired) /40 unknown? 06/22/41 MG Nicolae Şova (Under-Secretary of State for the Navy) 02/19/43 MG Constantin Voiculescu (acting; 10/06/43, Commanding General, 1st Mountain Division) 03/21/43 MG Constantin Popescu (in reserve?) 10/05/43 Col. Radu Korne [+ 8th Cavalry Division] 03/18/44 MG Radu Niculescu-Cociu (Inspector in Inspectorate-General of Pre-Military Preparation) 07/13/44 BG Petre Antonescu (Commander, Artillery, Fourth Army) 1015/44 BG Ioan Dumitriu 03/21/45 BG Gheorghe Gh. Marinescu (/45, after World War II, Commanding General, 1st Mountain Division; /46, in reserve; /50, arrested and condemned to 15 years imprisonment; /64, released) 04/15/45 BG Ion Dumitru.

A. **Deputy Commander, 1st Guards Division**: /41 Col. Octavian Georgescu (Commanding General, 10th Infantry Division) 11/08/41 Col. Ioan Beldiceanu (Deputy Commander, 1st Armored Division) /42

B. *Components* - **Royal Guard Division**
    1. **Guards Infantry Brigade**
    2. **Royal Horse Guard Regiment**

3. **Guards Artillery Brigade**
C. *Components - 1st Guard Division*
   1. **6th Guard Infantry Regiment**
   2. **2nd Guard Rifle Regiment**
   3. **9th Guard Rifle Regiment**
   4. **1st Guard Artillery Regiment**
   5. **2nd Guard Artillery Regiment**
D. **Infantry, 1st Guards Division**: /42 Col. Petre Camenita (Secretary-General to Under-Secretary of State for Land Forces) /42 unknown? /43 Col. Stefan Opriş (acting Commanding General, Guards Training Division) 08/23/44 unknown? /44 BG Stefan Opriş (/46, in reserve; /47, retired).
E. **Artillery, 1st Guards Division**: /42 Col. Alexandru Nasta (Deputy Commander, 1st Frontier Division) /42

2nd Guards Division (04/24/42, from **2nd Mixed Guard Brigade**; 03/20/43, disbanded; saw no combat): **2nd Mixed Guard Brigade** /40 Col. Vintila Davidescu [+ Commanding Officer, Oil Field Military Zone] (Commanding General, 31st Reserve Infantry Division) 01/11/41 BG Gheorghe Ionescu-Sinaia (Commanding General, 13th Infantry Division) 04/24/42 redesignated **2nd Guards Division** 04/24/42 BG Grigore Nicolau (Commanding General, 5th Infantry Division) 11/23/43 BG Petre Vasilescu (?) 03/20/43 disbanded.
A. *Components - 2nd Guard Division*
   1. **2nd Frontier Guard Regiment:**
   2. **3rd Frontier Guard Regiment**
   3. **4th Frontier Guard Regiment**
   4. **3rd Guard Artillery Regiment**
   5. **4th Guard Artillery Regiment**

1st Infantry Division (line division; pre-war; Home Station: Timişoara [Timisoara], VII Corps Area; 09/41, Eastern Front; 12/41, Romania; 03/42, Eastern Front; 02/43, Romania; 03/44, Eastern Front; 09/02/44, disbanded): 01/01/40 BG Emanoil Bârzotescu (retired; /45, recalled; /45, in reserve; /45 Commanding General, VI Territorial Corps Area) 05/10/42 BG Constantin Panaitiu (Commanding General, 9th Infantry Division) 08/01/42 BG Ioan Mihaescu (Chief of Staff, Inspectorate-General of the Army) 03/21/43 BG Alexandru Saidac (Soviet prisoner-of-war; 10/19/44, Commanding General, 1st Infantry Training Division) 09/02/44 disbanded.
A. **Deputy Commander, 1st Infantry Division**: /41 Col. Nicolae T. Petrescu (Commanding Officer, 1st Fortification Brigade) /41
B. **Infantry, 1st Infantry Division**: /42 Col. Alexandru Saidac (Commanding General, 1st Infantry Division) 03/21/43
C. **Artillery, 1st Infantry Division**: /42 Col. Ioan Mihaescu (Commanding General, 1st Infantry Division) 08/01/42
D. *Components - 1st Infantry Division*
   1. **5th Infantry Regiment**: /41 Col. Vasile Pascu (Prefect of Viasca) /41
   2. **17th Infantry Regiment**
   3. **55th Infantry Regiment**
   4. **57th Infantry Regiment**

5. **85th Infantry Regiment**: /40 Col. Emil Paraschivescu (retired; 01/03/45, Commanding General, 18th Infantry Brigade) /42
6. **93rd Infantry Regiment**
7. **1st Light Artillery Regiment**
8. **38th Howitzer Artillery Regiment**

2nd Infantry Division (line division; pre-war; Home Station: Craiova, I Corps Area; 09/41, Eastern Front; 12/41, Romania; 03/42, Eastern Front; 02/43, Romania; 03/44, Eastern Front; 08/44, disbanded and its troops were absorbed into the **14th Infantry Division**): /38 MG Ioan Popovici (in reserve; /41, retired) 11/15/41 BG Nicolae Ghineraru (Commanding General, Mobile Group, 1st Etape) 06/28/42 BG Dumitru Tudosie [09/13/44 to 09/30/44, acting Commanding General, IV Army Corps] (Commanding General, 2nd Rear Area) 10/18/44 BG Romulus Stănescu (wounded and in hospital; /45, Deputy Commander, VI Territorial Corps Area) 10/24/44 BG Mihail Voicu (/46, in reserve; /47, retired; /57, arrested and condemned to life imprisonment; /61, died in prison).
[**NOTE**: one source lists /42 Col. Ioan A. I. Georgescu (acting/Artillery Commander, VI Army Corps) /42]
A. **Infantry, 2nd Infantry Division**: /42 BG Constantin Iordachescu (Commanding General, 102nd Mountain Command) /44
B. **Artillery, 2nd Infantry Division**: /42 Col. Marin Ceausu (at disposal for I Army Corps) /42
C. *Components - 2nd Infantry Division*
    1. **1st Dorobanti Infantry Regiment**: /41 Col. Constantine Badescu (in reserve, /43, retired, /44 Commanding General, 11th Infantry Brigade) /44
    2. **26th Dorobanti Infantry Regiment**: /40 Col. Damian Raşcu (Chief of Staff, VI Army Corps) /42
    3. **31st Infantry Regiment**
    4. **4th Light Artillery Regiment**
    5. **14th Howitzer Artillery Regiment**: /39 Col. Marin Ceausu (Artillery Commander, 2nd Infantry Division) /42

3rd Infantry Division (line division; pre-war; Home Station: Piteşti [Pitesti], I Corps Area; 07/41, Eastern Front; 10/41, Romania; 03/44, Eastern Front; 08/24/44 redesignated **3rd Training Infantry Division**; 10/44, absorbed the remnants of the **13th Infantry Division**): **3rd Infantry Division (#1)** /39 BG Teodor Ionescu (Commanding General, I Army Corps) 06/12/40 unknown? 02/20/41 BG Ilie Şteflea (Chief of the General Staff) 01/21/42 BG Ioan Arhip (Vice Chief of the General Staff) 02/10/42 MG Ion Boiţeanu (Commanding General, I Army Corps) 03/21/43 MG Corneliu Calotescu (in reserve; /45, retired) 08/24/44 BG Ioan Tanasescu [+ Commanding General, 3rd Infantry Training Division] (04/07/45, Commanding General, 3rd Infantry Division) 09/06/44 BG Ioan Dumitriu [+ Commanding General, 3rd Infantry Training Division] [+ 10/15/44, Commanding General, 1st Guards Division] 11/03/44 BG Ioan D. Popescu (/48, retired) 04/07/45 BG Ioan Tanasescu.
A. **Deputy Commander, 3rd Infantry Division**: /41 Col. Ioan Arhip (Commanding General, 3rd Infantry Division) 01/21/42
B. *Components - 3rd Infantry Division*
    1. **4th Infantry Regiment**

2.   **11ᵗʰ Infantry Regiment** (transferred to 21ˢᵗ Infantry Division)
3.   **30ᵗʰ Infantry Regiment**
4.   **1ˢᵗ Rifle Regiment**
4.   **6ᵗʰ Light Artillery Regiment**: /41 Col. Gheorghe Cosma (Chief of Staff, Higher Technical Department) /41
5.   **15ᵗʰ Howitzer Artillery Regiment**

4ᵗʰ Infantry Division (line division; pre-war; Home Station: Bucharest, VII Corps Area; 03/42, Eastern Front; 12/42, temporary merged with **18ᵗʰ Infantry Division**; 02/43, Romania; 03/44, Eastern Front; 11/10/44, disbanded and its troops were absorbed into the **10ᵗʰ Infantry Division**): 02/20/41 MG Gheorghe Cialâk (Commanding General, VII Territorial Corps Area) 08/02/42 BG Barbu Alinescu (in reserve) 11/2842 Col. Ioan Dumitriu (Chief of Staff, Fourth Army) /43 BG Tudorance Ciurea [acting; 04/17/43, Commanding General, 4ᵗʰ Mountain Division] 04/30/43 BG Ioan Mihaescu (Chief of Staff, Third Army) 07/16/44 BG Dumitru Petrescu [+ 09/09/44, Commanding General, 4ᵗʰ Infantry Training Division] (in reserve?) 10/01/44 BG Platon Chirnoaga (German prisoner-of-war; /45, Minister of Defense, Government in Exile, Germany) 10/21/44 BG Mihail Voicu [+ 10/24/44, Commanding General, 2ⁿᵈ Infantry Division) 11/10/44 disbanded and remnants absorbed into **10ᵗʰ Infantry Division**.
[NOTE: acting Commanding General in /43 BG Alexandru Nasta [+ acting Commanding General, 24ᵗʰ Infantry Division] (Commanding General, 4ᵗʰ Mountain Division) /43]
A.   **Deputy Commander, 4ᵗʰ Infantry Division**: /41 Col. Dumitru Carlaonţ (Commandant of Iasi) /41 unknown? /43 Col. Sotir Mazareanu (Deputy Commander, 24ᵗʰ Infantry Division) /43
B.   **Infantry, 4ᵗʰ Infantry Division**: /42 Col. Ioan Dumitriu (Commanding Officer, 4ᵗʰ Infantry Division) 11/28/42
C.   *Components - 4ᵗʰ Infantry Division*
   1.   **5ᵗʰ Infantry Regiment**
   2.   **20ᵗʰ Infantry Regiment**
   3.   **21ˢᵗ Infantry Regiment**
   4.   **2ⁿᵈ Light Artillery Regiment**
   5.   **10ᵗʰ Howitzer Artillery Regiment**

5ᵗʰ Infantry Division (line division; pre-war; Home Station: Buzău [Buzau], V Corps Area; assigned to Poliesti oil field; 07/41, Eastern Front; 10/41, Romania; 01/15/42, assigned to V Corps, First Army; 10/42, Eastern Front; 12/42, assigned to Third Army; 12/42, virtually destroyed; rebuilt; 03/44, Eastern Front; 10/44, disbanded and its troops were absorbed into the **9ᵗʰ Infantry Division**): /41? BG [Retired '37] Victor Traian Iliescu (/42, Under-Secretary of State of Military of National Education) 05/11/41 BG Petre Vladescu (retired) 02/11/42 BG Nicolae Mazarini (Soviet prisoner-of-war; /48, retired) 11/23/43 BG Grigore Nicolau (Director, Department of Higher Administration of the Army) 10/15/44 vacant 10/26/44 disbanded and remnants absorbed into the **9ᵗʰ Infantry Division**.
A.   **Deputy Commander, 5ᵗʰ Infantry Division**: /41 BG Gheorghe R. Gheorghiu (Commanding Officer, 1ˢᵗ Fortifications Brigade) /42
B.   **Chief of Staff, 5ᵗʰ Infantry Division**: /42 Col. Nicolae Cambrea (Soviet prisoner-of-war; /43, Commanding Officer, Soviet Romanian Tudor Vladimierscu Volunteer

Division) /42

C. **Infantry, 5th Infantry Division**: /42 Col. Dumitru Tudosie (Commanding General, 2nd Infantry Division) 06/28/42

D. *Components - 5th Infantry Division*
    1. **8th Infantry Regiment**
    2. **9th Infantry Regiment**
    3. **32nd Infantry Regiment**
    4. **7th Light Artillery Regiment**: /39 LCol. Alexandru Nicolici (Commanding Officer, 15th Artillery Brigade) /42 Col. Platon Chirnoagă (Vice Chief of Staff, Third Army) /42
    5. **28th Howitzer Artillery Regiment**

6th Infantry Division (line division; pre-war; Home Station: Focşani {Focsani], V Corps Area; assigned to Poliesti oil field; 07/41, Eastern Front; 10/41, Romania; 10/42, Eastern Front; 12/42, assigned to Third Army; 11/30/42, virtually destroyed; rebuilt; 03/44, Eastern Front): /39 BG Gheorghe Leventi (acting Commanding General, First Army) /40 Col. Ioan D. Popescu (Assistant Chief, Central Information Service, Ministerial Council) 06/03/41 BG Romulus Ioanovici (in reserve; 01/11/42, Commanding General, 11th Infantry Division) 09/11/41 BG Vintila Davidescu (Secretary-General of the Minister of Defense) 02/11/42 BG Traian Stănescu (Soviet prisoner-of-war; /46, retired; /48, condemned to 25 years imprisonment by the Soviets; /55, Repatriated to Romania but prison sentence confirmed; /57, pardoned and released) 03/11/42 BG Mihail Lascăr (Soviet prisoner-of-war; 04/12/45, Commanding General, Soviet-Romanian Division Horia, Closca si Crisan) 11/30/42 destroyed; reformed 03/20/43 BG Gheorghe R. Gheorghiu 09/21/44 BG Stefan Balaban [+ Commanding General, 6th Infantry Training Division] 10/13/44 BG Alexandru Dumitrescu (in reserve?) 10/26/44 MG Gheorghe R. Gheorghiu (Commanding General, VI Army Corps) 10/29/44 BG Ion Spirea (?) 11/10/44 BG Mihail Corbuleanu (Commanding General, 18th Infantry Brigade) 12/16/44 BG Gheorghe Gh. Marinescu (Commanding General, 1st Guard Division) 03/29/45 BG Nicolae Hrisafi (in reserve?) 04/08/45 BG Ioan Dimulescu (in reserve; /47, retired) /46.

A. *Components - 6th Infantry Division*
    1. **10th Infantry Regiment**
    2. **15th Infantry Regiment**
    3. **27th "Dorobanti" Infantry Regiment**:
        a. **Deputy Commander, 27th "Dorobanti" Infantry Regiment**: /42 LCol. Iacob Teclu (Soviet prisoner-of-war; /43, Chief of Staff, Division Tudor Vladimirescu) /42
    4. **11th Light Artillery Regiment**
    5. **16th Howitzer Artillery Regiment**

7th Infantry Division (line division; pre-war; Home Station: Roman, IV Corps Area; 07/41, Eastern Front; 10/41, Romania; 10/42, Eastern Front; 12/42, assigned to Third Army; 01/29/43, virtually destroyed at Stalingard; rebuilt; 12/01/44, disbanded and its troops were absorbed into the **6th Infantry Division**): 03/10/40 BG Olimpiu Stavrat (Commanding General, I Territorial Corps Area) 08/02/42 BG Constantin Trestioreanu (in reserve; 10/06/43, Commanding General, 10th Infantry Division) 03/21/43 BG Alexandru Poenaru (in reserve; /44, retired; /49, arrested; /52, condemned to 20 years imprisonment as a war criminal; /56, released; /66, rehabilitated) 04/05/44 BG Agricola Filip [+ 09/18/44 to 09/29/44, Commanding General, 7th Infantry Training Division; 09/28/44 to 10/13/44, acting Commanding General VI Army Corps; + /44, Commanding General, 4th Mountain Division] (in reserve; 04/08/45, Commanding General, IV Army Corps) 12/01/44 disbanded and remnants absorbed into the **6th Infantry Division**.

A.   **Deputy Commander, 7th Infantry Division**: /41 Col. Grigore Nicolau (Artillery Officer, 7th Infantry Division) /42 unknown? 10/15/44 BG Ioan D. Popescu (Commanding General, 3rd Infantry Division) 11/03/44

B.   **Infantry, 7th Infantry Division**: /42 Col. Corneliu Serghievici (Commanding General, 20th Infantry Division) 03/21/43

C.   **Artillery, 7th Infantry Division**: /42 Col. Grigore Nicolau (Artillery Commander, IV Army Corps) /42

D.   *Components - 7th Infantry Division*
   1.   **14th Infantry Regiment**
   2.   **16th "Dorobanti" Infantry Regiment**: /37 Col. Vasile Cretoiu /39 unknown? /41 Col. Constantin Visarion (Chief of Staff, VI Territorial Corps Area) /42
   3.   **37th Infantry Regiment**
   4.   **4th Light Artillery Regiment**
   5.   **8th Light Artillery Regiment**: /39 Col. Gheorghe Mosiu (Chief of Staff, Rear Area East) /42 unknown? /43 Col. Nicolae Dragomir (Vice Chief of Staff, Fourth Army) /44
   6.   **9th Howitzer Artillery Regiment**

8th Infantry Division (line division; pre-war; Home Station: Cernăuţi [Cernauti], IV Corps Area; 07/41, Eastern Front; 10/41, Romania; /44, Eastern Front; 10/44, disbanded and its troops were absorbed into the **11th Infantry Division**): /39 BG H. Dimitriu (in reserve?) 03/15/41 BG Alexandru Orasanu (retired) 09/02/41 BG Dumitru Carlaonţ (Secretary-General, Ministry of War) 09/12/44 MG Petre Camenita (Commanding General, 18th Infantry Division) 10/14/44 vacant 10/26/44 disbanded and remnants absorbed into the **11th Infantry Division**.

A.   **Deputy Commander, 8th Infantry Division**: /41 Col. Savu Nedelea (Commanding General, 11th Infantry Division) 02/11/42

B.   *Components - 8th Infantry Division*
   1.   **29th Infantry Regiment**
   2.   **38th Infantry Regiment**
   3.   **42nd Infantry Regiment**
   4.   **69th Infantry Regiment**
   5.   **7th Rifle Regiment**
   6.   **8th Rifle Regiment**
   7.   **12th Light Artillery Regiment**
   8.   **17th Howitzer Artillery Regiment**

9th Infantry Division (line division; pre-war; Home Station: Constanţa [Constanta], II Corps Area; 10/42, Eastern Front; 02/43, Romania; 10/44, absorbs the remnants of the **5th Infantry Division**): 01/01/40 BG Hugo Schwab (Commanding General, IV Territorial Corps

Area) 01/11/42 BG Constantin Panaitiu (Commanding General, 1st Infantry Division) 04/24/42 BG Marin Manafu (Commanding General, VI Territorial Corps Area) 08/02/42 BG Constantin Panaitiu (in reserve; /43, retired; /49, arrested; /50, condemned to 8 years imprisonment; /57, released) 03/21/43 MG Costin Ionaşcu [+ 08/23/44 to 08/29/44, Commanding General, 9th Infantry Training Division] (Director of Artillery, Inspectorate-General of Artillery) 12/05/44 Col. Ioan Iucal 01/01/45 BG Ioan Stănculescu 03/21/45 Col. Ioan Iucal (in reserve; /47, retired) 04/09/45 BG Ioan Stănculescu (/48, retired) 05/12/45

A. **Artillery, 5th Infantry Division**: /42 Col. Costin Ionaşcu (Artillery Commander, V Army Corps) /42
B. *Components - 9th Infantry Division*
    1. **34th Infantry Regiment**
    2. **36th Infantry Regiment**
    3. **40th Infantry Regiment**
    4. **84th Infantry Regiment**
    5. **13th Light Artillery Regiment**
    6. **18th Howitzer Artillery Regiment**

10th Infantry Division (line division; pre-war; Home Station: Brăila [Braila], II Corps Area; 09/41, Eastern Front; 12/41, Romania; 03/42, Eastern Front; 04/44, virtually destroyed in Crimea; rebuilt; 10/44, absorbs the remnants of the **4th Infantry Division**): /39 BG J. Pleniceanu (in reserve?) 06/22/41? BG Gheorghe Avramescu (Commanding General, Mountain Corps) 06/03/41 BG Ionel Glogojanu (killed in action) 10/23/41 BG Nicolae Ghineraru (Commanding General, 2nd Infantry Division) 11/08/41 BG Octavian Georgescu (in reserve?) 03/25/42 BG Sava Caracas (in reserve; 08/23/44, Commanding General, 7th Infantry Training Division) 10/06/43 MG Constantin Trestioreanu (in reserve; 05/27/44, 10th Infantry Division) 03/23/44 BG Gheorghe Niculescu (Commandant, Mechanization Instruction Center) 05/27/44 MG Constantin Trestioreanu (acting Commanding General, II Army Corps) 11/14/44 BG Mihail Camarasu (Deputy Commander, V Territorial Corps Area) after 05/12/45

[NOTE: listed as acting Commanding Officer /41 Col. Constantin Panaitiu (Commandant, Chisinau; /41, Commanding Officer, 1st Frontier Sector; 01/11/42, Commanding General, 9th Infantry Division) /41

A. **Deputy Commander, 10th Infantry Division**: /41 Col. Constantin Trestioreanu (Commandant, Odessa) /41 Col. Constantin Panaitiu (acting Commanding Officer, 10th Infantry Division) /41
B. **Infantry, 10th Infantry Division**: /42 Col. Sava Caracas (Commanding General, 10th Infantry Division) 03/25/42 unknown? /43 Col. Gheorghe Niculescu (acting Commanding General, 10th Infantry Division) 03/23/44
C. *Components - 10th Infantry Division*
    1. **23rd Infantry Regiment**
    2. **33rd Infantry Regiment**: /41 Col. Constantin Iordachescu (Infantry Commander, 2nd Infantry Division) /42
    3. **38th Infantry Regiment**
    4. **50th Infantry Regiment**
    5. **3rd Light Artillery Regiment**
    6. **20th Howitzer Artillery Regiment**

7.   **34th Howitzer Artillery Regiment**

D.   **Artillery, 10th Infantry Division**: unknown? /42 Col. Paul Alexiu (in reserve; /44, Artillery Commander, First Army) /43

11th Infantry Division (pre-war; Home Station: Slatina, I Corps Area; 07/41, Eastern Front; 10/41, Romania; 10/42, Eastern Front; 12/42, assigned to Third Army; 12/19/42, virtually destroyed; 02/43, Romania for rebuilding; 03/44, Eastern Front; 10/44, absorbs the remnants of the **8th Infantry Division**): 01/01/40 BG David Popescu [+ 07/04/39, Interior Minister] 09/01/41 BG Iosif Teodorescu (Deputy Commander, V Army Corps) 01/11/42 BG Romulus Ioanovici (in reserve; /432, retired) 02/11/42 BG Savu Nedelea (Soviet prisoner-of-war; /46, Inspector-General for Mechanization; /47, Secretary-General, Ministry of Defense; /48, retired) 12/23/42 BG Manole Iliescu (in reserve?) 03/21/43 MG Radu Niculescu-Cociu (Commanding General, 24th Infantry Division) 04/12/43 BG Edgard Rădulescu 09/21/44 Col. Nicolae Alecu (acting) 09/26/44 BG Edgard Rădulescu (acting Commanding General, II Army Corps) 01/12/45 BG Constantin Badescu (Commanding General, 11th Infantry Brigade) 02/19/45 BG Edgard Rădulescu [+ 03/03/45 to 03/08/45, acting Commanding General, II Army Corps] (retired) 03/13/45 BG Constantin Badescu (retired) /47

A.   *Components - 11th Infantry Division*
    1.   **2nd Infantry Regiment**
    2.   **3rd "Dorobanti" Infantry Regiment**: /41 Col. Simion Coman (Deputy Commander, 2nd Mountain Division) /42
    3.   **19th Infantry Regiment**
    4.   **21st Light Artillery Regiment**
    5.   **26th Howitzer Artillery Regiment**

12th Infantry Division (pre-war; Home Station: Ismail, III Corps Area; 11/01/40, disbanded): /37 Col. Constantin Constantinescu-Klaps (Commanding General, X Army Corps) /39 unknown? 11/01/40 disbanded.

A.   *Components - 12th Infantry Division*
    1.`   **28th Infantry Regiment**
    2.   **35th Infantry Regiment**
    3.   **67th Infantry Regiment**
    4.   **68th Infantry Regiment**
    5.   **22nd Light Artillery Regiment**
    6.   **27th Howitzer Artillery Regiment**

13th Infantry Division (line division; pre-war; Home Station: Ploeşti [Ploesti], V Corps Area; assigned to Poliesti oil field; 07/41, Eastern Front; 10/41, Romania; 08/42, Eastern Front; 11/42, virtually destroyed at Stalingrad; rebuilt; 03/44, Eastern Front; 10/44, destroyed and its troops were absorbed into the **3rd Infantry Division**): /39 BG Traian Grigorescu (in reserve?) 09/18/40 BG Gheorghe Rozin (Director, Higher Military Education) 11/09/41 BG Gheorghe Zaharescu (08/02/42, Inspector-General of Engineers) 04/04/42 BG Agricola Filip (Chief of Staff, First Army) 04/24/42 BG Gheorghe Ionescu-Sinaia (Commanding General, Rear Area East) 03/21/43 BG Mircea Dumitriu (Commanding General, 13th Infantry Training Division) 10/15/44 BG Cristache Gherorghiu (retired) 10/26/44 disbanded and remnants absorbed into **3rd Infantry Division**.

A.   **Deputy Commander, 13th Infantry Division**: /41 Col. Agricola Filip (Infantry Commander, 13th Infantry Division) /42

B.   *Components* - **13th Infantry Division**
   1.   **7th Infantry Regiment**
   2.   **22nd Infantry Regiment**
   3.   **89th Infantry Regiment**: /36 Col. Agricola Filip (Head, Divisional Training Center, Iasi; /41, Deputy Commander, 13th Infantry Division) /40
   4.   **19th Howitzer Artillery Regiment**
   5.   **41st Light Artillery Regiment**

C.   **Infantry, 13th Infantry Division**: Col. Agricola Filip (Commanding General, 13th Infantry Division) 04/04/42

14th Infantry Division (line division; pre-war; Home Station: Bălţi [Balti], IV Corps Area; 07/41, Eastern Front; 10/41, Romania; 10/42, Eastern Front; virtually destroyed at Stalingrad; 02/43, Romania for rebuilding; 03/44, Eastern Front; 10/26/44, disbanded and its troops were absorbed into the **2nd Infantry Division**):/39? BG Cristache Popescu (Commanding General, 21st Infantry Division) 07/30/40 unknown? 01/21/41 BG Gheorghe Stavrescu (?) 03/21/43 BG Mihail Voicu (Commanding General, 4th Infantry Division) 10/14/44 vacant 10/26/44 disbanded and remnants absorbed into the **2nd Infantry Division**.

A.   *Components* - **14th Infantry Division**
   1.   **6th Infantry Regiment**
   2.   **13th Infantry Regiment**
   3.   **39th Infantry Regiment**:
   4.   **53rd Infantry Regiment**
   5.   **24th Light Artillery Regiment**
   6.   **29th Howitzer Artillery Regiment**

15th Infantry Division (line division; pre-war; Home Station: Chişinău [Chisinau], III Corps Area; 07/41, Eastern Front; 10/41, Romania; 10/42, Eastern Front; 11/24/42, virtually destroyed at Stalingrad; 02/43, Romania for rebuilding; 10/26/44, disbanded and its troops were absorbed into the **21st Infantry Division**): /40 MG Cosma Marin Popescu (Deputy Commander, III Army Corps) 08/02/42 BG Ioan Alecu Sion (killed in action) 11/24/42 destroyed; reformed 03/20/43 BG Ioan A. I. Georgescu (in reserve; /44, retired) 12/11/43 BG Ştefan Bardan (Vice Staff of the General Staff) 09/03/44 MG Ioan Arhip (Commanding General, 15th Infantry Training Division) 09/09/44 BG Scarlet Momiceanu (in reserve?) 10/26/44 disbanded and remnants absorbed into the **21st Infantry Division**.

A.   **Deputy Commander, 15th Infantry Division**: /41 Col. Mircea Dimitriu (Commanding General, Rear Area East) /42

B.   *Components* - **15th Infantry Division**
   1.   **10th Infantry Regiment**
   2.   **25th Infantry Regiment**
   3.   **35th Infantry Regiment**: /39 Alexandru Poenaru (Commandant, Sarata Instruction Center) /42 Col. Ion Constantinescu (Commanding Officer, 21st Infantry Brigade) /44

    4.   **47th Infantry Regiment**
    5.   **60th Infantry Regiment**
    6.   **23rd Light Artillery Regiment**
    7.   **25th Light Artillery Regiment**
    8.   **30th Howitzer Artillery Regiment**

C.   **Infantry, 15th Infantry Division**: Col. Grigore Mosteoru (Commanding Officer, Detachment 18, Oil Fields Zone) /43

16th Infantry Division (pre-war; Home Station: Dej (now in Hungary); /41, disbanded): /39 BG Teodor Şerb (Commanding General, Frontier Guards Corps) /40 Col. Radu Băldescu (Deputy Commander, 18th Infantry Division) 11/01/40 BG Constantin Papadopol (retired) /41 disbanded.

A.   *Components - 16th Infantry Division*
    1.   **81st Infantry Regiment**
    2.   **87th Infantry Regiment**
    3.   **88th Infantry Regiment**
    4.   **31st Light Artillery Regiment**
    5.   **32nd Howitzer Artillery Regiment**

17th Infantry Division (pre-war; Home Station: Oradea (Nagyvárad, now in Hungary) 11/01/40, disbanded): /39 BG Hariton Dragomirescu (in reserve?) /40 unknown? 11/01/40 disbanded.

A.   *Components - 17th Infantry Division*
    1.   **83rd Infantry Regiment**
    2.   **85th Infantry Regiment**
    3.   **86th Infantry Regiment**
    4.   **98th Infantry Regiment**
    5.   **33rd Light Artillery Regiment**
    6.   **34th Howitzer Artillery Regiment**

18th Infantry Division (line division; pre-war; Home Station: Sibiu, VI Corps Area; 07/41, Eastern Front; 12/42, temporary merged with **4th Infantry Division**; 02/43 Romania for rebuilding; 08/43, operational as a mountain division; virtually destroyed; reduced to a single artillery regiment, the 35th Field Artillery Regiment; 10/44, rebuilt by absorbing the remnants of the **20th Infantry Division**): <u>**18th Infantry Division (#1)**</u> /39 BG Dumitriu N. Gheorghiu (in reserve?) /41 MG Radu Gherghe (Prefect of Bucharest) 06/03/41 BG Iosif Teodorescu [+ Commanding General, 27th Reserve Infantry Division] (Commanding General, 8th Infantry Division) 09/01/41 BG Nicolae Costescu (Director of Higher Infantry Department) 01/06/42 BG Radu Baldescu (Commanding General, 18th Mountain Division) 8/43 redesignated **18th Mountain Division** 08/43 BG Radu Baldescu (In reserve; /44, Deputy Commander, VI Territorial Corps Area) 04/30/44 BG Vasile Pascu (?) [08/44 virtually destroyed; rebuilt] <u>**18th Infantry Division (#2)**</u> 10/10/44 Col. Demostene Gheorghiade (acting) 10/19/44 BG Petre Camenita (acting Commanding General VI Army Corps) 01/03/45 BG Mihail Corbuleanu (in reserve; /47, retired) 02/27/45 MG Petre Camenita (retired) 04/10/45 BG _[Retired '42] Emil Paraschivescu (/46, in reserve; /47, retired) 04/18/45 MG Paul Alexiu (in reserve?) 05/09/45 BG Gheorghe Cosma (/45, Commanding

General, 19th Infantry Division) 05/12/45.
A. **Deputy Commander, 18th Infantry Division**: 11/01/40 Col. Radu Bǎldescu (Commanding General, 18th Infantry Division) 01/06/42 unknown? 8/43 redesignated **Deputy Commander, 18th Mountain Division** 08/43 Col. Gheorghe Gh. Marinescu (in reserve; 09/06/44, Commanding General, 20th Infantry Training Division) /44
B. **Artillery, 18th Infantry Division**: /42 Col. Atanasie Petculescu (Commanding General, 19th Infantry Division) 03/21/43
C. *Components - 18th Infantry Division*
    1. **18th Infantry Regiment**
    2. **90th Infantry Regiment** : /39 Col. Vasile Chiţu (Chief of Staff, VII Territorial Corps Area) /41
    3. **92nd Infantry Regiment**
    4. **35th Light Artillery Regiment**
    5. **36th Howitzer Artillery Regiment**
D. *Components - 18th Mountain Division*
    1. **18th Mountain Jager Group**
    2. **90th Mountain Jager Group**
    3. **92nd Mountain Jager Group**
    4. **35th Light Artillery Regiment**
    5. **36th Howitzer Artillery Regiment**

19th Infantry Division (line division; pre-war; Home Station: Turnu Severin, VII Corps Area; 03/42, Eastern Front; 04/44, virtually destroyed): /38 Col. Grigore Georgescu (Inspector-General of Engineering) /40 BG Flores Mitrǎnescu [+ 03/25/41, Commanding General, VII Army Corps] 06/14/41 BG Carol Schmidt (Commanding General, VII Territorial Corps Area) 03/21/43 BG Atanasie Petculescu (Commanding General, 18th Artillery Brigade) 10/29/43 BG Mihail Lǎcǎtuşcu 04/02/44 BG Atanasie Petculescu (Artillery Officer, V Army Corps) 04/28/44 BG Mihail Lǎcǎtuşcu 02/07/45 BG Constantin Rosetti-Balanescu (Artillery Commander, V Army Corps) 02/17/45 BG Mihail Lǎcǎtuşcu (Commanding General, II Territorial Corps Area) 03/03/45 Gheorghe Mosiu (Artillery Commander, First Army; /45, Chief of Staff, First Army; /46, in reserve; /46, arrested, but released later that year; /47, retired; /48, arrested; /60, condemned to 22 years imprisonment; /64, released).
[**NOTE**: acting Commanding Officer /43 Col. Ioan Dimulescu [+ Artillery Commander, 19th Infantry Division]; also listed in one source: 09/17/44 BG Dumitru Drajna (Artillery Commander, VI Army Corps) /45]
A. **Artillery, 19th Infantry Division**: /42 Col. Edgar Rǎdulescu (Artillery Commander, II Army Corps) /42 Col. Ioan Dimulescu [+ /43, acting Commanding Officer, 19th Infantry Division] (Director of Artillery) /43
B. *Components - 19th Infantry Division*
    1. **94th Infantry Regiment**
    2. **95th Infantry Regiment**: /41 Col. Grigore Mosteoru (Infantry Commander, 15th Infantry Division) /43
    3. **96th Infantry Regiment**
    4. **37th Light Artillery Regiment**
    5. **42nd Howitzer Artillery Regiment**

20ᵗʰ Infantry Division (line division; pre-war; Home Station: Alba Iulia, VI Corps Area; 03/42, Eastern Front; 02/43, destroyed at Stalingrad; reformed; 02/44, Eastern Front; 10/26/44, disbanded and remnants were absorbed into the **18ᵗʰ Infantry Division**): /38 BG Pion [Pavel Ion] Georgescu [+ Commanding General, Somesului Fortress] (/40, Commanding General, VII Army Corps) /39 Col. Carol Schmidt (Commanding General, 19ᵗʰ Infantry Division) 06/14/41 MG Nicolae Dascalescu (Commanding General, 21ˢᵗ Infantry Division) 06/30/41 BG Gheorghe B. Georgescu (Director, Higher Infantry Department) 07/04/42 MG Nicolae Tataranu (in reserve; /43, Commanding General, Mountain Corps) 03/21/43 BG Corneliu Serghievici (killed in action) 04/29/44 BG Damian Raşcu (Soviet prisoner-of-war; /44, Romanian Liaison Officer to the Soviet Command in Moldova) 10/14/44 vacant 10/26/44 disbanded and remnants absorbed into the **18ᵗʰ Infantry Division**.

[NOTE: acting /43 BG Romulus Dimitriu (Soviet prisoner-of-war; 04/45, Deputy Commander, Soviet Horia Closca si Crisan Division) /43**]**

A. **Infantry, 20ᵗʰ Infantry Division**: /42 BG Romulus Dimitriu (acting Commanding General, 20ᵗʰ Infantry Division) /43

B. *Components* -**20ᵗʰ Infantry Division**
    1. **82ⁿᵈ Infantry Regiment**
    2. **83ʳᵈ Infantry Regiment**
    3. **83ʳᵈ Infantry Regiment**
    4. **91ˢᵗ Infantry Regiment**
    5. **39ᵗʰ Light Artillery Regiment**
    6. **40ᵗʰ Howitzer Artillery Regiment**

21ˢᵗ Infantry Division (line division; pre-war; Home Station: Galaţi [Galati], III Corps Area; 07/41, Eastern Front; 10/41, Romania; 09/43, absorbed remnants of **4ᵗʰ Mountain Division**): /39 BG S. Dimitriu (in reserve?) /40 Col. Correcu (acting) 07/31/40 MG Christache Popescu (retired) 06/30/41 MG Nicolae Dascalescu (Commanding General, II Army Corps) 11/02/41 BG Atanasie Trincu (Commandant of Bucharest Police) 02/11/42 BG Radu Niculescu-Cociu (in reserve; 03/21/43, Commanding General, 11ᵗʰ Infantry Division) 11/02/42 BG Atanasie Trincu (in reserve; 10/10/44, Commanding General, 2ⁿᵈ Rear Area) 08/26/44 Col. Virgil Georgescu (acting) 09/21/44 BG Dumitru Dumitrescu-Polihron (Deputy Commander, Capital Military Command) 11/28/44 Col. Ion Constantinescu (acting; /45, Inspector of II Territorial Corps Area) 12/19/44 BG Petre Antonescu (in reserve) 04/03/45 BG Marin Ciausu.

[NOTE: also listed in one source 03/20/43 Col. Dumitru Dumitrescu-Polihron [acting] (Director, Higher Military Education) /43**]**

A. **Deputy Commander, 21ˢᵗ Infantry Division**: /41 Col. Romulus Dimitriu (Commanding Officer, Reserves, V Army Corps) /41 unknown? /41 Col. Romulus Dimitriu (Deputy Commander, 35ᵗʰ Reserve Infantry Division) /41 Col. Petre Camenita (Infantry Commander, 1ˢᵗ Guards Division) /42 unknown? /44 Col. Ion Constantinescu (acting Commanding Officer, 21ˢᵗ Infantry Division) 11/28/44

B. **Artillery, 21ˢᵗ Infantry Division**: /42 Col. Mihail Voicu (Artillery Commander, IV Army Corps) 04/24/42

C. *Components* - **21ˢᵗ Infantry Division**

1. **11th Infantry Regiment**: /41 Col. Ştefan Bardan (Commandant Infantry Instruction Center) /41
2. **12th Infantry Regiment**
3. **24th Infantry Regiment**: /41 Col. Ghedeon Seracin (Commandant, Arad Reserve Officer School) /42
4. **41st Infantry Regiment**
5. **5th Howitzer Artillery Regiment**
6. **23rd Light Artillery Regiment** (transferred to 15th Infantry Division)
7. **30th Light Artillery Regiment**: /41 Col. Constantin Rosetti-Balanescu (Commanding General, 5th Artillery Brigade) /43

24th Infantry Division (04/11/43; 11/04/43, disbanded): MG Radu Niculescu-Cociu (Commanding General, 4th Mountain Division) 11/04/43 disbanded.
[NOTE: acting Commanding General in /43 BG Alexandru Nasta [+ acting Commanding General, 4th Infantry Division) /43]
A. **Deputy Commander, 24th Infantry Division**: /43 Col. Sotir Mazareanu (Deputy Commander, 4th Mountain Division) 11/04/43 dissolved.
B. *Components - 24th Infantry Division*
   1. **111th Infantry Regiment**
   2. **112th Infantry Regiment**
   3. **104th Field Artillery Regiment**

100th Infantry Division (/43, sometimes appears as **110th "Commandmentul" Infantry Division**): BG Romulus Stănescu (Soviet prisoner-of-war; 10/18/44, Commanding General, 2nd Infantry Division) /44
A. *Components - 100th Infantry Division*
   1. **123rd Infantry Regiment**
   2. **133rd Infantry Regiment**
   3. **138th Infantry Regiment**
   4. **5th Horse Artillery Regiment**

1st Frontier Guards (Graniceri) Division (line division; pre-war; Home Station: Timişoara [Timisoara], VII Corps Area; also known as **1st Graniceri Division** 09/41, Eastern Front; /42, virtually destroyed; Romania for rebuilding; Eastern Front; 03/20/43, disbanded and used to rebuild the **4th Infantry Division** and **18th Infantry Division**): 08/01/40 BG Emanoil Leoveanu (Commanding General, 35th Reserve Infantry Division) 06/22/41? BG Gheorghe Potopeanu (Commanding General, II Territorial Corps Area) 03/20/43 disbanded.
A. **Deputy Commander, 1st Frontier Division**: /41 Col. Atanasie Trincu (Commanding General, 35th Reserve Infantry Division) 07/19/41 Col. Ioan Mihaescu (Artillery Commander, 1st Infantry Division) /42 Col. Alexandru Nasta (Artillery Commander, VII Army Corps) /43
B. **Infantry, 1st Frontier Division**: /42 BG Tudorance Ciurea (acting Commanding General, 4th Infantry Division) /43
C. *Components - 1st Frontier Division* (06/41)
   1. **1st Frontier Guard (Graniceri) Regiment**: /40 Col. Ioan Iucal (Commandant, Reserve Officer School) /42

2. **2nd Frontier Guard (Graniceri) Regiment**: /41 Col. Sotir Mazareanu (Commanding Officer, Regional Battalion Group of Ardeal; /43, Deputy Commander, 4th Infantry Division) /43
3. **5th Frontier Guard (Graniceri) Regiment**: /39 Col. Cristache Gherorghiu (Prefect of Ilfov) /42
4. **1st Frontier Guard (Graniceri) Artillery Regiment**
5. **2nd Frontier Guard (Graniceri) Artillery Regiment**
6. **Bridge Battalion**

1st Fortress Division (12/41, from **1st Fortress Brigade**; 02/43, disbanded and use to rebuild the **6th Infantry Division**): unknown? 02/43 disbanded.
A.   **Infantry, 1st Fortress Division**: /42 BG Stefan Balaban (Commanding General, 6th Infantry Brigade) 02/43 disbanded.

1st Fortification Division (/42, from **1st Fortification Brigade**): **1st Fortification Brigade** /39 Col. Nicolae Scariat Stoenescu (Secretary-General, Ministry of National Defense) /40 unknown? /41 Col. Nicolae T. Petrescu (Commanding Officer, 2nd Engineer Brigade) /42 BG Gheorghe R. Gheorghiu (Commanding General, 1st Fortification Division) /42 redesignated **1st Fortification Division** BG Gheorghe R. Gheorghiu (Commanding General, 6th Infantry Division) 03/20/43

Soviet Romanian Infantry Divisions
[Released Soviet captured Romanian Prisoner-of-War Divisions]

Tudor Vladimirescu Volunteer (1ˢᵗ Romanian) Division (11/28/43, at Seletskiy Camp, Moscow Military District, the Soviet Union;, communist division, from Soviet captured prisoners-of-war. The division was led by a puppet Romanian prisoner-of-war; actual power held by Soviet Political Commissar; held in reserve until war progressed into Hungary; 05/07/44, received its flag and officially formed; 08/21/44, assigned to Soviet Second Ukrainian Front in Soviet Twenty-Seventh Army; 10/20/44, received honorific place-name title "Debrecenskikh"; 03/45, in reserve in Bucharest; after war, reorganized as an armored division): vacant 08/21/44 Col. Nicolae Cambrea (Vice Chief of the Romanian General Staff) /45 Col. Iacob Teclu (/47, Commanding General, Frontier Troops).

A.	**Chief of Staff, Tudor Vladimirescu Volunteer Division** (11/28/43): Col. Iacob Teclu (acting Commanding General, Tudor Vladimirescu Volunteer Division) /45

B.	*Components* - **Tudor Vladimirescu Volunteer Division**
1.	**1ˢᵗ Rifle Regiment**
2.	**2ⁿᵈ Rifle Regiment**
3.	**3ʳᵈ Rifle Regiment**
4.	**1ˢᵗ Artillery Regiment**

Horia Closca si Crisan (2ⁿᵈ Romanian) Division (03/20/45, in Odessa Military District, the Soviet Union; 04/12/45, second communist division formed; assigned to Soviet Ukrainian Front; 04/04/45, move to reserve in Bucharest; after war, redesignated a motorized infantry division): vacant 04/12/45 MG Mihail Lascăr (Commanding General, Fourth Army) 09/12/45.

A.	**Deputy Commander, Horia Closca si Crisan Division** (04/12/45): BG Romulus Dimitriu (Chief of Staff, Horia Closca si Crisan Division) /45.

B.	**Chief of Staff, Horia Closca si Crisan Division** (04/12/45): unknown? /45 BG Romulus Dimitriu.

C.	*Components* - **Horia Closca si Crisan Division**
1.	**4ᵗʰ Rifle Regiment**
2.	**5ᵗʰ Rifle Regiment**
3.	**6ᵗʰ Rifle Regiment**
4.	**2ⁿᵈ Artillery Regiment**

Reserve Infantry Divisions

25th Reserve Infantry Division (1941; disbanded to provide replacements for existing divisions): /39 BG Nicolae Dascalescu (Commanding General, 20th Infantry Division) /40 unknown? /41 disbanded.

A.   *Components - 25th Reserve Infantry Division*
   1. **48th Reserve Infantry Regiment**
   2. **49th Reserve Infantry Regiment**
   3. **72nd Reserve Infantry Regiment**
   4. **61st Reserve Field Artillery Regiment**
   5. **62nd Reserve Field Artillery Regiment**

26th Reserve Infantry Division (06/01/40; 11/01/40, disbanded): unknown? 11/01/40 disbanded.

27th Reserve Infantry Division (1941; disbanded to provide replacements for existing divisions): 06/22/41? BG Iosef Teodorescu [+ Commanding General, 11th Infantry Division] 09/01/41 disbanded.

A.   *Components - 27th Reserve Infantry Division*
   1. **74th Reserve Infantry Regiment**
   2. **75th Reserve Infantry Regiment**
   3. **76th Reserve Infantry Regiment**
   4. **67th Reserve Field Artillery Regiment**
   5. **68th Reserve Field Artillery Regiment**

30th Reserve Infantry Division (pre-war; 11/30/41; disbanded to provide replacements for existing divisions): 01/01/40 BG Nicolae Magereanu (in reserve?) 11/30/41 disbanded

A.   *Components - 30th Reserve Infantry Division*
   1. **41st Reserve Infantry Regiment**
   2. **66th Reserve Infantry Regiment**
   3. **71st Reserve Infantry Regiment**
   4. **51st Reserve Field Artillery Regiment**
   5. **52nd Reserve Field Artillery Regiment**

31st Reserve Infantry Division (01/11/41; 09/10/41, disbanded to provide replacements for existing divisions): 01/11/41 BG Vintila Davidescu Commanding General, 6th Infantry Division) 09/10/41 disbanded.

A.   *Components - 31st Reserve Infantry Division*
   1. **42nd Reserve Infantry Regiment**
   2. **43rd Reserve Infantry Regiment**
   3. **59th Reserve Infantry Regiment**
   4. **53rd Reserve Field Artillery Regiment**
   5. **54th Reserve Field Artillery Regiment**

32nd Reserve Infantry Division (1941; disbanded to provide replacements for existing divisions): /41 BG Ionel Glogojanu (Commanding General, 10th Infantry Division) 06/03/41 disbanded.

A.   *Components - 32nd Reserve Infantry Division*
1.   **46th Reserve Infantry Regiment**
2.   **73rd Reserve Infantry Regiment**
3.   **78th Reserve Infantry Regiment**
4.   **55th Reserve Field Artillery Regiment**
5.   **56th Reserve Field Artillery Regiment**

33rd Reserve Infantry Division (06/01/40; 11/01/40, disbanded): unknown? 11/01/40 disbanded.

34th Reserve Infantry Division (06/01/40; 11/01/40, disbanded): unknown? 11/01/40 disbanded.

35th Reserve Infantry Division (/41; 11/0841, disbanded to provide replacements for existing divisions): /41 BG Romulus Dimitriu [acting] (/42, Infantry Commander, 20th Infantry Division) /41 BG Emanoil Leoveanu (Director, General Policde Department) 06/21/41 BG Ermil Procopiescu (retired) 07/19/41 BG Atanasie Trincu (in hospital/Commanding General, 21st Infantry Division) 11/08/41 disbanded.

A.   **Deputy Commander, 35th Reserve Infantry Division**: /41 Col. Romulus Dimitriu (acting Commanding Officer, 35th Reserve Infantry Division) /41 Col. Alexandru Saidac (Infantry Commander, 1st Infantry Division) /42
B.   *Components - 35th Reserve Infantry Division*
1.   **50th Reserve Infantry Regiment**
2.   **55th Reserve Infantry Regiment**
3.   **67th Reserve Infantry Regiment**
4.   **63rd Reserve Field Artillery Regiment**
5.   **64th Reserve Field Artillery Regiment**

Mountain Divisions

1st Mountain Division (1939 as **1st Mixed [Mountain] Brigade**; Home Station: Sinaia, V Corps Area; 03/42, reorganized as **1st Mountain Division**; 10/26/44, disbanded and absorbed into **2nd Mountain Division**): **1st Mixed [Mountain] Brigade** /39 BG Balanescu (in reserve?) 01/10/41 BG Mihail Lascăr (Commanding General, 6th Infantry Division) 02/10/42 BG Constantin Văşiliu-Rascanu (Commanding General, 1st Mountain Division) 03/42 redesignated **1st Mountain Division** 03/42 BG Constantin Văşiliu-Rascanu (in reserve; 08/23/44, Commanding General, V Territorial Corps Area) 10/06/43 BG Constantin Voiculescu (08/23/44, Commanding General, III Territorial Corps Area) 05/06/44 BG Ioan Beldicesnu (/47, retired) 10/08/44 vacant 10/26/44 disbanded and absorbed into **2nd Mountain Division**.

A. **Deputy Commander, 1st Mountain Division**: /42 Col. Gheorghe Gh. Marinescu (Deputy Commander 18th Mountain Division) /43 Col. Scarlat Momiceanu (Commanding General, 15th Infantry Training Division) 08/23/44 BG Grigore Balan (killed in action) /44 unknown? /45 Col. Enache Juganaru.

B. *Components* - **1st Mountain Brigade** (04/41):
1. **1st Mountain Group**: /41 Col. Gheorghe Gh. Marinescu (Deputy Commander, 1st Mountain Division) /42
2. **2nd Mountain Group**

C. *Components* - **1st Mountain Division** (03/42):
1. **1st Mountain Rifle Regiment**
2. **2nd Mountain Rifle Regiment**
3. **1st Mountain Artillery Regiment**
4. **4th Mountain Engineer Battalion**

2nd Mountain Division (1939 as **2nd Mountain Mixed Brigade**; Home Station: Bistriţa [Bistrita] (now in Hungary); 03/42, reorganized as **2nd Mountain Division**; 10/26/44, absorbs **1st Mountain Division**): **2nd Mountain Brigade** /39 BG Nicolae Tataranu (/40, Vice Chief of the General Staff) /39 Col. Gheorghe Manoliu (01/10/41, Commanding General, 4th Mountain Brigade) /39 BG Ioan Dumitrache 10/10/40 BG Romulus Ioanovici (Commanding General, 6th Infantry Division) /41 BG Ioan Dumitrache (Commanding General, 2nd Mountain Division) 03/42 redesignated **2nd Mountain Division** 03/42 BG Ioan Dumitrache 09/26/42 Col. Radu Korne [+ Commanding Officer, 6th Motorized (Rosiori) Cavalry Regiment] 10/6/42 Col. Grigore Balan (acting; /43, Deputy Commander, 2nd Mountain Division) /43 BG Ioan Dumitrache (Commanding General, Mountain Corps) 08/16/44 Col. Gheorghe Bartolomeu (acting) 09/15/44 BG Constantin Iordachescu (in reserve; /47, retired; /50, arrested, but released later that year) /46.

A. **Deputy Commander, 2nd Mountain Mixed Brigade**: /41 Col. Leonard Mociulschi (Commanding General, 3rd Mountain Brigade) 01/01/42 Col. Simion Coman (Commanding Officer, Deputy Commander, 2nd Mountain Division) 03/42 redesignated **Deputy Commander, 2nd Mountain Division** 03/42 Col. Simion Coman (Commanding Officer, 5th Instruction Center) /43 Col. Grigore Balan (Deputy Commander, 1st Mountain Division) /44

B. *Components* - **2nd Mountain Brigade** (04/41):

1. **4th Mountain Group**
2. **5th Mountain Group**

C. *Components - 2nd Mountain Division* (03/42):
1. **4th Mountain Rifle Regiment**
2. **5th Mountain Rifle Regiment**
3. **2nd Mountain Artillery Regiment**
4. **1st Mountain Engineer Battalion**

3rd Mountain Division (1939 as **3rd Mountain Brigade**; Home Station: Aiud, VI Corps Area; 03/42, reorganized as **3rd Mountain Division**; 11/04/44, absorbs **4th Mountain Division**): **3rd Mountain Brigade** 02/20/41 BG Radu Fâlfănescu (Commanding General, 3rd Mountain Division or Commanding General, Mobile Group, 2nd Etape) 01/01/42 BG Leonard Mociulschi (Commanding General, 3rd Mountain Division) 03/42 redesignated **3rd Mountain Division** 03/42 BG Leonard Mociulschi (Commanding General, Mountain Corps (#2)) 03/09/45 BG Pompelus Demetrescu (/46, in reserve; /47, retired) /45.
[NOTE: one source lists /42 BG Radu Fâlfănescu (Commanding General, Mobile Group, 2nd Etape) /42]

A. **Deputy Commander, 3rd Mountain Division**: /42 Col. Vasile Pascu (Commanding General, 5th Frontier Brigade) /43
B. *Components - 3rd Mountain Brigade* (04/41):
1. **3rd Mountain Group**
2. **6th Mountain Group**
C. *Components - 3rd Mountain Division* (03/42):
1. **3rd Mountain Rifle Regiment**
2. **6th Mountain Rifle Regiment**
3. **3rd Mountain Artillery Regiment**
4. **3rd Mountain Engineer Battalion**

4th Mountain Division (1939 as **4th Mountain Brigade**; Home Station: Unknown?; 03/42, reorganized as **4th Mountain Division**; 11/04/44 disbanded and absorbed into **3rd Mountain Division**): **4th Mountain Brigade** 01/10/41 BG Gheorghe Manoliu (Commanding General, 4th Mountain Division) 03/42 redesignated **4th Mountain Division** 03/42 BG Gheorghe Manoliu (Commanding General, IV Territorial Corps Area) 03/21/43 BG Mihail Stănescu (?) 04/17/43 BG Tudorance Ciurea (Commanding General, Special Reparation Corps) 12/02/43 MG Radu Niculescu-Cociu (in reserve; 03/18/44, Commanding General, 1st Guards Division) 01/11/44 BG Alexandru Nasta (in reserve; /45, Deputy Commander, II Army Corps; /46, in reserve; /47, retired) 09/12/44 Col. Sotir Mazareanu (acting/Deputy Commander, 4th Mountain Division) 10/13/44 BG Ilie Crețulescu (Under-Secretary of State for Land Forces) /44 BG Agricola Filip (acting) [+ Commanding General, 7th Infantry Division] 11/04/44 disbanded and absorbed into **3rd Mountain Division**.

A. **Deputy Commander, 4th Mountain Division**: 11/04/43 Col. Sotir Mazareanu (acting Commanding General, 4th Mountain Division) 09/12/44 unknown? 10/13/44 Col. Sotir Mazareanu (/48, retired).
B. *Components - 4th Mountain Brigade* (04/41):
1. **8th Mountain Group**
2. **9th Mountain Group**

C.   *Components - 4th Mountain Division* (03/42):
1.   **8th Mountain Rifle Regiment**
2.   **9th Mountain Rifle Regiment**
3.   **4th Mountain Artillery Regiment**
4.   **4th Mountain Engineer Battalion**

103rd Mountain Division (09/06/44, from the trained reserves of the mountain divisions; 10/12/44, disbanded): BG Ilie Creţulescu (Commanding General, 4th Mountain Division) 10/12/44 disbanded.

A.   *Components - 103rd Mountain Command* (/44):
1.   **17th Infantry Rifle Regiment**
2.   **8th Frontier Guard Rifle Regiment**
3.   **11th Artillery Regiment**
4.   **16th Artillery Regiment**

Romanian Mountain Commands

[late 1943, the trained reserves of the mountain divisions were organized into Mountain Commands]

101st Mountain Command (1943): /43 BG Ioan Beldiceanu (Commanding General, 1st Mountain Division) 05/06/44

102nd Mountain Command (1943): /43 BG Nicolae Vladescu Director, Department of Higher Military Education) /44 BG Constantin Iordachescu (Commadning General, 2nd Mountain Division) 09/15/44 disbanded.

103rd Mountain Command (1943): BG Mihail Camarasu (Romanian Liaison Officer to XVII German Army Corps) 09/06/44 reformed as **103rd Mountain Division** - see **103rd Mountain Division**.

104th Mountain Command (09/06/44, disbanded: /43 BG Mihail Stănescu (Commanding General, Frontier Corps) /44 BG Ilie Crețulescu (Commanding General, 103rd Mountain Division) 09/06/44 disbanded.

Security Divisions

1st Security Division (08/30/41, Transnistria; 03/20/43, disbanded): unknown? 03/15/42 Col. Alexandru Nasta 03/20/43 disbanded.
A.   *Components - 1st Security Division*
   1.   **72nd Infantry Regiment**
   2.   **55th Artillery Regiment** (½ of regiment)

2nd Security Division (08/30/41, from **2nd Fortress Brigade**; Transnistria; 03/20/43, disbanded): unknown? 03/15/42 Col. Nicolae Vladescu (Commanding General, 4th Infantry Brigade) 03/20/43 disbanded.
A.   *Components - 2nd Security Division*
   1.   **28th Fortress Infantry Regiment**: /41 Col. Alexandru Batcu (Prefect of Dubasari) /43
   2.   **53rd Fortress Infantry Regiment**
   3.   **56th Artillery Regiment**

3rd Security Division (08/30/41, Transnistria; 03/20/43, disbanded): unknown? 03/15/42 Col. Dumitru Dumitrescu-Polihron (acting Commanding Officer, 21st Infantry Division) 03/20/43 disbanded.
A.   *Components - 3rd Security Division*
   1.   **Unknown? Infantry Regiment**
   2.   **55th Artillery Regiment** (½ of regiment)

Cavalry Divisions

1st Cavalry Division (Home Station: Arad, VI Corps Area; 03/42, from **1st Cavalry Brigade**; 08/41, Eastern Front; 02/01/43, largely destroyed at Stalingrad; /43, reformed; Eastern Front; 08/44, disbanded): **1st Cavalry Brigade** /39 Col. Petre Georgescu /39 unknown? 01/23/41 BG Marin Manafu (acting Commanding General, Cavalry Corps) 03/11/42 redesignated **1st Cavalry Division** 03/11/42 BG Gheorghe I. Georgescu (in reserve; /44, retired; 08/23/44, recall/Commanding General, 11th Infantry Training Division) 07/17/42 BG Constantin Brătescu (Soviet prisoner-of-war; /48, released and retired) 02/01/43 destroyed; rebuilt 03/20/43 BG Gheorghe Munteanu (in reserve; /44, retired) 07/17/44 Col. Vladimir Constantinescu (Deputy Commander, 8th Cavalry Division) 10/21/44 Col. Constantin Talpeş 12/01/44 BG Dumitru T. Popescu (in reserve; /45, Director, Army College; /46, in reserve; /47, retired) 01/06/45 Col. Constantin Talpeş (/48, retired).
[NOTE: also listed from one source: /43 Col. Hercule Fortunescu (acting/Deputy Commander, 8th Cavalry Division) /43]

A. **Deputy Commander, 1st Cavalry Brigade**: 07/25/41 Col. Gheorghe Munteanu (Commanding General, 7th Cavalry Brigade) 10/11/41 unknown? /43 Col. Dumitru T. Popescu (Commanding General, 9th Cavalry Division) 03/23/43

B. *Components* - **1st Cavalry Division**
    1. **1st Cavalry Brigade**
    2. **2nd Cavalry Brigade**
    3. **4th Cavalry Brigade**
    4. **3rd Light Infantry Battalion**
    5. **1st Horse Artillery Regiment**

C. *Components* - **1st Cavalry Division** (05/12/42)
    1. **11th Calarasi (Cavalry) Regiment**
    2. **1st Rosiori (Cavalry) Regiment**
    3. **2nd Rosiori (Cavalry) Regiment**
    4. **1st Horse Artillery Regiment**

5th Cavalry Division (03/42, from the **5th Cavalry Brigade**; 07/41, Eastern Front; 11/20/42, largely destroyed at Stalingrad; remnants transferred to **6th Cavalry Division**; /43, reformed; 07/43, becomes **5th Motorized**; soon reverted back to **5th Cavalry Division**; 11/29/44 disbanded and absorbed into the **1st Cavalry Division** and the **9th Cavalry Division**): **5th Cavalry Brigade** 01/10/41 Col. Vasile Mainescu (Commanding General, 5th Cavalry Division) 03/42 redesignated **5th Cavalry Division** 03/42 Col. Vasile Mainescu (Director, Higher Cavalry Department) 03/23/43 unknown? 07/16/43 BG Corneliu Carp (/45, Vice Chief of the General Staff) 11/29/44 disbanded and remnants absorbed into the **1st Cavalry Division** and the **9th Cavalry Division**.

A. **Deputy Commander, 5th Cavalry Division**: 03/42 Col. Dumitru T. Popescu (Deputy Commander, 1st Cavalry Division) /43 Col. Ilie Antonescu (Commanding General, 5th Cavalry Training Division) 04/15/44

B. *Components* - **5th Cavalry Division** (05/12/42)
    1. **6th (Motorized) Rosiori (Cavalry) Regiment**: /41 Col. Radu Korne [+ 09/26/42 to 10/06/42, acting Commanding Officer, 2nd Mountain Division]

(Commanding Officer, 8th Cavalry Division) 01/02/43
2. **7th Rosiori (Cavalry) Regiment**
3. **8th Rosiori (Cavalry) Regiment**: /42 Col. Vladimir Constantinescu (Commandant, Cavalry School) /42
4. **2nd Horse Artillery Regiment**

2nd Cavalry Division (Home Station: Iaşi [Iasi], IV Corps Area):
A. *Components - 2nd Cavalry Division*
1. **3rd Cavalry Brigade**
2. **5th Cavalry Brigade**
3. **9th Cavalry Brigade**
4. **2nd Light Infantry Battalion**
5. **2nd Horse Artillery Regiment**

3rd Cavalry Division (Home Station: Bucharest, II Corps Area):
A. *Components - 2nd Cavalry Division*
1. **6th Cavalry Brigade**
2. **7th Cavalry Brigade**
3. **8th Cavalry Brigade**
4. **1st Light Infantry Battalion**
5. **4th Horse Artillery Regiment**

6th Cavalry Division (03/42, from **6th Cavalry Brigade**; 07/41, Eastern Front; 09/12/44, disbanded and remnants absorbed into the **8th Cavalry Division**): **6th Cavalry Brigade** 09/01/40 MG Aurel Racovita (retired) 06/30/41 Col. Gheorghe Munteanu (Deputy Commander, 1st Cavalry Brigade) 07/25/41 Col. Ion Codreanu (Head, Historical Service, General Staff) 02/11/42 Col. Cristu Cantuniari (Commanding Officer, 6th Cavalry Division) 03/42 redesignated **6th Cavalry Division** 03/42 Col. Cristu Cantuniari 10/16/42 Col. Corneliu Teodorini 04/22/44 Col. Ioan Gaspar (acting) 05/04/44 BG Corneliu Teodorini (Commanding General, 8th Cavalry Division) 07/25/44 BG Ioan Eftimiu (Secretary-General, Ministry of War) 09/12/44 disbanded and remnants absorbed into the **8th Cavalry Division**.
A. **Deputy Commander, 6th Cavalry Brigade**: /41 Col. Dumitru T. Popescu [+ Commanding Officer, 5th Rosiori (Cavalry) Regiment] (Deputy Commander, 5th Cavalry Division) 03/42 redesignated **Deputy Commander, 6th Cavalry Division** 03/42 unknown? /43 Col. Hercule Fortunescu (Deputy Commander, 8th Cavalry Division) /44 BG Constantin Talpeş (Commanding General, 1st Cavalry Division) 10/21/44
B. *Components - 6th Cavalry Division* (05/12/42)
1. **10th (Motorized) Rosiori (Cavalry) Regiment**: /41 Col. Dumitru Dămăceanu (chief of Staff, Capital Military Command) /42
2. **5th Rosiori (Cavalry) Regiment**: /41 Col. Dumitru T. Popescu [+ Deputy Commander, 6th Cavalry Brigade] (Deputy Commander, 5th Cavalry Division) /42
3. **9th Rosiori (Cavalry) Regiment**
4. **4th Horse Artillery Regiment**

7ᵗʰ Cavalry Division (03/42, from the **7ᵗʰ Cavalry Brigade**; 07/41, Eastern Front; 03/20/43, disbanded and its regiment used to rebuild the **1ˢᵗ Cavalry Division**, the **5ᵗʰ Cavalry Division**, and the **8ᵗʰ Cavalry Division**): **7ᵗʰ Cavalry Brigade** /41 BG Mihail Ramniceanu (Commanding General, 9ᵗʰ Cavalry Division) 01/12/41 Col. Gheorghe Savoiu (retired; /44, Head, Special Information Service) 07/26/41 Col. Cristu Cantuniari 10/11/41 BG Gheorghe Munteanu (Commanding General, 7ᵗʰ Cavalry Division) 03/42 redesignated **7ᵗʰ Cavalry Division** 03/42 BG Gheorghe Munteanu (Commanding General, 1ˢᵗ Cavalry Division) 03/20/43 disbanded and its regiment used to rebuild the **1ˢᵗ Cavalry Division**, the **5ᵗʰ Cavalry Division**, and the **8ᵗʰ Cavalry Division**

A.   *Components - 7ᵗʰ Cavalry Division* (05/12/42)
  1.   **9ᵗʰ Calarasi (Cavalry) Regiment**
  2.   **11ᵗʰ Rosiori (Cavalry) Regiment**
  3.   **12ᵗʰ Rosiori (Cavalry) Regiment**
  4.   **5ᵗʰ Horse Artillery Regiment**

8ᵗʰ Cavalry Division (03/42, from the **8ᵗʰ Cavalry Brigade**; 07/41, Eastern Front; 11/42, largely destroyed at Stalingrad; reformed and in 1943, becomes **8ᵗʰ Motorized Division**): **8ᵗʰ Cavalry Brigade** 06/12/41 Col. Ioan Dănescu (killed in action) 10/28/41 Col. Corneliu Teodorini (Commanding Officer, 8ᵗʰ Cavalry Division) 03/42 redesignated **8ᵗʰ Cavalry Division** 03/42 Col. Corneliu Teodorini (Chief, Propaganda Section, General Staff) 05/10/42 Col. Corneliu Carp (Commandant, Cavalry Instruction Center) 01/02/43 Col. Radu Korne [+ 10/05/43 to 03/18/44, Commanding Officer, 1ˢᵗ Guard Division] 04/05/44 BG Vasile Mainescu (Director, Higher Cavalry Department) 07/25/44 BG Corneliu Teodorini (in reserve; /44, Directory of Cavalry) 11/04/44 Col. Ion Craciunescu (acting) 11/26/44 BG Hercule Fortunescu (Chief of Staff, Inspectorate-General of Cavalry) 03/13/45 BG Ioan Eftimiu (/46, in reserve; /47, retired).

A.   **Deputy Commander, 8ᵗʰ Cavalry Division**: /43 Col. Hercule Fortunescu (Deputy Commander, 6ᵗʰ Cavalry Division) /43 unknown? /44 Col. Hercule Fortunescu (Commanding General, 8ᵗʰ Cavalry Division) 11/26/44 Col. Vladimir Constantinescu (/46, in reserve; /47 retired) /45

B.   *Components - 8ᵗʰ Cavalry Division* (05/12/42)
  1.   **2ⁿᵈ Calarasi (Cavalry) Regiment**
  2.   **3ʳᵈ Calarasi (Cavalry) Regiment**: /38 LCol. Hercule Fortunescu (Chief of Staff, Higher Artillery Department) /41 Col. Constantin Talpeş (Commandant, Cavalry Instruction Center) /41
  3.   **4ᵗʰ Rosiori (Cavalry) Regiment**
  4.   **3ʳᵈ Horse Artillery Regiment**

9ᵗʰ Cavalry Division (03/42, from **Cavalry Brigade**; 09/41, Eastern Front; 11/29/44, absorbs some remnants of the **5ᵗʰ Cavalry Division**): **9ᵗʰ Cavalry Brigade** 01/12/41 BG Mihail Ramniceanu (in reserve?) 01/23/41 BG Traian Cocorascu (Commanding General, Cavalry Corps) 03/26/42 Col. Mihail Chiriacescu 03/21/43 BG Dumitru T. Popescu (Commanding General, 1ˢᵗ Cavalry Training Division) 10/31/44 Col. Dumitru Neferu 12/03/44 Col. Vasile Botezatu (acting) 12/18/44 BG Ilie Antonescu (in reserve) 05/12/45

A.   *Components - 9ᵗʰ Cavalry Division* (05/12/42)
  1.   **13ᵗʰ Calarasi (Cavalry) Regiment**

2. **3rd Rosiori (Cavalry) Regiment**
3. **13th Rosiori (Cavalry) Regiment**
4. **6th Horse Artillery Regiment**

Armored Divisions

1st Greater Romania Armored Division (1940, as **1st Armored Division**; Home Station: Targovişte [Targoviste], II Corps Area; 10/42, Eastern Front; virtually destroyed at Stalingrad; 12/19/42, reorganized as a battle group; 02/43, Romania to rebuild; 03/43, Eastern Front; 04/26/44, renamed **Greater Romania [Rumania Mare] Armored Division**; 08/44, Romania; 09/14/44, disbanded): **1st Armored Division** /41 BG Nicolae Scariat Stoenescu (Finance Minister) 01/27/41 BG Ioan Alecu Sion (08/02/42, Commanding General, 15th Infantry Division) 01/11/42 MG Radu Gherghe (Director, Higher Military Education Department) 03/21/43 MG Nicolae Scariat Stoenescu (Commanding General, IV Army Corps) 04/05/44 BG Radu Korne (Commanding General, Greater Romania Armored Division) 04/26/44 redesignated **Greater Romania Armored Division** 04/26/44 BG Radu Korne (in reserve; 10/21/44, arrested; 02/45, released; 03/24/48, arrested; /49, died in prison) /44 BG Gheorghe Niculescu (Commandant, Mechanization Instruction School) 09/14/44 disbanded.

A. **Deputy Commander, 1st Armored Division**: /42 BG Ioan Beldiceanu (Commanding General, 101st Mountain Command) /43
B. *Components - 1st Armored Division*
   1. **1st Armored Regiment**
   2. **2nd Armored Regiment**
   3. **1st Motorized Artillery Regiment**
   4. **3rd Motorized Infantry Regiment**
   5. **4th Motorized Infantry Regiment**
   6. **35th Motorized Infantry Regiment** (transferred)

2nd Armored Division (08/44, from **8th Motorized Division**; Romania; never took to the field as an armored division; 09/44, absorbed into short lived **Motorized-Mechanized Corps**): unknown? 09/44 absorbed into short lived **Motorized-Mechanized Corps**.

Niculescu Armored Detachment (08/24/44, from **Mechanized Training Center (Trigoviste)**; later absorbs Popescu Armored Detachment):

Popescu Armored Detachment (08/21/44, from **1st Training Armored Division**); absorbed by Niculescu Armored Division):

Motorized Divisions

5th Motorized Division (1943, from **5th Cavalry Division**; /43, never received adequate equipment and soon reverted back to **5th Cavalry Division**): unknown? /43 disbanded.

8th Motorized Division (1943, Eastern Front; 08/44, reorganized into **2nd Armored Division**,): unknown? 08/44 reorganized into **2nd Armored Division** - see **2nd Armored Division**.

Anti-Aircraft Artillery Divisions

1st Antiaircraft Artillery Division (01/01/45): BG Horia Roman (/46, in reserve; /47, retired).

Training Divisions
Infantry Training Divisions

Guards Training Division (08/23/44): BG Stefan Opriş (Soviet prisoner-of-war; /44, Infantry Commander, 1st Guards Division) 08/31/44 disbanded.

1st Infantry Training Division (08/24/44, from **1st Infantry Division**; 10/31/44, disbanded and its troops were absorbed into the **19th Infantry Division**) BG Vasile Chiţu (retired) 09/01/44 BG Gheorghe Posoiu (?) 10/19/44 BG Alexandru Saidac (acting Commanding General, Cavalry Corps) 10/24/44 Col. Ghedeon Seracin (in hospital; /49, condemned to 8 years imprisonment; /55 pardoned and released) 10/31/44 disbanded and absorbed into the **19th Infantry Division**.

2nd Infantry Training Division (08/23/44; 09/29/44, disbanded): Col. Nivolae Marinescu 08/27/44 Col. Ion Mustata 09/15/44 BG Pompeius Demetrescu (in reserve; 03/09/45, Commanding General, 3rd Mountain Division) 09/29/44 disbanded.

3rd Infantry Training Division (08/23/44; 10/44, disbanded): BG Ioan Tanasescu [+08/24/44, Commanding General, 3rd Infantry Division] (04/07/45, Commanding General, 3rd Infantry Division) 09/05/44 BG Ioan Dumitriu [+ Commanding General, 3rd Infantry Division] 10/44 disbanded.

4th Infantry Training Division (08/23/44; 09/30/44, disbanded): Col. Constantin Basta 09/09/44 BG Dumitru Petrescu [+ Commanding General, 4th Infantry Division] 09/30/44 disbanded.

5th Infantry Training Division (08/23/44; 10/06/44, disbanded): Col. Alexandru Batcu (Assistant Commandant of Bucharest) 08/31/44 Col. Enache Juganaru (Deputy Commandant, Infantry Instruction Center) 10/06/44 disbanded.

6th Infantry Training Division (08/23/44; 10/21/44, disbanded): BG Dumitru Drajna (Commanding General, 19th Infantry Division) 09/17/44 BG Stefan Balaban [09/21/44 to 10/13/44, Commanding General, 6th Infantry Division] (/47, in reserve) 10/21/44 disbanded.

7th Infantry Training Division (08/23/44; 10/15/44, disbanded): BG Sava Caracas (Commanding General, 20th Infantry Training Division) 09/18/44 BG Agricola Filip [+ Commanding General, 7th Infantry Division] (acting Commanding General, VI Army Corps) 09/29/44 BG Ioan D. Popescu (Deputy Commander, 7th Infantry Division) 10/15/44 disbanded.

8th Infantry Training Division (05/07/44; 10/20/44, disbanded): BG Alexandru Nicolici (retired; /52, arrested; /53, died in prison) 10/20/44 disbanded.

9th Infantry Training Division (08/23/44; 08/29/44, disbanded): MG Costin Ionaşcu [+ Commanding General, 9th Infantry Division] 08/29/44 disbanded.

11th Infantry Training Division (08/23/44; 09/20/44, disbanded): BG [Retired '44] Gheorghe I. Georgescu (in reserve, /45, retired) 09/20/44 disbanded.

13th Infantry Training Division (08/23/44; 10/26/44, disbanded): BG Cristache Gherorghiu (13th Infantry Division) 09/01/44 BG Mihail Corbuleanu (Commanding General, 18th Infantry Brigade) 10/16/44 MG Mircea Dumitriu (Soviet prisoner-of-war) 10/26/44 disbanded and absorbed into **3rd Infantry Division**.

14th Infantry Training Division (08/23/44; 10/25/44, disbanded): BG Constantin Teodorescu (in reserve?) 10/25/44 disbanded and absorbed into **2nd Infantry Division**.

15th Infantry Training Division (08/23/44; 10/06/44, disbanded): BG Scarlat Momiceanu (Commanding General, 15th Infantry Division) 09/11/44 BG Ioan Arhip (Director of Infantry) 10/06/44 disbanded.

18th Infantry Training Division (08/23/44; 09/05/44): Col. Virgil Citiriga 09/05/44 disbanded.

20th Infantry Training Division (08/23/44; 12/01/44, disbanded): MG Constantin Visarion (German prisoner-of-war; /47, retired) 09/06/44 BG Gheorghe Gh. Marinescu (Commanding General, 6th Infantry Division) 10/16/44 BG Sava Caracas (Commanding General, Rear Area 1) 12/01/44 disbanded.

21st Infantry Training Division (08/23/44; 09/21/44, disbanded): BG Simion Coman (Commanding General, 3rd Frontier Brigade) 09/21/44 disbanded.

Mountain Training Divisions

4ᵗʰ Mountain Training Division (08/23/44; 10/25/44, disbanded): Col. Alexandru Nicolescu 09/13/44 BG Alexandru Nasta (?) 10/14/44 Col. Ion Mazareanu 10/25/44 disbanded.

Cavalry Training Divisions

1ˢᵗ Cavalry Training Division (08/23/44; 10/31/44, disbanded) Col. Alexandru Plesoianu 10/31/44 BG Dumitru T. Popescu (12/01/44, Commanding General, 1ˢᵗ Cavalry Division) 10/31/44 disbanded.

5ᵗʰ Cavalry Training Division (04/15/44; 09/20/44, disbanded): BG Ilie Antonescu (Assistant Inspector-General of Cavalry) 09/20/44 disbanded.

Armored Training Divisions

1ˢᵗ Armored Training Division (08/24/44; 08/31/44, disbanded): Col. Otto Benedict 08/31/44 disbanded.

Unknown? Training Divisions

1ˢᵗ Training Division : BG Trifon Stoenescu

Royal Romanian Naval Commands

Asov Detachment (02/23/43, as an ad hoc formation; fate of this formation not known; probably withdrawn and disassembled): Col. Alexandru Nicolescu

Danube Division (Naval Command; 09/05/44, disbanded):
A. *Components*
    1. **River Naval Force**
        a. **Monitor Squadron** (3 ships)
        b. **Torpedo Boat Section** (2 ships)
        c. **the Landing Company**
        d. **the Underwater Defense Group**
        e. **the Service Group**
    2. **"Tulcea" Tactical Group**
        a. **River Group** (2 monitors & 4 torpedo boats)
        b. **the Underwater Defense Sector**
        c. **the Supply Convoy**

Brigades

1ˢᵗ Infantry Brigade: /44 BG Ghedeon Seracin (acting Commanding General, 1ˢᵗ Infantry Training Division) 10/24/44

2ⁿᵈ Infantry Brigade: /44 BG Pompeius Demetrescu (Commanding General, 2ⁿᵈ Training Infantry Division) 09/15/44

4ᵗʰ Infantry Brigade: 03/20/43 BG Nicolae Vladescu (Commanding General, 102ⁿᵈ Mountain Division) /43

5ᵗʰ Infantry Brigade: /44 Col. Enache Juganaru (acting Commanding Officer, 5ᵗʰ Infantry Training Division) 08/31/44

6ᵗʰ Infantry Brigade: /42 BG Traian Stănescu (Commanding General, 6ᵗʰ Infantry Division) 02/11/42 unknown? 02/43 BG Stefan Balaban (Commanding General, 6ᵗʰ Infantry Training Division) 09/17/44

8ᵗʰ Infantry Brigade: /43 Col. Scarlat Momiceanu (Deputy Commander, 1ˢᵗ Mountain Division) /43

9ᵗʰ Infantry Brigade: /42 BG Ilie Creţulescu (Commanding General, 104ᵗʰ Mountain Command) /44 Col. Ioan Iucal (Commanding Officer, 9ᵗʰ Infantry Division) 12/05/44

10ᵗʰ Infantry Brigade: /44 BG Grigore Mosteoru (Commanding General, 5ᵗʰ Frontier Brigade) /44

11ᵗʰ Infantry Brigade: /38 Col. Olimpiu Stavrat (Head, Military Transport Section, General Staff) /39 unknown? 01/12/45 BG ₍Retired '43₎ Constantin Badescu (Commanding General, 11ᵗʰ Infantry Division) 01/12/45 unknown? 02/19/45 BG ₍Retired '43₎ Constantin Badescu (Commanding General, 11ᵗʰ Infantry Division) 03/13/45

13ᵗʰ Infantry Brigade: /43 Col. Cristache Gherorghiu (Commanding General, 13ᵗʰ Infantry Training Division) 08/23/44

16ᵗʰ Infantry Brigade: /38 BG Constantin Papadopol (Commanding General, 16ᵗʰ Infantry Division) /40 disbanded.

18ᵗʰ Infantry Brigade: /37 Col. Grigore Georgescu (Commanding Officer, 19ᵗʰ Infantry Division) /38 unknown? 1016/44 BG Mihail Corbuleanu (Commanding General, 6ᵗʰ Infantry Division) 11/10/44 unknown? 12/16/44 BG Mihail Corbuleanu (Commanding General, 18ᵗʰ Infantry Division) 01/03/45 BG ₍Retired '42₎ Emil Paraschivescu (Commanding General, 18ᵗʰ Infantry Division) 04/10/45

19ᵗʰ Infantry Brigade: /44 BG Grigore Mosteoru (Commanding General, 10ᵗʰ Infantry

Brigade) /44

20th Infantry Brigade: /37 BG Nicolae Şova (Director, Personnel, Ministry of Defense) /39 unknown? /43 BG Damian Raşcu (Commanding General, 20th Infantry Division) 04/29/44

21st Infantry Brigade: /42 Col. Alexandru Poenaru (Commanding Officer, 7th Infantry Division) /43 unknown? /44 Col. Ion Constantinescu (Deputy Commander, 21st Infantry Division) /44

23rd Mountain Brigade: /41 BG Gheorghe B. Georgescu (Commanding General, 20th Infantry Division) 06/29/41

2nd Cavalry Brigade: /39 BG I. D. Zissu (retired) /39 disbanded.

1st Artillery Brigade: /37 BG Constantin Apostolescu

3rd Artillery Brigade: /42 BG Ioan D. Popescu (Artillery Officer, VI Army Corps) 03/20/43 Col. Gheorghe Mosiu (Government Representative for Evacuation of the Eastern Territories) /43

4th Artillery Brigade: /38 Col. Nicolae Scariat Stoenescu (Commanding Officer, 1st Fortification Brigade) /39 unknown? /44 BG Platon Chirnoagă (Commanding General, 4th Infantry Division) 10/01/44

5th Artillery Brigade: /43 BG Constantin Rosetti-Balanescu (Artillery Commander, I Army Corps) /44

9th Artillery Brigade: /35 Col. Constantin Trestioreanu (Deputy Commander, 10th Infantry Division) /41 unknown? /42 Col. Gheorghe Cosma (Commanding Officer, 13th Artillery Brigade) /43

10th Artillery Brigade: 04/05/44 BG Paul Leonida (/46, in reserve; /47, retired)

12th Artillery Brigade: /36 Col. Nicolae Dascalescu [+ /37 to /38, Secretary-General of Ministry of National Defense; + /38, Commanding Officer, 1st Anti-Aircraft Artillery Brigade] (Commanding General, 25th Reserve Infantry Division) /39

13th Artillery Brigade: /43 Col. Gheorghe Cosma (Artillery Officer, VII Army Corps) /43

14th Artillery Brigade: /43 BG Dumitru Drajna (Commanding General, 6th Infantry Training Brigade) 08/23/44

15th Artillery Brigade: /42 Col. Alexandru Nicolici (Commanding General, 8th Infantry Training Division) 05/07/44

18th Artillery Brigade: /43 BG Titus Gârbea (Romanian Liaison Officer to the German

General Staff) /44

19th Artillery Brigade: 10/29/43 Col. Atanasie Petculescu (Commanding General, 19th Infantry Division) 04/02/44

1st Anti-Aircraft Artillery Brigade: /38 Col. Nicolae Dascalescu [+ Commanding Officer, 12th Artillery Brigade] (Commanding General, 25th Reserve Infantry Division) /39 unknown? /43 BG Horia Roman (01/01/45, Commanding General, 1st Anti-Aircraft Division) /44

1st Anti-Aircraft Echelon: /41 Col. Gheorghe D. Marinescu (Deputy Commander, Anti-Aircraft Command) /41

1st Frontier Brigade: /41 Col. Petre Camenita (Deputy Commander, 21st Infantry Division) /41

3rd Frontier Brigade: 09/21/44 BG Simion Coman (Deputy Commander, IV Territorial Corps Area) /44

5th Fortress Brigade: /43 BG Vasile Pascu (Commanding General, 18th Infantry Division) 04/30/44 BG Grigore Mosteoru (/46, in reserve; /47, retired).

1st Fortress Brigade (02/01/40, Romania; 12/41, redesignated **1st Fortress Division**):/38 Col. Nicholae Ghineraru (Commanding General, 10th Infantry Division) 10/23/41 BG Stefan Balaban (Commanding General, 1st Fortress Division) 12/41 redesignated **1st Fortress Division** - see **1st Fortress Division**.
A.   *Components* - **1st Fortress Brigade** (06/41)
        1.   **1st Fortress Regiment**
        2.   **2nd Fortress Regiment**
        3.   **1st Fortress Artillery Regiment**

2nd Fortress Brigade (02/01/40, Romania; 12/41, redesignated **2nd Security Division**): 06/22/41? BG Iaon Arbore (Commanding General, 3rd Mixed Fortress Brigade) 12/41 redesignated **2nd Security Division** - see **2nd Security Division**.
A.   *Components* - **2nd Fortress Brigade**(06/41)
        1.   **28th Fortress Regiment**: /41 Col. Alexandru Batcu (Prefect of Dubasari) /43
        2.   **53rd Fortress Regiment**
        3.   **4th Fortress Artillery Regiment**

3rd Mixed Fortress Brigade: 12/41 BG Iaon Arbore (Chief of Staff, Third Army) /42

Commandant, Somesului Fortress: /37 BG Pion [Pavel Ion] Georgescu [+ /38, Commanding General, 20th Infantry Division] (/40, Commanding General, VII Army Corps) /39

1st Engineer Brigade: /41 Col. Barbu Alinescu [+ Inspector of Engineers] (Commanding General, 4th Infantry Division) 08/02/42 Col. Nicolae T. Petrescu (Chief of Signals) /42

2nd Engineer Brigade: /42 Col. Nicolae T. Petrescu (Commanding Officer, 1st Engineer Brigade) 08/02/42

3rd Engineer Brigade: /40 Col. Nicolae T. Petrescu (Deputy Commander, 1st Infantry Division) /41

5th Mountain Group: /41 Col. Grigore Balan (acting Commanding Officer, 2nd Mountain Division) /43

Mobile Group, 1st Etape: 06/28/42 BG Nicolea Ghineraru (Prefect of Botosani) /43

Mobile Group, 2nd Etape: /42 BG Radu Fâlfănescu (in reserve, Commanding General, III Territorial Corps Area) /43

Detachment Eftimiu (1941): Col. Constantin Eftimiu (Director of Studies, Higher War School; /42, Vice Chief of Staff, Third Army) /41

Commandant, Bucharest: /37 MG Victor Dombrovski (Mayor of Bucharest) /38 unknown? /45 BG Alexandru Batcu (/46, retired)
A.   **Assistant Commandant, Bucharest**: 08/31/44 Col. Alexandru Batcu (Commandant, Bucharest) /45
B.   **Mayor of Bucharest**: /38 MG Victor Dombrovski (retired) /40 unknown? /41 Gen. [Retired '40] Gheorghe Florescu (retired) /42 Gen. [Retired '21 & '32] Ioan Răşcanu (retired) /44 LG [retired '40] Victor Dombrovski.

Commandant, Dobrogei: /44 BG Ioan Dimulescu (in reserve; 04/08/45, Commanding General, 6th Infantry Division) /44

Commandant, Iasi: /41 Col. Dumitru Carlaonţ (Commanding General, 8th Infantry Division) 09/02/41

Commandant, Odessa: /41 BG Constantin Trestioreanu (Commanding General, 7th Infantry Division) 08/02/42
A.   **Deputy Commandant, Odessa**: /41 Col. Corneliu Carp (Commanding Officer, 8th Cavalry Division) 05/10/42

Prefect of Botosani: /43 BG Nicolea Ghineraru (arrested; condemned to 20 years imprisonment as a war criminal; /56, released) /44

Perfect of Braila: /41 Col. Edgar Rădulescu (Artillery Commander, 19th Infantry Division) /42

Prefect of Bucharest: 06/03/41 BG Radu Gherghe (Commanding General, 1st Armored Division) 01/11/42 unknown? /43 MG Nicolae Palangeanu (Commanding General, II Territorial Corps Area) /44

Prefect of Buzau: /41 Col. Mihail Voicu (Artillery Commander, 21st Infantry Division) /42

Prefect of Dubasari: /43 Col. Alexandru Batcu (Prefect of Tirapol) /44

Prefect of Iasi: /43 BG Constantin Talpeş (Deputy Commander, 6th Cavalry Division) /44

Prefect of Ilfov: /42 Col. Cristache Gherorghiu (Commanding Officer, 13th Infantry Brigade) /43

Prefect of Roman: /41 Col. Romulus Stănescu (Artillery Commander, I Army Corps) /42

Prefect of Timis-Torontal: /41 Col. Alexandru Nasta (in reserve; /42, Artillery Commander, 1st Guards Division) /41

Prefect of Tirapol: /44 Col. Alexandru Batcu (Commanding Officer, 5th Infantry Training Division) 08/23/44

Prefect of Tulcea: /41 Col. Costin Ionaşcu (Artillery Commander, 5th Infantry Division) /42

Prefect of Viasca: /41 Col. Vasile Pascu (Mayor of 2nd Sector of Black Bucharest; /42, Deputy Commander, 3rd Mountain Division) /41

5th Instruction Center: /43 Col. Simion Coman (Commanding General, 21st Infantry Training Division) 08/23/44

"Sulina" Naval Detachment (naval command; to defend the Danuba Delta 09/05/44, disbanded)
A.   *Components*
    1.   **"Sulina" Sector**
    2.   **"Periprava" Sector**
    3.   **"Chilia Veche" Sector**
    4.   **Patrol Boat Section**

Upper Danube Sector (naval command; from Cazane to Portile-de-Fier; 09/05/44, renamed **Upper Danube Detachment**):

"Liman" Naval Detachment 09/41; (naval command; disbanded):

"Odessa" Naval Detachment (09/41; naval command; disbanded):

Middle Danube Sector (1943; naval command 09/05/44, renamed **Middle Danube Detachment**):

Lower Danube Detachment (09/05/44; naval command):

Royal Romanian Air Force
June 1941
[Forţele Aeriene Regale ale Romaniei [FARR]]

In the Soviet Union

Combat Air Grouping (Gruparea Aeriana de Lupta):
A. **1st Bomber Flotilla**
    1. **1st Bomber Group**
        a. **71st Bomber Squadron**
        b. **72nd Bomber Squadron**
    2. **4th Bomber Group**
        a. **76th Bomber Squadron**
        b. **77th Bomber Squadron**
    3. **5th Bomber Group**
        a. **78th Bomber Squadron**
        b. **79th Bomber Squadron**
        c. **80th Bomber Squadron**
B. **2nd Bomber Flotilla**
    1. **2nd Bomber Group**
        a. **74th Bomber Squadron**
        b. **75th Bomber Squadron**
    2. **82nd Bomber Squadron**
    3. **18th Light Bomber Squadron**
C. **2nd Observation Flotilla**
        a. **11th Observation Squadron**
        b. **12th Observation Squadron**
        c. **13th Observation Squadron**
        d. **14th Observation Squadron**
D. **1st Fighter Flotilla**
    1. **5th Fighter Group**
        a. **51st Fighter Squadron**
        b. **52nd Fighter Squadron**
    2. **7th Fighter Group**
        a. **56th Fighter Squadron**
        b. **57th Fighter Squadron**
        c. **58th Fighter Squadron**
    3. **8th Fighter Group**
        a. **41st Fighter Squadron**
        b. **59th Fighter Squadron**
        c. **60th Fighter Squadron**
E. **1st Long Range Recon Squadron**

Romanian Third Army (Comandamentul Aero Armata III-A)
A.   4th Long Range Recon Squadron
B.   19th Observation Squadron
C.   20th Observation Squadron
D.   21st Observation Squadron
E.   115th Liaison Squadron

Romanian Fourth Army (Comandamentul Aero Armata IV-A)
A.   3rd Long Range Recon Squadron
B.   17th Observation Squadron
C.   22nd Observation Squadron
D.   114th Liaison Squadron

Romanian 1st Armored Division (Divizie 1. Blindate)
A.   15th Observation Squadron

In Romania

2ⁿᵈ Air Region (Regiunii II-A Aeriene)
A.   **3ʳᵈ Fighter Flotilla**
     1.   **43ʳᵈ Fighter Squadron**
     2.   **44ᵗʰ Fighter Squadron**
     3.   **45ᵗʰ Fighter Squadron**
B.   **4ᵗʰ Fighter Flotilla**
     1.   **46ᵗʰ Fighter Squadron**
     2.   **49ᵗʰ Fighter Squadron**
     3.   **50ᵗʰ Fighter Squadron**
C.   **112ᵗʰ Liaison Squadron**

3ʳᵈ Air Region (Regiunii III-A Aeriene)
A.   **2ⁿᵈ Fighter Flotilla**
     1.   **6ᵗʰ Fighter Group**
          a.   **61ˢᵗ Fighter Squadron**
          b.   **62ⁿᵈ Fighter Squadron**
B.   **113ᵗʰ Liaison Squadron**

in Dobruja (Comandamentul Aero Dobrogea)
A.   **101ˢᵗ Seaplane Squadron**
B.   **102ⁿᵈ Seaplane Squadron**
C.   **16ᵗʰ Observation Squadron**
D.   **53ʳᵈ Fighter Squadron**

Combat Air Grouping (Gruparea Aeriana de Lupta):

Romanian Third Army (Comandamentul Aero Armata III-A)
Romanian Fourth Army (Comandamentul Aero Armata IV-A)
1ˢᵗ Bomber Flotilla
2ⁿᵈ Bomber Flotilla
3ʳᵈ Bomber Flotilla (1943)
1ˢᵗ Fighter Flotilla
2ⁿᵈ Fighter Flotilla
3ʳᵈ Fighter Flotilla
4ᵗʰ Fighter Flotilla
2ⁿᵈ Observation Flotilla
In Dobruja (Comandamentul Aero Dobrogea)
Fighter Command (Commanda Aviaţiei de Vanatori)
Bombardment Command (Comanda de Aviaţiei de Bombardament)

Royal Romanian Navy

Ships

4 Destroyers:	*Mărăst, Mărăsesti, Regele Ferdinand, Regina Maria*
3 Gunboats:	*Capitan Dumitrescu Constantin, Locotenent-Comandor Stihi Eugen, Sublocotenent Ghiculescu Ion*
7 Monitors:	*Alexandru Lahovari, Ardeal, Basarabia, Bucovina, Ion C. Bratianu, Lascar Catargiu, Mihail Kogaliniceanu*
3 Minelayers:	*Amiral Murgescu, Cetetea Alba* (not completed), *Carol I, Dacia*
3 Submarines:	*Delfinul, Marsuinul, Rechinul*
6 Torpedo Boats:	*Naluca, Sborul, Smeul,* + 5 others
2 Royal Yachts:	*Luceatarul, Taifun*
Sail Training Ship:	*Mircea*
Submarine Depot Ships:	*Constanta*

Table of Equivalent Ranks

Romanian Army & Air Force	United States Army & Air Force
Maresal al România (Army only)	General of the Army
General de Armatâ (Army only)	General
General de Corp de Armatâ (Army only)	Lieutenant General
General de Divizie (Army) General Commandant (Air Force)	Major General
General de Brigadâ (Army) General de escadrá (Air Force)	Brigadier General
Colonel (Army) Comandor (Air Force)	Colonel
Locotenent-colonel (Army) Capitan-Comandor (Air Force)	Lieutenant Colonel
Major (Army) Locotenent-Comandor (Air Force)	Major
Câpitan (Army & Air Force)	Captain
Locotenent (Army & Air Force)	First Lieutenant
Sublocotenent (Army & Air Force)	Second Lieutenant

Table of Equivalent Ranks

Romanian Navy	United States Navy
	Fleet Admiral
Amiral	Admiral
Vice-amiral	Vice Admiral
Contra-amiral	Rear Admiral
	Commodore
Comandor	Captain
Câpitan-Comandor	Commander
Locotenent-Comandor	Lieutenant Commander
Câpitan de Marinâ	Lieutenant
Locotenent de Marinâ	Lieutenant (Junior Grade)
Aspritant de Marinâ	Ensign
Plutonier Maior	
Plutonier	Midshipman

Romanian Senior Officers

	Name	Rank	Date of Rank
1.	Prezan, Constantin	Marshall	1920?
2.	Antonescu, Ion Victor	Marshall	08/21/41
3.	Răşcanu, Ioan	General	1931?
4.	Bărbuneau, Petre [RRN]	Admiral	prior to 1937
5.	Ilasievici, Constantin	General	1939?
6.	Florescu, Gheorghe	General	1940?
7.	Dumitrescu, Petre	General	07/18/42
8.	Avramescu, Gheorghe	General	09/44
9.	Mihail, Gheorghe	General	11/11/44
10.	Atanasiu, Vasile	General	04/11/45
	Sichitiu, Ioan	Lt. Gen.	1937?
	Ilcuş, Ioan	Lt. Gen.	1939?
	Moţaş, Dumitru	Lt. Gen.	1939?
	Raşca, Eugeniu [RRN]	V. Adm (Eng)	prior to 1940
	Celăreanu, Constantin [RRAF]	Lt. Gen.	prior to 1940
	Ţenescu, Florea	Lt. Gen.	prior to 1940
	Dragalina, Corneliu	Lt. Gen.	prior to 01/40
	Ciupercă, Nicolae	Lt. Gen.	prior to 06/40
	Vartejanu, Eugeniu	Lt. Gen.	prior to 1941
	Leventi, Gheorghe	Lt. Gen.	prior to 03/41
	Popescu, Dumitru I.	Lt. Gen	prior to 03/41
	Iacobici, Iosif	Lt. Gen.	prior to 09/41
	Şteflea, Ilie	Lt. Gen.	prior to 01/42
	Constantinescu-Klaps, Constantin	Lt. Gen.	01/24/42
	Macici, Nicolae	Lt. Gen.	01/24/42
	Sănătescu, Constantin	Lt. Gen.	01/24/42
	Dascalescu, Nicolae	Lt. Gen.	07/18/42
	Ionescu, Teodor	Lt. Gen.	07/18/42
	Mitrănescu, Florea	Lt. Gen.	07/18/42
	Negulescu, Ion	Lt. Gen.	07/18/42
	Racovita, Mihail	Lt. Gen.	07/18/42
	Son, Aurelian	Lt. Gen.	07/18/42
	Pantazi, Constantin	Lt. Gen.	1942?
	Georgescu, Ioan [RRN]	V. Adm (Eng)	1942?
	Boiteanu, Ioan	Lt. Gen.	prior to 03/43
	Niculescu, Constantin	Lt. Gen.	prior to 03/43
	Leoveanu, Emanoil	Lt. Gen.	prior to 09/43
	Rozin, Gheorghe	Lt. Gen.	prior to 01/44
	Boiţeanu, Ion	Lt. Gen.	1943
	Şova, Nicolae	Lt. Gen.	01/24/44
	Teodorescu, Iosif	Lt. Gen.	01/24/44

Gherghe, Radu	Lt. Gen.	prior to 04/44
Popescu, Cosma Marin	Lt. Gen.	prior to 04/44
Schwab, Hugo	Lt. Gen.	after 08/16/44
Rădescu, Nicolae	Lt. Gen.	prior to 10/44
Argeşanu, Gheorghe	Lt. Gen.	unknown?

Romanian Military Units in Selected Campaigns

Romanian Forces in the Invasion of the Soviet Union, June 22, 1941

German Army Group South
    German Eleventh Army
        German XI Infantry Corps
            German 76th Infantry Division
            German 239th Infantry Division
            6th Romanian Infantry Division
            8th Romanian Infantry Division
            6th Romania Cavalry Division
        German XXX Infantry Corps
            German 198th Infantry Division
            14th Romanian Infantry Division
            5th Romanian Cavalry Brigade
        German LIV Infantry Corps
            German 50th Infantry Division
            German 170th Infantry Division
        Romanian Motorized Corps
            7th Romanian Infantry Division
            1st Romanian Mountain Brigade
            2nd Romanian Mountain Brigade
            4th Romanian Mountain Brigade
            8th Romanian Cavalry Division

      Romanian formations not under German Army Group South command

Third Romanian Army
    Mountain Corps
        1st Mountain Brigade
        2nd Mountain Brigade
        4th Mountain Brigade
    Cavalry Corps
        5th Cavalry Brigade
        6th Cavalry Brigade
        8th Cavalry Brigade

Fourth Romanian Army
        5th Romanian Infantry Division
        6th Romanian Infantry Division

7th Romanian Infantry Division
Romanian Guards Infantry Division
Frontier Brigade
Armor Brigade

By the end of 09/41, Fourth Romanian Army had been reinforced with the following divisions.

1st Infantry Division
2nd Infantry Division
3rd Infantry Division
8th Infantry Division
10th Infantry Division
13th Infantry Division
14th Infantry Division
15th Infantry Division
18th Infantry Division
21st Infantry Division
35th Reserve Division
1st Cavalry Brigade
7th Cavalry Brigade
9th Cavalry Brigade

After the fall of Odessa in 10/41, the Fourth Romanian Army was withdrawn except for:

1st Infantry Division
2nd Infantry Division
10th Infantry Division
18th Infantry Division

Romanian Army January 15, 1942

In Romania Reorganizing
- First Army
    - I Army Corps
        - 3rd Infantry Division
        - 11th Infantry Division
        - 7th Cavalry Division
    - V Army Corps
        - 5th Infantry Division
        - 6th Infantry Division
        - 13th Infantry Division
        - Guard Infantry Division
    - VII Army Corps
        - 19th Infantry Division
        - 20th Infantry Division
        - 2nd Mountain Division
        - 3rd Mountain Division
- Fourth Army
    - III Army Corps
        - 9th Infantry Division
        - 15th Infantry Division
        - 21st Infantry Division
    - IV Army Corps
        - 7th Infantry Division
        - 8th Infantry Division
        - 14th Infantry Division
- Army Troops
    - Mixed Guard Brigade
    - 1st Armored Division

Security Forces in Tranistria, Black Sea Coast and Bug-Dnieper Region
  Third Army
      II Army Corps
          2nd Infantry Division
          4th Infantry Division
          1st Fortress Brigade
          1st Cavalry Brigade
          9th Cavalry Brigade
      Army Corps
          5th Cavalry Brigade
          6th Cavalry Brigade
          90th Infantry Regiment
      Army Troops
          2nd Fortress Brigade
  Assigned to XI Army Corps
      VI Army Corps
          10th Infantry Division
          18th Infantry Division (less 90th Infantry Regiment)
      Mountain Corps
          1st Mountain Brigade
          4th Mountain Brigade
          8th Cavalry Brigade

HUNGARY

(German Ally)

Hungarian Government

Hungary joined the Tripartite Pact in November 1940 but remained reluctant to fight as part of the Axis. In April 1941 however she was forced to allow the passage of German troops en route for Yugoslavia and a new government subsequently agreed to participate in Operation Barbarossa. But Hungarian support became increasingly lukewarm and in March 1944 the Germans marched into Hungary and sat up a puppet government. But these men were distasteful to Regent Horthy who had maintained his position, and in August he dismissed them. The Germans intervened again and this time supported the creation of an overtly fascist regime which was not ousted until the Russians imposed their own nominees in April 1945.

Head of State

Regent: 03/01/20 Adm. Miklós Horthy de Nagybánya, Duke of Szeged and Otranto [HN] (resigned and arrested by the Germans; 10/16/44, deported by the Germans) 10/16/44 Governing Council [Regency] 11/03/44 Hungary then ruled by Prime Minister

Governing Council [Regency] (acting for absent Adm. Horthy to 11/03/44):

    CG Károly Beregfy [+ Defense Minister & Commander-in-Chief, Armed Forces & Chief of the General Staff]

    FERENC RAJNISS

    SÁNDOR CSIA

1.   **Chief Aide-de-Camp to Adm. Horthy de Nagybánya**: /28 Col. Miklós Koós (retired) /43

2.   **First Air Adjutant to the Regent**: /42 MG Gábor Gerlóczy (?) /44

3.   **Air Adjutant to the Regent**: /32 Maj. Gábor Gerlóczy (First Air Adjutant to the Regent) /42

Head of Government

Prime Minister: 05/14/38 BÉLA IMRÉDY de ÓMORAVICZA [+ 11/28/38 to 12/10/38, Foreign Minister] (resigned) 02/16/39 Count PÁL TELEKI de SZÉK [+ 01/27/41 to 02/15/41, Foreign Minister] (suicide) 04/03/41 LÁSZLÓ BÁRDOSSY de BÁRDOS [+ Foreign Minister] (resigned) 03/10/42 MIKLÓS KÁLLAY de NAGY-KÁLLÓ [+ 03/09/43 to 07/24/43, Foreign Minister] 03/23/44 CG Döme Sztójay [+ Foreign Minister] 08/29/44 CG Géza Lakatos de Csikszentsimon (arrested and interned at Sopronkohida Prison; 02/45, released; 04/01/45, arrested by the Soviets; 02/46, released) 10/15/44 FERENC SZÁLASI [+ 03/07/45, Religion & Education Minister] 03/29/45 see Provisional Government.

[NOTE: 12/28/44 CG Béla Miklós de Dalnoki (acting; in opposition to Szálasi**]**

A.   **Foreign Minister**: 01/05/36 KÁLMÁN KANYA 11/28/38 BÉLA IMRÉDY de ÓMORAVICZA [+ Prime Minister] 12/10/38 Count ISTVÁN CSÁKY 01/27/41 Count PÁL TELEKI de SZÉK [+ Prime Minister] 02/15/41 LÁSZLÓ BÁRDOSSY de BÁRDOS [+ 04/03/41, Prime Minister] 03/07/42 FERENC KERESZTES-FISCHER [+ Interior Minister] 03/09/42 MIKLÓS KÁLLAY de NAGY-KÁLLÓ [+ Prime Minister] 07/43 JENÖ GHYCZY 03/22/44 CG Döme Sztójay [+ Prime Minister] 08/29/44 CG Gusztáv Hennyey (arrested and interned in Sopronkohida Prison) 10/16/44 Baron

GÁBOR KEMÉNYI 03/28/45 see Provisional Government.

1. *Ambassadors*
   a. **Ambassador to Germany [Berlin]**: /33 MG Döme Sztójay (Prime Minister & Foreign Minister) 02/23/44

B. **Finance Minister**: 03/09/38 LAJOS REMÉNYI-SCHNELLER 03/27/45 see Provisional Government.

C. **Defense Minister**: 05/14/38 Gdl Jenö Rátz [+ Chief of the General Staff] (retired) 11/25/38 Mas.-Gen. of Ord. Károly Bartha vités Dálnokfalva (retired) 09/24/42 CG [Retired 02/41] Vilmos Nagybaczoni Nagy (retired; 10/16/44, arrested, interned at Sopronkohida Prison) 06/12/43 CG Lajos Csatay vités Csatai [+ 04/44 to 05/44, Commander-in-Chief, Armed Forces] (arrested; 11/19/44, committed suicide along with his wife) 10/16/44 CG Károlyi Beregfy [+ Commander-in-Chief, Armed Forces & Chief of the General Staff] (arrested; /46, sentenced to death; 03/12/46, publically executed by firing squad) 03/27/45 see Provisional Government.

D. **Interior Minister**: 105/13/38 CG [Retired 11/01/42] Lajos Keresztes-Fischer (arrested by the German and placed in Buchenwald Concentration Camp) 03/22/44 ANDOR JAROSS 08/14/44 MIKLÓS BONCZOS 10/12/44 PÉTER SCHELL 10/16/44 GÁBOR VAJNA 03/27/45 see Provisional Government.

E. **Justice Minister**: 03/09/38 ÖDÖN MIKECZ 11/15/38 ANDRÁS TASNÁDI NAGY 11/09/39 LÁSZLÓ RADOCSAY 03/2244 ISTVÁN ANTAL [+ Religion & Education Minister] 08/29/44 GÁBOR ULADÁR 10/16/44 LÁSZLÓ BUDINSZKY 03/27/45 see Provisional Government.

F. **Religion (Culture) & Education Minister**:05/14/38 Count PÁL TELEKI de SZÉK (Prime Minister) 02/16/39 BÁLINT HÓMAN 07/03/42 JENŐ SZINYEI MERSE 03/22/44 ISTVÁN ANTAL [+Justice Minister] 08/29/44 IVÁN RAKOVSKY 10/16/44 FERENC RAJNISS 03/07/45 FERENC SZÁLASI [+ Prime Minister] 03/27/45 see Provisional Government.

G. **Agriculture Minister**: 05/14/38 SÁNDOR SZTRANYAVSZKY 11/15/38 MIHÁLY TELEKI 12/30/40 DÁNIEL BÁNFFY 03/22/44 BÉLA JURCSEK 10/16/44 FIDÉL PÁLFFY 03/27/45 see Provisional Government.

H. **Minister of Food Supplies**: 10/16/44 CG Gábor Faraghió 03/27/45 .

I. **Ministers without Portfolio**
   09/15/41 MG [Retired '41] Sándor Györffy-Bengyel (retired) /42

J. **Crown Council** (an advisory body of military and political leaders):
   Members: 03/01/40 CG [Retired '40] Hugó Sónyi

German Occupation

Commander, German Army in Hungary (04/01/44): LG Hans von Greiffenberg [German] (?) 04/05/45 disbanded.

Hungarian Puppet Government under Germany

National Leader (11/04/44, Prime Minister): FERENC SZÁLASI 03/29/45 see Provisional Government.

A. **National Employment Commissioner** (10/16/44): LG Ferenc K. Farkas (Commander-in-Chief, Army Reserve) 01/45

B. **Hungarian High Commissioner to Germany** (11/44): CG [Retired 08/44] Sándor Magyarossy (in reserve)01/45

Inspector-General of Hungarian Troops (12/01/44, Germany; Head of Hungarian Armed Forces): CG Jëno Major (stayed in Germany after surrendered of Hungarian Forces) 05/08/45.

Commander-in-Chief, Army Reserve (01/45): CG Ferenc K. Farkas (fled to Germany after the war) 06/45

Allied Occupation

Commander, Soviet Troops in Hungary (10/19/44): MSU Semyon Konstantinovich Timoshenko [Russian] (?) 01/20/45 see **Chairman, Allied Control Council**.

Chairman, Allied Control Council.(01/20/45): MSU Kliment Yefremovich Voroshilov [Russian].

Provisional Government, April 1945

[This was a coalition of Russian nominees formed in December 1944 and usually referred to as the Debrecen Committee. In April 1945 it returned to Budapest to become the recognized government.]

Chairman, Provisional National Assembly (12/21/44): Dr. ISTVÁN VÁSÁRY (Finance Minister) 12/21/44 BÉLA ZSEDÉNYI LÖCSEI 01/26/45 dissolved.

Provisional Supreme Council (01/25/45):
Members (01/26/45 to 12/07/45):   BÉLA ZSEDÉNYI LÖCSEI
        Gen. Béla Miklós de Dalnoki
        ERNÖ GERÖ
        05/11/45 JÓZSEF RÉVAY
        09/27/45 MÁTYÁS RÁKOSI
Members (12/07/45 to 02/02/46):   FERENC NAGY
        ZOLTÁN TILDY (ex officio)
        LÁSZLÓ RAJK
        BÉLA VARGA 01/08/46

General Secretary of the Hungarian Worker's Party (MKP/MDP) (Communist Party) (02/45): MÁTYÁS RÁKOSI.

Prime Minister: 12/28/44 CG Béla Miklós de Dalnoki (/48, tried by a Hungarian military tribunal, his military rank taken from him; 11/21/48, died a broken man from a heart attack suffered two months earlier) 11/15/45 ZOLTÁN TILDY.

A. **Foreign Minister** (12/28/44; officially 03/27/45): Dr. JÁNOS GYÖNGYÖSSY.

B. **Finance Minister** (12/28/44; officially 03/27/45): Dr. ISTVÁN VÁSÁRY 07/21/45 IMRE OLTVÁNRY 11/15/45 FERENC GORDON.

C. **Defense Minister** (12/28/44; officially 03/27/45): CG János Vörös [+ Chief of the General Staff Provisional Government] (/48, imprisoned, accused of being an American spy) 11/15/45 CG Jenõ Tombor.

D. **Interior Minister** (12/28/44; officially 03/27/45): FERENC ERDEI 11/15/45 IMRE NAGY.

E. **Justice Minister** (12/28/44; officially 03/27/45): ÁGOSTON VALENTINY 07/21/45 ISTVÁN RIES.

F. **Religion (Culture) and Education Minister** (12/28/44; officially 03/27/45): GÉZA TELEKI 11/13/45 DEZSÕ KERESTURY.

G. **Agriculture Minister** (12/28/44; officially 03/27/45): IMRE NAGY (Interior Minister)

11/15/45 BÉLA KOVÁCS.

H.   **Minister of Food Supplies** (03/27/45): CG Gábor Faraghió.

Chief of the General Staff (12/28/44): CG János Vörös [Minister of Defense Provisional Government] (/48, imprisoned, accused of being an American spy) /45 MG Sándor András.

Ministry of Defense

Defense Minister: 01/12/36 Gdl Jenö Rátz [+ Chief of the General Staff] (retired) 11/15/38 Mas.-Gen. of Ord. Károly Bartha vités Dálnokfalva (retired) 09/24/42 CG [Retired 02/41] Vilmos Nagybaczoni Nagy (retired; 10/16/44, arrested, interned at Sopronkohida Prison) 06/12/43 CG Lajos Csatay vités Csatai [+ 04/44 to 05/44, Commander-in-Chief, Armed Forces] (arrested; 11/19/44, committed suicide along with his wife) 10/16/44 CG Károlyi Beregfy [+ Commander-in-Chief, Armed Forces & Chief of the General Staff] (arrested; /46, sentenced to death; 03/12/46, publically executed by firing squad) 03/45 see Provisional Government.

A.   **Deputy Defense Minister**: 05/13/38 LG Károly Bartha vités Dálnokfalva (Minister of Defense) 11/15/38 MG Miksa Nagyszombathy (?) /39 LG Emil Barabás [+ Chief, Group I, Organization & Mobilization, Ministry of Defense] (/41, retired; /44, Military Advisor to the Szálasi Government) 01/12/40 MG Sándor Györffy-Bengyel (retired; Minister without Portfolio) 09/15/41 LG András Littay (retired) 11/01/42 LG Imre Ruszkiczay-Rüdiger [+ to 02/43, Chief, Main Bureau of Supply Section, Ministry of Defense; + 04/44 to 05/44, Deputy Commander-in-Chief, Armed Forces & Deputy Chief of the General Staff] (arrested; interned at Sopronkohida Prison; 01/45, released & retired; 05/45, Soviet prisoner-of-war) 10/17/44 CG [Retired '42] Ferenc Feketehalmy-Czeydner [+ Deputy Commander-in-Chief, Armed Forces] (ill health - throat cancer, voice box removed; 03/45, Commanding General, German XVII Waffen-Infantry Corps of the SS [see Volume I]; /45, extradicted to Yugoslavia; /46, condemned to death and executed as a war criminal) 01/45

1.   **Group VII Legal and Civilian Affairs, Deputy Defense Minister, Ministry of Defense**:
       Political Secretary and Group Chief: /38 Dr. JÁNOS PRUZSINSKZKY /41 Dr. LAJOS SZENTGYÖRGYI.

       a.   **Deputy Political Secretary and Group Chief**: Dr. LÁSZLÓ BERNÁTH /43 Dr. BÉLA NAGY.

       b.   **Section 14. Contracts and Patents, Group VII Legal and Civilian Affairs, Deputy Defense Minister, Ministry of Defense**: unknown? /40 Dr. ARPÁD RÉNYI /43 Dr. JÓZSÉF SÁRKÁNY.

       c.   **Section 15. Legislation Agreements, Group VII Legal and Civilian Affairs, Deputy Defense Minister, Ministry of Defense**: unknown? /39 Dr. LAJOS SZENTGYÖRGYI (Political Secretary and Group Chief, Group VII Legal and Civilian Affairs, Deputy Defense Minister, Ministry of Defense) /41 Dr LÁSZLÓ BERNÁTH /43 Dr. ZOLTÁN PLÁNER.

       d.   **Section 16. Citizenship and Passports, Group VII Legal and Civilian Affairs, Deputy Defense Minister, Ministry of Defense**: unknown? /40 ISTVÁN SÁNDOR /44

       e.   **Section 18. Conscription Board, Group VII Legal and Civilian Affairs, Deputy Defense Minister, Ministry of Defense**: Dr. JÓZSÉF SÁRKÁNY /43 Dr. SÁNDOR HAVASSY-BAYER.

       f.   **Civilian Section, Group VII Legal and Civilian Affairs, Deputy Defense Minister, Ministry of Defense**: Dr. BARNA NAGY /43 Dr. ALAJOS PANTZ

2. **Section 13. Judge Advocate General, Group VIII, Commander of the Levente, Ministry of Defense**: unknown? /39 LG Arpád Ambrózy (retired) /40 MG Dezsö Kis (President, Supreme Military Tribune (Court)) /42 MG Mihály Cseh [+ Judge Advocate General] (retired) /44 MG [Retired '43] Nándor Leventeújváry [+ Judge Advocate General] (retired) 12/44 MG Oszkár Levente-Littomericzki

    a. **Deputy Chief, Section 13. Judge Advocate General, Group VIII, Commander of the Levente, Ministry of Defense**: /36 MG Arpád Ambrózy (Chief, Section 13. Judge Advocate General, Group VIII, Commander of the Levente, Ministry of Defense) /39

3. **Military Auditor Office, Deputy Defense Minister, Ministry of Defense**: unknown? /42 MG Géza Horvárth.

4. **Bureau of Welfare, Deputy Defense Minister, Ministry of Defense**: /38 MG [Retired] Jenö Deczky-Marsik (retired) /41 MG [Retired '41] Géza S. Kerner.

5. **Royal Hungarian Topographical Institute, Deputy Defense Minister, Ministry of Defense**: /38 MG Endre Somogyi.

6. **Royal Hungarian Military Archives, Deputy Defense Minister, Ministry of Defense**: unknown? /39 MG Béla Lukács (?) 08/11/42 MG Károly Bogányi (retired) /42 MG Mihály Cseke (/44, Vice President, Supreme Military Court) 10/42 MG Ferenc Farkas (retired).

    a. **Deputy Chief, Royal Hungarian Military Archives**: /38 MG Árpád Kossaczky (retired) /41

7. **Royal Hungarian Army Museum, Deputy Defense Minister, Ministry of Defense**: unknown? /43 MG [Retired] Aron Nagy von Szotyor (retired) /44

B. **Chancellery (Staff Group), Ministry of Defense**: unknown? 02/39 Col. Imre Németh (Commanding General, 6th Infantry Brigade) 12/24/40 MG Col. Béla Ebesfalvi Lengyel (Chief, Section 10 Enlisted Personnel, Group I Organization & Mobilization, Ministry of Defense) /41 MG Gábor Faraghió (Inspector of Gendarmes) /42 unknown? 05/43 Col. Zoltán Zsedényi [+ 06/01/44, Commanding General, 2nd Armored Division] 08/44 MG Dezsö Istóka (?) 10/11/44 MG Ferenc Deák.

1. **Deputy Chief of the Military Chancellery**: /36 Col. Antal Vattay [assigned LCol. Vilmos Czech] (Commanding Officer, 2nd Cavalry Brigade) 02/01/40 Col. Bèla Aggteleky [+ Commanding General, 1st Infantry Brigade] (10/01/42, Commanding General, II Army Corps) 12/24/40 Col. Elemér Mészöly [assigned Col. György Világny] 05/42 Col Zoltán Zsedényi (Chief, Chancellery, Ministry of Defense) 05/43 Col. Imre Pogány /44 Col. Gyula Kalkó 10/15/44 dissolved.

2. **Section A Regulations & Bulletins, Chancellery, Ministry of Defense** (until /41, dissolved and services incorporated into **Records Section**): unknown? /39 MG Alfréd Bántay (Commanding General, 6th Infantry Brigade) /40 LCol. Mihály Perlaky /41 Col. Zoltán Zsedényi (05/42, Deputy Chief of the Military Chancellery, Ministry of Defense /41

3. **Section B Military Attaché Group, Chancellery, Ministry of Defense** (to /41, when it was attached to Section 2 of the General Staff): /36 Col. Rezsö Andorka /39 Col. Gábor Faraghió (attached to Military Intelligence) /40 Col. Mihály Perlaky /41 moved to **Section 2 of the General Staff**.

    a. **Military Attaché Bulgaria**: /38 LCol. János Aday 02/15/41 see

Section 2 of the General Staff.

b.   **Military Attaché Czechoslovakia**: 02/01/38 LCol. Ulászló Solymossy (/39, Military Attaché Slovakia) /38 disbanded.

c.   **Military Attaché Estonia**: /34 Col. Béla Ebesfalvi Lengyel [+ Military Attaché Poland] /38 Col. Lászió N. Deseö [+ Military Attaché Finland, Latvia, Lithuania & Sweden] (Commanding Officer, 20th Field Artillery Detachment; /42, Artillery Commander, I Army Corps) /40 see **Section 2 of the General Staff**.

d.   **Military Attaché Finland**: /34 Col. Béla Ebesfalvi Lengyel [+ Military Attaché Poland] /38 Col. Lászió N. Deseö [+ Military Attaché Estonia, Latvia, Lithuania, & Sweden] (Commanding Officer, 20th Field Artillery Detachment; /42, Artillery Commander, I Army Corps) /40 see **Section 2 of the General Staff**.

e.   **Military Attaché France**: 10/01/38 Maj. László Karátsony /41 see **Section 2 of the General Staff**.

f.   **Military Attaché Germany**: 05/36 LCol. of RF Dr. Kálmán Hardy [HN] [+ 03/39, Military Attaché Netherlands & Military Attaché Sweden] (Commanding Officer, 12th Infantry Regiment; Commanding Officer, 19th Field Detachment; Aide-de-Camp to Chief of the General Staff) 03/01/40 unknown? /41 see **Section 2 of the General Staff**.

g.   **Military Attaché Greece**: 09/15/35 Col. József Vasváry [+ Military Attaché Yugoslavia] (/42, Chief, Section 2. Intelligence, Group I Executive Staff, General Staff) 05/13/41 disbanded.

h.   **Military Attaché Great Britain**: 05/22/37 Maj. Lóránd Utassy /40 disbanded.

i.   **Military Attaché Italy**: 06/15/32 Maj. László Szábó (08/42, Commanding General, 6th Light Infantry Division) /41 see **Section 2 of the General Staff**.

j.   **Military Attaché Latvia**: /34 Col. Béla Ebesfalvi Lengyel [+ Military Attaché Poland] /38 Col. Lászió N. Deseö [+ Military Attaché Estonia, Finland, Lithuania, & Sweden] (Commanding Officer, 20th Field Artillery Detachment; /42, Artillery Commander, I Army Corps) /40 see **Section 2 of the General Staff**.

k.   **Military Attaché Lithuania**: /34 Col. Béla Ebesfalvi Lengyel [+ Military Attaché Poland] /38 Col. Lászió N. Deseö [+ Military Attaché Estonia, Finland, Latvia, & Sweden] (Commanding Officer, 20th Field Artillery Detachment; /42, Artillery Commander, I Army Corps) /40 see **Section 2 of the General Staff**.

l.   **Military Attaché Netherlands**: 05/36 Col. of RF Dr. Kálmán Hardy [HN] [+ 03/39, Military Attaché Germany & Military Attaché Sweden] (Commanding Officer, 12th Infantry Regiment; Commanding Officer, 19th Field Detachment; Aide-de-Camp to Chief of the General Staff) 03/01/40

m.   **Military Attaché Poland**: /34 Col. Béla Ebesfalvi Lengyel [+ to /38, Military Attaché Estonia, Finland, Latvia, & Lithuania] (/40, Chief of Chancellery, Ministry of Defense) 09/39 LCol. Jenö Sárkány 09/39 disbanded.

n. **Military Attaché Portugal**: /38 Col. László Karátsony [+ Military Attaché Spain] /41 see **Section 2 of the General Staff**.

o. **Military Attaché Romania**: 35 Col. Oszkár Beodrai Baitz [+ /37 to /38, Military Attaché, Turkey] (/42, Deputy Commander, 1st Cavalry Division) /40 Maj. Jenö Szántay (/42, Military Attaché Spain & Military Attaché Portugal /41 see **Section 2 of the General Staff**.

p. **Military Attaché Slovakia**: unknown? /39 Col. Ulászlo Solymossy 08/01/41 see **Section 2 of the General Staff**.

q. **Military Attaché Soviet Union**: /35 LCol. László Deseö 09/24/39 MG Gábor Faraghó (11/15/42, Inspectorate of Gendarmerie [Secret Police]) 08/01/41 disbanded.

r. **Military Attaché Spain**: /38 Col. László Karátsony [+ Military Attaché Portugal] /41 see **Section 2 of the General Staff**.

s. **Military Attaché Sweden**: 05/36 Col. of RF Dr. Kálmán Hardy [HN] [+ 03/39, Military Attaché Germany & Military Attaché Netherlands] (Commanding Officer, 12th Infantry Regiment; Commanding Officer, 19th Field Detachment; Aide-de-Camp to Chief of the General Staff) 03/01/40 Col. Sándor Homlok [+ Military Attaché Estonia, Finland, Latvia & Lithuania) 01/14/41 see **Section 2 of the General Staff**.

t. **Military Attaché Switzerland**: unknown? /39 LCol. Jenö Sárkány 12/01/41 see **Section 2 of the General Staff**.

u. **Military Attaché Turkey**: /37 Col. Oszkár Beodrai Baitz [+ Military Attaché, Romania] /38 LCol. János Aday 02/15/41 see **Section 2 of the General Staff**.

v. **Military Attaché United States**: 05/22/37 Maj. Lóránd Utassy /40 disbanded.

w. **Military Attaché Yugoslavia**: 09/15/35 Col. József Vasváry [+ Military Attaché Greece] (/42, Chief, Section 2. Intelligence, Group I Executive Staff, General Staff) 05/13/41 disbanded.

4. **Records Section, Chancellery, Ministry of Defense**: unknown? /39 LCol. Gyula Keresztes /41 Col. Aladár Csatay /42 Col. Imre Pogány /43 Col. Kálmán Bartalitis /44 dissolved.

5. **Chaplain Section, Chancellery, Ministry of Defense**:

    1. **Royal Military Catholic Bishop**: /29 LCol. Dr, István Hász.

    2. **Royal Military Protestant Chaplain**: /23 LCol. Dr. Elemér Soltész.

C. **President's Bureau, Ministry of Defense**: unknown? /40 MG Gyözö Ankay-Anesini (attached to Field Training Courses; /41, Chief, Section 19, Ministry of Defense) /41 MG Gábor Faraghó (Inspector of Gendarmarie & Police) 11/15/42

    1. **President's Office, Ministry of Defense**: unknown? /42 Col. Irme Kálmán (Commanding General, 25th Light Infantry Division) 08/15/42

D. **Military Bureau, Ministry of Defense** (until 03/01/41 when it becomes **Bureau of Ground Forces**): 01/36 MG Károly Bartha vités Dálnokfalva (Deputy Minister of Defense) 10/38 MG Emil Zách (retired) 02/40 MG Sándor Györffy-Bengyel (Deputy Minister of Defense) 03/01/41 becomes **Bureau of Ground Forces**.

    1. **Group I Organization & Mobilization, Military Bureau, Ministry of**

Defense: see **Group I Organization & Mobilization, Bureau of Ground Forces, Ministry of Defense**.

2. **Group III Procurement and Supply, Military Bureau, Ministry of Defense**: see **Group III Procurement and Supply, Bureau of Supply, Ministry of Defense**.

E. **Bureau of Ground Forces, Ministry of Defense**: unknown? 03/01/41 LG Szilárd Schindler (retired) 10/01/42 MG István Náday [+ Commander-in-Chief, First Army] /43 MG Sándor Magyarossy (Commander-in-Chief , Air Force & Inspector of the Air Force) 11/01/43 MG György Rakovszky (?) 03/01/44 vacant 10/16/44

   10/16/44 MG Dr. Gyula Hankovzsky (Commanding General, VIII Army Corps) 12/18/44

   10/16/44 LG István Bánfalvy (?) 12/18/44

   12/18/44 MG Miklós Nagyöszy [+ Head, Bureau of Supply, Ministry of Defense].

   1. **Group I Organization & Mobilization, Bureau of Ground Forces, Ministry of Defense**: /38 MG Emil Barabás [+ /39, Deputy Minister of Defense] /40 MG Szilárd Schindler (Chief, Bureau of Ground Forces, Ministry of Defense) 03/01/41 MG István Náday [+ 08/01/42, Commander-in-Chief, First Army] (Chief, Bureau of Ground Forces, Ministry of Defense) 10/01/42 MG Mihály Cseke (Head, Royal Hungarian Military Archives, Deputy Defense Minister, Ministry of Defense) 03/01/43 MG Miklós Nagyöszy (Commanding General, VI Army Corps) 10/16/44

      a. **Deputy Chief, Group I Organization & Mobilization, Bureau of Ground Forces, Ministry of Defense**: unknown? /42 MG Chief Group I Organization & Mobilization, Bureau of Ground Forces, Ministry of Defense) 10/01/42 Col. Ágoston Gecsányi (Infantry Commander, 10th Infantry Division) /44

      b. **Section 1./a Peacetime Organization, Group I Organization & Mobilization, Bureau of Ground Forces, Ministry of Defense**: unknown? /39 Col. Béla Aggteleky /40 Col. Gyözö Jolsvay 05/01/44 Col. Ferenc Makay-Hollósy (?) 10/15/44 LCol. Endre Pesty. Col. **[NOTE: also found /39 Col. Dr. Gyula Hankovzsky (Chief of Staff, Third Army) /43]**

      c. **Section 1./b Wartime Organization, Group I Organization & Mobilization, Bureau of Ground Forces, Ministry of Defense**: unknown? /39 Col. Kálmán Török (Commanding General, 12th Infantry Division) 02/01/40 unknown? /42 MG Mihály Cseke (Deputy Chief, Group I Organization & Mobilization, Bureau of Ground Forces, Ministry of Defense) /42 Col. Miklós Nagyöszy (Commanding General, 27th Light Infantry Division) /42 Col. Ágoston Gecsányi (Deputy Chief, Group I Organization & Mobilization, Bureau of Ground Forces, Ministry of Defense) /43 unknown? /44 Col. Sándor Zachár 03/01/44 LCol. Aladár Gál-Zugi

         i. **Deputy Chief, Section 1./b Wartime Organization, Group I Organization & Mobilization, Bureau of Ground Forces, Ministry of Defense**: unknown? /39 Col. Dénés Dobák /42 unknown? 10/01/43 Maj. László Vértes /44

      d. **Section 1./Om Mobilization, Group I Organization & Mobilization,**

Bureau of Ground Forces, Ministry of Defense: unknown? /42 Col. Dénés Dobák 10/01/43 Col. Károly Chemez /44

e.   **Section 1./ny Replacements, Group I Organization & Mobilization, Bureau of Ground Forces, Ministry of Defense**: unknown? /43 Col. József Németh (II) /44

f.   **Section 8 Officers, Group I Organization & Mobilization, Military Bureau, Ministry of Defense**: under Group I until 03/01/41, then split into three sections and move to Group II Personnel

g.   **Section 9. Schools and Training, Group I Organization & Mobilization, Bureau of Ground Forces, Ministry of Defense**: unknown? /39 Col. Géza Fehér (/42, Commanding Officer, 43rd Infantry Regiment; /42, Commanding Officer, 8th Border Guard Brigade) /41 Col. Sándor Illy (attached to the Air Force High Command) /42 Col. Ferenc Karlóczy (Commanding Officer, 24th Infantry Division) /44

     i.   **Commandant, Technical War Institute**: unknown? /43 MG Zoltán K. Harmos

     ii.   **Commandant, Army Infantry School**: unknown? /42 MG Ferenc Lóskay (Commanding General, 19th Light Infantry Division) /42

         A.   **Attached to Army Infantry School**
            /40 Col. Ferenc Lóskay (Commandant, Army Infantry School) /42

     iii.   **Commandant, Hajmáskér Field Artillery School**: /36 Col. Lajos Csatay vités Csatai (Chief of Artillery Field Training) 05/37 Col. Imre Ruszkiczay-Rüdiger (Deputy Chief, Supply Group, Ministry of Defense) 07/38 unknown? 03/40 Col. Kálmán Ternegg (Artillery Field Training; /41, Commanding Officer; 101st Artillery Detachment; 10/42, Inspector of Field Artillery) /41

     iv.   **Commandant, Anti-Aircraft Artillery School**: /38 MG Gyözö Árvay (Commanding General, 2nd Anti-Aircraft Brigade) /42

     v.   **Commandant, Bolyai János Technical Academy**: unknown? 11/01/40 Col. Endre Schmoll (Chief Group III Procurement & Supply, Ministry of Defense) /41 unknown? /43 MG Gábor Nagy

     vi.   **Commandant, Non-Commissioned Officer School**: unknown? /43 MG János Markóczy (Commanding General, 24th Infantry Division) 06/01/44

     vii.   **Commandant, "Zrinyi Miklós" Military School**: unknown? /41 Col. Pái Magyar (Commanding Officer, 9th Infantry Regiment; /43, attached to V Army Corps) /42

     viii.   **Chief, "Miklós Toldi" Army Sports Institute**: /38 MG Ernö Kölley (attached to I Mobile [Rapid] Army Corps) 12/24/40 MG Alajos Béldy (Chief, Bureau of Pre-Military Training, Minister of Defense) /41

i.   **Section 10. Enlisted Personnel, Group I Organization & Mobilization, Bureau of Ground Forces, Ministry of Defense**: unknown? /39 Col. Aladar Pintér (retired; 10/01/41, Commanding General, 1st Mountain Brigade) /40 Col. Gyözö Materna Széchy /41

Col. Béla Ebesfalvi Lengyel (Commanding General, 16th Light Infantry Division) 08/01/42 unknown? /43 Col. Lajos Vincze /44

j.   **Section 19. Border Guards, Group I Organization & Mobilization, Bureau of Ground Forces, Ministry of Defense**: /38 Col. Ferenc Farkas (Commanding Officer, 8th Border Guard Brigade) /41 MG Gyözö Ankay-Anesini (Commanding General, 1st Armored Brigade) 11/01/41 Col. Antal Benda (Infantry Commander, 25th Infantry Division) /43 Col. János Hatnay

k.   **Section 21. Internees and Prisoners-of-War, Group I Organization & Mobilization, Bureau of Ground Forces, Ministry of Defense**: Col. Zoltán Baló /43 MG Szilárd Bakay (Commanding General, III Army Corps) 05/15/43 Col. Lóránd Utassy 10/15/44

2.   **Group II Personnel, Bureau of Ground Forces, Ministry of Defense**: 01/38 Col. István Náday (First Deputy Chief of the General Staff) 01/15/39 unknown? /41 Col. Ferenc Bardóczy (Deputy Inspector of Infantry) /43 MG Dezsö Istóka (Chief, Chancellery, Ministry of Defense) 03/01/44 Col. Sándor Szávay 10/15/44 Col. Dr. Mihály Bán.

a.   **Section 4. Retirees, widows, orphans, etc., Group II Personnel, Bureau of Ground Forces, Ministry of Defense**: unknown? /43 Col. István Soós /44

b.   **Section 8./e General Officer Attachments, Group II Personnel, Bureau of Ground Forces, Ministry of Defense**: /38 Col. Jëno Major (Commanding General, 1st Motorized Brigade) 03/01/40 Col. Ferenc Bardóczy (Chief, Group II Personnel, Ministry of Defense) /41 unknown? /42 Col. Dr. Mihály Bán /43 Col. Lajos Balikó

   i.   **Deputy Chief, Section 8./e General Officer Attachments, Group II Personnel, Bureau of Ground Forces, Ministry of Defense**: Maj. Károly Meggyes /44 Maj. Endre Kalmár.

c.   **Section 8./b Officer Assignments, Group II Personnel, Bureau of Ground Forces, Ministry of Defense**: unknown? /39 Col. László Molnár (Commanding General, 10th Light Infantry Division) 09/42 Col. Pál Szombathy (08/44, Deputy Commander, II Army Corps & Commanding General, II Military District) /43 Col. Ernö Godányi.

d.   **Section 8./ny Officer Records, Group II Personnel, Bureau of Ground Forces, Ministry of Defense**: unknown? /39 Col. Kálmán N. Máthé (Commanding Officer, 23rd Infantry Brigade) /42 Col. János Tusa /44

e.   **Section 20. Royal Gendarmerie, Group II Personnel, Bureau of Ground Forces, Ministry of Defense** (as of 03/01/41, under control of Group II): /38 Col. Farkas Damasy (Deputy Inspector-General, Gendarmerie) /41 Col. Endre Temesváry /43 Col. Ferenc Mátray.:

3.   **Group VI Civil Defense, Bureau of Ground Forces, Ministry of Defense**: unknown? /41 MG Nándor Komposcht [+ Chief, National Air Defense] (President, Central Inspecting Committee) /42 MG Lajos Szurmay (?) /44

a.   **Section 35. Conscription, Group VI Civil Defense, Bureau of Ground Forces, Ministry of Defense**: unknown? /42 Col. Attila

Selymessy /44

b. **Section 36. Air Defense, Group VI Civil Defense, Bureau of Ground Forces, Ministry of Defense**: /38 MG Dr. Dániel Fábry [+ Chief, National Anti-Aircraft Defense; + /39, Chief, Group XI Military Labor Force, Ministry of Defense; + /39, National Inspector, Military Labor Force, Ministry of Defense] (Secretary-General, Supreme Military Council) /40 unknown? /42 LCol. Julián Borsány /44

4. **Group X Casualty Administration, Bureau of Ground Forces, Ministry of Defense** (until 03/01/40, Casualty Administration Section; from 03/01/40 until 1943, Section 22): unknown? /39 MG József Horváth (retired) /41 MG Ernö Petrik (retired) /42 MG Arpád Tarnaváry (Commanding General, 4th Field Replacement Division) 08/44:

a. **Section 22./h Casualty Administration (Wounded, Invalids, etc.), Group X Casualty Administration, Bureau of Ground Forces, Ministry of Defense**: unknown? /39 Col. József Horváth (retired; /40 Military Commander, Csik-Háromszék County) /40 unknown? /43 Col. [Retired] Mihály Géczy /44

b. **Section 22./v Graves, Group X Casualty Administration, Bureau of Ground Forces, Ministry of Defense**: unknown? /43 Col. [Retired] Sándor Véry /44

F. **Main Bureau of the Air Force, Ministry of Defense**: 04/38 Col. Ferenc Feketehalmi-Czeydner (Commanding Officer, 6th Infantry Brigade) 01/23/39 unknown? 02/41 LG András Littay (Deputy Minister of Defense) 0/41 MG György Rakovszky (Commadning General, III Army Corps) /41 MG Sándor Magyarossy (Commander-in-Chief, acting Head, Bureau of the Ground Forces, Ministry of Defense) 08/01/44 LG István Bánfalvy [+Commander-in-Chief, Air Force] (acting Head, Bureau of Ground Forces, Ministry of Defense) 10/16/44 LG Kálmán Ternegg [+ Commander-in-Chief, Air Force & Inspector of the Air Force].

1. **Deputy, Main Bureau of the Air Force, Ministry of Defense**: unknown? /44 MG Vilmos Hellebronth (Chief, Group IX Armaments & Defense Industry, Main Bureau of Supply, Minister of Defense) /44

a. **Section 30. Legal Affairs and Administration, Main Bureau of the Air Force, Ministry of Defense**: LCol. Dr. Béla Csepreghy

2. **Group IV Organization and Training, Main Bureau of the Air Force, Ministry of Defense**: unknown? /40 Col. Aladár Szirmay (09/01/44, Commanding General, 1st Air Force Division) /43 Col. János Németh /44

a. **Section 37. Organization, Group IV Organization and Training, Main Bureau of the Air Force, Ministry of Defense**: unknown? /41 Col. Sándor András (Commanding Officer, 2nd Air Brigade) /42 LCol. János Németh /43 Maj. László Várkonyi /44

b. **Section 38. Personnel, Group IV Organization and Training, Main Bureau of the Air Force, Ministry of Defense**: Col. Kálmán Kazay /44

c. **Section 5/rep Training, Group IV Organization and Training, Main Bureau of the Air Force, Ministry of Defense** (assigned to Army General Staff):

      i.   **Deputy Chief, Section 5/rep Training, Group IV Organization and Training, Main Bureau of the Air Force, Ministry of Defense**: unknown? /40 Col. Károly Ertsay-Leitschaf (Chief Administration Officer, VII Army Corps) /41

    d.   **Section 7./rep Employment and Operations, Group IV Organization and Training, Main Bureau of the Air Force, Ministry of Defense** (assigned to Army General Staff):

3.   **Group V Procurement & Administration, Main Bureau of the Air Force, Ministry of Defense** (until 03/01/40, known as Group II of the Air Force): unknown? 03/01/41 MG Vilmos Hellebronth (Deputy Commander-in-Chief, Air Force) /44 Col. János Németh.

    a.   **Staff Section. General Administration, Group V Procurement & Administration, Main Bureau of the Air Force, Ministry of Defense**: unknown? /41 LCol. Emil Barkász 03/01/44 Maj. Miklós Balássy.

    b.   **Section 31. Technology, Group V Procurement & Administration, Main Bureau of the Air Force, Ministry of Defense**: Maj. György Jakab /42 Maj. Pál Németh /43 Maj. Viktor Prugerberger /44

    c.   **Section 32./a Flying Equipment, Group V Procurement & Administration, Main Bureau of the Air Force, Ministry of Defense**: unknown? /43 Col. Ernö Ojtozy

    d.   **Section 32./b Arms, Equipment, and Vehicles, Group V Procurement & Administration, Main Bureau of the Air Force, Ministry of Defense**: unknown? /43 Col. Ottó Szaich /44

    e.   **Section 32./eü Medical Service, Group V Procurement & Administration, Main Bureau of the Air Force, Ministry of Defense**: unknown? /43 LCol. Dr. Gusztáv Scholtz /44

    f.   **Section 33. Airfields & Installations, Group V Procurement & Administration, Main Bureau of the Air Force, Ministry of Defense**: unknown? /41 Col. Árpád Gálocsy (attached to Group III, Procurement & Supply, Main Bureau of Supply, Ministry of Defense)

    g.   **Section 34. Budget, Group V Procurement & Administration, Main Bureau of the Air Force, Ministry of Defense**: unknown? /42 Col. Dezsö Dobay /44

4.   **Anti-Aircraft Bureau, Main Bureau of the Air Force, Ministry of Defense**: unknown? 03/01/40 Col. Emil N. Justy (Deputy Commander-in-Chief, Air Force) 01/01/41

5.   **Attached to Air Force Bureau, Ministry of Defense**
       01/01/41 Col. Sándor András (Chief, Sectiuon 37., Ministry of Defense) /41

G.   **Main Bureau of Supply, Ministry of Defense** (until 03/01/41, known as Supply Group): unknown? /39 MG Sándor Györffy-Bengyel (Head, Military Bureau, Ministry of Defense) 02/40 MG Imre Ruszkiczay-Rüdiger [+ to 11/40, Chief, Group III Procurement & Supply, Main Bureau of Supply, Ministry of Defense] (Commanding General, I Army Corps) 03/01/41 MG József Heszlényi (?) 11/01/41 MG Frigyes Gyimesy (?) 02/43 MG János Vörös (sabbatical leave; 11/01/43, Commanding General, II Army Corps & II Military District) 08/43 unknown? 11/15/44 MG Miklós Nagyöszy [+ to 12/17/44, Commanding General, V Army Corps & V Military District;

+ 12/18/44, Head, Bureau of the Ground Forces, Ministry of Defense].

1.   **Deputy Chief (**and **Quarter Master General)**, **Main Bureau of Supply, Ministry of Defense Main Bureau of Supply, Ministry of Defense**: 07/38 Col. Imre Ruszkiczay-Rüdiger (02/40, Chief, Main Bureau of Supply Section, Ministry of Defense) /39 MG Antal Náray (Secretary-General of the Supreme Military Council) 10/11/40

2.   **Group III Procurement & Supply**, **Main Bureau of Supply, Ministry of Defense**: Col. Károly Beregfy (Military Archives; 11/38, Commanding Officer, 2nd Motorized Infantry Brigade) /38 unknown? /39 MG Sándor Györffy-Bengyel (Deputy Minister of Defense & Head, Military Bureau, Ministry of Defense) 02/40 MG Imre Ruszkiczay-Rüdiger [+ Chief, Bureau of Supply, Ministry of Defense] 11/40 MG József Heszlényi (Commanding General, IV Army Corps) 11/01/42 LG   Imre Ruszkiczay-Rüdiger [+ Deputy Minister of Defense] 08/01/43 MG Frigyes Gyimesi (retired) 11/01/44 MG Béla Ferenczy.
      [NOTE: also listed in one source /41 MG Endre Schmoll (?   ) 11/01/44**]**

   a.   **Deputy Chief, Group III Procurement & Supply**, **Main Bureau of Supply, Ministry of Defense**: unknown? /42 Col. [Retired '40] Árpád Denk-Doroszlay (National Inspector, War Supply Production) /43 Col. László Karátsony (Commanding General, 6th Infantry Division) 07/44 Col. Béla Ferenczy (Deputy Chief, Group III Procurement & Supply, Ministry of Defense) 11/01/44

   b.   **Staff Section. General Administration, Group III Procurement & Supply**, **Main Bureau of Supply, Ministry of Defense** (disbanded 11/01/44 and incorporated into Section 3 of the General Staff): unknown? /40 Col. Kázmér Kubicza /42 Col. László Zsigmondi 11/01/44 disbanded.

   c.   **Section 2./é Rations, Group III Procurement & Supply**, **Main Bureau of Supply, Ministry of Defense**: unknown? /39 Col. Dr. Pál Bodrogi /42 Col. Mihály Mózes /44

   d.   **Section 2./I Pay, Group III Procurement & Supply**, **Main Bureau of Supply, Ministry of Defense**: Col. János Szaladin /44

   e.   **Section 2./r Clothing, Group III Procurement & Supply**, **Main Bureau of Supply, Ministry of Defense**: unknown? /39 Col. József Lambert (retired) /41 Col. Jenö Kovalszky /44

   f.   **Section 3./a Weapons & Optics, Group III Procurement & Supply**, **Main Bureau of Supply, Ministry of Defense**: /38 Col. Vilmos Hellebronth (Chief, Group V Procurement & Administration, Ministry of Defense) 03/01/41 Col. Gyula Kovács (Chief, Field Officer Training Courses) /41 Col. Béla Ferenczy (Deputy Chief, Group III Procurement & Supply, Ministry of Defense) /44 LCol. Attila Noszticus.

   g.   **Section 3./b Motor Vehicles & Fuel, Group III Procurement & Supply**, **Main Bureau of Supply, Ministry of Defense**: /38 Col. József Futó (Chief of Staff, IV Army Corps) 11/39 Col. Ferenc Osztovics (10/01/43, Commanding Officer, 2nd Armored Division) /42 Col. Oszkár Levente-Littomericzki (Chief, Section 13 Chief of Judge Advocate General, Group VIII Commander of the Levente, Ministry of Defense) /44 LCol. Károly Kádas.

h.   **Section 3./c Ammunition and Explosives, Group III Procurement & Supply, Main Bureau of Supply, Ministry of Defense**: unknown? /40 Col. Árpád Denk-Doroszlay (retired; /41, Chief, Artillery Engineering Training Courses) /40 MG István Bánfalvy (Commanding General, Air Training Brigade) /41 Col. Géza Asztalos /44

i.   **Section 5. Animals and Vehicles, Group III Procurement & Supply, Main Bureau of Supply, Ministry of Defense**: unknown? /39 Col. György Vukováry (Commanding General, 201st Light Infantry Division) 11/05/42 Col. István Badzey /44

j.   **Section 6./k Budget, Group III Procurement & Supply, Main Bureau of Supply, Ministry of Defense**: /38 Col. József Keresö (retired) /40
        /40 Col. István Hlatky (retired) /41
        /40 Col. Gyula Karánsebsey (Quartermaster-General of the Army) /41
    /41 Col. Emil Boldvay /44

k.   **Section 11. Housing, Group III Procurement & Supply, Main Bureau of Supply, Ministry of Defense**: unknown? /39 Col. Sándor Csiby /40 /41 Col. Kálmán Vándorfy /43 Col. Gyula Ries /44

l.   **Section 12. Medical [Chief Medical Officer & Chief of the Army Medical Corps], Group III Procurement & Supply, Main Bureau of Supply, Ministry of Defense**: unknown? /39 MG Dr. Richard Frank (?) /42 MG Dr Antal Demkö [+ Chief, Army Medical Corps] (retired) /43 MG Béla Millián (retired?) /44

   i.   **Deputy Commander, Medical [Chief Medical Officer & Chief of the Army Medical Corps], Group III Procurement & Supply, Main Bureau of Supply, Ministry of Defense**: unknown? /43 Col. Jenö Jándy.

   ii. **Attached to Section 12. Medical [Chief Medical Officer & Chief of the Army Medical Corps], Group III Procurement & Supply, Main Bureau of Supply, Ministry of Defense**:
        /38 Col. Jenö Jándy (Deputy Commander, Medical [Chief Medical Officer & Chief of the Army Medical Corps], Group III Procurement & Supply, Main Bureau of Supply, Ministry of Defense) /43

m.   **Attached to Group III Procurement & Supply, Main Bureau of Supply, Ministry of Defense**:
    /44 Col. Árpád Gálocsy (retired) /45

n.   **Section 7./k Transport, Group I Executive Staff, General Staff** (subordinate to Bureau of Supply regarding matter of purchasing): see. **Section 7./k Transport, Group I Executive Staff, General Staff**.

o.   **Section 7./m Technical & Engineer Services, Group I Executive Staff, General Staff** (subordinate to Bureau of Supply regarding matter of purchasing): see .**Section 7./m Technical & Engineer Services, Group I Executive Staff, General Staff**.

p.   **Section 7./ö Communications, Group I Executive Staff, General**

Staff (subordinate to Bureau of Supply regarding matter of purchasing): see. **Section 7./ö Communications, Group I Executive Staff, General Staff**.

3. **Group IX Armaments & Defense Industry, Main Bureau of Supply, Ministry of Defense**: unknown? /42 MG Jenö Halmaji Bor (Commanding General, 4th Light Infantry Division) 06/01/43 MG Gyula Kézay (?) /44 LG Vilmos Hellebronth (?) 12/09/44 LG Jenö Halmaji Bor (Inspector of Hungarian Forces, Northern)

   a. **Deputy Head, Main Bureau of Supply, Ministry of Defense**: unknown? /40 Col. Jenö Halmaji Bor (Chief, Group IX Armaments & Defense Industry, Main Bureau of Supply, Ministry of Defense) /42

   b. **Section 3./v Government Owned Industry, Group IX Armaments & Defense Industry, Main Bureau of Supply, Ministry of Defense**: unknown? /43 Col. Andor Bartha (Chief, Gas Protection Laboratory, Military Technical Institute) /44

   c. **Section 17./a Mobilization & Air Defense, Group IX Armaments & Defense Industry, Main Bureau of Supply, Ministry of Defense**: unknown? /40 Col. Dr. Lajos Fábián (Chief, Civilian Sector, Group XII Military Labor Forces, Ministry of Defense & National Inspector of the Military Labor Forces, Ministry of Defense) /43 Col. Kálmán Szábó /44

   d. **Section 17./b Manufacture of War Material, Group IX Armaments & Defense Industry, Main Bureau of Supply, Ministry of Defense**: unknown? /39 Col. Gyula Kézay (Chief, Group IX Armaments & Defense Industry, Ministry of Defense) 06/01/43 Col. Béla Marcell.

   e. **Section 17./c Procurement of Raw Materials, Group IX Armaments & Defense Industry, Main Bureau of Supply, Ministry of Defense**: Col. Sándor Székely /44

   f. **Section 17./r Aviation Industry, Group IX Armaments & Defense Industry, Main Bureau of Supply, Ministry of Defense**: unknown? /44 Col. Emil Barkász /44 LCol. Brunó Hámory.

4. **Chief of the Administrative Office [Military Administrative Bureau], Main Bureau of Supply, Ministry of Defense**: 01/36 MG Vilmos Nagybaczoni Nagy (Commanding General, 1st Mixed Brigade & I Military District) 10/01/36 MG Emil Barabás [+ Chief Administration Officer, 4th Mixed Brigade] (Chief, Group I, Organization & Mobilization, Ministry of Defense) /38 unknown? /42 MG Gyula Karánsebessey (retired) /44

5. **Chief of the Engineer Corps, Main Bureau of Supply, Ministry of Defense**: unknown? /42 MG László Mattyasovszky.

6. **Chief of Remounts, Main Bureau of Supply, Ministry of Defense**: unknown? /42 Col. [Retired] Alfréd Adda

7. **Inspector General of the Armaments Industry, Main Bureau of Supply, Ministry of Defense** (1942): MG László Stirling

   a. **Officer-in-Charge of Sub-Machine Guns and Munition**: Col. Elemér Bátor

   b. **Officer-in-Charge of Rubber Production**:

   c. **Officer-in-Charge of Tank and Motor Vehicles**: Col.

Bartholomeidesz
- d. **Officer-in-Charge of Fuel**: Col. József Kutassy
- e. **Officer-in-Charge of Armaments Production**: unknown? /45 MG Károly Bézler
- f. **Hungarian State Wagon and Engineering Factory [Mágyar Allami Vaggon és Gépgyár (MÁVAG)] - Director**: KÁLMÁN BORBÉLY
8. **Industrial Materials Office, Main Bureau of Supply, Ministry of Defense**: Col. Lajos Károlyi

H. **Bureau of Training, Ministry of Defense**: unknown? /43 MG István Kudriczy (Commanding General, 10th Infantry Division) 08/10/43
  1. **Deputy Head, Bureau of Training, Ministry of Defense**: unknown? /42 Col. István Kudriczy (Head, Bureau of Training, Ministry of Defense) /43

I. **Adjutant, Ministry of Defense**: unknown? /40 Col. Jenö Sárkány /41 LCol. Sándor Makray (/43, Chief, 5th Section Troop Training, Group II Training Staff, General Staff) /42 Col. Kálmán Kéry [+ Military Attaché Slovakia] /43 Col. Otto Hatz /44 Col. Ferenc Makay-Hollósy.

J. **Main Labor Bureau & Chief of the Military Labor Corps, Ministry of Defense** (11/01/43): LG Gusztáv Hennyey (Minister of Foreign Affairs) 08/29/44
  - a. **Inspector of the Military Labor Forces**: unknown? 08/01/41 MG Jenö Röder (?)12/11/42
  - b. **Inspector of the Field Labor Force**: unknown? 09/42 MG Béla Tanitó (Deputy Commander, VI Army Corps & Commanding General, VI Military District) 06/01/43
  - c. **Chief of the Construction Corps of the Air Force**: Col. Elemér Póhly
  1. **Group XI Military Labor Forces - Military Sector & National Inspector of the Military Labor Forces, Main Labor Bureau, Ministry of Defense**: unknown? /39 MG Dr. Dániel Fábry [+ Chief, National Anti-Aircraft Defense; Chief, Section 36. Air Defense, Group VI Civil Defense, Bureau of Ground Forces, Ministry of Defense; + /39, National Inspector, Military Labor Force] (Secretary-General, Supreme Military Council) /03/01/40 Col. László Stemmer (01/42, Commanding General, 108th Infantry (Security) Brigade) /41 MG Ernö Horny [+ to /43, National Inspector, Military Labor Force] (Engineers Commander, I Army Corps) /44
    - a. **Section 41. Administration and Liaison, Group XI Military Labor Forces - Military Sector, Main Labor Bureau, Ministry of Defense**: unknown? /41 Col. Sándor Vályi (acting Commanding Officer, 13th Infantry Division) 11/20/44
    - b. **Section 42. Organization and Training, Group XI Military Labor Forces - Military Sector, Main Labor Bureau, Ministry of Defense**: Col. Gusztáv Hibbey /44
    - c. **Section 43. Operations, Group XI Military Labor Forces - Military Sector, Main Labor Bureau, Ministry of Defense**: Col. [Retired] Egen Gátföldy /44
    - d. **Section 44. Purchasing and Budget, Group XI Military Labor Forces - Military Sector, Main Labor Bureau, Ministry of Defense**: Col. János Heinrich /44

2. **Group XII Military Labor Force - Civilian Sector, Main Labor Bureau, Ministry of Defense**: unknown? /43 MG Dr. Lajos Fábián [+ /44, National Insoector, Military Labor Force, Ministry of Defense].

   a. **Section 45. Work Force Mobilization, Group XII Military Labor Force - Civilian Sector, Main Labor Bureau, Ministry of Defense**: Col. [Retired] Ernö Acs /44

   b. **Section 46. Women's Work Corps, Group XII Military Labor Force - Civilian Sector, Main Labor Bureau, Ministry of Defense**: unknown? /39 MG Dénes Sturm [+ National Inspector of Women's Work Corps] (?) /43 Col. Dénes Marton

K. **Bureau of Pre-Military Training, Minister of Defense**: unknown? /43 LG Alajos Béldy [+ National Leader of Pre-military Training & Athletics] /44 Capt. András Bak /44 vacant.

   1. **Secretary, Bureau of Pre-Military Training, Minister of Defense**: /34 Dr. IMRE RAJCZI.

   2. **Group VIII Commander of the Levente & National Commander of the Levente, Bureau of Pre-Military Training, Ministry of Defense** (Para-Military Youth Organization): unknown? 08/10/43 MG Ulászlo Solymossy (?) / 44

   a. **Section 40./e Organization, Group VIII Commander of the Levente, Bureau of Pre-Military Training, Ministry of Defense**: unknown? /41 Col. István Kudriczy (Deputy Head, Bureau of Training, Ministry of Defense) /42 LCol. Lázsló Lovass /43 LCol. Tibor Szurmay /44

   b. **Section 40./k Training, etc., Group VIII Commander of the Levente, Bureau of Pre-Military Training, Ministry of Defense**: unknown? /42 Col. János Pálossy /44 LCol. György Balassa.

       i. **Attached to Section 40./k Training, etc., Group VIII Commander of the Levente, Bureau of Pre-Military Training, Ministry of Defense**: /41 Col. Tibor Fráter (Commanding Officer, 2nd Air Force Brigade) /42

   c. **National Headquarters of the Levente**: unknown? /40 Col. József Benke /44

       i. **Deputy Chief, Levente Organization**: unknown? /44 Col. Alajos Haynal.

       ii. **Levente Organization, Budapest**: unknown? /43 Col. Alajos Haynal (Deputy Chief, Levente Organization) /44

   d. **Inspector, Levente Youth Organization**: /37 MG Kálmán Kiss (retired) /40

L. **Bureau VI, Ministry of Defense**

   1. **Group Operations, Bureau VI, Ministry of Defense**: /33 MG József D. Bajnóczy (Commanding General, 2nd Infantry Brigade) /36

M. *Inspectors*

   1. **Inspectorate of Infantry**: 07/01/37 MG József Böckl (?) 02/01/38 Gen./Inf. János Kiss (retired) 02/01/39 LG Vilmos Nagybaczoni Nagy (Commander-in-Chief, First Army) 03/01/40 unknown? 10/01/42 LG Gusztáv

Hennyey [+ President, Supreme Military Court] (Main Labor Bureau, Ministry of Defense) 11/01/43 LG József Németh (I) (retired) 04/30/44 LG Ferenc Bardóczy (Commanding General, 16th Infantry Division) 07/15/44 unknown? 08/44 MG Ferenc Bardóczy (Deputy Inspector of Infantry) /44 unknown? /4 MG Ferenc Bardóczy (Deputy Commander, IX Army Corps) 11/15/44 LG János Markóczy (retired) 03/01/45 LG Mihály Ibrányi (Inspector of Huszárs) /45.

a. **Deputy Inspectorate of Infantry**: unknown? /43 MG Ferenc Bardóczy (acting Inspector of Infantry) 04/30/44 unknown? /44 MG Ferenc Bardóczy (Inspector of Infantry) /44

b. **Chief, Field Infantry Training**: unknown? /40 Col. János Legeza (Commanding General, 1st Infantry Brigade) 11/01/41

2. **Inspectorate of Cavalry & [03/01/40] Commander-in-Chief, Cavalry**: 02/01/35 MG Gusztáv Denk (Deputy Commander-in-Chief, Armed Forces) 05/01/38 **Inspectorate of Rapid Mobile Forces and Cavalry** 05/01/38 Gen./Inf. Elemér Gorondy-Novák (Commander-in-Chief, Third Army) 03/01/40 unknown? 10/01/42 **Inspectorate of Cavalry** 10/01/42 LG Antal Vattay [+ to 07/18/44, Commanding General, 1st Cavalry Division; + 07/18/44, Commanding General, II Reserve Army Corps] (Chief of the Military Chancellery & Adjutant-General of the Military) 08/01/44 LG [Retired '43] Oszkár Beodrai Baitz (retired) /45 LG Mihály Ibrányi.

a. **Inspector of Remount, Ministry of Defense**:
/38 MG Elemér Fáy (Inspector, Military Horse Institutes) /41
/40 Col. Ottó Hager (retired) /41

b. **Inspector, Military Horse Institutes**: unknown? /41 MG Elemér Fáy (retired) /42

c. **Chief, Field Cavalry Training**: /38 Col. Ottó Hager (Inspector of Remount, Ministry of Defense) /40

3. **Inspectorate of Armored and Mobilized Forces** (10/01/42): MG Jëno Major [+ Commanding General, I Armored Corps] (Commander-in-Chief, Second Army (#2)) 10/16/44 unknown? 02/11/45 LG [Retired '44] Ferenc Bisza.

a. **Motorized Troops Field Training**: unknown? 03/01/40 Col. Sándor Horváth (attached to I Mobile [Rapid] Army Corps) /40

b. **Chief, Field Officer Training**: /41 MG Sándor Horváth (Commanding General, VII Army Corps) 05/01/42

4. **Inspectorate of Artillery**: 02/01/36 LG Kornél Rumpelles (?   ) 06/02/36 unknown? 08/01/36 LG Imre Bangha [+ Chief, Army Technical Staff; + /38, Inspector of Army Trains] (President, Army Technical Committee) 02/01/40 unknown? 10/01/42 MG Kálmán Ternegg (personal leave; 10/15/44, Commander-in-Chief, Home Army) 10/01/44 LG Jenö Kunczfalusy (retired) 03/01/45

a. **Deputy Inspector of Artillery**: unknown? /45 MG Gyula Királyehotai Lehoszky.

b. **Chief, Artillery Field Training**: unknown? 03/40 MG Lajos Csatay vités Csatai (Chief of Artillery, Third Army) /41

c. **Chief, Artillery Engineering Training Courses**: unknown? /41 Col. [Retired '40] Árpád Denk-Doroszlay (Deputy Chief, Group III Procurement

& Supply, Main Bureau of Supply, Ministry of Defense) /42

    d.   **Chief, Artillery Officer Training Courses**: /38 Col. Gyula Királyehotai Lehoszky (Artillery Officer, 2nd Armored Division) /42

5.   **Inspectorate of Anti-Aircraft Artillery & [05/01/35] Commanding General, Antiaircraft Artillery Corps**: 05/01/35 LG Oszkár Maliczki (?) 02/01/36 LG Jenö Ruszkay (10/01/38, Commanding General, 4th Mixed Army Brigade & Commanding General, IV Military District) 08/15/37 unknown? /40 MG Nándor Komposcht (Chief, National Anti-Aircraft Defense & Chief, Group VI Civil Defense, Bureau of Ground Forces, Ministry of Defense) /41 unknown? 10/42 LG Emil N. Justy (Commander-in-Chief, Air Force & Inspector of the Air Force) 12/44

6.   **Inspectorate of Engineers**: 02/01/34 LG Zoltán Zelenka (retired) 02/01/40 unknown? /42 MG László Kassay-Farkas (retired) 02/01/43 LG László Gertenyesi Hollósy-Kuthy (Commanding General, 25th Infantry Division) 10/16/44

    a.   **Chief, Engineer (Pioneer) Training Courses**: unknown? /41 MG László Kassay-Farkas (Inspector of Engineers) /42

7.   **Inspectorate of Fortifications**: unknown? /41 MG Teofil Hárosy

8.   **Inspectorate of Signal Troops**: unknown? /43 MG Ernö Vasady (?) /43 MG Henrik Hargittay.

9.   **Inspectorate of Gendarmerie (Secret Police) and Police**: 08/01/36 LG Lajos Folkhusházy (?) 02/01/38 LG László Falta (retired) 08/01/39 LG Márton Nemerey (retired?) 11/15/42 LG Gábor Faraghó (Minister of Food Supplies - Provisional Government) 10/16/44 LG József Finta.

    a.   **Deputy Inspector-General of Gendarmerie**: unknown? 08/01/39 MG Dezsö Bittó (Military Commander, Bihar County; /40, retired; /41 Military Commander, Szabadka) /40 unknown? /41 MG Farkas Damasy (retired) /43

    b.   **Assistant Inspector of Gendarmerie**:
    /43 MG Vilmos Poltáry
    /43 MG Ferenc Szabadhegyi

    c.   **Special Purposes General, Inspector of the Gendarmerie**: unknown? /40 MG Ágoston Huszár (retired) /42

    d.   **Commandant, Gendarmerie Officers School**: unknown? /39 MG Béla Balogh (Commandant, Gendarmerie Equipment Depot) /40

    e.   **Commandant, Gendarmerie Equipment Depot**: unknown? /40 MG Béla Balogh

    f.   **Chief of Gendarmerie, Máramarosszigeti**: unknown? /40 Col. Pál Hódosy (President, Gendarmerie Regulations Commission) /43

    g.   **President, Gendarmerie Regulations Commission**: unknown? /43 MG Pál Hódosy (retired; /44, National Inspector of Police) /44

    h.   **National Inspector of Police**: unknown? /44 MG [Retired '44] Pál Hódosy.

10.   **Inspectorate of the Air Force**: /38 MG Valdemár Kenese (retired; /40, Commander-in-Chief, Air Force) /40 unknown? 02/01/41 MG József Grassy [+ Commander-in-Chief, Air Force] (Commanding General, 15th Infantry Brigade) 03/01/41 LG Béla Rákosi (?) 42 MG Sándor András [+ Deputy Commander-in-Chief, Air Force; + Chief of the General Staff, Air Force]

(Deputy Commandant of the Royal Hungarian Military Academy) 08/01/43 LG Sándor Magyarossy [+ Commander-in-Chief, Air Force] (retired; 11/44, Hungarian High Commissioner to Germany) 10/16/44 MG Sándor Illy [+ acting Commander-in-Chief, Air Force] 12/44 CG Emil N. Justy [+ Commander-in-Chief, Air Force] (05/08/45, made his way to Germany after war) 01/01/45 CG Kálmán Ternegg [+ Commander-in-Chief, Air Force; + Head, Bureau of the Air Force, Ministry of Defense].

11. **Inspectorate of River Forces** (also known as Commander-in-Chief of River Forces from 03/01/40): 06/25/37 RA Armin Bauszern [HN] (?) 01/15/39 Capt. Guido Tasnády [HN] (?) 04/30/42 Capt. Gen. [RA] Dr. Kálman Hardy [HN] (arrested and interned in Sopronkohida Prison) 10/16/44 RA Ödön Trunkwalter [HN] (?) 12/15/44

12. **Inspectorate of Border Guards**: Col. Teofil Hárosy /39 MG István Schweitzer (Commanding General, II Army Corps & II Military District) 10/01/39 MG Károly Beregfy [+ Commandant, General Staff Academy] (Commanding General, VI Army Corps) 11/01/41 MG Dezsö László (?) 03/01/43 unknown? 10/01/44 MG József Finta (?) 01/16/45 LG Ferenc Bardóczy.

13. **Inspectorate of Troop Trains**: /38 MG Imre Bangha [+ Inspector of Artillery; + Chief, Army Technical Staff] (President, Army Technical Committee) 02/01/40 unknown? 10/01/42 MG András Király (retired) /43

14. **Inspectorate of Military Training Schools**: 05/38 LG Gusztáv Denk [+ Deputy Commander-in-Chief, Armed Forces & Commanding General, Garrison Troops, Northern Hungarian Recovered Territories] (retired) 03/01/40

15. **Inspector of War Production**
    a. **Attached to the Inspector of War Production**
       /43 MG Tibor Kovács (retired) /43

N. **National Inspector, Military Labor Force, Ministry of Defense**: unknown? /39 MG Dr. Dániel Fábry [+ Chief, National Anti-Aircraft Defense; Chief, Section 36. Air Defense, Group VI Civil Defense, Bureau of Ground Forces, Ministry of Defense; + /39, Chief, Group XI Military Labor Force, Ministry of Defense] (Secretary-General, Supreme Military Council) /40 unknown? /41 MG Ernö Horny [+ Chief, Group XI Military Labor Forces - Military Sector & National Inspector of the Military Labor Forces, Main Labor Bureau, Ministry of Defense] /43 unknown? 44 Col. Dr. Lajos Fábián [+ Chief, Civilian Sector, Group XII Military Labor Forces, Ministry of Defense].

O. **Central Receiving Committee**
   President, Central Receiving Committee: unknown? /43 MG Mihály Kanotay (?) /44
   1. **Vice-President, Central Receiving Committee**: unknown? /40 Col. Mihály Kanotay (President, Central Receiving Committee) /43

P. **Attached to Ministry of Defense**
   /42 MG Sándor Dákay [Quartermaster-General] (retired) /42

Q. **At Disposal of Ministry of Defense**
   12/01/44 LG Béla Ebesfalvi Lengyel (Commanding General, III Army Corps) /45

Armed Forces Supreme Command

Commander-in-Chief, Armed Forces (03/01/40, office of **Commander-in-Chief, Army** and **Chief of the General Staff** are merged together): Gen./Inf. [Retired '36] Henrik Werth [+ Chief of the German Staff] (dismissed; /45, arrested by the Soviet Union; 05/28/52, died in captivity) 0906/41 LG Ferenc Szombathelyi [+ Chief of the German Staff] (dismissed; 10/16/44, arrested, interned at Sopronkohida Prison; 05/45, sentenced to death by Yugoslavia; 11/04/46, possible death by impalement) 04/19/44 CG Lajos Csatay vités Csatai [+ Minister of Defense] 05/44 CG János Vörös [+ Chief of the General Staff] (dismissed; 12/44 Minister of Defense & Chief of the General Staff Provisional Government) 10/16/44 CG Károly Beregfy [+ Minister of Defense & Chief of the General Staff] (arrested; /46, sentenced to death by military tribunal; 03/12/46, publically executed by firing squad) 03/45 disbanded.

1.   **Aide-de-Camp, Commander-in-Chief, Armed Forces**: 07/36 Col. József Heszlényi (Commanding Officer, 23rd Infantry Brigade) 11/38

A.   **Deputy Commander-in-Chief, Armed Forces** (03/01/40): LG András Littay [+ Deputy Chief of the General Staff] (Chief of Main Bureau of the Air Force, Ministry of Defense) 02/41 vacant 05/01/41 LG Zoltán Decleva [+ Deputy Chief of the General Staff] (Commander-in-Chief, Third Army) 11/01/41 LG József Bajnóczy [+ Deputy Chief of the General Staff] (dismissed) 04/16/44 CG Imre Ruszkiczay-Rüdiger [+ Deputy Minister of Defense & Deputy Chief of the General Staff] 05/04/44 LG Dezsö László [+Deputy Chief of the General Staff] (Commander-in-Chief, First Army) 10/16/44 CG [Retired '42] Ferenc Feketehalmy-Czeydner [+ Deputy Minister of Defense & Deputy Chief of the General Staff] (ill health - throat cancer, voice box removed; 03/45, Commanding General, German XVII Waffen-Infantry Corps of the SS [see Volume I]; /45, extradicted to Yugoslavia; /46, condemned to death and executed as a war criminal) 01/45

B.   **Supreme Military Tribunal (Court)**
1.   **President, Supreme Military Tribunal (Court)**: unknown? /42 LG Ernö Gyimesi (Commanding General, VII Army Corps) /42 MG Dezsö Kis (retired) /43 LG Ernö Gyimesi (retired) /44 LG Szilárd Bakay (Commanding General, I Army Corps, + Commanding General, Budapest Corps) /44
2.   **Vice President, Supreme Military Court**: unknown? /44 MG Mihály Cseke (attached to III Military District) /44
3.   **Councilor, Supreme Military Tribunal (Court)**: unknown? /43 MG Dezsö Kiss
4.   **Member, Supreme Military Tribunal (Court)**:
/?? MG Livius Barzó (retired) /43
/44 MG [Retired '43] Livius Barzó.

C.   **National Inspector, War Supply Production**: unknown? /43 MG [Retired '40] Árpád Denk-Doroszlay

D.   **National Anti-Aircraft Defense**: /37 MG Dr. Dániel Fábry [+ Chief, Section 36. Air Defense, Group VI Civil Defense, Bureau of Ground Forces, Ministry of Defense; + /39, Chief, Group XI Military Labor Force, Ministry of Defense; + /39, National Inspector, Military Labor Force] (Secretary-General, Supreme Military Council) /40 unknown? /41 MG Nándor Komposcht [+ Chief, Group VI Civil Defense, Bureau of

Ground Forces, Ministry of Defense] (President, Central Inspecting Committee) /42

    1.   **Attached to Anti-Aircraft Artillery Command**

        /42 Col. László Kesseö (Commanding General, 1st Anti-Aircraft Artillery Brigade & Commanding Officer, Solt-Dunaegyhazai Bridgehead)

E.   **Attached to Commander-in-Chief, Armed Forces**

    11/44 MG Gyula Kovács [+ acting Chief of the General Staff] (Inspector of Combat Discipline) /45

Military High Command

Supreme Commander-in-Chief of Armed Forces: Adm. Miklós Horthy de Nagybánya, Duke of Szeged and Otranto [HN] (arrested; in exile in Germany) 10/16/44

Military Chancellery

Chief of the Military Chancellery [Magyarország Kormányzójának Katonai Irodája]: 01/16/35 MG Lajos Keresztes-Fischer (Chief of the General Staff) 05/24/38 LG Gusztáv Vitéz Jány [+ Adjutant General] (02/01/39, Commanding General, I Army Corps) 09/29/38 office combined with **Adjutant General** - see **Adjutant-General and Chief of the Military Chancellery**.

A.   **Deputy Chief of the Military Chancellery**: /35 Col. Sándor Horváth (Commanding General, 2nd Motorized Brigade) 01/39

Adjutant-General: 01/38 LG Gusztáv Vitéz Jány [+ 05/38, Military Chancellary] (02/01/39, Commanding General, I Army Corps) 09/29/38 office combined with **Chief of the Military Chancellery** - see **Adjutant-General and Chief of the Military Chancellery.**

Adjutant-General and Chief of the Military Chancellery (09/29/38): LG Lajos Keresztes-Fischer (retired; Minister of Interior) 11/11/42 LG Béla Miklós de Dalnoki (Commander-in-Chief, First Army) 07/29/44 MG Antal Vattay [+ to 08/20/44, Commanding General, II Reserve Army Corps] (arrest by the Germans; /49, arrested and imprisoned by the communist) 10/15/44 dissolved.

Royal Hungarian Army Supreme Command

Commander-in-Chief, Army (to 03/01/40 when it becomes **Commander-in-Chief, Armed Forces**): 09/05/38 Gen./Inf. Hugó Sónyi (retired; Member of the Crown Council) 03/01/40 becomes **Commander-in-Chief, Armed Forces** - see **Commander-in-Chief, Armed Forces**.

A. **Deputy Commander-in-Chief, Army** (to 03/01/40 when it becomes **Deputy Commander-in-Chief, Armed Forces**): /36 Gen. Richard Rapaich (?) 05/07/38 Gen. Gusztáv Denk [+ Commanding General, Garrison Troops, Northern Hungarian Recovered Territories & Inspector of Military Training Schools] (retired) 03/01/40 becomes **Deputy Commander-in-Chief, Armed Forces** - see **Deputy Commander-in-Chief, Armed Forces**.
    [**NOTE:** also listed in one source, /36 Col. Zoltán Decleva (Secretary-General of the Supreme Military Council) 05/38]

B. **Crown Council, Secretary-General, Supreme Military Council**: 05/38 MG Zoltán Decleva (Commanding General, I Army Corps) 03/01/40 MG Dr. Dániel Fábry (retired) 10/11/40 MG Antal Náray (?) 02/05/42 MG Kálmán N. Máthé (?) /43 MG Géza N. Vörös (Commanding General, VII Army Corps) 05/15/44 MG Elemér Mészöly (?) 10/16/44 disbanded.
    1. **Permanent Deputy Secretary General**: unknown? /43 Dr. IRME RÁKOCZY 10/16/44 dissolved.

C. **Crown Prosecutor of the Army**: /?? MG Nándor Leventeújváry (retired; /44, Chief, Section 13. Group VIII, Commander of the Levente, Ministry of Defense & Judge Advocate General) /43

D. **Supreme Military Court**:
    President, Supreme Military Court: /34 MG Lajos Karay (retired) /40 unknown? 10/01/42 MG Gusztáv Hennyey [+ Inspector of Infantry] (Main Labor Bureau, Ministry of Defense) 11/01/43 Col. Lajos Szalay 10/15/44 disbanded.
    1. **Vice President, Supreme Military Court**: unknown? 02/01/42 MG János Dömötör (Chief, Officer Training Course) /42 Col. Milkós Depóld (acting; Commanding General, 102nd Light Division) 05/26/42 unknown? /43 MG József Futó (Commanding General, VII Army Corps) /44 MG Milkós Depóld (attached to I Army Corps) /44

E. **President, Army Medical Council**: unknown? /40 MG Antal Demkö (Chief, Section 12 Medical, Group III Procurement & Supply, Ministry of Defense) /42 MG Géza Franz (Commanding General, 11th Army Hospital; /43, Chief Medical Officer, I Army Corps) /43?

F. **Chief, Central Inspection Committee**: unknown? 03/01/40 MG Ernö Gyimesi (President, Supreme Military Tribunal (Court)) /42 MG Nándor Komposcht (retired) /43 MG Ernö Billnitzer (Commandant, Hajmaskér Field Artillery School) /44

G. **Commissioner of Transportation**: unknown? /44 MG Imre Czlenner (acting).

H. **Attached to Commander-in-Chief, Army**
    /44 MG Ferenc Bardóczy (Commandant, Royal Hungarian Military Academy) /45

Chief of the General Staff

Chief of the General Staff (03/01/40, office of Commander-in-Chief, Armed Forces and Chief of the General Staff are merged together): 10/12/36 GdI Jenö Rátz [+ Defense Minister] (retired) 01/38 LG Lajos Keresztes-Fischer (Military Chancellary & Adjutant General) 05/24/38 Gen./Inf. [Retired'36] Henrik Werth [+ 03/01/40, Commander-in-Chief, Armed Forces] (dismissed; ; /45, arrested by the Soviet Union; 05/28/52, died in captivity) 09/06/41 LG Ferenc Szombathelyi [+ to 05/30/41, Commander-in-Chief, Armed Forces] (dismissed; 10/16/44, arrested, interned at Sopronkohida Prison; 05/45, sentenced to death by Yugoslavia; 11/04/46, possible death by impalement) 04/19/44 CG János Vörös [+ 05/44, Commander-in-Chief, Armed Forces] (dismissed; 12/44 Minister of Defense & Chief of the General Staff Provisional Government) 10/16/44 CG Károly Beregfy [+ Minister of Defense & Commander-in-Chief, Armed Forces] (arrested; /46, sentenced to death by military tribunal; 03/12/46, publically executed by firing squad) 03/45 disbanded.

[NOTE: acting Chief of the General Staff 11/44 LG Gyula Kovács [+ attached to Commander-in-Chief, Armed Forces] (Inspector of Combat Discipline) /45**]**

1.   **Aide-de-Camp, Chief of the General Staff**: /40 Col. of RF Kálmán Hardy [HN] (Commanding Officer, 26th Infantry Brigade) 08/41

A.   **First Deputy Chief of the General Staff**: unknown? 01/15/39 MG István Náday (Chief, Executive Staff, General Staff) 03/01/40 dissolved.

B   **Second Deputy Chief of the General Staff**: /36 Col. Zoltán Decleva (Secretary-General of the Supreme Military Council; 03/01/40, Commanding General, I Army Corps) 10/01/38 MG Ferenc Szombathelyi (Commanding General, VIII Army Corps) 01/15/39 unknown? 03/01/40 dissolved.

C.   **Deputy Chief of the General Staff**: unknown? 03/01/40 LG András Littay [+ Deputy Commander-in-Chief, Armed Forces] (Chief of Main Bureau of the Air Force, Ministry of Defense) 02/41 vacant 05/01/41 LG Zoltán Decleva [+ Deputy Commander-in-Chief, Armed Forces] (Commander-in-Chief, Third Army) 11/01/41 LG József Bajnóczy [+ Deputy Commander-in-Chief, Armed Forces] (dismissed) 04/16/44 CG Imre Ruszkiczay-Rüdiger [+ Deputy Minister of Defense & Commander-in-Chief, Armed Forces] 05/04/44 LG Dezsö László [+ Deputy Commander-in-Chief, Armed Forces] (Commander-in-Chief, First Army) 10/16/44 CG [Retired'42] Ferenc Feketehalmi-Czeydner [+ Deputy Minister of Defense & Deputy Commander-in-Chief, Armed Forces] (ill health - throat cancer, voice box removed; 03/45, Commanding General, German XVII Waffen-Infantry Corps of the SS [see Volume I]; /45, extradicted to Yugoslavia; /46, condemned to death and executed as a war criminal) 01/45

D.   **Group I Executive Staff, General Staff**: unknown? 03/01/40 MG István Náday (Chief Group I Organization & Mobilization, Ministry of Defense) 03/01/41 MG Dezsö László (Commanding General, 5th Infantry Brigade) 02/01/41 MG János Vörös (02/43, Head, Main Bureau of Supply, Ministry of Defense) /42 MG Géza N. Vörös (Secretary-General of the Supreme Military Council) /43 MG Dr. Gyula Hankovzsky (Commanding General, 13th Infantry Division) 04/01/44 MG Elemér Sáska.

1.   **Section 1. Operations, Executive Staff, General Staff**: 02/37 Col. Sándor Magyarossy (Commanding Officer, 2nd Border Guard Brigade; 03/01/40, Chief, Training, General Staff) 11/38 Col. Dezsö László (Commanding Officer, 5th Infantry Brigade) 02/01/41 Col. Elemér Sáska (Commanding Officer, 1st

Motorized Brigade) 05/01/42 Col. Elemér Mészöly /43 Col. Lajos Nádas 02/43 Maj. Ferernc Kovács.

    a.   **Section K Operations Planning, etc., Section 1. Operations, Executive Staff, General Staff**:

    b.   **Section E Organization, Weapons, Replacements, Section 1. Operations, Executive Staff, General Staff**:

2.   **Section 2. Intelligence, Group I Executive Staff, General Staff**: /38 unknown? /39 MG István Újszászy (/43, Commander, State Security Police; /44, arrested by the Gestapo; /45, arrested by the Soviet NKVD; /47, returned to Hungary but imprisoned; /48, disappeared, presumed dead) /42 MG József Vasváry (Commanding General, 15th Light Infantry Division) 08/01/43 Col. Gyula Kádár /44 Col. László Kuthy 10/44 MG András Zákó.

    a.   **Deputy Chief, Military Intelligence**: /42 Col. László Karátsony (Deputy Chief, Group III Procurement & Supply, Main Bureau of Supply, Ministry of Defense) /43

    b.   **Attaché Group, Section 2. Intelligence, Group I Executive Staff, General Staff** (attached 1941)

        i.   **Military Attaché Bulgaria**: unknown? 02/15/41 Col. Otto Hatz /44

        ii.   **Military Attaché Croatia**: unknown? 05/15/41 Maj. Lajos Keresztes-Karleusa /43 LCol. György Kollényi

        iii.   **Military Attaché Estonia**: unknown? 01/14/41 Col. Sándor Homlok [+ Military Attaché Finland, Latvia, Lithuania, & Sweden] (Military Attaché Germany & Switzerland) 11/03/41 LCol. Dr. László Rakolczai [+ Military Attaché Finland, Latvia, Lithuania, & Sweden] /43 Maj. Frigyes Kóbor [+ Military Attaché Finland, Latvia, Lithuania, & Sweden] /44

        iv.   **Military Attaché Finland**: unknown? 01/14/41 Col. Sándor Homlok [+ Military Attaché Estonia, Latvia, Lithuania, & Sweden] (Military Attaché Germany & Switzerland) 11/03/41 LCol. Dr. László Rakolczai [+ Military Attaché Estonia, Latvia, Lithuania, & Sweden] /43 Maj. Frigyes Kóbor [+ Military Attaché Estonia, Latvia, Lithuania, & Sweden] /44

        v.   **Military Attaché France**: /38 Col. László Karátsony [+ Military Attaché Portugal & Military Attaché, Spain] (Deputy Chief, Military Intelligence) /42 Maj. László Karátsony /43 Maj. Béla Sipos /44

        vi.   **Military Attaché Germany**: unknown? 12/01/41 MG Sándor Homlok [+ Military Attaché Switzerland] /44 MG Sándor Makray.

        vii.   **Military Attaché Italy**: unknown? /41 Col. László János Szábó (Commanding General, 5th Reserve Infantry Division) 10/43 Col. Dr. László Rakolczai /44

        viii.   **Military Attaché Latvia**: unknown? 01/14/41 Col. Sándor Homlok [+ Military Attaché Estonia, Finland, Lithuania, & Sweden] (Military Attaché Germany & Switzerland) 11/03/41 LCol. Dr. László Rakolczai [+ Military Attaché Estonia, Finland, Lithuania, & Sweden] /43 Maj. Frigyes Kóbor [+ Military Attaché

Estonia, Finland, Lithuania, & Sweden] /44

ix. **Military Attaché Lithuania**: unknown? 01/14/41 Col. Sándor Homlok [+ Military Attaché Estonia, Finland, Latvia, & Sweden] (Military Attaché Germany & Switzerland) 11/03/41 LCol. Dr. László Rakolczai [+ Military Attaché Estonia, Finland, Latvia, & Sweden] /43 Maj. Frigyes Kóbor [+ Military Attaché Estonia, Finland, Latvia, & Sweden] /44

x. **Military Attaché Mexico**: unknown? 09/29/41 Maj. Lóránd Utassy /51 disbanded.

xi. **Military Attaché Portugal**: /38 Col. László Karátsony [+ Military Attaché Spain & Military Attaché, France] (Deputy Chief, Military Intelligence) /42 MG Jenö Szántay [+ Military Attaché Spain].

xii. **Military Attaché Romania**: unknown? /42 Maj. Endre Bartha /44 disbanded.

xiii. **Military Attaché Slovakia**: unknown? 08/01/41 LCol. Kálmán Kéry [+ /42 to /43, Adjutant, Ministry of Defense] /44 Maj. Sándor Lipcsey-Magyar

xiv. **Military Attaché Spain**: /38 Col. László Karátsony [+ Military Attaché Portugal & Military Attaché, France] (Deputy Chief, Military Intelligence) /42 MG Jenö Szántay [+ Military Attaché Potugal].

xiv. **Military Attaché Sweden**: unknown? 01/14/41 Col. Sándor Homlok [+ Military Attaché Estonia, Finland, Latvia, & Lithuania] (Military Attaché Germany & Switzerland) 11/03/41 LCol. Dr. László Rakolczai [+ Military Attaché Estonia, Finland, Latvia, & Lithuania] /43 Maj. Frigyes Kóbor [+ Military Attaché Estonia, Finland, Latvia, & Lithuania] /44

xv. **Military Attaché Switzerland**: unknown? 12/01/41 MG Sándor Homlok [+ Military Attaché Germany] /44

xvi. **Military Attaché Turkey**: unknown? 02/15/41 Maj. Ottó Hatz 09/29/41 LCol. Kálmán /44

c. **Section Ny War Diary, Section 2. Intelligence, Group I Executive Staff, General Staff**:

d. **Section D Counter Intelligence, Section 2. Intelligence, Group I Executive Staff, General Staff**

e. **Attached to Military Intelligence**
/40 Col. Gábor Faraghó (Military Attaché Soviet Union) /40
/40 Col. Sándor Homlok (/40, Military Attaché Sweden [Stockholm]) /39

3. **Section 3. Quartermaster-General, Group I Executive Staff, General Staff**: /36 Col. János Dömötör (Commanding Officer, 11th Infantry Brigade) 02/01/39 Col. Árpád Denk-Doroszlay (Chief, Section 3./c Ammunition and Explosives, Group III Procurement & Supply, Main Bureau of Supply, Ministry of Defense) /40 Col. János Henkey /42 Col. Gyula Karánsebsey (Chief, Economic Administration, High Command) /44 Col. István Olchváry.

4. **Section 6. Information Propaganda, Group I Executive Staff, General Staff**: unknown? /41 LCol. Gyula Kádár /43 Col. Sándor Nagylucskay /44 Maj. László Kovács.

5. **Section 7./k Transport, Group I Executive Staff, General Staff**: unknown? /39 LCol. Kálmán Kéry (Military Attaché Slovakia) /41 Col. Imre Czlenner (Commanding Officer, 2nd Field Replacement Division) 08/44 LCol. Gyula Miklós /44 Col. Imre Czlenner (acting Commissioner of Transportation) /45 Maj Imre Kertész

6. **Section 7./m Technical & Engineer Services, Group I Executive Staff, General Staff**: unknown? /39 Col. Endre Schmoll (Commandant, Bolyai János Technical Academy) 11/01/40 Col. László Gertenyesi Hollósy-Kuthy (Commanding General, 22nd Light Infantry Division) 08/01/42 Col. Gusztáv Deseö (Commanding General, 1st Light Infantry Division) 08/10/43 LCol. Géza Bodiczy.

   a. **Army Technical Staff**: 08/01/36 MG Imre Bangha [+ Inspector pf Artillery; + /38, Inspector of Army Trains] (President, Army Technical Committee) 02/01/40

   b. **President, Army Technical Committee**: unknown? 02/01/40 MG Imre Bangha (retired) /40

   c. **Unknown? Section, Section 7./m Technical & Engineer Services, Group I Executive Staff, General Staff**: unknown? /40 Col. László Gertenyesi Hollósy-Kuthy (Chief, Section 7./m Technical & Engineer Services, Group I Executive Staff, General Staff) 11/01/40

7. **Section 7./ö Communications, Group I Executive Staff, General Staff**: unknown? /39 Col. János Vörös (Commanding Officer, 2nd Motorized Brigade) 10/31/40 Col. Ferenc Deák (Infantry Commander, 7th Infantry Division) 03/01/44 LCol. György Porzezinsky 10/16/44 Maj. Deszö Huba.

   a. **Section K Operations, Section 7./ö Communications, Group I Executive Staff, General Staff**:

   b. **Section E Organization, Section 7./ö Communications, Group I Executive Staff, General Staff**:

   c. **Section Supply, Section 7./ö Communications, Group I Executive Staff, General Staff**: unknown? /39 Col. István Kerényi.

   d. **Section Air Force, Section 7./ö Communications, Group I Executive Staff, General Staff**:

   e. **Liaison Officer to the Royal Hungarian Post, Section 7./ö Communications, Group I Executive Staff, General Staff**: unknown? /39 Col. Gyula Szita /40 Col. Károly Csabay /44

8. **Section 7. Rep Air Force Operations, Group I Executive Staff, General Staff**:

9. **Section 8./e General Officer Assignments, Group I Executive Staff, General Staff**:

E. **Group II Training Staff, General Staff**: unknown? /39 MG József Németh (I) [+ Commanding General, 1st Mountain Brigade & Chief, Section 5. Troop Training, Group II Training Staff, General Staff] (11/01/42, Commanding General, I Army Corps & I Military District) 03/01/40 Col. Sándor Magyarossy (leave of absence; Main Air Force Bureau, Ministry of Defense) 09/41 MG Sándor Horváth (Chief, Field Officer Training) /41 unknown? 11/15/42 MG József Grassy (joins the Waffen-SS; Commanding General, 25th Waffen-Grenadier-Division der SS Hunyadi; + /45,

Commanding General, 26th Waffen-Grenadier-Division der SS Hungaria; /45, extradited to Yugoslavia; /46, condemned to death and executed as a war criminal [See Volume I]) /44 vacant.

1. **Section 4. General Staff Training, Group II Training Staff, General Staff**: unknown? /39 Col. István Kiss (Commanding General, 23rd Light Infantry Division) 02/17/42 Col. Jenö Tömöry (09/23/44, Commanding Officer, 4th Field Replacement Division) /43 Col. Sándor Kiss (acting) /44 Col. László Huszkay (acting).

    a. **Section Regulations, Section 4. General Staff Training, Group II Training Staff, General Staff**:

2. **Section 5. Troop Training, Group II Training Staff, General Staff**: /37 Col. Béla Z. Zsombolyay (08/10/43, Commanding General, 25th Infantry Division) /39 MG József Németh (I) [+ Commanding General, 1st Mountain Brigade & Chief, II Training Staff, General Staff] (11/01/42, Commanding General, I Army Corps & I Military District) 03/01/40 Col. Ferenc Horváth (III) (Chief of Staff, IX Army Corps) 09/04/40 Col. Mikály Ibrányi (Commanding General, 17th Light Infantry Division) 08/01/42 unknown? 08/10/43 Col. Sándor Makray (Commanding General, 2nd Mountain Brigade) /44 Col. Ferenc Németh.

3. **Section 6. Military Training Outside the Army, Group II Training Staff, General Staff** (becomes Group VIII of the Ministry of Defense in 1941): unknown? /40 Col. István Kudriczy (acting Chief of Staff, I Army Corps) /41 unknown? /41 Col. István Kudriczy (Chief, Section 40./e Organization, Group VIII Commander of the Levente, Bureau of Pre-Military Training, Ministry of Defense) /41 becomes **Group VIII Commander of the Levente, Ministry of Defense** - see **Group VIII Commander of the Levente, Ministry of Defense**.

    a. **Attached to Section 6. Military Training Outside the Army, Group II Training Staff, General Staff**:

    /41 Col. Tibor Fráter (attached to Section 40./k Training, etc., Group VIII Commander of the Levente, Bureau of Pre-Military Training, Ministry of Defense) /41

4. **Section 5/rep Training, Group IV Organization and Training, Main Bureau of the Air Force, Ministry of Defense** (assigned to Army General Staff): unknown? /42 LCol. Pál Németh /44

5. **Section 7./rep Employment and Operations, Group IV Organization and Training, Main Bureau of the Air Force, Ministry of Defense** (assigned to Army General Staff): unknown? /42 Maj. Kázmér Jávorszky /43 LCol. Zoltán Aszódy /44

F. **Adjutant, General Staff**: /38 LCol. Kálmán Bartalis /41 Col. Dr. László Rakolczai /41 vacant /44 Maj. Ferenc Adonyi 06/19/44 Maj Albin Kapitánffy 10/15/44 disbanded.

1. **Chief, Disciplinary Section, General Staff**: unknown? /40 MG Iván Kishindi Hindy (attached to I Army Corps) /42

G. **Chiefs of Army Branches**

1. **Chief, Army Engineers**: unknown? /40 MG Gustáv Cziegler [+ Chief, Army Technical Institute] (retired) /43

2. **Chief, Army Technical Staff**: unknown? /44 MG Zoltán K. Harmos.

3. **Chief, Signal Corps**: /38 Col. Henrik Hargittay (Commanding Officer, 101st Signals Regiment; /43, Inspector of Signals) /41

4. **Chief, Army Medical Corps**: unknown? /42 MG Antal Demkö [+ Chief, Section 12 Medical, Group III Procurement & Supply, Ministry of Defense] (retired) /43 unknown? /44 MG Géza Franz.

5. **Chief, Army Veterinary Service**: MG Károly Halasi (retired) /43

H. **Army Chief Economical Director**: MG Sándor Dravay

1. **Chief, Economic Administration, High Command**: unknown? /45 MG Gyula Karánsebsey.

I. **Chief Army Auditor**: MG Gyula Elekes

J. *Schools*

1. **Commandant, General Staff Academy [Royal Hungarian Military Academy]**: /36 Col. István Schweitzer (Inspector of Border Guards) 10/01/39 Col. Károly Beregfy [+ Inspector of Border Guards] (Commanding General, VI Army Corps) 03/01/41 MG Dezsö László [+ /42, Commanding General, 7th Light Infantry Division] (Commanding General, VIII Army Corps) 03/01/43 MG Gyula Kovács (Commanding General, IX Army Corps) /44 Col. Imre Czlenner (Chief, Section 7./k Transport, Group I Executive Staff, General Staff) 10/01/44 Col. Sándor András (acting) /45 MG Ferenc Bardóczy.

   a. **Assistant Commandant, General Staff Academy [Royal Hungarian Military Academy]**: unknown? /44 MG Sándor András (Infantry Commander, 10th Infantry Division) /44

2. **Commandant, Ludovika Military Academy**: 08/01/36 Col. Ferenc Szombathelyi (Deputy Chief of the General Staff) 10/01/38 Col. Ferenc K. Farkas (Commanding General, VI Army Corps) 08/20/43 Col. Elemér Sáska [+ 04/01/44, Chief, Group I Executive Staff, General Staff] 10/31/44 Col. László Kocsis.

   a. **Instructor, Ludovika Military Academy**
   /34 Col. Béla Madaras (Deputy Commander, II Army Corps & Commanding General, II Military District) /40

   b. **Attached to Ludovika Military Academy**
   /40 Col. Ferenc Bisza (attached to Air Force High Command) /41

3. **Commandant, Hunyadi Mátyás Military School**: /38 MG József Finta (Deputy Commander, VII Army Corps & Commanding General, VII Military District) 08/01/42

4. **Commandant, Army Technical Institute**: /35 MG Gustáv Cziegler [+ /40, Chief, Army Engineers] (retired) 12/42 MG Zoltán K. Harmos (Chief, Army Technical Staff) /44

   a. **Deputy Commandant, Military Technical Institute**: unknown? /40 MG Zoltán K. Harmos (Commandant, Military Technical Institute) /42

5. **Commandant, Hajmaskér Field Artillery School**: unknown? /44 MG Ernö Billnitzer (Assault Artillery Commander, Group Budapest) /44

6. **Commandant, Riding & Driving Teacher Training School**: unknown? /41 MG Ottó Binder (Chief, Remount Training Staff; /43, retired) /42

7. **Commandant, "Kinizsi Pál" Non-Commissioned Officers' Training School**: /38 MG Lóránt Kiskéry (Deputy Commander, VI Army Corps &

Commanding General, VI Military District) 08/40

8. **Chief, Officer Training Course**: unknown? /39 MG Dezsö Füleky (retired) /41 unknown? /42 MG János Dömötör (Commanding General, III Army Corps) 07/15/42

9. **Chief, Administrative Training Courses**: /38 Col. Gyula Karánsebsey (Chief, Section 6./k Budget, Group III Procurement & Supply, Main Bureau of Supply, Ministry of Defense) /40

10. **Chief, Field Officer Training Courses**: unknown? /41 MG Gyula Kovács (Chief, Section I/a., Second Army) 07/01/42 MG Emil Lánghy (retired) /43

K. **Chief Medical Officer, General Staff**: /38 MG Pál Encsy (Commanding General, 1st Army Garrison Hospital; /45, retired) /43

Royal Hungarian Air Force

Commander-in-Chief, Air Force: /38 MG László Háry [+Commanding General, 1st Air Brigade] (/41, retired) 02/01/40
> 02/01/40 MG József Grassy [+ Inspector of the Air Force] (Commanding General, 15th Infantry Brigade) 03/01/41
> /40 LG [Retired '40] Valdemár Kenese (retired) /41

03/01/41 LG Béla Rákosi (?) 08/01/43 LG Sándor Magyarossy [+ Inspector of the Air Force] (retired; 11/44, Hungarian High Commissioner to Germany) 08/01/44 MG István Bánfalvy [+ Head, Air Force Bureau, Ministry of Defense] (acting Head, Bureau of Ground Forces, Ministry of Defense) 10/16/44 MG Sándor Illy [acting; + Inspector of the Air Force] 11/01/44 Col. Edgar Keksz (acting) 12/44 CG Emil N. Justy [+ Inspector of the Air Force] (05/08/45, made his way to Germany after war) 01/01/45 CG Kálmán Ternegg [+ Inspector of the Air Force; + Head, Bureau of the Air Force, Ministry of Defense].

A. **Deputy Commander-in-Chief, Air Force**: unknown? /40 Col. Sándor András (attached to the Air Force Bureau, Ministry of Defense) 01/01/41 MG Emil N. Justy (10/41, Commanding General, I Anti-Aircraft Artillery Corps) 04/41 unknown? /42 MG Sándor András [+ Chief of the General Staff, Air Force, Air Force; + Inspector of the Air Force] (Deputy Commandant of the Royal Hungarian Military Academy) /44 MG Vilmos Hellebronth (Deputy Head, Bureau of the Air Force, Ministry of Defense) /44

B. **Chief of the General Staff, Air Force**: unknown? /39 MG István Bánfalvy (Chief, Section 3./c Ammunition and Explosives, Group III Procurement & Supply, Main Bureau of Supply, Ministry of Defense) /41 unknown? /42 MG Sándor András [+ Deputy Commander-in-Chief, Air Force; + Inspector of the Air Force] (Deputy Commandant of the Royal Hungarian Military Academy]

C. **Chief Administration Officer, Air Force High Command**: unknown? /39 Col. Géza Csenky (attached to Air Force High Command) /41 unknown? /42 Col. Sándor Illy (Commanding General, 2nd Air Brigade) /43 Col. Tibor Fráter (Commanding Officer, 2nd Air Force Brigade) /43 MG Sándor Illy (Deputy Commander, 1st Air Division) /43

D. **Commandant, Miklós Horthy Air Force Academy**: unknown? /39 Col. Sándor Illy (Chief, Section 9. Schools and Training, Group I Organization & Mobilization, Bureau of Ground Forces, Ministry of Defense) /41

E. **Attached to Air Force High Command**:
> /41 Col. Ferenc Bisza (Commanding General, 2nd Motorized Brigade) /41
> /41 Col. Géza Csenky (retired) /43
> /42 Col. Sándor Illy (Chief Administration Officer, Air Force High Command) /42

Military Districts

I Military District (02/01/29; HQ: Budapest): 10/01/36 MG Vilmos Nagybaczoni Nagy [+ to 10/01/38, Commanding General, 1st Mixed Brigade; + 10/01/38, Commanding General, I Army Corps] (Inspector of Infantry) 02/01/39 MG Gusztáv Vitéz Jány [+ Commanding General, I Army Corps] (Commander-in-Chief, Second Army) 03/01/40 MG Zoltán Decleva [+ Commanding General, I Army Corps] 08/40 MG Artúr Horvay [+ Deputy Commander, I Army Corps] (retired) 02/41 LG Imre Ruszkiecay-Rüdiger [+ Commanding General, I Military District] (?) 11/01/42 LG József Németh (I) [+ Commanding General, I Army Corps] (Inspector of Infantry) 11/01/43 LG Béla Aggteleky [+ Commanding General, I Military District] (?) 08/01/44 LG Szilárd Bakay [+ Commanding General, I Military District & Commanding General, Budapest Corps] (arrested by the Germans; placed in Mauthausen Concentration Camp; /46, executed by the Soviets as a war criminal) 10/08/44 LG Béla Aggteleky [+ Commanding General, I Military District] (?) 10/16/44 LG Iván Kishindi Hindy [+ Commanding General, I Military District] (retired; /46, condemned to death and executed) 02/12/45 lost in Budapest.

A. **Commandant, Budapest**: unknown? /39 MG Gyözö Horváth (attached to IX Army Corps) /42

II Military District (02/01/29): 08/01/37 MG Milán Temessy [+ to 10/01/38, Commanding General, 2nd Mixed Brigade; + 10/01/38, Commanding General, II Army Corps] (?) 10/01/39 MG István Schweitzer [+ Commanding General, II Military District] 08/40 MG Béla Madaras [+ Deputy Commander, II Army Corps] (retired) 10/40 MG István Schweitzer [Commanding General, II Army Corps] (Commander-in-Chief, First Army) 02/01/41 MG Gusztáv Hennyey [+ Commanding General, II Army Corps] (Inspector of Infantry & President, Supreme Military Court) 10/01/42 LG Béla Aggteleky [+ Commanding General, II Army Corps] (?) 11/01/43 LG János Vörös [+ Commanding General, II Army Corps] (Chief of the General Staff) 04/19/44 vacant 05/15/44 LG István Kiss [+ Commanding General, II Army Corps] 08/44 MG Pál Szombathy [+ Deputy Commander, II Army Corps] (?) 11/15/44 LG István Kiss [+ Deputy Commander, II Army Corps].

A. **Gendarmerie, II Military District, Székesfehérvár**: unknown? /39 Col. Ágoston Huszár (Special Purposes General, Inspector to the Gendarmerie) /40

III Military District (10/01/28): 11/36 MG Gusztáv Vitéz Jány [+ Commanding General, 3rd Mixed Brigade] (Chief of the Military Chancellery & Adjutant-General) 05/25/38 vacant 10/01/38 MG László Belásfalvi Kiss [+ to 10/01/38, Commanding General, 3rd Mixed Brigade; + 10/01/38, Commanding General, III Army Corps] 08/40 MG Béla Pekle [+ Deputy Commander, III Army Corps] (retired) 02/41 László Belásfalvi Kiss [+ Commanding General, III Army Corps] (retired; /45, Commanding General, Defense Zone "F") 05/01/42 MG Imre Szécsy [+ Deputy Commander, III Army Corps; + 06/01/42 Deputy Commander, VIII Army Corps & Commanding General, VIII Military District] (Commanding General, 124th Light Infantry Division & Commanding General, Hungarian Occupation Group West) 10/01/42 MG Ottó Abt [+ Deputy Commander, III Army Corps] (at disposal of III Army Corps) 11/42 MG Endre Mezö [+ Deputy Commander, III Army Corps] (?) 02/01/43 MG Árpád Matláry [+ Deputy Commander, III Army Corps] (?) 05/16/43 LG Szilárd Bakay [+ Commanding General, III Army Corps] (President, Supreme Military Courts) 08/44 MG Árpád Matláry [+

Deputy Commander, III Army Corps] (?) /44 MG [Retired '42] Lászió Akay (?) 03/45 LG Ferenc Horváth (III) (American prisoner-of-war) 05/45.
A.   **Attached to III Military District**:
       /44 MG Mihály Cseke (retired) /45.

IV Military District (04/01/28): MG Henrik Worth [+ Commanding General, 4th Mixed Division] (retired) 12/01/35 MG László Falta [+ Commanding General, 4th Mixed Division] (Inspector of Gendarmerie) 10/01/38 MG Jenö Ruszkay [+ Commanding General, IV Army Corps] (?) 02/01/40 MG László Horváth [+ to 08/40, Commanding General, IV Army Corps] 08/40 MG Gyözö Materna Széchy [+ Deputy Commander, IV Army Corps] (Chief, Section 10 Enlisted Personnel, Group I Organization & Mobilization, Ministry of Defense) 10/40 MG László Horváth [+ Commanding General, IV Army Corps] (?) 08/01/41 MG Lajos Csatay vités Csatai [+ Commanding General, IV Army Corps] 05/01/42 MG Jenö Felkl [+ Deputy Commander, IV Army Corps] (?) 11/15/42 MG [Retired] Dr. Béla Remesy [+ Deputy Commander, IV Army Corps] (retired) 06/01/43 LG Jozséf Heszlényi [+ Commanding General, IV Army Corps] 07/01/44 MG [Retired] Dr. Béla Remesy [+ Deputy Commander, IV Army Corps] (retired) 09/15/44 MG László Molnár [+ Deputy Commander, IV Army Corps] (?) 11/15/44 LG Imre Kálmán.
A.   **Chief Medical Officer, IV Military District**: unknown? /42 MG [Retired '42] Antal Kábdebó (retired) /43

V Military District (12/07/25): 11/01/36 MG László Mérey [+ to 10/01/38, Commanding General, 5th Mixed Brigade; + 10/01/38, Commanding General, V Army Corps] (retired?) 08/01/39 MG Antal Silley [+ Commanding General, V Army Corps] 08/40 MG János Solymossy [+ Deputy Commander, V Army Corps] (retired) 10/40 MG Antal Silley [+ Commanding General, V Army Corps] (?) 08/01/41 MG Ferenc Feketehalmy-Czeydner [+ Commanding General, V Army Corps] (dismissed and retired; joined the German-SS, Deputy Commander, II SS Panzer Corps [see Volume I]; 10/16/44, Deputy Minister of Defense, Deputy Commander-in-Chief, Armed Forces, & Deputy Chief of the General Staff) 08/20/42 LG Frigyes Gyimesi [+ Commanding General, V Army Corps] (Head, Bureau of Supply, Ministry of Defense) 08/01/43 LG Pál Platthy [+ Commanding General, V Army Corps] (?) 04/01/44 vacant 06/01/44 LG Imre Kálmán (?) 09/15/44 LG Zoltán Algya-Pap [+ 09/15/44, Commanding General, V Army Corps] (?) 11/15/44 LG Miklós Nagyöszy [+ Commanding General, V Army Corps; + 11/15/44, Head, Bureau of Supply, Ministry of Defense] (Head, Bureau of the Ground Forces, Ministry of Defense) 12/17/44 LG Mihály Ibrányi [+ Commanding General, V Army Corps] (Inspector of Infantry) 03/01/45 LG József Vasváry [+ Commanding General, V Army Corps] 05/45 surrendered.
A.   **Gendarmerie, Military District V** (Szeged): unknown? /42 MG Lászió (?) /44
B.   **Attached to V Military District**
       09/44 MG Antal Benda (retired) /45.

VI Military District (10/01/28): 10/01/32 MG Géza Demény [+ Commanding General, 6th Mixed Brigade] (?) 05/01/36 MG Géza E. Siegler [+ to 10/01/38, Commanding General 6th Mixed Army Brigade; + 10/01/38, Commanding General, VI Army Corps] (?) 06/18/39 vacant 08/01/39 MG József Bajnóczy [+ to 08/40, Commanding General, VI Army Corps] 08/40 MG Lóránd Kiskéry [+ Deputy Commander, VI Army Corps] (retired) 12/40 MG József Bajnóczy [Commanding General, VI Army Corps] (Deputy Commander-in-Chief, Armed

Forces & Deputy Chief of the General Staff) 11/01/41 MG Károly Beregfy [Commanding General, VI Army Corps] 06/01/43 MG Béla Tanitó [+ to 11/15/44, Deputy Commander, VI Army Corps; + 08/01/43, Deputy Commander, VIII Army Corps & Commanding General, VIII Military District] (?   ) 03/04/45 dissolved.

VII Military District (07/01/28): 05/01/34 MG Hugó Sónyi [+ Commanding General, 7th Mixed Brigade] (Commander-in-Chief, Army Supreme Command) 09/05/38 vacant 10/01/38 MG András Littay [+ Commanding General, VII Army Corps] (Deputy Chief of the General Staff & Deputy Commander-in-Chief, Armed Forces) 03/01/40 MG Gyula S. Nágy [+ to 08/40, Commanding General, VII Army Corps] 08/40 MG Gyözö Beleznay [+ Deputy Commander, VII Army Corps] (Commanding General, 19th Infantry Brigade) 08/01/41 MG Gyula S. Nágy [Commanding General, VII Military District] (retired) 05/01/42 MG Károly Ertsay-Leitschaf [+ Deputy Commander, VII Army Corps] (Inspector, Military Stud; /45, retired) 08/01/42 MG József Finta [+ Deputy Commander, VII Army Corps] (Commanding General, 7th Replacement Division) 08/44 LG Géza N. Vörös [+ Commanding General, VII Army Corps] (?   ) 10/17/44 CG János Markóczy [+ Commanding General, VII Army Corps] (?   ) 11/15/44 dissolved.
A.   **Chief Administration Officer, VII Military District**: unknown? /44 MG _[Retired '42] Elemér Hunfalvay.

VIII Military District (01/15/39): MG Ferenc Szombathelyi [+ to 08/40, Commanding General, VIII Military District] 08/40 MG Iván Szilassy [+ Commanding General, VIII Military District] (?   ) 10/40 MG Ferenc Szombathelyi [+ Commanding General, VIII Army Corps; + 06/22/41, Commanding General, Carpathian Battle Group] 08/01/41 MG Géza Lakatos de Csikszentsimon [+ Commanding General, VIII Army Corps] 06/01/42 MG Imre Szécsy [+ Deputy Commander, VIII Army Corps; + to 10/01/42, Deputy Commander, III Army Corps & Commanding General, III Military District; + 10/01/42, Commanding General, 124th Light Infantry Division & Commanding General, Hungarian Occupation Group West] (retired) 08/01/43 MG Béla Tanitó [+ Deputy Commander, VIII Army Corps; + Commanding General, VI Military District; + to 11/15/44, Deputy Commander, VI Army Corps] (?   ) 03/04/45 LG Dr. Gyula Hankovszky [+ Commanding General, VIII Army Corps] 05/45 dissolved.
A.   **Attached to VIII Military District**
        /43 Col. Lajos Burget (Artillery Commander, I Armored Corps) /43

IX Military District (09/04/40): MG László Stirling [+ Commanding General, IX Army Corps] (Inspector-General of the Armaments Industry, Main Bureau of Supply, Ministry of Defense) 02/01/42 MG Béla Miklós de Dalnoki [+ Commanding General, IX Army Corps] (Adjutant-General & Head of the Military Chancellery) 10/14/42 MG Lajos Veress [+ Commanding General, IX Army Corps] (Commander-in-Chief, Second Army (#2)) 08/28/44 vacant 09/01/44 MG Gyula Kovács [+ Commanding General, IX Army Corps] (acting Chief of the General Staff & attached to Commander-in-Chief of the Armed Forces) 11/44 MG Frigyes Vasváry [+ Commanding General, IX Army Corps] 05/45 disbanded.

Armies

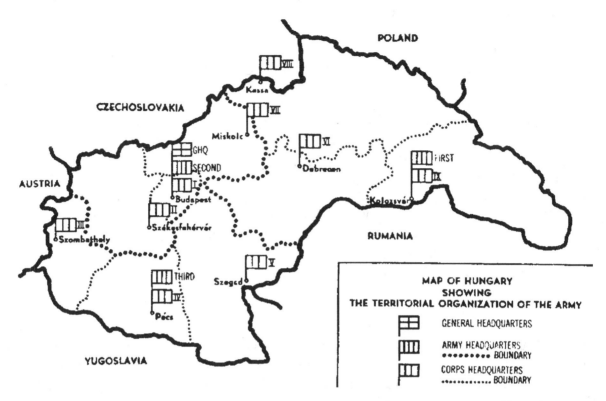

First Army (03/01/40; HQ: Kolozsvár; originally **Hungarian Home Army**; redesignated **First Army** on activation of Second Army; did not see any action until 05/44; fought against the Soviet Union until the end of the war): MG Vilmos Nagybaczoni Nagy (retired; 09/24/42, Minister of Defense) 02/01/41 LG István Schweitzer (removed; 11/42, retired; /47, tried by Hungarian military tribunal and sentenced to death; 11/26/47, executed by firing squad) 08/01/42 LG István Náday [+ 10/01/42 to 11/01/43, Head, Bureau of the Ground Forces, Ministry of Defense] (replaced; 07/44, retired; 09/44, sent to Italy as an emissary of VA Horthy to the Western Allies to try to negotiate Hungary's withdrawal from the war) 04/01/44 CG Géza Lakatos de Csikszentsimon (placed on leave; 08/29/44, appointed Prime Minister) 05/26/44 LG Károly Beregfy (Commander-in-Chief, Replacement Army) 07/25/44 LG Ferenc K. Farkas [acting; + Commanding General, VI Army Corps] 08/01/44 LG Béla Miklós de Dalnoki (left command, made his way to the Soviets lines, following the coup and appointed Prime Minister of the Provisional Government; replaced) 10/16/44 CG Dezsö László (06/08/49, executed after being tried by a military tribunal) 05/08/45 surrenderes in Bohmia, Czechoslovakia.

[NOTE: acting Commanding General, First Army 04/45, MG László Karátsony]

A.   **Chief of Staff, First Army** (03/01/40): MG Ferenc Feketehalmi-Czeydner (Commanding General, V Army Corps) 08/41 Col. János Vörös (Chief of Operations Section, General Staff) 11/41 unknown? 10/01/42 MG István Kiss (Commanding General, VII Army Corps) 05/01/43

B.   *Components* - **First Army** (07/43)
1.   **I Army Corps**

2. **VI Army Corps**
3. **VII Army Corps**
C. *Components* - **First Army** (04/18/44)
1. **VI Army Corps**
2. **VII Army Corps**
3. **German XI Army Corps**
4. **20th Infantry Division**
D. **Artillery, First Army** (03/01/40): unknown? /44 MG Jenö Kunczfalusy (Inspector of Field Artillery) 10/01/44 MG Gyula Királyehotai Lehoszky (Deputy Inspector of Artillery) /45
E. **Rear Area, First Army** (03/01/40): unknown? /42 MG Géza Fehér (Commanding General, 23rd Reserve Infantry Division) /44
F. **Military Discipline, First Army** (03/01/40): unknown? /44 MG János Testhali Jordán (Artillery Commander, Third Army) /44
G. **Attached to Commanding General, First Army**
/44 MG Gyözö Árvay (Commanding General, 5th Light Division) /44

Second Army (#1) (03/01/40; HQ: Budapest; 07/42, arrived on Eastern Front; 01/43, all but destroyed north of Stalingrad): LG Gusztáv Vitéz Jány (Commander-in-Chief, Second Army (#2); 04/05/44, retired; /47, condemned to death and executed) 02/43 virtually destroyed. **[NOTE:** short time in /42 MG Lajos Csatay vités Csatai [+ Commanding General, IV Army Corps]]
A. **Chief of Staff, Second Army** (03/01/40): MG Géza Lakatos de Csikszentsimon (Commanding General, VIII Army Corps) 08/01/41 unknown? /42 MG Gyula Kovács (Commandant, Royal Hungarian Military Academy) 03/01/43 dissolved.
B. *Components* - **Second Army (#1)** (02/42)
1. **III Army Corps**
2. **IV Army Corps**
3. **VII Army Corps**
4. **1st Armored Division**
5. **2nd Air Brigade**
C. **Quartermaster-General, Second Army** (03/01/40): MG Sándor Dákay (Quartermaster-General attached to Ministry of Defense) /42
D. **Chief Medical Officer, Second Army**: /42 MG József Bandenburg [+ Chief Medical Officer, II Army Corps] /43
E. **Chief Veterinary Officer, Second Army** (03/01/40) MG Ernö Friedl (retired) /43
F. **Section I/a., Second Army** (03/01/40): unknown? /42 MG Gyula Kovács (Chief of Staff, Second Army (#2)) /42
G. **Training, Second Army (#1)** (03/01/40): unknown? 02/43 MG János Legeza (retired; /45, Commanding General, Defense Zone "B") /45
H. **Attached to Second Army**
/42 Col. Oszkár Ginszkey (Commanding General, 6th Light Division) 11/15/42
/43 MG Ferenc Lóskay (Commanding General, 10th Infantry Division) /43

Hungarian Occupation Forces Command [H. O. F. C.] (05/01/43, from **Second Army (#1)**): 12/42 LG Ernö Gyimesi (President, Supreme Military Tribunal (Court)) 05/01/43 MG

Géza Lakatos de Csikszentsimon (Commander-in-Chief, Second Army) 08/43 redesignated **Second Army (#2)** 08/43 CG Géza Lakatos de Csikszentsimon (Commander-in-Chief, First Army) 04/01/44 relieved by **Hungarian Occupation Command [H. O. C.]**, the Headquarters Staff was transported back to Hungary and used for other purposes 04/01/44 LG Lajos Vörös von Dalnoki (replaced) 04/07/44 disbanded.

A.   **Chief of Staff, Second Army (#2)** (08/43):
B.   *Components* - **Hungarian Occupation Forces Command** (05/43)
     1.   **VII Army Corps**
     2.   **VIII Army Corps**

Second Army (#3) (08/2844, reformed from **IX Army Corps**): CG Lajos Veress (arrested and interned in Sopronkohida Prison; put on trail for his life; received 15-year prison term; escaped; 05/45, arrested by the Soviets; 12/45, released; /47, arrested and tried by a Hungarian Military Tribunal, sentenced to death for anti-Government activities; sentence commuted to life imprisonment; /56, released from prison during Hungarian Uprising and fled to England) 10/16/44 LG Jëno Major (dispatched to Germany; Inspector-General of the Hungarian Army) 11/13/44 disbanded and used to form **Inspector-General of the Hungarian Army**.

A.   *Components* - **Second Army (#2)** (08/44)
     1.   **II Army Corps**
     2.   **IX Army Corps**

Inspector-General of the Hungarian Army (11/13/44, from **Second Army (#3)**): CG Jëno Major.

Third Army (03/01/40; HQ: Pécs; 06/12/43, inactivated; 08/01/43, activated; 05/15/44, disbanded; 09/10/44, reformed from **IV Army Corps**): **Third Army (#1)** 03/01/40 LG Elemér Gorondy-Novák (dismissed; retired by 02/42) 11/01/41 LG Zoltán Decleva (retired) 12/01/42 LG Lajos Csatay vités Csatai (Minister of Defense) 06/12/43 inactivated, position not filled; **Third Army (#2)** 08/01/43 LG Károly Beregfy (Commander-in-Chief, First Army) 05/15/44 disbanded, reformed **Third Army (#3)** 09/19/44 LG József Heszlényi (committed suicide) 05/08/45 surrendered in Styria, Austria.

A.   **Chief of Staff, Third Army**: unknown? /43 Col. Dr. Gyula Hankovzsky (Chief, Group I Executive Staff, General Staff) /43
B.   *Components* - **Third Army** (07/43)
     1.   **I Army Corps**
     2.   **VI Army Corps**
     3.   **VII Army Corps**
C.   *Components* - **Third Army** (04/41)
     1.   **I Army Corps**
     2.   **IV Army Corps**
     3.   **V Army Corps**
     4.   **Mobile [Rapid] Corps**
D.   **Chief Administration Officer, Third Army**: unknown/ /45 MG László Bokross.
E.   **Artillery, Third Army** (03/10/40): unknown? /41 LG Lajos Csatay vités Csatai (Commanding General, IV Army Corps) 08/01/41 unknown? /44 MG Vilmos

Maasfeldi Hanke (?) /44 MG János Testhali Jordán (retired)
/45 MG Lajos Burget.
/45 MG János Lajtay.
F.   **Rear Area, Third Army**
1.   **Military Administration, Rear Area, Third Army**: unknown? /44 MG [Retired '44]
Aladár Asztalossy

Home Army (10/16/44): LG Kálmán Ternegg (Commander-in-Chief, Air Force & Inspector of the Air Force & Chief, Main Bureau of the Air Force, Ministry of Defense) 01/01/45

Replacement Army (07/25/44): LG Károly Beregfy (Minister of Defense, Commander-in-Chief, Armed Forces; & Chief of the General Staff) 10/16/44

Army Battle Group

Carpathian Battle Group (06/22/41; Ukraine; 07/09/41, withdrawn back to Hungary; 11/0141, disbanded and redesignated **Hungarian Occupation Command**): MG Ferenc Szombathelyi [+ to 08/01/41, Commanding General, VIII Army Corps & VIII Military District] (Commander-in-Chief, Armed Forces & Chief of the General Staff) 09/06/41 vacant 11/01/41 disbanded and redesignated **Hungarian Occupation Command** - see **Hungarian Occupation Command**.

A.   *Components* - **Carpathian Group** (06/22/41)
  1.   **VIII Army Corps**
  2.   **Mobile Corps**

Group Budapest
A.   **Assault Artillery, Group Budapest**: /44 MG Ernö Billnitzer.

Corps

Army Corps

I Army Corps (10/01/38; HQ: Budapest; from **1ˢᵗ Mixed Brigade**; Hungary; 04/07/41, Third Army; 04/17/41, Hungary; 08/30/44, Second Army; 11/12/44, Third Army; 02/12/45, destroyed in Budapest): MG Vilmos Nagybaczoni Nagy [+ Commanding General, I Military District] (Inspector of Infantry) 02/01/39 MG Gusztáv Vitéz Jány [+ Commanding General, I Military District] (Commander-in-Chief, Second Army) 03/01/40 MG Zoltán Decleva [+ to 08/40, Commanding General, I Military District] (Deputy Chief of the General Staff) 05/01/41 LG Imre Ruszkiczay-Rüdiger [+ 02/41, Commanding General, I Military District] (Deputy Minister of Defense & Chief, Main Bureau of Supply Section, Ministry of Defense) 11/01/42 LG József Németh (I) [+ Commanding General, I Military District] (Inspector of Infantry) 11/01/43 LG Béla Aggteleky [+ Commanding General, I Military District] (?) 08/01/44 LG Szilárd Bakay [+ Commanding General, Budapest Corps & Commanding General, I Military District] (arrested by the Germans; placed in Mauthausen Concentration Camp; /46, executed by the Soviets as a war criminal) 10/08/44 LG Béla Aggteleky [+ Commanding General, I Military District] (?) 10/16/44 LG Iván Kishindi Hindy [+ Commanding General, I Military District] (retired; /46, condemned to death and executed) 02/12/45 lost in Budapest.

A. **Deputy Commander, I Army Corps** (08/01/38): unknown? 08/40 MG Artúr Horvay [+ Commanding General, I Military District] (retired) 02/41

B. **Chief of Staff, I Army Corps** (08/01/38): unknown? /40 Col. István Kudriczy (acting; Chief, Section 6. Military Training Outside the Army, Group II Training Staff, General Staff) /41

C. *Components - I Army Corps*
   1. **1ˢᵗ Infantry Brigade**
   2. **2ⁿᵈ Infantry Brigade**
   3. **3ʳᵈ Infantry Brigade**

D. *Components - I Army Corps* (04/41)
   1. **1ˢᵗ Infantry Brigade**
   2. **13ᵗʰ Infantry Brigade**
   3. **14ᵗʰ Infantry Brigade**

E. *Components - I Army Corps* (06/41)
   1. **1ˢᵗ Infantry Division**
   2. **7ᵗʰ Infantry Division**
   3. **1ˢᵗ Rapid Division**

F. **Chief Administration Offiecr, I Army Corps** (10/01/38):
     10/01/38 Col. Kálmán Ditrói Csiby (Commanding Officer, 32ⁿᵈ Infantry Regiment)
     10/01/38 Col. Artúr Horvay (Deputy Commander, I Army Corps) 08/40
   /41 MG Károly Bogányi (Commanding General, 102ⁿᵈ Light Division) /41

G. **Artillery, I Army Corps** (10/01/38): unknown? /40 Col. László Kassay-Farkas (Chief, Engineer (Pioneer) Training Courses) /41 unknown? /42 Col. László Deseö (Artillery

Commander, III Army Corps) /42 Col. László Bokross (Artillery Commander, V Army Corps) /43

H. **Anti-Aircraft Artillery, I Army Corps** (10/01/38): Col. Emil N. Justy (Chief, Anti-Aircraft Bureau, Ministry of Defense) 03/01/40 Col. Nándor Komposcht (Chief, Anti-Aircraft Artillery Section, Ministry of Defense) /40 MG Egon Barczaujfalusy (Commanding General, 1st Anti-Aircraft Brigade) /41

I. **Engineers, I Army Corps** (10/01/38): unknown? /44 MG Ernö Horny (retired) /45.

J. **Quartermaster-General, I Army Corps** (10/01/38): Col. István Hlatky (Chief, Section 6./k Budget, Group III Procurement & Supply, Main Bureau of Supply, Ministry of Defense) /40 unknown? /41 MG Vince Derestey (retired) /43

K. **Chief Medical Officer, I Army Corps** (10/01/38): unknown? /43 MG Géza Franz (Chief, Army Medical Staff) /44

L. **Chief Veterinary Officer, I Army Corps** (10/01/38): MG Ernö Friedl (Chief Veterinary Officer, Second Army) /40

M. **Attached to I Army Corps**

/42 Col. László Gerlóczy (Commanding Officer, 3rd Anti-Aircarft Brigade) /42

/42 MG Iván Kishindi Hindy (Commanding General, I Army Corps & Commanding General, I Military District) /10/16/44

/42 MG Gyözö Horváth (retired; /44, Commanding General, 25th "Székler" Infantry Division) /43

/44 MG Milkós Depóld (Vice-President, Supreme Military Council) /44

/44 MG Milkós Depóld.

II Army Corps (10/01/38; HQ: Székesfehérvár; from **2nd Mixed Brigade**; Hungary; 08/30/44, Second Army (#2), Eastern Front; 10/18/44, German Sixth Army; 10/23/44, Third Army): 10/01/38 MG Milán Tenessy [+ Commanding General, II Military District] (?) 01/10/39 MG István Schweitzer [+ to 08/40, Commanding General, II Military District; + 10/40, Commanding General, II Military District] (Commander-in-Chief, First Army) 02/01/41 MG Gusztáv Hennyey [+ Commanding General, II Military District] (Inspector of Infantry & President, Supreme Military Court) 10/01/42 LG Béla Aggteleky [+ Commanding General, II Military District] (?) 11/01/43 LG János Vörös [+ Commanding General, II Military District] (Chief of the General Staff) 04/19/44 vacant 05/15/44 LG István Kiss [+ to 08/44, Commanding General, II Military District] (Deputy Commander, II Army Corps & Commanding General, II Military District) 11/15/44 LG István Kudriczy 05/08/45 surrendered in Styria, Austria.

A. **Deputy Commander, II Army Corps** (10/01/38): unknown? 08/40? MG Béla Madaras [+ Commanding General, II Military District] (retired) 10/40 unknown? 08/44 MG Pál Szombathy [+ Commanding General, II Military District] (?) 11/15/44 LG István Kiss [+ Commanding General, II Military District].

B. **Chief of Staff, II Army Corps** (10/01/38): Col. Aladár Szirmay (Chief, Group IV Organization & Training, Main Bureau of the Air Force, Ministry of Defense) /40

C. *Components - II Army Corps*
1. **4th Infantry Brigade**
2. **5th Infantry Brigade**
3. **6th Infantry Brigade**

D. *Components - II Army Corps* (08/44)
1. **2nd Armored Division**

2. **7th Field Replacement Division**
3. **9th Field Replacement Division**
4. **1st Replacement Mountain Brigade**
5. **2nd Replacement Mountain Brigade**

E. *Components* - II Army Corps (06/41)
1. **2nd Infantry Division**
2. **8th Infantry Division**
3. **10th Infantry Division**

F. **Chief Administration Officer, II Army Corps** (10/01/38): unknown? 02/01/40 MG József Benke (retired) /40

G. **Artillery, II Army Corps** (10/01/38): Col. László Kassay-Farkas (Artillery Commander, I Army Corps) /40? unknown? /42 MG Ernö Billnitzer (Chief, Central Inspection Committee) /43 unknown? /44 Col. János Lajtay (Artillery Officer, Third Army) /45

H. **Anti-Aircraft Artillery, II Army Corps** (10/01/38): Col. Nándor Komposcht (Anti-Aircraft Artillery Commander, I Army Corps) /40

I. **Chief Engineer Officer, II Army Corps** (10/01/38): MG Zoltán Gergely (Chief of Danube Fortifications; /44, Commanding General, 203rd Infantry Brigade) /44

J. **Chief Medical Officer, II Army Corps**: /42 MG József Bandenburg [+ to /43, Chief Medical Officer, Second Army] (retired) /44

III Army Corps (10/01/38; HQ: Szombathely; from **3rd Mixed Brigade**; Hungary; 04/10/42, Second Army, Eastern Front; 04/30/42, German Army Group South; 04/30/42; German Army Group "B"; 07/09/42, Second Army; 05/43, Hungary; 08/04/44, First Army; 03/45, disbanded): 10/01/38 MG László Belásfalvi Kiss [+ to 08/40, Commanding General, III Military District; + 10/40, Commanding General, III Military District] (retired; /45 Commanding General, Defense Zone "F") 08/01/41 MG Ödön Domaniczky [+ to 05/01/42, Commanding General, III Military District] (retired) 06/15/42 LG György Rakovszky (11/01/43, Head, Bureau of the Ground Forces, Ministry of Defense) 07/15/42 LG János Dömötör (retired) 12/05/42 LG Count Marcell Stomm (Soviet prisoner-of-war; captured at Stalingrad) 02/01/43 vacant 05/15/43 LG Szilárd Bakay [+ Commanding General, III Military District] (President, Supreme Military Court) 08/01/44 LG Béla Aggteleky (?) 10/08/44 LG László Gertenyesi Hollósy-Kuthy (?) 10/31/44 LG József Vasváry (Commanding General, V Army Corps & V Military District) 01/45 LG Ferenc Horváth (III) (Commanding General, III Military District) 03/45 LG Béla Ebesfalvi Lengyel (retired) /45 disbanded.

A. **Deputy Commander, III Army Corps** (10/01/38): unknown? 08/40? MG Béla Pekle [+ Commanding General, III Military District] (retired) 02/41 unknown? 05/01/42 MG Imre Széchy [+ Commanding General, III Military District; + 06/01/42, Deputy Commander, VIII Army Corps & Commanding General, VIII Military District] (Commanding General, 124th Light Infantry Division & Commanding General, Hungarian Occupation Group West) 10/01/42 MG Ottó Abt + Commanding General, III Military District] (at disposal of III Army Corps) 11/09/42 MG Endre Mezö [+ Commanding General, III Military District] (?) 02/01/43 MG Árpád Matláry [+ Commanding General, III Military District] (?) 05/16/43 unknown? 08/44 MG Árpád Matláry [+ Commanding General, III Military District] (?) 03/45 dissolved.

B. **Chief of Staff, III Army Corps** (10/01/38): Col. Gyözö Ankay-Anesini (Head, President's Bureau, Ministry of Defense) /40 Col. Gyula Kovács (Chief, Section 3./a

Weapons & Optics, Group III Procurement & Supply, Main Bureau of Supply, Ministry of Defense) /41 unknown? /43 MG Dr. Gyula Hankovzsky (Chief, Group I Executive Staff, General Staff) /43

C. ***Components* - III Army Corps**
    1. **7th Infantry Brigade**
    2. **8th Infantry Brigade**
    3. **9th Infantry Brigade**
D. ***Components* - I Army Corps** (06/41)
    1. **3rd Infantry Division**
    2. **4th Infantry Division**
    3. **12th Infantry Division**
    4. **2nd Rapid Division**
E. ***Components* - III Army Corps** (02/42)
    1. **6th Light Infantry Division**
    2. **7th Light Infantry Division**
    3. **9th Light Infantry Division**
F. **Artillery, III Army Corps** (10/01/38): MG Lászió Akay (retired; /44 Commanding General, 3rd Military District) /42 MG Gábor Marton (?) /42 Col. Vilmos Maasfeldi Hanke (in reserve; /43, Artillery Commander, IX Army Corps) /42 Col. László Deseö (Soviet prisoner-of-war) /43 Col. János Testhali Jordán (Chief, Military Discipline, First Army) /44
G. **Chief Engineer Officer, III Army Corps** (10/01/38): Col. Zoltán Gergely (Chief Engineer Officer, IX Army Corps) /41
H. **At Disposal of III Army Corps**:
    11/09/42 MG Ottó Abt (retired; /46, condemned to death as a war criminal by the Soviets and executed; /91 rehabilitated) /43

IV Army Corps (10/01/38; HQ: Pécs; from **4th Mixed Brigade**; Hungary; 04/03/41, Third Army; 04/17/41, Hungary; 04/10/42, Second Army, Eastern Front; 04/30/42, German Army Group South; 07/07/42, German Army Group "B"; 07/09/42, Second Army; 05/43, Hungary; 08/04/44, Third Army; 09/19/44, disbanded and used to form **Third Army (#3)**): 10/01/38 MG Jenö Ruszkay [+ Commanding General, IV Military District] (?) 02/01/40 MG László Horváth [+ to 08/40, Commanding General, IV Military District; +10/40 Commanding General, IV Military District] (?) 08/01/41 MG Lajos Csatay vités Csatai [+ to 05/42, Commanding General, IV Military District; + /42, acting Commanding General, Second Army] (Commander-in-Chief, Third Army) 10/01/42 MG János Legeza (Commanding General, VII Army Corps) 12/03/42 MG József Heszlényi [+ 06/01/43 to 07/01/43, Commanding General, IV Military District] (Commander-in-Chief, Third Army) 09/10/44 vacant 09/19/44, disbanded and used to form **Third Army (#3)** - see **Third Army (#3)**.

A. **Deputy Commander, IV Army Corps** (10/01/38): unknown? 08/40? MG Gyözö Materna Széchy [+ Commanding General, IV Military District] (Chief, Section 10 Enlisted Personnel, Group I Organization & Mobilization, Ministry of Defense) 10/40 unknown? 05/01/42 MG Jenö Felkl [+ Commanding General, IV Military District] (?) 11/15/42 MG _[Retired] Dr. Béla Remesy [+ Commanding General, IV Military District] (retired) 06/01/43 unknown? 07/01/44 MG _[Retired] Dr. Béla Remesy [+ Commanding General, IV Military District] (retired) 09/15/44 MG László Molnár [+

Commanding General, IV Military District] (?   ) 11/15/44

B. **Chief of Staff, IV Army Corps** (10/01/38): unknown? /40 Col. József Futó (Commanding Officer, 13th Field Artillery Detachment; /42, Artillery Commander, V Army Corps) /41 Col. Ágoston Gecsányi (Section 1./b Wartime Organization, Group I Organization & Mobilization, Bureau of Ground Forces, Ministry of Defense)

C. *Components - IV Army Corps*
1. **10th Infantry Brigade**
2. **11th Infantry Brigade**
3. **12th Infantry Brigade**: /38 Col. Ottó Abt (Deputy Commander, 8th Infantry Brigade) /41

D. *Components - IV Army Corps* (04/41)
1. **2nd Infantry Brigade**
2. **10th Infantry Brigade**
3. **12th Infantry Brigade**

E. *Components - I Army Corps* (06/41)
1. **5th Infantry Division**
2. **6th Infantry Division**
3. **9th Infantry Division**

F. *Components - IV Army Corps* (05/42)
1. **10th Light Infantry Division**
2. **12th Light Infantry Division**
3. **13th Light Infantry Division**

G. **Infantry, IV Army Corps** (10/01/38): Col. József Benke (Commanding General, 12th Infantry Brigade) 01/23/39

H. **Artillery, IV Army**: /42 Col. Gyula Királyehotai Lehoszky (acting Commanding Officer, 20th Light Infantry Division) /43

I. **Chief Medical Officer, IV Army Corps** (10/01/38): unknown? /39 MG Antal Kábdebó (retired; /42, Chief Medical Officer, IV Military District) /42 MG György Csongor

V Army Corps (10/01/38; HQ: Szeged; from **5th Mixed Brigade**; Hungary; 04/03/41, Third Army; 04/17/41, Hungary; 08/04/44, First Army): 10/01/38 MG László Mérey [+ Commanding General, V Military District] (retired?) 08/01/39 MG Antal Silley [+ to 08/40, Commanding General, V Military District; + 10/40, Commanding General, V Military District] (?   ) 08/01/41 MG Ferenc Feketehalmy-Czeydner [+ Commanding General, V Military District] (dismissed and retired; joined the German-SS, Deputy Commander, II SS Panzer Corps [see Volume I]; 10/16/44, Deputy Minister of Defense, Deputy Commander-in-Chief, Armed Forces, & Deputy Chief of the General Staff) 08/20/42 LG Frigyes Gyimesi [+ Commanding General, V Military District] (Head, Bureau of Supply, Ministry of Defense) 08/01/43 LG Pál Platthy [+ Commanding General, V Military District] (?   ) 04/01/44 vacant 06/01/44 disbanded; reformed 09/01/44 LG Zoltán Algya-Pap [+ 09/15/44, Commanding General, V Military District] (?   ) 11/15/44 LG Miklós Nagyöszy [+ Commanding General, V Military District; + 11/15/44, Head, Bureau of Supply, Ministry of Defense] (Head, Bureau of the Ground Forces, Ministry of Defense) 12/17/44 LG Mihály Ibrányi [+ Commanding General, V Military District] (Inspector of Infantry) 03/01/45 LG József Vasváry [+ Commanding General, V Military District] 05/45 surrendered in Austria.

A. **Deputy Commander, V Army Corps** (10/01/38): unknown? 08/40? MG János Solymossy [+ Commanding General, V Military District] (retired) 10/40

B. **Chief of Staff, V Army Corps** (10/01/38): Col. László Gertenyesi Hollósy-Kuthy (Chief, Unknown? Section, Section 7./m Technical & Engineer Services, Ministry of Defense) /40 MG Dezsö Istóka (Chief, Group II Personnel, Bureau of Ground Forces, Ministry of Defense) /43

C. *Components - V Army Corps*
   1. **13th Infantry Brigade**
   2. **14th Infantry Brigade**
   3. **15th Infantry Brigade**

D. *Components - V Army Corps* (04/41)
   1. **14th Infantry Brigade**
   2. **19th Infantry Brigade**
   3. **2nd Cavalry Brigade**

E. *Components - I Army Corps* (06/41)
   1. **14th Infantry Division**
   2. **15th Infantry Division**
   3. **4th Cavalry Brigade**

F. **Infantry, V Army Corps** 910/01/38): MG Alfréd Friedrich (Commanding General, 16th Infantry Brigade) /40

G. **Artillery, V Army Corps** (10/01/38): unknown? /42 MG József Futó /43 Col. László Bokross (Commanding Officer, 103rd Independent Motorized Artillery Detachment; /44, Commanding Officer, 101st Independent Motorized Artillery Detachment; /45, Chief Administration Officer, Third Army) /44

H. **Quartermaster, V Army Corps** (10/01/38): MG Géza Horvárth (Military Auditor Office, Deputy Defense Minister, Ministry of Defense) /42

I. **Attached to V Army Corps**
   /43 Col. Pái Magyar (Commanding General, 23rd Light Division) 07/01/43
   07/01/43 MG Milkós Depóld (attached to I Army Corps) /44

VI Army Corps (10/01/38; HQ: Debrecen; from **6th Mixed Brigade**; Hungary; 04/18/44, First Army, Eastern Front; 10/13/44, Third Army; 11/12/44, disbanded): 10/01/38 MG Géza Siegler [+ Commanding General, VI Military District] (?) 06/18/39 vacant 08/01/39 MG József Bajnóczy [+ to 08/40, Commanding General, VI Military District; + 12/40, Commanding General, VI Military District] (Deputy Commander-in-Chief, Armed Forces & Deputy Chief of the General Staff) 11/01/41 MG Károly Beregfy [+ to 06/01/43, Commanding General, VI Military District] (Commander-in-Chief, Third Army) 06/12/43 vacant 08/21/43 MG Ferenc K. Farkas [+ 08/44, temporary Commanding General, First Army] (National Employment Commissioner) 10/16/44 MG Milós Nagyöszy (Head, Bureau of Supply, Ministry of Defense & Commanding General, V Army Corps and V Military District) 11/15/44 disbanded.

A. **Deputy Commander, VI Army Corps** (10/01/38): unknown? 08/40 MG Lóránd Kiskéry [+ Commanding General, VI Army Corps] (retired) 12/40 unknown? 06/01/43 MG Béla Tanitó [+ Commanding General, VI Army Corps; + 08/01/43, Deputy Commander, VIII Army Corps & Commanding General, VIII Military District] 11/15/44 dissolved.

B. **Chief of Staff, VI Army Corps** (10/01/38): Col. Mikály Ibrányi (Section 5. Troop

Training, Group II Training Staff, General Staff) 03/01/40 Col. Ferenc Horváth (III) (Chief of Staff, IX Army Corps) 09/04/40 MG Mihály Cseke (Chief, Section 1./b Wartime Organization, Group I Organization & Mobilization, Bureau of Ground Forces, Ministry of Defense) /42

C. **Components - VI Army Corps**
   1. **16th Infantry Brigade**
   2. **17th Infantry Brigade**
   3. **18th Infantry Brigade**
D. **Components - VI Army Corps** (04/18/44)
   1. **25th Infantry Division**
   2. **27th Light Infantry Division**
   3. **201st Light Infantry Division**
E. **Chief Administration Officer, VI Army Corps** (10/01/38): Col. Ferenc Horváth (II) (retired) /40
F. **Artillery, VI Army Corps** (10/01/38): Col. Károly Bogányi (Chief Administration Officer, I Army Corps) /41 unknown? /42 MG Sándor Berecz (retired) /43 Col. János Lajtay (Artillery Officer, II Army Corps) /44
G. **Air Defense, VI Army Corps** (10/01/38): unknown? /39 MG Egon Barczaujfalusy (Commanding Officer, Anti-Aircraft Artillery, I Army Corps) /40
H. **Chief Medical Officer, VI Army Corps** (10/01/38): MG Ferenc Horváth (I) (retired) /40
I. **Attached to VI Army Corps**
   05/01/42 MG Gyözö Ankay-Anesini (retired) /43

VII Army Corps (10/01/38; HQ: Miskolc; ; from **7th Mixed Brigade**; Hungary; 04/07/41, Third Army; 04/17/41, Hungary; 04/10/42, Second Army, Eastern Front; 05/01/43, Army of Occupation; 08/15/43, Second Army; 04/01/44, First Army; 08/01/44, German Panzer Army 1; 09/13/44, German Reserves, Army Group North Ukraine; 09/18/44, Second Army, 09/23/44, Third Army): 10/01/38 MG András Littay [+ Commanding General, VII Military District] (Deputy Chief of the General Staff & Deputy Commander-in-Chief, Armed Forces) 03/01/40 MG Gyula S. Nágy [+ to 08/40, Commanding General, VII Military District; + 12/40, Commanding General, VII Military District] (retired) 05/01/42 MG Sándor Horváth (retired) 05/21/42 LG Ernö Gyimesi (Commanding General, Hungarian Occupation Army) 12/03/42 MG János Legeza (Chief, Training, Second Army) 02/43 LG Ernö Gyirnesi (retired) 05/01/43 MG István Kiss (Commanding General, II Army Corps) 05/15/44 LG Géza N. Vörös [+ Commanding General, VII Military District] (?) 08/26/44 MG István Kudriczy (Commanding General, II Army Corps) 10/17/44 LG János Markóczy [+ Commanding General, VII Military District] (Inspector of Infantry) 11/15/44 MG József Futó (retired) /44 dissolved.

A. **Deputy Commander, VII Army Corps** (10/01/38): unknown? 08/40 MG Gyözö Beleznay [+ Commanding General, VII Military District] (08/01/41, Commanding General, 19th Infantry Brigade) 12/40 unknown? 05/01/42 Col. Károly Ertsay-Leitschaf [+ Commanding General, VII Military District] (Inspector, Military Stud; /45, retired) 08/01/42 MG József Finta [+ Commanding General, VII Military District] (Commanding General, 7th Replacement Division) 08/31/44
B. **Chief of Staff, VII Army Corps** (10/01/38): unknown? /40 Col. István Kozma (Commanding Officer, Transylvania Units, IX Army Corps) /42

C. *Components - VII Army Corps*
    1. **19th Infantry Brigade**
    2. **20th Infantry Brigade**
    3. **21st Infantry Brigade**
D. *Components - VII Army Corps* (05/42)
    1. **19th Light Infantry Division**
    2. **20th Light Infantry Division**
    3. **23rd Light Infantry Division**
E. *Components - VII Army Corps* (05/43)
    1. **1st Light Infantry Division**
    2. **5th Light Infantry Division**
    3. **9th Light Infantry Division**
    4. **12th Light Infantry Division**
    5. **23rd Light Infantry Division**
F. *Components - VII Army Corps* (04/18/44)
    1. **16th Infantry Division**
    2. **18th Light Infantry Division**
G. **Artillery, VII Army Corps** (10/01/38): Col. Tibor Kovács (attached to the Inspector of War Production) /42 unknown? /43 Col. Gyula Királyehotai Lehoszky (Artillery Officer, First Army) 10/01/44
H. **Chief Administration Officer, VII Army Corps** (10/01/38): unknown? /41 Col. Károly Ertsay-Leitschaf (Deputy Commander, VII Army Corps) 05/01/42

VIII Army Corps (01/15/39; HQ: Kassa; Hungary; 06/22/41, temporary redesignated **Carpathian Battle Group**, German Seventeenth Army; 07/09/41, redesignated **VIII Army Corps**, with German Army Group South; 11/01/41, Hungary; 05/18/43, Army of Occupation; 08/15/43, Second Army; 04/05/44 Hungary; 05/01/44, redesignated **II Reserve Army Corps**, Ostland & German Army Group Mitte; 05/15/44, German Second Army; 07/27/44, German, Ninth Army; 09/22/44, redesignated **VIII Army Corps**; 12/10/44, Third Army; 05/45, disbanded): **VIII Army Corps** 01/15/39 MG Ferenc Szombathelyi [+ to 08/40, Commanding General, VIII Military District; + 10/40, Commanding General, VIII Military District; + 06/22/41 to 11/41, Commanding General, Carpathian Army Group] 08/01/41 MG Géza Lakatos de Csikszentsimon (Commanding General, Hungarian Army of Occupation) 05/01/43 LG Dezsö László (Deputy Commander-in-Chief, Armed Forces & Deputy Chief of the General Staff) /43 MG Jenö Halmaji Bor Commanding General, 12th Reserve Division) /44 unknown? 05/04/44 redesignated **II Reserve Army Corps** 05/04/44 LG Jenö Halmaji Bor (12/01/44, Commanding General, VIII Army Corps (#2)) 07/18/44 MG Antal Vattay [+ to 08/01/44, Inspector of Cavalry; + 07/29/44, Chief of the Military Chancellery & Adjutant-General of the Military] 08/20/44 LG Béla Ebesfalvi Lengyel (Commanding General, II Reserve Corps) 09/22/44 redesignated **VIII Army Corps (#2)** 09/22/44 LG Béla Ebesfalvi Lengyel (at disposal of Ministry of Defense) 12/01/44 LG Jenö Halmaji Bor (Head, Group IX Armaments & Defense Industry, Main Bureau of Supply, Ministry of Defense) 12/09/44 LG Dr. Gyula Hankovszky [+ 03/45, Commanding General;, VIII Military District] 05/45 disbanded.
A. **Deputy Commander, VIII Army Corps** (01/15/39): unknown? 08/40 MG Iván Szilassy [+ Commanding General, VIII Military District] (?) 10/40 unknown? 06/01/42 MG Imre Szécsy [+ Commanding General, VIII Military District; + to

10/01/42, Deputy Commander, III Army Corps & Commanding General, III Military District; + 10/01/42, Commanding General, 124th Light Infantry Division & Commanding General, Hungarian Occupation Group West] (retired) 08/01/43 MG Béla Tanitó [+ Commanding General, VIII Military District & Commanding General, VI Military District; + to 11/15/44, Deputy Commander, VI Army Corps] (?) 03/04/45

B. **Components - VIII Army Corps**
1. **22nd Infantry Brigade**
2. **23rd Infantry Brigade**
3. **24th Infantry Brigade**

C. **Components - VIII Army Corps** (06/41)
1. **1st Mountain Brigade**
2. **8th Border Guard Brigade**

D. **Components - VIII Army Corps** (05/43)
1. **18th Light Infantry Division**
2. **19th Light Infantry Division**
3. **21st Light Infantry Division**
4. **201st Light Infantry Division**

E. **Artillery Commander, VIII Army Corps (#1)** (01/15/39): Col. Kálmán Ternegg (Commandant, Hajmásker Field Artillery School) 03/40 unknown? 09/22/44 **Artillery Commander, VIII Army Corps (#2)** 09/22/44 Col. Lajos Burget (Artillery Commander, Third Army) /45

IX Army Corps (09/04/40; HQ: Kolozsvár; Hungary; 04/15/44, First Army; 08/28/44 used to form **Second Army (#3);** 09/01/44, reformed; 09/05/44, Second Army (#2), Eastern Front; 09/16/44, German Reserves, German Eighth Army; 10/03/44, Second Army; 10/18/44, German Eighth Army): **IX Army Corps (#1)** 09/04/40 MG László Stirling [+ Commanding General, IX Military District] (Inspector-General of the Armaments Industry, Main Bureau of Supply, Ministry of Defense) 02/01/42 MG Béla Miklós de Dalnoki [+ Commanding General, IX Military District] (Adjutant-General & Head of the Military Chancellery) 10/14/42 MG Lajos Veress [+ Commanding General, IX Military District] (Commander-in-Chief, Second Army (#2)) 08/28/44 used to form **Second Army (#3);** reformed **IX Army Corps (#2)** 09/01/44 MG Gyula Kovács [+ Commanding General, IX Military District] (acting Chief of the General Staff & acting Commander-in-Chief of the Armed Forces) 11/44 MG Frigyes Vasváry [+ Commanding General, IX Military District] 05/45 disbanded.

A. **Deputy Commander, IX Army Corps** (09/04/40): unknown? 11/15/44 MG Ferenc Bardóczy (attached to the Staff of the Commander-in-Chief of the Army) /44

B. **Chief of Staff, IX Army Corps (#1)** (09/04/40): Col. Ferenc Horváth (III) (Commanding General, 1st Armored Field Division) 12/06/42

C. **Components - IX Army Corps (#1)**
1. **25th Infantry Brigade**
2. **26th Infantry Brigade**
3. **27th Infantry Brigade**

D. **Components - IX Army Corps (#2)** (09/01/44)
1. **2nd Field Replacement Division**
2. **25th Infantry Division**

3.   **27th Light Infantry Division**
4.   **9th Border Guard Brigade**

E.   **Chief Administration Officer, IX Army Corps** (09/04/40): unknown? 10/15/40 MG Brunó Berkovich (retired) /41

F.   **Artillery, IX Army Corps** (09/04/40): unknown? /43 MG Vilmos Maasfeldi Hanke (Artillery Commander, Third Army) /44

G.   **Chief Engineer Officer, IX Army Corps** (09/04/40): unknown? /41 Col. Zoltán Gergely (Chief Engineer Officer, II Army Corps) /44

H.   **Transylvania Units, IX Army Corps** (09/04/40): unknown? /42 Col. István Kozma (Commanding General, 27th Light Infantry Division) 11/15/42

I.   **Attached to IX Army Corps**
/42 MG Gyözö Horváth (attached to I Army Corps) /42
/43 MG Aladár Asztalossy (retired; /44 Chief, Military Administration, 3rd Army Rear Area) /44

Anti-Aircraft Artillery Corps (05/01/35; + Inspector of Anti-Aircraft Artillery): MG Oszkár Maliczki (?   ) 02/01/36 LG Jenö Ruszkay (?   ) 08/15/37 unknown? 10/41 MG Emil N. Justy (Commander, Anti-Aircraft Forces & Inspector of Anti-Aircraft Artillery) 10/42

A.   **Attached to I Anti-Aircraft Corps**
/42 Col. László Kesseö (attached to Anti-Aircraft Artillery Command) /42

Garrison Troops, Northern Hungarian Recovered Territories: 05/01/38 MG Gustáv Denk [+ Deputy Commander-in-Chief, Armed Forces & Inspector of Military Training Schools] (retired) 03/01/40

Mobile [Rapid] Army Corps (03/01/40; Hungary; 04/05/41, Reserve, Third Army; 04/13/41, Third Army; 04/20/41, Hungary; 06/27/41, Carpathian Battle Group; 07/09/41, German Reserve, German Army Group South; 07/19/41, German Kempf Battle Group, German Seventeenth Army; 08/12/41, German Kempf Battle Group, German Panzer Army 1; 09/12/41, German Reserve, German Army Group South; 09/22/41, German von Roques Battle Group, German Army Group South; 10/08/41, German Reserve, German Army Group South; 10/12/41, German Seventeenth Army; 06/12/41, Hungary; 10/01/42, redesignated **I Armored Corps**): MG Béla Miklós de Dalnoki (Commanding General, IX Army Corps) 02/01/42 vacant 04/01/42 MG Jëno Major (Commanding General, 1st Armored Division) 10/01/42 MG Lajos Veress (Commanding General, IX Army Corps) 09/15/42 MG Jëno Major [+ Inspector of Armored and Mobilized Forces] (Commanding General, I Armored Corps) 10/01/42 redesignated **I Armored Corps** - see **I Armored Corps**.

A.   *Components - Mobile [Rapid] Army Corps* (04/41)
1.   **1st Cavalry Brigade**
2.   **1st Motorized Brigade**
3.   **2nd Motorized Brigade**

B.   **Chief Administration Officer, I Mobile [Rapid] Army Corps** (03/01/40): unknown? 08/01/41 MG Alajos Lemberkovics (Commanding General, 18th Light Division) 04/01/42

C.   **Attached to I Mobile [Rapid] Army Corps**
/40 Col. Sándor Horváth (Chief, Training Section, General Staff) /41
12/24/40 MG Ernö Kölley (?   ) /42

I Armored Corps (10/01/42; from **Mobile [Rapid] Army Corps**; it was a training and coordination command; Hungary): MG Jëno Major [+ Inspector of Armored and Mobilized Forces] 11/01/44 LG _[Retired '44] Ferenc Bisza (Inspector of Tanks & Motorized Troops) 02/11/45 disbanded.

A. **Artillery, I Armored Corps** (03/01/42): Col. Lajos Burget (Artillery Commander, VIII Army Corps (#2))

B. **Attached to I Armored Corps**:
    10/01/43 MG Ferenc Bisza (retired; 11/01/44, Commanding General, I Armored Corps) /44

Hungarian Occupation Command [H. O. C.] (10/06/41, by VIII Army Corps; German Army Group South; Soviet Union; 02/09/42, split into two commands **Hungarian Occupation Group East** and **Hungarian Occupation Group West**): MG Károly Olgyay [+ Commanding General, 18th Infantry Brigade] 02/09/42 split into two commands **Hungarian Occupation Group East** and **Hungarian Occupation Group West** - see **Hungarian Occupation Group East** and **Hungarian Occupation Group West**.

Hungarian Occupation Group East [H. O. G. East] (02/09/42, Soviet Union; German Army Group South; 07/01/42, German Army Group "B"; 02/09/43, Second Army; 05/18/43, disbanded and absorbed into **VIII Army Corps**): MG Károly Bogányi (Chief, Military Archives) 08/11/42 MG Szilárd Bakay Chief, 21st Section, Bureau of Ground Forces, Ministry of Defense) 05/01/43 disbanded.

Hungarian Occupation Group West [H. O. G. East] (02/09/42, Ukraine; 02/09/43, Second Army; 05/18/43, disbanded and absorbed into **VIII Army Corps**): MG Ödön Sziklay [+ to 02/27/42, Commanding General, 124th Infantry (Security) Brigade; + 02/17/42, Commanding General, 124th Light Infantry Division] (Commanding General, 11th Light Infantry Division) 10/15/42 MG Imre Szécsy [+ Commanding General, 124th Light Infantry Division; + Deputy Commander, VIII Army Corps & Commanding General, VIII Military District] 05/01/43 disbanded.

Hungarian Occupation Group [H. O. G.] (04/01/44, by VIII Army Corps; Ostland; 05/01/44, disbanded and absorbed by the **II Reserve Army Corps**): LG Dezsö László [+] 04/05/44 LG Jenö Halmaji Bor (Commanding General, VIII Army Corps) 05/01/44 disbanded.

Budapest Corps (08/01/44): LG Szilárd Bakay [+ Commanding General, I Army Corps & Commanding General, Western Military District] (arrested by the Germans; placed in Mauthausen Concentration Camp; /46, executed by the Soviets as a war criminal) 10/08/44

Miscellaneous Units (Corps Status)

Commandant, Old Castle of Budapest: /44 LG Károly Csiktaplóczai Lázár (arrested by the Germans and deported to Mauthausen Concentration Camp) 10/44

National Fortifications Command
A.   **Attached to National Fortifications Command**
        /44 MG Gusztáv Deseö

Corps Group "Kálmán": 05/44 MG Irme Kálman (Commanding General, 5th Field Replacement Division) 08/44

Defense Zone "B" (1945): LG [Retired '43] János Legeza.

Defense Zone "F" (1945): LG [Retired '41] László Belásfalvi Kiss.

Mixed Army Brigades

[The term "Mixed Army Brigade" was somewhat of a misnomer, being in reality the cover name for an Army Corps. Such a cover was required to get a round the restrictions imposed by the Treaty of Trianon. In the case of mobilization, the Mixed Brigades were to be converted into Army Corps. Within each Mixed Brigade were a number of smaller Brigades-in-the-making. To maintain a cover, the commander of' each such unit was designated an Infantry Commander within the Mixed Brigade,. so for example, Infantry Commander 3/1 was in actual fact the Commander of the 3rd Infantry Brigade in the 1st Mixed Brigade.]

1st Mixed Army Brigade (HQ: Budapest; 10/01/38, redesignated **I Army Corps**): 10/01/36 MG Vilmos Nagybaczoni Nagy [+ Commanding General, I Military District] (Commanding General, I Army Corps) 10/01/38 redesignated **I Army Corps** - see **I Army Corps**.
- A. **Chief of Staff, 1st Mixed Army Brigade**: 05/36 LCol. Sándor Magyarossy (Chief, Operations Section, General Staff) 02/37 LCol. Dezsö László (Chief, 1 Section Operations, Group I Executive Staff, General Staff) 10/01/38 dissolved.
- B. *Components - 1st Mixed Army Brigade*
    1. **Infantry Commander 1** - 01/23/39 becomes **1st Infantry Brigade**.
    2. **Infantry Commander 2** - 01/23/39 becomes **2nd Infantry Brigade**.
    3. **Infantry Commander 3** - 01/23/39 becomes **3rd Infantry Brigade**.
- C. **Chief Administration Officer, 1st Mixed Army Brigade**: /36 Col. Artúr Horvay (Chief Administration Officer, I Army Corps) 10/01/38 dissolved.
- D. **Infantry, 1st Mixed Brigade**: /37 Col. László Horváth (Commanding General, 2nd Infantry Brigade) 10/01/38 dissolved.
- E. **Anti-Aircraft Artillery, 1st Mixed Army Brigade**: 02/38 Col. Emil N. Justy (Commander, Anti-Aircraft Artillery, I Army Corps) 10/01/38 dissolved.

2nd Mixed Army Brigade (HQ: Székesfehérvár; 10/01/38, redesignated **II Army Corps**): 08/01/37 MG Milán Temessy [+ Commanding General, II Military District] (Commanding General, II Army Corps) 10/01/38 redesignated **II Army Corps** - see **II Army Corps**.
- A. *Components - 2nd Mixed Army Brigade*
    1. **Infantry Commander 1** - 01/23/39 becomes **4th Infantry Brigade**.
    2. **Infantry Commander 2** - 01/23/39 becomes **7th Infantry Brigade**.
    3. **Infantry Commander 3** - 01/23/39 becomes **5th Infantry Brigade**.
- B. **Artillery, 2nd Mixed Army Brigade**: /38 Col. László Kassay-Farkas (Artillery Commander, II Army Corps) 10/01/38 dissolved.

3rd Mixed Army Brigade (HQ: Szombathely; 10/01/38, redesignated **III Army Corps**): 11/36 MG Gusztáv Vitéz Jány [+ Commanding General, III Military District] (Chief of the Military Chancellery & Adjutant-General) 05/25/38 vacant 10/01/38 MG László Belásfalvi Kiss [+ Commanding General, III Military District] (Commanding General, III Army Corps)10/01/38 redesignated **III Army Corps** - see **III Army Corps**.
- A. *Components - 3rd Mixed Army Brigade*
    1. **Infantry Commander 1** - 01/23/39 becomes **8th Infantry Brigade**.

2.	**Infantry Commander 2** - 01/23/39 becomes **10th Infantry Brigade**.
3.	**Infantry Commander 3** - 01/23/39 becomes **9th Infantry Brigade**.

B.	**Infantry, 3rd Mixed Army Brigade**:
/36 Col. Dezsö Füleky (Chief, Officer Training Courses) 10/01/38 dissolved.
/38 Col Brunó Berkovich (Commanding General, 1st Border Guard Brigade) 10/01/38 dissolved.

C.	**Artillery, 3rd Mixed Army Brigade**: /37 MG Lászió Akay (Artillery Commander, III Army Corps) 10/01/38 dissolved.

D.	**Chief Engineer Officer, 3rd Mixed Army Brigade**: /38 Col. Zoltán Gergely (Chief Engineer Officer, III Army Corps) 10/01/38 dissolved.

4th Mixed Army Brigade (HQ: Pécs; 10/01/38, redesignated **IV Army Corps**): 09/01/31 MG Henrik Worth [+ Commanding General, IV Military District] (retired) 12/01/35 MG László Falta [+ Commanding General, IV Military District] (Inspector of Gendarmerie) 02/01/38 MG Jenö Ruszkay [+ Commanding General, IV Military District] (Commanding General, IV Army Corps) 10/01/38 redesignated **IV Army Corps** - see **IV Army Corps**.

A.	*Components - 4th Mixed Army Brigade*
1.	**Infantry Commander 1** - 01/23/39 becomes **13th Infantry Brigade**.
2.	**Infantry Commander 2** - 01/23/39 becomes **11th Infantry Brigade**.
3.	**Infantry Commander 3** - 01/23/39 becomes **12th Infantry Brigade**.

B.	**Chief Administration Officer, 4th Mixed Brigade**: /35 MG Emil Barabás [+ /36, Head, Bureau of Military Administration, Ministry of Defense] (Chief, Group I, Organization & Mobilization, Ministry of Defense) 10/01/38 dissolved.

C.	**Infantry, 4th Mixed Brigade**; /37 Col. József Benke (Infantry Commander, IV Army Corps) 10/01/38 dissolved.

D.	**Artillery, 4th Mixed Brigade**: /35 Col. Ernö Gyimesi (Commanding Officer, 6th Border Guard Brigade) 10/01/38 dissolved.

5th Mixed Army Brigade (HQ: Szeged; 10/01/38, redesignated **V Army Corps**): 01/11/36 MG László Mérey [+ Commanding General, V Military District] (Commanding General, V Army Corps) 10/01/38 redesignated **V Army Corps** - see **V Army Corps**.

A.	*Components - 5th Mixed Army Brigade*
1.	**Infantry Commander 1** - 01/23/39 becomes **14th Infantry Brigade**.
2.	**Infantry Commander 2** - 01/23/39 becomes **16th Infantry Brigade**.
3.	**Infantry Commander 3** - 01/23/39 becomes **18th Infantry Brigade**.

B.	**Infantry, 5th Mixed Brigade**: /38 Col. Alfréd Friedrich (Commanding General, Infantry Commander, V Army Corps) 10/01/38 dissolved.

C.	**Signals, 5th Mixed Brigade**: /37 Col. Henrik Hargittay (Chief, Signal Corps) 10/01/38 dissolved.

6th Mixed Army Brigade (HQ: Debrecen; 10/01/38, redesignated **VI Army Corps**): 10/01/32 MG Géza Demény [+ Commanding General, VI Military District] (?) 05/01/36 Géza E. Siegler [+ Commanding General, VI Military District] (Commanding General, VI Army Corps) 10/01/38 redesignated **VI Army Corps** - see **VI Army Corps**.

A.	*Components - 6th Mixed Army Brigade*
1.	**Infantry Commander 1** - 01/23/39 becomes **17th Infantry Brigade**.

144

2. **Infantry Commander 2**: /36 Col. Sándor Eötvös (Commanding General, 22nd Infantry Brigade) 01/23/39 becomes **22nd Infantry Brigade**.
3. **Infantry Commander 3** - 01/23/39 becomes **15th Infantry Brigade**.
B. **Infantry, 6th Mixed Army Brigade**: /38 Col Dezsö Bittó (Commanding Officer, 17th Infantry Brigade) 10/01/38 dissolved.
C. **Chief Medical Officer, 6th Mixed Brigade**: /35 Col. Ferenc Horváth (I) (Chief Medical Officer, VI Army Corps) 10/01/38 dissolved.

7th Mixed Army Brigade (HQ: Miskolc; 10/01/38, redesignated **VII Army Corps**): 05/01/34 MG Hugó Sónyi [+ Commanding General, VII Military District] (Commander-in-Chief, Army Supreme Command) 09/05/38 vacant 10/01/38 MG András Littay (Commanding General, VII Army Corps) 10/01/38 redesignated **VII Army Corps** - see **VII Army Corps**.
A. **Chief of Staff, 7th Mixed Army Brigade**: 11/36 Col. Géza Lakatos de Csikszentsimon (Commanding Officer, 3rd Infantry Brigade) 05/38 unknown? 10/01/38 dissolved.
B. *Components - 7th Mixed Army Brigade*
1. **Infantry Commander 1**: /38 Col. József Csatáry (Commanding General, 19th Infantry Brigade) 01/23/39 becomes **19th Infantry Brigade**.
2. **Infantry Commander 2** - 01/23/39 becomes **20th Infantry Brigade**.
C. **Artillery, 7th Mixed Brigade**: /33 MG Imre Bangha (Inspector of Artillery & Chief, Army Technical Staff) /36 unknown? 10/01/38 dissolved.

Light Infantry Divisions

1st Light Infantry Division (02/17/42; from **1st Infantry Brigade**; HQ: Budapest; 12/31/43 Hungarian Occupation Group East; 05/01/43, VIII Army Corps, Eastern Front; 04/01/44, Hungarian Occupation Command; 05/01/44, II Reserve Army Corps; 05/10/44, disbanded): MG János Legeza (Commanding General, IV Army Corps) 10/01/42 MG Károly Ungár (Commanding General, 13th Infantry Division) 08/10/43 MG Gusztáv Deseö (Commanding General, 23rd Reserve Infantry Division) 05/10/44 disbanded.

A. *Components - 1st Light Infantry Division*
   1. **1st Infantry Regiment**
   2. **31st Infantry Regiment**
   3. **1st Artillery Regiment**

3rd Light Infantry Division (02/17/42; HQ: Budapest; IV Army Corps; 09/42, Soviet Union; 01/43, virtually annihilated): unknown? 01/43 virtually annihilated.

A. *Components - 3rd Light Infantry Division*
   1. **15th Infantry Regiment**
   2. **45th Infantry Regiment**
   3. **3rd Artillery Regiment**

4th Light Infantry Division (02/17/42, from **4th Infantry Brigade**; HQ: Székesfehérvár; Hungary; 08/43, disbanded): MG Gyula Vargyassy (Commanding General, 23rd Light Infantry Division) 09/10/42 MG Imre Kolossváry (retired) 01/01/43 MG Dezsö Pötze (04/05/44, Commanding General, 12th Reserve Infantry Division) 06/01/43 MG Jenö Halmaji Bor (Commanding General, 12th Light Infantry Division) 08/10/43 disbanded.

A. *Components - 4th Light Infantry Division*
   1. **3rd Infantry Regiment**
   2. **33rd Infantry Regiment**
   3. **4th Artillery Regiment**

5th Light Infantry Division (06/43, from **105th Light Infantry Division**; HQ: Györ; VIII Army Corps, Eastern Front; 10/01/43, redesignated **5th Reserve Infantry Division**): MG Zoltán Algya-Papp (Commanding General, V Army Corps) 10/01/43 redesignated **5th Reserve Infantry Division** - see **5th Reserve Infantry Division**.

A. *Components - 5th Light Infantry Division*
   1. **16th Infantry Regiment**
   2. **46th Infantry Regiment**
   3. **5th Artillery Regiment**

6th Light Infantry Division (02/17/42, from **6th Infantry Brigade**; HQ: Komárom; Hungary; 03/24/42, III Army Corps, Eastern Front; 05/25/42, Reserve, Second Army; 06/08/42, III Army Corps; 06/18/42 VII Army Corps; 07/09/42, III Army Corps; 02/11/43, Reserve, Second Army; 05/01/43, Hungarian Occupation Group East; 06/43, Hungary; 08/43, redesignated **6th Infantry Division**): Col. János Gödry 08/42 MG László Szábó (Commanding General, 7th Light Infantry Division) 08/20/42 MG Dr. Béla Temesy (06/01/43,

Commanding General, 11th Light Infantry Division) 11/15/42 MG Oszkár Ginszkey (Commanding General, 6th Infantry Division) 08/43 redesignated **6th Infantry Division** - see **6th Infantry Division**.

A.   *Components* - **6th Light Infantry Division**
1.   **22nd Infantry Regiment**: unknown? /41 Col. Alajos Haynal (Commanding Officer, 20th Light Infantry Division) /42
2.   **52nd Infantry Regiment**
3.   **6th Artillery Regiment**

7th Light Infantry Division (02/17/42, from **7th Infantry Brigade**; HQ: Sopron; Hungary; 03/24/42, III Army Corps, Eastern Front; 09/02/42, IV Army Corps; 02/11/43, Reserve, Second Army; 03/04/43, Hungarian Occupation Group East; /43, Hungary; 08/10/43, redesignated **7th Infantry Division**): MG Endré Mezö (?   ) 10/42 MG Dezsö László [acting; + Commandant, Royal Hungarian Military Academy] 10/42 MG László Szábó (Commanding General, 7th Infantry Division) 08/10/43 redesignated **7th Infantry Division** - see **7th Infantry Division**.

A.   *Components* - **7th Light Infantry Division**
1.   **4th Infantry Regiment**
2.   **34th Infantry Regiment**
3.   **7th Artillery Regiment**

9th Light Infantry Division (02/17/42, from **9th Infantry Brigade**; HQ: Nagykanizsa; Hungary; 03/24/42, III Army Corps, Eastern Front; 02/27/43, Reserve, Second Army; 03/04/43, Hungarian Occupation Group East; 05/18/43, VIII Army Corps; 08/10/43, redesignated **9th Reserve Infantry Division**): MG Imre Szécsy (Deputy Commander, III Army Corps & Commanding General, III Military District) 05/01/42 MG Jenö Újlaky [+ 10/01/42, Commanding General, 18th Light Infantry Division] 11/15/42 MG Kornél Oszlányi (06/15/44, Commanding General, 10th Infantry Division) 08/10/43 redesignated **9th Reserve Infantry Division** - see **9th Reserve Infantry Division**.

A.   *Components* - **9th Light Infantry Division**
1.   **17th Infantry Regiment**
2.   **47th Infantry Regiment**
3.   **9th Artillery Regiment**

10th Light Infantry Division (02/17/42, from **10th Infantry Brigade**; HQ: Kaposvár; Hungary; 03/24/42, IV Army Corps, Eastern Front; 07/15/42, VII Army Corps; 07/29/42, IV Army Corps; 02/03/43, Reserve, Second Army; 06/43, Hungary; 08/10/43 redesignated **10th Infantry Division**): MG Jenó Felkl (Deputy Commander, IV Army Corps & Commanding General, IV Military District) /42 MG Pál Platthy (Commandfing General, 15th Light Division) 05/01/42 Col. Belá Tanitó (Inspector of the Field Labor Force, Ministry of Defense) 09/42 MG László Molnár (09/15/44, Deputy Commander, IV Army Corps & Commanding General, VI Military District) 08/10/43 redesignated **10th Infantry Division** - see **10th Infantry Division**.

A.   *Components* - **10th Light Infantry Division**
1.   **6th Infantry Regiment**
2.   **36th Infantry Regiment**

3. **10th Artillery Regiment**

11th Light Infantry Division (02/17/42, from **11th Infantry Brigade**; HQ: Pécs; Hungary; 08/10/43, disbanded): MG Zoltán Álgya-Pap (Commanding General, 105th Light Infantry Division) 10/15/42 MG György Sziklay (retired) 11/01/42 vacant 11/15/42 MG Kálmán Ditrói Csiby (retired) 06/01/43 MG Dr. Béla Temesy (08/44, Commanding General, 8th Field Replacement Division) 08/10/43 disbanded.

A. *Components* - **11th Light Infantry Division**
    1. **8th Infantry Regiment**
    2. **38th Infantry Regiment**
    3. **11th Artillery Regiment**

12th Light Infantry Division (02/17/42, from **12th Infantry Brigade**; HQ: Szekszárd; Hungary; 03/24/42, IV Army Corps, Eastern Front; 09/17/42, VII Army Corps; 10/08/42, IV Army Corps; 12/22/42, VII Army Corps; 02/11/43, Second Army; 03/04/43, Hungarian Occupation Group East; 05/18/43, VIII Army Corps; 08/10/43, redesignated **12th Reserve Infantry Division**): MG Gábor Illéházy (retired) 08/08/42 Col. Elemér Sáska (Commanding Officer, 1st Armored Field Division) 09/23/42 vacant 10/01/42 MG Uászló Solymossy (Chief, Group VIII, Bureau of Pre-Military Training, Ministry of Defense & National Commander of the Levente Youth Organization) /43 MG Jenö Halmaji Bor (Commanding General, VIII Army Corps) 08/10/43 redesignated **2th Reserve Infantry Division** - see **12th Reserve Infantry Division**.

A. *Components* - **12th Light Infantry Division**
    1. **18th Infantry Regiment**: /38 Col. Elemér Hunfalvay (Commanding General, 16th Infantry Brigade) 03/01/40
    2. **48th Infantry Regiment**
    3. **12th Artillery Regiment**

13th Light Infantry Division (02/17/42; from **13th Infantry Brigade**; HQ: Kecskemét; Hungary; 03/24/42, IV Army Corps, Eastern Front; 02/01/43, virtually destroyed Eastern Front; 03/01/43, reformed; 03/04/43, Hungarian Occupation Group East; 06/43, Hungary; 08/10/43 redesignated **13th Infantry Division**): **13th Light Infantry Division (#1)** 02/17/42 MG Pál Platthy (Commanding General, 10th Light Infantry Division) 04/01/42 MG József Grassy (Chief, Group II Training Staff, General Staff) 11/15/42 MG László Gertenyesi Hollósy-Kuthy (Inspector of Engineers) 02/01/43 destroyed; reformed **13th Light Infantry Division (#2)** 05/15/43 MG Frigyes Vasváry (Commanding General, 20th Infantry Division) 08/10/43 redesignated **13th Infantry Division** - see **13th Infantry Division**.

A. *Components* - **13th Light Infantry Division**
    1. **7th Infantry Regiment**
    2. **37th Infantry Regiment**
    3. **13th Artillery Regiment**

14th Light Infantry Division (02/17/42; from **14th Infantry Brigade**; HQ: Szeged; Hungary; 08/10/43, disbanded): MG Count Marcell Stomm (Commanding General, III Army Corps) 10/42 Col. Zontán N. Kozma (Infantry Commander, 16th Infantry Division) 08/10/43 disbanded.

A.	**Components - 14th Light Infantry Division**
1.	**9th Infantry Regiment**
2.	**39th Infantry Regiment**
3.	**14th Artillery Regiment**

15th Light Infantry Division (02/17/42; from **15th Infantry Brigade**; HQ: Kiskunhalas; Hungary; 08/10/43, disbanded): MG József Grassy (Commanding General, 13th Light Infantry Division) 04/01/42 MG Pál Platthy (Commanding General, V Army Corps & V Military District) 08/01/43 MG József Vasváry (01/01/44, Commanding General, 18th Reserve Infantry Division) 08/10/43 disbanded.
A.	**Components - 15th Light Infantry Division**
1.	**20th Infantry Regiment**
2.	**50th Infantry Regiment**
3.	**15th Artillery Regiment**

16th Light Infantry Division (02/17/42, from **16th Infantry Brigade**; HQ: Szolnok; Hungary; 03/10/43, redesignated **16th Infantry Division**): MG Béla Tanitó (Commanding General, 10th Light Infantry Division) 05/01/42 MG Gyözö Beleznay (retired) 08/01/42 MG Béla Lengyal (Commanding General, 16th Infantry Division) 03/10/43 redesignated **16th Infantry Division** - see **16th Infantry Division**.
A.	**Components - 16th Light Infantry Division**
1.	**10th Infantry Regiment**: unknown? /42 Col. József Kisfaludy (Infantry Commander, 20th Infantry Division) /43
2.	**40th Infantry Regiment**
3.	**16th Artillery Regiment**

17th Light Infantry Division (02/17/42, from **17th Infantry Brigade**; HQ: Debrecen; Hungary; 08/10/43, disbanded): MG Szilárd Bakay (Commanding General, Hungarian Occupation Group East) 08/01/42 MG Mikály Ibrányi (Commanding General, 18th Reserve Infantry Division) 08/10/43 disbanded.
A.	**Components - 17th Light Infantry Division**
1.	**11th Infantry Regiment**
2.	**41st Infantry Regiment**
3.	**17th Artillery Regiment**

18th Light Infantry Division (02/17/42, from **18th Infantry Brigade**; HQ: Békéscsaba; Hungary; 04/04/43, VIII Army Corps, Eastern Front; 08/10/43, redesignated **18th Reserve Infantry Division**): MG Károly Olgyay (retired) 04/01/42 MG Alajos Lemberkovics (retired; /44, Chief of Administration, Bihar County; /44, Military Commander, Pest County) 08/01/42 Col. Ulázló Solymossy (Commanding General, 12th Light Infantry Division) 10/01/42 MG Jenö Újlaky (?   ) 08/10/43 redesignated **18th Reserve Division** - see **18th Reserve Infantry Division**.
A.	**Components - 18th Light Infantry Division**
1.	**19th Infantry Regiment**
2.	**49th Infantry Regiment**
3.	**18th Artillery Regiment**

19th Light Infantry Division (02/17/42, from **19th Infantry Brigade**; HQ: Miskole; Hungary; 03/24/42, VII Army Corps, Eastern Front; 07/04/42, VIII Army Corps; 07/09/42, VII Army Corps; 02/11/43, Second Army; 03/04/43, Hungarian Occupation Group West; 05/01/43, VII Army Corps; 08/10/43, redesignated **19th Reserve Infantry Division**): MG Gyözö Beleznay (Commanding General, 16th Light Infantry Division) 05/01/42 Col László Deák 08/42 Col. Ferenc Szász (02/01/43, Commanding General, 9th Border Guard Brigade) 10/01/42

      10/01/42 MG Aladár Asztalossy (attached to IX Army Corps) 08/10/43

      /42 MG Ferenc Lóskay (attached to Second Army) /43

08/10/43 redesignated **19th Reserve Infantry Division** - see **19th Reserve Infantry Division**.

A.   *Components* - **19th Light Infantry Division**
      1.   **13th Infantry Regiment**
      2.   **43th Infantry Regiment**
      3.   **19th Artillery Regiment**

20th Light Infantry Division (02/17/42, from **20th Infantry Brigade**; HQ: Eger; Hungary 03/24/42, VII Army Corps, Eastern Front; 07/20/42, IV Army Corps; 07/29/42, III Army Corps; 01/12/43, IV Army Corps; 02/03/43, Reserve, Second Army; 05/43, Hungary; 08/10/43, redesignated **20th Infantry Division**): MG Károly Kovács (retired) 08/21/42 Col. Géza Nagy 10/03/42

      10/03/42 MG Frigyes Vasváry (Commanding General, 13th Light Infantry Division)
          05/15/43

      /42 Col. Alajos Haynal (Chief, Levente Organization, Budapest) /

05/15/43 Col. Gyula Királyehotai Lehoszky (acting; Artillery Officer, VII Army Corps) /43 Col. Béla Németh (Commanding General, 9th Reserve Infantry Division) 08/10/43 redesignated **20th Infantry Division** - see **20th Infantry Division**.

A.   *Components* - **20th Light Infantry Division**
      1.   **14th Infantry Regiment**: unknown? /39 Col. Károly Kovács (Commanding General, 20th Infantry Brigade) 08/01/41
      2.   **44th Infantry Regiment**
      3.   **20th Artillery Regiment**

22nd Light Infantry Division (02/17/42, from **22nd Infantry Brigade**; HQ: Szatmárnémeti; Hungary; 08/10/43, disbanded): MG Aladár Máriay (?) 08/01/42 MG László Gertenyesi Hollósy-Kuthy (Commanding General, 13th Light Infantry Division) 09/15/42 vacant 05/15/43 Col. Mihály Veskóczi Budaházy (Infantry Commander, 24th Infantry Division) 08/10/43 disbanded.

A.   *Components* - **22nd Light Infantry Division**
      1.   **12th Infantry Regiment**: unknown? /41 Col. Zontán N. Kozma (Commanding Officer, 14th Light Infantry Division) 10/42
      2.   **42nd Infantry Regiment**
      3.   **22nd Artillery Regiment**

23rd Light Infantry Division (02/17/42, from **23rd Infantry Brigade**; HQ: Kassa; Hungary; 03/24/42, VII Army Corps, Eastern Front; 02/11/43, Reserve, Second Army; 03/04/43,

Hungarian Occupation Group East; 05/18/43, VIII Army Corps; 08/10/43, redesignated **23rd** **Reserve Infantry Division**): MG István Kiss (Chief of Staff, First Army) 10/01/42 MG Gyula Vargyassy (?) 06/01/43 MG Milkós Depóld (attached to V Army Corps) 07/01/43 MG Pál Magyar (Commanding General, 23rd Reserve Infantry Division) 08/43 redesignated **23rd** **Reserve Infantry Division** - see **23rd Reserve Infantry Division**.

A. *Components* - **23rd Light Infantry Division**
   1. **21st Infantry Regiment**
   2. **51st Infantry Regiment**
   3. **23rd Artillery Regiment**: unknown? /41 Col. János Testhali Jordán (Artillery Commander, 1st Armored Division) /42

25th Light Infantry Division (02/17/42, from **25th Infantry Brigade**; HQ: Nagyvárad; Hungary; 04/11/43, Hungarian Occupation Group East; 05/01/43, VIII Army Corps; 08/10/43, redesignated **19th Reserve Infantry Division**): MG Béla Góthay (retired) 08/15/42 MG Irme Kálman (Commanding General, 19th Reserve Infantry Division) 08/10/43, redesignated **19th Reserve Infantry Division** - see **19th Reserve Infantry Division**.

A. *Components* - **25th Light Infantry Division**
   1. **25th Infantry Regiment**: unknown? /40 Col. Imre Kálman (Chief, President's Officer, Ministry of Defense) /42
   2. **55th Infantry Regiment**
   3. **58th Infantry Regiment**
   4. **25th Artillery Regiment**

26th Light Infantry Division (02/17/42, from **26th Infantry Brigade**; HQ: Kolozsvár; Hungary; 03/01/43, disbanded): Col. of RF Dr. Kálmán Hardy _[HN] (Commander-in-Chief, River Forces & Inspector of River Forces) 04/01/42 MG János Mindszenty (08/44, Commanding General, 9th Field Replacement Division) 08/10/43 vacant 03/01/44 disbanded.

A. *Components* - **26th Light Infantry Division**
   1. **26th Infantry Regiment**
   2. **56th Infantry Regiment**
   3. **59th Infantry Regiment**
   4. **26th Artillery Regiment**

27th Light Infantry Division (02/17/44, from **27th Infantry Brigade**; HQ: Marosvásárhely; Hungary; 03/21/44, VI Army Corps; 04/15/44, IX Army Corps; 04/17/44, VI Army Corps; 07/21/44, Reserve, First Army; 08/15/44, VI Army Corps; 09/11/44, IX Army Corps, Eastern Front; 10/16/44, redesignated **Command Székler**): MG Ferenc Kolthay (retired) 11/15/42 MG István F. Kozma (Commanding General, Command Székler) 02/01/43 MG Miklós Nagyöszy [+ Chief, Group I Organization & Mobilization, Bureau of Ground Forces, Ministry of Defense] 10/01/43 Col. András Zákó (Commanding Officer, 27th "Székler" Infantry Division) 10/16/44 redesignated **Command Székler** - see **Command Székler**.

A. *Components* - **27th Light Infantry Division**
   1. **27th Infantry Regiment**
   2. **57th Infantry Regiment**
   3. **60th Infantry Regiment**

4. **27th Artillery Regiment**

102nd Light Infantry Division ((02/17/42, from **102nd Infantry (Security) Brigade**; HQ: Budapest; Hungarian Occupation Group East; 05/01/43, VIII Army Corps; 07/01/43, disbanded and remnants absorbed by **23rd Light Infantry Division**): /41 MG Károly Bogányi (Commanding General, Hungarian Occupation Group East) 05/26/42 MG Milkós Depóld (Commanding General, 23rd Light Infantry Division) 07/01/43 disbanded.

A. *Components - 102nd Light Infantry Division*
  1. **2nd Infantry Regiment**: /38 Col. Imre Kolossváry (Commanding General, 5th Infantry Brigade) 03/01/41
  2. **32nd Infantry Regiment**: unknown? /42Col. Kálmán Ditrói Csiby (Commanding Officer, 108th Light Division) /42
  3. **2nd Artillery Regiment**

105th Light Infantry Division (02/17/42, from **105th Infantry (Security) Brigade**; HQ: Györ; Hungarian Occupation Command; 05/01/42, Hungarian Occupation Group East; 05/01/43, VIII Army Corps; 06/43, redesignated **5th Light Infantry Division**): MG Imre Kolossváry (Commanding General, 4th Light Infantry Division) 10/01/42 MG Zoltán Algya-Papp (Commanding General, 5th Light Infantry Division) 06/43 redesignated **5th Light Infantry Division** - see **5th Light Infantry Division** .

A. *Components - 105th Light Infantry Division*
  1. **16th Infantry Regiment**
  2. **46th Infantry Regiment**: /42 Col. [Retired '42] Géza Ehrlich (Commanding General, 124th Light Division) /43
  3. **5th Artillery Regiment**

108th Light Infantry Division (02/17/42, from **108th Infantry (Security) Brigade**; HQ: Szombathely; Hungary Occupational Group West; 05/01/43, VII Army Corps; 08/10/43, disbanded) MG Ottó Abt (Deputy Commander, III Corps) 11/42 MG Kálmán Csiby (Commanding General, 11th Light Division) 11/15/42 MG István Makay 03/43 unknown? 06/43 MG István Makay (/44, killed by a mine) 08/10/43 disbanded.

A. *Components - 108th Light Infantry Division*
  1. **5th Infantry Regiment**
  2. **35th Infantry Regiment**
  3. **8th Artillery Regiment**

121st Light Infantry Division (02/17/42, from **121st Infantry (Security) Brigade**; HQ: Losonc; Hungarian Occupation Group West; 05/01/43, VII Army Corps, Eastern Front; 04/19/44, Reserve, First Army; 05/15/44, disbanded and remnants transferred to **18th Reserve Infantry Division**): MG Béla Tarnay (?) 06/01/43 Col. Géza Pusztakürthy 08/01/43 MG [Retired '42] Géza Ehrlich (?) 01/44 MG László Miskey (Commanding General, 19th Reserve Infantry Division) 03/44 vacant 05/15/44 disbanded.

A. *Components - 121st Light Infantry Division*
  1. **23rd Infantry Regiment**
  2. **53rd Infantry Regiment**
  3. **21st Artillery Regiment**

124th Light Infantry Division (02/17/42, from **124th Infantry (Security) Brigade**; HQ: Ungvár; Hungarian Occupation Group West; 05/01/43, Hungarian Occupation Group East; 05/18/43, VIII Army Corps; 08/10/43, redesignated **24th Infantry Division**): MG György Sziklay [+ Commanding General, Hungarian Occupation Group West] (Commanding General, 11th Light Infantry Division) 10/15/42 MG Imre Szécsy [+ Commanding General, Hungarian Occupation Group West; + Deputy Commander, III Army Corps & Commanding General, III Military District] 06/01/43 MG Ferenc Lóskay (Commanding General, 1st Mountain Brigade) /43 MG [Retired '42] Géza Ehrlich (Commanding General, 121st Light Division) 08/10/43 redesignated **24th Infantry Division** - see **24th Infantry Division**.

A.   *Components* - **124th Light Infantry Division**
    1.   **24th Infantry Regiment**
    2.   **54th Infantry Regiment**
    3.   **24th Artillery Regiment**

201st Light Infantry Division (11/05/42, new unit, Hungary; 01/01/43, Hungarian Occupation Group West; 05/01/43, VII Army Corps, Eastern Front; 04/15/44, Reserve, First Army; 05/26/44, disbanded): MG Gyorgy Vukováry (08/44, Commanding General, 6th Field Replacement Division) 07/01/43 Col. László Miskey (Commanding General, 121st Light Infantry Division) 01/44 MG József Kisfaludy (Commanding General, 10th Infantry Division) 05/26/44 disbanded.

Infantry Divisions

6th Infantry Division (08/10/43, from **6th Light Infantry Division**, Hungary; 05/18/44, III Military District; 06/23/44, IV Military District; 08/16/44, III Army Corps; 12/09/44, disbanded and remnants transferred to **16th Infantry Division**): 08/10/43 MG Oszkár Ginszkey (died from a disease) 03/07/44 MG Ferenc Horváth (III) (Commanding General, Székely Border Garrison) 07/44 MG László Karátsony (Commanding General, 16th Infantry Division) /44 Col. István Baumann (Commanding General, 12th Infantry Division) 12/09/44 disbanded.
- A.   **Infantry, 6th Infantry Division** (08/10/43): unknown? /44 Col. István Baumann (Commanding General, 6th Infantry Division) 12/09/44 dissolved/

7th Infantry Division (08/10/43, from **7th Light Infantry Division;** Hungary; 05/10/44, III Military District;06/03/44, West Hungary; 06/13/44, Reserve, First Army; 08/26/44, disbanded and remnants transferred to **24th Infantry Division**): MG László Szábó (?) 06/15/44 MG István Kudriczy (Commanding General, VII Army Corps) 08/26/44 disbanded.
- A.   **Infantry, 7th Infantry Division** (08/10/43): unknown? /44 Col. Ferenc Deák (Commanding General, 25th Infantry Division) 08/26/44 dissolved.

10th Infantry Division (08/10/43, from **10th Light Infantry Division**; Hungary; 07/22/44, III Army Corps; 09/16/44, VI Army Corps; 10/14/44, Reserve, First Army; 10/23/44, V Army Corps; 10/31/44, VII Army Corps; 11/12/44, I Army Corps; 02/12/45, destroyed in Budapest): MG Ferenc Lóskay (Commanding General, 124th Light Infantry Division) /43 MG István Kudriczy (Commanding General, 7th Infantry Division) /44 MG Kornél Oszlányi (?) 05/26/44 MG József Kisfaludy (Commanding General, 7th Replacement Infantry Division) 12/44 MG Sándor András (Chief of General Staff, Provisional National Government) 02/12/45 destroyed.
- A.   **Infantry, 10th Infantry Division**: unknown? /44 MG Sándor András (Commanding General, 10th Infantry Division) 12/44 Col. Ágoston Gecsányi

12th Infantry Division (08/23/43; from **12th Reserve Division**; VIII Army Corps; 04/01/44, Hungarian Occupation Command; 05/01/44, II Reserve Army Corps; 08/31/44, VII Army Corps; 10/28/44, VI Army Corps; 11/27/44, I Army Corps; 02/12/45, destroyed in Budapest): MG Jenö Bor (Commanding General, Hungarian Occupation Group Ukraine) 04/05/44 MG Dézsö Pötze (?) 05/44 MG Béla Németh (?) 09/28/44 Col. Jenö Tömöry (Commanding General, 20th Infantry Division) 10/26/44 MG Ferenc Mikófalvy (?) 12/06/44 MG István Baumann (?) 02/12/45 destroyed.

13th Infantry Division (08/10/43, from **13th Light Infantry Division**; Hungary; 07/22/44 III Army Corps; 08/31/44, Reserve, First Army; 09/28/44, V Army Corps;11/27/44, disbanded and its remnants transferred to **24th Infantry Division**): MG Károly Ungár (?) 03/30/44 Col. János Markóczy (acting) 04/01/44 vacant 08/01/44 MG Dr. Gyula Hankovszky (Head, Bureau of Ground Forces, Ministry of Defense) 10/16/44 MG Jenö Sövényhazi-Herdiczky (?) 11/20/44 Col. Sándor Vályi (acting) 11/27/44 disbanded.

16th Infantry Division (08/10/43, from **16th Light Infantry Division**; Hungary; 01/06/44,

First Army; 04/15/44, VII Army Corps, Eastern Front; 08/20/44, Reserves, First Army; 08/30/44, VII Army Corps; 09/19/44, III Army Corps;09/28/44, Reserve, First Army; 10/05/44, VI Army Corps; 10/14/44, Reserve, First Army; 11/26/44, V Army Corps; 05/45, surrendered to Red Army at Olmütz, Czechoslovakia): MG Béla Lengyal (Commanding General, II Reserve Army Corps) 07/44 MG Ferenc Bardóczy (acting Inspector of Infantry) 08/01/44 MG József Vasváry (Commanding General, III Army Corps) 11/01/44 MG Elemér Mészöly (?) 12/09/44 MG László Karátsony (?) 03/45 Col. Gyula Keresztes (acting Commanding General, First Army) 04/45 Col. Alajos Pápay (Soviet prisoner-of-war) 05/45 surrendered.

A. **Infantry, 16th Infantry Division** (08/10/43): Col. Zontán N. Kozma (retired) 05/45 dissolved.

20th Infantry Division (08/10/43, from **20th Light Infantry Division**; Hungary; 03/21/44, VII Military District; 04/05/44, First Army, Eastern Front; 04/15/44, IX Army Corps; 07/24/44, VII Army Corps; 09/16/44, IV Army Corps; 09/27/44, VIII Army Corps; 11/26/44, II Army Corps; 12/03/44, Reserve, Third Army; 01/06/45, II Army Corps; 05/45, surrendered to the British in southern Austria and northern Croatia): MG Frigyes Vasváry (Commanding General IX Army Corps & IX Military District) 12/05/44 MG Jenö Tömöry (?) 03/45 MG Ferenc Tilger (British prisoner-of-war) 05/45 surrendered.

A. **Infantry, 20th Infantry Division** (08/10/43): Col. József Kisfaludy (Commanding General, 201st Light Infantry Division) 01/44

24th Infantry Division (08/10/43, from **124th Light Infantry Division**; VIII Army Corps; 08/15/43, VII Army Corps; 10/21/43, Hungary; 01/06/44, First Army; 04/18/44, German XI Army Corps, Eastern Front; 07/24/44, VII Army Corps; 08/08/44, III Army Corps; 09/27/44, VI Army Corps; 10/20/44, Reserve, First Army; 12/31/44, V Army Corps; 05/45, surrendered to the Red Army in Bohemia, Czechoslovakia): MG [Retired '40] Aldár Pintér (retired) 06/01/44 MG János Markóczy (Commanding General, VII Army Corps) 10/15/44 Col. Ferenc Karlóczy 11/44 Col. Gyula Keresztes (Commanding Officer, 16th Infantry Division) 03/45 Col. Lajos Rumy (Soviet prisoner-of-war) 05/45 surrendered.

A. **Infantry, 24th Infantry Division**: 08/10/43 Col. Mihály Veskóczi Budaházy (Military Commander, Sopron County; /45, retired) /44

25th Infantry Division (08/10/43, new unit, Hungary; 08/15/43, VIII Army Corps; 10/01/43, Hungary; 03/21/44, VI Army Corps; 04/15/44, IX Army Corps; 07/24/44, VI Army Corps, Eastern Front; 08/15/44, Reserve, First Army; 09/05/44, II Army Corps; 10/18/44, VII Army Corps; 10/23/44, II Army Corps; 04/45, surrendered to the partisans in Yugoslavia): MG Béla Z. Zsombolyay (?) 01/01/44 MG Milály Ibrányi (Commanding General, 1st Cavalry Division) 07/01/44 MG István F. Kozma (Commander-in-Chief, Home Guard) 07/29/44 MG Antal Benda (attached to V Military District) /44 MG Ferenc Deák (Commanding General, Field Replacement Division) 09/44 MG László Gertenyesi Hollósy-Kuthy (Commanding General, III Army Corps) 10/10/44 MG Ferenc Horváth (III) (Commanding General, III Army Corps & Commanding General, III Military District) 12/44 Col. Gyula Kalkó (prisoner-of-war) 04/45 surrendered.

A. **Infantry, 25th Infantry Division** (08/10/43): Col. Antal Benda (Commanding General, 25th Infantry Division) 07/29/44

Szt László Infantry Division (10/12/44, at Pápa; Reserve, Third Army; 12/19/44, *German LVII Panzer Corps, German Eighth Army*; 03/15/45, *German XXII Army Corps, German Panzer Army 2*; 03/19/45, II Army Corps; 04/12/45, *German XXII Army Corps, German Panzer Army 1*; 05/08/45, surrendered to British forces at Preitenegg, Austria): MG Zoltán Szügyi (?) 05/08/45 surrendered.

Command Székler (10/16/44, from **27th Light Infantry Division**; IX Army Corps; 03/45, virtually destroyed; 05/45, surrendered to the Red Army nerar Vienna, Austria): Col. András Zákó (Chief, Section 2. Intelligence, Group I, Executive Staff, General Staff) 10/44 MG [Retired '43] Gyözö Horváth (Soviet prisoner-of-war) 03/45 virtually destroyed 05/45 surrendered.

Reserve Infantry Divisions

5th Reserve Infantry Division (10/43, from **5th Light Infantry Division**, VIII Army Corps; 04/01/44, Hungarian Occupation Command; 05/01/44, II Reserve Army Corps; 09/25/44, Hungary; 05/45, surrendered to the Red Army in Zlin, Czechoslovakia): MG Gyözö Árvay (on leave; /45, retired) /44 MG László János Szábó (prisoner-of-war) 05/45 surrendered.

9th Reserve Infantry Division (08/10/43, from **9th Light Infantry Division**; VIII Army Corps; 04/01/44, Hungarian Occupation Command; 04/15/44, disbanded and remnants transferred to the **5th Reserve Infantry Division**, the **12th Reserve Infantry Division**, and the **23rd Reserve Infantry Division**): MG Béla Németh (Commanding General, 12th Infantry Division) 04/15/44 disbanded.

12th Reserve Infantry Division (08/10/43, from **12th Light Infantry Division**; VIII Army Corps; 08/23/43, redesignated **12th Infantry Division**): MG Jénö Halmaji Bor (Commanding General, II Reserve Corps) 08/23/43 redesignated **12th Infantry Division** - see **12th Infantry Division**.

18th Reserve Infantry Division (08/10/43, from **18th Light Infantry Division**; VII Army Corps; 08/15/43, VIII Army Corps; 10/15/43, VII Army Corps; 05/10/44, VI Army Corps; 08/01/44, disbanded and remnants transferred to the **16th Infantry Division**): MG Mihály Ibrányi (Commanding General, 25th Infantry Division) 01/01/44 MG József Vasváry (Commanding General, 16th Infantry Division) 08/01/44 disbanded.

19th Reserve Infantry Division (08/10/43; from **19th Light Infantry Division**; VII Army Corps; 05/10/44, VI Army Corps; 07/21/44, Reserve, First Army; 08/44, disbanded and remnants transferred to the **20th Infantry Division**): Col. Imre Kálman (Commanding General, Corps Group "Kálmán") 05/44 MG László Miskey (Commanding General, 5th Field Replacement Division) 08/44 disbanded.

23rd Reserve Infantry Division (08/43, from **23rd Light Infantry Division**; VIII Army Corps; 04/01/44, Hungarian Occupation Command; 05/01/44, II Reserve Army Corps; 09/09/44, VIII Army Corps; 11/07/44, II Army Corps; 01/07/45, Reserve, Third Army; 03/02/45, VIII Army Corps; 05/06/45, surrendered to the Red Army in Styria, Austria): MG Pál Magyar (retired) 01/30/44 Col. Jenö Sövényhazi-Hediczky (10/16/44, Commanding General, 13th Infantry Division) 05/10/44 MG Gusztáv Deseö (?) 10/44 MG Ferenc Osztovics (?) 10/20/44 unknown? 11/44 MG Géza Fehér (?) 04/45 Col. István Milóssy (Soviet prisoner-of-war) 05/06/45 surrendered.

26th Reserve Infantry Division (06/43, from **1st Light Infantry Division**; saw no combat):

Field Replacement Divisions

2ⁿᵈ Field Replacement Division (05/01/44, Field Replacement Army; 08/44, Hungary; 09/02/44, Székler Border Command; 10/44, IX Army Corps, Eastern Front; 10/23/44, Reserve, Second Army; 11/13/44, Reserve, Third Army; 12/31/44, II Army Corps; 01/45, disbanded and remnants transferred to **20ᵗʰ Infantry Division**): vacant 08/44 Col. Imre Czlenner (Commandant, Royal Hungarian Military Academy) 10/13/44 Col. Dénes Dobák 01/45 disbanded.

3ʳᵈ Field Replacement Division (05/01/44, Field Replacement Army; 08/26/44, Hungary; 09/02/44, Székler Border Command; 10/44, Reserve, Third Army; 12/31/44, II Army Corps; 04/45, surrendered to Red Army in Czechoslovakia): unknown? 04/45 surrendered.

4ᵗʰ Field Replacement Division (05/01/44, Field Replacement Army; 08/26/44, Hungary; 09/02/44, II Army Corps; 10/26/44, disbanded and remnants transferred to **12ᵗʰ Reserve Infantry Division**): vacant 08/44 MG Árpád Tarnaváry (?) 09/23/44 Col. Jenö Tömöry (acting/Commanding Officer, 12ᵗʰ Infantry Division) 09/28/44 Col. Ferenc Mikófalvy (Commanding General, 12ᵗʰ Infantry Division) 10/26/44 disbanded.

5ᵗʰ Field Replacement Division (05/01/44, Field Replacement Army; 08/26/44, Hungary; 10/23/44, VIII Army Corps; 11/44, disbanded and remnants transferred to **20ᵗʰ Infantry Division**): vacant 08/44 MG Imre Kálman (Deputy Commander, V Army Corps & Commanding General, V Military District) 11/15/44 MG László Miskey (?) 11/44 disbanded.

6ᵗʰ Field Replacement Division (05/01/44, Field Replacement Army; 08/26/44, Hungary; 08/31/44, Reserve, Third Army; 09/16/44, IV Army Corps; 09/28/44, VIII Army Corps; 10/12/44, disbanded and remnants transferred to **Szt László Infantry Division**): vacant 08/44 MG György Vukováry (?) 10/12/44 disbanded.

7ᵗʰ Field Replacement Division ((05/01/44, Field Replacement Army; 08/26/44, Hungary; 09/05/44, II Army Corps; 09/18/44, Finta Group, Second Army; 11/13/44, Reserves, Third Army; 03/45, disbanded and remnants transferred to **Szt László Infantry Division**): vacant 08/44 MG József Finta (Inspector of Gendarmerie) 10/16/44 unknown? 12/44 MG József Kisfaludy (?) 03/45 disbanded.

8ᵗʰ Field Replacement Division ((05/01/44, Field Replacement Army; 08/26/44, Hungary; 08/31/44, VIII Army Corps; 12/31/44, II Army Corps; 03/45, disbanded and remnants transferred to **Szt László Infantry Division**): vacant 08/44 MG Dr. Béla Temesy (?) 03/09/45 Col. Sándor Martsa 03/45 disbanded.

9ᵗʰ Field Replacement Division (05/01/44, Field Replacement Army; 08/26/44, Hungary; 08/31/44, II Army Corps; 10/18/44, IX Army Corps; 11/29/44, II Army Corps; 01/07/45, disbanded): vacant 08/44 MG János Mindszenty (?) 10/44 Col. János Fónagy 11/44 vacant 01/45 disbanded.

Field Replacement Division: /44 MG Ferenc Deák (Commanding General, 1st Armored Division) 09/23/44

Cavalry Units

Cavalry Division

1st Cavalry (later Huszár) Division (10/01/42; from **1st Cavalry Brigade** and **2nd Cavalry Brigade**, Hungary; 06/15/44, II Reserve Army Corps; 09/44, redesignated **1st Huszár Division**; from **1st Cavalry Brigade** and **2nd Cavalry Brigade**; 10/08/44, Reserve, Third Army; 01/31/45, VIII Army Corps;04/45, surrendered at Styria, Austria to United States and Soviet Union Troops): MG Antal Vattay [+ Inspector of Cavalry] (Commanding General, II Reserve Army Corps) 07/18/44 Col. Zoltán Schell (acting) 07/31/44 MG Mihály Ibrányi (Commanding General, 1st Huszár Division & Inspector of Huszár (Cavalry)) 09/44 redesignated **1st Huszár Division** 09/44 MG Mihály Ibrányi (Commanding General, V Army Corps) 11/04/44 Col. Attila Makay (acting) 11/13/44 Col. Zoltán Schell (Prisoner-of-war) 04/45 surrendered.

A. **Deputy Commander, 1st Cavalry Division** (10/01/42): Col. Oszkár Beodrai Baitz (retired; /44, Inspector of Cavalry) /43

Cavalry Brigades

1st Cavalry Brigade (10/01/37, from **2nd Cavalry Brigade**, Hungary; 04/05/41, Mobile [Rapid] Corps; 06/10/41, Hungary; 10/01/42, merged with **2nd Cavalry Brigade** and redesignated **1st Cavalry Division**): Col. Elemér Gorondy-Novák (Inspector of Rapid Mobile Forces and Cavalry) 05/01/38 Col. Béla Miklós de Dalnoki (Commanding General, Mobile [Rapid] Corps) 03/01/40 MG Lajos Veress (Commanding General, 2nd Armored Division) 10/01/41 Col. András Király (Inspector of Troop Trains) 10/01/42, merged with **2nd Cavalry Brigade** and redesignated **1st Cavalry Division** - see **1st Cavalry Division**.

A. *Components - 1st Cavalry Brigade* (03/15/42)
    1. **1st Cavalry Regiment**: unknown? /39 Col. Milkós Depóld (acting Vice-President, Supreme Military Court) /42
    2. **2nd Cavalry Regiment**: /38 Col. András Király (Commanding Officer, 1st Cavalry Brigade) 10/01/41

2nd Cavalry Brigade (#1) (10/01/37, from **1st Cavalry Brigade**, Hungary; 04/05/41, Mobile [Rapid] Corps; 04/20/41, V Army Corps; 01/01/42, Hungary; 10/01/42, merged with **1st Cavalry Brigade** and redesignated **1st Cavalry Division**): MG Alajos Béldy (Chief, "Miklós Toldi" Army Sports Institute) 12/24/40 Col. Antal Vattay (Commanding General, 1st Cavalry Division & Inspector of Cavalry) 10/01/42, merged with **1st Cavalry Brigade** and redesignated **1st Cavalry Division** - see **1st Cavalry Division**.

A. **Artillery Commander, 2nd Cavalry Brigade**: 05/38 Col. Kálmán Ternegg (Artillery Commander VIII Army Corps) 01/15/39 Col. László Kesseö (attached to I Anti-Aircraft Artillery Corps) /42

3rd Cavalry Brigade: unknown?

A.   ***Components* - 3rd Cavalry Brigade** (03/15/42)

     1.   **3rd Cavalry Regiment**

4th Cavalry Brigade: unknown?

A.   ***Components* - 4th Cavalry Brigade** (03/15/42)

     1.   **8th Cavalry Regiment**

1st Cavalry Field Replacement Brigade (05/01/44, Hungary; 08/26/44, Reserve, Second Army; 09/18/44, IV Cavalry Corps; 09/28/44, Viii Army Corps; 10/18/44, Reserve, Third Army; 10/23/44, disbanded): Col. von Auerhammer 10/23/44 disbanded.

Armored Divisions

1ˢᵗ Armored Field Division (04/15/42, as ad-hoc unit; Hungary; 05/42, Second Army, Eastern Front; 06/24/42, IV Army Corps; 07/04/42, Reserve, Second Army; largely destroyed; 02/21/43, Hungary, remnants joined **1ˢᵗ Armored Division**): MG Lajos Veress (Commanding General, I Armored Corps) 08/42 MG Jëno Major (Commanding General, 1ˢᵗ Armored Division; Commanding General, I Armored Corps & Inspector of Armored and Mechanized Forces) 10/01/42 Col. Elemér Sáska (08/20/43, Commandant, Royal Hungarian Ludovica Academy) 12/06/42 MG Ferenc Horváth (III) (Commanding General, 1ˢᵗ Armored Division) 04/01/43 disbanded.

A. **Components - 1ˢᵗ Armored Field Division**
    1.   **1ˢᵗ Cavalry Brigade**
    2.   **2ⁿᵈ Cavalry Brigade**

1ˢᵗ Armored Division (10/01/42; Hungary; exited only on paper until 04/43 as it's components were attached to **1ˢᵗ Armored Field Division**; used as a training and replacement unit until mid-44; 08/01/44, IV Military District; 09/01/44, IV Army Corps, Third Army; 09/23/44, Reserve, Third Army; 10/05/44, VIII Army Corps, Third Army; 10/23/44, VI Army Corps, Third Army; 11/12/44, I Army Corps, Third Army; 02/12/45, destroyed at Budapest): MG Jëno Major [+ Commanding General, I Armored Corps & Inspector-General Motorized & Armored] 11/15/42 vacant 04/01/43 MG Ferenc Horváth (III) (Commanding General, 6ᵗʰ Infantry Division) 03/07/44 Col. Ferenc Koszorus 09/23/44 MG Ferenc Deák (Chief of the Military Chancellery) 10/10/44 Col. Béla Tiszay (acting) 10/21/44 Col. Zoltán Schell 11/13/44 Col. Ernö Mike 12/44 Col. Vértessy 02/12/45 destroyed.

A. **Artillery, 1ˢᵗ Armored Division** (10/01/42): Col. János Testhali Jordán (Artillery Commander, VIII Army Corps) /43

2ⁿᵈ Armored Division (10/01/42; Hungary; 03/27/44, Reserve, First Army; 03/27/44, III Army Corps; 04/18/44, German XI Army Corps, Eastern Front; 05/44, III Army Corps; 08/31/44, Reserve, First Army; 09/05/44, II Army Corps, II Army Corps; 10/23/44, Reserve, First Army; 11/05/44, Reserve, Third Army; 04/04/45 VIII Army Corps; 04/45, surrendered to Red Army in Styria, Austria): MG Lajos Veress (Commanding General, 1ˢᵗ Armored Field Division) 04/15/42 MG Aladár Asztalossy (Commanding General, 19ᵗʰ Light Division) 10/01/42 MG Ferenc Bisza (attached to I Armored Corps) 10/01/43 Col. Ferenc Osztovics (10/44, Commanding General, 23ʳᵈ Reserve Infantry Division) 06/01/44 MG Zoltán Zsedényi (Soviet prisoner-of-war) 04/45 surrendered.

A. **Deputy Commander, 2ⁿᵈ Armored Brigade**: /40 Col. Antal Benda (Chief, Section 19. Border Guards, Group I Organization & Mobilization, Bureau of Ground Forces, Ministry of Defense) /41

B. **Artillery, 2ⁿᵈ Armored Division** (10/01/42): Col. Gyula Királyehotai Lehoszky (Artillery Officer, IV Army Corps) /42

Miscellaneous Divisions

Royal Life Guard (Brigade status; /42, changed to division status): /36 Col. Károly Csiktaplóczai Lázár /42 upgraded to division status /42 MG Károly Csiktaplóczai Lázár (Commandant, Old Castle of Budapest) /44

9th Border Guard Division (/45, from **9th Border Guard Brigade**; 04/45, surrendered to United States troops in Munich, Germany): MG Ferenc Lóskay (United States prisoner-of-war) 04/45 surrendered.

Székely Border Garrison (02/01/43; 10/44, disbanded): 02/01/43 MG István F. Kozma (Commanding General, 25th Infantry Division) 08/01/44 MG Ferenc Horváth (III) (Commanding General, 25th Infantry Division) 10/10/44 disbanded.

Soviet Sponsored Hungarian Divisions [December 1944]

Hungary was taken in October 1944, a Soviet sponsored Hungarian Government was set up in the city. Conferences between the Soviet and Hungarian military officer resulted in an agreement to form two different types of Hungarian Divisions by January 9, 1945, the regular infantry division (16,000 men) and the light division (10,000 men). The first Hungarian units formed under Soviet auspices were not infantry divisions but railroad support units to move troops through Hungary. This was a problem for Hungary throughout World War II.

Railroad Units

1st Hungarian Railroad Brigade (12/28/44; 01/11/45, attached to the Soviet 27th Railroad Brigade, Soviet Second Ukrainian Front):

3rd Hungarian Railroad Brigade (02/05/45, attached to the Soviet 47th Railroad Brigade):

Infantry Divisions

1st Hungarian Infantry Division (12/22/44, Debrecen, Hungary; 75% of unit coming from Soviet held Hungarian prisoners-of-war; 02/45, assigned to Soviet Second Ukrainian Front; although it did not go to the front until 05/01/45, and assigned to the Soviet Twenty-Sixth Army):

3rd Hungarian Infantry Division (04/14/45, Debrecen, Hungary; barely started forming when the war in Europe ended in May):

5th Hungarian Infantry Division (02/45, Segede and Khaimash, Hungary; formed on a Hungarian "Light Division"; never completed forming before the war ended):

6th Hungarian Infantry Division (02/45, Debrecen, Hungary; 04/01/45, assigned to Soviet Third Ukrainian Front; fought in the last three weeks of war):

7th Hungarian Infantry Division (02/45, Mishkeltse, Hungary; no indication that this division was ever even partially formed before the war ended in Europe):

Infantry Brigades

1st Infantry Brigade (01/23/39, from **Infantry Commander 1, 1st Mixed Army Brigade**, Hungary; 04/07/41, I Army Corps; 04/17/41, Hungary; 02/17/42, redesignated **1st Light Infantry Division**): Col. József Makay (?) 02/01/40 MG Béla Aggtelekey [+ to 12/24/40, Deputy Chief of Chancellery, Ministry of Defense] (10/01/42, Commanding General, II Army Corps) 11/01/41 MG János Legeza (Commanding General, 1st Light Infantry Division) 02/17/42 redesignated **1st Light Infantry Division** - see **1st Light Infantry Division.**

2nd Infantry Brigade (01/23/39, from **Infantry Commander 2, 1st Mixed Army Brigade**; 04/07/41, I Army Corps; 04/17/41, Hungary; 10/01/41, Hungarian Occupation Command; 02/09/42, Hungarian Occupation Group East; 12/01/42, redesignated **102nd Infantry (Security) Division**): /36 MG József D. Bajnóczy (Chief, Field Officer Training; /39 Commanding General, VI Army Corps) /38 MG László Horváth (Commanding General, IV Army Corps) 03/01/40 Col. Géza Heim 10/41 MG Károly Bogányi (Commanding General, 102nd Infantry (Security) Brigade) 12/01/41 redesignated **102nd Infantry (Security) Brigade** - see **102nd Infantry (Security) Brigade.**

3rd Infantry Brigade (01/23/39, from **Infantry Commander 3, 1st Mixed ArmyBrigade**, Hungary; 04/07/41, I Army Corps; 04/17/41, Hungary; 08/01/41, disbanded): Col. Géza Lakatos de Csikszentsimon (Chief of Staff, Second Army) 03/01/41 MG Károly Osskó (?) /41 MG Aladár Asztalossy (Commanding General, 2nd Motorized Infantry Brigade) 08/01/41 disbanded.

4th Infantry Brigade (01/23/39, from **Infantry Commander 1, 2nd Mixed Army Brigade**, Hungary; 02/17/42, redesignated **4th Light Infantry Division**): MG Dezsö Thold (retired) 10/17/39 MG Emö Paksy (?) 08/01/41 MG Gyula Vargyassy (Commanding General, 4th Light Infantry Division) 02/17/42 redesignated **4th Light Infantry Division** - see **4th Light Infantry Division.**

5th Infantry Brigade (01/23/39, from **Infantry Commander 3, 2nd Mixed Army Brigade**, Hungary; 10/01/41, Hungarian Occupation Command; 12/01/41, redesignated **105th Infantry (Security) Brigade**): Col. Gusztáv Hennyey (Commanding General, II Army Corps) 02/01/41 Col. Dezsö László (Chief, 1 Section Operations, Group I Executive Staff, General Staff & Commandant, Royal Hungarian Military Academy) 03/01/41 MG Imre Kolossváry (Commanding General, 105th Infantry (Security) Brigade) 12/01/41 redesignated **105th Infantry (Security) Brigade** - see **105th Infantry (Security) Brigade.**

6th Infantry Brigade (01/23/39, new unit, Hungary; 02/17/42, redesignated **6th Light Infantry Division**): Col. Ferenc Feketehalmy-Czeydner (Chief of Staff, First Army) 03/01/40 MG Alfréd Bántay (retired) 12/24/40 MG Imre Németh (?) 08/01/41 Col. Gyula Pajtás 01/27/42 vacant 02/17/42 redesignated **6th Light Infantry Division** - see **6th Light Infantry Division.**

7th Infantry Brigade (01/23/39, from **Infantry Commander 2, 2nd Mixed Brigade**, Hungary;

02/17/42, redesignated **7ᵗʰ Light Infantry Division**): MG Károly Zalay (retired) 01/01/41 MG Endré Mezö (Commanding General, 7ᵗʰ Light Infantry Division) 02/17/42 redesignated **7ᵗʰ Light Infantry Division** - see **7ᵗʰ Light Infantry Division**.

8ᵗʰ Infantry Brigade (01/23/39, from **Infantry Commander 1, 3ʳᵈ Mixed Army Brigade**, Hungary; Eastern Front; 10/01/41, redesignated **108ᵗʰ Infantry (Security) Division**): MG Gyözö Weinmann (retired) 02/01/41 MG Ottó Abt (Commanding General, 108ᵗʰ Infantry (Security) Brigade) 10/41 redesignated **108ᵗʰ Infantry (Security) Brigade** - see **108ᵗʰ Infantry (Security) Brigade.**
A.   **Deputy Commander, 8ᵗʰ Infantry Brigade**: /41 Col. Ottó Abt (Commanding General, 8ᵗʰ Infantry Brigade) 02/01/41

9ᵗʰ Infantry Brigade (01/23/39, from **Infantry Commander 3, 3ʳᵈ Mixed Army Brigade**, Hungary; 02/17/42, redesignated **9ᵗʰ Light Infantry Division**): MG János Székely (?) 08/01/41 MG Imre N. Szécsy (Commanding General, 9ᵗʰ Light Infantry Division) 02/17/42 redesignated **9ᵗʰ Light Infantry Division** - see **9ᵗʰ Light Infantry Division**.

10ᵗʰ Infantry Brigade (01/23/39, from **Infantry Commander 2, 3ʳᵈ Mixed Army Brigade**, Hungary; 04/05/41, IV Army Corps; 04/17/41, Hungary; 02/17/42, redesignated **10ᵗʰ Light Infantry Division**): 08/01/39 MG Frigyes Gyimesi (Chief of Staff, Third Army) 03/01/40 MG Ferenc Peterdy (?) 10/01/41 MG Jenö Felkl (Commanding General, 10ᵗʰ Light Infantry Division) 02/17/42 redesignated **10ᵗʰ Light Infantry Division** - see **10ᵗʰ Light Infantry Division**.

11ᵗʰ Infantry Brigade (01/23/39, from **Infantry Commander 2, 4ᵗʰ Mixed Army Brigade**, Hungary; 04/05/41, IV Army Corps; 04/17/41, Hungary; 02/17/42, redesignated **11ᵗʰ Light Infantry Division**):
     /38 MG Alajos Lemberkovics (Commanding General, 11ᵗʰ Infantry Brigade) 03/01/40
     /39 MG Kálmán Pèchy (?) 02/01/39
     02/01/39 MG János Dömötör (Vice President, Supreme Military Court) 02/01/42
02/01/42 MG Zoltán Álgya-Pap (Commanding General, 11ᵗʰ Light Infantry Division) 02/17/42 redesignated **11ᵗʰ Light Infantry Division** - see **11ᵗʰ Light Infantry Division**.

12ᵗʰ Infantry Brigade (01/23/39, from **Infantry Commander 3, 4ᵗʰ Mixed Army Brigade**, Hungary; 04/05/41, IV Army Corps; 04/17/41, Hungary; 02/17/42, redesignated **12ᵗʰ Light Infantry Division**): MG József Benke (Chief Administration Officer, II Army Corps) 02/01/40 MG Kalmán Török (?) 08/01/41 MG Gábor Illésházy (Commanding General, 12ᵗʰ Light Infantry Division) 02/17/42 redesignated **12ᵗʰ Light Infantry Division** - see **12ᵗʰ Light Infantry Division**.

13ᵗʰ Infantry Brigade (01/23/39, from **Infantry Commander 1, 4ᵗʰ Mixed Army Brigade**, Hungary; 04/05/41, V Army Corps; 04/17/41, Hungary; 02/17/42, redesignated **13ᵗʰ Light Infantry Division**): MG Gyula S. Nágy (Commanding General, VII Army Corps & VII Military District) 03/01/40 MG Pál Platthy (Commanding General, 13ᵗʰ Light Infantry Division) 02/17/42 redesignated **13ᵗʰ Light Infantry Division** - see **13ᵗʰ Light Infantry Division**.

14th Infantry Brigade (01/23/39, from **Infantry Commander 1, 5th Mixed Army Brigade**, Hungary; 04/05/41, V Army Corps; 04/17/41, Hungary; 02/17/42, redesignated **14th Light Infantry Division**): MG Antal Silley (Commanding General, V Army Corps & V Military District) 08/01/39 MG Count Marcell Stomm (Commanding General, 14th Light Infantry Division) 02/17/42 redesignated **14th Light Infantry Division** - see **14th Light Infantry Division**.

15th Infantry Brigade (01/23/39, from **Infantry Commander 3, 6th Mixed Army Brigade**, Hungary; 04/05/41, I Army Corps; 04/17/41, Hungary; 02/17/42, redesignated **15th Light Infantry Division**): Col. Lajos Veress (Commanding General, 2nd Cavalry Brigade) 03/01/40 MG Alajos Lemberkovics (Chief Administration Officer, I Mobile [Rapid] Army Corps) 08/01/41 Col. József Grassy (Commanding General, 15th Light Infantry Division) 02/17/42 redesignated **15th Light Infantry Division** - see **15th Light Infantry Division**.

16th Infantry Brigade (01/23/39, from **Infantry Commander 2, 5th Mixed Army Brigade**, Hungary; 02/17/42, redesignated **16th Light Infantry Division**): MG Alfréd Friedrich (retired) 03/01/40 MG Elemér Hunfalvay (retired) 02/01/42 Col. Béla Tanitó (Commanding General, 16th Light Infantry Division) 02/17/42 redesignated **16th Light Infantry Division** - see **16th Light Infantry Division**.

17th Infantry Brigade (01/23/39, from **Infantry Commander 1, 6th Mixed Army Brigade**, Hungary; 02/17/42, redesignated **17th Light Infantry Division**): Col. Dezsö Bittó (Deputy Inspector-General of the Gendarmerie) 08/01/39 MG Szilárd Bakay (Commanding General, 17th Light Infantry Division) 02/17/42 redesignated **17th Light Infantry Division** - see **17th Light Infantry Division**.

18th Infantry Brigade (01/23/39, from **Infantry Commander 3, 5th Mixed Army Brigade**, Hungary; 02/17/42, redesignated **18th Light Infantry Division**): MG Károly Olgyay [+ 10/06/41, Commanding General, Hungarian Occupation Command] (Commanding General, 18th Light Infantry Division) 02/17/42 redesignated **18th Light Infantry Division** - see **18th Light Infantry Division**.

19th Infantry Brigade (01/23/39, from **Infantry Commander 1, 7th Mixed Army Brigade**, Hungary; 04/07/41, VII Army Corps; 04/17/41, Hungary; 02/17/42, redesignated **19th Light Infantry Division**): MG József Csatáry (retired) 08/01/41 MG Gyözö Beleznay (Commanding General, 19th Light Infantry Division) 02/17/42 redesignated **19th Light Infantry Division** - see **19th Light Infantry Division**.

20th Infantry Brigade (01/23/39, from **Infantry Commander 2, 7th Mixed Army Brigade**, Hungary; 04/05/41, VII Army Corps; 04/17/41, Hungary; 02/17/42, redesignated **20th Light Infantry Division**): MG Ödön Domaniczky (Commanding General, III Army Corps) 08/01/41 MG Károly Kovács (Commanding General, 20th Light Infantry Division) 02/17/42 redesignated **20th Light Infantry Division** - see **20th Light Infantry Division**.

21st Infantry Brigade (01/23/39, new unit, Hungary; 04/05/41, VII Army Corps; 04/17/41, Hungary; 09/01/41, Hungarian Occupation Command; 10/41, redesignated **121st Infantry**

(Security) Division): MG Jenö Röder (Inspector of the Military Labor Force, Ministry of Defense) 08/01/41 MG Ferenc Tilger (Commanding General, 121st Infantry (Security) Brigade) 10/41 redesignated **121st Infantry (Security) Brigade** - see **121st Infantry (Security) Brigade**.

22nd Infantry Brigade (01/23/39, from **Infantry Commander 2, 6th Mixed Army Brigade**, Hungary; 02/17/42, redesignated **22nd Light Infantry Division**): MG Sándor Eötvös (retired) 11/01/40 MG Aladár Máriay (Commanding General, 22nd Light Infantry Division) 02/17/42 redesignated **22nd Light Infantry Division** - see **22nd Light Infantry Division**.

23rd Infantry Brigade (01/23/39, new unit, Hungary; 02/17/42, redesignated **23rd Light Infantry Division**): 11/38 Col. József Heszlényi (Commanding Officer, 2nd Motorized Brigade) 03/01/40 MG Kálmán N. Máthé (Secretary-General, Supreme Military Council) 02/11/42 vacant 02/17/42 redesignated **23rd Light Infantry Division** - see **23rd Light Infantry Division**.
A.   **Attached to 23rd Infantry Brigade**
     /?? Col. Gábor Illèsházy (Commanding Officer, 12th Infantry Division) 08/01/41

24th Infantry Brigade (01/23/39, new unit, Hungary; 08/30/41, VIII Army Corps; 10/41, redesignated **124th Infantry (Security) Division**): MG Andor Vásárhelyi (?   ) 08/01/41 MG György Sziklay (Commanding General, 124th Infantry (Security) Brigade) 10 /41 redesignated **124th Infantry (Security) Brigade** - see **124th Infantry (Security) Brigade**.

25th Infantry Brigade (09/15/40, new unit, Hungary; 02/17/42, redesignated **25th Light Infantry Division**): MG Béla Góthay (Commanding General, 25th Light Infantry Division) 02/17/42 redesignated **25th Light Infantry Division** - see **25th Light Infantry Division**.

26th Infantry Brigade (09/15/40, new unit, Hungary; 02/17/42, redesignated **26th Light Infantry Division**): vacant 11/15/40 MG Béla Marschalkó (retired) 08/01/41 Col. of RF Dr. Kálmán Hardy [HN] (Commanding General, 26th Light Infantry Division) 02/17/42 redesignated **26th Light Infantry Division** - see **26th Light Infantry Division**.

27th Infantry Brigade (09/15/40, new unit, Hungary; 02/17/42, redesignated **27th Light Infantry Division**): MG Ferenc Kolthay (Commanding General, 27th Light Infantry Division) 02/17/42 redesignated **27th Light Infantry Division** - see **27th Light Infantry Division**

203rd Infantry Brigade: /44 MG Zoltán Gergely.

Unknown? Infantry Brigade: /39 MG Ferenc Falka

Security Brigades

102nd Infantry (Security) Brigade (12/01/41, from **2nd Infantry Brigade**, Hungarian Occupation Group East; 02/17/42, redesignated **102nd Light Infantry Division**): 12/01/41 MG Károly Bogányi (Commanding General, 102nd Light Infantry Division) 02/17/42 redesignated **102nd Light Infantry Division** - see **102nd Light Infantry Division.**

105th Infantry (Security) Brigade (12/01/41, from **5th Infantry Brigade**, Hungarian Occupation Command; 02/17/42, redesignated **105th Light Infantry Division**): MG Imre Kolossváry (Commanding General, 105th Light Infantry Division) 02/17/42 redesignated **105th Light Infantry Division** - see **105th Light Infantry Division.**

108th Infantry (Security) Brigade (10/41, from **8th Infantry Brigade**, Hungarian Occupation Command; 02/09/42, Hungarian Occupation Group, West; 02/17/42, redesignated **108th Light Infantry Division**): MG Ottó Abt 01/42 MG László Stemmer (?) 02/42 MG Ottó Abt (Commanding General, 108th Light Infantry Division) 02/17/42 redesignated **108th Light Infantry Division** - see **108th Light Infantry Division.**

121st Infantry (Security) Brigade (10/41, from **21st Infantry Brigade**; Hungarian Occupation Command; 02/09/42, Hungarian Occupation Group West; 02/17/42, redesignated **121st Light Infantry Division**): MG Ferenc Tilger (03/45, Commanding General, 20th Infantry Division) 02/17/42 redesignated **121st Light Infantry Division** - see **121st Light Infantry Division**.

124th Infantry (Security) Brigade (10/01/41, from **24th Infantry Brigade**; Hungarian Occupation Command; 02/09/42, Hungarian Occupation Group West; 02/17/42, redesignated **124th Light Infantry Division**,): MG György Sziklay [+ 02/09/42, Commanding General, Hungarian Occupation Group West] (Commanding General, 124th Light Infantry Division) 02/17/42 redesignated **124th Light Infantry Division** - see **124th Light Infantry Division**.

Mountain Brigades

1st Mountain Brigade (09/15/39, Hungary; 06/06/41, Carpathian Battle Group; 07/09/41, VIII Army Corps; 12/01/41, Hungary; 01/06/44, IX Army Corps; 04/18/44, German XI Army Corps, Eastern Front; 04/21/44; VI Army Corps; 09/14/44, V Army Corps; 01/25/45, Reserve, First Army; 02/01/45, 24th Infantry Division, First Army; 02/21/45, First Army; 05/45, surrendered to United States forces in Styria, Austria): MG József Németh (I) [+ Chief, Group II Training Staff, General Staff & Chief, Section 5 Troop Training, Group II, Training Staff, General Staff] (11/01/42, Commanding General, I Army Corps & I Military District) 12/01/40 Col. Jenó Felkl (Commanding General, 10th Infantry Brigade) 10/01/41 MG [Retired '40] Aladár Pintér (Commanding General, 24th Infantry Division) 08/10/43 MG Ferenc Lóskay (Commanding General, 9th Border Guard Brigade) 11/10/44 Col. Lajos Barátosy 04/45 Col. Sándor Kossuth 05/45 surrendered.

A. **Attached to 1st Mountain Brigade**
    /39 Col. Ferenc Lóskay (attached to the Army Infantry School) /40

2nd Mountain Brigade (1941; 10/01/42, disbanded; 08/10/43, reformed from **8th Border Guard Brigade**, Hungary; 01/06/44, IX Army Corps; 04/18/44, German XI Army Corps, Eastern Front; 04/21/44, VI Army Corps; 09/14/44, III Army Corps; 10/31/44, First Army; 12/03/44, V Army Corps; 12/07/44, First Army; 12/31/44, VIII Army Corps; 01/21/45, First Army; 08/44, IX Army Corps; 05/45, surrendered to Soviet forces in Styria, Austria): **2nd Mountain Brigade (#1)** /41 MG Ferenc Bisza (Commanding General, 2nd Armored Division) 10/01/42 disbanded, reformed **2nd Mountain Brigade (#2)** 08/10/43 MG Géza Fehér (Commanding General, Rear Area, First Army) 05/44 MG Sándor Makray (Military Attaché Germany [Berlin]) 09/44 Col. Lajos Rumy 11/44 Col. Endre Dósa 11/44 unknown? 05/45 surrendered.

6th Mountain Brigade (1941):

1st Mountain Replacement Brigade (05/01/44, Field Replacement Army; 08/26/44, Hungary; 09/02/44, II Army Corps; 10/05/44, Finta Group, Second Army; 11/07/44, disbanded and remnants transferred to the **1st Mountain Brigade**): unknown? 11/07/44 disbanded.

2nd Mountain Replacement Brigade (05/01/44, Field Replacement Army; 08/26/44, Hungary; 09/02/44, Reserves, Second Army; 10/05/44, Finta Group, Second Army; 11/07/44, disbanded and remnants transferred to the **2nd Mountain Brigade**): unknown? 11/07/44 disbanded.

Motorized Brigades

1st Armored Brigade (also known as **1st Motorized Brigade**; 10/10/38; HQ: Budapest; Hungary; 03/01/41, Mobile [Rapid] Corps; 06/42, disbanded): MG Ödön Zay (retired) 03/01/40 Col. Jëno Major (Commander of Infantry Field Training; + 05/42, acting Commanding General, I Mobile [Rapid] Army Corps) 11/01/41 MG Gyözö Ankay-Anesini (attached to VI Army Corps) 05/01/42 Col. Elemér Sáska (Commanding Officer, 12th Light Infantry Division) 06/42 disbanded.

A.   **Deputy Commander, 1st Motorized Brigade**: unknown? /39 Col. Ferenc Bisza (attached to Ludovika Military Academy) /40

B.   **Artillery, 1st Armored Brigade**: /39 Col. Sándor Berecz (Artillery Commander, VI Army Corps) /42

    a.   **Light Artillery Detachment**: /38 LCol. Mihály Kanotay (Vice-President, Central Receiving Committee) /40

2nd Motorized Brigade (10/01/38; HQ: Budapest; Hungary; 03/01/41, Mobile [Rapid] Corps; 12/01/41, Hungary; 10/01/42, disbanded): Col. Károly Beregfy (Commandant, General Staff Academy) 01/15/39 Col. Sándor Horváth (Chief, Motorized Troops Field Training) 03/01/40 Col. József Heszlényi (Chief, Main Supply Bureau, Ministry of Defense) 10/29/40 Col. János Vörös [+ 08/41, Chief of Staff, First Army] /41 MG Aladár Asztalossy (Commanding General, 2nd Armored Division) 12/01/41 Col. Ferenc Bisza (Commanding General, 2nd Armored Division) 10/01/42 disbanded.

Miscellaneous Brigades

1st Anti-Aircraft Artillery Brigade: /41 MG Egon Barczaujfalusy (retired) /42 unknown? /45 MG László Kesseö [+ Commanding General, Solt-Dunaegyhazai Bridgehead] (Hungarian General with 17th German Military District) /45 MG Ákos Gesztessy.

2nd Anti-Aircraft Artillery Brigade: /42 Col. Ákos Gesztessy (Commanding Officer, Air Defenses Budapest) /42 MG Gyözö Árvay (Commanding General, Anti-Aircraft Brigade, Transylvania Army Detachment) /44 MG Ákos Gesztessy (Commanding General, 1st Anti-Aircraft Brigade) /45

3rd Anti-Aircraft Brigade: /42 Col. László Gerlóczy (retired) /45

Anti-Aircraft Brigade (/44, Transylvania Army Detachment): /44 MG Gyözö Árvay (attached to Commanding General, 1st Army) /44

Air Defenses Budapest: /42 Col. Ákos Gesztessy (Commanding General, 2nd Anti-Aircraft Brigade) /44

Székesfehérvár Military Hospital: unknown? /39 Col. József Bandenburg (Chief Medical Officer, Second Army & Chief Medical Officer, II Army Corps) /42

Debrecen Military Hospital: unknown? /44 MG János Kopniczky

Border Guard Brigades

1st Border Guard Brigade (01/23/39, Hungary; 11/15/40, disbanded): MG Brunó Berkovich (Chief Administration Officer, IX Army Corps) 11/15 /40 disbanded.

2nd Border Guard Brigade (01/23/39, Hungary; 11/15/40, disbanded): /39 Col. Sándor Magyarossy (Chief, Group II Training Staff, General Staff) 03/01/40 Col. Béla Góthay (Commanding Officer, 25th Infantry Brigade) 11/15/40 disbanded.

3rd Border Guard Brigade (01/23/39, Hungary; 11/15/40, disbanded): Col. Emil Lánghy (Commanding General, 9th Border Guard Brigade) 11/15/40 disbanded.

4th Border Guard Brigade (01/23/39, Hungary; 11/15/40, disbanded): Col. Jenö Felkl (Commanding Officer, 1st Mountain Brigade) 11/15/40 disbanded.

5th Border Guard Brigade (01/23/39, Hungary; 11/15/40, disbanded): Col. Ferenc Kolthay (Commanding General, 27th Infantry Brigade) 09/15/40 disbanded.

6th Border Guard Brigade (01/23/39, Hungary; 11/15/40, disbanded): /38 Col. Ernö Gyimesi (Chief Central Inspection Committee) 03/01/40 unknown? 11/15/40 disbanded.

7th Border Guard Brigade (01/23/39, Hungary; 11/15/40, disbanded): /38 Col. Ferenc Bisza (Deputy Commander, 1st Motorized Brigade) 01/23/39 Col. Sándor Bodor 12/18/39 Col. Béla Marschalkó (Commanding General, 26th Infantry Brigade) 11/15/40 disbanded.

8th Border Guard Brigade (01/23/39, Hungary; 06/06/41, Carpathian Battle Group; 07/09/41, VIII Army Corps; 12/01/41, Hungary; 08/10/43, disbanded): MG Endre Szücs (?) 02/01/41 MG György Rakovszky (Head, Bureau of the Air Force, Ministry of Defense) 08/01/41 Col. Fenerc Farkas (Head, Royal Military Archives, Ministry of Defense) 10/42 Col. Géza Fehér (Commanding General, 2nd Mountain Brigade) 08/10/43 disbanded.

9th Border Guard Brigade (11/15/40, in IX Military District; 02/01/43, Székler Command; 09/16/44, Reserve, Second Army; 10/23/44, IX Army Corps, Eastern Front; 11/17/44, Reserve, First Army; 12/17/44, Reserve, Third Army; 01/45, redesignated **9th Border Guard Division**): MG Emil Lánghy (Chief, Field Officer Training Courses) 07/01/42 MG Dezsö Tolnay (?) 02/01/43 MG Ferenc Szász (retired) 11/10/44 MG Ferenc Lóskay (Commanding General, 9th Border Guard Division) 01/45 redesignated **9th Border Guard Division** - see **9th Border Guard Division**.

Royal Hungarian Air Force Units
Air Force Divisions

1ˢᵗ Air Force Division (HQ: Budapest): /43 MG István Bánfalvy [+ Inspector of the Air Force] (Commander-in-Chief, Air Force & Head, Air Force Bureau, Ministry of Defense) 08/01/44 MG Aladár Szirmay

A.   **Deputy Commander, 1ˢᵗ Air Force Division**: /43 MG Sándor Illy (Commanding General, Home Air District) /44

B.   *Components - 1ˢᵗ Air Force Division* (09/01/44)
   1.   **101ˢᵗ Fighter Interceptor Brigade**
   2.   **102ⁿᵈ Air Force Brigade**
   3.   **Air Force Training Brigade**

Air Force Brigades

1ˢᵗ Air Force Brigade: /38 MG László Háry [+ Commander-in-Chief, Air Force] (retired) 02/01/40 unknown? 07/09/41? LCol. B. Orosz

A.   **Chief of Staff, 1ˢᵗ Air Brigade**: /39 LCol. Sándor András (Deputy Chief of the General Staff of the Air Force) /40

2ⁿᵈ Air Force Brigade (05/42, Second Army, Eastern Front): /42 Col. Sándor András (Chief of the General Staff, Air Force) /42 Col. Sándor Illy (/43, Chief Administration Officer, Air Force High Command) /42 Col. Tibor Fráter (Chief Administration Officer, Air Force High Command) /43 unknown? /43 Col. Tibor Fráter (Commanding Officer, 3ʳᵈ Air District) /44

Home Air District: /44 MG Sándor Illy (Commander-in-Chief, Air Force & Inspector, Air Force) /44

1ˢᵗ Air District (HQ: Veszprém): 09/01/44? unknown?

2ⁿᵈ Air District (HQ: Budapest): 09/01/44? unknown?

3ʳᵈ Air District (HQ: Debrecen): /39 Col. Tibor Fráter (attached to Section 6. Military Training Outside the Army, Group II Training Staff, General Staff) /40 unknown? /44 Col. Tibor Fráter (Commanding Officer, 3ʳᵈ Bomber Regiment; /45, retired) /44

101ˢᵗ Fighter Interceptor Brigade: 09/01/44? unknown?

102ⁿᵈ Air Force Brigade: 09/01/44? unknown?

Air Force Training Brigade: /41 MG István Bánfalvy (Inspector of the Air Force & Commanding General, 1st Air Division) /43 unknown?

Table of Equivalent Ranks

Hungarian Army & Air Force	United States & British Armies
Tábornagy (Field Marshal)	General of the Army (United States) Field Marshal (Britain)

[4 Star]

[created 08/41] Vezérezredes (Colonel General)	General

[3 Star]

[the following four ranks are replaced by 08/41]

Tüzérségi tábornok (General of Artillery)	Lieutenant General
Lovassági tábornok (General of Cavalry)	
Gyalogsági tábornok (General of Infantry	
Táborszernagy (Master-General of Ordnance)	

[2 Star]

Altábornagy (Lieutenant-Field Marshal) [Lieutenant-General]	Major General

[1 Star]

Vezérõrnagy (Major General)	Brigadier General (United States)
Vezérkapitágy (Major General - River Forces)	Brigadier (Britain)
Ezredes	Colonel
Alezredes	Lieutenant Colonel
Örnagy	Major
Százados	Captain
Fõhadnagy	First Lieutenant
Hadnagy	Second Lieutenant

Table of Equivalent Ranks

Hungarian Navy	United States & British Navies
	Fleet Admiral (United States) Admiral of the Fleet (Britain)
	Admiral
Altengernagy (Vice Admiral) Vezérfökapitány (Captain-General)	Vice Admiral
Ellentengernagy	Rear Admiral
	Commodore
Fötözskapitány	Captain
Törzsalkapitány	Captain (Junior Grade) (Britain) No Equivalent in the United States Navy
Törzsalkapitány	Commander
Kapitány	Lieutenant Commander
Föhajónagy	Lieutenant
Hajónagy	Lieutenant (Junior Grade)
Folyam zászlós	Ensign

Hungarian Senior Commanders

Colonel Generals

Name	Rank	Date of Rank	Command End of War
Jenö Rátz	General of Infantry	1936?	retired
Hugó Sónyi	General of Infantry	09/05/36	retired 03/01/40
Gusztáv Denk	General of Cavalry	05/38	retired 03/01/40
Károly Bartha vités Dálnokfalva	Master-Gen. of Ordnance	11/38	retired 09/24/42
Henrik Werth	General of Infantry	1939	retired 09/41
Lajos Keresztes-Fischer	General of Artillery	05/40	retired 02/43
András Littay	General of Infantry	09/40	retired 02/42
Vilmos Nagybaczoni Nagy	General of Infantry	1940	arrested 10/16/44
Gusztáv Vitéz Jány	General of Infantry	05/01/41	retired 11/43
Ferenc Szombathelyi	Colonel General	09/41	arrested 10/16/44
Elemér Gorondy-Novák	Colonel General	1941	retired by 02/42
István Náday	Colonel General	11/42	retired 07/44
Zoltán Decleva	Colonel General	12/42	retired 12/01/42
Lajos Csatay vités Csatai	Colonel General	02/43	committed suicide 11/19/44
József Bajnóczy	Colonel General	1943?	retired 10/16/44
János Vörös	Colonel General	05/44 (back-dated to 08/43)	Provisional Government Minister of Defense, Chief of the General Staff
Imre Ruszkiczay-Rüdiger	Colonel General	08/43	retired 01/45
Döme Sztójay	Colonel General	prior 1944	Prime Minister
Lajos Veress	Colonel General	08/44	arrested 10/16/44, escaped
Gusztáv Hennyey	Colonel General	08/44	arrested 10/16/44
Károly Beregfy	Colonel General	10/44?	German Puppet Government Minister of Defense, Chief of the General Staff, & Commander-in-Chief, Armed Forces
Dezsö László	Colonel General	11/44	CinC, First Army
Feketehalmi-Czeydner	Colonel General	11/44	German Puppet Government Deputy Minister of Defense, Deputy Commander-in-Chief, Armed Forces, & Deputy Chief of the General Staff
József Heszlényi	Colonel General	11/44	CinC, Third Army
Jëno Major	Colonel General	11/44	Inspector-General of the Hungarian Army
Ferenc K. Farkas	Colonel General	11/44	CinC, Reserve Army
Sándor Magyarossy	Colonel General	11/44	in reserve 01/45
Kálmán Ternegg	Colonel General	11/44	CinC, Hungarian Air Force
Emil N. Justy	Colonel General	11/44	retired 12/31/44
Lakatos de Csikszentsimon	Colonel General	1944	arrested 10/16/44
Béla Miklós de Dalnoki	Colonel General	1944	Provisional Government Prime Minister
Gábor Faraghió	Colonel General	1944	Provisional Government Minister of Food Supplies
Fenenc, Feketehalmy-Czeydner	Colonel General	1944	Deputy Defense Minister & Deputy Commander-in-Chief, Armed Forces
Jenö Tombor	Colonel General	1945?	Provisional Government Minister of Defense

Captain General

Name	Rank	Date of Rank	Command End of War
Miklós Horthy [HN]	Admiral	prior to 1920	arrested 10/16/44
Kálmán Hardy [HN]	Captain-General	01/01/44	arrested 10/16/44

Royal Hungarian Navy

The Hungarian Navy had no major ships prior or during World War II. A major ship is consider a cruiser or larger. The Hungarian Navy consisted of:

Danube Flotilla

7 River Patrol Vessels	*Gödöllö; Györ, Debrecen; Sopron; Szeged; Kecskemét*
10 Motor Launches	*Honvéd; Huszár, Tüzér, Mecsek; Galya; PM 1; PM 2; PM 3; PM 4; PM 5*
11 Minelayers	*Baja; Maros; AM 1; AM 2; AM 3; AM 4; AM 5; AM 6; AM 7; PAM 1; PAM 2*
1 Depot Ship	*Csobánc*
1 Training Vessel	*Badacsony*
3 Auxiliary Vessels	*Körös; Bükk; Vulkán*
7 Motor Yachts	*Anikó; Ágnes; Gerti; Lily; Magdi; Irma; Nóra*
4 Sailing Boats	*Albatrosz; Daru; Fecske; Pingvin*
8 Large Motor Boats	*Jolán; Juliska; Gizi; Sári; Vera; Sólyom; Emma; Erzsi*
13 Small Motor Boats	*Etel; Enikö; Guszti; Hédi; Hilda; Ica; Ilona; Irén; Kató; Klára; Paula; Piri; Zsuzsi*
2 Steam Boats	*Gözbárka I; Gözbárka II*
4 Barracks Ships	
4 Pontoon Ships	
9 Tug Boats	

BULGARIA

(German Ally)

Bulgarian Government

Head of State

King: BORIS III {Boris Klemens Robert Maria Pius Ludwig Stanislaus Xaver [Boris Clement Robert Mary Pius Louis Stanislaus Xavier], House of Saxe-Coburg and Gotha}(died of apparent heart failure) 08/28/43 SIMEON II [Simeon Borisov of Saxe-Coburg-Gotha] (with Counsel of Regency)

    a.   **Adjutant-General to the King**: /35 LG Stefan Tsanev Tsanev (　?　) /40 unknown? /44 MG Rafail Knev Zhechev (/45, executed)

    b.   **Aide-de-Camp to the King**:

        /35 Col. Rafail Knev Zhechev (Adjutant-General to the King) /44

        /44 MG Gancho Manchev Ivanov.

        /44 MG [Retired '31] Hristro Marholev.

Council of Regency to serve King Simeon II (three members)

Head: 08/43 LG Prince Kiril Preslavski [Brother of King Boris III] (02/01/45, condemned to death and executed by Bulgarian People's Court) /44

Members:

    08/43 BOGDAN DIMITROV FILOV (02/01/45, executed by firing squad)

    08/43 LG Nikola Mihailov Mihov [Michoff] (arrested; 02/01/45, condemned to death and executed; /96, rehabilitated) /44

Head of Government

Prime Minister: 05/19/34 Gen.Inf. Kimon Stoyanov Georgiev (09/09/44, Prime Minister) 01/22/35 LG Pencho [Petko] Ivanov Zlatev [+ War Minister] 04/21/35 ANDREY SLAVOV TOSHEV 11/23/35 GEORGI IVANOV KYOSEIVANOV [+ Foreign Minister] (resigned) 02/15/40 BOGDAN DIMITROV FILOV [+ 04/42, Foreign Minister; 08/43, Member, Council of Regents] 09/09/43 PETAR HRISTOV [DIMITROV] GABROVSKI (acting; executed by the communist) 09/14/43 DOBRI BOZHILOV [KHADZHIYANAKEV] (resigned; arrested, tried, sentenced to death, and 02/01/45, executed) 06/01/44 IVAN IVANOV BAGRYANOV [+ to 06/44, Foreign Minister] (removed) 09/02/44 KONSTANTINE "KOSTA" VLADOV MURAVIEV (overthrown by a coup) 09/09/44 CG Kimon Stoyanov Georgiev.

[NOTE: in opposition to CG Kimon Stoyanov Georgiev, in exile in Germany, 09/09/44 ALEKSANDUR TSOLOV TSANKOV 05/45.**]**

    A.   **Foreign Minister**: /34 Gen.Inf. Kimon Stoyanov Georgiev (Prime Minister) 05/19/34 KOSTA BATALOV 11/23/35 GEORGI IVANOV KYOSEIVANOV[+ Prime Minister] 02/16/39 IVAN VLADIMIR POPOV 06/06/41 ALEKSANDER NIKOLAIEOV 04/11/42 BOGDAN DIMITROV FILOV [+ Prime Minister; 08/43, Member, Council of Regents] 09/09/43 SAVIA KIROV 10/43 DIMITUR SHISHMANOV 06/01/44 IVAN IVANOV BAGRYANOV [+ Prime Minister] 06/12/44 PURVAN DAGRANOV /44 KONSTANTIN "KOSTA" VLADOV MURAVIEV (Prime Minister) 09/02/44 PETRO STAINOV

    B.   **Finance Minister**: /34 PETAR TODOROV /35 MIHAIL KALENDAROV [+ Justice Minister] /35 MARKO RYAZKOV /35 STOYCHO MUSHANOV /35 KIRIL GUNEV 11/38 DOBRI BOZHILOV [KHADZHIYANAKEV] [+ 09/09/43, Prime Minister]

06/01/44 DIMITAR SAVOV 09/44 ALEKSANDUR GIRGINOV 09/44 PETRO STOYANOV

C. **War Minister**: /34 LG Pencho [Petko] Ivanov Zlatev [+ Prime Minister] (?   ) 04/21/35 LG Boyan Tsanev (?   ) /35 LG Hristo Lukov /38 LG Theodosi Petrov Daskalov (retired; 02/01/45, condemned to death and executed by Bulgarian People's Court) 04/42 LG Nikola Mihailov Mihov [Michoff] (one of three regents for King Simeon III) 08/43 LG Rusi Hristov Rusev (retired; /45, condemned to life imprisonment by Bulgarian People's Court; 02/01/45, died in prison) /44 LG Ivan Krystev Marinov [Marinoff] (Commander-in-Chief, Armed Forces) 05/44 CG [Retired '28] Damian Velchev.

    1.   **Under-Secretary of State for Air**: /41 MG Dimitar Vasilev Ayryanov [+ Commanding General, Air Force] (retired; /50, condemned to death by Bulgarian People's Court and executed as a war criminal) /44

D. **Home Affairs [Interior] Minister:** /34 LG Petur Midilev (?   ) /35 LG Krum Kolev (?   ) /35 LG Rasko Atanasov (?   ) /35 LG Georgi Sapov (?   ) /36 IVAN KRASNOVSKY /38 LCol. Nikola Nikolaev /38 MG [Retired '36] Nikota Dimitrov Nedev (retired) 02/15/40 PETAR HRISTOV [DIMITROV] GABROVSKI (Prime Minister) 09/09/43 LG Ivan Rusev (02/01/45, condemned to death and executed by Bulgarian People's Court) /43 DOCHO HRISTOV /44 ALEKSANDUR STANISHEV /44 VIRGIL DIMOV /44 ANTON TANEV YUGOV.

E. **Justice Minister**: /34 Col. Kimon Georgiev Stoyanov /35 MIHAIL KALENDAROV [+ Finance Minister] /35 LYUBEN DIKOV /35 VASIL KARADZOZOV /35 DIMITUR PESHEV /36 VASIL KARADZOZOV /37 ALEKSANDUR OGNYANOV /38 ILCHO KOZUHAROV /38 N. YOTOV /39 VASIL MITAKOV /42 KONSTANTIN PARTOV /44 RUSTI RUSHEV /44 ALEKSANDUR STALIYSKY /44 BORIS PAVLOV /44 MINCHO NEYCHEV.

F. **Commerce Minister**:

G. **Agriculture & State Property Minister**:

F. **Representative of the Government to the Allied Control Commission**: /44 Gen.Art. [Retired '41] Georgi Nikolov Popov.

German Diplomatic Representative

(in charge of all relations with the Bulgarian authorities)

Envoys Extraordinary and Minister Plenipotantiary: /39 HERBERT Baron von RICHTHOFEN [German] /41 SS-LG Adolf Heinz Beckerle [German] (?) /44 dissolved.

Head, Bureau of the Office of Foreign Affairs for Bulgaria and Romania (1944): GÜNTHER ALTENBURG [German].

National Bulgarian Government in Germany

(After the Soviet invasion, hardliners in collaboration with Germany, withdrew to Berlin and established a National Government that lasted to May 1945.)

Prime Minister, Minister of Foreign Affairs, & Finance Minister (09/09/44): ALEKSANDUR TSOLOV TSANKOV 05/45.]

Allied Occupation 1944 to 1947

Commander of Soviet [Third Ukrainian Front] Forces: MSU Fyodor Ivanovich Tolbukhin [Russian].

A.   **Political Commissars**: CG Aleksej Sergeevich Sheltov [Russian] /45 MG Vladimir Makarovich Layoli [Russian]

Chairman, Allied Control Commission (10/28/44): MSU Fyodor Ivanovich Tolbukhin [Russian] [+ to 05/45, Commander-in-Chief, Third Ukrainian Front; + 05/45, Commander-in-Chief, Southern Group of Forces] 04/46 LG Aleksandr Ivanovich Cherepanov [Russian] 09/15/47 dissolved.

[NOTE: acting for MSU Fyodor Ivanovich Tolbukhin [Russian] 10/28/44 to 04/46, LG Sergey Semyonovich Biriuzov [Russian] [+ Head, Soviet Military Mission to Bulgaria]]

Military High Command
Ministry of War

War Minister: /34 LG Pencho [Petko] Ivanov Zlatev [+ Prime Minister] (?) 04/21/35 unknown? /38 LG Theodosi Petrov Daskalov (retired; 02/01/45, condemned to death and executed by Bulgarian People's Court) 04/42 LG Nikola Mihailov Mihov [Michoff] (one of three regents for King Simeon III) 08/43 LG Rusi Hristov Rusev (retired; /45, condemned to life imprisonment by Bulgarian People's Court; 02/01/45, died in prison) /44 LG Ivan Krystev Marinov [Marinoff] (Commander-in-Chief, Armed Forces) 05/44 CG [Retired '28] Damian Velchev.

A. **Under-Secretary of State for Air**: unknown? /41 MG Dimitar Vasilev Ayryanov [+ Commanding General, Air Force] (retired; /50, condemned to death by Bulgarian People's Court and executed as a war criminal) /44

B. **Deputy Minister of War**: unknown? /44 MG Blagoi Ivanov Ivanov (/49, Minister of Construction & Roads) /44 LG Krum Lekarski.

C. **Chancellery, Ministry of War** (in /41, becomes **Chancellor, Ministry of War**): unknown? /39 MG Hristo Ivanov Velchev (retired) /40 Col. Rusi Hristov Rusev (Inspector of Armaments) /41 Col. Vasil Tsankov Balarev [+ /43?, Commander of Cavalry, Ministry of War] (retired; /44, arrested; /54, condemned to 5 years imprisonment by Bulgarian People's Court) /44 MG Ivan Nedialkov Koev (?) /44 LG Petr Hristov Iliev (Head, Bulgarian Liaison Mission to Soviet Third Ukrainian Front) /45 LG Nikola Konstadinov Genchev (imprisoned) /46.

D. **Chief of Cabinet, Ministry of War**: unknown? /44 MG Kiril Dimitrov Yanchulev (Chief of the General Staff) /44 MG Dimitr Georgiev Tomov (acting Head, Military Supplements, Ministry of War) /45

E. **Commander of Cavalry, Ministry of War**: unknown? /43? MG Vasil Tsankov Balarev [+ Chief, Chancellery, Ministry of War] (retired) /44

F. **Chief of Communications, Ministry of War**: unknown? /41 MG Atanas Pavlov Zhilkov (?) /44

G. **Supply Department, Ministry of War**: unknown? /42 MG Rusi Hristov Rusev (War Minister) 08/43 unknown? /45 MG Dimitr Georgiev Tomov (acting; /47, Head, Military Industry Department, Ministry of Defense; /48, arrested and executed) /45 LG Boyan Georgiev Uruman.

H. *Military Attachés*
   1. **Military Attaché France**: /36 LCol. Ivan Krystev Marinov [Marinoff] (Chief of Staff, Third Army) /39
   2. **Military Attaché Greece**: /35 LCol. Georgi Hristov Ivanov (/44, Commandant, Reserve Officer School) /3?
   3. **Military Attaché Germany**: /36 LCol. Asen Nikolov Sirakov [Sierakoff] (Chief, Unknown? Section, General Staff; /41, Commanding Officer, Belomorska Detachment) /38
   4. **Military Attaché Hungary**: /35 LCol. Asen Nikolov Sirakov [Sierakoff] (Military Attaché Germany) /36

I.   **OPD**: /43 LG Asen Petrov Krasnovski (Inspector of Artillery) /44

Armed Forces

Commander-in-Chief, Armed Forces: 09/44 LG Ivan Krystev Marinov [Marinoff] (Chief Inspector of the Army) /45

A.   **Commander-in-Chief, Political Affairs**:
1.   **Deputy Commander-in-Chief, Political Affairs**: /44 LG Ferdinand Todorov Kozovski

B.   **Bulgarian Military Mission to Soviet Third Ukrainian Front**: /45 LG Marko Atanasov Kolev.

C.   **Bulgarian Liaison Mission to Soviet Third Ukrainian Front**: /45 LG Petr Hristov Iliev.

D.   **Council of National Defense**:
1.   **Secretary, Council of National Defense**: /36 Col. Asen Stefanov Kraev (Commanding Officer, 3rd Infantry Defense) /38

E.   *Army Components* (06/22/41)
1.   **First Army**
2.   **Second Army**
3.   **Third Army**
4.   **Fourth Army**
5.   **Fifth Army**
6.   **Bulgarian Royal Air Force**
7.   **Bulgarian Royal Navy**
8.   **1st Cavalry Division**
9.   **2nd Cavalry Division**
10.   **16th Infantry Division**
11.   **Armored Regiment**
12.   **Railroad Regiment**
13.   **Air Defense Regiment**

Chief of the General Staff: /38 LG Nikola Nikolov Hadzhipetkov (retired) /41 LG Vasil Tenev Boydev [Boideff] (Commanding General, Fifth Army) /41 LG Konstantin Ludvig Lukash (Chief Inspector of the Army) /44 MG Trifon Yordanov Trifonov (retired; 03/15/45, condemned to death and executed by Bulgarian People's Court) /44 LG Raycho Boev Slavkov (Commanding General, Third Army) /44 MG Kiril Dimitrov Yanchulev (retired) /44 LG Ivan Atanasov Kinov [Russian].

A.   **Deputy Chief of the General Staff**: /38 MG Nikola Nikolov Hadzhipetkov (Chief of the General Staff) /38 unknown? /42 MG Kiril Dimitrov Yanchulev (Chief of the Cabinet, Ministry of War) /44 MG Angel Georgiev Dotsev (Commanding General, 11th Infantry Division) /44

B.   **Intendant-General**: unknown? /39 MG Konstantin Ivanov Bekyarov /40 Col. Stefan Khristov Boyadzhiev (acting; /42, Intendant-General) /40 MG Konstantin Ivanov Bekyarov (Director, Civilian Mobilization Sector) /42 MG Stefan Khristov Boyadzhiev [+ /43 to /44, Inspector of Artillery].

C.   **Operations, General Staff**: /35 Col. Atanas Atanasov Stefanov [Stefanoff] (Commandant, Infantry School) /35 LCol. Vladimir Antonov Ketskaro (/44, Chief,

VUZ) /37 Col. Trifon Yordanov Trifonov (Commanding Officer, 22nd Infantry Regiment) /39 unknown? /39 Col. Trifon Yordanov Trifonov [+ Chief Mobilization, General Staff] (Commanding Officer, 16th Infantry Division) /41 Col. Ivan Konstantinov Popov (?) /44

D. **Mobilization, General Staff**: /36 Col. Trifon Yordanov Trifonov (Chief, Operations, General Staff) /37 unknown? /39 Col. Trifon Yordanov Trifonov [+ Chief, Operations, General Staff] (Commanding Officer, 16th Infantry Division) /41

E. *Schools*

    1. **Commandant, Military Academy**: /36 Col. Asen Stefanov Kraev (Secretary, Council of National Defense) /36 unknown? /38 Col. Nikola Mihailov Mihov [Michoff] (Commanding General, Fifth Army) or Col. Kiril Dimitrov Yanchulev (Commanding Officer, 22nd Infantry Regiment) /40 Col. Ivan Konstantinov Popov (Chief, Operations, General Staff) /41 Col. Boris Ivanov Dimitrov (Commandant of Sofia) /42

    2. **Commandant, Infantry School**: /35 Col. Atanas Atanasov Stefanov [Stefanoff] (Commanding Officer, 5th Infantry Division) /36

        a. **Assistant Commandant, Infantry School**: unknown? /39 LCol. Nikola Khristov Aleksiev (Commanding Officer, 4th Infantry Regiment) /40

    3. **Commandant, Artillery School**: /37 Col. Dimitar Mitrov Stanchev (Deputy Inspector of Artillery) /38

    4. **Commandant, Officer School**: unknown? /41 Col. Georgi Atanasov Mladenov (Commanding Officer, 3rd Infantry Division) /41

    5. **Commandant, Reserve Officers School**: unknown? /42 Col. Petar Tsankov (killed?) /44 Col. Georgi Hristov Ivanov.

        a. **Deputy Commandant, Reserve Officers School**: /38 LCol. Petar Dimitrov Karov [Karoff] (attached to the Infantry Inspectorate) /39 Col. Petar Tsankov (Commandant, Reserve Officers School) /42

    6. **Commandant, Military Workshops**: unknown? /40 Col. Boniu Bonev Gochev /44

    7. **Officers Training Courses**: /36 MG Nikola Nikolov Hadzhipetkov (Deputy Chief of the General Staff) /38

F. **National Gendarmerie**: unknown? /44 MG Boris Ivanov Dimitrov

G. **Directorate of Civilian Mobilization**: unknown? /39 MG Sava Dimitrov Bakyrdzhiev (retired) /42 MG Konstantin Ivanov Bekyarov (retired) /44

    1. **Supply Department, Directorate of Civilian Mobilization**: unknown? /39 Col. Ivan Krystev Marinov [Marinoff] (Commanding Officer, 6th Infantry Division) /40

H. **Military Factories**: unknown? /42 LG Asen Petrov Krasnovski (Chief, ODP) /43

    1. **Kazalik Military Factory**: unknown? /39 MG Asen Petrov Krasnovski (Commanding General, Military Factories) /42 unknown? /44 MG Ivan Dimitrov Dzhangozov.

        a. **Attached to Kazalik Military Factory**:

            /42 Col. Ivan Dimitrov Dzhangozov (Director, Kazalik Military Factory) /44

            /43 MG Ivan Genchev Ivanov (?) /44

I. **Compulsory Labor Corps**: /38 Col. Anton Stefanov Ganev (09/14/44, killed) /43

J.   **Commanding General, Air Force**: /36 MG Vasil Tenev Boydev [Boideff] (Chief of the Army General Staff) /41 MG Dimitar Vasilev Ayryanov [+Under-Secretary of State for Air] (retired) /44 MG Gancho Ivanov Manchev.

    1.   *Components - Air Force* (06/22/41)
        a.   **2nd Dive Bomber Ground Support Attack Group**
        b.   **5th Bomber Torpedo Group**
        c.   **8th Fighter Interceptor Group**
        d.   **Reconnaissance Group**
        e.   **Air Warning Group**

K.   **Air Defense**: unknown? /40 MG Dimitar Mitrov Stanchev

L.   **Military Training**: unknown? /41 Col. Aleksandr Popdimitrov (Commanding Officer, 14th Infantry Division) /42 MG Ivan Histrov Sapundzhiev (Commanding General, 17th Infantry Division) /44 LG Hristo Hristov Stoykov.

M.   **Director of Sanitary Service**: unknown? /43 MG Khristo Bosnev

N.   **Army Legal Service**: unknown? /43 MG Asen Stoev Karov [Karoff] (killed) 10/09/44 MG Hristo Trifonov Lilkov.

    1.   **Supreme Military Court**: /34 Col. Nikfor Iordanov Nikiforov (?) /43
    2.   **Military Court of Cassation**:
        a.   **Members**: /37 LCol. Asen Stoev Karov [Karoff] (Chief, Army Legal Service) /43

O.   **VUZ**: /44 MG Vladimir Antonov Ketskaro.

Chief Inspector of the Army: unknown? /44 LG Konstantin Ludvig Lukash (retired; 03/15/45, condemned to death as a war criminal by Bulgarian People's Court) /44 unknown? /45 LG Ivan Krystev Marinov [Marinoff].

A.   **Inspector of Infantry**: /38 MG Nikola Totev Markov (retired) /41 Col. Petar Dimitrov Karov [Karoff] (retired) /44

    1.   **Attached to Infantry Inspectorate**:
        /39 Col. Petar Dimitrov Karov [Karoff] (Commanding Officer 12th Infantry Division) /41
        /42 Col. Ivan Popov Rafailov (Commanding Officer, 25th Infantry Division) /43

B.   **Inspector of Armor**:

    1.   **Attached to Armor Inspectorate**
        /39 Col. Ivan Dimitrov Dzhangozov (attached to the Kazalik Military Factory) /42

C.   **Inspector of Cavalry**: /36 MG Atanas Pavlov Zhilkov (Chief of Communications, Ministry of War) /41 unknown? /42 MG Petr Georgiev Penev (?) /44 MG Georgi Nikolov Genev (?) /44 MG Marko Atanasov Kolev (Head, Bulgarian Military Mission to Soviet Third Ukrainian Front)

D.   **Inspector of Artillery**: unknown? /39 Col. Nikola Georgiev Stoychev (Commanding General, Third Army) /41 unknown? /42 MG Ivan Histrov Sapundzhiev (Chief, Military Training) /42 MG Stefan Khristov Boyadzhiev [+ Intendant-General] /44 LG Asen Petrov Krasnovski (retired) /44

    1.   **Deputy Inspector of Artillery**: /38 Col. Dimitar Mitrov Stanchev (Chief, Air Defense) /40

E.   **Inspector of Engineers**: /35 Col. Dimitar Vasilev Ayryanov (Commanding Officer,

4th Infantry Division) /38 Col. Nikola Hristov Hristov (/44, Commanding General, Third Army) /43 MG Hristo Bozhilov Peev (?) /44

F. **Inspector of Signals**: unknown? /43 MG Vasil Kitin Mirchev.

G. **Inspector of Air Defense Artillery**: /36 Col. Asen Dobrev Nikolov [Nikoloff] (Commanding Officer, 2nd Infantry Division) /38

H. **Inspector of Armaments**: /36 Col. Rusi Hristov Rusev (Head, Chancellery, Ministry of War) /40 unknown? /41 MG Rusi Hristov Rusev (Head, Supply Department, Ministry of War) /42

   1. **Deputy Inspector of Armaments**: /36 LCol. Nikola Georgiev Stoychev (Inspector of Artillery) /39

I. **Inspector of Mobilization**: unknown? /44 MG Dimitr Georgiev Tomov (Chief of Cabinet, Ministry of War) /44 MG Boris Bogdanoff (?) /45 MG Todor Lazov Krstev.

J. **Inspector of Border Guards**: /38 MG Georgi Yordanov Yordanov (Commanding General, 10th Infantry Division) /39 unknown? /40 MG Asen Stefanov Kraev (?) /41 unknown? /43 MG Boris Bogdanoff (Inspector of Mobilization) /44

Governor-General of Dobrogea: /40 LG Georgi Nikolov Popov (retired) /41

Commander-in-Chief, Navy: /35 RA Sava Ivanov [BN] (?) /37 RA Ivan Variklechkov [BN] (?) /39

Army Corps

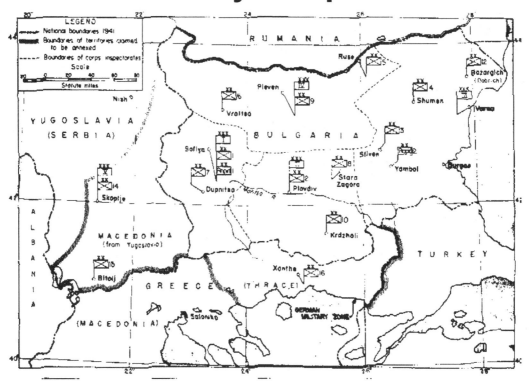

Map of Bulgaria, showing corps inspectorates, corps headquarters, and home stations of divisions.

First Army (from **First Army Inspectorate**; HQ: Sofia): /38 MG Konstantin Ludvig Lukash (Chief of the General Staff) /41 LG Nikola Mihailov Mihov [Michoff] (War Minister) /42 MG Nikola Kochev Nakov [Nakoff] (?   ) /44 MG Kostantin Biberov Stoyanov [Stojanoff] (retired; /44, committee suicided) /44 CG [Retired '35] Vladimir Dmitrov Stoychev (Bulgarian Representative to the United Nations) /45

A. **Chief of Staff, First Army**: /38 Col. Rafail Stoianov Banov (Chief, Unknown? Section, Unknown? Military School; /43 Commanding General, 6th Infantry Division) /42 Col. Dilhovski

B. **Components - First Army** (06/22/41)
  1. **1st Infantry Division**
  2. **7th Infantry Division**
  3. **1st Border Guard Regiment**
  4. **1st Border Guard Regiment**
  5. **1st Army Artillery Regiment**: unknown? /39 Col. Ivan Histrov Sapundzhiev (Artillery, Fourth Army) /40
  6. **1st Engineer Regiment**

C. **Artillery, First Army**: unknown? /39 Col. Kostantin Biberov Stoyanov [Stojanoff] (Commanding Officer, 10th Infantry Division) /40 unknown? /42 MG Zlatiu Tsonev Teptsiev (?   ) /44

D. **Chief Signal Officer, First Army**: unknown? /40 Col. Vasil Kitin Mirchev (Inspector of Signals) /43

194

E.   **Border Guards, First Army**: unknown? /44 MG Todor Stoianov Antonov (retired) /44

Second Army (from **Second Army Inspectorate**; HQ: Plovdiv): /36 MG Georgi Markov Markov (retired) /41 LG Ivan Hristov Markov [Merkoff] (retired?) /43 LG Nikola Georgiev Stoychev (/45, condemned to death and executed) /44 LG Kiril Nikilov Stanchev (Commanding General, Fifth Army) 09/44 MG Nikola Konstadinov Genchev (Head, Chancellery, Ministry of War) /45.
A.   **Chief of Staff, Second Army**: unknown? /40 Col. Kiril Nikolov Popbozhilov (Commanding General, 2nd Infantry Division) /43
B.   *Components* - Second Army (06/22/41)
    1.   2nd **Infantry Division**
    2.   8th **Infantry Division**
    3.   10th **Infantry Division**
    4.   3rd **Border Guard Regiment**
    5.   4th **Border Guard Regiment**
    6.   2nd **Army Artillery Regiment**
    7.   2nd **Engineer Regiment**: /35 Col. Vasil Kitin Mirchev (Commanding Officer, Signals Regiment; /40, Chief of Signals, First Army) /39
C.   **Chief Signal Officer, Second Army**: unknown? /39 Col. Konstantin Ivanov Bekyarov (Intendant-General) /39

Third Army ((from **Third Army Inspectorate**; HQ: Varna): /35 MG Georgi Nikolov Popov (Governor-General of Dobrogea) /40 unknown? /41 MG Nikola Georgiev Stoychev (Commanding General, Second Army) /43 unknown? /44 LG Nikola Hristov Hristov (killed) 09/08/44 MG Asen Ivkov Krstev (Bulgarian Liaison Officer to 3rd Ukrainian Front; /44, Commanding General, Fourth Army) /44 LG Raycho Boev Slavkov (retired) /45 MG Stefan Dimitrov Taralezhkov.
A.   **Chief of Staff, Third Army**: /36 Col. Kiril Dimitrov Yanchulev (Commandant, Military Academy) /38 unknown?/39 Col. Ivan Krystev Marinov [Marinoff] (Head, Supply Department, Directorate of Civilian Mobilization) /39 unknown? /40
            /40 Col. Angel Georgiev Dotsev (Chief, Unknown? Section, General Staff; /44, Deputy Chief of the General Staff) /42
            /40 MG Frigyes Gyimesi (Commanding General, V Army Corps) 08/20/42
B.   *Components* - Third Army (06/22/41)
    1.   3rd **Infantry Division**
    2.   4th **Infantry Division**
    3.   5th **Border Guard Regiment**
    4.   6th **Border Guard Regiment**
    5.   3rd **Army Artillery Regiment**
    6.   3rd **Engineer Regiment**
C.   **Artillery, Third Army**: unknown? /41 MG Zlatiu Tsonev Teptsiev (Artillery Commander, First Army) /42

Fourth Army ((from **Fourth Army Inspectorate**; HQ: Pleven): /36 LG Theodosi Petrov Daskalov (Minister of War) /38 Col. Petar Tsankov (acting; Chief, Unknown? Section, Fourth

Army; /39, Deputy Commandant, Reserve Officers School) /38 MG Ivan Hristov Markov [Merkoff] (Commanding General, Second Army) /41 MG Atanas Atanasov Stefanov [Stefanoff] (killed) 09/12/44 MG Aleksandr Popdimitrov (?) /44 MG Asen Nikolov Sirakov [Sierakoff] (retired) /44 LG Boyan Georgiev Urumov (Commanding General, Unknown? Army; /45, Head, Military Supplements Department, Ministry of War) 12/44 MG Asen Ivkov Krstev (Commanding General, Auxiliary Troops) /45.

A. **Deputy Commander, Fourth Army**: unknown? /44 MG Boris Dikov Kopchev (/50, Commandant, Military-Technical Academy)

B. **Chief of Staff, Fourth Army**: unknown? /39 Col. Nikola Ivanov Grozdanov (Commanding Officer, 3rd Infantry Regiment) /40

C. *Components* - **Fourth Army** (06/22/41)
    1. **5th Infantry Division**
    2. **6th Infantry Division**
    3. **9th Infantry Division**
    4. **7th Border Guard Regiment**
    5. **8th Border Guard Regiment**
    6. **4th Army Artillery Regiment**
    7. **4th Engineer Regiment**

D. **Artillery, Fourth Army**: unknown? /40 Col. Ivan Histrov Sapundzhiev (Inspector of Artillery) /42

E. **Chief Engineer, Fourth Army**: unknown? /39 Col. Hristo Bozhilov Peev (Commandant of Air Force Base; /43, Inspector of Engineers) /42

Fifth Army (/41, new unit; 09/44, fought with Russians; HQ: Skoplje, Macedonia): MG Nikola Mihailov Mihov [Michoff] (Commanding General, First Army) /41 MG Vasil Tenev Boydev [Boideff] (retired) 09/44 LG Kiril Nikilov Stanchev

A. **Chief of Staff, Fifth Army**: /41 Col. Nicho Georgiev Georgiev (Commanding Officer, 10th Infantry Division) /42 Col. Savov

B. *Components* - **Fifth Army** (06/22/41)
    1. **14th Infantry Division**
    2. **15th Infantry Division**

People's Liberation Partisan Army:
A. **Chief of Staff, People's Liberation Partisan Army**: MG Blagoi Ivanov Ivanov (Deputy Minister of War) /44

I Occupation Corps (/1942; HQ: Niska Banja, Serbia; also known as **Serbian Occupation Corps**; possibly now the **VI Army Corps**): /42 MG Asen Dobrev Nikolov [Nikoloff] (/45, condemned to death by Bulgarian People's Court and executed as a war criminal) /44

A. **Chief of Staff, I Occupation Corps**: /42 Col. Naidenov

B. *Components* - **I Occupation Corps**
    1. **22nd Infantry Division**
    2. **24th Infantry Division**
    3. **27th Infantry Division**

II Occupation Corps (1942; HQ: Xanthe, Thrace; also known as **Aegean Command**): /42

MG Murnov (?) /43 MG Trifon Yordanov Trifonov (Chief of the General Staff) /44 MG Asen NIkolov Sirakov [Sierakoff] (Commanding General, Fourth Army) /44 MG Trifon Yordanov Trifonov (chief of the General Staff) /44
A.   **Chief of Staff, II Occupation Corps**:
B.   ***Components* - II Occupation Corps**
    1.   **11th Infantry Division**
    2.   **16th Infantry Division**

Divisions

Infantry Divisions

1st Infantry Division (1935, from **1st Infantry Regiment**): MG Konstantin Ludvig Lukash (Commanding General, 1st Army Inspectorate) /38 Col. Nikola Kochev Nakov [Nakoff] (Commanding General, First Army) /42 MG Dimitri Rushev (?) /43 MG Kostantin Biberov Stoyanov [Stojanoff] (Commanding General, First Army) /44 MG Todor Stefanov Toshev.

A. **Deputy Commander, 1st Infantry Division**: /43 Col. Boris Ivanov Dimitrov (Commanding General, National Gendarmerie) /44

B. **Chief of Staff, 1st Infantry Division**: /38 LCol. Hristofor Stoyanov Serafimov [Serafinoff] (Commanding Officer, 5th Infantry Division) /41 Col. Raycho Boev Slavkov (Chief of the General Staff) /44

C. *Components - 1st Infantry Division* (02/42)
    1. **1st Infantry Regiment**
    2. **6th Infantry Regiment**: /35 Col. Aleksandr Popdimitrov (Chief, Military Training) /39 Col. Georgi Atanasov Mladenov (Commandant, Officer School) /41 Col. Nikola Khristov Aleksiev (Commanding General, 17th Infantry Division) /43
    3. **41st Infantry Regiment**
    4. **4th Artillery Regiment**: /39 Col. Nikola Khristov Boev [Bojeff] (Commanding Officer, 15th Infantry Division) /41

2nd Infantry Division (1935, from **2nd Infantry Regiment**; HQ: Plovdiv): /36 Col. Ivan Hristov Markov [Merkoff] (Commanding General, Fourth Army) /38 Col. Asen Dobrev Nikolov [Nikoloff] (Commanding General, I Occupation Corps) /42 unknown? MG Kiril Nikolov Popbozhilov (?) /44 MG Nikola Konstadinov Genchev (Commanding General, Third Army) /45.

A. **Chief of Staff, 2nd Division**: LCol. Kiril Nikolov Popbozhilov (Chief, Unknown? Section, General Staff; /40, Chief of Staff, Second Army) /39 LCol. Ivan Popov Rafailov (Commanding Officer, 29th Infantry Regiment) /41

B. *Components - 2nd Infantry Division* (02/42)
    1. **9th Infantry Regiment**
    2. **21st Infantry Regiment**
    3. **27th Infantry Regiment**
    4. **3rd Artillery Regiment**

3rd Infantry Division (1935, from **3rd Infantry Regiment**; HQ: Sliven): /36 Col. Georgi Markov Markov (Commanding General, Second Army) /36 Col. Nikola Mihailov Mihov [Michoff] (Commandant, Military Academy) /38 Col. Asen Stefanov Kraev (Inspector of Border Guards) /40 Col. Kiril Dimitrov Yanchulev (Chief, Unknown? Section, General Staff; /42, Deputy Chief of the General Staff) /41 Col. Georgi Atanasov Mladenov (?) /44

A. *Components - 3rd Infantry Division* (02/42)
    1. **11th Infantry Regiment**

2. **24th Infantry Regiment**: /35 LCol. Todor Lazov Krstev (Commanding General, 28th Infantry Division) /44
3. **29th Infantry Regiment**: /41 Col. Ivan Popov Rafailov (attached to the Infantry Inspectorate) /42
4. **6th Artillery Regiment**: /35 Col. Stefan Khristov Boyadzhiev (Intendant-General) /40 unknown? /41 Col. Bonyu Stoev Pironkov (Commanding General, 5th Infantry Division) /44

4th Infantry Division (1935, from **4th Infantry Regiment**; HQ: Schumen): Col. Nikola Totev Markov (Inspector of Infantry) /38 Col. Dimitar Vasilev Ayryanov (Under-Secretary of State for Air & Commanding General, Air Force) /41 Col. Georgi Hristov Kovachev [Kovatscheff] (?) /43 unknown? /45 MG Tsonyu Stoev Ganev.
A. **Chief of Staff, 4th Infantry Division**: /38 LCol. Dimitar Ivanov Yanchev (Commanding Officer, 18th Infantry Regiment) /39
B. *Components - 4th Infantry Division* (02/42)
   1. **7th Infantry Regiment**: /39 Col. Georgi Hristov Kovachev [Kovatscheff] (Commanding Officer, Belomorska Detachment) /41
   2. **8th Infantry Regiment**: /38 Col. Georgi Atanasov Mladenov (Commanding Officer, 13th Infantry Regiment) /39
   3. **19th Infantry Regiment**
   4. **5th Artillery Regiment**: /36 Col. Zlatiu Tsonev Teptsiev (Artillery Commander, Third Army) /41

5th Infantry Division (1935, from **5th Infantry Regiment**; HQ: Russe): MG Theodosi Petrov Daskalov (Commanding General, Fourth Army) /36 Col. Atanas Atanasov Stefanov [Stefanoff] (Commanding General, Fourth Army) /41 Col. Hristofor Stoyanov Serafimov [Serafinoff] (?) /44 MG Bonyu Stoev Pironkov
A. *Components - 5th Infantry Division* (02/42)
   1. **5th Infantry Regiment**
   2. **18th Infantry Regiment**: /35 Col. Sava Dimitrov Bakyrdzhiev (Head, Civilian Mobilization Section) /39 Col. Dimitar Ivanov Yanchev (Commanding Officer, 9th Infantry Division) /40
      a. **Deputy Commander, 18th Infantry Regiment**: /38 LCol. Nikola Khristov Aleksiev (Assistant Commandant, Infantry School) /39
   3. **33rd Infantry Regiment**
   4. **1st Artillery Regiment**: /36 Col. Petr Iliev Ilinov (Commanding General, 6th Infantry Division) /39

6th Infantry Division (1935, from **6th Infantry Regiment**; HQ: Vraca): /39 MG Petr Iliev Ilinov (retired) /40 Col. Ivan Krystev Marinov [Marinoff] (Commanding General, 15th Infantry Division) /42 MG Nikola Khristov Boev [Bojeff] (?) /43 MG Rafail Stoianov Banov (retired; /45, condemned to death by Bulgarian People's Court and executed as a war criminal) /44 MG Mihail Iliev Zahariev (?) /45 MG Angel Georgiev Dotsev (retired) /46
A. **Deputy Commander, 6th Infantry Division**: /36 Col. Asen Ivkov Krstev (Commanding General, Third Army) /44
B. *Components - 6th Infantry Division* (02/42)
   1. **3rd Infantry Regiment**: /40 Col. Nikola Ivanov Grozdanov (Commanding

Officer, 12th Infantry Regiment) /40

2. **15th Infantry Regiment**
3. **35th Infantry Regiment**: /39 Col. Simeon Grigorov Simov (Commanding General, 24th Infantry Division) /43
4. **2nd Artillery Regiment**

7th Infantry Division (1935, from **7th Infantry Regiment**): /38 Col. Petr Georgiev Penev (Commanding Officer, 1st Mobile [Rapid] Division) /39 Col. Boris Bogdanoff (Inspector of Border Guards) /43 MG Nikola Ivanov Grozdanov (Commanding General, 25th Infantry Division) /43 MG Ivan Popov Rafailov (?) /44

A. *Components - 7th Infantry Division* (02/42)
1. **13th Infantry Regiment**: /39 Col. Georgi Atanasov Mladenov (Commanding Officer, 6th Infantry Regiment) /40
2. **14th Infantry Regiment**
3. **39th Infantry Regiment**
4. **7th Artillery Regiment**
B. **Attached to 7th Infantry Division**: /44 Col. Stefan Dimitrov Taralezhkov (attached to 27th Infantry Division) /44

8th Infantry Division (1935, from **8th Infantry Regiment**; HQ: Stara Zagora): Col. Asen Krstev Daskalov (retired) /41 Col. Asen NIkolov Sirakov [Sierakoff] (Commanding General, II Occupation Corps) /44 MG Nikola Ivanov Grozdanov (?) /44 MG Boris Mitev Harzianov.

A. *Components - 8th Infantry Division* (02/42)
1. **12th Infantry Regiment**: /40 Col. Nikola Ivanov Grozdanov (attached to 8th Infantry Division) /42
2. **23rd Infantry Regiment**
3. **30th Infantry Regiment**: /43 Col. Stefan Dimitrov Taralezhkov (attached to 7th Infantry Division) /44
4. **8th Artillery Regiment**
B. **Attached to 8th Infantry Division**: /42 Col. Nikola Ivanov Grozdanov (Commanding General, 24th Infantry Division) /43

9th Infantry Division (1936, new unit; HQ: Pleven): /39 Col. Konstantin Dimitrov Kotsev (retired) /40 Col. Dimitar Ivanov Yanchev (?) /44 MG Mihail Iliev Zahariev (Commanding General, 6th Infantry Division) /44

A. **Intendant, 9th Infantry Division**: /39 Col. Boris Ivanov Dimitrov (Commandant, Military Academy) /41
B. *Components - 9th Infantry Division* (02/42)
1. **4th Infantry Regiment**: /40 Col. Nikola Khristov Aleksiev (Commanding Officer, 6th Infantry Regiment) /41
2. **34th Infantry Regiment**
3. **36th Infantry Regiment**
4. **9th Artillery Regiment**: /36 LCol. Nikola Khristov Boev [Bojeff] (Commanding Officer, 4th Artillery Regiment) /39

10th Infantry Division (1936, new unit; HQ: Kirdzali): /39 MG Georgi Yordanov Yordanov (retired) /40 Col. Kostantin Biberov Stoyanov [Stojanoff] (/43, Commanding General, 1st Infantry Division) /42 Col. Nicho Georgiev Georgiev (Chief, Unknown? Section, General Staff; /45, condemned to death by Bulgarian People's Court and executed as a war criminal) /44

A.   **Deputy Commander, 10th Infantry Division**: /44 Col. Ivan Iordanov Hubenov (Commanding Officer, 10th Infantry Regiment) /44

B.   *Components - 10th Infantry Division* (02/42)
  1.   **10th Infantry Regiment**: unknown? /44 Col. Ivan Iordanov Hubenov.
  2.   **44th Infantry Regiment**
  3.   **47th Infantry Regiment**
  4.   **10th Artillery Regiment**

11th Infantry Division (1941, as a reserve unit; disbanded; 01/43, reformed; 07/44?, disbanded): /44 MG Angel Georgiev Dotsev (Commanding General, 6th Infantry Division) /45

A.   *Components - 11th Infantry Division (#1)* (02/42)
  1.   **22nd Infantry Regiment**: /39 Col. Trifon Yordanov Trifonov (Chief, Operations & Mobilization, General Staff) /39 unknown? /40 Col. Kiril Dimitrov Yanchulev (Commanding Officer, 3rd Infantry Division) /40
  2.   **25th Infantry Regiment**: Col. Ignat Tainiianski Iliev (attached to 14th Infantry Division) /4?
  3.   **42nd Infantry Regiment**
  4.   **11th Artillery Regiment**

B.   *Components - 11th Infantry Division (#2)* (01/43)
  1.   **42nd Infantry Regiment**
  2.   **70th Infantry Regiment**
  3.   **80th Infantry Regiment**
  4.   **11th Artillery Regiment**

C.   **Attached to 11th Infantry Division**:
  /45 MG Stefan Dimitrov Taralezhkov (Commanding General, Third Army) /45

12th Infantry Division (1941, as a reserve unit): Col. Petar Dimitrov Karov [Karoff]

A.   *Components - 12th Infantry Division* (02/42)
  1.   **31st Infantry Regiment**: /36 LCol. Dimitar Ivanov Yanchev (Chief of Staff, 4th Infantry Division) /38 unknown? /40 Col. Hristo Lazarov Kozarov (Commanding General, 27th Infantry Division) /43
  2.   **32nd Infantry Regiment**
  3.   **46th Infantry Regiment**:
  4.   **12th Artillery Regiment**

13th Infantry Division (1941, as a reserve unit; disbanded):

14th Infantry Division (1941, as a reserve unit; HQ Skoplje, Macedonia): 12/41 MG Peneff /42 Col. Aleksandr Popdimitrov (Commanding General, V Army Corps) /44

A.   *Components - 14th Infantry Division* (03/15/42)
  1.   **51st Infantry Regiment**

  2. **52nd Infantry Regiment**
  3. **15th Infantry Brigade**
  4. **1st Cavalry Brigade**
  5. **14th Cavalry Regiment**
B. **Attached to 14th Infantry Division**: /4? Col. Ignat Tainiianski Iliev.

15th Infantry Division (1941, as a reserve unit; HQ: Bitolji, Macedonia): /41 Col. Nikola Khristov Boev [Bojeff] (Commanding General, 6th Infantry Division) /42 MG Ivan Krystev Marinov [Marinoff] (Minister of War) /44 MG Mihail Petrov Mateev.
A. *Components - 15th Infantry Division* (07/15/44)
  1. **45th Infantry Regiment**
  2. **54th Infantry Regiment**
  3. **55th Infantry Regiment**
  4. **15th Artillery Regiment**

16th Infantry Division (12/41, as a reserve unit): 12/41 Col. Trifon Yordanov Trifonov (Commanding General, II Occupation Corps) /43 unknown? /44 Col. Tsonyu Stoev Ganev (Commanding General, 4th Infantry Division) /45
A. *Components - 16th Infantry Division* (11/06/43)
  1. **22nd Infantry Regiment**
  2. **57th Infantry Regiment**
  3. **59th Infantry Regiment**
  4. **62nd Infantry Regiment**
  5. **3rd Cavalry Regiment**
  6. **16th Artillery Regiment**

17th Infantry Division (12/41, as a reserve unit; Yugoslavia for occupation duty): unknown? /43 MG Nikola Khristov Aleksiev (retired; /54, condemned to 5 years imprisonment by Bulgarian People's Court) /44 MG Ivan Histrov Sapundzhiev
A. *Components - 17th Infantry Division* (07/15/44)
  1. **49th Infantry Regiment**
  2. **56th Infantry Regiment**
  3. **63rd Infantry Regiment**
  4. **17th Artillery Regiment**

18th Infantry Division: WAS NEVER FORMED.

19th Infantry Division: WAS NEVER FORMED.

20th Infantry Division: WAS NEVER FORMED.

21st Infantry Division (12/41, as a reserve unit; /43, disbanded): MG of Res. [Retired '34] Vasil Stefanov Manov [Manoff]
A. *Components - 21st Infantry Division* (02/42)
  1. **69th Infantry Regiment**
  2. **2nd Infantry Regiment**: /34 LCol. Mihail Iliev Zahariev (Commanding

General, 9th Infantry Division) /44
  3.   **34th Artillery Regiment**

22nd Infantry Division (1943, as a reserve unit):
A.   *Components - 22nd Infantry Division* (09/44)
  1.   **63rd Infantry Regiment**
  2.   **66th Infantry Regiment**
  3.   **103rd Infantry Regiment**
  4.   **22nd Artillery Regiment**

23rd Infantry Division: WAS NEVER FORMED.

24th Infantry Division (01/43, Yugoslavia for occupation duty): MG Nikola Ivanov Grozdanov (Commanding General, 7th Infantry Division) /43 MG Simeon Grigorov Simov [+ Commanding General, Bulgarian Occupation Force, Greece] (/45, condemned to death by Bulgarian People's Court and executed) /44
A.   *Components - 24th Infantry Division* (07/15/44)
  1.   **61st Infantry Regiment**
  2.   **64th Infantry Regiment**
  3.   **108th Infantry Regiment**
  4.   **24th Artillery Regiment**

25th Infantry Division (01/43): unknown? /43 Col. Ivan Popov Rafailov (Commanding General, 7th Infantry Division) /43 MG Nikola Ivanov Grozdanov (Commanding General, 8th Infantry Division) /44
A.   *Components - 25th Infantry Division* (07/15/44)
  1.   **69th Infantry Regiment**
  2.   **70th Infantry Regiment**
  4.   **25th Artillery Regiment**

26th Infantry Division: WAS NEVER FORMED.

27th Infantry Division (01/43): MG Hristo Lazarov Kozarov (?) /44
A.   *Components - 27th Infantry Division* (07/15/44)
  1.   **122nd Infantry Regiment**
  2.   **123rd Infantry Regiment**
  4.   **27th Artillery Regiment**
B.   **Attached to 27th Infantry Division**: /44 Col. Stefan Dimitrov Taralezhkov (attached to 11th Infantry Division) /45

28th Infantry Division (12/43): MG Stanimir Khristov Grnev (?) /44 MG Todor Lazov Krstev (Inspector of Mobilization) /45
A.   *Components - 28th Infantry Division* (11/06/43)
  1.   **10th Infantry Regiment**
  2.   **58th Infantry Regiment**
  3.   **6th Cavalry Regiment**

    4.   **28th Artillery Regiment**

29th Infantry Division (1944):
A.   *Components - 29th Infantry Division* (07/15/44)
    1.   **3rd Infantry Regiment**
    2.   **50th Infantry Regiment**
    3.   **52nd Infantry Regiment**

Frontier Command: 12/41 MG Bosadschieff

1st Guards Division: /44 MG Dimitr Nikolov Popov.

Mobile Divisions

1st Mobile [Rapid] Division (1939): /39 Col. Petr Georgiev Penev /40 MG Georgi Nikolov Genev (Commanding General, Belomorska Detachment) /41 MG Petr Georgiev Penev (Inspector of Cavalry) /42
A.   *Components - 1st Mobile [Rapid] Division* (1939)
    1.   **1st Cavalry Brigade**
    2.   **4th Cavalry Brigade**
    3.   **1st Armored Brigade**
    4.   **1st Horse Artillery Regiment**

2nd Mobile [Rapid] Division (1939): unknown? /39 Col. Georgi Nikolov Genev
A.   *Components - 2nd Mobile [Rapid] Division* (1939)
    1.   **2nd Cavalry Brigade**
    2.   **3rd Cavalry Brigade**
    3.   **1st Motorized Infantry Brigade**
    4.   **2nd Horse Artillery Regiment**

1st Cavalry Division: /36 MG Atanas Pavlov Zhilkov (Inspector of Cavalry) /36 unknown? /44 MG Marko Atanasov Kolev (Inspector of Cavalry) /44
A.   *Components - 1st Cavalry Division* (02/28/42)
    1.   **1st Cavalry Brigade**
        a.   *Components - 1st Cavalry Brigade*
            i.   **3rd Cavalry Regiment**: /38 Col. Mihail Genchev Minchov (Commanding General, 2nd Cavalry Brigade) /43
    2.   **2nd Cavalry Brigade**: unknown? /43 MG Mihail Genchev Minchov (Commanding General, 2nd Cavalry Division) /44
    3.   **1st Motorized Infantry Regiment**
    4.   **1st Horse Artillery Regiment**

2nd Cavalry Division: 12/41 Col. Genoff /44 MG Mihail Genchev Minchov
A.   *Components - 2nd Cavalry Division* (02/28/42)
    1.   **3rd Cavalry Brigade**: /39 Col. Georgi Nikolov Genev (Commanding General, 1st Rapid Division) /40
        a.   *Components - 3rd Cavalry Brigade*
            i.   **Guards Cavalry Regiment**: /38 Col. Todor Stoianov Antonov (Commanding General, 4th Cavalry Brigade) /41
    2.   **4th Cavalry Brigade**: /41 MG Todor Stoianov Antonov (Commanding General, Border Guards, First Army) /44
        a.   *Components - 4th Cavalry Brigade*
            i.   **10th Cavalry Regiment**: /38 Col. Georgi Nikolov Genev (Commanding Officer, 3rd Cavalry Brigade) /39
    3.   **2nd Motorized Infantry Brigade**
    4.   **2nd Horse Artillery Regiment**

Miscellaneous Units

Commandant of Sofia: /42 Col. Boris Ivanov Dimitrov (Deputy Commander, 1st Infantry Division) /43 unknown? /44 CG [Retired '35] Vladimir Dmitrov Stoychev (Commanding General, First Army) /44

Commandant of Stolichata: /35 Col. Georgi Yordanov Yordanov (Inspector of Border Guards) /38

Belomorska Detachment: /41 Col. Georgi Hristov Kovachev [Kovatscheff] (Commanding General, 4th Infantry Division) /41 Col. Asen Nikolov Sirakov [Sierakoff] (Commanding Officer, 8th Infantry Division) /41 MG Georgi Nikolov Genev (Inspector of Cavalry) /44

Brigades

1st Armored (Independent) Brigade: /44 MG Stoyan Konstantinov Trendafilov (Chief of Armored Forces) /45
A. *Components - 1st Armored (Independent) Brigade* (01/28/42)
    1. **1st Armored Regiment**: /41 LCol. Genoff (Commanding Officer, 2nd Cavalry Division) 12/41
    2. **1st Motorized Infantry Regiment**
    3. **1st Motorized Artillery Regiment**

2nd Armored Brigade: /44 MG Dimitr Nikolov Popov (Commanding General, 1st Guards Division) /44

15th Infantry Brigade
A. *Components -15th Infantry Brigade* (03/15/42)
    1. **54th Infantry Regiment**
    2. **55th Infantry Regiment**

Mountain Brigade (1941; disbanded; 01/43, reformed; 09/44?, disbanded):

Fortress Force (02/23/44, Strumamundung-Dedagatsch region):

Frontier Forces

1st Frontier Brigade (pre-war)
A.   ***Components - 1st Frontier Brigade*** (07/15/44)
    1.   **1st Frontier Regiment**
    2.   **5th Frontier Regiment**

2nd Frontier Brigade (pre-war)
A.   ***Components - 2nd Frontier Brigade*** (07/15/44)
    1.   **2nd Frontier Regiment**
    2.   **6th Frontier Regiment**

3rd Frontier Brigade (pre-war)
A.   ***Components - 3rd Frontier Brigade*** (07/15/44)
    1.   **3rd Frontier Regiment**
    2.   **7th Frontier Regiment**

4th Frontier Brigade (pre-war)
A.   ***Components - 4th Frontier Brigade*** (07/15/44)
    1.   **4th Frontier Regiment**
    2.   **8th Frontier Regiment**

Table of Equivalent Ranks

Bulgarian Army & Air Force	United States & British Armies
	General of the Army (United States) Field Marshal (Britain)
	General
General	Lieutenant General
General-leytenant	Major General
General-major	Brigadier General (United States) Brigadier (Britain)
Polkovnik	Colonel
Podpolkovnik	Lieutenant Colonel
Major	Major
Kapitan	Captain
Porucik	First Lieutenant
Podporucik	Second Lieutenant

Table of Equivalent Ranks

Bulgarian Navy	United States Navy
	Fleet Admiral
Admiral	Admiral
Vitse-admiral	Vice Admiral
Kontra-admiral	Rear Admiral
	Commodore
Kapitan I	Captain
Kapitan II	Commander
Kapitankeitenant	Lieutenant Commander
Michman I	Lieutenant
Michman II	Lieutenant (Junior Grade)
	Ensign

Senior Commanders

1.	Kutinchev, Vasil	General of Infantry	10/25/18
2.	Savov, Sava	General of Infantry	07/29/19
3.	Ivanov, Nikola	General of Infantry	05/06/36
4.	Kovachev, Stilian	General of Infantry	05/06/36
5.	Popov, Georgi Nikolov	General of Artillery	08/06/41
	recalled as a	Colonel General	10/09/44
6.	Velchev, Damian	Colonel General	05/06/45
7.	Daskalov, Theordosi Petrov	Colonel General	unknown?
8.	Rusev, Rusi Hristov	Colonel General	unknown?
9.	Georgiev, Kimon Stoyanov	Colonel General	unknown?

Bulgarian Military Units in Selected Campaigns

Bulgarian Army February 1942

First Army
- 1st Infantry Division
- 7th Infantry Division
- 11th Infantry Division
- **First Army Troops**
  - 1st Replacement Regiment
  - 1st Motorized Army Artillery Regiment
  - 1st Anti-Tank Regiment

Second Army
- 2nd Infantry Division
- 8th Infantry Division
- 10th Infantry Division
- **Second Army Troops**
  - 2nd Replacement Regiment
  - 2nd Motorized Army Artillery Regiment
  - 2nd Anti-Tank Regiment

Third Army
- 3rd Infantry Division
- 4th Infantry Division
- 12th Infantry Division
- **Third Army Troops**
  - 3rd Replacement Regiment
  - 3rd Motorized Army Artillery Regiment
  - 3rd Anti-Tank Regiment

Fourth Army
- 5th Infantry Division
- 6th Infantry Division
- 9th Infantry Division
- **Fourth Army Troops**
  - 4th Replacement Regiment
  - 4th Motorized Army Artillery Regiment
  - 4th Anti-Tank Regiment

Fifth Army
- 14th Infantry Division
- 15th Infantry Division

General Command, I Corps

       6th Infantry Division

       17th Infantry Division

       21st Infantry Division

Independent Formations

       16th Infantry Division

       2nd Cavalry Division

       Armored Brigade

Frontier Command

       Unknown Brigade

       3rd Brigade

       4th Brigade

Army Troops

       1st Railroad Regiment

Bulgarian Navy

Bulgarian Navy (HQ: Sofia)

A.   **Black Sea Flotilla** (HQ: Varna)
  1.   **Torpedoboat Squadron** (HQ: Varna)
       a.   **1ˢᵗ Torpedoboat Division** (*Drski*, *Khrabry*, *Strogi*, *Smely*)
       b.   **2ⁿᵈ Torpedoboat Division** (*F-1*, *F-2*, *F-3*, *F-4*)
       c.   **Gunboat Half-division** (*Chernomorec*, *Belomorec*)
  2.   **Minelayer Squadron** (HQ: Varna)
  3.   **Varna Fortress Garrison**
  4.   **Maine Infantry Battalion**
  5.   **Varna Coast Artillery Regiment**
  6.   **Burgas Coast Artillery Regiment**
B.   **Danube Flotilla** (HQ: Ruse)
  1.   **Gunboat Half-division** (*Maritza*, *Vardar*)
  2.   **Minelayer Company**
  3.   **Maintenance Unit**
  4.   **Danube River Police**
C.   **Aegean Sea Flotilla** (HQ: Dede Agatch)
  1.   **Marine Infantry Battalion**
  2.   **Kavála Artillery Regiment**
  3.   **Dede Agatch Coast Artillery Regiment**
D.   **2-Training Sail Ships** (*Assen*, *Kamcia*)

SLOVAKIA
[SLOVAK REPUBLIC]

(German Puppet State)

Slovakian Government
(Slovak Republic 1939 - 1945)
Map of Slovakia 1939 and present day.

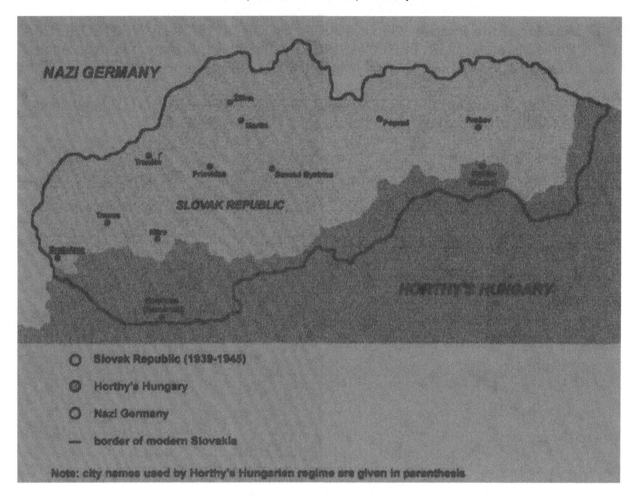

Head of State
President: 03/14/39 Dr. JOZEF TISO [+ to 10/29/39, Prime Minister of Slovak Republic] (went into exile in Germany; surrendered to United States troops) 04/03/45 dissolved.

Head of Government
Prime Minister: 10/07/38 Dr. JOSEF TISO 03/09/39 JOZEF SIVÁK 03/11/39 Dr. JOZEF TISO 03/11/39 Dr. KAROL SIDOR 03/14/39 Dr. JOZEF TISO [+ President of Slovak Republic] 10/29/39 Dr. VOJTECH TUKA [+ /40. Minister of Foreign Affairs] 09/02/44 ŠTEFAN TISO [+ Minister of Foreign Affairs & Minister of Justice] 04/03/45 dissolved.

A. **Minister of Foreign Affairs**: /39 Dr. FERDINAND DURCANSKY [+ Minister of the Interior] 10/26/39 Dr. VOJTECH TUKA [+ Prime Minister & Minister of Justice] 09/02/44 ŠTEFAN TISO

B.   **Minister of Finance**: /39 MIKULÁŠ PRUŽINSKÝ 04/03/45 dissolved.

C.   **Minister of Defense**: LG Ferdinand Čatloš [+ Chief of the Army General Staff] (deserted to the Resistance; arrested by the Germans) 09/02/44 ŠTEFAN HAŠŠIK 04/03/45 dissolved.

D.   **Minister of the Interior**: /36 Dr. KAROL SIDOR 10/26/39 Dr. VOJTECH TUKA (Prime Minister) /39 Dr. FERDINAND DURCANSKY [+ Minister of Foreign Affairs] 10/26/39 ALEXANDER "ŠANO" MACH 04/03/45 dissolved.

E.   **Minister of Justice**: /39 GEJZA FRITZ 09/02/44 ŠTEFAN TISO [+Prime Minister & Minister of Justice] 04/03/45 dissolved.

German Forces in Slovakia

German Envoys and Ministers Plenipotentiary: 07/39 HANS BERNARD [German] 07/29/40 SA-Gen. Manfred Freiherr [Baron] von Killinger [German] (?) 01/19/41 SA-Gen. Hans Elard Ludin [German] (?) 04/04/45 disbanded.

Reich Governor for Slovakia: KONRAD HENLEIN [German] 04/04/45 disbanded.

German General with Slovak Defense Ministry and Head of Military Mission (05/01/39): LG Franz Barckhausen [German] (German Inspector at the Armaments Inspectorate, Greater East, Cracow) [see Volume I] 11/08/39 unknown? 02/27/42 MG Franz Schliepper [German] (Commanding General, German 32nd Infantry Division) [see Volume I] 02/01/44 GdPzTr Dr. Alfred Ritter [Knight] von Hubicki [German] (?) 04/04/45 disbanded.

German Regional Commander, Security Zone Slovakia (04/01/43): GdFl Karl Barlen [German-Luft] [+ Air Defense, Slovakia] [see Volume I] 08/29/44 redesignated **German Occupation Forces. Slovakia**.

Higher SS and Police Leaders and Commanders in Slovakia [HSSPf Slovakia]: 08/29/44 SS-Gen. Gottlob Berger [German] (Chief, Prisoner-of-War Affairs, Armed Forces High Command [O. K. W.]) [see Volume I) 09/20/44 SS-Gen. Hermann Hoefle [Höfle] [German] (?) 04/03/45 disbanded.

Military High Command

Chief of the Army General Staff: LG Ferdinand Čatloš [+ Minister of Defense] (arrested by the Germans) 09/44 LG Ján Golian (Commander-in-Chief, Slovakian National Raising; /44, arrested and placed in German prison; /45, executed by the Germans) /44

A.   **Inspector of Slovakian Army School**: /40 MG Augustin Malár (Commanding General, 1st Slovak Infantry Division "Janošík") /40

B.   **Military Attaché, Berlin, Rome, Budapest**: /42 MG Augustin Malár (Commanding General, I Slovakian Army Corps) /44

Slovakia Resistance

Head of all Partisan Units (10/44): Col. Aleksey Nikitich Asmolov.

Slovakian Communist Party

Chairman of the Presidium of the Slovak Communist Party (KSS) (09/17/44): KAROL ŠMIDKE 08/12/45 VILIAM SIROKÝ.

Slovak National Council

A. **President of the Slovak National Council** (09/05/44):
    Co-Chairmen 09/05/44 to 10/27/44 KAROL ŠMIDKE and VARVRO JÁN ŠROBÁR
    10/27/44 to 04/11/45 vacant
    04/11/45 to 02/26/48 JOZEF LETTRICH and vacant to 09/14/45
    09/14/45 to 07/14/50 KAROL ŠMIDKE and JOZEF LETTRICH (to 02/26/48)

B. **Board of the Slovak National Council** (09/05/44):
    VARVRO JÁN ŠROBÁR (representing the non-Communist groups)
    KAROL ŠMIDKE (representing the Slovak Communist Party)
    GUSTÁV HUSÁK (representing the Slovak Communist Party)
    DANIEL ERTL (representing the Slovak Communist Party)
    JOZEF LETTRICH (representing the non-Communist groups)
    JÁN URSÍNY (representing the non-Communist groups)

Council of Plenipotentiaries

A. **Chairman of the Council of Plenipotentiaries [Board of Commissioners]** (09/05/44): GUSTÁV HUSÁK 09/17/45 KAROL ŠMIDKE 08/14/46 GUSTÁV HUSÁK 05/04/50
B. **Plenipotentiary for National Defense** (09/05/44): Col. Mikuláš Ferjencik
C. **Plenipotentiary for Home Affairs** (09/05/44): GUSTÁV HUSÁK
D. **Plenipotentiary for Justice** (09/05/44): JOZEF SOLTESZ
E. **Plenipotentiary for Finance** (09/05/44): VILIAM PAULINY

Board for the Defense of Slovakia [Rada na Obrranu Slovenska] (Highest military authority during the Uprising of 1944):
MG Ján Golian (to 10/07/44, Chairman of the Underground Army Headquarters and of the Defense of Slovakia)
MG Rudolf Viest [Czech], (10/07/44, Chairman of the Underground Army Headquarters and of the Defense of Slovakia & Commanding General, First Czechoslovak Army in Slovakia)
Capt. (Army) Milan Polak
Maj. Jozef Marko
Col. Mikuláš Ferjencik (Plenipotentiary for National Defense in the S. N. R.)
KAROL ŠMIDKE (representing the Slovak Communist Party)
RUDOLF SALZMANN [RUDOLF SLÁNSKÝ] [Czech] (representing the Czechoslovak Communist Party in exile)
PETER ZATKO (representing the non-Communist Parties)
Col. Aleksey Nikitich Asmolov (representing the Partisans) **[NOTE**: after the Germans had quelled the uprising, he continued the struggle as head of all partisan units.**]**

Soviet Occupation (from 08/04/45)

Commander of Soviet Occupation Forces in Slovakia: 08/06/44 CG Ivan Yefimovich Petrov [Russian] [+ Commander-in-Chief, Soviet Fourth Ukrainian Front] (Chief of Staff, Soviet First Ukrainian Front) 03/24/45 CG Andrei Ivanovich Yeremenko [Russian] [+ Commander-in-Chief, Soviet Fourth Ukrainian Front] 07/45 **[NOTE**: See Volume 5 - The Union of Soviet Socialist Republic**]**

Slovakian Army (Slovenské Armáda)
Corps

Field Army Bernolák (09/39, a Slovakian Army infantry unit that took part in the invasion of Poland; 10/39, returned to Slovakia and upgraded to a full motorized division, **Fast Troops Group "Kalinčiak"**): LG Ferdinand Čatloš [+ Minister of Defense & Chief of the Army General Staff] 10/39 upgraded to **Fast Troops Group "Kalinčiak"** - see **Fast Troops Group "Kalinčiak"**.

Slovakian Forces in the Field (1941): MG Antonin Pulanich

I Slovakian Army Corps (1944): MG Augustin Malár (participated in Slovakian National Raising; /44, arrested and placed in German prison) /44

Military Districts

Military District 1: 08/31/39? MG Antonin Pulanich [+ Commanding General, 1st Infantry Division "Jánošík"] (/41, Commanding General, Slovakian Forces in the Field) /40 MG Augustin Malár (Commanding General, Slovak Security Division) 11/19/41

Military District 2: 08/31/39? MG Alexandr Čunderlik [+ Commanding General, 2nd Infantry Division "Škultéty"]

Military District 3: 08/31/39? MG Augustin Malár [+ Commanding General, 3rd Infantry Division "Rázus"] (Inspector of Slovakian Army School) /40

Divisions

1st Slovak Infantry Division (#1) "Janošík" [Vyšší Vojenskí Velitseltsvi 1 "Janošík"] (1939, Military District 1; 09/05/39, Field Army; 07/01/41, Expeditionary Army Group): 08/31/39? MG Antonin Pulanich [+ Commanding General, Military District 1] (/41, Commanding General, Slovakian Forces in the Field) /40 MG Augustin Malár (Commanding General, Slovak Security Division) 07/01/41 Col. Josef Turanec 08/41 disbanded and reformed as **Slovak Fast Division** - see **Slovak Fast Division**.

A.   **Chief of Staff**: 08/31/39? Maj. Lavotha

B.   *Components - 1st Slovak Infantry Division (#1) "Janošík"*

1.   **1st Infantry Regiment** (07/01/41, Expeditionary Army Group)

2.   **2nd Infantry Regiment** (07/01/41, Expeditionary Army Group)

3.   **3rd Infantry Regiment** (07/01/41, Expeditionary Army Group)

4.   **4th Infantry Regiment**: 08/31/39? LCol. Bodieky

5.   **5th Infantry Regiment**: 08/31/39? Col. Lofka 09/05/39 transferred to 2nd Slovak Infantry Division "Cunderlik".

6.   **6th Infantry Regiment** (09/05/41):

7.   **35th Infantry Regiment** (09/05/41):

8.   **1st Artillery Regiment** (07/01/41, Expeditionary Army Group): 08/31/39? Maj. Vesel

9.   **2nd Artillery Regiment**: 08/31/39? Maj. Majercik 09/05/39 transferred to 2nd Slovak Infantry Division "Cunderlik".

10.   **153rd Anti-Aircraft Artillery (Mobile) Regiment**: 08/31/39? LCol. Pozesky 09/05/39 transferred to Field Army.

1st Slovak Infantry Division (#2) "Janošík" (08/01/43, from **Slovak Fast Division**; 07/44, disbanded): unknown? 07/44 disbanded.

2nd Slovak Infantry Division (#1) "Škultéty" [Vyšší Vojenskí Velitseltsvi 2 "Škultéty"] (1939, Military District 2; 09/05/39, Field Army; 07/01/41, Expeditionary Army Group; 09/01/41, redesignated **Slovak Security Division**): Col. Ivan Imro (Commanding Officer, 2nd Infantry Division (#2) "Škultéty") 08/31/39? MG Alexandr Čunderlik [+ Commanding General, Military District 2] (?   ) 07/01/41 MG Augustin Malár 09/01/41 redesignated **Slovak Security Division** - see **Slovak Security Division**.

A.   **Chief of Staff, 2nd Slovak Infantry Division (#1) "Škultéty"**: 08/31/39? Maj Tatarko

B.   *Components - 2nd Slovak Infantry Division (#1) "Škultéty"*

1.   **3rd Infantry Regiment**: 08/31/39? LCol. Imrc 07/01/41 transferred to 1st Slovak Infantry Division "Janošík".

2.   **4th Infantry Regiment** (07/01/41, Expeditionary Army Group):

3.   **5th Infantry Regiment** (09/05/39, from 1st Slovak Infantry Division "Janošík"; 07/01/41, Expeditionary Army Group): Col. Lofka

4.   **6th Infantry Regiment** (07/01/41, Expeditionary Army Group):

5.   **21st Infantry Regiment** (09/05/39): by 07/01/41 transferred.

6.   **2nd Artillery Regiment** (09/05/39, from 1st Slovak Infantry Division "Janošík"):

Maj. Smutny
7. **52nd Artillery Regiment** (removed by 09/05/39): 08/31/39? Maj Lendvay

2nd Slovak Infantry Division (#2) "Škultéty" (08/01/43, from **Slovak Security Division**; transferred to Italy; redesignated **2nd Technical Division**): Col. Rudolf Pilfousek 07/01/44 Col. Ivan Imro (deserted to American forces) 07/30/44 Col. Veselý /45? redesignated **2nd Technical Division** /45
A. **Chief of Staff, 2nd Slovak Infantry Division (#2) "Škultéty"** (08/01/44): Capt. Hujs (deserted to the American forces) 07/30/44 unknown?.
B. *Components - 2nd Slovak Infantry Division (#2) "Škultéty"*
   1. **4th Infantry Regiment**:
   2. **5th Infantry Regiment**:
   3. **6th Infantry Regiment**:
   4. **2nd Artillery Regiment**:

3rd Slovak Infantry Division "Rázus" [Vyšší Vojenskí Velitseltsvi 3 "Rázus"] (1939, Military District 3; 09/05/39, Field Army): 08/31/39? MG Augustin Malár (Inspector of Sloviakian Army School) /40
A. **Chief of Staff, 3rd Slovak Infantry Division "Rázus"**: 08/31/39? Maj. Krnac
B. *Components - 3rd Slovak Infantry Division "Rázus"*
   1. **1st Infantry Regiment**: 08/31/39? LCol. Kunn
   2. **2nd Infantry Regiment**: 08/31/39? Maj. Stenzinger
   3. **18th Infantry Regiment** (09/05/39)
   3. **3rd Artillery Regiment**: 08/31/39? LCol. Dotzauer
   4. **4th Artillery Regiment**: 08/31/39? Maj. Perko 09/05/39 transferred

Slovak Fast Division (08/41, from **Pilfousek Brigade** and **Fast Troops Group "Kalinčiak"**; 08/01/43 reorganized as **1st Slovak Infantry Division**): 08/41 MG Augustin Malár (Military Attaché to Rome, Berlin, & Budapest) 11/19/41 MG Štefan Jurech (/44, Deputy Commander, First Czechoslovakian Army) 08/01/43 reorganized as **1st Slovak Infantry Division** - see **1st Slovak Infantry Division**.
A. *Components - Slovak Fast Division*
   1. **20th Infantry Regiment (Motorized)**
   2. **21st Infantry Regiment (Motorized)**
   3. **11th Artillery Regiment**

Slovak Security Division (09/01/41, from **2nd Slovak Infantry Division (#1) "Škultéty"**; northern Ukraine and Belorussia for fighting the partisans; 08/01/43, redesignated **2nd Slovak Infantry Division**): MG Augustin Malár (Commanding Officer, Slovak Fast Division) 11/19/41 Col. Kuna 06/42 Col. Rudolf Pilfousek 08/01/43 redesignated **2nd Slovak Infantry Division** - see **2nd Slovak Infantry Division**.
A. *Components - Slovak Security Division*
   1. **101st Security Regiment**
   2. **102nd Security Regiment**
   3. **31st Artillery Regiment**

2nd Technical Division (/45, from **2nd Slovak Infantry Division (#2) "Škultéty"**):

Brigades

Fast Troops Group "Kalinčiak" (10/39, from **Field Army Bernolák**; 06/41, took part in Operation Barbarossa under German Army Group South; 08/01/43, merged with **Pilfousek Brigade** to form **1st Slovak Infantry Division "Janošík"**): 10/39 Col. Ivan Imro (07/01/44, Commanding Officer, **2nd** Slovak Infantry Division "Škultéty") 08/01/43 merged with **Pilfousek Brigade** to form **1st Slovak Infantry Division "Janošík"** - see **1st Slovak Infantry Division "Janošík"**.

Pilfousek Brigade (06/41, from the merging of all the motorized units of the **Slovakian Expeditionary Army Group** that joined the German forces in the invasion of the Soviet Union; 08/41, upgraded to **Slovak Fast Division**): Col. Rudolf Pilfousek (Commanding Officer, Slovak Fast Division) 08/41 upgraded to **Slovak Fast Division** - see **Slovak Fast Division**.

A.   *Components - Pilfousek Brigade*
   1.   **6th Infantry Regiment (Motorized)**
   2.   **Armored Regiment**

Slovakian Air Force
(Slovenské Vzdusné Zbrane (SUZ))

Reconnaissance Squadrons

1st Latka

2nd Letka

3rd Letka

Fighter Squadrons

11th Letka

12th Letka

13th Letka

Table of Equivalent Ranks

Slovakian Army & Air Force	United States & British Armies
	General of the Army (United States) Field Marshal (Britain)
	General
General I Triedy	Lieutenant General
General II Triedy	Major General
	Brigadier General United States) Brigadier (Britain)
Plukovnik	Colonel
Podplukovnik	Lieutenant Colonel
Major	Major
Stotnik	Captain
Nadporocik	First Lieutenant
Porocik	Second Lieutenant

CROATIA

(German Puppet State)

Independent State of Croatia
[Nezavisna Država Hrvatska (NDH)]
Map of the Independent State of Croatian, 1941-1945

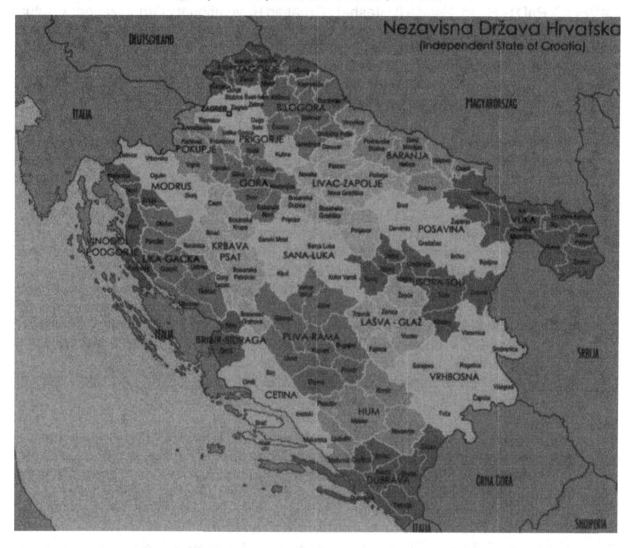

Croatian Government

King (04/10/41; Italian Duke of Aosta; never actually visited Croatia): TOMISLAV II, King of Croatia, Prince of Bosnia and Herzegovina, Voivode of Dalmatia, Tuzla and Knin, Duke of Aosta, Prince of Cisterna and of Belriguardo, Marquess of Voghera, and Count of Ponderano [AIMONE [Italian] , DUKE OF AOSTA] 07/25/43 abdicated 10/43 renounced his title.

Actual Head of Government: 04/10/41 Poglavnik (Chief) Dr. ANTE PAVELIĆ, PhD [+ Head, Ustaša [Ustašha] - Croatian Revolutionary Organization; + to /44, Prime Minister;

+ to 06/09/41, Foreign Minister; + 1/04/43 to 09/02/43, Minister of Armed Forces] (escaped to Argentina; /57, wounded in an assassination attempt in Buenos Aires; /59, died in Madrid, Spain from wound) 05/06/45 office abolished.

Prime Minister (President of the Government): 04/16/41 Poglavnik (Chief) Dr. ANTE PAVELIĆ, PhD [+ Head, Ustaša [Ustaša] - Croatian Revolutionary Organization; + Actual Head of Government; + to 06/09/41, Foreign Minister; + 1/04/43 to 09/02/43, Minister of Armed Forces] 09/02/44 Dr. NIKOLA MANDIĆ (captured by the British; turned over to Yugoslav authorities and tried and executed) 05/06/45 office abolished.
   1. **Adjutant to Primer Minister**: /41? BG Victor I. Prebeg (Deputy Commandant, Military Academy) /4?

A. **Vice President** (04/16/41): Dr. OSMAN KULENOVIĆ (attached to Ministry of Foreign Affairs] 11/41 DŽAFER-beg KULENOVIĆ [+ President, Yugoslav Moslem Organization] (escaped to Syria) 05/06/45 office abolished.

B. **Foreign Minister** (04/16/41): Poglavnik (Chief) Dr. ANTE PAVELIĆ, PhD [+ Head, Ustaša [Ustaša] - Croatian Revolutionary Organization; + Actual Head of Government; + Prime Minister] 06/09/41 BG Dr. Mladen Lorković (Minister of Internal Affairs) 04/28/43 STIJEPO PERIĆ 05/43 Dr. MILE BUDAK [+ Deputy Head, Ustaša [Ustaša] - Croatian Revolutionary Organization] (captured by the British; turned over to Yugoslav authorities and tried; 06/07/45, executed) 05/44 Dr. MEHMED ALAJBEGOVIĆ (/47, executed by Yugoslavia) 05/06/45 office abolished.
   1. **Croatian Ambassador to Germany** (04/16/41): unknown? 11/41 Dr. MILE BUDAK (Minister of Foreign Affairs) 04/43
   2. **Attached to Ministry of Foreign Affairs**
      11/41 Dr. OSMAN KULENOVIĆ (retired) /43

C. **Minister of Interior** (04/16/41): Dr. ANDRIJA ARTUKOVIĆ (Minister of Justice) 10/10/42 ANTE NIKŠIĆ 04/29/43 Dr. ANDRIJA ARTUKOVIĆ (Secretary of State) 11/01/43 BG Dr. Mladen Lorković (arrested for the Lorković-Vokić coup and jailed in Lepoglava prison; 04/30/45, executed by the Ustaša) 08/30/44 Dr. MATE FRKOVIĆ (escaped to Argentina; /80, died in Argentina) 05/06/45 office abolished.

D. **Minister of Armed Forces (also known as Minister of War [Defense] and Minister of Croatian Home Guard (Hrvatsko Domobranstvo) [Home Defense Army]** (04/24/41): FM Slavko Kvarternik [+ Deputy Head, Ustaša [Ustaša] - Croatian Revolutionary Organization; + Commander-in-Chief, Armed Forces; + Minister of Traffic] (retired and exile to Slovakia; /45, tried and sentence to death by Yugoslav officials; 06/07/47, executed) 01/04/43 Poglavnik (Chief) Dr. ANTE PAVELIĆ, PhD [+ Head, Ustaša [Ustaša] - Croatian Revolutionary Organization; + Actual Head of Government; + Prime Minister] 09/02/43 Gen. Miroslav Navratil [CAF] (retired and moved to Austria; extradited to Yugoslavia post war; /47, executed) 01/29/44 BG Dr. Ante Vokić (arrested for the Lorković-Vokić coup and jailed in Lepoglava prison; 04/30/45, executed by the Ustaša [Ustaša]) 08/30/44 RA Nikola Steinfl [Steinfel] [CN] [+ Commander-in-Chief, Croatian Navy] (afer war, executed) 05/06/45 office abolished.

1. **Deputy Defense Minister** (04/16/41): CG Vilko Begić (?) /43
2. **Commander-in-Chief, Armed Forces**
3. **Air Force of the Independent State of Croatia**
4. **Navy**
5. **Ustaša [Ustašha] Army (Ustaška Vojnica)**
6. **Gendarmes (Secret Police)**
7. **Head, Personnel Department, Ministry of Armed Forces** (04/24/41): Col. Jovan Iskrić (Commanding Officer, 1st Domobran Labor Regiment) 08/44
8. **Head, Counter-Intelligence Department, Ministry of Armed Forces**: /4? BG Rudolf Wanner (?) 05/45.
9. **Head, Supply Section, Ministry of Armed Forces** (04/24/41): BG Kosta Bader (retired; died shortly after retirement) /44
10. **Head, Arms & Ammunitions Department, Ministry of Armed Forces** (04/24/41): BG Josip Lemesić (retired) /44
11. **Advocate General**, **Ministry of Armed Forces**:
    a. **Head Judge, Advocate General, Ministry of Armed Forces**: /41 BG Milan von Praunsperger (Head, Military Archives) /43
12. **Head, Legal Department, Ministry of Armed Forces**: /43 BG Mirko Vuković (condemned to death and executed) 05/45.
13. **Head, Health Department, Ministry of Armed Forces** (04/24/41): BG Mile Sertić (?) 01/42 BG Rudolf Herceg (?)
14. **Head, Military Archives**: /43 BG Milan von Praunsperger (?) 05/45.
15. **President, Office of Promotions & Decorations, Ministry of Armed Forces:** LG Istvan von Percevié (condemned to death and executed) 05/45.
16. **Military Attaché, Germany (Berlin)**: 01/43 BG Milan Desović (condemned to 15 years imprisonment) 05/45.
17. **Military Attaché, Romania (Bucharest)**: MG Miroslav Navratil (Minister of the Armed `Forces] 08/43

E. **Minister of Religion (Culture) and Education** (04/16/41): Dr. MILE BUDAK (Croatian Ambassador to Germany) 11/41 VLADIMIR KOŠAK /43? ANTON FILIPANČIĆ /44? DRAGUTIN TOTH 05/06/45 office abolished.

F. **Minister of Traffic** (04/16/41): FM Slavko Kvarternik [+ Deputy Head, Ustaša [Ustašha] - Croatian Revolutionary Organization; + Minister of the Armed Forces; + Commander-in-Chief, Armed Forces] (retired and exile to Slovakia; /45, tried and sentence to death by Yugoslav officials; 06/07/47, executed) 01/04/43 HILMIJA BEŠLAGIĆ 10/11/43 BG Dr. Ante Vokić (Minister of Armed Forces) 01/29/44 JOZO DUMANDŽIĆ 05/06/45 office abolished.

G. **Minister of Justice** (04/16/41): Dr. MIRKO PUK (Secretary of State) 10/10/42 Dr. ANDRIJA ARTUKOVIĆ (Minister of Interior) 04/29/43 unknown? 05/06/45 office abolished.

H. **Minister of Economy** (00/10/41): Dr. LOVRO ŠUŠIĆ [+ /43 to /44, Minister of Association] 05/06/45 office abolished.

I.   **Minister of Trade** (also known as **Labor**) (04/16/41):MARIJAN ŠIMIĆ /42? DRAGUTIN TOTH /43? JOSIP CABAS /44? Maj. Vjekoslav Vrančič (escaped to Argentina; /90, died in Argentina) 05/06/45 office abolished.

J.   **Minister of Health** (04/16/41): IVAN PETRIĆ (moved to South America) /42 JANKO TORTIĆ [+ /44?, Minister of Association] 05/06/45 office abolished.

J.   **Minister of Forestry and Mining** (04/16/41): Ing. IVICA FRKOVIĆ /43? JOSIP BALEN 05/06/45 office abolished.

L.   **Minister of Association** (04/16/41): JOZO DUMANDŽIĆ /43? Dr. LOVRO ŠUŠIĆ [+ Minister of Economy] /44? JANKO TORTIĆ [+ Minister of Health] 05/06/45 office abolished.

M.   **Minister of Rurual Economy and Food (Agriculture)** (unknown?): STJEPAN HEFER 05/06/45 office abolished.

N.   **Minister of Welfare for Perished Lands** (11/11/43): MEHMED ALAJEGOVIĆ (Foreign Minister) 05/44 MEHO MEHIČIĆ 05/06/45 office abolished.

O.   **Minister for Liberated Lands** (unknown?): Dr. EDO BULAT 05/06/45 office abolished.

P.   **Ministers without Protfolio**:
       Dr. ANDRIJA ARTUKOVIĆ
       SAVO BESAROVIĆ
        Dr. EDO BULAT
       ŽIVAN KUVEŽEDIĆ
       04/28/41 BG Dr. Mladen Lorković (Minister of Interior) 11/11/43 **[NOTE:** during this
              time period, he was **Minister for Relations with German Army]**
       Dr. MIRKO PUK
       LJUDEVIT ŠOLC
       JANKO TORTIĆ
       Maj. Vjekoslav Vrančić
       MILOVAN vitez [Knight] ŽANIĆ

Q.   **Secretary of State** (04/16/41): unknown? 10/10/42 Dr. MIRKO PUK (/45, possible suicide) 11/11/43 Dr. ANDRIJA ARTUKOVIĆ (captured by the British, avoided extradition to Yugoslavia, and moved to Switzerland) 05/06/45 office abolished.

R.   **President, Legislative Committee** (04/16/41): MILOVAN vitez [Knight] ŽANIĆ

S.   **State Chief of Labor Services** (04/16/41): BG Dušan Palčić (?   ) 05/45.

Ustaša [Ustašha] - Croatian Revolutionary Organization (Ustaša [Ustašha] - Hrvatska Revolucionarna Organizacija [UHRO]) (/30): Poglavnik (Chief) Dr. ANTE PAVELIĆ, PhD + [04/15/41, Actual Head of Government & to /43, Prime Minister; + to 06/09/41, Foreign

Minister; + 1/04/43 to 09/02/43, Minister of Armed Forces] (escaped to Argentina) 05/06/45.

A. **Deputy Head, Ustaša [Ustašha] - Croatian Revolutionary Organization**: FM Slavko Kvarternik [+ Minister of Croatian Home Guard; + Commander-in-Chief, Armed Forces; + Minister of Traffic] (retired and exile to Slovakia; /45, tried and sentence to death by Yugoslav officials; 06/07/47, executed) 01/04/43 unknown? 05/43 Dr. MILE BUDAK [+ Minister of Foreign Affairs](captured by the British; turned over to Yugoslav authorities and tried; 06/07/45, executed) 05/45.

B. **Ustaša [Ustašha] Army (Ustaška Vojnica)** (Military Wing of the Ustaša [Ustašha] - Croatian Revolutionary Organization)

    1.   **Ustaša [Ustašha] Black Legion [Crna Legija]**: Col. Jure Francetić (severely wounded, when plane shot down; captured by Partisan villagers; taken to NOVJ General Staff Hospital where he died) 12/28?/42 and Col. Rafael vitez [Knight] Boban 12/28/42 Col. Rafael vitez [Knight] Boban [+ Commanding Officer, 5th Ustaša [Ustašha] Brigade] (5th Croatian Infantry Division) 12/01/44

    2.   **Poglavnik Bodyguard Battalion [Poglavnikov Tjelesni Bojna]**

C. **Gendarmes (Secret Police)**: /41 BG Milan Miesler (?) /42 BG Kvintiljan Tartalja (?) /45 BG Slavko Skoliber (?) 05/45.

    1.   **Inspector-General of Gendarmes**: /43 BG Viktor Novak (?) 05/45.

D. **Ustaša [Ustašha] Surveillance Service [Ustaška Nadzoma Služba (UNS)]**: 04/41 BG Vjekoslav "Maks" Luburić (Commanding General, II Ustaša [Ustašha] Corps) 04/45

    1.   *Components* - **Ustaša [Ustašha] Surveillance Service**

        a.   **1st Ustaša [Ustašha] Guard Brigade** (01/42; 03/45, transferred to II Ustaša [Ustašha] Corps)

        b.   **2nd Ustaša [Ustašha] Guard Brigade (07/42 to 12/43)**

        c.   **1st Domobran Volunteer Regiment (1. Domobranska Dobrovoljačka Pukovnija)**: 09/42 Col. Franjo Šimić (12/01/43, 6th Ustaša [Ustašha] Brigade) 10/43 disbanded.

    2.   **Concentration Camps**:

        a.   **Danica Concentration Camp** (Spring /41, near Koprivnica)

        b.   **Pag Concentration Camp** (Spring /41)

        c.   **Jadovno Concentration Camp** (prior to 05/41, near Gospić): LCol. Juco Rukavina (02/45, Commanding Officer, 11th Croatian Infantry Division) /4? LCol. Jurica Frković /4? LCol. Stjepan Rubinić

        d.   **Kruščica Concentration Camp** (Spring /41, near Vitez and Travnik, Bosnia)

        e.   **Dakovo Concentration Camp** (Spring /41)

        f.   **Loborgrad Concentration Camp** (Spring /41, in Zagorje)

        g.   **Tenja Concentration Camp** (Spring /41, near Osijek)

        h.   **Jasenovac [Yasenovatz] Concentration Camp** (08/41; largest, as actually a complex of 5 subcamps; 04/45, dismantled) unknown? 12/41 LCol. Ivica Matković 03/43 LCol. Ivica Brkljačić 04/44 LCol. Dinko Šakić (04/45, fled to Argentina, eventually extradited; /99, tried and sentenced to 20 years in Remetinec Priooson; 2008, died in Remetinec Prison) 11/44 unknown? 04/45 dismantled

     i.   **Assistant Commandant, Jasenovac [Yasenovatz] Concentration Camp**: 12/41 Capt. Dinko Šakić (Commandant, Jasenovac [Yasenovatz] Concentration Camp) 04/44
     i.   **Dulag 183** (09/41, Šabac, Serbia; 09/44, dismantled)
     j.   **Stara-Gradiška Concentration Camp** (09/41?; 04/45, dismantled): unknown? 10/42 LCol. Father Miroslav Filipović [Roman Catholic priest, later known as Tomislav Filipović; Tomislav Filipović-Majstorović; or Miroslav Majstorović] (/46, captured by Yugoslav Communist forces, tried and executed) 03/27/43
     k.   **Sajmište Concentration Camp** (12/41, German run; 09/44, dismantled)
     l.   **Lepoglava** (unknown?)
     m.   **Jastrebarsko Concentration Camp** (/42, for children; /42, dismantled))

German Occupation of Croatia

Reich Minister for Croatia: SIEGFRIED KASCHE [German]

Head of German Military Mission to Croatia: 04/21/41 LG Dr. H. C. Edmund Glaise von Horstenau [German] (retired) 11/01/42 redesignated **Regional Commander of German Troops in Croatia** 11/01/42 Gdl Rudolf Lüters [German] (German XV Mountain Corps) 08/24/43

Military High Command

Commander-in-Chief, Armed Forces (04/24/41): FM Slavko Kvarternik [+ Deputy Head, Ustaša [Ustaŝa] - Croatian Revolutionary Organization;+ Minister of Croatian Home Guard (retired; /45, tried and sentence to death by Yugoslav officials; 06/07/47, executed) 01/04/43 LG Matija Čanić (?) 05/45 LG Vjekoslav "Maks" Luburić (fled to Spain; /69, assassinated) 05/45.

A.   **Chief, High Command** (04/24/41): LG August Marić (retired) /42

B.   **Inspector-General of Armed Forces**: /41? BG Slavko vitez [Knight] Štanzer [Stancer] [+ 05/42 to 03/43, Commanding General, Zagreb Garrison Command] (President Military Court) /4?

C.   **President Military Court**: /4? BG Slavko vitez [Knight] Štanzer [Stancer] (?) 05/45.

D.   *Schools*
  1.   **Commandant, Military Academy**:
    a.   **Deputy Commandant, Military Academy**: /4? BG Victor I. Prebeg (condemned to death and executed) 05/45.
  2.   **Commandant Military Schools** (04/24/41): BG Karlo Klaić (retired) 01/43
    a.   **Commandant, Domobran Central School (Domobranska Središnja Škola)** (07/41, Zagreb): unknown? 01/43 LCol. Ivan Babić 04/43 unknown? 01/44 Col. Zdenko Begić (02/45, Commanding Officer, 4th Croatian Infantry Division) 09/22/44 closed.
    b.   **Domobran Cadet School (Domobranska Zastavnička Škola)** (07/20/41, Zagreb): Col. Viktor Pavičić 07/42 Col. Milivoj Durbešić 12/42 unknown? 12/43 school status unknown?

E.   *Liaison Officers*
  1.   **Croatian Liaison Officer to Second Italian Army**: 10/41 BG Mihajlo Lukić (Commanding General, III Domobran Corps) 11/41 unknown? /43 LG Dragutin Rumler (?) 05/45
  2.   **Croatian Liaison Officer to German XV Army Corps**: 08/42 Col. Ivan Tomašević (Commanding General, 10th Croatian Infantry Division) 12/01/44
  3.   **Croatian Liaison Officer to 13th Croatian Volunteer Waffen-SS Division "Handchar"**: BG Muhamed Hromić (condemned to death and executed) 05/45.
  4.   **Croatian Liaison Officer between the Croatian Armed Forces and the SS-Police in Croatia**: /43 Col. Junuz Ajanović (Commanding Officer, 3rd Mountain Regiment; /45, arrested by Yugoslav Partisan forces and executed in Zagreb) /44

Commander-in-Chief of the Army (04/24/41): LG August Marić (Chief, High Command) 04/16/41 BG Slavko vitez [Knight] Štanzer [Stancer] (Inspector-General of Armed Forces) /41 LG Vladimir Laxa (?) /44 BG Đorde [Djuro] F. Gruić [+ Chief, Army General Staff] (condemned to death for treason/executed by firing squad in 1945) 05/45.

A.   **Deputy Commander-in-Chief of the Army** (04/24/41): BG Vladimir Laxa [+ 07/31/41 to 08/16/41, Commanding General, Knin Brigade] (Commander-in-Chief of the Army) /41

B. **Chief, Army General Staff, Croatia** (04/24/41): 08/01/41 BG Ivan Prpić (?) 12/42 BG Tomislav Sertić (1945, condemned to death and executed) /43 CG Fedor Dragojlov (?) /44 BG Đorde [Djuro] F. Gruić [+ Commander-in-Chief of the Army] (condemned to death for treason/executed by firing squad in 1945) 05/45.

C. **Head, Organization Department, Army General Staff**: /43 BG Đorde [Djuro] F. Gruić (Commander-in-Chief of the Army & Chief, Army General Staff) /44

D. *Inspector-Generals*
   1. **Inspector-General of Infantry**: 08/01/41 BG Mihajlo Lukić [+ Commanding General, Lika Brigade] (Croatian Liaison Officer, Second Italian Army) 10/41 unknown? /43 BG Franjo Nikolić (Assistant Commandant, Zagreb) 02/43 BG Artur Gustović (Commanding General, III Ustasha Corps) 03/15/45
   2. **Inspector-General of Cavalry**: /43 BG Zvonimir Stimaković (Commanding Officer, 4th Jäeger Brigade) 02/44
   3. **Inspector-General of Artillery**: Col. Slavko Cesarić (Commanding General, 12th Croatian Infantry Division) 12/01/44 BG Antum Prohaska (?) 05/45.

Commander-in-Chief, Croatian Air Force (04/24/41): BG Vladimir Kren [CAF] (retired) 09/14/43 BG Adalbert Rogulja [CAF] (after war, died in Yugoslavia jail) 06/04/44 MG [Retired 09/43] Vladimir Kren [CAF] (escaped to Austria; /47, arrested and extradited to Yugoslavia; sentenced to death; /48, executed) 05/45.

Commander-in-Chief, Croatian Navy (04/24/41): RA Djuro Jakčin [CN] (Head, Diplomatic Representation of Croatian Navy in Sofia, Bulgaria) /43 RA Edgar Angeli [CN] (?) 01/44 RA Nikola Steinfl [Steinfel] [CN] [+ 08/44, Minister of the Armed Forces] (after war, executed) 05/45.

A. **Diplomatic Representation of Craotian Navy in Sofia, Bulgaria**: 01/44 RA Djuro Jakčin [CN] (died of natural causes) 02/44

Army Headquarters (MINDOM)
A. *Components - Army Headquarters*
   1. **Zagreb Cavalry Regiment** 11/41 see Cavalry Regiments 08/14/43 transferred to III Territorial Corps.
   2. **Knin Brigade** (07/31/41 to 10/41)
   3. **Lika Brigade** (07/31/to 10/41)
   4. **Sanski Brigade** (07/31/to 10/41)
   5. **Gračac Brigade** (08/41 to 09/41)
   6. **Kordun Brigade** (08/41; 10/41, transferred to I Domobran Corps)
   7. **Lovinac Domobran Brigade** (08/41 to 09/41)
   8. **Combined Gendarmerie-Domobran Regiment** (07/41; 11/41, transferred to I Domobran Corps; may also be known as 2nd **Composite Brigade**): 07/41 unknown? 09/41 Col. Ivan Tomašević 11/41 transferred to I Domobran Corps.
   9. **1st Croatian Istrian Regiment** (07/41; 11/41, transferred to I Domobran Corps): LCol. Stjepan Sertić 11/41
   10. **I Cavalry Group** (07/41 to 11/41) - see Cavalry Regiments
   11. **II Cavalry Group** (07/41 to 11/41) - see Cavalry Regiments
   12. **Independent Cavalry Group** (07/41 to 11/41) - see Cavalry Regiments

Army Corps
(November 1941 to March 1945)

I Domobran Corps (I. Domobranski Zbor) [Vrbas Military District] (11/01/41; HQ: Sisak; 08/14/43, merged with **I Domobran Territorial Corps** and forms **I Territorial Corps**): 11/01/41 LG Dragutin Rumler (Croatian Liaison Officer to Second Italian Army) 04/43 LG Ivan Brozović [+ Commanding General, Banja Luka Brigade (#1)] (Commanding General, I Territorial Corps) 08/14/43 merged with **I Domobran Territorial Corps** and forms **I Territorial Corps** - see **I Territorial Corps**.

A. *Components - I Domobran Corps*
1.   **1ˢᵗ Infantry Division** (11/41 to 05/43)
2.   **Kordun Brigade** (11/41 to 08/42)
3.   **Utinjski Brigade** (01/42 to 05/42)
4.   **Petrinja Brigade** (02/42 to 02/43)
5.   **Kalnik Brigade** (04/42 to 05/01/42)
6.   **4ᵗʰ Ustaša [Ustašha] Brigade** (08/42; 08/14/43, transferred to I Territorial Corps)
7.   **Paški Brigade** (05/43 to 05/43)
8.   **Combined Gendarmerie-Domobran Regiment**: 09/41 Col. Ivan Tomašević [+ Commanding Officer, Karlovac Garrison Command] (Commanding Officer, 2ⁿᵈ Infantry Division) 11/41 unknown? 05/42 disbanded.
9.   **1ˢᵗ Croatian Istrian Regiment** (11/41 to 05/42): 11/41 LCol. Stjepan Sertić 03/45
10. **2ⁿᵈ Infantry Regiment**: 07/43 Col. Čihak 08/14/43, transferred to I Territorial Corps.
11. **3ʳᵈ Infantry Regiment**: 08/43 unknown? 08/14/43, transferred to I Territorial Corps.
12. **I Cavalry Group** (11/41 to 08/14/43) - see Cavalry Regiments.

II Domobran Corps (II. Domobranski Zbor) [II Military District] (11/01/41; HQ Slavonski Brod; 08/14/43, merged with **II Domobran Territorial Corps** and forms **II Territorial Corps**): 11/01/41 BG Zvonimir Stimaković (temporary/1943, Inspector-General of Cavalry) /42? LG Djuro Izer (retired) 08/14/43 merged with **II Domobran Territorial Corps** and forms **II Territorial Corps**.

A. **Deputy District Officer, II Military District**: Col. Rudolf Wanner (Head, Counter-Intelligence Department, Ministry of Armed Forces) /4?
B. *Components - II Domobran Corps*
1.   **Banja Luka Brigade (#1)** (11/41 to 03/43)
2.   **Gradiška Brigade** (02/42 to 06/42)
3.   **Syrmian Brigade** (03/15/42; 08/14/43, transferred to II Territorial Corps)
4.   **II Ustaša [Ustašha] Brigade** (07/42; 08/14/43, transferred to II Territorial Corps)
5.   **Slavonian Brigade** (08/42 to 08/43)
6.   **Tuzla Brigade** (04/43; 08/14/43, transferred to II Territorial Corps)

7. **Domdo Regiment Banja Lake** (03/43; 08/13/43, transferred to II Territorial Corps)
8. **II Cavalry Group** (11/41 to 08/14/43) - see Cavalry Regiments

III Domobran Corps (III. Domobranski Zbor) [III Military District] (11/01/41; HQ: Sarajevo; 08/14/43, merged with **III Domobran Territorial Corps** and forms **III Territorial Corps**): BG Mihajlo Lukić (retired/1945, condemned to 10 years imprisonment) 04/43 Gen. Anton Prohaska (Commanding General, III Territorial Corps) 08/14/43 merged with **III Domobran Territorial Corps** and forms **III Territorial Corps**.

A. *Components - III Domobran Corps*
1. **Independent Cavalry Group** (11/41 to 05/42) - see Cavalry Regiments
2. **1st Ustaša [Ustaša] Brigade** (07/42; 08/14/43, transferred to III Territorial Corps)
3. **5th Ustaša [Ustaša] Brigade** (07/42; 08/14/43, transferred to III Territorial Corps)

Territorial Corps

I Domobran Territorial Corps [I. Domobranski Zborno Područja] (11/01/41; HQ: Petrinja): 11/01/41 Col. Franjo Dolacki [+ Artillery Commander, 3rd Division] (Assistant Commandant, Zagreb) 08/14/43 disbanded and consolidated with the **I Domobran Corps** to form the **I Territorial Corps**.

A. *Components - I Domobran Territorial Corps*
1. **1st Infantry Division** (11/01/41 to 08/14/43)
2. **2nd Infantry Division** (11/01/41 to 08/14/43
3. **1st Mountain Division** (04/42 to 08/14/43
4. **5th Mountain Brigade** (02/15/43 to 08/14/43)
5. **1st Domobran Labor Regiment**: 09/42 unknown? 08/14/43 transferred to I Territorial Corps.

B. *Mobilization Commands (Popunidbena Zapovjedništva)* (Commands existed to the end of the war or until each area had been occupied by Partisan forces. In 08/14/45, Mobilization Commands transferred to the I Territorial Corps)
1. **Mobilization Command Bjelovar**
2. **Mobilization Command Karlovac**
3. **Mobilization Command Knin**
4. **Mobilization Command Otočac**
5. **Mobilization Command Petrinja**
6. **Mobilization Command Sinj**
7. **Mobilization Command Varaždin**
8. **Mobilization Command Zagreb**

C. *Garrison Commands (Mjestno Zapovjedništvo)* (Established in key cities and towns in 1941 to perform a variety of administration duties. Larger locations are I Class, towns are either II Class or "without Class". In 08/14/45, Garrison Commands transferred to the III Territorial Corps)
1. **Bihać Garrison Command** (II Class command):
2. **Bjelovar Garrison Command** (II Class command): 09/41 LCol. Asim Tanović 10/43 LCol. Fingerhut
3. **Drniš Garrison Command** (without class):
4. **Gospić Garrison Command** (without class): 07/41 LCol. Antun Pihler 11/42 Maj. Stjepan Milinković
5. **Karlovac Garrison Command** (I Class command): 09/41 Col. Ivan Tomašević [+ to 11/41, Commanding Officer, Combined Gendarmerie-Domobran Regiment; + 11/41, Commanding Officer, Commanding Officer, 2nd Infantry Division] 01/42 Col. Pajić [Paić] (Commanding Officer, Varaždin Garrison Command) 05/42 Col. Ivan Grospić (Commanding Officer, Zemun Garrison Command) 05/42 LCol. Dragutin Culebić
   a. **Crikvenica Garrison Command** (without class; subordinated to Karlovac Garrison Command):
   b. **Deinice Garrison Command** (without class; subordinated to Karlovac Garrison Command):
   c. **Ogulin Garrison Command** (without class; subordinated to Karlovac Garrison Command):

    d.   **Senj Garrison Command** (without class; subordinated to Karlovac Garrison Command):

    e.   **Vrovsko Garrison Command** (without class; subordinated to Karlovac Garrison Command):

6.   **Knin Garrison Command** (II Class command):

7.   **Koprivnica Garrison Command** (without class): 12/41 LCol. Julije Reš (Commanding Officer, Paški Brigade) 05/01/43

8.   **Križevci Garrison Command** (without class): 02/44 LCol. Sulejman Torlić

9.   **Otočac Garrison Command** (II Class command): 12/41 Maj Muhamed-beg Sulejmanpačić

10.   **Petrinja Garrison Command** (I Class command):

11.   **Šibenik Garrison Command** (without class): 11/01/43 Maj. Davorin Vinković

12.   **Sinj Garrison Command** (without class): 07/41 LCol. Buble

13.   **Sisak Garrison Command** (I Class command): 07/41 Col. Ivan Matagić [+ Commanding Officer, 11th Infantry Regiment] (killed in action) 10/03/41 unknown? 07/43 LCol. Josip Aleksić (Commanding Officer, 11th Croatian Infantry Division) 12/01/44

14.   **Slavonski Brod Garrison Command** (I Class command):

15.   **Varaždin Garrison Command** (II Class command): 07/41 Col. Ivan Markulj (Commandant, Zagreb) 12/41 Col. Petruhar 04/42 Col. Rudolf Štaufer [Štamfer] (Commanding Officer, Kalnik Brigade) 04/42 LCol. Aurel Schlacher [Schlaher; Šlaher] (02/43, Commanding Officer, Zagreb Cavalry Regiment) 06/42 Col. Pajić [Paić] 10/42 Col. Eduard Boroš

16.   **Zagreb Garrison Command** (I Class command; also found as **Headquarters, Zagreb City Command**): 05/42 BG Slavko vitez [Knight] Štanzer [Stancer] [+ Inspector-General, Armed Forces] 03/43 BG Ivan Markulj [+ Commandant, Zagreb] (Commanding General, III Domobran Corps) 08/31/44

    a.   *Components* - HQ Zagreb City Command

        i.   **Zagreb Garrison Brigade** (07/20/43; 04/01/44, transferred to I Territorial Corps)

        ii.   **Ustasha-Domobran Regiment Poglavnik Dr. Ante Pavelić (Ustaško-Domobranska Pukovnija Poglanika Dra Ante Pavelića)** (10/21/41): unknown? 06/42 LCol. Rudolf Šimić 04/01/44 disbanded.

II Domobran Territorial Corps [II. Domobranski Zborno Područja] (11/01/41; HQ: Banja Luka): 11/01/41 Col. Vilko Lukić 08/14/43 disbanded and consolidated with the **II Domobran Corps** to form the **II Territorial Corps**.

A.   *Components* - II Domobran Territorial Corps

    1.   **3rd Infantry Division** (11/01/41 to 08/14/43

    2.   **4th Infantry Division** (11/01/41 to 08/14/43

    3.   **2nd Domobran Labor Regiment**: 09/42 Col. Kljajić 08/14/43 transferred to II Territorial Corps.

    4.   **Domdo Regiment Hadžiefendić** (08/41; also known as **Domdo Regiment Tuzla, Moslem Legion**): 08/41 unknown? 08/42 Col. Muhamed Hadžiefendić 08/14/43 disbanded and used to form **Dombo Regiment**

"**Bosanski Planinci**" - see II Territorial Corps.

B. *Mobilization Commands (Popunidbena Zapovjedništva)* (Commands existed to the end of the war or until each area had been occupied by Partisan forces. In 08/14/45, Mobilization Commands transferred to the II Territorial Corps)
1. **Mobilization Command Banja Luka**
2. **Mobilization Command Hrvatska Mitrovica**
3. **Mobilization Command Osijek**
4. **Mobilization Command Ruma**
5. **Mobilization Command Slavonska Požega**
6. **Mobilization Command Tuzla**

C. *Garrison Commands (Mjestno Zapovjedništvo)* (Established in key cities and towns in 1941 to perform a variety of administration duties. Larger locations are I Class, towns are either II Class or "without Class". In 08/14/45, Garrison Commands transferred to the III Territorial Corps)
1. **Banja Liku Garrison Command** (I Class command): 10/43 Col. Medlan (Commanding Officer, Split Garrison Command) 04/44
2. **Bijeljina Garrison Command** (without class):
3. **Brćko Garrison Command** (without class):
4. **Doboj Garrison Command** (II Class command):
5. **Hrvatska Mitrovica Garrison Command** (without class):
6. **Konjić Garrison Command** (without class):
7. **Osijek Garrison Command** (II Class command): 07/44 Col. Djuro Gebauer (Commanding Officer, 1st Popular-Ustaša [Ustaša] Regiment "Baranja") 11/44
8. **Petrovaradin Petrinja Garrison Command** (II Class command): LCol. Franjo Pirć
9. **Ruma Garrison Command** (without class):
10. **Slavonska Požega Garrison Command** (II Class command): 08/44 Maj. Strelić 12/44 Capt. Josip Kurtović
11. **Tuzla Garrison Command** (II Class command):
12. **Vinkovci Garrison Command** (II Class command):
13. **Zemun Garrison Command** (II Class command): 05/42 Col. Ivan Grospić
14. **Zvornik Garrison Command** (without class):

III Domobran Territorial Corps [III. Domobranski Zborno Područja] (11/01/41; HQ: Travnik): 11/01/41 Col. L. Kozel 08/14/43 disbanded and consolidated with the **III Domobran Corps** to form the **III Territorial Corps**.
A. *Components - I Domobran Territorial Corps*
1. **5th Infantry Division** (11/01/41 to 08/14/43
2. **6th Infantry Division** (11/01/41 to 08/14/43
3. **Zagreb Cavalry Regiment** 11/41 see Cavalry Regiments 08/14/43 transferred to III Territorial Corps.
4. **3rd Domobran Labor Regiment**: 09/42 unknown? 08/14/43 transferred to III Territorial Corps.

B. *Mobilization Commands (Popunidbena Zapovjedništva)* (Commands existed to the end of the war or until each area had been occupied by Partisan forces. In 08/14/45, Mobilization Commands transferred to the III Territorial Corps)

1. **Mobilization Command Mostar**
2. **Mobilization Command Sarajevo**
3. **Mobilization Command Trebinje**
4. **Mobilization Command Travnik**

C. *Garrison Commands (Mjestno Zapovjedništvo)* (Established in key cities and towns in 1941 to perform a variety of administration duties. Larger locations are I Class, towns are either II Class or "without Class". In 08/14/45, Garrison Commands transferred to the III Territorial Corps)

1. **Bileća Garrison Command** (without class):
2. **Bosanska Dubica Garrison Command** (without class): 05/42 Maj. Šarkan
3. **Dubrovnik Garrison Command** (II Class command): 01/43 Col. Stjepan Zuech (Commanding Officer, 9th Garrison Brigade) 04/01/44
4. **Imotski Garrison Command** (without class):
5. **Mostar Garrison Command** (II Class command):
6. **Nevesinje Garrison Command** (without class):
7. **Nova Gradiška Garrison Command** (without class):
8. **Sarajevo Garrison Command** (I Class command): 01/42 Col. Franjo Knezević
9. **Split Garrison Command** (without class): 04/44 Col. Medlan 10/44 Maj. Prijić
10. **Travnik Garrison Command** (I Class command): 01/43 Maj. Šel
11. **Trebinje Garrison Command** (II Class command):
12. **Višegrad Garrison Command** (without class):

I Territorial Corps (I. Zbornog Područja) (08/14/43, from merger of **I Domobran Corps** and **I Domobran Territorial Corps**): 08/14/43 LG Ivan Brozović (Commanding General, I Ustasha Corps) 03/15/45 disbanded.

A. *Components - I Territorial Corps*
1. **1st Croatian Assault Division** (12/01/44; 03/15/45, transferrred to I Ustaša [Ustašha] Corps)
2. **2nd Croatian Infantry Division** (12/01/44; 03/15/45, transferrred to I Ustaša [Ustašha] Corps)
3. **4th Croatian Infantry Division** (12/01/44; 03/15/45, transferrred to IV Ustaša [Ustašha] Corps)
4. **5th Craotain Assault Division** (12/01/44; 03/15/45, transferrred to I Ustaša [Ustašha] Corps)
5. **19th Craotain Infantry Division** (12/01/44; 03/15/45, transferrred to V Ustaša [Ustašha] Corps)
6. **11th Croatian Infantry Division** (12/01/44; 03/15/45, transferrred to V Ustaša [Ustašha] Corps)
7. **13th Croatian Infantry Division** (12/01/44; 03/15/45, transferrred to I Ustaša [Ustašha] Corps)
8. **16th Croatian Replacement Division** (12/01/44; 03/15/45, transferrred to I Ustaša [Ustašha] Corps)
9. **2nd Jäger Brigade** (04/43 to 12/01/44)
10. **1st Mountain Brigade** (08/12/43; 12/01/44, transferred to 7th Croatian Mountain Division)

11. **4th Ustaša [Ustasha], Brigade** (08/14/43; 12/01/44, transferred to 11th Croatian Infantry Division)
12. **5th Ustaša [Ustasha] Brigade** (02/44; 12/01/44, transferred to 5th Croatian Infantry Division)
13. **1st (Domobran) Replacement Brigade** (02/44 to 11/30/44)
14. **7th Ustaša [Ustasha] Brigade** (04/44; 12/01/44, transferred to 10th Croatian Infantry Division)
15. **1st Garrison Brigade** (04/01/44 to 11/30/44)
16. **2nd Garrison Brigade** (04/01/44 to 11/30/44)
17. **3rd Garrison Brigade** (04/01/44 to 11/30/44)
18. **4th Garrison Brigade** (04/01/44 to 11/30/44)
19. **Zagreb Garrison Brigade** (04/01/44 to 11/30/44)
20. **Ustaša [Ustasha] Garrison Brigade Zagreb** (04/44 to 12/01/44)
21. **8th Ustaša [Ustasha] Brigade** (05/44; 12/01/44, transferred to 4th Croatian Infantry Division)
22. **10th Ustaša [Ustasha] Brigade** (08/44; 12/01/44, transferred to 6th Croatian Infantry Division)
23. **Mobile [Fast] Brigade** (11/44; 03/15/45, transferred to I Ustasha Corps)
24. **15th Ustaša [Ustasha] Brigade** (11/20/44; 12/01/44, transferred to 2nd Croatian Infantry Division)
25. **17th Ustaša [Ustasha] Brigade** (11/20/44; 12/01/44, transferred to 13th Croatian Infantry Division)
26. **18th Ustaša [Ustasha] Brigade** (11/20/44; 12/01/44, transferred to 11th Croatian Infantry Division)
27. **2nd Infantry Regiment**: 08/14/43 unknown? 10/43 Col. Čihak (Commanding Officer, 1st Garrison Brigade) 04/01/44 redesignated **1st Garrison Brigade**.
28. **3rd Infantry Regiment**: 08/14/43 unknown? 04/44 redesignated **2nd Garrison Brigade**.
29. **1st Domobran Labor Regiment**: 08/14/43 unknown? 08/44 Col. Jovan Iskrić (retired) 09/44 disbanded.
30. **I Cavalry Group** (08/14/43 to 04/01/44) - see Cavalry Regiments.

II Territorial Corps (II. Zbornog Područja) (08/14/43, from merger of **II Domobran Corps** and **II Domobran Territorial Corps**): 08/14/43 BG Emil Radl (temporary) 10/26/43 LG Matija Čanić (Commander-in-Chief, Armed Forces) 01/31/44 LG Franjo Pacak (?) 03/15/45 disbanded.

A. **Components - II Territorial Corps**
1. **3rd Croatian Infantry Division** (12/01/44; 03/15/45, transferrred to III Ustaša [Ustasha] Corps)
2. **6th Croatian Infantry Division** (12/01/44; 03/15/45, transferrred to IV Ustaša [Ustasha] Corps)
3. **7th Croatian Mountain Division** (12/01/44; 03/15/45, transferrred to III Ustaša [Ustasha] Corps)
4. **12th Croatian Infantry Division** (12/01/44; 03/15/45, transferrred to IV Ustaša [Ustasha] Corps)
5. **14th Croatian Infantry Division** (12/01/44; 03/15/45, transferrred to II Ustaša [Ustasha] Corps)

6. **15th Croatian Infantry Division** (12/01/44; 03/15/45, transferrred to II Ustaša [Ustašha] Corps)
7. **18th Croatian Assault Division** (12/01/44; 03/15/45, transferrred to III Ustaša [Ustašha] Corps)
8. **1st Jäger Brigade** (05/01/43 to 10/44)
9. **3rd Jäger Brigade** (05/01/43 to 12/01/44)
10. **4th Jäger Brigade** (07/43 to 12/01/44)
11. **3rd Mountain Brigade** (08/12/43; 12/01/44, transferred to 12th Croatian Infantry Division)
12. **4th Mountain Brigade** (08/12/43; 12/01/44, transferred to 7th Croatian Mountain Division)
13. **Syrmian Brigade** (08/14/43 to 04/01/44)
14. **Tuzla Brigade** (08/14/43 to 10/43)
15. **2nd Ustaša [Ustašha] Brigade** (08/14/43; 12/01/44, transferred to 3rd Croatian Infantry Division)
16. **2nd (Domobran) Replacement Brigade** (02/44 to 11/30/44)
17. **5th Garrison Brigade** (04/01/44 to 11/30/44)
18. **6th Garrison Brigade** (04/01/44 to 11/30/44)
19. **7th Garrison Brigade** (04/01/44 to 11/30/44)
20. **10th Garrison Brigade** (04/01/44 to 11/30/44)
21. **12th Ustaša [Ustašha] Brigade** (07/44; 12/01/44, transferred to 12th Croatian Infantry Division)
22. **Banja Luka Brigade (#2)** (10/44 to 11/44)
23. **13th Ustaša [Ustašha] Brigade** (11/20/44; 12/01/44, transferred to 3rd Croatian Infantry Division)
24. **14th Ustaša [Ustašha] Brigade** (11/20/44; 12/01/44, transferred to 14th Croatian Infantry Division)
25. **16th Ustaša [Ustašha] Brigade** (11/20/44; 12/01/44, transferred to 15th Croatian Infantry Division)
26. **2nd Domobran Labor Regiment**: 08/14/43 Col. Kljajić 08/44 disbanded.
27. **Domdo Regiment Banja Luka** (08/14/43 to 09/14/43)
28. **Domdo Regiment "Bosanski Planinci"**: 08/14/43 TOPČIĆ [a Moslem school teacher] 04/01/44 incorporated into the **10th Garrison Brigade**.
29. **II Cavalry Group** (08/14/43 to 04/01/44) - see Cavalry Regiments.

III Territorial Corps (III. Zbornog Područja) (08/14/43, from merger of **III Domobran Corps** and **III Domobran Territorial Corps**): 08/14/43 Gen. Anton Prohaska (?) 08/31/44 LG Ivan Markulj (1945, condemned to death and executed) 03/15/45 disbanded.
A. *Components - III Territorial Corps*
   1. **6th Infantry Division** (08/14/43 to 04/01/44)
   2. **8th Croatian Infantry Division** (12/01/44; 03/15/45, transferrred to III Ustaša [Ustašha] Corps)
   3. **9th Croatian Mountain Division** (12/01/44; 03/15/45, transferrred to III Ustaša [Ustašha] Corps)
   4. **17th Croatain Assault/Infantry Division** (12/01/44; 03/15/45, transferrred to III Ustaša [Ustašha] Corps)
   5. **4th Jäger Brigade** (05/01/43; 07/43, transferred to II Territorial Corps)

6. **1st Mountain Brigade** (08/12/43; 12/01/44, transferred to 9th Croatian Mountain Division)
7. **1st Ustaša [Ustasha] Brigade** (08/14/43; 12/01/44, transferred to 8th Croatian Infantry Division)
8. **5th Ustaša [Ustasha] Brigade** (08/14/43; 02/44, transferred to I Territorial Corps)
9. **6th Ustaša [Ustasha] Brigade** (12/43; 12/01/44, transferred to 9th Croatian Mountain Division)
10. **3rd (Domobran) Replacement Brigade** (02/44 to 11/30/44)
11. **Mobile [Fast] Brigade** (04/01/44; 11/44, transferred to I Territorial Corps)
12. **8th Garrison Brigade** (04/01/44 to 11/30/44)
13. **9th Garrison Brigade** (04/01/44 to 11/30/44)
14. **9th Ustaša [Ustasha] Brigade** (05/44; 12/01/44, transferred to 9th Croatian Mountain Division)
15. **11th Ustaša [Ustasha] Brigade** (08/44; 12/01/44, transferred to 8th Croatian Infantry Division)
16. **7th Jäger Brigade** (11/13/44; 12/01/44, transferred to 4th Croatian Infantry Division)
17. **Zagreb Cavalry Regiment** (08/14/43 to 04/01/44) - see Cavalry Regiments
18. **3rd Domobran Labor Regiment**: 08/14/43 unknown? 03/45 disbanded.

Army Corps
(March 1945 to May 1945)

Poglavnik Bodyguard Corps [Poglavnikov Tjelesni Zbor] (03/15/45; HQ: Zagreb):
Poglavnik Bodyguard Battalion [Poglavnikov Tjelesni Bojna] /41 LCol. Anta Moškov
[+ 04/42 to 05/15/42, Commanding Officer, Utinjski Brigade] (Commanding Officer,
Poglavnik Bodyguard Brigade) 08/42 redesignated **Poglavnik Bodyguard Brigade
[Poglavnikov Tjelesni Zdrug]** 08/42 Col. Anta Moškov (Commanding General, 1st
Croatian Assault Division) 10/09/44 Col. Mirko Gregurić (Commanding General, 2nd
Croatian Infantry Division) 11/15/44 redesignated **Poglavnik Bodyguard Division
[Poglavnikov Tjelesni Divizija]** 11/15/44 BG Vjekoslav Servatzy [+ Commandant, Zagreb]
02/45 BG Antun Nardeli (1945, condemned to death and executed) 03/15/45 redesignated
Poglavnik Bodyguard Corps 03/15/45 BG Anta Moškov (?) 05/45
A. *Components - Poglavnik Bodyguard Corps*
   1. **2nd Croatian Infantry Division** (03/15/45 to 05/08/45)
   2. **5th Croatian Assault Division** (03/15/45 to 05/08/45)
   3. **16th Croatian Replacement Division** (03/15/45 to 05/08/45)
   4. **Mobile [Fast] Brigade** (04/15/45 to 05/45)

I Ustasha Corps [I. Ustaški Zbor] (03/15/45; HQ: Zagreb? Varaždin? Bjelovar?): LG Ivan
Brozović (?) 05/45
A. *Components - I Ustasha Corps*
   1. **1st Croatian Assault Division** (03/15/45 to 04/15/45)
   2. **2nd Croatian Infantry Division** (03/15/45; 04/15/45, transferred to Poglanik
      Bodyguard Corps)
   3. **5th Croatian Assault Division** (03/15/45; 04/15/45, transferred to Poglanik
      Bodyguard Corps)
   4. **13th Croatian Infantry Division** (03/15/45 to 05/08/45)
   5. **16th Croatian Replacement Division** (03/15/45; 04/15/45, transferred to
      Poglanik Bodyguard Corps)
   6. **Mobile [Fast] Brigade** (03/15/45; 04/15/45, transferred to Poglavnik
      Bodyguard Corps)

II Ustasha Corps [II. Ustaški Zbor] (03/15/45; HQ: Sisak): LG Vjekoslav "Maks" Luburić
(Commander-in-Chief, Armed Forces) 05/45
A. *Components - II Ustasha Corps*
   1. **14th Croatian Infantry Division** (03/15/45 to 05/08/45)
   2. **15th Croatian Infantry Division** (03/15/45; 04/15/45, transferred to IV
      Ustasha Corps)
   3. **18th Croatian Assault Division** (04/01/45 to 05/08/45)
   4. **1st Ustaša [Ustasha] Guard Brigade** (03/45 to 05/06/45)

III Ustasha Corps [III. Ustaški Zbor] (03/15/45; HQ: Nova Gradiška): LG Artur Gustović
(condemned to death and executed 05/45.

A. *Components - III Ustasha Corps*
1. **3rd Croatian Infantry Division** (03/15/45 to 05/08/45)
2. **7th Croatian Mountain Division** (03/15/45 to 05/08/45)
3. **8th Croatian Infantry Division** (03/15/45 to 05/08/45)
4. **9th Croatian Mountain Division** (03/15/45 to 05/08/45)
5. **17th Croatian Assault/Infantry Division** (03/15/45 to 05/08/45)

IV Ustasha Corps [IV. Ustaški Zbor] (03/15/45; HQ: Kostajnica): LG Josip Metzger (condemned to death and executed) 05/45.
A. *Components - IV Ustasha Corps*
1. **4th Croatian Infantry Division** (03/15/45 to 05/08/45)
2. **6th Croatian Infantry Division** (03/15/45 to 05/08/45)
3. **12th Croatian Infantry Division** (03/15/45 to 05/08/45)
4. **15th Croatian Infantry Division** (04/15/45 to 05/08/45)

V Ustasha Corps [V. Ustaški Zbor] (03/15/45; HQ: Karlovac): LG Ivan Herenčić (?) 05/45
A. *Components - V Ustasha Corps*
1. **10th Croatian Infantry Division** (03/15/45 to 05/08/45)
2. **11th Croatian Infantry Division** (03/15/45 to 05/08/45)

Infantry Divisions
(April 1, 1941 to November 30, 1944)

1ˢᵗ Infantry Division (08/01/41; from **Savska Division** formed 04/24/41; HQ: Zagreb; Bjelovar; 11/41, I Domobran Territorial Corps): **Savska Division** 04/24/41 Col. Emanuel Balley (Commanding Officer, 1ˢᵗ Division) 08/01/41 redesignated **1ˢᵗ Infantry Division** 08/01/41 Col. Emanuel Balley 04/42 Col. Ivan Pavić 08/42 Col. Matija Murković 12/42 Col. Stjepan vitez [Knight] Peričić (Commanding General, 1ˢᵗ Mountain Brigade) 07/43 Col. Mirko Zgaga [+ Commanding Officer, 4ᵗʰ Ustaŝha [Ustaŝa] Brigade] (Commandant, Gospić, I Domobran Territorial Corps [I Territorial Corps]) 08/43 disbanded.

- A. **Components - Savska Division** (04/24/41 to 06/29/41)
    1. **Delnice Infantry Regiment**
    2. **Karlovac Infantry Regiment**
    3. **Varaždin Infantry Regiment**
    4. **Zagred Infantry Regiment**
    5. **Zagreb Cavalry Regiment** 04/41 see Cavalry Regiments 08/41 transferred to General Headquarters (MINDOM) Zagreb.
- B. **Components - Savska Division** (06/29/41 to 08/01/41)
    1. **1ˢᵗ Infantry Regiment**: 06/29/41 Col. Walzl 08/01/41 transferred to 1ˢᵗ Infantry Division.
    2. **2ⁿᵈ Infantry Regiment**: 06/29/41 Col. Matija Murković 08/01/41 transferred to 1ˢᵗ Infantry Division.
    3. **3ʳᵈ Infantry Regiment**: 06/29/41 unknown? 08/01/41 transferred to 2ⁿᵈ Infantry Division.
- C. **Components - 1ˢᵗ Infantry Division** (08/01/41 to 05/43)
    1. **1ˢᵗ Infantry Regiment**: 08/01/41 Col. Walzl (08/42, acting Commanding Officer, 2ⁿᵈ Infantry Division) 10/41 Col. Mravinec 05/42 Col. Ivan Severović 05/43 renamed **1ˢᵗ Jäger Regiment**.
    2. **2ⁿᵈ Infantry Regiment**: 08/01/41 Col. Matija Murković (Commanding Officer, 5ᵗʰ Infantry Division) 11/41 LCol. Josip Ŝolc (acting; 04/42, Commanding Officer, 1ˢᵗ Mountain Brigade) 12/41 Col. Milutin Stipetić 07/43 direct control of I Territorial Corps.
    3. **11ᵗʰ Infantry Regiment**: 08/01/41 Col. Ivan Matagić [+ Commanding Officer, Sisak Garrison Command] (killed in action) 10/03/41 vacant 08/04/41 Col. Mario Zlobec (killed in action) 05/16/43 Col. Antun Nardeli (12/01/44, Commanding General, 4ᵗʰ Croatian Infantry Division) 08/01/43 renamed **11ᵗʰ Mountain Regiment** and transferred to 3ʳᵈ Mountain Brigade.

2ⁿᵈ Infantry Division (08/01/41; from **Vrbaska Division** formed 04/24/41; HQ: Banja Luka; I Domobran Territorial Corps; 04/42, Bihać; 09/42, Bos Novi; 11/07/42 Kostajnica; 07/15/43, Topusko): **Vrbaska Division** 04/24/41 BG Dragutin Rumler (Commanding Officer, 2ⁿᵈ Division) 08/01/41 redesignated **2ⁿᵈ Infantry Division** 08/01/41 BG Dragutin Rumler [+ 07/31/41 to 08/41, Commanding General, Sanski Brigade] (Commanding

General, I Domobran Corps [Vrbas Military District]) 11/41 Col. Ivan Tomašević [+ to 01/42, Commanding Officer, Karlovac Garrison Command] (Croatian Liaison Officer to German XV Army Corps) 8/42 Col. Walzl (acting) 09/42 Col. Matija Čanić 11/42 Col. Mirko Gregurić (Commanding General, 3rd Mountain Brigade) 08/01/43 reorganized and renamed **3rd Mountain Brigade**.

A.   *Components* - **Vrbaska Division** (04/24/41 to 06/29/41)
1.   **Banja Luka Infantry Regiment**
2.   **Bihać Infantry Regiment**
3.   **Otočac Infantry Regiment**
4.   **Sisak Infantry Regiment**

B.   *Components* - **Vrbaska Division** (06/29/41 to 08/01/41)
1.   **10th Infantry Regiment**: 06/29/41 unknown? 08/01/41 transferred to 2nd Infantry Division.
2.   **11th Infantry Regiment**: Col. Ivan Matagić [+ 07/41, Commanding Officer, Sisak Garrison Command] 08/01/41 transferred to 1st Infantry Division.
3.   **12th Infantry Regiment**: 06/29/41 unknown? 08/01/41 transferred to 2nd Infantry Division.

C.   *Components* - **2nd Infantry Division** (08/01/41)
1.   **3rd Infantry Regiment**: 08/01/41 unknown? 10/41 Col. Liberai Defar 01/42 unknown? 08/43 direct control I Territorial Corps.
2.   **10th Infantry Regiment**: 08/01/41 unknown? 12/41 transferred to 4th Infantry Division.
3.   **12th Infantry Regiment**: 08/01/41 unknown? 12/41 Col. Walzl (acting Commanding Officer, 2nd Infantry Division) 08/42 LCol. Jurković /42 LCol. Vuksan (killed in action) 11/27/42 unknown? 08/01/43 transferred to 3rd Mountain Brigade.
4.   **15th Infantry Regiment**

3rd Infantry Division (08/01/41; from **Osijek Division** formed 04/24/41; HQ Osijek; II Domobran Territorial Corps; 04/42 Vinkovci; 06/42 Tuzla): **Osijek Division** 04/24/41 BG Mihajlo Lukić (Inspector-General of Infantry & Commanding General, Lika Brigade) 08/01/41 redesignated **3rd Infantry Division** 08/01/41 Col. Emil Radl (Commanding General, II Military District) 08/43 disbanded.

A.   *Components* - **Osijek Division** (04/24/41 to 06/29/41)
1.   **Bjelovar Infantry Regiment**
2.   **Osijek Infantry Regiment**

B.   *Components* - **Osijek Division** (06/29/41 to 08/01/41)
1.   **4th Infantry Regiment**: 06/29/41 Col. Stjepan Binder 08/01/41 transferred to 3rd Infantry Division.
2.   **5th Infantry Regiment**: 06/29/41 Col. Milivoj Durbešić 08/01/41 transferred to 3rd Infantry Division.
3.   **6th Infantry Regiment**: 06/29/41 Col. Andrija [Andro] Grum (12/41, Commanding Officer, 4th Infantry Regiment) 08/01/41 transferred to 3rd Infantry Division.

C.   *Components* - **3rd Infantry Division** (08/01/41)
1.   **4th Infantry Regiment**: 08/01/41 Col. Stjepan Binder 12/41 Col. Andrija [Andro] Grum (Commanding Officer, Slavonian Brigade) /42 Col. Stjepan

Binder 01/02/43 Col. Andrija [Andro] Grum [+ to 03/43, Commanding Officer, Slavonian Brigade] (/45, Commanding Officer, 14th Croatian Infantry Division) 05/43 redesignated **4th Jäger Regiment**, and transferred to 1st Jäger Brigade.

    2.   **5th Infantry Regiment**: 08/01/41 Col. Milivoj Durbešić (07/42, Commandant, Domobran Cadet School) 10/41? transferred to 4th Infantry Division.

    3.   **6th Infantry Regiment**: 08/01/41 Col. Mriesa 11/41 Col. Franjo Djoić 12/41 unknown? 05/43 redesignated **6th Jäger Regiment** and transferred to 1st Jäger Brigade.

B.   **Artillery, 3rd Division** (08/01/41): Col. Franjo Dolacki [+ Commanding Officer, I Domobran Territorial Corps] (Assistant Commandant, Zagreb) 08/43

4th Infantry Division (08/01/41; HQ Doboj; II Domobran Territorial Corps): Col. Franjo Nikolić (Assistant Co) 10/41 Col. Artur Gustović (Commanding Officer, 1st Mountain Division) 04/42 Col. Bogdan Majetić (/44, Commanding Officer, 2nd Mountain Brigade) 08/43 dissolved to form other units.

A.   *Components - 4th Infantry Division* (06/29/41)

    1.   **5th Infantry Regiment**:10/41 Col. Ivan Šarnbek (12/42, Commanding Officer, 6th Infantry Division) 01/42 Col. Ivan Šulentić 05/43 redesignated **5th Jäger Regiment** and transferred to 3rd Jäger Brigade.

    2.   **10th Infantry Regiment**: 12/41 unknown? 06/42 Col. Josip Bučar (06/43, Commanding Officer, 2nd Jäger Brigade) 03/43 Col. Juraj Čordašić (Commanding Officer, 2nd Jäger Brigade) 05/43 renamed **10th Jäger Regiment** and assigned to 2nd Jäger Brigade.

5th Infantry Division (08/01/41; from **Bosanska Division** formed 04/24/41; HQ Sarajevo; III Domobran Territorial Corps; 08/01/43, reorganized and renamed **2nd Mountain Brigade**): **Bosanska Division** 04/24/41 Col. Pero Blašković (Commanding General, Bosnia Divisional Area) 08/01/41 redesignated **5th Infantry Division** 08/01/41 vacant 10/41 Col. Matija Murković (08/42, Commanding Officer, 1st Division) 11/41 Col. Antun Prohaska (Commanding Officer, 3rd Jäeger Brigade) 02/43 Col. Roman Domanik (12/01/44, Commanding General, 8th Croatian Infantry Division) 08/01/43 reorganized and renamed **2nd Mountain Brigade**.

A.   *Components - Bosanska Division* (04/24/41 to 06/29/41)

    1.   **Sarajevo Infantry Regiment**

    2.   **Tuzia Infantry Regiment**

    3.   **Infantry Regiment**

B.   *Components - Bosanska Division* (06/29/41 to 08/01/41)

    1.   **7th Infantry Regiment**: 06/29/41 unknown? 08/01/41 transferred to 5th Infantry Division.

    2.   **8th Infantry Regiment**: 06/29/41 Col. Mirko Paja 08/01/41 transferred to 5th Infantry Division.

    3.   **9th Infantry Regiment**: 06/29/41 Col. Artur Gustović (08/01/41 transferred to 5th Infantry Division.

C.   *Components - 5th Infantry Division* (08/01/41)

    1.   **7th Infantry Regiment**: 08/01/41 unknown? 04/42 Col. Sulejman beg

Filipović (04/43, Commanding Officer, Tuzla Brigade) 09/42 LCol. Vladimir Metikoš (Commanding Officer, 4th Jäger Brigade) 02/11/43 unknown? 04/43 redesignated **7th Jäger Regiment** and transferred to 4th Jäger Brigade.

2.   **8th Infantry Regiment**: 08/01/44 Col. Mirko Paja (10/01/43, Commanding Officer, 3rd Jäger Brigade) 12/41 Col. Stjepan Mifek (10/01/43, Commanding Officer, 3rd Jäger Brigade) 01/43 unknown? 08/43 redesignated **8th Jäger Regiment** and transferred to 3rd Jäger Brigade.

3.   **9th Infantry Regiment**: 08/01/41 Col. Artur Gustović (Commanding Officer, 4th Infantry Division) 10/41 Col. Franjo Šimić (Commanding Officer, 1st Domobran Volunteer Regiment) 08/42 unknown? 12/42 Maj. Jaroslav Schell (acting) 12/42 unknown? 08/01/43 renamed **6th Mountain Regiment** and assigned to 2nd Mountain Brigade.

6th Infantry Division (08/01/41; from **Jadranska Division** formed 04/24/41; HQ Mostar; III Domobran Territorial Corps; 09/43, Dubrovnik; III Territorial Corps; 04/01/44 renamed **9th Garrison Brigade**): **Jadranska Division** 04/24/41 BG Ivan Prpić (Chief, General Staff, Croatia) 08/01/41 redesignated **6th Division** 08/01/41 BG Djuro Izer (Commanding General, II Domobran Corps) 11/41 Col. Franjo Pacak (01/31/44, II Domobran Corps) 12/42 Col. Ivan Šarnbek (Commanding General, 2nd (Domobran) Replacement Brigade) 04/44 renamed **9th Garrison Brigade**.

A.   *Components* - Jadranska Division (04/24/41 to 06/29/41)
1.   **Benkovac Infantry Regiment**
2.   **Knin Infantry Regiment**
3.   **Mostar Infantry Regiment**
4.   **Sinj Infantry Regiment**

B.   *Components* - Jadranska Division (06/29/41 to 08/01/41
1.   **13th Infantry Regiment**: 06/29/41 unknown? 08/01/41 transferred to 6th Infantry Division.
2.   **14th Infantry Regiment**: 06/29/41 unknown? 08/01/41 transferred to 6th Infantry Division.
3.   **15th Infantry Regiment**: 06/29/41 Col. Juraj Čordašić (Commanding Officer, Knin Brigade) 08/01/41 transferred to 6th Infantry Division.

C.   *Components* - 6th Infantry Division
1.   **13th Infantry Regiment**: 08/01/41 unknown? 12/41? Col. Stjepan Gaščić (Commanding Officer, 4th Jäger Brigade) 02/18/43 renamed **13th Jäger Regiment** and transferred to 4th Jäger Brigade.
2.   **14th Infantry Regiment**: 08/01/41 unknown? 11/43 Col. Juraj Čordašić (Commanding Officer, 8th Garrison Brigade) 03/31/44 incorporated into 9th Garrison Brigade.
3.   **15th Infantry Regiment**: 08/01/41 LCol. Ivaništević 12/41 Col. Ivo Stipkovic 01/42 Col. Petar Tomac /42 Col. Josip Kopačin (killed in action) 06/43 unknown?04/01/44 incorporated into 3rd Garrison Brigade.

1st Mountain Division (04/42; HQ: Kostajnica; I Domobran Territorial Corps; 06/42 Petrinja; 10/42, Popovača; 01/26/43, Daruvar): Col. Stjepan vitez [Knight] Peričić (12/42, 1st Division) 06/42 Col. Artur Gustović (Inspector-General of Infantry) 02/43 Col. Matija

Čanić (Commanding General, 4th Mountain Brigade) 08/12/43 disbanded.

A.   ***Components - 1st Mountain Division***
   1.   **1st Mountain Brigade** (04/42; 08/12/43, transferred to I Territorial Corps)
   2.   **2nd Mountain Brigade** (04/42; 08/12/43, transferred to III Territorial Corps)
   3.   **3rd Mountain Brigade** (04/42; 08/12/43, transferred to II Territorial Corps)
   4.   **4th Mountain Brigade** (04/42; 08/12/43, transferred to II Territorial Corps)

Adriatic Divisional Area (04/24/41): BG Djuro Izer (Commanding General, 6th Division) 08/01/41

Bosnia Divisional Area (08/01/41): BG Pero Blašković (retired/1944, in prison/1945, died in prison) /41

Commandant, Zagreb: /42 BG Ivan Markulj [+ 03/43, Commanding General, Zagreb Garrison Command] (Commanding General, III Domobran Corps) 08/31/44 BG Vjekoslav Servatzy [+ 11/15/44 to 02/45, Commanding General, Poglavnik Bodyguard Division] (condemned to death and executed) 05/45.

A.   **Assistant Commandant, Zagreb**: 10/43 BG Franjo Nikolić (Commanding General, 1st Jäger Brigade) 07/44 BG Franjo Dolacki (1950, died in prison) 05/45.

Travnik Military District: BG Oton Cus (retired/1949 condemned to death and executed) /44

Croatian Divisions
(December 1944 to May 1945)

1st Croatian Assault Division (I. Hrvatian Udarna Divizija) (10/09/44; HQ: Unknown?; I Territorial Corps; 03/15/45, I Ustaša [Ustasha] Corps): BG Ante Moškov (Commanding General, Poglavnik Bodyguard Divisional Group) 03/45 Col. Josep Šolc (condemned to death and executed) 05/45.

A.   *Components - 1st Croatian Assault Division*
    1.   **20th Assault Regiment** (10/09/44 to 04/15/45)
    2.   **21st Assault Regiment** (10/09/44 to 04/15/45)
    3.   **22nd Assault Regiment** (01/45 to 04/15/45)

2nd Croatian Infantry Division (II. Hrvatian Pješačka Divizija) (11/15/44; HQ: Zagreb; I Territorial Corps; 03/15/45, I Ustaša [Ustasha] Corps; 04/15/45, Poglavnik Bodyguard Corps): BG Mirko Gregurić (1945, condemned to death and executed) 03/45 BG Adolf Sabljak (condemned to death and executed) 04/45 BG Božidar Zorn (?   ) 05/45.

A.   *Components - 2nd Croatian Infantry Division*
    1.   **15th Ustaša [Ustasha] Brigade** (12/01/44 to 05/08/45)
    2.   **20th Domobran Brigade** (12/01/44 to 04/29/45)
    3.   **26th Infantry Regiment** (04/29/45)
    4.   **27th Infantry Regiment** (04/29/45)

3rd Croatian Infantry Division (III. Hrvatian Pješačka Divizija) (12/01/44, II Territorial Corps; HQ: Vinkovci; 03/15/45, III Ustaša [Ustasha] Corps): BG Stjepan Mifek (condemned to death and executed) 05/45.

A.   *Components - 3rd Croatian Infantry Division*
    1.   **2nd Ustaša [Ustasha] Brigade** (12/01/44 to 05/08/45)
    2.   **13th Ustaša [Ustasha] Brigade** (12/01/44 to 05/08/45)
    3.   **8th Jäger Brigade** (12/01/44 to 05/45)

4th Croatian Infantry Division (IV. Hrvatian Pješačka Divizija) (12/01/44, I Territorial Corps; HQ: Dvor; 03/15/45, IV Ustaša [Ustasha] Corps): BG Antun Nardeli (Commanding General, Poglavnik Bodyguard Divisional Group) 02/45 Col. Zdenko Begić.

A.   *Components - 4th Croatian Infantry Division*
    1.   **8th Ustaša [Ustasha] Brigade** (12/01/44 to 05/08/45)
    2.   **7th Jäger Brigade** (12/01/44 to 05/02/44?)
    3.   **14th Domobran Brigade** (12/01/44 to 05/08/45)

5th Croatian Assault Division (V. Hrvatian Udarna Divizija) (12/01/44 as **5th Croatian Infantry Division (V. Hrvatian Pješačka Divizija)**; I Territorial Corps; HQ: Bjelovar; 03/15/45, I Ustaša [Ustasha] Corps; 03/45 redesignated **5th Croatian Assault Division**; 04/15/45, Poglavnik Bodyguard Corps): **5th Croatian Infantry Division** 12/01/44 BG Rafael vitez [Knight] Boban (Commanding General, 5th Croatian Assault Division) 03/45 redesignated **5th Croatian Assault Division** 03/45 BG Rafael vitez [Knight] Boban.

A. **Assistant Commander, 5th Croatian Assault Division**: /45 BG [Retired '44] Franjo Nikolić (condemned to death and executed) 05/45.
B. *Components - 5th Croatian Infantry/Assault Division*
    1. **5th Ustaša [Ustašha] Brigade** (12/01/44 to 05/08/45)
    2. **11th Domobran Brigade** (12/01/44 to 05/45)
    3. **23rd Assault Regiment** (11/21/44 to 05/08/45)
    4. **24th Assault Regiment** (11/21/44 to 05/08/45)
    5. **25th Assault Regiment** (11/21/44 to 05/08/45)

6th Croatian Infantry Division (VI. Hrvatian Pješačka Divizija) (12/01/44, II Territorial Corps; HQ: Banja Luka; 03/15/45, IV Ustaša [Ustašha] Corps): BG Vladimir Metikoš (sentenced to death by the Supreme Court of Yugoslavia) 05/45.
A. *Components - 6th Croatian Infantry Division* (11/21/44 to 05/08/45)
    1. **10th Ustaša [Ustašha] Brigade** (12/01/44 to 05/08/45)
    2. **15th Domobran Brigade** (12/01/44 to 05/45)

7th Croatian Mountain Division (VII. Hrvatian Gorska Divizija) (12/01/44; HQ: Nova Kapela & Batrina; II Territorial Corps; 03/15/45, III Ustaša [Ustašha] Corps): BG Stjepan vitez [Knight] Peričić.
A. *Components - 7th Croatian Mountain Division*
    1. **1st Mountain Brigade** (12/01/44 to 05/45)
    2. **4th Mountain Brigade** (12/01/44 to 05/45)

8th Croatian Infantry Division (VIII. Hrvatian Pješačka Divizija) (12/01/44; HQ: Sarajevo; III Territorial Corps; 03/15/45, III Ustaša [Ustašha] Corps): BG Roman Domanik (Commanding General, 17th Croatian Infantry Division) 03/45
A. *Components - 8th Croatian Infantry Division*
    1. **1st Ustaša [Ustašha] Brigade** (12/01/44 to 05/08/45)
    2. **11th Ustaša [Ustašha] Brigade** (12/01/44; 03/01/45, transferred to 17th Croatian Infantry Division)
    3. **18th Domobran Brigade** (12/01/44 to 05/45)

9th Croatian Mountain Division (IX. Hrvatian Gorska Divizija) (12/01/44; HQ: Mostar; III Territorial Corps; 03/15/45, III Ustaša [Ustašha] Corps): BG Božidar Zorn (2nd Croatian Infantry Division) 04/45 Col. Mihi Bajd /45 BG Stjepan Grlić (?) 05/45.
A. *Components - 9th Croatian Mountain Division*
    1. **2nd Mountain Brigade** (12/01/44 to 05/45)
    2. **6th Ustaša [Ustašha] Brigade** (12/01/44 to 05/08/45)
    3. **9th Ustaša [Ustašha] Brigade** (12/01/44 to 05/08/45)

10th Croatian Infantry Division (X. Hrvatian Pješačka Divizija) (12/01/44; Bihać; I Territorial Corps; 03/15/45, V Ustaša [Ustašha] Corps): BG Ivan Tomašević (condemned to death and executed) 03/45 Col. Dušan Rajković 05/45.
A. *Components - 10th Croatian Infantry Division*
    1. **7th Ustaša [Ustašha] Brigade** (12/01/44 to 05/08/45)
    2. **10th Jäger Brigade** (12/01/44 to 05/02/45?)

11ᵗʰ Croatian Infantry Division (XI. Hrvatian Pješačka Divizija) (12/01/44; HQ: Gospić; I Territorial Corps; 03/15/45, V Ustaša [Ustasha] Corps): Col. Josip Aleksić 02/45 Col. Jučo Rukavina 05/45.

A.   *Components - 11ᵗʰ Croatian Infantry Division*
  1.   **4ᵗʰ Ustaša [Ustasha] Brigade** (12/01/44 to 05/08/45)
  2.   **18ᵗʰ Ustaša [Ustasha] Brigade** (12/01/44 to 05/08/45)
  3.   **13ᵗʰ Domobran Brigade** (12/01/44 to 05/08/45)

12ᵗʰ Croatian Infantry Division (XII. Hrvatian Pješačka Divizija) (12/01/44; HQ: Brčka; II Territorial Corps; 03/15/45, IV Ustaša [Ustasha] Corps): Col. Slavko Cesarić (?   ) 05/45.

A.   *Components - 12ᵗʰ Croatian Infantry Division*
  1.   **3ʳᵈ Mountain Brigade** (12/01/44 to 05/08/45)
  2.   **12ᵗʰ Ustaša [Ustasha] Brigade** (12/01/44 to 05/08/45)

13ᵗʰ Croatian Infantry Division (XIII. Hrvatian Pješačka Divizija) (12/01/44; HQ: Karlovac; I Territorial Corps; 03/15/45, I Ustaša [Ustasha] Corps): BG Tomislav Rolf (committed suicide) 05/45.

A.   *Components - 13ᵗʰ Croatian Infantry Division*
  1.   **3ʳᵈ Ustaša [Ustasha] Brigade** (12/01/44 to 05/08/45)
  2.   **17ᵗʰ Ustaša [Ustasha] Brigade** (12/01/44 to 05/08/45)
  3.   **12ᵗʰ Domobran Brigade** (12/01/44 to 05/0845)
  4.   **28ᵗʰ Infantry Regiment**
  5.   **29ᵗʰ Infantry Regiment**

14ᵗʰ Croatian Infantry Division (XIV. Hrvatian Pješačka Divizija) (12/01/44; HQ: Slavonski Brod; II Territorial Corps; 03/15/45, II Ustaša [Ustasha] Corps): Col. Jaroslav Šotola /45 Col. Milivoj Durbešić [acting/+ 16ᵗʰ Croatian Infantry Division] /45 Col. Andrija [Andro] Grum 05/45.

A.   *Components - 14ᵗʰ Croatian Infantry Division*
  1.   **14ᵗʰ Ustaša [Ustasha] Brigade** (12/01/44 to 05/08/45)
  2.   **19ᵗʰ Domobran Brigade** (12/01/44 to 05/08/45)

15ᵗʰ Croatian Infantry Division (XV. Hrvatian Pješačka Divizija) (12/01/44; HQ: Doboj; II Territorial Corps; 03/15/45, II Ustaša [Ustasha] Corps; 04/15/45, IV Ustaša [Ustasha] Corps): Col. Zorko Čudina 05/45.

A.   *Components - 15ᵗʰ Croatian Infantry Division*
  1.   **16ᵗʰ Ustaša [Ustasha] Brigade** (12/01/44 to 05/08/45)
  2.   **16ᵗʰ Domobran Brigade** (21/01/44 to 05/08/45)

16ᵗʰ Croatian Replacement Division (XVI. Hrvatian Doknadna Divizija) (12/01/44; HQ: Zagreb; I Territorial Corps; 03/15/45, I Ustaša [Ustasha] Corps; 04/15/45 Poglavnik Bodyguard Corps): Col. Milivoj Durbešić 05/45.

A.   *Components - 16ᵗʰ Croatian Replacement Division*
  1.   **21ˢᵗ (Domobran) Replacement Brigade** (12/01/44 to 04/45)
  2.   **23ʳᵈ (Domobran) Replacement Brigade** (12/01/44 to 04/45)

3. **20th Ustaša [Ustašha] Replacement Brigade** (12/01/44 to 05/08/45)
4. **21st Ustaša [Ustašha] Replacement Brigade** (04/45 to 05/08/45)
5. **22nd Ustaša [Ustašha] Replacement Brigade** (04/45 to 05/08/45)
6. **Ustaša [Ustašha] Training Brigade** (04/45 to 05/08/45)

17th Croatian Infantry Division (XVII. Hrvatian Pješačka Divizija) (03/01/45; HQ: Zenica; sometimes known as **17th Croatian Assault Division (XVII. Hrvatian Udarna Divizija)**; III Territorial Corps; 03/15/45, III Ustaša [Ustašha] Corps): BG Roman Domanik (?) 05/45.
A. *Components - 17th Croatian Infantry Division*
1. **11th Ustaša [Ustašha] Brigade** (03/01/45 to 05/08/45)
2. **17th Domobran Brigade** (12/01/44 to 05/08/45)

18th Croatian Infantry Division (XVIII. Hrvatian Udarna Divizija) (03/22/45; HQ: Sisak; II Ustasha Corps): BG Julije Fritz (condemned to death and executed) 05/45.
A. *Components - 18th Croatian Assault Division*
1. **14th Infantry Brigade** (12/01/44 to 05/08/45)
2. **XI Ustasha Brigade** (12/01/44 to 05/08/45)
3. **XIX Ustasha Brigade** (12/01/44 to 05/08/45)
4. **30th Assault Regiment** (11/21/44 to 05/08/45)
5. **31st Assault Regiment**
6. **32nd Assualt Regiment**

Croatian Command "Istok"
A. *Components - Croatian Command "Istok"*
1. **Popular-Ustaša [Ustašha] Brigade**

Brigades
Composite, Territorial & Tactical Brigades

Knin Brigade (Kninski Zdrug) (07/31/41, Army Headquarters (MINDOM) Zagreb; HQ: Knin; a composite tactical formation; 10/41, disbanded): 07/31/41 BG Vladimir Laxa [+ Deputy Commander-in-Chief of the Army] 08/16/41 Col. Juraj Čordašić (03/43, Commanding Officer, 10th Infantry Regiment) 10/41 disbanded.

Lika Brigade (Lički Zdrug) (07/31/41, Army Headquarters (MINDOM) Zagreb; HQ: Bihać; a composite tactical formation; 10/41, ordered disbanded but used to form **IV Ustasha Brigade**): 07/31/41 BG Mihailo Lukić [+ Inspector-General of the Army] (Croatian Liaison Officer to Second Italian Army) 10/41 ordered disbanded but used to form **IV Ustasha Brigade**.

Sanski Brigade (Sanski Zdrug) (07/31/41, Army Headquarters (MINDOM) Zagreb; HQ: Prijedor; a composite tactical formation; 10/41, disbanded): 07/31/41 BG Dragutin Rumler [+ Commanding General, 2nd Infantry Division] 08/41 unknown? 10/41 disbanded.

Gračac Brigade (Gračački Domobranski Zdrug) (08/41 Army Headquarters (MINDOM) Zagreb; a composite tactical formation; 09/41, disbanded): 08/41 unknown? 09/41 disbanded.

Kordun Brigade (Kordunski Zdrug) (08/41, Army Headquarters (MINDOM) Zagreb; HQ: Karlovac; a composite Tactical formation; 11/41, I Domobran Corps); 08/01/42, renamed **III Ustasha Brigade**): 08/41 unknown? 08/01/42 renamed **III Ustasha Brigade**.

Lovinac Domobran Brigade (Lovinački Domobranski Zdrug) (08/41, Army Headquarters (MINDOM) Zagreb; HQ: Lovinac; a composite tactical formation; 09/41, probably disbanded): 08/41 unknown? 09/41 probably disbanded.

Banja Luka Brigade (#1) (Banjalučki Zdrug (#1)) (10/41, II Domobran Corps; HQ: Banja Lake; a composite tactical formation; 02/28/43, disbanded): 10/41 BG Ivan Brozović (Commanding General, I Domobran Corps) 02/28/43 disbanded.

Nova Gradiška Brigade (Nova Gradiška Zdrug) (also known as the **1st Domobran-Ustaša [Ustasha] Slavonian Brigade Ustaša [Ustasha] Brigade (I. Domobransko-Ustaški Slavonski Zdrug)**; 01/42, HQ: unknown?; a composite tactical formation; 06/43?, disbanded?): 03/42 Col. Slavko Skoliber (/45, Commanding General, Gendarmes (Secret Police)) 06/43? disbanded?

Utinjski Brigade (Utinjski Zdrug) (01/42; I Domobran Corps; HQ: unknown?; a composite tactical formation; 05/15/42, disbanded): 01/42 Col. Stjepan vitez [Knight] Peričić (10/42, Commanding General, 1st Mountain Division) 04/42 Col. Mirko Zgaga (acting; 03/43, Commanding Officer, 4th Ustaša [Ustaša] Brigade) 04/42 LCol. Ante Moškov [+ Commanding Officer, Poglavnik Bodyguard Regiment] 05/15/42 disbanded.

Gradiška Brigade (Gradiški Zdrug) (02/42, II Domobran Corps; HQ: unknown?; a composite tactical formation; 05/15/42, probably disbanded): 02/42 unknown? 05/15/42 probably disbanded.

Petrinja Brigade (Petrinjski Zdrug) (02/42, I Domobran Corps; HQ: Petrinja; a composite tactical formation; 02/15/43, renamed **5th Mountain Brigade**): 02/42 Col. Ivan Mrak [CAF] 09/42 Col. Milan Desović (Military Attaché, Germany) 01/43 Col. Lalić (Commanding Ofrficer, 5th Mountain Brigade) 02/15/43 renamed **5th Mountain Brigade**.

Syrmian Brigade (Sremski Zdrug) (03/15/42, II Domobran Corps; HQ: Ruma; a territorial & operational formation; 08/14/43, II Territorial Corps; 04/01/44, renamed **7th Garrison Brigade**): 03/15/42 Maj. Strecker /42 Col. Zvonimir Stimaković 08/43 unknown? 12/43 Col. Gjurgjević (Commanding Officer, 7th Garrison Brigade) 04/01/44 renamed **7th Garrison Brigade**.

Kalnik Brigade (Kalnički Zdrug) (04/10/42, I Domobran Corps; HQ: Varaždin; a composite tactical formation; 05/01/42, probably disbanded): 04/10/42 Col. Rudolf Štaufer [Štamfer] 05/01/42 probably disbanded.

Slavonian Brigade (Slavonski Zdrug) (08/42, II Domobran Corps; HQ: Osijek; a composite tactical formation; 08/43, disbanded): 08/42 unknown? /42 Col. Andrija [Andro] Grum [+ 01/02/43, Commanding Officer, 4th Infantry Regiment] 03/43 Col. Tomislav Bosnić 08/43 disbanded.

Tuzla Brigade (Tuzlanski Zdrug) (03/43, II Domobran Corps; HQ: Tuzla; a territorial & operational formation; 08/14/43, II Territorial Corps; 10/06/43, disbanded): 03/43 Col. Sulejman beg Filipović 10/06/43 disbanded.

Paški Brigade (Paški Zdrug) (05/01/43, I Domobran Corps; HQ: Karlobag; a territorial & operational formation; 05/31/43, disbanded): 05/01/43 LCol. Julije Reš (07/44, Commanding Officer, 4th Jäger Brigade) 05/31/43 disbanded.

Banja Luka Brigade (#1) (Banjalučki Zdrug (#1)) (09/44, II Territorial Corps; HQ: Banja Luka; a composite tactical formation; 12/01/44, disbanded): 09/44 BG Vladimir Metikoš (Commanding General, 6th Croatian Infantry Division) 12/01/44 disbanded.

Nova Gradiška Brigade

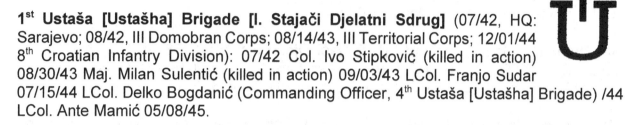

Ustaša [Ustasha] Brigades

1ˢᵗ Ustaša [Ustasha] Brigade [I. Stajači Djelatni Sdrug] (07/42, HQ: Sarajevo; 08/42, III Domobran Corps; 08/14/43, III Territorial Corps; 12/01/44 8ᵗʰ Croatian Infantry Division): 07/42 Col. Ivo Stipković (killed in action) 08/30/43 Maj. Milan Sulentić (killed in action) 09/03/43 LCol. Franjo Sudar 07/15/44 LCol. Delko Bogdanić (Commanding Officer, 4ᵗʰ Ustaša [Ustasha] Brigade) /44 LCol. Ante Mamić 05/08/45.

2ⁿᵈ Ustaša [Ustasha] Brigade [II. Stajači Djelatni Sdrug] (07/42, HQ: Hrv. Mitrovica; 08/42, II Domobran Corps; 08/14/43, II Territorial Corps;12/01/44, 3ʳᵈ Croatian Infantry Division): 07/42 LCol. Antun Ilik 09/23/43 unknown? 10/43 LCol. Ivan Štir 05/08/45.

3ʳᵈ Ustaša [Ustasha] Brigade [I. Stajači Djelatni Sdrug] (07/42, HQ: Karlovac; 08/42, I Domobran Corps; 08/14/43, I Territorial Corps; 12/01/44, 13ᵗʰ Croatian Infantry Division): 08/42 Col. Josip Metzger (12/01/44, Commanding General, Popular-Ustaša [Ustasha] Brigade) 11/42 LCol. Antun Magaš /43 LCol. Vladimir Rogoz 05/44 Col. Tomislav Rolf (Commanding General, 13ᵗʰ Croatian Infantry Division) 12/01/44 Capt. Božidar Katušić 03/45 unknown? 05/08/45.

4ᵗʰ Ustaša [Ustasha] Brigade [I. Stajači Djelatni Sdrug] (07/42, HQ: Bihać; 08/42, I Domobran Corps; 08/14/43, I Territorial Corps; 12/01/44, 13ᵗʰ Croatian Infantry Division): Col. Tomičić 11/42 Col. Vjekoslav Servatzy 03/43 Col Mirko Zgaga [+ 07/43 to 08/43, Commanding Officer, 1ˢᵗ Infantry Division; + 08/43, Commandant, Gospić, I Domobran Territorial Corps [I Territorial Corps]] (killed in action) 10/43 Col. Čiril Čudina (Commanding Officer, 6ᵗʰ Ustaša [Ustasha] Brigade) 08/09/44 LCol. Delko Bogdanić 05/08/45.

5ᵗʰ Ustaša [Ustasha] Brigade [I. Stajači Djelatni Sdrug] (07/42, HQ: Bugojno; 08/42, III Domobran Corps; 08/14/43, III Territorial Corps; 02/44, I Territorial Corps; 12/01/44, HQ: Koprivnica, and 5ᵗʰ Croatian Infantry Division; 03/45, 5ᵗʰ Croatian Assault Division): 08/42 Col. Rafael vitez [Knight] Boban [+ Commanding Officer, Ustaša [Ustasha] Black Legion] (Commanding General, 5ᵗʰ Croatian Infantry Division)12/01/44 unknown? 05/06/45.

6ᵗʰ Ustaša [Ustasha] Brigade [I. Stajači Djelatni Sdrug] (12/43, HQ: Imotski, Dalmatia; 12/01/44, 9ᵗʰ Croatian Mountain Division): 12/01/43 Col. Franjo Šimić (killed in action) 08/09/44 Col. Čiril Čudina 05/06/45.

7ᵗʰ Ustaša [Ustasha] Brigade [I. Stajači Djelatni Sdrug] (04/44, HQ: Ražanac, Dalmatia; 04/44, I Territorial Corps; 12/01/44, 10ᵗʰ Croatian Infantry Division): Col. Emil Kečet (killed in action) 08/01/44 08/01/44 vacant 08/02/44 Col. Tomislav Brajković 01/45 Maj. Petar Mikrut /45 Capt. Miroslav Markotić 05/06/45.

8th Ustaša [Ustaša] Brigade [I. Stajači Djelatni Sdrug] (05/44, HQ: Kostajnica, I Territorial Corps; 12/01/44, 4th Croatian Infantry Division) 05/44 unknown? 09/44 Maj. Petar Dujić [Duić] (01/45, Commanding Officer, 12th Ustaša [Ustaša] Brigade) 11/44 Maj. Josip Kurelac 12/44 unknown? 05/06/45.

9th Ustaša [Ustaša] Brigade [I. Stajači Djelatni Sdrug] (05/44, HQ: Makarska-Hutovo, Dalmatia, III Territorial Corps; 12/01/44, 9th Croatian Mountain Division): unknown? 03/45 LCol. Vladimir vitez [Knight] Majer 05/06/45.

10th Ustaša [Ustaša] Brigade [I. Stajači Djelatni Sdrug] (08/44, HQ: Zagreb, by renaming the **1st Traffic Control Brigade**; I Territorial Corps; 12/01/44, 6th Croatian Infantry Division): unknown? 02/45 LCol. Petar Dujić [Duić] 05/06/45.

11th Ustaša [Ustaša] Brigade [I. Stajači Djelatni Sdrug] (08/44, HQ: Sarajevo, by renaming the **2nd Traffic Control Brigade**; III Territorial Corps; 12/01/44, 8th Croatian Infantry Division; 03/01/45, 17th Croatian Infantry Division): LCol. Krešimir Kuraja 05/06/45.

12th Ustaša [Ustaša] Brigade [I. Stajači Djelatni Sdrug] (07/44, HQ: Tuzla, Bosnia; 08/44, II Territorial Corps; 12/01/44, 12th Croatian Infantry Division): 07/44 LCol. Avdag Hasić 01/45 Maj. Petar Dujić [Duić] (acting; Commanding Officer, 10th Ustaša [Ustaša] Brigade) 02/45 Maj. Dragutin Vudy 05/06/45.

13th Ustaša [Ustaša] Brigade [I. Stajači Djelatni Sdrug] (11/20/44, HQ: Privlaka, Syrmia, II Territorial Corps; 12/01/44, 3rd Croatian Infantry Division; 04/45, consolidated with the **16th Ustaša [Ustaša] Brigade**): 11/20/44 LCol. Petar Pavić 04/45 consolidated with the **16th Ustaša [Ustaša] Brigade**.

14th Ustaša [Ustaša] Brigade [I. Stajači Djelatni Sdrug] (11/20/44, HQ: Nova Gradiška, II Territorial Corps; 12/01/44, 14th Croatian Infantry Division; 04/26/45, HQ: Sisak): 11/20/44 unknown? 05/06/45.

15th Ustaša [Ustaša] Brigade [I. Stajači Djelatni Sdrug] (11/20/44, HQ: Zabok, I Territorial Corps; 12/01/44, 2nd Croatian Infantry Division; 04/29/45, disbanded): 11/20/44 unknown? 04/29/45 disbanded.

16th Ustaša [Ustaša] Brigade [I. Stajači Djelatni Sdrug] (11/20/44, HQ: Derventa, II Territorial Corps; 12/01/44, 15th Croatian Infantry Division): 11/20/44 unknown? 02/45 Maj. Viktor [Vinko] Tomić 05/06/45.

17th Ustaša [Ustaša] Brigade [I. Stajači Djelatni Sdrug] (11/20/44, HQ: Ogulin, I Territorial Corps; 12/01/44, 13th Croatian Infantry Division; 04/28/45, disbanded): 11/20/44 Maj. Vinko Ferček 04/28/45 disbanded.

18th Ustaša [Ustaša] Brigade [I. Stajači Djelatni Sdrug] (11/20/44, HQ: Otočac, I Territorial Corps; 12/01/44, 11th Croatian Infantry Division): 11/20/44 unknown? 05/06/45.

19th Ustaša [Ustasha] Brigade [I. Stajači Djelatni Sdrug] (12/01/44, HQ: Petrinja, 4th Croatian Infantry Division; 04/01/45, 18th Croatian Assault Division): 12/01/44 Maj. Hajdinović 05/06/45.

20th Ustaša [Ustasha] Brigade [I. Stajači Djelatni Sdrug] (12/01/44, HQ: Zagreb, 2nd Croatian Infantry Division): 12/01/44 Col. Branko Rukavina 05/06/45.

23rd Ustaša [Ustasha] Brigade [I. Stajači Djelatni Sdrug] (12/01/44, HQ: Zagreb, 16th Croatian Replacement Division; 03/15/45, HQ: Kraljevica): 12/01/44 unknown? 03/45 Maj. Jeronim Katić 05/06/45.

Mobile Brigades

Mobile [Fast] Brigade (Zdrug) (04/01/44, using **Zagreb Cavalry Regiment** as core, III Territorial Corps; 11/44, I Territorial Corps; 03/15/45, I Ustasha Corps; 04/15/45, Poglavnik Bodyguard Corps): 04/01/44 Col. Aurel Schlacher [Schlaher; Šlaher].
A.   **Deputy Commander, Mobile [Fast] Brigade**: 04/01/44 LCol. Josip Klobučarić.

Cavalry Regiments

Zagreb Cavalry Regiment (Zagrebački Konjanička Zdrug) (04/24/41, Zagreb; Savska Division; 07/41 General HQ (MINDOM) Zagreb; 11/41, III Domobran Territorial Corps; 08/01/43, III Territorial Corps; 04/01/44, renamed the **Mobile [Fast] Brigade**): 04/24/41 LCol. Stajić 06/41 LCol. Djuro Sivoš (12/01/44, Commanding Officer, 12th Domobran Brigade) 05/42 LCol. Ljubomir Rajman 02/43 LCol. Aurel Schlacher [Schlaher; Šlaher] (Commanding Officer, Mobile [Fast] Brigade 04/01/44 renamed the **Mobile [Fast] Brigade**.

I Cavalry Group (I. Konjanička Sklop) (08/41; HQ: Zagreb; General Headquarters (MINDOM) Zagreb; 11/41, I Domobran Corps; 08/14/43, I Territorial Corps; 04/01/44, incorporated into the **Mobile Brigade**): 08/41 unknown? 04/42? LCol. Oto Egelsdorfer 04/01/44 incorporated into the **Mobile Brigade**.

II Cavalry Group (II. Konjanička Sklop) (07/41; HQ: Virovitica; General Headquarters (MINDOM) Zagreb; 11/41, II Domobran Corps; 08/14/43, II Territorial Corps; 04/01/44, incorporated into the **Mobile Brigade**): 08/41 unknown? 05/43 Maj. Pintarić 09/43 Col. Bona Bunić 04/01/44 incorporated into the **Mobile Brigade**.

Independent Cavalry Group (Samostalni Konjanička Sklop) (04/24/41?; HQ: Brus General Headquarters (MINDOM) Zagreb; 11/41, III Domobran Corps; 05/42 incorporated into the **Zagreb Cavalry Regiment**): unknown? 05/42 incorporated into the **Zagreb Cavalry Regiment**.

Jäger Brigades

1st Jäger Brigade (1. Lovački Zdrug) (05/01/43, II Territorial Corps; 10/44, disbanded): 05/43 unknown? 10/43 BG Franjo Nikolić (retired) 10/44 disbanded.
A.   *Components - 1st Jäger Brigade*
    1.   **4th Jäger Regiment** (05/01/43)
    2.   **6th Jäger Regiment** (05/01/43)

2nd Jäger Brigade (2. Lovački Zdrug) (04/43, I Territorial Corps; 12/01/44, renamed **10th Jäger Brigade**): 04/43 Col. Juraj Čordašić (11/43, Commanding Officer, 14th Infantry Regiment) 06/43 Col. Josip Bučar (04/01/44, Commanding Officer, 5th Garrison Brigade) 11/43 Col. Zinković 12/01/44, renamed **10th Jäger Brigade** - see **10th Jäger Brigade**.
A.   *Components - 2nd Jäger Brigade*
    1.   **1st Jäger Regiment** (05/01/43)
    2.   **10th Jäger Regiment**

3rd Jäger Brigade (3. Lovački Zdrug) (05/01/43, II Territorial Corps; 12/01/44, disbanded and used to form **8th Jäger Brigade**): 05/43 Col. Stjepan Mifek (04/01/44, Commanding Officer, 4th Garrison Brigade) 09/29/43 vacant 10/01/43 Col. Mirko Paja 11/43 Col. Julije Fritz (03/22/45, Commanding General, 18th Croatian Infantry Division) 12/01/44 disbanded and used to form **8th Jäger Brigade** - see **8th Jäger Brigade**.
A.   *Components - 3rd Jäger Brigade*
    1.   **5th Jäger Regiment**: (05/01/43; 12/01/44, transferred to 8th Jäger Brigade)
    2.   **8th Jäger Regiment** (08/43)

4th Jäger Brigade (4. Lovački Zdrug) (02/11/43, III Territorial Corps; 07/43, II Territorial Corps; 11/13/44, disbanded and used to form **7th Jäger Brigade**): 02/11/43 Col. Vladimir Metikoš (10/44, Commanding General, Banja Luka Brigade (#2)) 04/43 Col. Stjepan Gaščić 02/44 Col. Zvonimir Stimaković 07/44 Col. Julije Reš (acting) 08/02/44 unknown? 11/13/44 disbanded and used to form **7th Jäger Brigade** - see **7th Jäger Brigade**.
A.   *Components - 4th Jäger Brigade*
    1.   **7th Jäger Regiment** (05/01/43)
    2.   **13th Jäger Regiment** (02/18/43; 11/13/44, transferred to 7th Jäger Brigade)

7th Jäger Brigade (7. Lovački Zdrug) (11/13/44, from **4th Jäger Brigade**, assigned to II Territorial Corps; 12/44, 4th Croatian Infantry Division; 05/02/45?, destroyed): LCol. Aleksander Kolaković 05/02/45? destroyed.
A.   *Components - 7th Jäger Brigade*
    1.   **13th Jäger Regiment**

8th Jäger Brigade (8. Lovački Zdrug) (12/01/44, from **3rd Jäger Brigade**, assigned to 3rd Croatian Infantry Division): 12/01/44 Col. Isović 01/45 Maj. Čado (acting) 02/45 Col. Janko Milčić.
A.   *Components - 8th Jäger Brigade*
    1.   **5th Jäger Regiment**

10th Jäger Brigade (10. Lovački Zdrug) (12/01/44, from **2nd Jäger Brigade**, assigned to 10th Croatian Infantry Division; 05/02/45?, dissolved.): 12/01/44 Col. Dušan Rajković (Commanding Officer, 10th Croatian Infantry Division) 03/45 unknown? 05/02/45? Dissolved.

Mountain Brigades

1ˢᵗ Mountain Brigade (1. Gorski Zdrug) (04/42, 1ˢᵗ Mountain Division; 08/43 I Territorial Corps; 12/01/44, 7ᵗʰ Croatian Mountain Division): 04/42 Col. Josip Šolc [+ 07/30/43, Commanding Officer, Zagreb Garrison Brigade] 08/43 Col. Stjepan vitez [Knight] Peričić (Commanding General, 7ᵗʰ Croatian Mountain Division) 12/44 LCol. Petar Gregurić.

A. **Components - 1ˢᵗ Mountain Brigade**
   1. **1ˢᵗ Mountain Regiment** (04/42 to 05/45)
   2. **5ᵗʰ Mountain Regiment** (04/42 to 05/45)

2ⁿᵈ Mountain Brigade (2. Gorski Zdrug) (04/42, 1ˢᵗ Mountain Division; 08/43 III Territorial Corps; 12/01/44, 9ᵗʰ Croatian Mountain Division): 04/42 Col. Božidar Zorn (acting) 08/42 Col. Arnold Redelstein (06/43, acting Commanding Officer, 3ʳᵈ Mountain Brigade) 10/42 unknown? 09/43 Col. Bogdan Majetić 10/43 unknown? 02/44 Col. Božidar Zorn (Commanding General, 9ᵗʰ Croatian Mountain Division) 12/01/44 unknown? 02/45 Col. Pletikoš [Pletikose] 05/45

A. **Components - 2ⁿᵈ Mountain Brigade**
   1. **2ⁿᵈ Mountain Regiment** (04/42 to 05/45)
   2. **6ᵗʰ Mountain Regiment** (04/42 to 05/45)

3ʳᵈ Mountain Brigade "Bosnian Mountaineers" (3. Gorski Zdrug) (04/42, 1ˢᵗ Mountain Division; 08/12/43 II Territorial Corps; 12/01/44, 12ᵗʰ Croatian Infantry Division): 03/21/42 Col. Dragutin Rubčić 06/42 unknown? 01/43 Col. Franjo Gjoić 05/43 Col. Milan Kereković (acting) 06/43 Col. Arnold Redelstein (acting) 06/43 unknown? 09/01/43 Col. Stjepan Grlić (Commanding Officer, 4ᵗʰ Mountain Brigade) 10/26/43 BG Mirko Gregurić (Commanding General, Poelavnik Bodyguard Corps) 09/18/44 unknown? 12/01/44 LCol. Andjelko Švab.

A. **Components - 3ʳᵈ Mountain Brigade**
   1. **3ʳᵈ Mountain Regiment** (04/42 to 05/45)
   2. **11ᵗʰ Mountain Regiment** (04/42 to 05/45)
   3. **12ᵗʰ Infantry Regiment**: 08/01/43 unknown? 04/17/44 disbanded, remnants absorbed into 3ʳᵈ Mountain Brigade.

4ᵗʰ Mountain Brigade (4. Gorski Zdrug) (04/42, 1ˢᵗ Mountain Division; 08/12/43 II Territorial Corps; 12/01/44, 7ᵗʰ Croatian Mountain Division): 03/21/42 unknown? 01/43 Col. Stjepan Grlić (09/01/43, Commanding Officer, 3ʳᵈ Mountain Brigade) 02/43 unknown? 08/07/43 BG Matija Čanić (Commanding General, II Territorial Corps) 10/26/43 Col. Stjepan Grlić (/45, Commanding General, 9ᵗʰ Croatian Mountain Division) 09/44 unknown? 11/44 Col. Viktor Marković.

.   **Components - 4ᵗʰ Mountain Brigade**
   1. **4ᵗʰ Mountain Regiment** (04/42 to 05/45)
   2. **8ᵗʰ Mountain Regiment** (04/42 to 05/45)

5ᵗʰ Mountain Brigade (5. Gorski Zdrug) (02/15/43, I Domobran Territorial Corps): 02/15/43 Col. Lalić (Partisans prisoner-of-war) 05/29/43 LCol. Dragutin Brkić (04/01/44, Commanding Officer, 3ʳᵈ Garrison Brigade) 08/01/43 disbanded.

6th Mountain Brigade (6. Gorski Zdrug): NOT FORMED. Formation was planned, but, no evidence that it was ever formed.

7th Mountain Brigade (7. Gorski Zdrug) (10/42, and transport by train for training in Austria; 04/43?, disbandedat Stockerau, Austria and all personnel incorporated into **373rd German-Croatian Legion Division** [see Volume I - Germany]): 10/42 unknown? 04/43? disbandedat Stockerau, Austria and all personnel incorporated into **373rd German-Croatian Legion Division** - see Volume I - Germany.

Garrison Brigades

1st Garrison Brigade (1. Posadni Zdrug) (04/01/44, from **2nd Infantry Regiment**, assigned to I Territorial Corps; HQ: Križevci; 12/01/44, reformed as the **11th Domobran Brigade**): 04/01/44 Col. Cihak (Commanding Officer, 1st (Domobran) Replacement Brigade) 09/01/44 Col. Hinko Karl 12/01/44 reformed as the **11th Domobran Brigade** - see **11th Domobran Brigade**.

2nd Garrison Brigade (2. Posadni Zdrug) (04/01/44, from **3rd Infantry Regiment**, assigned to I Territorial Corps; HQ: Karlovac; 12/01/44, reformed as the **12th Domobran Brigade**): 04/01/44 LCol. Slavko Miletić 09/44 LCol. Dragutin Cubelić 12/01/44 reformed as the **12th Domobran Brigade** - see **12th Domobran Brigade**.

3rd Garrison Brigade (3. Posadni Zdrug) (04/01/44, I Territorial Corps; HQ: Gospić; 12/01/44, reformed as the **13th Domobran Brigade**): 04/01/44 Col. Dragutin Brkić 07/23/44 unknown? 09/44 Sub-Maj. Japunčić (acting) 09/44 unknown? 12/01/44 reformed as the **13th Domobran Brigade** - see **13th Domobran Brigade**.

4th Garrison Brigade (4. Posadni Zdrug) (04/01/44, I Territorial Corps; HQ: Sisak; 12/01/44, reformed as the **14th Domobran Brigade**): 04/01/44 Col. Stjepan Mifek (12/01/44 reformed as the **14th Domobran Brigade** - see **14th Domobran Brigade**.

5th Garrison Brigade (5. Posadni Zdrug) (04/01/44, II Territorial Corps; HQ: Nova Gradiška; 12/01/44, reformed as the **15th Domobran Brigade**): 04/01/44 Col. Josip Bučar 12/01/44 reformed as the **15th Domobran Brigade** - see **15th Domobran Brigade**.

6th Garrison Brigade (6. Posadni Zdrug) (04/01/44, II Territorial Corps; HQ: Doboj; 12/01/44, reformed as the **16th Domobran Brigade**): 04/01/44 unknown? 12/01/44 reformed as the **16th Domobran Brigade** - see **16th Domobran Brigade**.

7th Garrison Brigade (7. Posadni Zdrug) (04/01/44, II Territorial Corps; HQ: Hrvatska Mitrovica; 12/01/44, reformed as the **17th Domobran Brigade**): Col. Gjurgjević 12/01/44 reformed as the **17th Domobran Brigade** - see **17th Domobran Brigade**.

8th Garrison Brigade (8. Posadni Zdrug) (04/01/44, III Territorial Corps; HQ: Sarajevo; 12/01/44 reformed as the **18th Domobran Brigade**): 04/01/44 Col. Juraj Čordašić 12/01/44 reformed as the **18th Domobran Brigade** - see **18th Domobran Brigade**.

9th Garrison Brigade (9. Posadni Zdrug) (04/01/44, III Territorial Corps; HQ: Dubrovnik; 12/01/44, absorbed into **9th Croatian Mountain Division**): 04/01/44 Col. Stjepan Zuech 12/01/44 absorbed into **9th Croatian Mountain Division**.

10th Garrison Brigade (10. Posadni Zdrug) (04/01/44, II Territorial Corps; HQ: Tuzla; 12/01/44, absorbed into **3rd Mountain Brigade "Bosnian Mountaineers"**): 04/01/44 LCol. Andjelko Švab (Commanding Officer, 3rd Mountain Brigade) 11/30/44 absorbed into 3rd

Mountain Brigade "Bosnian Mountaineers".

Zagreb Garrison Brigade (Zagrebački Posadni Zdrug) (07/20/43, HQ Zagreb City Command; 04/01/44, I Territorial Corps; 12/01/44, reformed as **20th Domobran Brigade**): 07/20/43 Col. Josip Šolc (03/45, Commanding Officer, 1st Assault Division) 08/44 unknown? 12/01/44, reformed **20th Domobran Brigade** - see **20th Domobran Brigade**.

Ustaša [Ustaša] Garrison Brigade Zagreb (Zagrebačka Ustaška Posadna Zdrug) (04/44, HQ: Zagreb, I Territorial Corps; 12/01/44, renamed **20th Ustaša [Ustaša] Brigade**): 04/44 unknown? 12/01/44 renamed **20th Ustaša [Ustaša] Brigade** - see **20th Ustaša [Ustaša] Brigade**.

Domobran Brigades

11ᵗʰ Domobran Brigade (11. Pješački Zdrug) (12/01/44, from **1ˢᵗ Garrison Brigade**, and assigned to 5ᵗʰ Croatian Infantry Division; 03/45, 5ᵗʰ Croatian Assault Division; HQ: Križevci): 12/01/44 unknown?

12ᵗʰ Domobran Brigade (12. Pješački Zdrug) (12/01/44, from **2ⁿᵈ Garrison Brigade**, and assigned to the 13ᵗʰ Croatian Infantry Division; HQ: Karlovac): 12/01/44 Col. Djuno Sivoš.

13ᵗʰ Domobran Brigade (13. Pješački Zdrug) (12/01/44, from **3ʳᵈ Garrison Brigade**, and assigned to the 11ᵗʰ Croatian Infantry Division; HQ: Gospić area): 12/01/44 unknown?

14ᵗʰ Domobran Brigade (14. Pješački Zdrug) (12/01/44, from **4ᵗʰ Garrison Brigade**, and assigned to the 11ᵗʰ Croatian Infantry Division; HQ: Sisak): 12/01/44 Col. Sočarin.

15ᵗʰ Domobran Brigade (15. Pješački Zdrug) (12/01/44, from **5ᵗʰ Garrison Brigade**, and assigned to the 6ᵗʰ Croatian Infantry Division; HQ: Nova Gradiška): 12/01/44 Col. Josip Bućar.

16ᵗʰ Domobran Brigade (16. Pješački Zdrug) (12/01/44, from **6ᵗʰ Garrison Brigade**, and assigned to the 15ᵗʰ Croatian Infantry Division; HQ: Doboj): 12/01/44 LCol. Djordjo Novak 02/45

17ᵗʰ Domobran Brigade (17. Pješački Zdrug) (12/01/44, from **7ᵗʰ Garrison Brigade**, and assigned to the 11ᵗʰ Croatian Infantry Division; HQ: Syrmia): 12/01/44 unknown?

18ᵗʰ Domobran Brigade (18. Pješački Zdrug) (12/01/44, from **8ᵗʰ Garrison Brigade**, and assigned to the 18ᵗʰ Croatian Infantry Division; HQ: Sarajevo): 12/01/44 unknown?

19ᵗʰ Domobran Brigade (19. Pješački Zdrug) (12/01/44, from railway security battalions, and assigned to the 14ᵗʰ Croatian Infantry Division; HQ: Virovitica): 12/01/44 unknown?

20ᵗʰ Domobran Brigade (20. Pješački Zdrug) (12/01/44, from **4ᵗʰ Garrison Brigade**, and assigned to the 2ⁿᵈ Croatian Infantry Division; HQ: Zagreb; 04/29/45, disbanded and used to form the new **26ᵗʰ Infantry Regiment** and the **27ᵗʰ Infantry Regiment**): 12/01/44 unknown? 04/29/45 disbanded and used to form the new **26ᵗʰ Infantry Regiment** and the **27ᵗʰ Infantry Regiment**.

Replacements Brigades

1st (Domobran) Replacement Brigade (1. Doknadni Zdrug) (02/44, by expanding the **2nd Recruit Regiment**, I Territorial Corps; HQ: Zagreb; 12/01/44, redesignated **21st (Domobran) Replacement Brigade**): 02/44 LCol. K. Zivanević 05/44 Col. Stjepan Mateša 09/01/44 Col. Cihak (Commanding Officer, 21st (Domobran) Replacement Brigade) 12/01/44 redesignated **21st (Domobran) Replacement Brigade** - see **21st (Domobran) Replacement Brigade**.

2nd (Domobran) Replacement Brigade (2. Doknadni Zdrug) (02/44, by expanding the **1st Recruit Regiment**, II Territorial Corps; HQ: Vinkovci; 12/01/44, disbanded): 02/44 vacant 03/44 BG Ivan Šarnbek (retired) 10/44 Maj. Skaldini (acting) 11/44 LCol. Dorwhaide 10/44 12/01/44 disbanded.

3rd (Domobran) Replacement Brigade (3. Doknadni Zdrug) (02/44, by expanding the **3rd Recruit Regiment**, III Territorial Corps; HQ: Sarajevo; 12/01/44, redesignated **23rd (Domobran) Replacement Brigade**): 02/44 unknown? 12/01/44 redesignated **23rd (Domobran) Replacement Brigade** - see **23rd (Domobran) Replacement Brigade**.

21st (Domobran) Replacement Brigade (21. Doknadni Zdrug) (12/01/44, from **1st (Domobran) Replacement Brigade**, assigned to the 16th Croatian Replacement Division; HQ: Zagreb; 04/45, redesignated **XXI Ustasha Replacement Brigade**): 12/01/44 Col. Cihak 04/45 redesignated **XXI Ustasha Replacement Brigade** - see **XXI Ustasha Replacement Brigade**.

22nd (Domobran) Replacement Brigade (22. Doknadni Zdrug): NOT FORMED. This Brigade was suppose to be formed on 12/01/44, but no evidence has been found that this was carried out.

23rd (Domobran) Replacement Brigade (23. Doknadni Zdrug) (12/01/44, from **3rd (Domobran) Replacement Brigade**; HQ: Sarajevo; 04/45, redesignated **XXII Ustasha Replacement Brigade**): 12/01/44 unknown? 04/45 redesignated **XXII Ustasha Replacement Brigade** - see **XXII Ustasha Replacement Brigade**.

20th Ustaša [Ustasha] Replacement Brigade (20. Ustaški Doknadni Zdrug) (12/01/44, 16th Croatian Replacement Division; 04/15/45, redesignated **Ustaša [Ustasha] Training Brigade**): 12/01/44 unknown? 04/45 redesignated **Ustaša [Ustasha] Training Brigade** - see **Ustaša [Ustasha] Training Brigade**.

21st Ustaša [Ustasha] Replacement Brigade (21. Ustaški Doknadni Zdrug) (04/45, from **21st (Domobran) Replacement Brigade**, 16th Croatian Replacement Division):04/45 unknown?

22nd Ustaša [Ustasha] Replacement Brigade (22. Ustaški Doknadni Zdrug) (04/45, from **23rd (Domobran) Replacement Brigade**, 16th Croatian Replacement Division):04/45 unknown?

Ustaša [Ustašha] Training Brigade (Ustaški Nastavni Zdrug) (04/15/45, from **20th Ustaša [Ustašha] Replacement Brigade**, 16th Croatian Replacement Division): 04/15/45 unknown? 05/06/45.

Miscellaneous Units (Brigade Status)

Territorial Defense Command (04/24/41) BG Julio Sach (killed in action) /44

Bosnia-Herzegovian Department (04/24/41): Col. Matija Čanić [+ to 05/29/41, Commanding Offiecr, Expeditionary Regiment] (Commanding Officer, 2nd Infantry Division) 09/42
A.   *Components - Bosnia-Herzegovian Department*
    1.   **Expeditionary Regiment** (04/20/41, in Zagreb; 05/29/41, disbanded in Sarajevo): Col. Matija Čanić [+ 04/24/41, Commanding Officer, Bosnia-Herzegovian Department] 05/29/41 disbanded.

1st Traffic Control Brigade Ustaša [Ustašha] Militia (I. Prometna Zdrug Ustaška Vojnica) (02/43, HQ: Zagreb; 08/44, redesignated **10th Ustaša [Ustašha] Brigade**): 02/43 unknown? 08/44 redesignated **10th Ustaša [Ustašha] Brigade** - see **10th Ustaša [Ustašha] Brigade**.

2nd Traffic Control Brigade Ustaša [Ustašha] Militia (II. Prometna Zdrug Ustaška Vojnica) (02/43, HQ: Sarajevo; 08/44, redesignated **11th Ustaša [Ustašha] Brigade**): 02/43 unknown? 05/44 LCol. Krešimir Kuraja (Commanding Officer, 11th Ustaša [Ustašha] Brigade) 08/44 redesignated **11th Ustaša [Ustašha] Brigade** - see **11th Ustaša [Ustašha] Brigade**.

Popular-Ustaša [Ustašha] Brigade (Pučko-Ustaška Zdrug) (12/01/44, in Vinkovci from the **2nd replacement Brigade** and remnants of the **7th Garrison Brigade**; 12/44, Croatian Command "Istok"; 03/45, disbanded.): 12/01/44 BG Josip Metzger (Commanding General, IV Ustaša [Ustašha] Corps) 03/45 disbanded.
A.   *Components - Popular-Ustaša [Ustašha] Brigade*
    1.   **1st Popular-Ustaša [Ustašha] Regiment "Baranja"**: 12/01/44 Col. Djuro Gebauer
    2.   **2nd Popular-Ustaša [Ustašha] Regiment "Vuka"**: 12/01/44 LCol. Rudolf Jagić
    3.   **3rd Popular-Ustaša [Ustašha] Regiment "Posavlje"**: 12/01/44 Col. Vladimir Klaić

Ustaša [Ustašha] Demi-Brigade Zadar (Ustaška Zadarski Poluzdrug) (07/44, HQ: Donji Zemunik; 09/44, disbanded): 07/44 LCol. Petar Zelić 09/44 disbanded.

1st Ustaša [Ustašha] Guard Brigade (1. Ustaška Obrabena Zdrug) (01/42, HQ: Lipik, Ustaša [Ustašha] Surveillance Service; 03/45 II Ustaša [Ustašha] Corps): 01/42 Col. Slavko Skoliber (Commanding Officer, Nova Gradiška Brigade) 03/42 LCol. Frane Primorac (Commanding Officer, 2nd Ustaša [Ustašha] Guard Brigade) 07/42 unknown? 01/43 Col. Marko Pavlović 04/44 unknown? 05/06/45.

2nd Ustaša [Ustašha] Guard Brigade (2. Ustaška Obrabena Zdrug) (07/42, HQ:

unknown?, Ustaša [Ustašha] Surveillance Service; 12/43, disbanded): 07/42 LCol. Frane Primorac 12/43 disbanded.

Air Force of the Independent State of Croatia

Roundel 41-44   Roundel 44-45

[Zrakoplovstvo Nezavisne Države Hrvatske (ZNDH)]

Commander-in-Chief, Croatian Air Force (04/24/41; HQ: Zagreb): BG Vladimir Kren [CAF] (retired) 09/14/43 BG Adalbert Rogulja [CAF] (after war, died in Yugoslavia jail) 06/04/44 MG [Retired 09/43] Vladimir Kren [CAF] (escaped to Austria; /47, arrested and extradited to Yugoslavia; sentenced to death; /48, executed) 05/45.

A.   **Air Force Wing** (HQ: Zagreb):
1.   **1st Air Force Group** (HQ: Zagreb-Borongaj):
2.   **2nd Air Force Group** (HQ: Sarajevo-Rajlovač):
3.   **3rd Air Force Group** (HQ: Mostar):
4.   **4th Air Force Group** (HQ: Zemun):
5.   **5th Air Force Group** (HQ: Banialuka):

B.   **Air Defense Wing** (HQ: Zagreb):
1.   **1st Air Defense Group** (HQ: Unknown?):
2.   **2nd Air Defense Group** (HQ: Unknown?):
3.   **3rd Air Defense Group** (HQ: Jasenovač):
4.   **4th Air Defense Group** (HQ: Sisak):
5.   **5th Air Defense Group** (HQ: Brod na Savi):

C.   **Croatian Air Force Training Wing** (07/21/44; from **Croatian Air Force Legion**, formed in 1941, when it was disbanded): **Croatian Air Force Legion** /41 Col. Ivan Mrak [CAF] (02/42, Commanding Officer, Petrinja Brigade) 07/21/44 disbanded; reformed as **Croatian Air Force Training Wing** 07/21/44 Col. Franjo Džal [CAF] 05/45.
1.   **4th Fighter Wing**: Maj. Franjo Džal [CAF] (Commanding Officer, Croatian Air Force Training Wing) 07/21/44
2.   **5th Bomber Wing**: Maj. Vjekoslav Vicević [CAF] /4? Maj. Vladimir Graovać [CAF] 05/45.

Croatian Air Force Legion [Hrvatska Zrakoplovna Legija (HZL)] (/41, Eastern Front; /43, transferred back to Croatia): BG Ivan Mrak [CAF] (**?**)

A.   *Components* - **Croatian Air Force Legion**
1.   **4th Fighter Wing**: /41 Maj. Franjo Džal [CAF] 07/21/44 Transferred to Croatian Air Force Training Wing.
2.   **5th Bomber Wing**: Maj. Vjekoslav Vicević [CAF] /4? Maj. Vladimir Graovać [CAF] 07/21/44 Transferred to Croatian Air Force Training Wing.

Croatian Navy

Commander-in-Chief, Croatian Navy (04/24/41; HQ: Zagreb): RA Djuro Jakčin [CN] (?) /43 RA Edgar Angeli [CN] (?) 01/44 RA Nikola Steinfl [Steinfel] [CN] [+ 08/44, Minister of the Armed Forces] (after war, executed) 05/45.

A. **Coast & Maritime Traffic Command** (HQ: Split):
    1. **North Adriatic Naval Command** (HQ: Crikvenica):
        a. **Kraljevica Naval District:**
        b. **Senij Naval District:**
    2. **Central Adriatic Naval Command** (HQ: Makarska):
        a. **Omis Naval District:**
        b. **Supertar Naval District:**
        c. **Makarska Naval District:**
        d. **Metkovic Naval District:**
        e. **Hvar Naval District:**
    3. **South Adriatic Naval Command** (HQ: Dubrovnik):
        a. **Trpanji Naval District:**
        b. **Orebic Naval District:**
        c. **Dubrovnik Naval District:**
B. **River & River Traffic Command** (HQ: Sisak):
    1. **River Flotilla Command** (HQ: Zemun; Flag: River Tugboat *Vrbas*):
        a. **1st Patrol Group:** River Patrol Boat *Sava*, River Gunboat *Ustaša [Ustašha]*, River Minelayer *Zagreb*, + 3 Motor Boats
        b. **2nd Patrol Group:** River Patrol Boat *Bosna*, River Gunboat *Bosut*, River Minelayer *Zrinski*, + 3 Motor Boats

Croatian Naval Legion (04/24/41): Capt. Andro Urkljan [CN] 01/42 Capt. Stjepan Rumenović [CN] 05/45.

Table of Equivalent Ranks

Croatian Army & Air Force	United States & British Army
Vojskovodja	General of the Army [U. S.] Field Marshal [Brit.]
Pukovnik General	General
General Pješastva (Infantry) General Topništva (Artillery) General Konjaništva (Cavalry)	Lieutenant General
Podmaršal	Major General
General	Brigadier General [U. S.] Brigadier [Brit.]
Pukovnik	Colonel
Podpukovnik	Lieutenant Colonel
Bojnik	Major
Nadstnik (Sub-major)	No equalivent
Satnik	Captain
Oberleutnant	First Lieutenant [U.S.] Lieutenant [Brit.]
Leutnant	Second Lieutenant

Table of Equivalent Ranks

Croatian Navy	United States & British Navy
	Fleet Admiral [U. S.] Admiral of the Fleet [Brit.]
Admiral	Admiral
Viceadmiral	Vice Admiral
Kontraadmiral	Rear Admiral
Kapetan Bojnog broda	Commodore
Kapetan fregate	Captain
Kapetan korvete	Commander
Natporucnik bojnog broda	Lieutenant Commander
Porucnik fregate	Lieutenant [U.S.] Lieutenant (Senior) [Brit.]
Porucnik korvete	Lieutenant (Junior Grade) [U.S.] Lieutenant (Junnior) [Brit]
Brodski Zastavnik	Ensign [U.S.] Sub-Lieutenant [Brit.]

SERBIA

(German Puppet State)

Serbian Government

Commissary Government
April 30, 1941 to August 29, 1941
[First Puppet Government of German occupied Serbia during World War II]

OO Serbia, 1941-1944

O Banat region with special status, administered by local German minority

— borders within Axis-controled Europe

President & Prime Minister of Commissary Government (04/30/41): MILAN AĆIMOVIĆ [+ Commissary for Interior Affairs] (Minister of Interior Affairss, Government of National Salvation Serbia) 08/29/41 Government becomes **Government of National Salvation Serbia**.

A. **Commissary for Interior Affairs** (04/30/41): MILAN AĆIMOVIĆ [+ President & Prime Minister] 08/29/41 disbanded.

    1. **First Deputy, Commissary for Interior Affairs** (07/11/41): TANASIJE DINIĆ (11/10/42, Minister of Internal Affairs, Government of National Salvation Serbia) 08/29/41 disbanded.

    2. **Second Deputy, Commissary for Interior Affairs** (07/11/41): ĐORĐE PERIĆ 08/29/41 disbanded.

B. **Commissary for Finance** (04/30/41): DUŠAN LETICA 08/29/41 (10/07/41, Minister for Finances, Government of National Salvation Serbia) disbanded.

    1. **Deputy, Commissary for Finance** (07/11/41): MILAN HORVATSKI 08/29/41 disbanded.

C. **Commissary for Justice** (04/30/41): MOMČILO JANKOVIĆ 08/29/41 disbanded.

    1. **Deputy, Commissary for Justice** (07/11/41): Dr. ĐURA KOTUR 08/29/41 disbanded.

D. **Commissary for Education** (04/30/41): RISTO JOJIĆ 07/11/41 VELIBOR JONIĆ 08/29/41 disbanded.

    1. **Deputy, Commissary for Education** (07/11/41): VLADIMIR VELMAR-JANKOVIĆ 08/29/41 disbanded.

E. **Commissary for Post Offices & Telegraph** (04/30/41): DUŠAN PANTIĆ 08/29/41 disbanded.

    1. **Deputy, Commissary for Post Offices & Telegraph** (07/11/41): MILORAD DIMITRIJEVIĆ 08/29/41 disbanded.

F. **Commissary for People's Economy** (04/30/41): MILOSAV VASILJEVIĆ 08/29/41 disbanded.

    1. **Deputy, Commissary for People's Economy** (07/11/41): Dr. MIHAJLOVIĆ 08/29/41 disbanded.

G.   **Commissary for Traffic** (04/30/41): Dr. LAZAR KOSTIĆ 07/11/41 RANISAV AVRAMOVIĆ 08/29/41 disbanded.

     1.   **Deputy, Commissary for Traffic** (07/11/41): NIKOLA ĐURIĆ 08/29/41 disbanded.

H.   **Commissary for Social Policy** (04/30/41): Dr. STEVAN IVANIĆ (Commissary for Social Policy and People's Health) 07/11/41 renamed **Commissary for Social Policy and People's Health** 07/11/41 Dr. STEVAN IVANIĆ 08/29/41 disbanded.

     1.   **Deputy, Commissary for Social Policy and People's Health** (07/11/41): BOŽIDAR-DARKO PETROVIĆ 08/29/41 disbanded.

I.   **Commissary for Buildings** (04/30/41): STANISLAV JOSIFOVIĆ 08/29/41 disbanded.

     1.   **no deputy**

J.   **Commissary for Food** (04/30/41): JEREMIJA PROTIĆ 07/11/41 BUDIMIR CVIJANOVIĆ 08/29/41 disbanded.

     1.   **no deputy**

Government of National Salvation Serbia

August 29, 1941 to October 1944

[Second Puppet Government of German occupation Serbia during World War II]

President, Prime Minister, & President of the Council of Ministers of the Government of National Salvation Serbia (08/29/41): Gen. Milan Dj. Nedić [+ /43, Minister of Home Affairs, Serbia] (1946, committed suicide) 12/44

A. **Minister of Interior Affairs** (08/29/41): MILAN AĆIMOVIĆ 11/10/42 TANASIJE DINIĆ (Minister of Social Policy and People's Health) 11/06/43 Gen. Milan Dj. Nedić [+ President, Prime Minister & President of the Council of Ministers of the Government of National Salvation Serbia] (1946, committed suicide) 10/44 dissolved.

B. **Minister of Finances** (08/29/41): Dr. LJUBIŠA MIKIĆ 10/07/41 DUŠAN LETICA 11/10/42 DUŠAN ĐORĐEVIĆ 10/44 dissolved.

C. **Minister of Justice** (08/29/41): Dr. ČEDOMIR MARJANOVIĆ 11/10/42 BOGOLJUB KUJUNDŽIĆ 10/44 dissolved.

D. **Minister of Education** (08/29/41): Dr. MILOŠ TRIVUNAC 10/07/41 VELIBOR JONIĆ 10/44 dissolved.

E. **Minister of Post Offices, Telegraphs & Telephones** (08/29/41): JOSIF KOSTIĆ 10/44 dissolved.

F. **Minister of People's Economy** (08/29/41): MIHAILO OLĆAN 11/10/42 Dr. MILORAD NEDELJKOVIĆ 10/44 dissolved.

G. **Minister of Social Policy and People's Health** (08/29/41): Dr. JOVAN MIJUŠKOVIĆ 11/10/42 STOJIMIR DOBROSAVLJEVIĆ 11/06/43 TANASIJE DINIĆ 10/44 dissolved.

H. **Minister of Buildings** (08/29/41): OGNJEN KUZMANOVIĆ 10/44 dissolved.

I. **Minister of Agriculture and Food** (08/29/41): Dr. MILOŠ RADOSAVLJEVIĆ 11/10/42 RADOSAV VESELINOVIĆ 10/44 dissolved.

J. **Minister of Labor** (08/29/41): PANTA DRAŠKIĆ 10/07/41 dissolved.

K. **Minister of Traffic (Transportation)** (10/07/41): BG Đura Dokić (?   ) 10/44 dissolved.

L. **Minister within Presidency of the Council of Ministers** (08/29/41): MOMČILO JANKOVIĆ 10/07/41 dissolved.

German Forces in Serbia

German Regional Commander, Serbia (04/19/41; HQ: Belgrade) GdFl Hellmuth Förster [GAF] [+ 05/15/41, Commanding General, German I Air Corps] 06/03/41 GdFk Ludwig von Schröder [GAF] (?) 07/29/41 GdFl Heinrich Danckelmann [GAF] (retired/officer reserve pool) 09/16/41 GdA Paul Bader [German] [+ Commanding General, German LXV Corps Command] (Commanding General, German XXI Mountain Corps) 08/25/43 redesignated Military Regional Commander Southeast

A. **German Deputy Commander, Serbia**: 07/19/41 GdA Paul Bader [German] [+ Commanding General, German LXV Corps Command] (German Regional Commander, Serbia) 09/16/41

B. **German LXV Corps Command**: GdI Hans G. Felber [German] (Commanding General, German XIII Army Corps) 10/25/40 GdI Franz Böhme [German] (Commanding General, German XVIII Mountain Corps) 05/25/41 GdI Paul Bader [German] [+ 07/19/41, German Deputy Commander, Serbia; + 09/16/41, German Regional Commander, Serbia] 04/10/42 disbanded.

    1. Chief of Staff, German LXV Corps Command: LCol. Bode [German]

Italian Forces in Serbia

Italian Commander-in-Chief (Italian Second Army): Gen. Vittorio Ambrosio [Ital] (Chief of the Italian Army General Staff) [see Volume VI - Italy and France] 01/42 LG Mario Roatta [Ital] (Commander-in-Chief, Italian Sixth Army) [see Volume VI - Italy and France] 02/43 LG Mario Robotti [Ital] (?) [see Volume VI - Italy and France] 09/08/43 disbanded.

Serbian Armed Forces
Overall Command

Serbian Volunteer Corps of the SS: /41 MG Dimitrije Ljotić (auto accident; /45, died from injuries in from the auto accident) 04/23/44

Corps

Serbian Chetnik's (05/41): MG Kosta Milovanović Pećanac (assassinated by Yugoslavian Chetniks) 06/06/41

Serbian Volunteer Command (09/17/41; 11/22/41, becomes **Šumadija Corps**): Col. Konstantin Mušicki (Commanding General, Šumadija Corps) 11/22/41 becomes **Šumadija Corps**.
1.　　**Education Department, Serbian Volunteer Command**: RATKO PAREŽANIN (journalist)

Šumadija Corps (11/22/41, from **Serbian Volunteer Command**; 01/01/43, redesignated **Serbian Volunteer Corps**) MG Konstantin Mušicki (arrested by the Germans; 11/42, released) 12/09/41 BG Ilija Kukić (　?　) 11/42 MG Konstantin Mušicki (Commanding General, Serbian Volunteer Corps) 01/01/43 redesignated **Serbian Volunteer Corps**.

Serbian Volunteer Corps [Sprski Dobrovoljački Korpus] (01/01/43, from **Šumadija Corps**; 05/05/45, surrendered to the British): MG Konstantin Mušicki (08/24/45, captured by the British; turned over to Yugoslavia; sentenced fro war crimes; /46, executed) 03/27/45 MG Damjanović 05/05/45 surrendered to the British.
A.　　**Deputy Commander, Serbian Volunteer Corps**: unknown? 06/43 Maj. Pavle Đurišić
B.　　*Components* - Serbian Volunteer Corps
　　1.　　**1st Volunteer Regiment** (HQ: Valijevo): 01/01/43 Maj. Ilija Mićašević
　　2.　　**2nd Volunteer Regiment** (HQ: Kragujevac): 01/01/43 Maj. Marisav Petrović
　　3.　　**3rd Volunteer Regiment** (HQ: Šabac): 01/01/43 Maj. Jovan Dobrosavljević
　　4.　　**4th Volunteer Regiment** (HQ: Smederevo)): 01/01/43 Maj. Vojislav Dimitrijević
　　5.　　**5th Volunteer Regiment** (HQ: Kruševac):

Serbian State Guard [Srpska Držauna Straža] (03/03/42; 10/44, merged with the **Serbian Frontier Guard** to form the **1st Serbian Shock Corps**): unknown? 10/44 merged with the **Serbian Frontier Guard** to form the **1st Serbian Shock Corps**.
A.　　*Components* - Serbian State Guard
　　1.　　**Danube Regiment**
　　2.　　**Drina Regiment**

1st Serbian Shock Corps (10/44, formed from the merger of the **Serbian State Guard** and the **Serbian Frontier Gurad**; 05/45, surrendered to the British): unknown? 05/45 surrendered to the British.

Russian Corps (05/41; anti-communist Russian emigres living in Serbia; 05/12/45, surrendered to the British): MG Mikhail Pavlovich Skorodumov [Russian] (arrested by the Germans) 09/12/41 MG Boris Shteifon [Russian] (died of a heart attack) 04/30/45 Col. Anatoli Ivanovich Rogozhin [Russian] 05/12/45 surrendered to the British.

A.   ***Components* - Russian Corps**
       5 regiments

FINLAND

(Co-Belligerent)

Finland Government

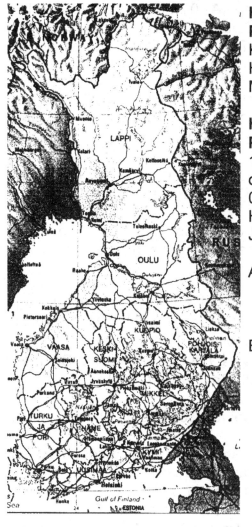

Head of State
President: 03/01/37 KYÖSTI KALLIO 03/12/37 AIMO KAARLO CAJANDER 12/01/39 11/27/40 RISTO HEIKKI RYTI [+ to 01/41, Prime Minister] 08/04/44 Marshal of Finland Carl Gustaf Emil Mannerheim.

Head of Government
Prime Minister: 03/12/37 AIMO KAARLO CAJANDER 12/01/39 RISTO HEIKKI RYTI [+ 11/27/40, President of Finland] 01/04/41 JOHANNES VILHELM RANGELL 03/05/43 EDWIN LINKOMIES 09/08/44 ANTTI HACKZELL 10/21/44 URHO CASTREN 11/17/44 JUHO KUSTI PAASIKIVI.

A.   **Deputy Prime Minister**: 03/12/37 unknown? 12/19/40 Gdl [Retired '20] Karl Rudolf Walden [+ Defense Minister] 01/04/41

B.   **Council of State Minister** (11/17/44):
11/17/44 MAUNO PEKKALA [+ 04/17/45, Defense Minister].
04/27/45 EERO A. WUORI [+ to 09/29/45, Transport & Public Works Minister; + to 0929/45, Deputy Social Affairs Minister; + to 09/29/45, Deputy People's Service Minister].
10/15/45 EINO KILPI [+ Social Affairs Minister].
1.   **Information Department, State Council**: unknown? /41 MG [Retired '37] Kaarle Heikki Kekoni (retired) /44

C.   **Foreign Affairs Minister**: 03/12/37 RUDOLF HOLSTI 11/16/38 VÄINÖ VOIONMAA [+ Deputy Foreign Minister] 12/01/38 vacant 12/12/38 ELJAS JUHO ERKKO 12/01/39 VÄINÖ TANNER (People's Service Minister) 03/27/40 ROLF WITTING 03/05/43 CARL HENRIK RAMSAY 09/08/44 CARL ENCKELL.
1.   **Deputy Foreign Affairs Minister**: 03/12/37 VÄINÖ VOIONMAA [+ 11/16/38 to 12/01/38, acting Foreign Minister] 12/01/39 unknown? 01/04/41 CARL HENRIK RAMSAY [+ 08/03/42, People's Service Minister] (Foreign Affairs Minister) 03/05/43 unknown? 10/21/44 MG Ilmari Armas-Eino Martola (Commanding General, Uusimaa Military District) 11/17/44 REINHOLD SVENTO.
2.   *Ambassadors*
a.   **Ambassador to Germany [Berlin]**: /38 TOIVO MIKAEL KIVIMÄKI
b.   **Ambassador to the Union of Social Socialist Republics**

[Moscow]: /38 JUHO KUSTI PAASIKIVI [+ 12/01/39 to 03/27/40, Minister without Portfolio] (11/44, Prime Minister) /41

D. **Justice Minister**: 03/18/37 ARVI AHMAVAARA 01/11/38 ALBIN EWALD RAUTAVAARA 10/13/39 JOHANNES OTTO SÖDERERHJELM 03/27/40 OSKARI LEHTONEN 08/08/44 vacant 09/08/44 ERNST VIKTOR LORENTZ von BORN 11/17/44 URHO KEKKONEN.

E. **Interior Minister**: 03/12/37 URHO KEKKONEN (11/17/44, Justice Minister) 12/01/39 ERNST VIKTOR LORENTZ von BORN (09/08/44, Justice Minister) 05/13/41 TOIVO HORELLI 03/05/43 LEO EHRNROOTH 09/08/44 KAARLO KILLILÄ 04/17/45 YRJÖ LEINO.
   1. **Deputy Interior Minister**: unknown? 03/27/40 EEMIL LUUKKA [+ 11/17/44 to 04/17/45, Agriculture Minister; + 04/17/45, Deputy Finance Minister; + 04/17/45, Deputy Agriculture Minister].
   2. **Chief of the Civil Defense, Ministry of Interior**: /38 LG Aarne Sihvo (Commander-in-Chief, Antiaircraft Defense, Headquarters) /41 unknown? /44 LG Aarne Sihvo.

F. **Defense Minister**: 03/12/37 JUHO NIUKKANEN 03/27/40 GdI [Retired '20] Karl Rudolf Walden [+ 12/19/40, Deputy Prime Minister] 12/01/44 LG Väinö Lahja Richard Valve 04/17/45 MAUNO PEKKALA [+ Council of State Minister].
   1. **First Secretary of the Ministry of Defense**: /38 Col. Oiva Oskar Olenius.
   2. **Chairman, Defense Council**: /30 GdI Carl Gustaf Emil Mannerheim (Commander-in-Chief, Armed Forces) 11/39
   3. **Command Section, Ministry of Defense**: /38 Col. Kustaa Anders Tapola (Chief of Staff, Isthmus Army) /39
   4. **Organization Section, Ministry of Defense**: /38 Col. Einar Nikolai Mäkinen (Head, Organization Department, General Headquarters) /39
   5. **Military Affairs Section, Ministry of Defense**: /34 LCol. Einar Nikolai Mäkinen (Chief, Organization Section, Ministry of Defense) /38
   6. **War Economic Department, Ministry of Defense**: /38 MG Leonard August Mathias "Lennart" Grandell [+ Inspector of War Economics] (retired) /44
      a. **Assistant Head, War Economics Department, Ministry of Defense**: /39 MG [Retired '30] Paavo Juho Talvela (Chief of Staff, Armaments Council) /40
   7. **Chairman, Weapon Design Board, Ministry of Defense**: /37 LG Vilho Petter Nenonen (Head, Finnish War Material Procurement Delegation in the United States) /40
   8. **Intendant-General Department, Ministry of Defense**: /28 Col. Gustaf Verner Jeremias Gustafsson (Intendant-General, General Headquarters) /40
   9. **Medical Department, Ministry of Defense**: /31 Col. Väinö Felix Lindén [+ to 1939, Chief Medical Officer of the Armed Forces] (retired) /41
   10. **Armaments Council**
      a. **Chief of Staff, Armaments Council**; /39 MG [Retired '30] Paavo Juho Talvela (Commanding General, Talvela Group) /39
   11. **Head, Finnish War Material Procurement Delegation in the United**

States: /40 LG Vilho Petter Nenonen (Inspector-General of Artillery) /40

12. **Attached to Ministry of Defense**
/45 MG Antti Kääriäinen (acting Commanding General, Savo-Karelia Military District) /45

G. **Finance Minister**: 03/12/37 VÄINÖ TANNER (Foreign Affairs Minister) 12/01/39 MAUNO PEKKALA (11/17/44, Council of State Minister) 05/22/42 VÄINÖ TANNER 09/08/44 OMNI ALFRED HILTUNEN (Deputy Transport & Public Works Minister) 11/17/44 JOHANNES HELO (Education Minister) 04/17/45 SAKARI TUOMIJA 07/17/45 RALF TÖRNGREN.
1. **Deputy Finance Minister**: unknown? 03/27/40 JUHO PILPPULA 01/04/41 JUHO KOIVISTO 03/05/43 TYKO REINIKKA 09/08/44 OLLI PALOHEIMO 10/21/44 unknown? 11/17/44 SAKARI TUOMIJA [Finance Minister] 04/17/45 EEMIL LUUKKA [+ Deputy Interior Minister; + Deputy Agriculture Minister].

H. **Education Minister**: 03/12/37 UUNO HANNULA 03/27/40 ANTTI KUKKONEN [+ to 08/15/40, Agriculture Minister] 03/05/43 KALLE KAUPPI 11/17/44 UUNO TAKKI (Deputy Trade & Industry Minister & Deputy People's Service Minister) 04/17/45 JOHANNES HELO 12/28/45 EINO PEKKALA.

I. **Agriculture Minister**: 03/12/37 PEKKA HEIKKINEN 03/27/40 ANTTI KUKKONEN [+ Education Minister] 08/15/40 VILJAMI KALLIOKOSKI 11/17/44 EEMIL LUUKKA [+ Deputy Interior Minister] (Deputy Agriculture Minister & Deputy Finance Minister) 04/17/45 KALLE JUTILA 09/29/45 VIHTORI VESTERINEN.
1. **Deputy Agriculture Minister**: 03/12/37 JUHO KOIVISTO (01/04/41, Deputy Finance Minister) 03/27/40 unknown? 01/04/41 TOIVO IKONEN (Deputy Transport & Public Works Minister) 03/05/43 NILS OSARA 09/08/44 unknown? 04/17/45 EEMIL LUUKKA [+ Deputy Interior Minister; + Deputy Finance Minister].

J. **Transport & Public Works Minister**: 03/12/37 HANNES RYÖMÄ 09/02/39 VÄINÖ SALOVAARA 11/17/44 EERO A. WUORI [+ 04/27/45, Council of State Minister] 09/29/45 ONNI PELTONEN.
1. **Deputy Transport & Public Works Minister**: 03/12/37 VÄINÖ SALOVAARA (Transport & Public Works Minister) 09/02/29 PIETARI SALMENOJA 12/01/39 unknown? 03/27/40 KARL-ERIK EKHOLM 01/04/41 VILHO ANNALA 03/05/43 TOIVO IKONEN 01/13/44 VÄINÖ KAASALAINEN 09/08/44 unknown? 10/21/44 EERO A. WUORI (Transport & Public Works Minister) 11/17/44 ONNI ALFRED HILTUNEN (02/14/46, Deputy Transport & Public Works Minister; Deputy Social Affairs Minister; & Deputy People's Service Minister) 04/17/45
04/17/45 YRJÖ MURTO.
11/22/45 KAARLO HILLILÄ [+ People's Service Minister; + Deputy Social Affairs Minister].
02/14/46 ONNI ALFRED HILTUNEN [+ Deputy Social Affairs Minister; + Deputy People's Service Minister].
2. **Chief, National Work Force, Ministry of Transport & Public Works**:

299

08/01/43 MG Einar Nikolai Mäkinen (Commanding General, II Army Corps) 08/14/44

K.   **Trade & Industry Minister**: 03/12/37 VÄINÖ VOIONMAA [+ Deputy Foreign Affairs Minister] 12/01/39 VÄINÖ KOTILAINEN (People's Service Minister) 09/15/40 TOIVO SALMIO 08/03/41 VÄINÖ TANNER (Finance Minister) 05/22/42 UUMO TAKKI (Education Minister) 11/17/44 ÅKE GARTZ [+ 04/27/46, Deputy Foreign Affairs Minister].
   1.   **Deputy Trade & Industry Minister**: unknown? 04/17/45 UUNO TAKKI [+ Deputy People's Service Minister].

L.   **Social Affairs Minister**: 03/12/37 JAAKKO KETO 11/09/37 KARL-AUGUST FAGERHOLM (10/21/44, Social Affairs Minister) 12/17/43 ALEKSI AALTONEN 10/21/44 KARL-AUGUST FAGERHOLM 11/17/44 RALF TÖRNGREN (07/17/45, Finance Minister) 04/17/45 EINO KILPI [+ 10/15/45, Council of State Minister].
   1.   **Deputy Social Affairs Minister**: 03/12/37 OSKARI REINIKAINEN 12/01/39 unknown? 11/17/44 YRJÖ LEINO (Interior Minister) 04/17/45
       04/17/45 MATTI JANHUNEN.
       04/27/45 EERO A. WUORI [+ Council of State Minister & Transport; + Public Works Minister; + Deputy People's Service Minister] 09/29/45
       11/22/45 KAARLO HILLILÄ [+ People's Service Minister; + Deputy Transport & Public Works Minister].
       02/14/46 ONNI ALFRED HILTUNEN [+ Deputy Transport & Public Works Minister; + Deputy People's Service Minister].

M.   **People's Service Minister** (09/20/39): RAINER von FIEANDT 03/27/40 VÄINÖ TANNER (08/03/41, Trade & Industry Minister) 09/15/40 VÄINÖ KOTILAINEN 04/16/41 VÄINÖ AROLA 08/03/42 CARL HENRIK RAMSAY [+ Deputy Foreign Affairs Minister] (Foreign Affairs Minister) 03/05/43 KAARLE ELLILÄ 04/17/45 KAARLO HILLILÄ [+ Deputy Transport & Public Works Minister; + Deputy Social Affairs Minister].
   1.   **Deputy People's Service Minister**: unknown? 03/27/40 TOIVO SALMIO [+ 09/15/40, Trade & Industry Minister] 01/04/41 unknown/ 03/05/43 JALO AURA 04/17/45
       04/17/45 UUNO TAKKI [+ Deputy Trade & Industry Minister].
       04/27/45 EERO A. WUORI [+ Council of State Minister; + Transport & Public Works Minister; + Deputy Social Affairs Minister] 09/29/45
       02/14/46 ONNI ALFRED HILTUNEN [+ Deputy Transport & Public Works Minister; Deputy Social Affairs Minister].

N.   **Minister without Portfolio** (10/13/39): ERNST VIKTOR LORENTZ von BORN (Interior Minister) 12/01/39 JUHO KUSTI PAASIKIVI [+ Ambassador to the Union of Social Socialist Republics] 03/27/40

German Military Mission to Finland

Head of German Military Mission to Finland (04/01/40): GdI Waldemar Erfurth [German]

A.   **Chief of Staff, German Military Mission to Finland**: LCol. Hölter [German]

Military High Command

Commander-in-Chief, Armed Forces [Defense Forces]: /33 MG Hugo Viktor Österman (Commanding General, Army of the Karelian Isthmus) 11/39 Marshal of Finland Carl Gustaf Emil Mannerheim (retired; President of Finland) 12/44 GdI Axel Erik Heinrichs (?) /45 LG Jari Fritjof Lundqvist.

    1.   **Advisor & Confident to Marshall of Finland**: 09/44 GdA [Retired '30] Paavo Juho Talvela (retired) /44

A.   **Chief of Staff, Armed Forces High Command**: /38 Col. Woldemar [Voldemar] Oinonen (Deputy Chief of the General Staff) /39

B.   **Chief of Finnish General Staff**:

C.   **General Headquarters**

D.   **Home Troops**

E.   **Chief of the Civil Guard [Suojeluskunta]**

F.   **Commander-in-Chief, Finnish Air Force**

G.   **Commander-in-Chief, Finnish Naval Forces**

H.   **Operational Department, Armed Forces High Command**: unknown? /40 Col. Kustaa Anders Tapola (Chief of Staff, Army of Karelia) /41

I.   **Communications, Armed Forces High Command**: unknown? /40 Col. Leo Aleksander Ekberg.

J.   **Welfare Section, Armed Forces**

K.   **Inspector of Territorial Organization, Armed Forces High Command**: unknown? /40 Col. Einar Nikolai Mäkinen (Head, Organization Department, General Headquarters) /41 unknown? 12/03/44 MG Einar Nikolai Mäkinen (Deputy Chief of the General Staff) /45.

L.   **Plenipotentiary of Marshal of Finland Mannerheim to the German Fuhrer Headquarters**: /40 MG [Retired '30] Paavo Juho Talvela (Commanding General, VI Army Corps) 06/41

M.   **Representative of General Headquarters at the State Council** (1939): GdI [Retired '20] Karl Rudolf Walden (Defense Minister) 03/40

N.   **Representative of the Finnish Commander-in-Chief to the German High Command (O. K. W.) & German Army High Command (O. K. H.)**: /41 LG Harald Öhquist (Commanding General, IV Army Corps) 02/01/42 LG [Retired '30] Paavo Juho Talvela (Commanding General, II Army Corps) 02/44 LG Hugo Viktor Österman (Chief Inspector of the Infantry) /44 LG [Retired '30] Paavo Juho Talvela (Advisor & Confident of Marshal of Finland Mannerheim) 09/44

O.   *Special Envoys, Armed Forces High Command*

    1.   **Special Envoy of the Commander-in-Chief to Toronto, in matters of**

Foreign Volunteers: /39 LG Johannes Ferdinand "Hannes" Ignatius (/41, died) /40

2. **Special Envoy of the Commander-in-Chief**: /41 LG [Retired '24] Oscar Paul Enckell [+ /41, Special Envoy of the Commander-in-Chief to Paris & London in matters on Foreign Volunteers] (retired) /44

3. **Special Envoy of the Commander-in-Chief to Paris & London in matters on Foreign Volunteers**: /40 LG [Retired '24] Oscar Paul Enckell [+ /41, Special Envoy of the Commander-in-Chief] (retired) /44

P. *Special Duties by the Commander-In-Chief, Armed Forces*

/39 GdI [Retired '26] Karl Fredrik Wilkama (retired) /44

/39 GdI [Retired '25] Paul Martin Wetzer (retired) /44

/39 MG [Retired '37] Kaarle Heikki Kekoni [+ Head, Foreign Volunteers Bureau] (Head, Information Department of the State Council) /44

/41 Col. Eino Iisakki Järvinen (Commanding Officer, Lake Ladoga Sea Defense) /41

08/07/42 MG Välinö Henrik Palojärvi (Commanding General, 8ᵗʰ Division) 01/09/43

11/08/42 MG Selim Engelbert Isakson (Commanding General, 7ᵗʰ Division) 01/28/44

02/17/43 MG Välinö Henrik Palojärvi (acting Chief, Welfare Section, Armed Forces High Command) /44

/44 MG Lars Rafael Melander (Employment on special duties of the Fortification Planning staff) /44

06/17/44 MG Juhani "Jussi" Sihvo (attached to Inspector-General, Defense Forces) /44

06/26/44 MG Paavo Johannes Paalu (retired).

/44 MG Välinö Henrik Palojärvi (Commanding General, Kymi Military District) /45.

/44 Col. Eino Iisakki Järvinen (Commanding Officer, 1ˢᵗ Coastal Division) 07/13/44

Chief of Finnish General Staff: /30 MG Karl Lennart Oesch [+ /32, Minister of the Interior; + /40, Commanding General, Group Coast] (Commanding General, Army of Karelian Isthmus) /40 LG Edvard Fritjof Hanell (Commanding General, Fortification Works) 02/41 LG Axel Erik Heinrichs [+ Commanding General, Army of Karelia] **[NOTE**: filling in for LG Heinrichs: /41 MG Vilijo Einar Tuompo [acting; + Chief, Command Section, General Headquarters] /41 MG Edvard Fritjof Hanell [acting; + Chief, Fortification Works, General Headquarters] /42 MG Vilijo Einar Tuompo [acting; + Chief, Fortification Works, General Headquarters]] 01/29/42 GdI Axel Erik Heinrichs (Commander-in-Chief, Armed Forces) 10/06/44 LG Karl Lennart Oesch (Commander-in-Chief, Finnish Ground Forces) 12/44 LG Aksel Fredrik Airo.

A. **Deputy Chief of the General Staff**: unknown? /39 Col. Woldemar [Voldemar] Oinonen (Commanding Officer, 23ʳᵈ Division) /40 MG Aksel Frederik Airo [+ Quartermaster General] (Chief of the General Staff) 12/44 unknown? /45 MG Einar Nikolai Mäkinen.

B. **Command Department, General Staff**: unknown? /40 Col. Viktor Alonzo Sundman [+ Head, Training Department, General Staff] (Commanding Officer, 2ⁿᵈ Jäger Brigade) /40 MG Välinö Henrik Palojärvi (Chief, Command Department, General Headquarters) /41

C. **Foreign Countries Department, General Staff**: /33 LCol. Antero Johannes Svensson [+Chief, Statistics Department, General Staff] (Commanding Officer, Karelian Guards Regiment; /39, Commanding Officer, 2ⁿᵈ Brigade) /37 unknown?

/40 Col. Lars Rafael Melander (Head, 2nd (Intelligence) Department, General Headquarters) /41

D. **Organization Department, General Staff**: /36 Col. Woldemar [Voldemar] Oinonen (Chief of Staff, Armed Forces High Command) /38

E. **Supply Department, General Staff**: /39 Col. Harald Vilhelm Roos [+ to 40, Commandant, Reserve Officer School] (Chief, Supply & Transport, General Headquarters) 44

F. **Training Department, General Staff**: unknown? /40 Col. Viktor Alonzo Sundman [+ Head, Command Department, General Staff] (Commanding Officer, 2nd Jäger Brigade) /41

G. **Statistics Department, General Staff**: /33 LCol. Antero Johannes Svensson [+Chief, Foreign Countries Department, General Staff] (Commanding Officer, Karelian Guards Regiment; /39, Commanding Officer, 2nd Brigade) /37 unknown?

General Headquarters

A. **Chief Administration Officer, General Staff [General Headquarters]**: unknown? /41 Col. Johan Viktor Arajuuri (Chief Administration Officer, Eastern Karelia) /42

B. **Command Department, General Headquarters**: unknown? /41 MG Välinö Henrik Palojärvi (Commanding General, Division J) /41 MG Vilijo Einar Tuompo [+ /41, acting Chief of General Staff; + /42, acting Chief of General Staff] (Instructor, Military Academy) /44

C. **1st Department, General Staff [General Headquarters]**: unknown? /39 Col. Einar Nikolai Mäkinen (Inspector of the General Staff Regional Organization)

D. **2nd Department (Intelligence), General Staff [General Headquarters]**: unknown? /39 Col. Lars Rafael Melander (Head, Foreign Department, General Staff) /40 unknown? /41 Col. Lars Rafael Melander (acting Commanding Officer, Cavalry Brigade) /42

E. **Operations, Department, General Headquarters**: unknown? 06/29/41 Col. Einar Nikolai Mäkinen (Commanding Officer, I Army Corps) 08/08/41

   1. **Assigned to Operations Section, General Headquarters**
/40 Col. Kustaa Anders Tapola [+ assigned to Organization Section, General Headquarters] (Chief, Operations Department, General Staff) /40

F. **Organization Department, General Headquarters**: /39 Col. Einar Nikolai Mäkinen (Inspector of Territorial Organization, Armed Force High Command) /40 Col. Selim Engelbert Isakson (acting Inspector of Military Schools) /41 Col. Einar Nikolai Mäkinen (Head, Operations Department, General Headquarters) 06/29/41

   1. **Assigned to Organization Section, General Staff [General Headquarters]**
/40 Col. Kustaa Anders Tapola [+ assigned to Operations Section, General Headquarters] (Chief, Operations Department, General Staff) /41

G. **Supply & Transport, General Headquarters**: unknown? /41 Col. Harald Vilhelm Roos (retired) /44

   1. **Chief, Supply Department, General Headquarters**: unknown? /41 Col. Harald Vilhelm Roos (Chief of Supply & Transport, General Headquarters) /41

      a. **Chief, Supply Department Section III, General Headquarters**: unknown? /39 Col. Harald Vilhelm Roos (Head, Supply Department, General Staff) /40

H. **Antiaircraft, General Headquarters**: unknown? /41 LG Aarne Sihvo (Chief of the Civil Defense, Ministry of Interior) /44

I. **Artillery, General Headquarters**: unknown? /39 MG Välinö Vilhelm Svanström (Chief Weapons Staff) /42 unknown? /45 MG Aaro Olavi Pajari.

J. **Corps of Engineer, General Headquarters**: unknown? /39 MG Unio Bernhard Sarlin [+ Inspector of Technical Services].
    1. **Military Research Center**: unknown? /44 MG Johan Woldemar Hägglund (retired) /45.

K. **Fortification Works**: unknown? /39 MG Edvard Fritjof Hanell (Commanding General, Group Hamina) /40 MG Juho Henrik Heiskanen [+ Assistant Chief Inspector of the Defense Force] /40 MG Edvard Fritjof Hanell (Chief, General Staff) /40 MG Juho Henrik Heiskanen [+ Assistant Chief Inspector of the Defense Force] /40 Col. Eino Iisakki Järvinen (Inspector of Fortifications, General Headquarters) /40 MG Edvard Fritjof Hanell [+ /41, Acting Chief of Finnish General Staff].
    1. **Fortification Planning Staff**: unknown? /44 MG Johan Woldemar Hägglund (Chief, Military Research Center) /44
        a. **Employment on Special Duties, Fortification Planning Staff** /44 Col. Lars Rafael Melander (acting Commanding General, Cavalry Brigade) /44

L. **Intendent-General, General Headquarters**: unknown? /40 MG Gustaf Verner Jeremias Gustafsson.

M. **Inspector-General, Defense Forces**: unknown? /40 LG Harald Öhquist (Representative of the Commander-in-Chief by the German High Command) /41 unknown? 06/16/43 LG Johan Woldemar Hägglund (Chief, Fortification Planning Staff) /44
        a. **Assigned to Inspector-General, Defense Forces**: /44 Col. Juhani "Jussi" Sihvo (attached to Military District Supervisory Office) /44
    1. **Assistant Chief Inspector, Defense Forces**: unknown? /39 MG Juho Henrik Heiskanen [in /40, acting Commanding General, Fortification Works] (in reserve; /41, Commandant of Viipuri) /41
    2. **Chief Inspector of Infantry**: /38 MG Axel Erik Heinrichs (Commanding General, III Army Corps) /39 unknown? /44 LG Hugo Viktor Österman.
        a. **Inspector of Infantry**: unknown? /45 LG Harald Öhquist [+ Inspector-General of Military Training].
    3. **Inspector-General of Artillery**: unknown? /40 LG Vilho Petter Nenonen.
        a. **Inspector of Artillery**: /37 Col. Väinö Vilhelm Svanström (Commanding General, Artillery, General Headquarters) /39
    4. **Inspector of Fortification Works**: unknown? /40 Col. Eino Iisakki Järvinen (Special Purposes Officer, III Army Corps) /41 unknown? /42 LG Edvard Fritjof Hanell (retired) /44
    5. **Inspector of Technical Services**: /20 Col. Unio Bernhard Sarlin [+ /39, Chief, Corps of Engineers, General Headquarters].
    6. **Inspector of Depots**: unknown? /45 MG Väinö Vilhelm Svanström.
    7. **Inspector of War Economics**: /38 MG Leonard August Mathias "Lennart" Grandell [+ Head, War Economic Department, Ministry of Defense] (retired) /44

8. **Chief Inspector of Military Schools**: /33 MG Edvard Fritjof Hanell [+ Commandant, Military Academy] (Commanding General, Hanell Group) /39 unknown? /42 MG Selim Engelbert Isakson (acting; Employment on special duties to the Commander-in-Chief) 11/08/42 LG Hjalmar Fridolf Siilasvuo (Commanding General, III Army Corps) 02/25/44 unknown? /45 GdI Kustaa Anders Tapola.

9. **Chief Inspector of Military Training**: unknown? /40 LG Hugo Viktor Österman [+ Chairman of the Service Regulations Committee] (Representative of the Commander-in-Chief by the German High Command) 05/04/44 LG Harald Öhquist [+ /45, Inspector of Infantry].
   a. **Special Duties to the Inspector-General of Military Training**
      /41 MG Juho Henrik Heiskanen (retired) /44

N. **Quartermaster General**: unknown? /39 MG Aksel Fredrik Airo [+ /40, Deputy Chief of the General Staff] (Chief of the General Staff) 12/44 MG Woldemar [Voldemar] Oinonen.

O. **Communications (Chief Signal Officer), General Headquarters**: unknown? /39 Col. Leo Aleksander Ekberg (Chief, Communications, Armed Forces High Command) /40

P. **Weapons Staff**: unknown? /42 MG Välinö Vilhelm Svanström (in reserve; /45, Inspector of Depots, General Staff) /44

Q. **Chief Medical Officer of the Defense Forces**: /30 Col. Väinö Felix Lindén [+ 1931, Head, Medical Department, Ministry of Defense] /39 MG [Retired '20] Eino E. Suolahti (retired) /44

R. **Foreign Volunteers Bureau, General Headquarters**: /39 MG [Retired '37] Kaarle Heikki Kekoni [+ employment on Special Duties to the Commander-in-Chief, Armed Forces] (Head, Information Department of the State Council) /44

S. *Military Schools*
   1. **Commandant, Military Academy**: /30 MG Edvard Fritjof Hanell [+ /33, Inspector of Military Schools] (Commanding General, Group Hanell) /39
      a. **Deputy Commandant, Military Academy**: /37 Col. Harald Vilhelm Roos (Commandant, Reserve Officer School) /38
      b. **Instructor, Military Academy**:
         /44 MG Viljo Einar Tuompo (retired) /45
   2. **Commandant, Reserve Office School**: /38 Col. Harald Vilhelm Roos [+ /39 Head, Supply Department III Section, General Headquarters] (Head, Supply Department, General Staff) /40

T. **Chairman, Service Regulations Committee**: unknown? /40 LG Hugo Viktor Österman [+ Inspector-General of Military Training] (Representative of the Commander-in-Chief to the German High Command) /44

U. *Military Attaché*
   1. **Military Attaché to Berlin, Rome & Budapest**: /37 Col. Viktor Alonzo Sundman (Chief, Command Department, General Staff & Chief, Training Section, General Staff) /40
   2. **Military Attaché to Stockholm, Copenhagen & Oslo**: /37 MG Välinö Henrik Palojärvi (Head Command Department, General Staff) /40

V. *Liaisons*
   1. **Finnish Liaison to German Twentieth Mountain Army**: /41 Col. Oiva

Willamo.

Home Troops (1939): LG Kaarlo Lauri Torvald Malmberg [+ Commander of the Civil Guard [Suojeluskunta]] (in reserve; /45, retired) /44 MG Woldemar [Voldemar] Oinonen (acting; Quartermaster-General) /44 unknown?.
A.   **Chief of Staff, Home Troops** (1939): Col. Ilmari Armas-Eino Martola [+ Chief of Staff, Civil Guard [Sujeluskunta]] (Commanding Officer, 1st Division) /40 vacant /40 Col. Ilmari Armas-Eino Martola (Commanding Officer, 2nd Division) 04/29/42 MG Woldemar [Voldemar] Oinonen (acting Commander-in-Chief, Home Troops) /44
B.   **Military District Supervisory Office**:
    1.   **Attached to Military District Supervisory Office**:
        /44 MG Juhani "Jussi" Sihvo.

Chief of the Civil Guard [Suojeluskunta]: /28 MG Kaarlo Lauri Torvald Malmberg [+ 1939, Commander-in-Chief, Home Troops] (in reserve; /45, retired) /44
A.   **Chief of Staff, Civil Guard [Suojeluskunta]**: /33 Col. Ilmari Armas-Eino Martola [+ 1939, Chief of Staff, Home Troops] (Commanding Officer, 1st Division) /40

Commander-in-Chief, Ground Forces: /40 LG Axel Erik Heinrichs (Chief of the General Staff) /40 unknown? 12/44 LG Karl Lennart Oesch.
A.   **Chief of Staff, Ground Forces**: /40 Col. Kustaa Anders Tapola (assigned to Operations & Organization Section, General Headquarters) /40
B.   **Supply Section, Ground Forces**: /40 Col. Ernst Ruben Lagus (Commanding Officer, Bicycle Brigade) /40

Commander-in-Chief, Finnish Air Force: /32 Col. Jari Fritjof Lundqvist (Commander-in-Chief, Armed Forces) /45.

Commander-in-Chief, Finnish Naval Forces: /27 Col. Väinö Lahja Richard Valve (retired; Defense Minister) 11/44
A.   **Chief of Staff, Naval Forces**: /38 Cdr. Ragnar Hakola [FinN] /40 Commo. [Retired '38] Svante August Sundman [FinN].
B.   **Commander of Finnish Navy**: unknown? /40 Commo. Eero Akseli Rahola [FinN].
    1.   **Chief of Staff, Commander, Finnish Navy**: unknown? /41 Capt. Eino Huttunen [FinN] /42 Capt. Eino Pukkila [FinN] /44 Capt. Aimo Saukkonen [FinN].
C.   **Inspector of Naval Artillery, Naval Staff**: unknown? /45 MG Eino Iisakki Järvinen.

Armies

Isthmus Army (1939): LG Hugo Viktor Österman (Chief Inspector, Military Training) /40 LG Karl Lennart Oesch (Commanding General, II Army Corps) /40 LG Axel Erik Heinrichs (Commander-in-Chief, Finnish Ground Forces) /40 disbanded.
- A. **Chief of Staff, Isthmus Army** (1939): Col. Kustaa Anders Tapola (Chief of Staff, Ground Forces) /40 dissolved.
- B. **Supply Section, Isthmus Army** (1939): Col Ernst Ruben Lagus (acting Commanding Officer, 14th Infantry Regiment) /40

Army of Karelia (Karjalan Armeija) (06/29/41): LG Axel Erik Heinrichs [+ Chief of Finnish General Staff] 01/29/42 LG Karl Lennart Oesch (temporary) 03/01/42 disbanded, headquarters used to form **Olonets Group** - see **Corps**.
- A, **Chief of Staff, Army of Karelia** (06/29/41): Col. Kustaa Anders Tapola (Chief of Staff, Aunus Group) 03/01/42
- B. *Components* - **Army of Karelia** (06/41)
  - 1. **VI Army Corps**
  - 2. **VII Army Corps**
  - 3. **Task Force Oinonen**
  - 4. **1st Division**

HQ of the Commander of the Isthmus Forces (Kannaksen Joukkojen Komentajan Esikunta) (06/14/44): LG Karl Lennart Oesch (Chief of the General Staff) 10/06/44 disbanded.

Army Corps

Army Corps (to 1939; disbanded): /33 LG Harald Öhquist (Commanding General, II Army Corps) /39 disbanded.

I Army Corps [I Armeijakunta] (1940; redesignated **V Army Corps**, 02/01/42): MG Taavetti "Pappa" Laatikainen (Commanding General, V Army Corps) 06/29/41 MG Einar Nikolai Mäkinen (Commanding Officer, V Army Corps) 02/01/42 see - **V Army Corps.**

II Army Corps [II Armeijakunta] (06/05/41; became **Maaselkä Group (Maaselän Ryhumä)**; also known as **Maaselän Front**; 03/01/42; then reformed as **IV Army Corps**, 03/04/44; disbanded 12/03/44): **II Army Corps** /39 LG Harald Öhquist (Chief Inspector, Military Training) /40 LG Karl Lennart Oesch (Commanding General, IV Army Corps) 06/05/41 unknown? /44 MG Välinö Henrik Palojärvi (Commanding General, Kymi Military District) /41 MG [Retired '30] Paavo Juho Talvela (Commanding General, VI Army Corps) 06/29/41 MG Taavetti "Pappa" Laatikainen (acting Commanding General, IV Army Corps) 08/25/41 MG Aarne Leopold Blick [acting; + Commanding General, VI Army Corps] 08/30/41 MG Taavetti "Pappa" Laatikainen (Commanding General, Maaselkä Group) 03/01/42 redesignated **Maaselkä Group** 03/01/42 LG Taavetti "Pappa" Laatikainen (Commanding General, IV Army Corps) 02/44 MG [Retired '30] Paavo Juho Talvela (Commanding General, II Army Corps) 03/04/44 redesignated **II Army Corps** 03/04/44 LG [Retired '30] Paavo Juho Talvela (Commanding General, Olonets Group) 06/14/44 MG Einar Nikolai Mäkinen (Inspector of Territorial Organization, Armed Forces High Command) 12/03/44 disbanded.
- A.   **Components - II Army Corps** (06/41)
    1.   **2nd Division**
    2.   **15th Division**
    3.   **18th Division**

III Army Corps [III Armeijakunta] (1939; headquarters existed without a commander 11/08/42 to 02/25/44; disbanded 11/28/44): LG Axel Erik Heinrichs (Commanding General, Army of Karelian Isthmus) /40 MG Hjalmar Fridolf Siilasvuo (Commanding General, V Army Corps) /40 MG [Retired '30] Paavo Juho Talvela (Finnish Liaison Officer to the German Army) /40 MG Woldemar [Voldemar] Oinonen (acting; Commanding General, Oinonen Group) 06/10/41 MG Hjalmar Fridolf Siilasvuo (Chief Inspector of Military Schools) 11/08/42 unknown? 02/25/44 LG Hjalmar Fridolf Siilasvuo (Commanding General, Lapland Force) 11/28/44 disbanded.
- A.   **Components - III Army Corps** (06/41)
    1.   **3rd Division**
    2.   **6th Division**
    3.   **Division J** (08/41)
    4.   **Group F** (09/41)
    5.   **Group J** (09/41)
- B.   **Special Purposes Officer, III Army Corps**: unknown? /40 Col. Aarne Leopold Blick (Commanding Officer, 3rd Division) /40 unknown? /41 Col. Eino Iisakki Järvinen (employment on Special Duties to Commander-in-Chief, Armed Forces) /41

IV Army Corps [IV Armeijakunta] (06/18/41; 03/11/42, became **Isthmus Group (Kannaksen Ryhmä)**; also known as **Karelian Isthmus Front**; then reformed as **IV Army Corps**, 03/04/44; disbanded 12/03/44): **IV Army Corps** /39 MG Juho Henrik Heiskanen (Assistant Chief Inspector of the Defense Forces) /39 MG Johan Woldemar Hägglund (Commanding General VII Army Corps) 06/18/41 LG Karl Lennart Oesch 08/25/41 MG Taavetti "Pappa" Laatikainen [acting; + Commanding General, II Army Corps] 08/30/41 LG Karl Lennart Oesch (Commanding General, Aunus [Olonets] Group) 02/01/42 LG Harald Öhquist (Commanding General, Isthmus Group) 03/01/42 redesignated **Isthmus Group** 03/01/42 LG Harald Öhquist (Chief Inspector of Military Training) 03/04/44 redesignated **IV Army Corps** 03/04/44 LG Taavetti "Pappa" Laatikainen (Commanding General, 3rd Division) 12/03/44 disbanded.

A.   *Components - IV Army Corps* (06/41)
   1.   **4th Division**
   2.   **8th Division**
   3.   **10th Division**
   4.   **12th Division**
   5.   **2nd Coastal Brigade**
B.   **Artillery, IV Army Corps**: /39 Col. Aarne Otto Snellman (acting Commanding Officer, 12th Division) /40

V Army Corps [V Armeijakunta] (06/22/41; became **VI Army Corps**, 06/29/41; reformed 02/01/42 from **I Army Corps**; disbanded 12/05/44): /40 MG Hjalmar Fridolf Siilasvuo Commanding General, III Army Corps) 06/22/41 MG Taavetti "Pappa" Laatikainen (Commanding General, VI Army Corps) 06/29/41 disbanded; reformed 02/01/42 MG Einar Nikolai Mäkinen (Chief, National Work Force, Ministry of Transport & Public Works) 08/01/43 MG Antero Johannes Svensson (Commanding General, Light Brigade) 12/05/44 disbanded.

VI Army Corps [VI Armeijakunta] (06/29/41, from **V Army Corps**; disbanded 11/30/44): MG [Retired '30] Paavo Juho Talvela (Representative of the Commander-in-Chief by the German High Command & German Army High Command) 08/25/41 unknown? 01/15/42 MG Antero Johannes Svensson [acting; + Commanding General, 7th Division] 02/01/42 MG Aarne Leopold Blick 09/29/43 MG Ernst Ruben Lagus [acting; + Commanding General, 1st Armored Division] 10/12/43 MG Aarne Leopold Blick (replaced; Commanding General, 2nd Division) 0706/44 MG Ilmari Armas-Eino Martola (Deputy Minister of Foreign Affairs) 09/21/44 MG Kustaa Anders Tapola (Commanding General, South Häme Military District) 11/30/44 disbanded.

A.   *Components - VI Army Corps* (06/41)
   1.   **5th Division**
   2.   **11th Division**

VII Army Corps [VII Armeijakunta] (06/20/41; disbanded 06/16/43): MG Johan Woldemar Hägglund (Inspector-General of the Armed Forces) 06/16/43 disbanded.

A.   *Components - VII Army Corps* (06/41)
   1.   **7th Division**
   2.   **19th Division**

Aunus [Olonets] Group (Aunuksen Ryhmä) (03/01/42 from **Headquarters, Army of Karelia**; also known as **Svir Front**; disbanded 07/18/44): LG Karl Lennart Oesch (HQ of the Commander of the Isthmus Forces) 06/14/44 LG [Retired '30] Paavo Juho Talvela (Representative of the Commander-in-Chief by the German High Command) 07/18/44

A.   **Chief of Staff, Aunus Group** (03/01/42): MG Kustaa Anders Tapola (Commanding General, 5th Division) /42

Salla Front (1940): GdK [Retired '20] Ernst Linder [+ Commanding General, Swedish Volunteer Corps]

Swedish Volunteer Corps (1940): GdK [Retired '20] Ernst Linder [+ Commanding General, Salla Front]

Task Force Oinonen (also known as **Oinonen Group (Ryhmä Oinonen)**; 06/18/41; disbanded 04/29/42): MG Woldemar [Voldemar] Oinonen (Chief of Staff, Home Troops) 04/29/42 disbanded.

A.   *Components -* **Task Force Oinonen** (06/41)
   1.   **1st Light Infantry (Jäger) Brigade**
   2.   **2nd Light Infantry (Jäger) Brigade**
   3.   **Cavalry Brigade**

Finnish Coastal Fleet: /36 Commo. Eero Akseli Rahola [FinN] (Commander of Finnish Navy) /40 Capt. Ragnar Hakola [FinN] (?   ) 07/41 Commo. Ragnar Göransson [FinN]

A.   **Chief of Staff, Finnish Coastal Fleet**: /39 Cdr. Oiva Koivisto [FinN] /40 Cdr. Bror Willberg [FinN],

Border Guards: /35 Col. Viljo Einar Tuompo (Commanding Officer, North Finland Group) /39 unknown? /40 MG Viljo Einar Tuompo (Chief of Command Staff at General Headquarters) /41 unknown? /44 MG Erkki Johannes Raappana.

Groups

Group (Detachment) Hanell (1939): MG Edvard Fritjof Hanell (Commanding General, Fortification Works) /40 disbanded
A.   *Components - **Group (Detachment) Hanell***
    1.   **22nd Infantry Regiment** (12/09/39 transferred to 6th Division (#1))

Lapland Group (1939): MG Kurt Martti Wallenius (Commanding General, Coast Group) /40 disbanded; reformed 11/28/44 LG Hjalmar Fridolf Siilasvuo (Commanding General, 1st Division) /44 disbanded.

Moulaa Group (1939): Col. Antti Kääriäinen (Commanding Officer, 3rd Brigade) /39

North Finland Group (1939): MG Viljo Einar Tuompo (Commanding General, Border Guards) /40 disbanded.

Pajari Detachment (1939): Col. Aaro Olavi Pajari (Commanding Officer, Group Talvela) /40 disbanded.

Group Sihvo (1939): Col. Juhani "Jussi" Sihvo (Commanding Officer, 1st Division) /40 disbanded.

Detachment (Group) Talvela (1939): MG [Retired '30] Paavo Juho Talvela (Commanding General, III Army Corps) /40 Col. Aaro Olavi Pajari (Commanding Officer, 14th Division) /40 disbanded.
A.   *Components - **Detachment Talvela***
    1.   **16th Infantry Regiment** (12/08/39 transferred from 6th Division (#1); 01/01/40 renumbered **7th Infantry Regiment** and transferred to 3rd Division)

Group Uusikirkko (1939): MG Georg Fredrik Palmroth [+ Commanding General, Cavalry Brigade] /40 disbanded.

Group Coast (1940): LG Karl Lennart Oesch [+ Chief of the General Staff] /40 MG Kurt Martti Wallenius (in reserve; /41, retired) /40 disbanded.

Group Hamina (1940): LG Edvard Fritjof Hanell (Commanding General, Fortification Works) /40 disbanded.

Kilpa Group (1940): Col. Frans Uno Fagernäs (Commanding Officer, 15th Division) /40 disbanded.

Group North Karelia (1940): Col. Erkki Johannes Raappana (Commanding Officer 9th Division) /40 disbanded.

Detachment Paalu (Group) (1940): Col. Paavo Johannes Paalu (Commanding Officer, 23rd Division) /40 disbanded.

Detachment Lagus (07/25/41): Col. Ernst Ruben Lagus (Commanding General, Armored Brigade) 06/28/42

Group F (08/09/41, III Army Corps; disbanded 08/07/42): LCol. Arne Somwersalo

Group J (08/09/41, III Army Corps; disbanded 08/07/42): LCol. Johannes Turtola

Battle Group Pajari (1942): MG Aaro Olavi Pajari [+ Commanding General, 18th Division] /42 disbanded; reformed **Group Pajari** 10/21/44 MG Aaro Olavi Pajari (attached to Civil Guard; /44, Commanding General, Savo-Karelin Military District) /44 disbanded.

Group Raappana (12/11/44): MG Erkki Johannes Raappana (Commanding General, Border Guards) /44 disbanded.

Divisions

Division J [Divisioona J] (08/09/41, III Army Corps; disbanded 08/07/42): MG Välinö Henrik Palojärvi (Employment for special duties at General Headquarters) 08/07/42 disbanded.

1ˢᵗ Division (10/39; 06/27/41, Army of Karelia): /38 Col. Taavetti "Pappa" Laatikainen /39 Col. Niilo Viktor Hersalo (Commanding Officer, 21ˢᵗ Division) 10/39 MG Viljo Einar Tuompo (Commanding General, North Finland Group) 11/30/39 MG Taavetti "Pappa" Laatikainen (Commanding General, I Army Corps) /40 Col. Johannes "Jussi" Sihvo (Commanding Officer, Päijänne Military District) /40 Col. Ilmari Armas-Eino Martola (Chief of Staff, Home Troops) /40 unknown? 06/18/41 Col. Paavo Johannes Paalu (Commanding General, 18ᵗʰ Division) 11/02/43 MG Frans Uno Fagernäs (?) 11/23/44 disbanded; reformed /44 Hjalmar Fridolf Siilasvuo.

A.   ***Components - 1ˢᵗ Division*** (11/30/39)
1.   **1ˢᵗ Brigade**
2.   **2ⁿᵈ Brigade**

B.   ***Components - 1ˢᵗ Division*** (06/20/41)
1.   **35ᵗʰ Infantry Regiment**
2.   **56ᵗʰ Infantry Regiment**
3.   **60ᵗʰ Infantry Regiment**
4.   **5ᵗʰ Artillery Regiment**

2ⁿᵈ Division (01/01/40; 06/27/41, II Army Corps): /34 Col. Johan Woldemar Hägglund (Commanding General, IV Army Corps) /39 disbanded 06/10/41 Col. Aarne Leopold Blick (Commanding General, VI Army Corps) 08/25/42 Col. Armas Kemppi (acting) 08/30/41 Col. Aarne Leopold Blick (Commanding General, VI Army Corps) 02/01/42 MG Hannu Esa Hannuksela (died of a heart attack) 05/12/42 MG Ilmari Armas-Eino Martola (Commanding General, VI Army Corps) 07/06/44 MG Aarne Leopold Blick (Commanding General, East Savo Military District) 11/19/44 MG Aarne Leopold Blick (Commanding General, 3ʳᵈ Division) 12/3044 MG Ernst Ruben Lagus.

A.   ***Components - 2ⁿᵈ Division*** (01/01/40)
1.   **4ᵗʰ Infantry Regiment** (01/01/40, renumbered from **31ˢᵗ Infantry Regiment**):
2.   **5ᵗʰ Infantry Regiment** (01/01/40, renumbered from **32ⁿᵈ Infantry Regiment**):
3.   **6ᵗʰ Infantry Regiment** (01/01/40, renumbered from **33ʳᵈ Infantry Regiment**):
4.   **2ⁿᵈ Field Artillery Regiment** (01/01/40, renumbered from **11ᵗʰ Field Artillery Regiment**):

B.   ***Components - 2ⁿᵈ Division*** (06/20/41)
1.   **7ᵗʰ Infantry Regiment**
2.   **28ᵗʰ Infantry Regiment**
3.   **46ᵗʰ Infantry Regiment**
4.   **15ᵗʰ Artillery Regiment**

3ʳᵈ Division (01/01/40, from **6ᵗʰ Division (#1)**; 06/27/41, III Army Corps): /34 Col. Juho Henrik Heiskanen (Commanding General, IV Army Corps) /39 Col. Aarne Leopold Blick (Commanding Officer, East [Itä] Savo Military District) /40 Col. Paavo Johannes Paalu

313

(Commanding Officer, Detachment Paalu) 06/16/41 Col. Frans Uno Fagernäs (Commanding General, 1st Division) 10/21/43 MG Aaro Olavi Pajari (Commanding General, Group Pajari) 10/21/44 Col. Aloys Kuistio 12/03/44 MG Taavetti "Pappa" Laatikainen (Inspector of Armed Forces) 01/45 MG Aarne Leopold Blick.

A. **Components - 3rd Division** (01/01/40)
1. **7th Infantry Regiment** (01/01/40, renumbered from **16th Infantry Regiment**): Col. Kaarlo Aleksanteri Heiskanen (Commanding Officer, 13th Division) /40
2. **8th Infantry Regiment** (01/01/40, renumbered from **17th Infantry Regiment**): unknown? /41 Col. Pietari Aleksanteri Autti (Commanding Officer, 3rd Brigade) /42
3. **9th Infantry Regiment** (01/01/40, renumbered from **18th Infantry Regiment**):
4. **3rd Field Artillery Regiment** (01/01/40, renumbered from **6th Field Artillery Regiment**): /38 Col. Aarne Otto Snellman (Commanding Officer, 12th Division) /39

B. **Components - 3rd Division** (06/20/41)
1. **11th Infantry Regiment**
2. **32th Infantry Regiment**
3. **53rd Infantry Regiment**
4. **16th Artillery Regiment**

4th Division (1939-40; 06/27/41, IV Army Corps): 11/30/39 Col. B. Nordenswan (replaced) 12/06/39 Col. A. Kaila /40 Col. Claes Bertil Napoleon Winell (Commanding Officer, Gulf of Finland Military District) /40 Col. Johan Viktor Arajuuri [+ Chief of Helsinki Police] /40 unknown? 06/18/41 Col. Kaarlo Ilmari Viljanen (killed in action) 04/24/42 vacant 05/22/42 Col. Yrjö Takkula 03/05/43 Col. Pietari Aleksanteri Autti (Commanding Officer, North Perä Military District) 11/27/44 disbanded.

A. **Components - 4th Division** (11/30/39)
1. **10th Infantry Regiment**
2. **11th Infantry Regiment**
3. **12th Infantry Regiment**
4. **4th Field Artillery Regiment**

B. **Components - 4th Division** (06/20/41)
1. **5th Infantry Regiment**
2. **25th Infantry Regiment**
3. **46th Infantry Regiment**
4. **1st Artillery Regiment**

5th Division (1939-40; 06/27/41, VI Army Corps): 11/30/39 Col. Selim Engelbert Isakson (Head, Organization Department, General Headquarters) /40 unknown? 06/18/41 Col. Eino Koskimies 07/11/41 Col. Ernst Ruben Lagus (temporary; Commanding Officer, Detachment Lagus) 07/25/41 Col. Ilmari Karhu 06/16/42 MG Kustaa Anders Tapola (Commanding General, VI Army Corps) 09/21/44 disbanded.

A. **Components - 5th Division** (11/30/39)
1. **13th Infantry Regiment**: /42 Col. Viktor Alonzo Sundman (Commanding Officer, 17th Division) /42
2. **14th Infantry Regiment** (12/09/39 detached to 1st Division): /40 Col. Ernst

Ruben Lagus (Chief, Supply Section, Ground Forces) /40

      3.   **15th Infantry Regiment**

      4.   **5th Field Artillery Regiment**

B.   ***Components - 5th Division*** (06/20/41)

      1.   **2nd Infantry Regiment**: 06/20/41 Col. Antti Kääriäinen (Commanding Officer, 3rd Brigade) 03/05/43

      2.   **23rd Infantry Regiment**

      3.   **44th Infantry Regiment**

      4.   **3rd Artillery Regiment**

6th Division (#1) (1939-40; 01/01/40, redesignated **3rd Division**; 06/27/41, III Army Corps): 11/30/39 Col. Paavo Johannes Paalu (Commanding Officer, 3rd Division) 01/01/40 redesignated **3rd Division** - see **3rd Division**.

A.   ***Components - 6th Division (#1)*** (11/30/39)

      1.   **16th Infantry Regiment** (12/08/39 transferred to Detachment Talvela)

      2.   **17th Infantry Regiment** (01/01/40 renumbered **8th Infantry Regiment** and transferred to 3rd Division): /39 Col. Kaarlo Aleksanteri Heiskanen (Commanding Officer, 7th Infantry Regiment) /40

      3.   **18th Infantry Regiment** (01/01/40 renumbered **9th Infantry Regiment** and transferred to 3rd Division)

      4.   **22nd Infantry Regiment** (12/09/39 transferred from Detachment Hanell)

      5.   **6th Filed Artillery Regiment** (01/01/40 renumbered **3rd Field Artillery Regiment** and transferred to 3rd Division)

6th Division (#2): 06/15/41 Col. Verner Viikla 12/18/41 MG Einar August Vihma [Wihma] (killed in action) 08/05/44 Col. Albert Puroma 11/24/44 Col. A. Kurenmaa 11/24/44 disbanded.

A.   ***Components - 6th Division (#2)*** (06/20/41)

      1.   **12th Infantry Regiment**

      2.   **33rd Infantry Regiment**

      3.   **54th Infantry Regiment**

      4.   **14th Artillery Regiment**

7th Division (01/01/40 from **10th Division**; 06/27/41, VII Army Corps): 11/30/39 Col. Aarne Leopold Blick (Commanding Officer, Taipale Sector; /40, acting Commanding Officer, 21st Division) /40 Col. Einar August Vihma [Wihma] (Commanding Officer, Helsinki Military District) /40 unknown? 06/17/41 Col. Antero Johannes Svensson (Commanding General, V Army Corps) 08/01/43 Col. William Häkli 01/28/44 MG Selim Engelbert Isakson (Commanding General, Savo-Karelia Military District) 11/15/44 disbanded.

A.   ***Components - 7th Division*** (01/01/40)

      1.   **19th Infantry Regiment**

      2.   **20th Infantry Regiment**

      3.   **21st Infantry Regiment**

      4.   **7th Field Artillery Regiment**

B.   ***Components - 7th Division*** (06/20/41)

      1.   **9th Infantry Regiment**

2. **30th Infantry Regiment**
3. **51st Infantry Regiment**
4. **2nd Artillery Regiment**

8th Division (1939-40; 06/27/41, IV Army Corps): 11/30/39 unknown? /41 Col. Claes Bertil Napoleon Winell (died of a heart attack) 01/09/43 MG Välinö Henrik Palojärvi (Special Employment by Commander-in-Chief at General Headquarters) 02/17/43 Col. Antti Kääriäinen (acting Commanding Officer, Kymi Military District) 11/15/44 disbanded.

A.   *Components - 8th Division* (11/30/39)
1. **22nd Infantry Regiment**
2. **23rd Infantry Regiment** (12/08/39 transferred to 10th Division)
3. **24th Infantry Regiment**
4. **8th Field Artillery Regiment**

B.   *Components - 8th Division* (06/20/41)
1. **4th Infantry Regiment**
2. **24th Infantry Regiment**
3. **45th Infantry Regiment**
4. **11th Artillery Regiment**

9th Division (1939-40): 11/30/39 MG Hjalmar Fridolf Siilasvuo (06/10/41, Commanding General, III Army Corps) /40 Col. Claes Bertil Napoleon Winell (Commanding Officer, 4th Division) /40 Col. Erkki Johannes Raappana (Commanding Officer, Kainuu Military District) /40 disbanded.

A.   *Components - 9th Division* (11/30/39)
1. **25th Infantry Regiment** (12/06/39 transferred to Kuhmo; 12/08/39 renamed **Brigade Vuokko**): /39 Col. Aarne Leopold Blick (Commanding Officer, Detachment Blick) /39
2. **26th Infantry Regiment** (11/30/39 detached to 8th Division): /39 Col. Aarne Leopold Blick (Commanding Officer, 7th Division) /39
3. **27th Infantry Regiment** (12/07/39 detached to North Finland Group)
4. **9th Field Artillery Regiment**

10th Division (#1) (1939-40; 01/01/40, redesignated **7th Division**): 11/30/39 Col. V. Kuappila 12/10/39 Col. Aarne Leopold Blick (Commanding Officer, 7th Division) 01/01/40 redesignated **7th Division** - see **7th Division**.

A.   *Components - 10th Division (#1)* (11/30/39)
1. **23rd Infantry Regiment** (12/08/39 transferred from 8th Division)
2. **28th Infantry Regiment** (01/01/40 renumbered **19th Infantry Regiment** and transferred to 7th Division)
3. **29th Infantry Regiment** (01/01/40 renumbered **20th Infantry Regiment** and transferred to 7th Division)
4. **30th Infantry Regiment** (01/01/40 renumbered **21st Infantry Regiment** and transferred to 7th Division)
5. **10th Field Artillery Regiment** (01/01/40 renumbered **7th Field Artillery Regiment** and transferred to 7th Division)

10th Division (#2) (06/27/41, IV Army Corps): 06/18/41 Col. Johannes "Jussi" Sihvo (relieved; employment to special duties to the Commander-in-Chief) 06/17/44 Col. Kai Savonjousi 12/04/44 disbanded.
A.   *Components - 10th Division (#2)* (06/20/41)
1.   **1st Infantry Regiment**
2.   **22nd Infantry Regiment**
3.   **43rd Infantry Regiment**
4.   **9th Artillery Regiment**

11th Division (#1) (1939-40; 01/01/40, redesignated **2nd Division**) 06/27/41, VI Army Corps): 11/30/39 Col. Eino Koskimies (06/18/41, Commanding Officer, 5th Division) 01/01/40 redesignated **2nd Division** - see **2nd Division**.
A.   *Components - 11th Division (#1)* (11/30/39)
1.   **31st Infantry Regiment** (01/01/40 renumbered **4th Infantry Regiment** and transferred to 2nd Division)
2.   **32nd Infantry Regiment** (01/01/40 renumbered **5th Infantry Regiment** and transferred to 2nd Division)
3.   **33rd Infantry Regiment** (01/01/40 renumbered **6th Infantry Regiment** and transferred to 2nd Division)
4.   **11th Field Artillery Regiment** (01/01/40 renumbered **2nd Field Artillery Regiment** and transferred to 2nd Division)

11th Division (#2) (06/27/41, VI Army Corps): /40 Col. Woldemar [Voldemar] Oinonen (acting Commanding Officer, III Army Corps) 06/18/41 Col. Kaarlo Aleksanteri Heiskanen (Commanding General, Central Finland Military District) 11/12/44 disbanded.
A.   *Components - 11th Division (#2)* (06/20/41)
1.   **8th Infantry Regiment**
2.   **29th Infantry Regiment**
3.   **50th Infantry Regiment**
4.   **4th Artillery Regiment**

12th Division (1939-40; 06/27/41, IV Army Corps): 11/30/39 Col. L. Tiainen /40 Col. Antero Johannes Svensson (Commanding Officer Savo-Karjala Military District) /40 Col. Aarne Otto Snellman (Commanding Officer, Kajaani Military District) /40 unknown? 06/16/41 Col. Einar August Vihma [Wihma] (Commanding General, 6th Division) 12/18/41 Col. Per Ekholm 01/42 disbanded and used to form **3rd Brigade** - **3rd Brigade**.
A.   *Components - 12th Division* (11/30/39)
1.   **34th Infantry Regiment**
2.   **35th Infantry Regiment**
3.   **36th Infantry Regiment** (12/12/39 detached to 13th Division)
4.   **12th Field Artillery Regiment**
B.   *Components - 12th Division* (06/20/41)
1.   **26th Infantry Regiment**
2.   **47th Infantry Regiment**
3.   **55th Infantry Regiment**
4.   **7th Artillery Regiment**

13th Division (1939-40): 11/30/39 Col. Hannu Esa Hannuksela (Commanding Officer, Artillery, Armor Forces; /40, Commanding Officer, South Pohjanmaa Military District) /40 Col. Kaarlo Aleksanteri Heiskanen (Commanding Officer, Keski-Pohjanmaa Military District) /40 disbanded

A.   *Components - 13th Division* (11/30/39)
   1.   **37th Infantry Regiment**
   2.   **38th Infantry Regiment** (12/08/39 transferred to 10th Division)
   3.   **39th Infantry Regiment**: 11/30/39 Col. Pietari Aleksanteri Autti (Commanding Officer, 8th Infantry Brigade) /
   4.   **13th Field Artillery Regiment**

14th Division (05/40): Col. Aaro Olavi Pajari (Commanding Officer, North [Pojois] Häme Military District) /40 unknown? 06/16/41 Col. Erkki Johannes Raappana (Commanding General, Group Raappana) 01/42 Col. Josse Olavi Hannula 12/11/44 disbanded.

A.   *Components - 14th Division* (06/20/41)
   1.   **10th Infantry Regiment**
   2.   **31st Infantry Regiment**
   3.   **52nd Infantry Regiment**
   4.   **18th Artillery Regiment**

15th Division (05/40; 06/27/41, II Army Corps): /40 Col. Frans Uno Fagernäs (Commanding Officer, North Pohjanmas) /40 unknown? 06/18/41 Col. Niilo Viktor Hersalo (Commanding General, Satakunta Military District) 11/27/44 disbanded.

A.   *Components - 15th Division* (06/20/41)
   1.   **15th Infantry Regiment**
   2.   **36th Infantry Regiment**
   3.   **57th Infantry Regiment**
   4.   **12th Artillery Regiment**

17th Division (05/40): /40 Col. Aarne Otto Snellman (Commanding Officer, Kajaani Military District) /40 unknown? 06/11/41 Col. Aarne Otto Snellman (wounded/; later died from his wounds) 04/13/42 Col. Viktor Alonzo Sundman (Commandant, Helsinki Garrison) 11/28/44 disbanded.

A.   *Components - 17th Division* (06/20/41)
   1.   **13th Infantry Regiment**
   2.   **34th Infantry Regiment**
   3.   **61st Infantry Regiment**
   4.   **8th Artillery Regiment**

18th Division (05/40; 06/27/41, II Army Corps): 06/18/41 Col. Aaro Olavi Pajari [+ 1942, Commanding General, Battle Group Pajari] (Commanding General, 3rd Division) 10/21/43 MG Paavo Johannes Paalu (relieved; employment on Special Duties for Commander-in-Chief, General Headquarters) 06/26/44 Col. Otto Gustaf "Gösta" Snellman 07/31/44 Col. Väinö Oinonen 12/16/44 disbanded.

A.   *Components - 18th Division* (06/20/41)
   1.   **6th Infantry Regiment**

2.   **27th Infantry Regiment**
3.   **48th Infantry Regiment**
4.   **19th Artillery Regiment**

19th Division (05/40; 06/27/41, VII Army Corps): 06/20/41 Col. Hannu Esa Hannuksela (Commanding Officer, 2nd Division) 02/01/42 disbanded.

A.   ***Components - 19th Division*** (06/20/41)

1.   **16th Infantry Regiment**: /39 Col. Aaro Olavi Pajari (Commanding Officer, Pajari Detachment) /39 Col. Kaarlo Ilmari Viljanen (Chief of Staff, Häme Military District) /40
2.   **37th Infantry Regiment**
3.   **58th Infantry Regiment**
4.   **10th Artillery Regiment**

21st Division (1939-40; formed as a training/replacement division): Col. Niilo Viktor Hersalo (Commanding Officer, Satakunta Military District) /40 Col. Aarne Leopold Blick (Special Purposes Officer, III Corps) /40 disbanded.

23rd Division (1940; formed as a training/replacement division): Col. Paavo Johannes Paalu (Commanding Officer, West Finland [Varsinals-Suomi] Military District) /40 Col. Woldemar [Voldemar] Oinonen (Commanding Officer, 11th Separate Division) /40 disbanded.

Armored Divisions

1st Armored Division (08/43; disbanded 12/30/44): **Armored Brigade** 06/28/42 MG Ernst Ruben Lagus (Commanding General, 1st Armored Division) 08/43 redesignated **1st Armored Division** 08/43 MG Ernst Ruben Lagus [+ 09/29/43 to 10/21/43, acting Commanding General, VI Army Corps] (Commanding General, 2nd Division) 12/30/44 disbanded.

Military Districts

Satakunta-Häme Military District (1933): LCol. Selim Engelbert Isakson (Commanding Officer, Tuurunmaa Military District) /38 Col. Paavo Johannes Paalu (Commanding Officer, 6th Reserve Division) /39

South [Etelä] Pohjanmaa Military District (1933): Col. Claes Bertil Napoleon Winell (Commanding Officer, 9th Division) /40 Col. Hannu Esa Hannuksela (Commanding Officer, 19th Division) 06/20/41

North Pohjanmaa Military District (1934): Col. Hjalmar Fridolf Siilasvuo (Commanding General, 9th Division) /39 unknown? /40 Col. Frans Uno Fagernäs (Commanding Officer, 3rd Division) 06/06/61

Savo Military District (1934): Col. Hannu Esa Hannuksela (Commanding Officer, 13th Division) 11/30/39

Tuurunmaa Military District (1937): Col. Taavetti "Pappa" Laatikainen (Commanding Officer, 1st Division) /38 Col. Selim Engelbert Isakson (Commanding Officer, 5th Division) /39

Central [Keski] Pohjanmaa Military District (1940): Col. Kaarlo Aleksanteri Heiskanen (Commanding Officer, 11th Division) 06/18/41

Gulf of Finland Military District (1940): Col. Claes Bertil Napoleon Winell (Commanding Officer 8th Division) 06/10/41

Helinski Military District (1940): Col. Einar August Vihma [Wihma] (Commanding Officer, 12th Division) 06/16/41 redesignated **Commandant of Helsinki** 06/16/41 MG Harry Uno Alfthan (?) 11/28/44 MG Viktor Alonzo Sundman.
A.   **Chief of Police, Helsinki**: /34 LCol. Johan Viktor Arajuuri (Commanding Officer, 4th Division) /40 unknown /43 MG Johan Viktor Arajuuri (?) /44

Kainuu Military District (1940): Col. Erkki Johannes Raappana (Commanding Officer, 14th Division) 06/16/41

Kajaani Military District (1940): Col. Aarne Otto Snellman (Commanding Officer, 17th Division) 06/11/41

North [Pojois] Häme Military District (1940): Col. Aaro Olavi Pajari (Commanding Officer, 18th Division) 06/18/41
A.   **Chief of Staff, Häme Military District**: /40 Col. Kaarlo Ilmari Viljanen (Commanding Officer, Salpausselkä Military District) /41

Päijänne Military District (1940): Col. Johannes "Jussi" Sihvo (Commanding Officer, 10th Division) 06/18/41

Salpausselkä Military District (1941): Col. Kaarlo Ilmari Viljanen (Commanding Officer, 4th Division) 06/18/41

Satakunta Military District (1940): Col. Niilo Viktor Hersalo (Commanding Officer, 15th Division) 06/18/41 unknown? 11/27/44 MG Niilo Viktor Hersalo.

Satakunta East [Itä] Savo Military District (1940): Col. Aarne Leopold Blick (Commanding Officer, 2nd Division) 06/10/41 unknown? /44 MG Aarne Leopold Blick (Commanding General, 2nd Division) 11/19/44

Savo-Karjala Military District (1940): Col. Antero Johannes Svensson (Commanding Officer, 7th Division) 06/17/41

Southwest Finland [Lounai-Suomi] Military District (1940): Col. Paavo Johannes Paalu (Commanding Officer, 1st Division) 06/18/41 unknown? 11/23/44 MG Frans Uno Fagernäs (Commanding General, North Finland Military District) /44 MG Lars Rafael Melander.

West Finland [Varsinals-Suomi] Military District (1940): Col. Paavo Johannes Paalu (Commanding Officer, Southwest Finland [Lounai-Suomi] Military District) /40

Commandant of Viipuri (1941): MG Juho Henrik Heiskanen (employment on special duties to the Inspector-General of Military Training) /41

Central Finland Military District (1944): MG Kaarlo Aleksanteri Heiskanen (Chief, Unknown? Section, Armed Forces High Command) /45 MG Frans Uno Fagernäs.

Kymi Military District (1944): MG Antti Kääriäinen (acting Savo-Karelia Military District) /44 MG Selim Engelbert Isakson (retired) ?45 MG Antti Kääriäinen (Commanding General, Savo-Karelia Military District) /45 MG Välinö Henrik Palojärvi.

North Finland Military District (1944): unknown? /44 MG Frans Uno Fagernäs (Commanding General, Central Finland Military District) /45

North Perä Military District: 11/27/44 Col. Pietari Aleksanteri Autti.

Savo-Karelia Military District (1944): MG Selim Engelbert Isakson (Commanding General, Kymi Military District) /44 MG Antti Kääriäinen (acting; attached to Ministry of Defense) /44 MG Aaro Olavi Pajari (Chief of Artillery, Armed Forces High Command) /45 MG Antti Kääriäinen (acting; Commanding General, Kymi Military District) /45 unknown? /45 MG Antti Kääriäinen.

South Häme Military District: /44 MG Kustaa Anders Tapola (Inspector of Military Schools) /45

Uusimaa Military District (1944): MG Ilmari Armas-Eino Martola.

Brigades

1st Brigade (11/30/39, 1st Division): /39 Col. Einat August Vihma [Wihma] (Commanding Officer, 7th Division) 11/30/39 Col. Einar August Wihma (Commanding Officer, 7th Division) /39

2nd Brigade (11/30/39, 1st Division): /39 Col. Antero Johannes Svensson (Commanding Officer, 12th Division) /40 Col. Antti Kääriäinen (Commanding Officer, 2nd Infantry Regiment) /41

3rd Brigade (01/42, from **12th Division**): /39 Col. Aarne Leopold Blick (Commanding Officer, 26th Infantry Regiment) /39 Col. Antti Kääriäinen (Commanding Officer, 2nd Brigade) /40 unknown? /42 Col. Pietari Aleksanteri Autti (Commanding Officer, 4th Division) 03/05/43 Col. Antti Kääriäinen (Commanding Officer, 8th Division) 02/17/44

4th Brigade: /39 Col. Juhani "Jussi" Sihvo (Commanding Officer, Sihvo Group) /39

7th Brigade
A.   ***Components - 7th Brigade***
    1.   **13th Infantry Regiment**
    2.   **34th Infantry Regiment**
    3.   **44th Infantry Regiment**

8th Brigade: /40 Col. Pietari Aleksanteri Autti (Commanding Officer, 8th Infantry regiment) /41

12th Brigade:

15th Brigade:

Brigade Vuokko (12/08/39, from **25th Infantry Regiment**):

Bicycle Brigade (/40): Col. Ernst Ruben Lagus (Commanding Officer, Light Infantry (Jäger) Brigade) /40

Light Infantry (Jäger) Brigade (1940): Col. Ernst Ruben Lagus (Commanding Officer, 1st Light Infantry (Jäger) Brigade) 06/27/41 disbanded.

1st Light Infantry (Jäger) Brigade (06/27/41, Task Force Oinonen): Col. Ernst Ruben Lagus

2nd Light Infantry (Jäger) Brigade (06/27/41, Task Force Oinonen): Col. Viktor Alonzo Sundman (Commanding Officer, 13th Infantry Regiment) /42

Light Brigade (12/05/44): MG Antero Johannes Svensson.

Cavalry Brigade (06/27/41, Task Force Oinonen): /27 LCol. George Fredrik Palmroth [+ /39

to /40, Commanding General, Group Uusikirkko] (retired) /41 Col. Harry Uno Alfthan (Commandant, Helsinki Military District) /41 unknown? /42 Col. Lars Rafael Melander (employment on Special Needs to the Commander-in-Chief, Armed Forces) /44 unknown? /44 MG Lars Rafael Melander (Commanding General, Southwest Finland Military District) /44

A. *Components* - **Cavalry Brigade** (1939)
    1. **Häme Cavalry Regiment**
    2. **Uusimaa Dragoon Regiment**: /28 LCol. Harry Uno Alfthan (Commanding Officer, Cavalry Brigade) /40

2ⁿᵈ Coastal Brigade (06/27/41, IV Army Corps):

Gulf of Finland Coastal Brigade:

Finnish White Guard: /36 Col. Einar August Vihma [Wihma] (Commanding Officer, 1ˢᵗ Brigade) /39

Viipuri Civil Guard District: /38 Col. Juhani "Jussi" Sihvo (Commanding Officer, 4ᵗʰ Brigade) /39

Detachment Blick (1939): Col. Aarne Leopold Blick (Commanding Officer, 3ʳᵈ Brigade) /39 disbanded.

Finnish Air Force

East Finland Air Defense District: /33 Col. Eino Iisakki Järvinen [+ Commanding Officer, 3rd Coastal Artillery Regiment] (Commanding Officer, Lake Lagoda Sea Defense) /39

1st Regiment: 11/30/39 LCol. Y. Opas [FinAF] 03/13/40 unknown? 05/03/42 LCol. V. Rekola [FinAF] 09/04/44.

2nd Regiment: 11/30/39 LCol. R. Lorenz [FinAF] 03/13/40 unknown? 06/25/41 LCol. R. Lorenz [FinAF] 06/16/43 LCol. J. Harju-Jeanty [FinAF] 09/04/44.

3rd Regiment: 06/25/41 LCol. E. Nuotui [FinAF] 05/27/43 LCol. G. Magnussion [FinAF] 09/04/44.

4th Regiment: 11/30/39 LCol. T. Somerto [FinAF] 03/13/40 unknown? 06/25/41 LCol. T. Somerto [FinAF] 04/02/42 LCol. O. Sarko [FinAF] 06/27/44 LCol. B. Gabrielsson [FinAF] 09/04/44.

5th Regiment: 11/04/42 Maj. K. Ilanko [FinAF] 09/04/44.

Finnish Navy

1st Coast Division (07/13/44): Col. Pekka Enkainen 09/09/44 MG Eino Iisakki Järvinen (Commanding Officer, Turku Coastal Artillery Regiment; /45, Inspector of Navy Artillery, Naval Staff) 11/30/44

Äänis Coastal Brigade (1943): Col. Eino Iisakki Järvinen (employment on special duties to Commander-in-Chief, Armed Forces)

Lagoda Coastal Brigade (1941): Col. Eino Iisakki Järvinen (Commanding Officer, Äänis Coastal Brigade) /43

Lake Lagoda Sea Defense: /39 Col. Eino Iisakki Järvinen (Chief, Fortifications Works, General Headquarters) /40 unknown? /41 Col. Eino Iisakki Järvinen (Commanding Officer, Lagoda Coastal Brigade) /41

The Finnish Navy had no major ships prior or during World War II. A major ship is consider a cruiser or larger. The Finnish Navy consisted of:

1 Coast Defense Ship	*Väinämöinen*	
4 Gunboats	*Uusimaa*; *Hämeenmaa*; *Karjala*; *Turunmaa*	
5 Submarines	*Vesikko*; *Vetehinen*; *Vesihiisi*; *Iku-Turso*; *Saukko*	

7 Minelayers
18 Motor Minesweepers
9 Motor Patrol Boats
4 Motor Torpedo Boats
3 Torpedo Boats
1 Cadets' Training Ship
1 Sail Training Ship
1 Submarine Depot Ship & Icebreaker *Sisu*
5 Icebreakers   *Otso*; *Tarmo*; *Sampo*; *Apu*; *Murtaja*

Table of Equivalent Ranks

Finnish Army	Translation	United States & British Army
Suomen Marsalkka	Marshal of Finland	General of the Army [U. S.] Field Marshal [Brit.]
Sotamarsalkka	General Field Marshal	General
Kenraali	Colonel General	Lieutenant General
Kenraaliluutnantti	Lieutenant General	Major General
Kenraalimajuri	Major General	Brigadier General [U. S.] Brigadier [Brit.]
Eversti	Colonel	Colonel
Everstiluutnantti	Lieutenant Colonel	Lieutenant Colonel
Majuri	Major	Major
Hauptmann	Captain	Captain
Oberfähnrich	First Lieutenant	First Lieutenant [U. S.] Lieutenant [Brit.]
Fähnrich	Lieutenant	Second Lieutenant

Senior Military Officers

Name	Rank	Date of Rank	Status at end of war
01. Karl Gustaf Emil Mannerheim	Marshal of Finland	Jun 04 42	President of Finland
02. Paul Martin Wetzer	General of Infantry	May 16 28	Special duties for CinC
03. Karl Fredrik Wilkama	General of Infantry	May 16 28	Special duties for CinC
04. Ernst Linder	General of Cavalry	Mar 25 40	CG, Swedish Volunteer Corps
05. Axel Erik Heinrichs	General of Infantry	Oct 03 41	CinC, Armed Forces
06. Vilho Petter Nenonen	General of Artillery	Oct 03 41	Inspector-General, Artillery
07. Karl Rudolf Walden	General of Infantry	Jun 03 42	Defense Minister to 11/44
08. Oiva Oskar Olenius	General of Infantry	unknown?	First Secretary, Ministry of Defense
09. Paavo Juho Talvela	General of Artillery	unknown?	Advisor & Confident to Marshal of Finland Mannerheim
09. Oscar Paul Enckell	Lieutenant General	Sep 18 24	Special Envoy for CinC
10. Johannes Ferdinand Ignatius	Lieutenant General	May 16 28	died 1941
11. Aarne Sihvo	Lieutenant General	Aug 14 30	Chief of Civil Defense
12. Hugo Viktor Österman	Lieutenant General	May 16 35	Chief Inspector of Infantry
13. Kaarlo Lauri Torvald Malmberg	Lieutenant General	May 16 36	CinC, Home Troops + CinC, Civil Guard
14. Karl Lennart Oesch	Lieutenant General	Dec 06 36	CinC, Ground Forces
15. Harald Öhquist	Lieutenant General	Dec 06 36	Chief Inspector of Military Training
16. Edvard Fritjof Hanell	Lieutenant General	Apr 11 40	CG, Fortification Works
17. Väinö Lahja Richard Valve	Lieutenant General	Apr 09 41	Defense Minister
18. Jarl Frithiof Lundqvist	Lieutenant General	Oct 03 41	CinC, Finnish Air Force
19. Viljo Einar Tuompo	Lieutenant General	Dec 11 41	Chief of Command Staff
20. Johan Woldemar Hägglund	Lieutenant General	Jan 16 42	Inspector-General, Armed Forces
21. Taavetti "Pappa" Laatikainen	Lieutenant General	Jan 16 42	CG, IV Army Corps
22. Unio Bernhard Sarlin	Lieutenant General	Jan 16 42	Chief Corps of Engineers, General HQ
24. Aksel Fredrik Airo	Lieutenant General	Jun 03 42	12/44, Chief, General Staff
25. Leonard August Mathias Grandell	Lieutenant General	Jul 03 42	Inspector, War Economics
26. Hjalmar Fridolf Siilasvuo	Lieutenant General	Jul 03 42	CG, 1st Division
27. Einar Nikolai Mäkinen	Lieutenant General	Jan 08 45	CG II Army Corps

Finnish Military Units in Selected Campaigns

The Finnish Army, November 30, 1939

Finnish Army
    Army of the Isthmus
        II Corps
                1st Infantry Division
                4th Infantry Division
                5th Infantry Division
                11th Infantry Division
                23rd Infantry Division
        III Corps
                8th Infantry Division
                10th Infantry Division
                21st Infantry Division
        Reserves, Army of the Isthmus
                6th Infantry Division
                9th Infantry Division
    General Headquarters (control)
        IV Corps
                2nd Infantry Division
                7th Infantry Division
                12th Infantry Division
                13th Infantry Division
        V Corps
                Nine independent battalions
        Group Talvela
        North Karelian Group
        North Finland Group
        Lapland Group

Finnish Forces for the Invasion of Russia, June 22, 1941

(fought under the of the German Army of Norway)

Southern Front
    South-East Army
        II Army Corps
            2nd Infantry Division
            10th Infantry Division
            15th Infantry Division
            18th Infantry Division
        IV Army Corps
            4th Infantry Division
            8th Infantry Division
            17th Infantry Division
    Army of Karelia
        VI Army Corps
            1st Infantry Division
            5th Infantry Division
            11th Infantry Division
            163rd German Infantry Division
        VII Army Corps
            7th Infantry Division
            19th Infantry Division
        Southern Front Reserves
            12th Infantry Division
            14th Infantry Division

Finnish Forces at the End of the Continuation War, 1944

Finnish Army
- **Karelian Isthmus**
  - V Army Corps
    - 10th Infantry Division
    - 11th Infantry Division
    - 17th Infantry Division
  - IV Army Corps
    - 4th Infantry Division
    - 6th Infantry Division
    - 18th Infantry Division
  - III Army Corps
    - 2nd Infantry Division
    - 15th Infantry Division
  - Reserve
    - 3rd Infantry Division
    - 1st Armored Division
- **Northern Karelia**
  - VI Army Corps
    - 5th Infantry Division
    - 8th Infantry Division
  - II Army Corps
    - 1st Infantry Division
    - 7th Infantry Division
  - Reserve
    - 14th Infantry Division

Lapland War, August 1944

Finnish Army
- III Army Corps
  - 1st Infantry Division
  - 3rd Infantry Division
  - 6th Infantry Division
  - 11th Infantry Division
  - 1st Armored Division

PART 2

IMPERIAL JAPAN's ALLY and PUPPET STATES

Thailand [Siam]

Great Empire of Manchukuo [Manchuria]

Mengjiang [Inner Mongolia]

Republic of China-Nanjing

State of Burma

Second Philippine Republic

Azad Hind [Provisional Government of Free India]

Empire of Vietnam

Kingdom of Cambodia

Kingdom of Luang Phra Bang [Laos]

THAILAND
[SIAM]

(Japanese Ally)

Thailand Government

King: 03/02/35 ANANDA MAHIDOL [RAMA VIII] {exiled in Switzerland until 12/05/45} (died) 06/09/46 BHUMIBOL ADULYADEJ [RAMA IX].

Regent: 03/02/35 Col. Prince Oscar Anuwatjaturong [Anuvatana] [+ President, Council of Regency] 08/12/35 LCdr. Prince Arthit Thip-apha [Prince Aditya Dibabha] [+ President, Council of Regency] 06/44 PRIDI BANOMYONG [+ President, Council of Regency].

Council of Regency:
A. **President**: 03/02/35 Col. Prince Oscar Anuwatjaturong [Anuvatana] [+ Regent] 08/12/35 LCdr. Prince Arthit Thip-apha [Prince Aditya Dibabha] [+ Regent] 06/44 PRIDI BANOMYONG [+ Regent].
B. **Members**:
/34 LCdr. Prince Arthit Thip-apha [Prince Aditya Dibabha] (Regent & President, Council of Regency) 08/12/35
03/02/35 CHAO PHRAYA [Duke] YOMMARAJ [PUN SUKHUM]
/35 Gen. Chao Phraya [Duke] Pichayenyothin (?) /42

Prime Minister: 06/24/33 Gen. Phraya [Marquis] Phahol Phonphayuhasena [+ Commander-in-Chief, Royal Thai Army; + /37, Inspector-General, Royal Thai Armed Forces] (resigned) 12/26/38 MG Plaek Luang [Viscount] Phibunsongkhram [+ to /40, Commander-in-Chief, Royal Thai Army; + /40, Supreme Commander, Royal Thai Armed Forces] 08/01/44 Maj. Luang [Viscount] Khuang Arhaiwong (resigned) 08/17/45 vacant 08/31/45 THAWI BOONYAKET 09/17/45 SENI PRAMOJ.
A. **Foreign Affairs Minister**: /35 PRIDI BANOMYONG (12/38, Finance Minister) /37 DIREK JAYANAMA (Ambassador to Japan) /42 MG Luang [Viscount] Wichit Wichitwathakan [nee Kim Liang] (Ambassador to Japan) /43
　1. **Ambassador to Japan**: /42 DIREK JAYANAMA /43 MG Luang [Viscount] Wichit Wichitwathakan [nee Kim Liang] (/51, Finance Minister) /45.
　1. **Ambassador to the United States**: /41? SENI PRAMOJ (Prime Minister) 09/17/45
B. **Defense Minister (Minister of Armed Forces)**: Gen. Plaek Luang [Viscount] Phibunsongkhram (Prime Minister) /41 LG Mangkorn Phromyothi (Minister of the Interior) /42 unknown? /43 LG Luang [Viscount] Kriengsakphichit (Commander-in-Chief, Royal Thai Army) /44 unknown? /45 LG Jira Wichitsongkhram (?) /45 LG Chit Mansion Sinadyotharak (?) /46 LG Luang [Viscount] Promyothi /47 LG Luang [Viscount] Chartnakrob.

1. **Undersecretary, Ministry of Defense**: LG Phra [Count/Earl] Prachonpadchanuk (Commanding General, Second Army) /43
2. **Supreme Commander, Royal Thai Armed Forces**: /40 FM Plaek Luang [Viscount] Phibunsongkhram [+ Prime Minister] (Supreme Advisor to Royal Thai Armed Forces) 08/01/44 Gen. Phraya [Marquis] Phahol Phonphayuhasena.

C. **Finance Minister**: 12/38 PRIDI BANOMYONG (resigned; 06/44, Regent & President , Council of Regency) 12/41

D. **Interior Minister**: /41 Gen. Luang [Viscount] Chawengsaksongkhram (/46, Minister of the Interior) /42 Gen. Mangkorn Phromyothi (/45, detained as a war criminal; released; /48, Minister of Education) /44

E. **Trade & Commerce Minister**: /42 LG Jarun Rattanakuln Seriroengrit (/45, detained as a war criminal) /44

F. **Director General, Department of Fine Arts [Propaganda Minister]**: /38 MG Luang [Viscount] Wichit Wichitwathakan [nee Kim Liang] (Foreign Affairs Minister) /42

Japanese Forces in Thailand

Commander, Japanese Forces in Thailand (12/08/41): **{Japanese} Fifteenth Army** 12/08/41 LG Shojiro Iida [Japanese] [see Volume IV - Japan] 01/04/43 Japanese Fifteenth Army replaced by **{Japanese} Thailand (Siam) Garrison Army** (formed) 01/04/43 LG Aketo Nakamura [Japanese] (Commanding General, Thirty-Ninth Japanese Army) [see Volume IV - Japan] 12/20/44 redesignated **{Japanese} Thirty-Ninth Army** 12/20/44 LG Aketo Nakamura [Japanese] (Commanding General, 18th Japanese Area Army) [see Volume IV - Japan] 07/14/45 redesignated **{Japanese} 18th Area Army** 07/14/45 LG Aketo Nakamura [Japanese] (?) [see Volume IV - Japan] 08/15/45

Military High Command

Supreme Commander, Royal Thai Armed Forces: /40 FM Plaek Luang [Viscount] Phibunsongkhram [+ Prime Minister] (Supreme Advisor to Royal Thai Armed Forces) 08/01/44 Gen. Phraya [Marquis] Phahol Phonphayuhasena [+ 08/24/44, Commander-in-Chief, Royal Thai Army].

1. **Military Secretary to FM Plaek Phibunsongkhram**: /41 MG Chai Pratipasen [+ to /44, Member, Joint Thai-Japanese Military Commission] 08/01/44

A. **Supreme Advisor to Royal Thai Armed Forces** (08/01/44): FM Plaek Luang [Viscount] Phibunsongkhram (detained as a war criminal, but released by courts shortly afterwards; /47, Commander-in-Chief, Royal Thai Army) /45.

1. **Military Secretary to FM Plaek Phibunsongkhram**: /44 MG Chai Pratipasen.

B. **Deputy Supreme Commander, Royal Thai Armed Forces**: 08/01/44 LG Chit Mansin Sinadyotharak (Minister of Defense) /45

C. **Commander-in-Chief, Royal Thai Army**: /32 Gen. Phraya [Marquis] Phahol Phonphayuhasena [+ 06/24/33, Prime Minister; + /37, Inspector-General, Royal Thai Armed Forces] 12/26/38 Gen. Plaek Luang [Viscount] Phibunsongkhram [+ Prime Minister] 08/06/44 LG Luang [Viscount] Kriengsakphichit (?) 08/24/44 Gen. Phraya [Marquis] Phahol Phonphayuhasena [+ Supreme Commander, Royal Thai Armed Forces].

D. **Commander-in-Chief, Royal Thai Navy**: 05/01/34 RA Phraya [Marquis] Wichanworajak [RTN] (?) /38 Adm. Sin Kamonnawin [RTN].

E. **Commander-in-Chief, Royal Thai Air Force**: /37 AM Munee Mahasanthana Vejayantarungsarit [RTAF] (?) /41 AM Lunag Atuegtevadej [RTAF] (?) /43 AM Luang [Viscount] Tevaritpanluek [RTAF].

F. **Liaison Officer, Franco-Thai Joint Committee**: /41 MG Chai Pratipasen (Member, Joint Thai-Japanese Military Commission)

G. **Joint Thai-Japanese Military Commission**:
1. **Members, Joint Thai-Japanese Military Commission**:
   /41 MG Prayoon Pamornmontri [+ to /43, Head, Yuwachon Movement] (/45, detained as war criminal) /44
   /41 MG Chai Pratipasen [+ Military Secretary, FM Plaek Luang [Viscount] Phibunsongkhram] /44

H. **Military Mission to Kandy (Sri Lanka [Ceylon])** (/45):
1. **Head, Military Mission to Kandy (Sri Lanka [Ceylon])** (/45): LG Luang [Viscount] Senanarong (Deputy Commander-in-Chief, Royal Thai Army) /46.
2. **Member, Military Mission to Kandy (Sri Lanka [Ceylon])** (/45): LG Phraya [Marquis] Aphaisongkhram

Inspector-General, Royal Thai Armed Forces: /37 Gen. Phraya [Marquis] Phahol Phonphayuhasena [+ to 12/26/38, Prime Minister] (Supreme Commander, Royal Armed Forces) 08/01/44

Army High Command

Commander-in-Chief, Royal Thai Army: /32 Gen. Phraya [Marquis] Phahol Phonphayuhasena [+ 06/24/33, Prime Minister; + /37, Inspector-General, Royal Thai Armed Forces] 12/26/38 Gen. Plaek Luang [Viscount] Phibunsongkhram [+ Prime Minister] /40 unknown? /44 LG Luang [Viscount] Kriengsakphichit (?) 08/24/44 Gen. Phraya [Marquis] Phahol Phonphayuhasena [+ Supreme Commander, Royal Thai Armed Forces].

A. **Deputy Commander-in-Chief, Royal Thai Army**: /33 LG Plaek Luang [Viscount] Phibunsongkhram (Prime Minister & Commander-in-Chief, Royal Thai Army) 12/26/38 unknown? /41 MG Chit Mansin Sinadyotharak (Deputy Supreme Commander, Royal Thai Armed Forces) 08/01/44

B. **Assistant Deputy Commander-in-Chief, Royal Thai Army**: /43 MG Luang [Viscount] Senanarong (Head, Thai Military Mission to Kandy) /45

C. **Chief of Staff, Royal Thai Army**: /39 LG Jira Wichitsongkhram (Commanding General, Phayap Army) /42 unknown? /43 LG Luang [Viscount] Prasityutthasin (Commanding General, Phayap Army) 12/43 LG Luang [Viscount] Chartnakrob [+ /44, Commanding General, Second Army] (/47, Minister of Defense) /45.

D. **Quartermaster-General, Royal Thai Army**: /38 MG Phra [Count/Earl] Prachonpadchanuk (Undersectary, Ministry of Defense) /42 unknown? /44 MG Luang [Viscount] Buranasongkhram.

E. **Director, 4ᵗʰ Department, Royal Thai Army General Staff**: MG Luang [Viscount] Saranuchit (Chief of Staff, Phayap Army)

F. **Member, General Staff**:
/44 LG Phin Choonhavan (/48, Commander-in-Chief, Royal Thai Army).

G. *Military Governors*
1. **Military Governor, Federated Shan States** (08/42): MG Phin Choonhavan (Deputy Commander, Phayap Army) /43 unknown? /43 MG Phin Choonhavan (Member, General Staff) /44
2. **Military Governor, Siamese Malaya**: /44 LG Luang [Viscount] Phairirayordej (/48, Director, Thai Armed Forces' Veterans' Association) /45.

H. **Head, Yuwachon Movement**: /38 Col. Prayoon Pamornmontri [+ /41, Member, Joint Thai-Japanese Military Commission] /43

I. **Lopburi Province**: /37 MG Phra [Count/Earl] Wichaiyutthadechakhani (/43, Commanding General, Phayap Army) /39

Navy High Command

Commander-in-Chief, Royal Thai Navy: 05/01/34 RA Phraya [Marquis] Wichanworajak [RTN] (?) /38 Adm. Sin Kamonnawin [RTN].

A.　　**Chief of Naval Staff**: RA Luang [Viscount] Sindhu [RTN]

Air Force High Command

Commander-in-Chief, Royal Thai Air Force: /37 AM Munee Mahasanthana Vejayantarungsarit [RTAF] (?) /41 AM Lunag Atuegtevadej [RTAF] (?) /43 AM Luang [Viscount] Tevaritpanluek [RTAF].

A.　　**Chief of the Air Staff**: 12/41? GC Khun [Baron] Ronnaphakasd [RTAF]

Armies

First Army: /40 LG Mangkorn Phromyothi (Commanding General, Buraphia Army) 10/40

Burapha Army (10/40; French-Thai War; 05/09/41, disbanded): LG Mangkorn Phromyothi (Minister of Defense) 05/09/41 disbanded.
A.   **Deputy Commander, Burapha Army**: /40 MG Luang [Viscount] Phairirayordej (Commanding General, 2nd Infantry Division) 12/40 MG Jarun Rattanakuln Seriroengrit (Commanding General, Phayap Army) 05/09/41 dissolved.

Isaan Army (10/40; French-Thai War; 05/09/41, disbanded): LG Luang [Viscount] Kriengsakphichit (Minister of Defense) 05/09/41 disbanded.
A.   **Deputy Commander, Isaan Army**: /40 MG Phin Choonhavan (/42, Commanding General, 3rd Infantry Division)05/09/41 dissolved.

Phayap [Northwest] Army (10/41; HQ: Lampang): LG Jarun Rattanakuln Seriroengrit (Minister of Trade & Commerce) /42 LG Jira Wichitsongkhram (/45, Minister of Defense) /43 LG Decha Bunyakhup (?) /43 LG Phra [Count/Earl] Wichaiyutthadechakhani (?) /44 LG Luang [Viscount] Prasityutthasin.
A.   **Deputy Commander, Phayap Army** (10/41): MG Decha Bunyakhup (Commanding General, Phayap Army) /43 LG Phin Choonhavan (Military Governor, Federated Shan States) /43 unknown? /44 MG Luang [Viscount] Sutthisanronnakorn (Commanding General, 4th Infantry Division) /45
B.   **Chief of Staff, Phayap Army** (10/41): MG Luang [Viscount] Chartnakrob (Chief of Staff, Royal Thai Army) /43 MG Luang [Viscount] Buranasongkhram (Quartermaster-General, Royal Thai Army) /44 LG Luang [Viscount] Haansongkhram (Commanding General, 37th Independent Infantry Division) /45 MG Luang [Viscount] Saranuchit (/48, Director, Royal Thai Armed Forces Education Department).
C.   *Components - Phayap [Northwest] Army*
     1.   **2nd Infantry Division**
     2.   **3rd Infantry Division**
     3.   **4th Infantry Division**
     4.   **Cavalry Division**

Second Army (09/43; HQ: Lopburi): LG Phra [Count/Earl] Prachonpadchanuk (/50, Director, Thai Armed Forces' Veterans' Association) /44 LG Luang [Viscount] Chartnakrob [+Chief of Staff, Royal Thai Army] (/47, Minister of Defense) /45
A.   *Components - Second Army*
     1.   **7th Infantry Division**
     2.   **20th Infantry Regiment**

Divisions

1ˢᵗ Guards Division: /42 MG Khun [Baron] Plotprarapak (?   ) /44 MG Luang [Viscount] Winwaththayothin.

1ˢᵗ Infantry Division (10/41, HQ: Bangkok): /39 MG Luang [Viscount] Kriengsakphichit (Commanding General, Isaan Army) /40 unknown? /43? MG Khun [Baron] Plodpornpaks
A.   ***Components - 1ˢᵗ Infantry Division***
    1.   **1ˢᵗ Infantry Regiment**
    2.   **2ⁿᵈ Infantry Regiment**
    3.   **12ᵗʰ Infantry Regiment**

2ⁿᵈ Infantry Division (10/41, HQ: Prachinburi; 12/41, assigned to Phayap Army; HQ: Chiang Mai): /41 MG Luang [Viscount] Phairirayordedj (/44, Military Governor, Siamese Malaya) /43 unknown? /44 MG Mom Luang [Viscount] Chuang Seniwong (Commanding General, 5ᵗʰ Army Area) /45.
A.   ***Components - 2ⁿᵈ Infantry Division***
    1.   **4ᵗʰ Infantry Regiment**
    2.   **5ᵗʰ Infantry Regiment**
    3.   **12ᵗʰ Infantry Regiment**

3ʳᵈ Infantry Division (10/41, HQ: Nakhon Ratchasima; 12/41, assigned to Phayap Army; HQ: Chiang Rai): /41 MG Phin Choonhavan (Military Governor, Federated Shan States) /42 MG Luang [Viscount] Shamnanyuthasart (?   ) /43 MG Luang [Viscount] Haansongkhram (Chief of Staff, Phayap Army) /44 MG Luang [Viscount] Kraichingrith.
A.   ***Components - 3ʳᵈ Infantry Division***
    1.   **7ᵗʰ Infantry Regiment**
    2.   **8ᵗʰ Infantry Regiment**: Col. Luang [Viscount] Winwaththayothin (Commanding General, 1ˢᵗ Guards Division) /44
    3.   **9ᵗʰ Infantry Regiment**

4ᵗʰ Infantry Division (10/41, HQ: Nakhon Sawan 12/41, assigned to Phayap Army; HQ: Nakhon Sawan): /41 Col. Luang [Viscount] Haansongkhram (Commanding General, 3ʳᵈ Infantry Division) 12/43 MG Luang [Viscount] Kriengdetphichai (?   ) /45 MG Luang [Viscount] Sutthisanronnakorn (Commanding General, 2ⁿᵈ Infantry Division) /46.
A.   **Deputy Commander, 4ᵗʰ Infantry Division**: /41 MG Luang [Viscount] Sutthisanronnakorn (Deputy Commander, Phayap Army) /44
B.   ***Components - 4ᵗʰ Infantry Division***
    1.   **3ʳᵈ Infantry Regiment**: /41 Col. Luang [Viscount] Kriengdetphichai (Commanding General, 4ᵗʰ Infantry Division) 12/43
    2.   **11ᵗʰ Infantry Regiment**
    3.   **13ᵗʰ Infantry Regiment**

5ᵗʰ Infantry Division (10/41, HQ: Phetchaburi):

6th Infantry Division (10/41, HQ: Nakhon Sri Thammarat): /41 MG Luang [Viscount] Senanarong (Assistant Deputy Commander-in-Chief, Royal Thai Army)

A. **Deputy Commander, 6th Infantry Division**: /41 Col. Mom Luang [Viscount] Chuang Seniwong (Commanding General, 2nd Infantry Division) /44

B. *Components - 6th Infantry Division*
   1. **15th Infantry Regiment**
   2. **17th Infantry Regiment**
   3. **18th Infantry Regiment**

7th Infantry Division (09/43): MG Dedj Dejapradit

A. *Components - 7th Infantry Division*
   1. **20th Infantry Regiment**
   2. **21st Infantry Regiment**
   3. **33rd Infantry Regiment**

37th Independent Infantry Division (02/45): LG Luang [Viscount] Haansongkhram.

Independent Phayap Infantry Division: /40 MG Luang [Viscount] Haansongkhram (Commanding General, 4th Infantry Division) /41

A. **Chief of Staff, Phayap Independent Infantry Division**: /40 Col. Luang [Viscount] Sutthisanronnakorn (Deputy Commander, 4th Infantry Division) /41

Bangkok Infantry Division: /40 MG Khun [Baron] Plotprarapak (/42, Commanding General, 1st Guards Division) /41

Southern Peninsular Infantry Division: /40 MG Luang [Viscount] Senanarong (Commanding General, 6th Infantry Division) /41

Surin Infantry Division: /40 Col. Luang [Viscount] Winwaththayothin (Commanding Officer, 8th Infantry Regiment) /41

Cavalry Division (/41;12/41, assigned to Phayap Army; /43, disbanded) : LCol. Thwuan Wichaikhatkha /43 disbanded.

A. *Components - Cavalry Division*
   1. **35th Cavalry Regiment**
   2. **46th Cavalry Regiment**

Royal Thai [Siamese] Air Force

5th Air Wing (10/41, HQ: Nakhon Sri Thammarat): WC Mom Luang [Viscount] Pravasd Chumsai [RTAF]

80th Combined Wing

Royal Thai [Siamese] Navy

Bangkok Naval Station (HQ: Bangkok):

Sattahip Naval Station (HQ: Sattahip):

Table of Equivalent Ranks

Royal Thai Army	United States Army	British Army
Chom Phon	General of the Army	Field Marshal
Phon Ek	General	General
Phon Tho	Lieutenant General	Lieutenant General
Phon Tri	Major General	Major General
Phan Ek Phiset	Brigadier General	Brigadier
Phan Ek	Colonel	Colonel
Phan Tho	Lieutenant Colonel	Lieutenant Colonel
Phan Tri	Major	Major
Roi Ek	Captain	Captain
Roi Tho	First Lieutenant	Lieutenant
Roi Tri	Second Lieutenant	Sub Lieutenant
Nak Rian Nai Roi	Army Cadet	Officer Cadet

Table of Equivalent Ranks

Royal Thai Air Force	United States Air Force	Royal Air Force
Phon Akat Ek Phon Akat Tho	General of the Air Force General	Marshal of the RAF Air Chief Marshal
Phon Akat Tri	Lieutenant General	Air Marshal
Nawa Akat Ek Phiset	Major General	Air Vice Marshal
Nawa Akat Ek	Brigadier General	Air Commodore
Nawa Akat Tho	Colonel	Group Captain
Nawa Akat Tri	Lieutenant Colonel	Wing Commander
Ruea Akat Ek	Major	Squadron Leader
Ruea Akat Tho	Captain	Flight Lieutenant
Ruea Akat Tri	First Lieutenant	Flying Officer
Nak Rian Nai Ruea Akat	Second Lieutenant	Pilot Officer
	Air Cadet	Officer Cadet

Table of Equivalent Ranks

Royal Thai Navy	United States Navy	British Navy
Chom Phon Ruea	Fleet Admiral	Admiral of the Fleet
Phon Ruea Ek	Admiral	Admiral
Phon Ruea Tho	Vice Admiral	Vice Admiral
Phon Ruea Tri	Rear Admiral	Rear Admiral
Nawa Ek Phiset	Commodore	Commodore
Nawa Ek	Captain	Captain
Nawa Tho	Commander	Commander
Nawa Tri	Lieutenant Commander	Lieutenant Commander
Ruea Ek	Lieutenant	Lieutenant
Ruea Tho	Lieutenant (Junior Grade)	Sub-Lieutenant
Ruea Tri	Ensign	Acting Sub-Lieutenant
Nak Rian Nai Ruea	Naval Cadet	Midshipman

GREAT EMPIRE of MANCHUKUO
[Manchuria]

(Japanese Puppet State)

Great Empire of Manchukuo Government
[Manchuria or Manchu State]
(02/18/32 to 08/15/45)

[Captial: Xinjing [Hsinking or Chiangchun]

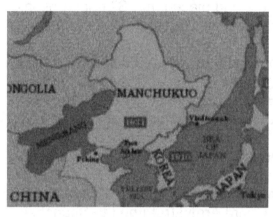

Head of State
Emperior of Manchukuo ((03/01/34): Emperior KANG-DE [AISINGIORO PU-YI] (captured by the Soviets; extradited to communist China; imprisoned for 10 years as war criminal in Fushun War Criminals Management Center) 08/16/45 dissolved.
    1.   **Chamberlain & Aide-de-Camp to Emperior Puyi**: LG Chǔ Kudō
A.   **Privy Council**
B.   **General Affairs State Council** (de facto executive administrative branch):
    1.   **Premier**
    2.   **Cabinet Ministers**
C.   **Legislative Council** (ceremonial body, rubber-stamped decisions by State Council):
    1.   **President of the Senate**: 05/21/35 ZANG SHIYI [TSANG SHIH-YI] (Minister of Home Affairs) /4?

General Affairs State Council

Head of Government

Premier (03/09/32): Zheng Xiaoxu [Chang Hsiao-hisn] (resigned from office; 03/28/38, died suddenly under unclear circumstances) 05/21/35 Gen. Zhang Jinghui [Chang Ching-hui] (captured by the Soviets and placed in a Siberian prison; extradited to communist China; died in captivity in Fushun War Criminals Management Center) 08/15/45 dissolved.

A. **Minister of Home Affairs**: unknown? /36 LG Xi Qia [Hsi Hsia; Xi Xia] (08/45, captured by the Soviets and placed in a Siberian prison; extradited to communist China; died in captivity in Fushun War Criminals Management Center) /4? ZANG SHIYI [TSANG SHIH-YI] (captured by the Soviets and placed in a Siberian prison; extradited to communist China; died in captivity in Fushun War Criminals Management Center) 08/15/45 dissolved.

B. **Minister of Foreign Affairs**: XIE JIESHI (Ambassador to Japan) 06/19/35 ZHANG YANQING
   1. **Vice Foreign Minister**: CHIUNE SUGIHARA [Japanese]
   2. **Ambassador to Japan**: 06/19/35 XIE JIESHI Ministry of Industry & Agriculture) /37

C. **Minister of Defense**: 04/32 Gen. Zhang Jinghui [Chang Ching-hui] (Premier) 05/21/35 unknown?

D. **Minister of War**: 10/10/31 Gen. Ma Zhanshan [Ma Chan-shan] [Chinese] [+ Commander-in-Chief, Heilungjiang Province & Heilungjiang Guard Army] (returned to Shanghai, rebelled against the Japanese, returned to the Nationalist Government, formed Northeast Anti-Japanese National Salvation Army) [see Volume VIII - China] 04/07/33

E. **Minister of Finance**: unknown? /34 LG Xi Qia [Hsi Hsia; Xi Xia] (Minister of Home Affairs) /36 unknown?
   1. **Vice Finance Minister**: HOSHINO NAOKI [Japanese]

F. **Minister of Military Affairs**: YU ZHISHAN

G. **Minister of Industry & Agriculture**: DING JIANXIU /37 XIE JIESHI (left government service for private sector; 08/45, arrested by Communist China government as a Japanese collaborator and traitor; /46, died in a Beijing prison) 08/17/45 dissolved.

G. **Minister of Transportation & Communications**: LI SHAOGENG

H. **Minister of Justice**: unknown?

I. **Minister of Civil Affairs**: LÜ RONGHUAN
   1. **Vice Minister of Civil Affairs**: MASAHIKO AMAKASU [Japanese]

J. **Minister of Education**: RUAN ZHENDUO

K. **Minister of Mongolian Affairs**: YUAN JINKAI

Provinces in Manchukuo under Japanese

A. **Governor, Kirin Province** (09/23/31): LG Xi Qia [Hsi Hsia; Xi Xia] [+ Commanding General, Kirin Guard (Provincial) Army] (removed by the Japanese) 04/32

B. **Committee for the Maintenance of Peace and Order** (09/24/31; Fengtien Province): LG Yuan Chin-hai [Chinese]

C. **Chairman, Heilungkiang Provisional Government**: 10/10/31 LG Ma Zhanshan [Chinese] [+ Minister of War, Manchukuo Government] (returned to Shanghai, rebelled against the Japanese, and returned to Nationalist Government; /37, rumored to be a commander in the Soviet Army during the Xinjing War; /37, Commanding General, Cavalry Army, National Revolutionary Army [also see Volume VIII - China]) 03/07/33

D.   **Self-Government Association** (01/01/32; Heilungkiang Province): Governor CHANG CHING-HUI [Chinese]

E.   **Governor, Rehe Province**: 03/33 LG Zhang Haipeng [Chang Hai-peng] [+ Commanding General, Rehe Guard Army] (Commanding General, 5th District Army "Chengde") 11/34

Japanese Commanders and Ambassadors in Manchukuo

Ambassador to Manchukuo and Commander-in-Chief, Kwantung Army (04/12/19; upgraded to So-Gun class; 10/01/42; Manchuria): 08/01/31 Gen. Baron Shigeru Honjo [Japanese] [see Volume IV - Japan] (Military Councilor) 08/08/32 FM Nobuyoshi Muto [Japanese] [see Volume IV - Japan] (died) 07/27/33 vacant 07/29/33 Gen. Takashi Hishikari [Japanese] [see Volume IV - Japan] (retired) 12/10/34 Gen. Jiro Minami [Japanese] [see Volume IV - Japan] (retired; 08/05/36, Governor-General of Chosen [Korea]) 03/06/36 Gen. Kenkichi Ueda [Japanese] [see Volume IV - Japan] (attached Army General Staff/retired) 09/07/39 Gen. Yoshijiro Umezu [Japanese] [see Volume IV - Japan] 07/41 LG. Tomoyoki Yamashita [Japanese] [see Volume IV - Japan] [+ Commanding General, Twenty-Fifth Army] (acting) 11/06/41 Gen. Yoshijiro Umezu [Japanese] [see Volume IV - Japan] (Chief of the Army General Staff & Military Councilor) 07/18/44 Gen. Otozō Yamada [Japanese] [see Volume IV - Japan] [+ Governor-General, Kwantung Leased Territory] (1949, condemned to 25 years imprisonment as a war criminal; 1956 released) 08/11/45. disbanded.

Soviet Military Governor

Soviet Military Governor (08/15/45): MSU Aleksandr Mikhailovich Vasilevskiy [Soviet Union] [+ Commander-in-Chief, Far East Command] [see Volume V, Books a & B - The Union of Soviet Socialist Republics] 05/46

Manchukuo Armed Forces

Commander-in-Chief, Manchukuo Armed Forces: Gen. Oda Takeshi

Manchukuo Imperial Army

Armies

Fengtien Guard Army (02/18/32; /34, reorganized and designated **1st District Army "Fengtien"**): <u>Fengtien Guard Army</u> 02/18/32 unknown? 34 reorganized and designated **<u>1st District Army "Fengtien"</u>** /34 LG Yu Chih-shan

A.　　*Components - Fengtien Guard Army* (1932)
1.　　**1st Mixed Brigade**
2.　　**2nd Mixed Brigade**
3.　　**3rd Mixed Brigade**
4.　　**4th Mixed Brigade**
5.　　**5th Mixed Brigade**
6.　　**6th Mixed Brigade**
7.　　**7th Mixed Brigade**
8.　　**1st Cavalry Brigade**
9.　　**2nd Cavalry Brigade**
10.　　**1st Teaching Unit**

Kirin Guard (Provincial) Army (02/18/32; /34, reorganized and designated **2nd District Army "Kirin"**): <u>Kirin Guard (Provincial) Army</u> 02/18/32 LG Xi Qua [Hsi Hsia; Xi Xia [+ to 4/32, Governor, Kirin Province for Japanese] (Minister of Finance) 34 reorganized and designated **<u>2nd District Army "Kirin"</u>** /34 LG Chi Hsing

A.　　*Components - Kirin Guard (Provincial) Army* (1932)
1.　　**1st Infantry Brigade**
2.　　**2nd Infantry Brigade**
3.　　**3rd Infantry Brigade**
4.　　**4th Infantry Brigade**
5.　　**5th Infantry Brigade**
6.　　**6th Infantry Brigade**
7.　　**7th Infantry Brigade**
8.　　**8th Infantry Brigade**
9.　　**1st Cavalry Brigade**
10.　　**2nd Cavalry Brigade**
11.　　**3rd Cavalry Brigade**
12.　　**4th Cavalry Brigade**
13.　　**2nd Teaching Unit**
14.　　**Infantry Detachment**

15.   **Cavalry Detachment**
16.   **Yilan Unit**

Heilungjiang Guard Army (02/18/32; /34, reorganized and designated **3rd District Army "Qiqihar"**): <u>Heilungjiang Guard Army</u> 02/18/32 LG Ma Zhanshan [Ma Chan-shan] [Chinese] [also see Volume VIII - China] [+ Minister of War] (rebelled against the Japanese, formed Northeast Anti-Japanese National Salvation Army to fight them) 04/32 unknown? 34 reorganized and designated **3rd District Army "Qiqihar"** /34 LG Chang Wen-tao

A.   *Components - Heilungjiang Guard Army* (1932)
    1.   **1st Mixed Brigade**
    2.   **2nd Mixed Brigade**
    3.   **3rd Mixed Brigade**
    4.   **4th Mixed Brigade**
    5.   **5th Mixed Brigade**
    6.   **1st Cavalry Brigade**
    7.   **2nd Cavalry Brigade**
    8.   **3rd Cavalry Brigade**
    9.   **3rd Teaching Unit**

Hsingan Army (02/18/32; /34, reorganized and designated **4th District Army "Harbin"**): <u>Hsingan Army</u> 02/18/32 unknown? /34 reorganized and designated **4th District Army "Harbin"** /34 Gen. Yu Cheng-shen

A.   *Components - Hsingan Army* (1932)
    1.   **South Hsingan Garrison**
        a.   **3rd Cavalry Regiment**
        b.   **4th Cavalry Regiment**
    2.   **South Hsingan Garrison**
        a.   **5th Cavalry Regiment**
        b.   **6th Cavalry Regiment**
    3.   **South Hsingan Garrison**
        a.   **7th Cavalry Regiment**
        b.   **8th Cavalry Regiment**

Taoliao Army (02/18/32, from the **Hsingan Reclamation Army**, formed 10/31; 03/33, redesignated **Rehe Guard Army**; /34, reorganized and designated **5th District Army "Chengde"**): <u>Hsingan Reclamation Army</u> 10/31 LG Zhang Haipeng [Chang Hai-peng] (Commanding General, Taoliao Army) 02/18/32 redesignated <u>Taoliao Army</u> 02/18/32 Gen. Zhang Haipeng [Chang Hai-peng] (Commanding General, Rehe Guard Army) 03/33 redesignated <u>Rehe Guard Army</u> 03/33 LG Zhang Haipeng [Chang Hai-peng] [+ Governor of Rehe Province] (Commanding General, 5th District Army "Chengde") 11/34 reorganized and designated <u>5th District Army "Chengde"</u> 11/34 LG Zhang Haipeng [Chang Hai-peng] (retired; /45, went into hiding; /49, found and executed by the People's Republic of China for treason) /41

Mauchukuo Forces around Doulon (/33, defending fortifications around Doulon): MG Li Shouxin [Li Shou-hsin] [Chinese] (Commanding General, Manchukuoan Mongol Irregulars helping Prince DEWANG [THE WANG or DEMCHUGDONGRUB] in Inner Mongolia)[see

Volume VIII - China] /35 dissolved.

National Salvation Army (/33, Japanese puppet force in southeast Manchukuo): MG Li Chi-chun (disappeared, reports have him retired to the Japanese Concession in Tianjin) 05/31/33 disbanded by the Japanese after the Tanggu Truce.

East Hingganling Guard Army (1934, Independent unit):

West Hingganling Guard Army (1934, Independent unit):

North Hingganling Guard Army (1934, Independent unit):

South Hingganling Guard Army (1934, Independent unit):

Seian Guard Army (1934, Independent unit):

Mauchukuoan Mongol Irregulars (/35; assisting Prince DEWANG [THE WANG or DEMCHUGDONGRUB] in Inner Mongolia): LG Li Shouxin [Li Shou-hsin] [Chinese] (transferred his allegiance to Prince DEWALD, and becomes Chief of Staff, Inner Mongolian Army [see Inner Mongolian Army under Mengjiang Armies this volume and Volume VIII - China] 02/36 dissolved.

Manchukuo Imperial Guards

Formed in 1933, and copied after the Japanese Imperial Guard. Formed to protect the Emperior and senior members of the Manchukuo civil government. Initially it consisted of 200 men. Later, an independent brigade called the **Chinganyuchitui [Special Guard Corps]** was formed.

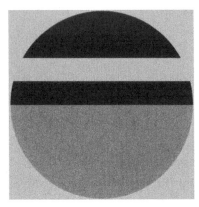

Manchukuo Imperial Air Force

Established 02/37, with initially 30 men selected from the Manchukuo Imperial Army and trained by the Japanese Kwantung Army. Up until 1940, only Japanese pilots were deployed. After 1940, the Japanese allowed native ethnic Manchus to receive pilot training. In 1944, the Manchukuo Imperial Air Force came under the command of the Japanese Second Air Army. It had around 100 to 120 combat aircraft and around 400 men.

Manchukuo Imperial Navy

The Manchukuo Imperial Navy was formally established April 15, 1932. Emperior KANG-DE [AISINGIORO PU-YI] assumed the role of Supreme Commander. The flagship of the fleet was the destroyer *Hai Wei* [ex-*Kashi*] of the Japanese Imperial Navy. The coastal defense for Manchukuo remained largely with the Japanese Imperial Navy's Third China (North) Fleet; with the rivers of Manchukuo the responsibility of the Manchukuo Imperial Navy. In November 1938, Japanese Imperial Navy units were withdrawn from Manchukuo because of the ongoing political conflict between the Japanese army and navy over who controlled Manchukuo. In November 1939, the navy officially came under control of the Manchukuo Imperial Army, and was renamed **River Force**.

Manchukuo Navy Coastal Defense Forces

Headquarters (Yingkou Naval Base, Fentieng; Secondary Base: Hulutao Naval Base, Fengtieng): Flagship: destroyer *Hai Wei* [ex-*Kashi*]

2nd Patrol Division (Sea):
A.   ***Components - 2nd Patrol Division***
  1.   district patrol vessel *Hai Lung*
  2.   district patrol vessel *Hai Feng*
  3.   district patrol vessel *Li Sui*
  4.   district patrol vessel *Lin Chi*

3rd Patrol Division (Sea):
A.   ***Components - 3rd Patrol Division***
  1.   district patrol vessel *Kuen Ning*
  2.   district patrol vessel *Kuan Ching*
  3.   district patrol vessel *Chian Tung*

4th Patrol Division (Sea):
A.   ***Components - 4th Patrol Division***
  1.   district patrol vessel *Hai Kuang*
  2.   district patrol vessel *Hai Jui*
  3.   district patrol vessel *Hai Jung*
  4.   district patrol vessel *Hai Hua*

5th Patrol Division (Sea):
A.   ***Components - 5th Patrol Division*** (Sea):

361

1. district patrol vessel *Daichii*
2. district patrol vessel *Kaihen*
3. district patrol vessel *Kaini*
4. district patrol vessel *Ta Tung*
5. district patrol vessel *Li Ming*

Manchukuo Navy River Defense Patrol

1st Patrol Division (Sungari River; Yingkou and Antung Base, Fengtieng):

A.   ***Components - 1st Patrol Division***
1. river gunboat *Ting Pien*
2. river gunboat *Ching Hen*
3. river gunboat *Shun Tien*
4. river gunboat *Yan Ming*

Manchukuo [Manchuria] Guerilla Forces
Anti-Japanese Volunteer Armies

Jilin Self-Defense Army (01/32; Harbin [also see Volume VIII - China]): LG Ting Chao [Ding Chao] [Chinese] (Chairman of Jilin Province) /32 LG Li Du [Li Tu] [Chinese] 12/24/32 retreated into the Union of Soviet Socialist Republics and disbanded.

Lower Sungari Garrison (1932 [also see Volume VIII - China]): Li Du [Li Tu] [Chinese] (Commanding General, Jilin Self-Defense Army) /32 merged with **Jilin Self-Defense Army** - see **Jilin Self-Defense Army**.

Chinese People's National Salvation Army [NAS] (02/08/32; southwest Kirin [also see Volume VIII - China]): LG Wang Delin [Chinese] 01/13/33 retreated into the Union of Soviet Socialist Republics and disbanded.
A.   **Deputy Commander, Chinese People's National Salvation Army**: /32 MG Kong Xianrong [Chinese] 01/13/33 dissolved.
B.   **Chief of Staff, Commander, Chinese People's National Salvation Army** (02/08/32): MG Li Yanlu [Chinese] 01/13/33 dissolved.

Northeastern People's Revolutionary Army (Communist) ([also see Volume VIII - China]):

Northeastern Loyal and Brave Army (02/32 [also see Volume VIII - China]): LG Feng Zhanhai [Feng Chan-hai] [Chinese] (Commanding General, 4th Route Army) 09/32 disbanded, most join **Chahar People's Anti-Japanese Army** [see Mengjiang Guerilla Forces and Volume VIII - China].

Northeastern Volunteer Righteous & Brave Fighters (03/32 [also see Volume VIII - China]): LG Wang Fengge [Chinese] (captured by the Japanese and executed) /37

Northeast People's Anti-Japanese Volunteer Army (pre 05/32 [also see Volume VIII - China]): LG Tang Juwu [Chinese] (joins the Chahar People's Anti-Japanese Army) /32 retreated into the Union of Soviet Socialist Republics and disbanded.

Northeast Anti-Japanese National Salvation Army (05/32 [also see Volume VIII - China]): LG Ma Zhanshan [Ma Chan-shan; Ma Chan-san; Muazzam Husain] [Chinese] (/33, returned to China; /37, rumored to be a commander in the Soviet Army during the Xinjing War; /37, Commanding General, Cavalry Army, National Revolutionary Army) 11/28/32 retreated into the Union of Soviet Socialist Republics and disbanded.

Heilungkiang National Salvation Army (09/27/32 [also see Volume VIII - China]): LG Su Bingwen [Chinese] 11/28/32 retreated into the Union of Soviet Socialist Republics and disbanded.

Anti-Japanese Army for the Salvation of the Country (/32 [also see Volume VIII - China]): LG Hai-ching [Chinese]

Northeast Anti-Japanese United Army (Communist) (1935 [also see Volume VIII - China]): LG Zhao Shangzhi [Chinese Communist] (captured by the Japanese; died) 02/12/42

A.   *Components - Northeast Anti-Japanese United Army*

1.   **1st Route Army** (02/36, Fengtien Province; formed as **1st Army**; 06/36, redesignated **1st Route Army**): **1st Army** 02/36 LG Yang Jingyu [Chinese Communist] (Commanding General, 1st Route Army) 06/36 redesignated **1st Route Army** 02/36 LG Yang Jingyu [Chinese Communist] (died) 02/23/40

2.   **2nd Route Army** (06/36; Kirin Province): LG Zhou Baozhong [Chinese Communist] 07/42 retreated into the Union of Soviet Socialist Republics and disbanded.

3.   **3rd Route Army** (06/36; Heilungkiang Province): LG Li Zhaolin [Li Chaolin] [Chinese Communist] 11/41 retreated into the Union of Soviet Socialist Republics and disbanded.

MENGJIANG
[INNER MONGOLIA]

(Japanese Puppet State)

Mengjiang [Inner Mongolia]
Mongol Military Government
(05/12/36 to 10/37)

[On April 24, 1934, the Mongols in Inner Mongolia established the autonomous Mongolian Federation or League. On December 22, 1935, they declared themselves an independent country. The Mongol Military Government was formed on May 12, 1936, operating under nominal Chinese sovereignty and Japanese control. In October 1937, the Mongol Military Government was renamed the Mongol United Autonomous Government]

Chairman, Autonomous Political Council (04/23/34): Prince DEWANG [THE WANG or DEMCHUGDONGRUB] [+ 05/12/36 to 10/37, Head of State, Mongol Military Government; + 10/37 to 09/01/39, Head of State, Mongol United Autonomous Government; + 09/01/37, Head of State, Mengjing United Autonomous Government] (Chairman, Inner Mongolia Federation) 12/08/37 dissolved.

Head of State, Mongol Military Government (05/12/36): Prince DEWANG [THE WANG or DEMCHUGDONGRUB] [+ Chairman, Autonomous Political Council] (Head of State, Mongol United Autonomous Government) 10/37 dissolved.

Japanese Advisor to Mongol Military Government: TOYONORI YAMAUCHI [Japanese]

369

Mongol United Autonomous Government (10/37 to 09/01/39)

[The predominantly Han Chinese governments of South Chahar and North Shanxi were merged on 09/01/39 with the Mongol United Autonomous Government, creating the new Mengjiang United Autonomous Government]

Head of State, Mongol United Autonomous Government (05/12/36): Prince DEWANG [THE WANG or DEMCHUGDONGRUB] [+ to 12/08/37, Chairman, Autonomous Political Council; + 12/08/37, Chairman, Mingjiang [Inner Mongolia] Federation] (Head of State, Mengjiang United Autonomous Government) 09/01/39 merged with South Chahar and North Shanxi to form **Mengjiang United Autonomous Government** - see **Mengjiang United Autonomous Government**.

Chairman, Mingjiang [Inner Mongolia] Federation (12/08/37): Prince DEWANG [THE WANG or DEMCHUGDONGRUB] [+ to 09/01/39, Head of State, Mongol Military Government; + 09/01/39 to 08/04/41, Head of State, Mengjiang United Autonomous Government; + 08/04/41 to 08/15/45, Head, Mongolian Autonomous Federation] (08/15/45, Chinese prisoner; 08/49, released) 12/49 dissolved.

Mengjiang United Autonomous Government
[Méngjiāng Liánhé Zìzhì Zhèngfǔ]
(09/01/39 to 08/04/41)

[Mengjiang [Mengchaing or Mengkiang], also known in English as Mongol Border Land, was an autonomous area in Inner Mongolia, operating under nominal Chinese sovereignty and Japanese control. After WANG JINGWEI formed the new government of the Republic of China-Nanjing, Mengjiang was placed under its control, though it remained completely autonomous. It was renamed on August 4, 1941, Mongolian Autonomous Federation]

Head of State, Mengjiang United Autonomous Government (09/01/39): Prince DEWANG [THE WANG or DEMCHUGDONGRUB] [+ Chairman, Mingjiang [Inner Mongolia] Federation] (Head, Mongolian Autonomous Federation) 08/04/41 dissolved.

Mongolian Autonomous Federation
(08/04/41 to 08/15/45)

Head, Mongolian Autonomous Federation (08/04/41): Prince DEWANG [THE WANG or DEMCHUGDONGRUB] [+ Chairman, Mingjiang [Inner Mongolia] Federation] (Chinese prisoner; 08/49, released) 08/15/45 dissolved.

Japanese Commanders in Mengjiang

Army Group Command

Commander-in-Chief, Kwantung Army (04/12/19; upgraded to So-Gun class; 10/01/42; Manchuria): 08/01/31 Gen. Baron Shigeru Honjo [Japanese] [see Volume IV - Japan] (Military Councilor) 08/08/32 FM Nobuyoshi Muto [Japanese] [see Volume IV - Japan] (died) 07/27/33 vacant 07/29/33 Gen. Takashi Hishikari [Japanese] [see Volume IV - Japan] (retired) 12/10/34 Gen. Jiro Minami [Japanese] [see Volume IV - Japan] (retired; 08/05/36, Governor-General of Chosen [Korea]) 03/06/36 Gen. Kenkichi Ueda [Japanese] [see Volume IV - Japan] (attached Army General Staff/retired) 09/07/39 Gen. Yoshijiro Umezu [Japanese] [see Volume IV - Japan] 07/41 LG. Tomoyoki Yamashita [Japanese] [see Volume IV - Japan] [+ Commanding General, Twenty-Fifth Army] (acting) 11/06/41 Gen. Yoshijiro Umezu [Japanese] [see Volume IV - Japan] (Chief of the Army General Staff & Military Councilor) 07/18/44 Gen. Otozō Yamada [Japanese] [see Volume IV - Japan] [+ Governor-General, Kwantung Leased Territory] (1949, condemned to 25 years imprisonment as a war criminal; 1956 released) 08/11/45. disbanded.

Corps Command

Mongolia Garrison Army (12/28/37; Mongolia): LG Shigeru Hasunuma [Japanese] [see Volume IV - Japan] (Chief Aide-de-Camp to the Emperor) 08/31/39 Gen. Hajime Sugiyama [Japanese] [see Volume IV - Japan] [+ Commander-in-Chief, Northern China Area Army] (Military Councilor) 09/12/39 LG Nosaburō Okabe [Japanese] [see Volume IV - Japan] (Director of the Technical Headquarters) 09/29/40 LG Masataka Yamawaki [Japanese] [see Volume IV - Japan] (09/05/42, Commander-in-Chief, Borneo Garrison Army) 01/20/41 LG Shigetarō Amakasu [Japanese] [see Volume IV - Japan] (retired) 03/02/42 LG Ichiro Shichida [Japanese] [see Volume IV - Japan] (Commanding General, Second Army) 05/28/43 LG Yoshio Kozuki [Japanese] [see Volume IV - Japan] (Commanding General, Eleventh Army) 11/22/44 LG Hiroshi Nemoto [Japanese] [see Volume IV - Japan] (Commander-in-Chief, Northern China Area Army) 08/19/45

Mengjiang Armies

Inner Mongolian Army (/29, as personal bodyguard to protect the prince; by /36, it expanded to 9 divisions): Prince DEWANG [THE WANG or DEMCHUGDONGRUB]

A.   **Chief of Staff, Inner Mongolian Army** (02/36): LG Li Shouxin [Li Shou-hsin] [Chinese] (Commanding General, Mengjiang National Army)[see Volume VIII - China] 08/37 dissolved.

Grand Han Righteous Army (/36; a collaborationist Chinese army of about 6000 men; made up of 4 brigades; after 01/37, disbanded by the Japanese): MG Wang Ying [Minguo] [Chinese] (forms a small puppet army, independent of Mangjiang in Western Suiyuan)) 01/37 disbanded by the Japanese.

Mengjiang National Army (08/37, rebuilt from remnants of Inner Mongolian Army after Suiyuan Campaign): LG Li Shouxin [Li Shou-hsin] [Chinese] [see Volume VIII - China] (defected back to the Chinese Nationalist [Kuomintang]; Commanding General, Chinese 10th Route Army) 07/45 unknown? 08/17/45 disbanded.

Japanese East Asia Affined Army (1939): MG Bai Fengxiang (poisoned by a Japanese doctor when planning an up-rising [also see Volume VIII - China]) /39 disbanded.

Mengjiang [Inner Mongolia] Guerilla Forces
Anti-Japanese Volunteer Armies

People's Revolutionary Army (/33? [also see Volume VIII - China]):
A.   **1st Army**: /33 Col. Li Shengzong (Chief of Staff, 19th Route Army) /36

10th Counter-Rebel Army (/33?, Yúnnán [Yunnan] Province [also see Volume VIII - China]):
A.   **Chief of Staff, 10th Counter-Rebel Army**: /30 MG Li Shihan (/37, Superintendent, Mengzi Customs Bureau; /38?, Instructor, Yúnnán [Yunnan] Military Academy) /3?

Resisting-Japan and Saving-China Army (/33 [also see Volume VIII - China]): /33 LG Fang Zhenwu [Fang Cheh-wu] (Director, Cháhār [Chahar; Chaha'er; Chakhar; Qahar] People's Anti-Japanese Army) /33 dissolved and helps form the **Cháhār [Chahar; Chaha'er; Chakhar; Qahar]**

People's Anti-Japanese Army [also see Volume VIII - China].
A.   *Components* - **Resisting-Japan and Saving-China Army**
       1.   **1st Army, Resisting-Japan and Saving-China Army**
       2.   **4th Army**
       3.   **5th Army**

Commander-in-Chief, Cháhār [Chahar; Chaha'er; Chakhar; Qahar] People's Anti-Japanese Army (/33? [also see Volume VIII - China]): Gen. 2nd Rank Feng Yuxiang [Feng Yu-hsiang] (Vice President, National Military Council) /33
A.   *Components* - **Cháhār [Chahar; Chaha'er; Chakhar; Qahar] People's Anti-Japanese Army**
       1.   **4th Route Army**
       2.   **Cavalry Army**
       3.   **4th Division**

Northwestern Army [also see Volume VIII - China]: /32 MG Ji Hongchang [Communist] (Commanding General, 2nd Army, Cháhār [Chahar; Chaha'er; Chakhar; Qahar] People's Anti-Japanese Army) /33 dissolved and helps form the **Cháhār [Chahar; Chaha'er; Chakhar; Qahar] People's Anti-Japanese Army**.
A.   *Components* - **Northwestern Army**
       1.   **25th Division**
       2.   **5th Cavalry Division**
       3.   **1st New Division**

Jehol [Rèhé; Rehe] Anti Japanese Militia or 18th Army [XVIII Corps] [also see Volume VIII - China]: see 18th Army.

Cháhār [Chahar; Chaha'er; Chakhar; Qahar] Self-Defense Army [also see Volume VIII - China]: MG Zhang Lisheng *
A.   *Components - Cháhār [Chahar; Chaha'er; Chakhar; Qahar] Self-Defense Army*
    1.   1st Division, Cháhār [Chahar; Chaha'er; Chakhar; Qahar] Self-Defense Army
    2.   2nd Division, Cháhār [Chahar; Chaha'er; Chakhar; Qahar] Self-Defense Army
    3.   3rd Division, Cháhār [Chahar; Chaha'er; Chakhar; Qahar] Self-Defense Army
    4.   1st Detachment, Cháhār [Chahar; Chaha'er; Chakhar; Qahar] Self-Defense Army
    5.   2nd Detachment, Cháhār [Chahar; Chaha'er; Chakhar; Qahar] Self-Defense Army

1st Army, Resisting-Japan and Saving-China Army (/33 [also see Volume VIII - China]): MG Zhang Renjie *
A.   *Components - 1st Army, Resisting-Japan and Saving-China Army*
    1.   *Unknown?* Division, 1st Army, Resisting-Japan and Saving-China Army
    2.   *Unknown?* Division, 1st Army, Resisting-Japan and Saving-China Army
    3.   *Unknown?* Division, 1st Army, Resisting-Japan and Saving-China Army
    4.   *Unknown?* Brigade, 1st Army, Resisting-Japan and Saving-China Army
    5.   Cavalry Brigade, 1st Army, Resisting-Japan and Saving-China Army

Ethnic-Mongol Army [also see Volume VIII - China]: MG Teh Wang
A.   *Components - 1st Army, Ethnic-Mongol Army*
    1.   1st Cavalry, Ethnic-Mongol Army
    2.   2nd Cavalry, Ethnic-Mongol Army
    3.   Self Defense Army

Bandit & Former Puppet Troops [also see Volume VIII - China]
A.   *Components - Bandit & Former Puppet Troops*
    1.   1st Route
    2.   6th Route

Cavalry Army (/33, Cháhār [Chahar; Chaha'er; Chakhar; Qahar] People's Anti-Japanese Army [also see Volume VIII - China]): /33 MG Sun Liangcheng [Sun Liang-cheng] (/39, Committee Member, Héběi [Hebei; Hopeh; Hopei] Provincial Government & Commanding General, Guerilla Warfare, Héběi [Hebei; Hopeh; Hopei] War Area) /33

REPUBLIC of CHINA-NANJING

(Japanese Puppet State)

List of Japanese Puppet Governments of China (prior to 03/30/40)

[During the Second Sino-Japanese War, Japan advanced from its bases in Manchukuo [Manchuria] to occupy much of North-East and Central China. Several puppet states were organized in areas occupied by the Japanese Army, including the Provisional Government of the Republic of China at Peking in 1937, and the Reformed Government of the Republic of China, in 1938. These governments were merged into the Republic of China-Nanjing in 1940. The new government was also known as the Wang Jingwei Government.]

Chairman, East Hebei Autonomous Council (11/25/35 to 02/01/38) (11/25/35 at Tungchow, northern China; also known as **East Ji Autonomous Council** and **East Hebei Anti-Communist Council** 12/14/37, absorbed into the collaboration **Provisional Government of China**): YIN JU-KENG (captured by the Japanese Army and exiled; /42, allowed back into China; 08/45, arrested by the Republic of China; tried for treason; 11/08/47, sentenced to death; 12/01/47, executed by firing squad) 12/14/37 absorbed into the collaboration **Provisional Government of China** 02/01/38 dissolved.

Chairman, Provisional Government of China (12/14/37, North China, from **East Hebei Autonomous Council**, at Peking; 03/30/40, merged into **Republic of China-Nanjing**): WENG KEMIN (Interior Affairs Minister & Chairman, North China Political Council) 03/30/40 merged into **Republic of China-Nanjing** - see **Republic of China-Nanjing**.

Dadao Municipal Government of Shanghai (12/05/37 to 05/03/38) (12/05/37, at Pudong; 04/38, **Reformed Government of the Republic of China** asserted its authority over **Dadao Municipal Government of Shanghai** by establishing a Supervisory Yamen): SU XIWEN (Head, Supervisory Yamen over Shanghai) 04/38 **Reformed Government of the Republic of China** asserted its authority over **Dadao Municipal Government of Shanghai** by establishing a Supervisory Yamen; absorbed into **Reformed Government of the Republic of China** 05/03/38 dissolved.

Chairman, Reformed Government of the Republic of China (03/28/38, Central China;

03/30/40 at Nanjing, renamed and merged into **Republic of China-Nanjing**): LIANG HONGZHI (08/15/45, arrested by the Republic of China; tried for treason; sentenced to death; 11/09/46, executed by firing squad) 03/30/40 renamed and merged into **Republic of China-Nanjing** - see **Republic of China-Nanjing**.

A.   **Supervisory Yamen over Shanghai** (04/38): vacant 05/03/38 SU XIWEN 10/16/38 dissolved.

B.   **Mayor of Shanghai** (10/16/38): FU XIAOAN

Reformed Government of China and Provisional Government of China Military Units

Eastern Hénán [Henan; Honan] Communist Suppression Army (/38, Japanese Puppet Army): LG Zhang Lanfeng (joins Wang Jingwei's Government; Member, National Military Council of Republic of China-Nanjing; Deputy Commander, Jiāngsū [Jiangsu]-Henen Border Area Suppression Headquarters; Commanding General, 1ˢᵗ Army, National Salvation Army; & Head, Military Officers Training Group) 03/30/40 merged into **Republic of China-Nanjing Military** and disbanded.

Japanese Commanders in China

Army Group Command

China Expeditionary Force (China): 09/15/38 LG Otozō Yamada [Japanese] [see Volume IV - Japan] (Inspectorate-General of Military Training) 09/22/39 Gen. Juzo [Toshizou] Nishio [Japanese] [see Volume IV - Japan] (Military Councilor) 03/01/41 FM Shunroku Hata [Japanese] [see Volume IV - Japan] (Inspector-General of Military Training) 11/23/44 Gen. Yasuji Okamura [Japanese] [see Volume IV - Japan] (?   ) 09/09/45.

Southern Army (11/06/41, Southern Operations, excluding China) FM Count Hisaichi Terauchi [Japanese] [see Volume IV - Japan] (retired; 06/12/46, died of cerebral hemorrhage) 11/30/45 surrendered.

Army Command

Central China Area Army (10/30/37 from **Shanghai Expeditionary Force** and **Tenth Army**; China): Gen. [Retired 08/34] Iwane Matsui [Japanese] [see Volume IV - Japan] (retired/Privy Councilor) 02/14/38 Gen. Shunroku Hata (Military Councilor) [Japanese] [see Volume IV - Japan] 12/14/38 upgraded to **China Expeditionary Force** - see **China Expeditionary Force**.

Northern China Area Army (08/26/37; China): Gen. Count Hisaichi Terauchi [Japanese] [see Volume IV - Japan] (Military Councilor) 12/09/38 Gen. Hajime Sugiyama [Japanese] [see Volume IV - Japan] [+ 08/39, Commander-in-Chief, Mongolia Garrison Army] (Military Councilor) 09/12/39 Gen. Hayao Tada [Japanese] [see Volume IV - Japan] (?   ) 07/07/41 Gen. Yasuji Okamura [Japanese] [see Volume IV - Japan] (Commanding General, 6th Area Army) 08/25/44 Gen. Nosaburō Okabe [Japanese] [see Volume IV - Japan] (Commanding General, 6th Area Army) 11/22/44 LG Sadamu Shimomura [Japanese] [see Volume IV - Japan] (Minister of War & Inspector-General of Military Training) 08/19/45 LG Hiroshi Nemoto [Japanese] [see Volume IV - Japan].

Southern China Area Army (02/10/40; China): LG Rikichi Ando [Japanese] [see Volume IV - Japan] (retired) 10/05/40 LG Jun Ushiroku [Japanese] [see Volume IV - Japan] (Chief of Staff, China Expeditionary Army) 06/26/41 disbanded.

Corps Command

Shanghai Expeditionary Force (08/15/37; China): 08/15/37 Gen. [Retired 08/34] Iwane Matsui [Japanese] [see Volume IV - Japan] (Commanding General, Central China Area Army) 12/02/37 Gen. Prince Yasuhiko Asaka [Japanese] [see Volume IV - Japan] [+ Military Councilor &] 02/14/38 combined with **Tenth Army** to form **Central China Area Army**; disbanded.

Central District Army (HQ: Osaka; 08/02/37 as **Central Defense Command**; renamed **Central Army** 08/01/40; renamed **Central District Army** 02/01/45): **Central Defense Command** 08/02/37 LG Kesaware Nakashima [Japanese] [see Volume IV - Japan] (Commanding General, 16ᵗʰ Division) 08/26/37 LG Shigeru Hasunuma [Japanese] [see Volume IV - Japan] (Commander-in-Chief, Mongolia Garrison Army) 12/28/37 LG Hisao Tani [Japanese] [see Volume IV - Japan] (in reserve) 08/01/39 LG Waichiro [Ichiro] Sonobe [Japanese] [see Volume IV - Japan] (?) 03/09/40 LG Yoshio Iwamatsu [Japanese] [see Volume IV - Japan] (Commanding General, Central Army) 08/01/40 renamed **Central Army** 08/01/40 LG Yoshio Iwamatsu [Japanese] [see Volume IV - Japan] (Commanding General, First Army) 06/20/41 LG Yoji Fujii [Japanese] [see Volume IV - Japan] (in reserve/retired) 08/17/42 LG Jun Ushiroku [Japanese] [see Volume IV - Japan] (Vice Chief of Naval General Staff) 02/21/44 LG Shojiro Iida [Japanese] [see Volume IV - Japan] (retired) 12/01/44 Gen. Masakasu Kawabe [Japanese] [see Volume IV - Japan] (Commander-in-Chief, Central District Army) 02/01/45 renamed **Central District Army** 02/01/45 Gen. Masakasu Kawabe [Japanese] [see Volume IV - Japan] [+ Commanding General, 15ᵗʰ Area Army] (Commander-in-Chief, Air General Army) 04/07/45 LG Eitaro Uchiyama [Japanese] [see Volume IV - Japan] [+ Commanding General, 15ᵗʰ Area Army] (Commander-in-Chief, 2ⁿᵈ Demobilization Command; 1946, arrested; 1949, condemned to 40 years imprisonment; 1958, released) 09/12/45 deactivated.

Ambassadors to the Republic of China-Nanjing

Japanese Ambassador and Representative, Republic of China-Nanjing (03/30/40): KUMATARO HONDA [Japanese]

German Ambassador, Republic of China-Nanjing (03/30/40): Dr. ERNST WÖRMANN [German]

Republic of China-Nanjing Government (03/30/40 to 08/15/45)

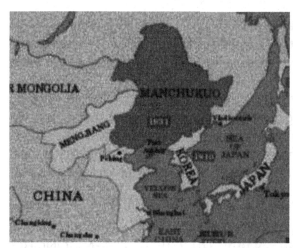

[The Republic of China-Nanjing Government had no real power, and its main role was to act as a propaganda tool for the Japanese. This government had a strained relationship with the Japanese from the beginning. Wang insisted that his regime was the true Nationalist government of China and in replicating all the symbols of the Kuomintang [KMT], the Nationalist government of his arch rival Generalissimo Chiang Kei-shak [Jiǎng Jièshi; Jiǎng Zhōngshèng], led to frequent conflicts with the Japanese. The most prominent conflict being the issue of the regime's flag, which was identical to that of the Republic of China.

The actual borders of the Republic of China-Nanjing, changed as the Japanese gained territory during the war]

Head of State, Republic of China-Nanjing (03/30/40): WANG JINGWEI (died) 11/10/44 vacant 11/20/44 CHEN GONGBO [CHENG KUNG-PO] (fled to Japan; 10/03/45, extradited back to China by the United States; tried for treason; 06/03/46, executed by firing squad) 09/09/45 dissolved.

Executive Yuan, Republic of China-Nanjing (03/30/40)
A.   **President, Executive Yuan** (03/30/40): WANG JINGWEI [+ Head of State, Republic of China-Nanjing] (died) 11/10/44 CHEN GONGBO [CHENG KUNG-PO] (fled to Japan; 10/03/45, extradited back to China by the United States; tried for treason; 06/03/46, executed by firing squad) 09/09/45 dissolved.
B.   **Vice President, Executive Yuan** (03/30/40): ZHOU FOHAI [CHOU FO-HAI] [+ Foreign Affairs Minister, Executive Yuan; Finance Minister, Executive Yuan; & Treasury Minister, Executive Yuan; + 11/20/44, Mayor of Shanghai] (captured by the Republic of China; tried for treason; sentenced to death but commuted to life imprisonment; 02/28/48, died in prison from heart & stomach problems) 09/09/45 dissolved.
C.   **Foreign Affairs Minister, Executive Yuan** (03/30/40): ZHOU FOHAI [CHOU FO-HAI] [+ Vice President, Executive Yuan; Finance Minister, Executive Yuan; & Treasury Minister, Executive Yuan; + 11/20/44, Mayor of Shanghai] (captured by the Republic of China; tried for treason; sentenced to death but commuted to life imprisonment; 02/28/48, died in prison from heart & stomach problems) 09/09/45

dissolved.

    1.   **Ambassador to Japan** (03/30/40, in Yokohama, Japan): CHU MINYI

D.   **Finance Minister, Executive Yuan** (03/30/40): ZHOU FOHAI [CHOU FO-HAI] [+ Vice President, Executive Yuan; Foreign Affairs Minister, Executive Yuan; & Treasury Minister, Executive Yuan; + 11/20/44, Mayor of Shanghai] (captured by the Republic of China; tried for treason; sentenced to death but commuted to life imprisonment; 02/28/48, died in prison from heart & stomach problems) 09/09/45 dissolved.

E.   **Military Affairs Minister, Executive Yuan** (03/30/40): MG Bao Wenyue

F.   **Interior Affairs Minister, Executive Yuan** (03/30/40): WENG KEMIN [+ Chairman, North China Political Council] (arrested by Republic of China; 12/26/45, committed suicide) 09/09/45 dissolved.

G.   **Treasury Minister, Executive Yuan** (03/30/40): ZHOU FOHAI [CHOU FO-HAI] [+ Vice President, Executive Yuan; Foreign Affairs Minister, Executive Yuan; & Finance Minister, Executive Yuan; + 11/20/44, Mayor of Shanghai] (captured by the Republic of China; tried for treason; sentenced to death but commuted to life imprisonment; 02/28/48, died in prison from heart & stomach problems) 09/09/45 dissolved.

Legislative Yuan, Republic of China-Nanjing (03/30/40):

A.   **Head, Legislative Yuan, Republic of China-Nanjing** (03/30/40): CHEN GONGBO [CHENG KUNG-PO] [+ Mayor of Shanghai] (Head of State, Republic of China-Nanjing & President, Executive Yuan, Republic of China-Nanjing) 11/20/44

Mayor of Shanghai (03/30/40): CHEN GONGBO [CHENG KUNG-PO] [+ Head, Legislative Yuan, Republic of China-Nanjing] (Head of State, Republic of China-Nanjing & President, Executive Yuan, Republic of China-Nanjing) 11/20/44 ZHOU FOHAI [CHOU FO-HAI] [+ Vice President, Executive Yuan; Foreign Affairs Minister, Executive Yuan; Finance Minister, Executive Yuan; & Treasury Minister, Executive Yuan] (captured by the Republic of China; tried for treason; sentenced to death but commuted to life imprisonment; 02/28/48, died in prison from heart & stomach problems) 09/09/45 dissolved.

Chairman, North China Political Council (03/30/40): WENG KEMIN [+ Interior Affairs Minister, Executive Yuan] (arrested by Republic of China; 12/26/45, committed suicide) 09/09/45 dissolved.

North China Political Affairs Committee:

A.   **Chief of Military Staff, North China Political Affairs Committee**: /38 LG He Fenglin

Republic of China-Nanjing Armed Forces

Military Affairs Minister (03/30/40): MG Bao Wenyue
A.   **Minister of Navy** (03/30/40): MG Ren Yuandao
B.   **General Chief of Staff** (03/30/40): MG Xiao Shuxuan or MG Yang Kuiyi
C.   **Minister of Military Training** (03/30/40): MG Yang Kuiyi or MG Xiao Shuxuan

National Military Council
A.   **Members, National Military Council**
/40 MG Liu Peixu (Deputy Chief of the General Staff) /40
/40 LG Zhang Lanfeng [+ to /42, Deputy Commander, Jiāngsū [Jiangsu]-Hénán [Henan; Honan] Communist Suppression Area; + to /42, Commanding General, 1st Army, Nationalist Salvation Army; + Head, Military Officers Training Group] (Commander-in-Chief, 2nd Army Group also see Volume VIII - China]) /43
/43 LG Sun Dianying [+ Deputy Commander-in-Chief, 24th Army Group; + Commanding General, 6th Front Army; + Commanding General, Yubei Security Headquarters] (rejoins the National Revolutionary Army; /45, Commanding General, 6th Route Army [also see Volume VIII - China]) /45

Reformed Government of China Army (03/28/38; 03/30/40, renamed **National Government of China-Nanjing Army**): Reformed Government of China Army 03/28/38 unknown? 03/30/40 renamed **National Government of China-Nanjing Army** 03/30/40 unknown?
A.   **Chief of the General Staff**: unknown? /42 LG Liu Yufen (died of an illness) /43
B.   **Deputy Chief of the General Staff**: unknown? /40 MG Liu Peixu (Head, Training Department, Central Military Academy) /40
C.   *Schools*
    1.   **Central Military Academy**:
        a.   **Training Department, Central Military Academy**: unknown? /40 MG Liu Peixu (removed from office after planning an assassination of Wang Jingwei; /41, Commanding General, 2nd Provisional Army) /41
    2.   **Officers Training Corps**: /40 LG Zhang Lanfeng [+ Member, National Military Council; + to /42, Deputy Commander, Jiāngsū [Jiangsu]-Hénán [Henan; Honan] Communist Suppression Area; + to /42, Commanding General, 1st Army, Nationalist Salvation Army] (Commander-in-Chief, 2nd Army Group also see Volume VIII - China]) /43
        a.   **Deputy, Officers Training Corps**: /39 MG Liu Peixu (Member, National Military Council) /40

Reformed Government of China Air Force (03/28/38; 03/30/40, renamed **National Government of China-Nanjing Air Force**): Reformed Government of China Air Force 03/28/38 unknown? 03/30/40 renamed **National Government of China-Nanjing Air**

Force 03/30/40 unknown?

Reformed Government of China Navy (03/28/38; 03/30/40, renamed **National Government of China-Nanjing Navy**): Reformed Government of China Navy 03/28/38 unknown? 03/30/40 renamed **National Government of China-Nanjing Navy** 03/30/40 unknown?

National Government of China-Nanjing Military Units

Front Armies (Army Status)

2nd Front Army (03/30/40 [also see Volume VIII - China]): unknown? /42 LG Sun Liangcheng [Sun Liang-cheng] (Commanding General, Kaifeng Pacification Headquarters) /42

A. **Chief of Staff, 2nd Front Army**: unknown? /44 LG Gan Lichu [Kan Li-chu] (Chief of Staff, Guǎngzhōu [Guangzhou, Kwangchou; Canton] Field Headquarters) /45.

B. *Components - 2nd Front Army*
   1. **4th Army**

C. **3rd Department, 2nd Front Army**: unknown? /45 Col. Li Hanchong.

4th Front Army (03/30/40 [also see Volume VIII - China): unknown? /44 LG Zhang Lanfeng (rejoins the Nationalist Government; /45, Commanding General, 3rd New Route Army) /45.

A. **Chief of Staff, 4th Front Army**: unknown? /45 MG Qiu Weida (Commanding General, 51st Division) /45

6th Front Army (03/30/40 [also see Volume VIII - China]): unknown? /43 LG Sun Dianying [+ Member, National Military Council; + Deputy Commander-in-Chief, 24th Army Group; + Commanding General, Yubei Security Headquarters] (rejoins the National Revolutionary Army; /45, Commanding General, 6th Route Army) /45

Army Groups and Pacification Headquarters (Army Status)

2nd Army Group (03/30/40, 1st War Area; 04/40, 5th War Area [also see Volume VIII - China]): 09/30/37 MG Sun Lianzhong [Sun Lian-chung] [+ to 03/40, Commander-in-Chief, 3rd Army Corps; + /39, Deputy Commander-in-Chief, 5th War Area; + /43, Commander-in-Chief, 6th War Area] /43 LG Zhang Lanfeng (Commander-in-Chief, 4th Front Army) 12/44 LG Liu Ruming [Liu Ju-ming] [+ Commander-in-Chief, Western Hénán [Henan; Honan] Left Force].

A. **Deputy Commander-in-Chief, 2nd Army Group** (03/30/40):
/40 LG Tian Zhennan [Tien Chen-nan].
/43 MG Gong Lingxun [Kong Lingxun; Kung Ling-hsun] (Commanding General, Shānxī [Shanxi; Shensi] Province Army Area)
/43 LG Cao Fulin [Tsao Fu-lin] [+ Commanding General, 55th Army] (Deputy Commander, 4th Pacification Area) /45.

B. **Chief of Staff, 2nd Army Group**: 03/20/33? MG Lu Ji (?) /43 MG Song Yuxiu (Chief of Staff, 4th Pacification Area) /45.

C. **Senior Staff Officer, 2nd Army Group** (03/30/40): unknown? /42 MG Ren Panian (Senior Staff Office, 2nd War Area) /44 MG He Zhanghai [+ Commanding General, Rear Area, 2nd Army Group] (attached to Ministry of National Defense) /45.

D. **Chief of Staff Section, 2nd Army Group** (03/30/40): MG Song Yuxiu (Chief of Staff, 2nd Army Group) /43

E. **Rear Area, 2nd Army Group**: unknown? /44 MG He Zhanghai [+ Senior Staff Officer, 2nd Army Group] (attached to Ministry of National Defense) /45.

24th Army Group (03/30/40 [also see Volume VIII - China]): 12/38 LG Pang Bingxun [Pang Ping-hsun (joins Wang Jingwei's Government [see Volume VII - Germany's & Imperial Japan's Allies and Puppet States]]) /41

A. **Deputy Commander, 24th Army Group**:unknown? /42 MG Ma Fawu [Ma Fa-wu] [+ Commanding General, 40th Army] (Deputy Commander-in-Chief, Héběi [Hebei; Hopeh; Hopei] War Area)
/43 MG Liu Jin [Liu Chin] (Head, 21st Reserve Officer Corps & Commanding General, Bǎojī [Baoji] Garrison) /45.
/43 LG Sun Dianying [+ Member, National Military Council; + Commanding General, 6th Front Army; + Commanding General, Yubei Security Headquarters] (rejoins the National Revolutionary Army; /45, Commanding General, 6th Route Army) /45.

B. **Chief of Staff, 24th Army Group**: unknown? /43 MG Qiu Weida (Chief of Staff, 4th Front Army) /45

C. *Components - 24th Army Group*
1. **7th Provisional Army** (/43 to end of World War II)

D. **Senior Staff Officer, 24th Army Group**:

E. **Adjutant-General Section, 24th Army Group**: /39 Col. Si Yuanjoy (Commanding Officer, 46th Independent Brigade) /42

F. **Military Judge Advocate Section, 24th Army Group**: /41 MG Chen Wenming

(Councilor, National Military Council) /41

1. **Vice Chief, Military Judge Advocate Section, 24ᵗʰ Army Group**: /38 Col. Chen Wenming (Chief, Military Judge Advocate Section, 24ᵗʰ Army Group) /41

National Salvation Army:
A. *Components* - **National Salvation Army**
1. **1ˢᵗ Army**

Kāifēng [Kaifeng] Pacification Headquarters (03/30/40 [also see Volume VIII - China]): unknown? /42 LG Sun Liangcheng [Sun Liang-cheng] (Commanding General, Northern Jiāngsū [Jiangsu] Pacification Headquarters) /42

Northern Hénán [Henan; Honan] Pacification Headquarters (03/30/40 [also see Volume VIII - China]): unknown? /41 MG Liu Changyi [Liu Chang-yi] [+ Commanding General, 21ˢᵗ Provisional Division] (escapes and returns to Nationalist China [also see Volume VIII - China]) /42

Northern Jiāngsū [Jiangsu] Pacification Headquarters (03/30/40 [also see Volume VIII - China]): unknown? LG Sun Liangcheng [Sun Liang-cheng] (rejoins the nationalist Government; /45, Commanding General, 2ⁿᵈ New Route Army) /45.

Armies and Suppression Headquarters (Corps Status)

1st Army, National Salvation Army (03/30/40): LG Zhang Lanfeng [+ Deputy Commander, Jiāngsū [Jiangsu]-Hénán [Henan; Honan] Communist Suppression Area; + Head, Military Officers Training Group] /43

4th Army, 2nd Front Army (03/30/40, 4th War Area; 08/41, 9th War Area [also see Volume VIII - China]): 07/38 MG Ou Zhen [Ou Chen] [+ /44, Commanding General, Army Ou Chen; + /45, Commanding General, 99th Division] /42 MG Zhao Yunxiang [/44, dismissed by Nationalist Government] (rejoins Nationalist Government; /45, Commanding General, 1st Army, 2nd Route Army) /45

A.　**Deputy Commander, 4th Army**: unknown? /39 MG Bai Huizhang [+ Commanding General, 102nd Division; + /43, Commanding General, Gannan Division Area] (Deputy Commander, 88th Army) /44 MG Shen Jiucheng.

.　**Training, 4th Army**

　1.　**Military Officers Training Group, 4th Army**: unknown? /45 MG Li Yikuang.

2nd Provisional Army (03/30/40; 08/41, 9th War Area [also see Volume VIII - China]): unknown? /41 LG Liu Peixu (retired) /43 unknown? 12/44 MG Shen Fazao [Shen Fa-tsao].

A.　**Political Department, 2nd Provisional Army**: /39 Col. Chen Gan (II) (Planning Commissioner, Political Department, National Military Council) /40

7th Provisional Army (03/30/40 [also see Volume VIII - China]; /43, 24th Army Group): unknown? /42 MG Liu Yueting (joins Nationalist Government; /45, Commanding General, 3rd Provisional Column; /47 captured by the People's Liberation Army; /51, executed as a counter-revolutionary) /45

Heping National Salvation Army (03/30/40, Japanese Puppet Army):

A.　*Components* - **Heping National Salvation Army**

　1.　**3rd Division**

Jiāngsū [Jiangsu]-Hénán [Henan; Honan] Communist Suppression Headquarters (03/30/40 [also see Volume VIII - China]):

A.　**Deputy Commander, Jiāngsū [Jiangsu]-Hénán [Henan; Honan] Communist Suppression Headquarters**: /40 LG Zhang Lanfeng [+ Commanding General, 1st Army, Nationalist Salvation Army; + Head, Military Officers Training Group] /42

Divisions and Brigades

3rd Division: /39 MG Song Kebin (rejoins the Nationalist Government; /40, Deputy Commander, 7th Division) /40

21st Provisional Division (/41): MG Liu Changyi [Liu Chang-yi] [+ Commanding General, Northern Hénán [Henan; Honan] Pacification Headquarters] (escapes and returns to Nationalist China [also see Volume VIII - China]) /42

Yubei Security Headquarters (03/30/40 [also see Volume VIII - China]): unknown? /43 LG Sun Dianying [+ Member, National Military Council; + Deputy Commander-in-Chief, 24th Army Group; + Commanding General, 6th Front Army] (rejoins the National Revolutionary Army; /45, Commanding General, 6th Route Army [also see Volume VIII - China]) /45

Independent Garrison Brigade (Nanjing): /42 MG Liu Yi (arrested but subsequently released)

National Government of China-Nanjing Navy Fleet

[Imperial Japanese Navy provided some captured warships for the collaborationist navy]

light cruiser: *Isojima* (ex-Chinese Navy *Ning Hai*)
                                 Yasojima (ex-Chinese Navy *Ping Hai*)

patrol boat: *PB-101* (ex-HMS *Thracian*)
                                 PB-102 (ex-USS *Stewart*)

gunboat: *Suma* (ex-HMS *Moth*)
                                 Tatara (ex-USS *Wake*)
                                 Karatsu (ex-USS *Luzon*)
                                 Narumi (ex-RM *Ermanno Carlotto*)
                                 Okitsu (ex-RM *Lepanto*)
                                 Nan-Yo (ex-Chinese Navy *The Hsing*)

STATE of BURMA

(Japanese Puppet State)

State of Burma Government (08/01/43 to 05/03/45)

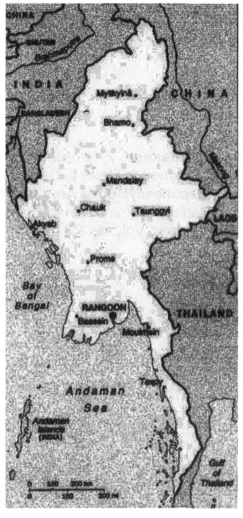

[On September 25, 1943, Japan ceded all of the Shan states to the State of Burma, except for Kengtung and Mongpan, which were given to Thailand. Basically an independent puppet nation under Japanese Control.]

Head, Burmese Administration (08/01/42, Provisional Civilian Government under Japanese military Authority): Dr. BA MAW (Chief of State, State of Burma) 08/01/43 dissolved.

Chief of State, State of Burma (08/01/43): Dr. BA MAW [+ Prime Minister] (fled to Japan and captured later that year; held in Sugamo Prison, Tokyo until 1946) 05/03/45 converted back to British Territory.

Prime Minister (08/01/43): Dr. BA MAW [+ Chief of State]

A. **Deputy Prime Minister** (08/01/43): THAKIN MYA
B. **Minister of Home Affairs** (08/01/43): BA WIN
C. **Minister of Foreign Affairs** (08/01/43): THAKIN NU
   1. **Ambassador to Japan**: /44? Dr. THEIN MAUNG
D. **Minister of Finance** (08/01/43): Dr. THEIN MAUNG (Ambassador to Japan) /44? U SET
E. **Minister of Defense** (08/01/43): MG Aung San
F. **Minister of Justice** (08/01/43): Dr. THEIN MAUNG
G. **Minister of Education and Health** (08/01/43): HLA MIN
H. **Minister of Agriculture** (08/01/43): THAKIN THAN TUN (Minister of Transport) /44?
I. **Minister of Commerce and Industry** (08/01/43): U MYA
J. **Minister of Communications and Irrigation** (08/01/43): THAKIN LAY MAUNG
K. **Minister of Welfare and Publicity** (08/01/43): BANDULA U SEIN
L. **Minister of Co-Operation with Japan** (08/01/43): TUN AUNG
M. **Public Works Recovery Minister** (08/01/43): THAKIN LUN BAW
N. **Minister of Transport**: /44? THAKIN THAN TUN

Japanese Military Commanders

Army Group

Southern Army (11/06/41, Southern Operations, excluding China) FM Count Hisaichi Terauchi [Japanese] [see Volume IV - Japan] (retired; 06/12/46, died of cerebral hemorrhage) 11/30/45 surrendered.

Army

Japanese Military Commanders in Burma (04/20/42): **{Japanese} Fifteenth Army** 04/20/42 LG Shojiro Iida [Japanese] [see Volume IV - Japan] (assigned to General Defense Command) 03/18/43 Japanese Fifteenth Army replaced by **{Japanese} Burma Area Army** 03/18/43 LG Masakazu Kawabe [Japanese] [see Volume IV - Japan] (Commander-in-Chief, Central District Army) 08/30/44 LG Heitaro Kinura [Japanese] [see Volume IV - Japan] 08/15/45.

British Governors of Burma

Governor of Burma: 05/08/36 Sir ARCHIBALD DOUGLAS COCHRANE [British] 05/06/41 Sir REGINALD HUGH DORMAN-SMITH [British] {05/42 to 10/45, in exile at Simla, India} 08/31/46.

Allied Military Governors

Allied Military Governor (01/01/44): Adm. The Right Honorable Lord Louis (Francis Albert Victor Nicholas) Mountbatten, Duke of Mountbatten [British] [see Volume II - The British Commonwealth & Volume III - The United States] [+ Supreme Commander, Allied South-East Asia Command] 10/45 MG Sir Hubert Elvin Rance [British] [see Volume II - The British Commonwealth] 08/31/46.

Burmese Military

Burma Independent Army [BIA] (12/26/41, Japanese Puppet Army, formed in Thailand; 04/42, disbanded): unknown? 04/42 disbanded.

Burma Defense Army [BFA] (07/42, Japanese Puppet Army; 08/01/43, redesignated **Burma National Army**): Col. Aung San [+ Minister of Defense] (Commanding General, Burma National Army) 08/01/43 redesignated **Burma National Army**.

Burma National Army [BNA] (08/01/43, Japanese Puppet Army; 03/27/45, switched to the Allies side and launch an uprising against the Japanese; 05/15/45, redesignated **Patriotic Burmese Forces**): MG Aung San [+ Minister of Defense] (Commanding General, Patriotic Burmese Forces) 05/15/45 redesignated **Patriotic Burmese Forces**.

Patriotic Burmese Forces [BPF] (05/15/45): LG Aung San [+ Minister of Defense].

Arakan Defense Army (Japanese Puppet Army in Rakhine area of Burma; the Japanese gave Rakhine autonomy rule; 03/27/45, switched to the Allies side and with the Burma National Army fought against the Japanese):

Burma's Resistance Movement Against Japan

Anti-Fascist Organization (AFO) (08/44): THAKIN SOE 08/19/45 reorganized as the **Anti-Fascist People's Freedom League (AFPFL)**

Anti-Fascist People's Freedom League (AFPFL) (08/19/45): THAKIN SOE and LG Aung San.

SECOND PHILIPPINE REPUBLIC

(Japanese Puppet State)

Second Philippine Republic
(10/14/43 to 08/17/45)

[President Manuel Luis Quezon, of the Commonwealth of the Philippines, declared Manila an "open city". The Japanese entered the city on 01/02/42 and established it as their capital, even thought Japan didn't fully capture the Philippines until 05/06/42.

Therefore before listing the government of the Second Philippine Republic, we have to look at the Commonwealth of the Philippines.]

Commonwealth of the Philippines Government

[see Volume IX - Allied Nations]

[The Philippines was a Commonwealth of the United States prior to World War II. After the war, it was granted it's independence as a nation, from the United States on July 4, 1946.]

Executive Branch

President, Commonwealth of the Philippines (11/15/35): MANUEL LUIS QUEZON ANTONIO y MOLINA [in exile in Washington, D. C. from 01/03/42] 08/01/44 SERGIO OSMEÑA [in exile in Washington, D. C. to 10/20/44] 05/28/46 MANUEL ROXAS y ACUÑA.

A. **Mayor of Manila**: /41? JORGE BARTOLOMÉ VARGAS y CELIS (Chairman, Philippine Executive Council) 01/21/43

Secretaries

Secretary of Justice: /34 JOSÉ YULO (Speaker Philippine National Assembly) /38 JOSÉ ABAD SANTOS (Chief Justice, Supreme Court, Commonwealth of the Philippines) /4?

Secretary of Interior: JOSÉ ZULUETA (06/09/45, Speaker, Philippine National Assembly)

Secretary of Agriculture & Commerce: /38 BENIGNO SIMEON AQUINO y QUIAMBAO Sr. (Director, KALIBAPI) /41

Legislative Branch

Philippine National Assembly
Speaker, Philippine National Assembly: 01/24/39 JOSÉ YULO (Chief Justice, Supreme Court, Second Philippine Republic) 12/30/41 vacant & dissolved - see **Speaker, Philippine National Assembly, Second Philippine Republic**

Judicial Branch

Chief Justice, **Supreme Court, Commonwealth of the Philippines**: /4? JOSÉ ABAD SANTOS /42 dissolved - see **Chief Justice, Supreme Court, Second Philippine Republic**

Associate Justice, **Supreme Court, Commonwealth of the Philippines**: 02/29/36 JOSÉ PACIANO LAUREL y GARCIA (02/05/42 dissolved.

United States High Commissioners for the Philippine Commonwealth

United States High Commissioner (11/15/35):

   11/15/35 WILLIAM FRANCIS "FRANK" MURPHY [American] 12/31/36

   05/13/36 J. WELDON JONES [American] [acting for Murphy to 01/01/37] 04/26/37

   04/26/37 PAUL VORIES McNUTT [American] 07/12/39

   05/39 J. WELDON JONES [American] [acting for McNutt to 07/12/39] 10/21/39

   10/21/39 FRANCIS BOWES SAYRE [American] [from 03/42 in Washington, D. C.]
      10/12/42

   10/13/42 HAROLD L. ICKES [American] [United States Interior Secretary, in charge of
      high commissioner's functions, in D. C.] 09/14/45

   09/15/45 PAUL VORIES McNUTT [American] 07/04/46

[Japanese General Masaharu Honma dissolved the Commonwealth of the Philippines and established the Philippine Executive Commission, a caretaker government until the Second Philippine Republic was formed. On 12/08/42, all political parties were banned and replaced by the non-partisan "Organization in the Service of the New Philippines" {Kapisanan sa Paglilingkod sa Bagong Pilipinas [KALIBAPI]}.]

Second Philippine Republic Government

Philippine Executive Commission (01/23/43):
Chairman, Philippine Executive Commission (01/23/43): JORGE BARTOLOMÉ VARGAS y CELIS (Ambassador to Japan) 10/14/43

A.   **Organization in the Service of the New Philippines [Kapisanan sa Paglilingkod sa Bagong Pilipinas [KALIBAPI]]**
    Director, KALIBAPI: BENIGNO SIMEON AQUINO y QUIAMBAO Sr.
    1.   **Preparatory Commission for Independence** (06/19/43; a committee of 20 members from the KALIBAPI to draft a Constitution for a new republic controlled by the Japanese): JOSÉ PACIANO LAUREL y GARCIA (President, Second Philippine Republic) 09/07/43 dissolved after Constitution was ratified by KALIBAPI.

[On 09/20/43, the KALIBAPI's representative groups in the country's provinces and cities elected from among themselves 54 members of the Philippine National Assembly, the national legislature, and 54 governors and city mayors.]

Executive Branch

President, Second Philippine Republic (10/14/43): JOSÉ PACIANO LAUREL y GARCIA (arrested for collaboration with the Japanese; /46, charged with 132 counts of treason; /48, never brought to trial, granted an general amnesty) 08/17/45

Vice President, Second Philippine Republic (10/14/43): BENIGNO SIMEON AQUINO y QUIAMBAO Sr. (fled to Japan, arrested and imprisoned at Sugamo Prison when Japan surrendered; 08/25/46, flown back to Philippines for treason charges; 12/20/47, died of heart attack) 08/17/45 dissolved.
RAMÒN AVANCEÑA

Legislative Branch

Philippine National Assembly, Second Philippine Republic (09/23/43):
Speaker, Philippine National Assembly (09/23/43): BENIGNO SIMEON AQUINO y QUIAMBAO Sr. 02/02/44

Judicial Branch

Chief Justice, Supreme Court, Second Philippine Republic: /42 JOSÉ YULO 08/17/45 dissolved.

JORGE BOCOBO

Japanese Military Commanders
Army Group

Southern Army (11/06/41, Southern Operations, excluding China) FM Count Hisaichi Terauchi [Japanese] [see Volume IV - Japan] (retired; 06/12/46, died of cerebral hemorrhage) 11/30/45 surrendered.

Japanese Military Commanders and Military Governors

Japanese Military Commander (01/03/42, Manila; 08/01/42, renamed **Japanese Military Governor**): **Fourteenth Army** LG Masaharu Honma [Japanese] [see Volume IV - Japan] (in reserve/retired; 1946, condemned to death and executed as a war criminal) 08/01/42 renamed **Japanese Military Governor** 08/01/42 LG Shizuichi Tanaka [Japanese] [see Volume IV - Japan] (attached Army General Staff) 05/19/43 LG Shigenori Kuroda [Japanese] [see Volume IV - Japan] (Commanding General, 14th Area Army) 07/28/44 upgraded to **14th Area Army** 07/28/44 LG Shigenori Kuroda [Japanese] [see Volume IV - Japan] (replaced/in reserve) 09/26/44 Gen. Tomoyuki "Tiger of Malaya" Yamashita [Japanese] [see Volume IV - Japan] (1946, condemned to death and hanged as a war criminal) 08/17/45.

AZAD HIND
[PROVISIONAL GOVERNMENT of FREE INDIA]

(Japanese Puppet State)

Azad Hind
[Provisional Government of Free India]
(10/21/43 to 08/18/45)

[Azad Hind was established by Indian nationalists-in-exile during the second half of World War II, in Singapore with monetary, military and political assistance from Imperial Japan, to fight against British rule in India. It's capital was Port Blair, located on Nicobar Island, even though the government operated in Singapore from 10/21/43 to 11/43; in Rangoon, Burma, 11/43 to 11/44; Singapore, from 11/44 to 01/10/45; Rangoon, Burma, from 01/10/45 to 04/24/45; Bangkok, Thailand, from 04/24/45 to 05/45; Kuala Lumpur, Malaya, from 05/45 to 08/12/45; and Singapore, from 08/12/45 to 08/18/45.]

Prior to Azad Hind

Indian Independence League (03/29/42, by Indian nationalist-in-exile): RASH BEHARI BOSE (01/21/45, died) /4? LCol. Jaganath Rao. Bhonsle [+ Director, Military Bureau] (Minister of the Armed Forces) 07/04/43 NETAJI SUBHAS CHANDRA BOSE (Chief of State, Azad Hind, Prime Minister, Azad Hind, Minister of Foreign Affairs, Azad Hind, & Minister of War, Azad Hind) 10/21/43 becomes the **Azad Hind** and dissolved - see **Azad Hind**.

Indian National Army (#1) [Azad Hind Fauj] (09/42, Singapore; 40,000 men): Capt. Mohan Singh (arrested by the Japanese and exiled to Pulau Ubia) 12/42 disbanded.
A.   **Director, Military Bureau** (09/42): LCol. Jaganath Rao. Bhonsle [+ Head, Indian Independence League] (Director, Military Bureau, Azad Hind) 10/21/43 dissolved.

Azad Hind
[Provisional Government of Free India]

Chief of State, Azad Hind (10/21/43): NETAJI SUBHAS CHANDRA BOSE [+ Prime Minister, Minister of Foreign Affairs, & Minister of War] (presumed dead from a plane crash over Taiwan) 08/18/45 dissolved.

Prime Minister, Azad Hind (10/21/43): NETAJI SUBHAS CHANDRA BOSE [+ Head of State, Minister of Foreign Affairs, & Minister of War] (presumed dead from a plane crash over Taiwan) 08/18/45 dissolved.

A. **Minister of Foreign Affairs** (10/21/43): NETAJI SUBHAS CHANDRA BOSE [+ Head of State, Prime Minister, & Minister of War] (presumed dead from a plane crash over Taiwan) 08/18/45 dissolved.

B. **Minister of War** (10/21/43): NETAJI SUBHAS CHANDRA BOSE [+ Head of State, Prime Minister, & Minister of Foreign Affairs] (presumed dead from a plane crash over Taiwan) 08/18/45 dissolved.

C. **Minister of Finance** (10/21/43): LCol. A. C. Chatterjee 08/18/45 dissolved.

D. **Minister-in-Charge of Women's Organization** (10/21/43): Capt. Dr. Lakshmi Swaminathan [later married to LAKSHMI SEHGAL] 08/18/45 dissolved.

E. **Minister of Armed Forces** (10/21/43): LCol. Aziz Ahmed /43 LCol. N. S. Bhagat 07/04/43 LCol. Jaganath Rao. Bhonsle /4? LCol. Guizara Singh /4? LCol. Mohammed Zaman Kiani /4? LCol. A. D. Loganathan /4? LCol. Ehsan Qadir /4? LCol. Shah Nawaz Khan 08/18/45 dissolved.

F. **Minister of Publicity and Propaganda** (10/21/43): SHRI S. A. AYER

G. **Minister of Unknown? Cabinet Post** (10/21/43): JOHN ALOYSIUS THIVY

H. **Secretary to Netaji Subhas Chandra Bose** (Ministerial Rank; 10/21/43): A. N. SAHAY 08/18/45 dissolved.

I. **Legal Advisor to Netaji Subhas Chandra Bose** (Ministerial Rank; 10/21/43): A. N. SARKAR 08/18/45 dissolved.

J. *Other Secretaries and Advisory officials* (Ministerial Rank; 10/21/43):
    1. **Advisor from Burma**: KARIM GHANI
    2. **Advisor from Thailand**: DEBNATH DAS
    3. **Advisor from Thailand**: SIRDAR ISHER SINGH
    4. **Advisor from Hong Kong**: D. M. KHAN
    5. **Advisor from Singapore**: A. YELLAPA
    6. **Advisor from Singapore**: A. N. SARKAR

K. **Governorship, Andaman [Shaheed] & Nicobar [Swaraj] Islands**: LCol. A. D. Loganathan

Azad Hind Armed Forces

Indian National Army (#2) [Azad Hind Fauj] (02/15/43, Singapore; 40,000 men): LCol. Mohammed Zaman Kiani (Commanding General, 1st Azad Hind Division)

Director, Military Bureau (02/15/43): LCol. Jaganath Rao. Bhonsle [+ to 07/04/43, Head, Indian Independence League] ·

Chief of the General Staff: LCol. Shah Nawaz Khan /4? MG Mohammed Zaman Kiani (surrendered) 08/2545 dissolved.
A.   **Military Secretary, to Netaji Subhas Chandra Bose**: Maj Prem Kumar Sahgal
B.   **Commandant, Officer Training School**: Maj. Habib Ur Rahman (11/46, tried for treason, but released) 08/25/45 dissolved.
C.   **Head, Enlightment & Culture Department**: LCol. A. C. Chatterjee (Minister of Finance) /43 Maj A. D. Jahangir

Azad Hind Divisions

1st Azad Hind Division: MG Mohammed Zaman Kiani (Chief of the General Staff) /45
A.   *Components - 1st Azad Hind Division*
    1.   **1st Guerrilla Regiment** or **Subhas Brigade**
    2.   **2nd Guerrilla Regiment** or **Gandhi Brigade**
    3.   **3rd Guerrilla Regiment** or **Azad Brigade**
    4.   **4th Guerrilla Regiment** or **Nehru Brigade**

2nd Azad Hind Division: Col. N. S. Bhagat /4? MG Shah Nawaz Khan (surrendered; 11/46, tried for treason, but released) 08/25/45 dissolved.
A.   *Components - 2nd Azad Hind Division*
    1.   **5th Guerrilla Regiment** or **2nd Infantry Regiment**

3rd Azad Hind Division: unknown?

Groups

Bahadur Group (part of 1st Azad Hind Division): /44 Col. Shaukat Hayat Malik

Azad Hind Regiments

1st Guerrilla Regiment or **Subhas Brigade** (02/43): Col. Shah Nawaz Khan (Commanding General, 2nd Azad Hind Division)

2nd Guerrilla Regiment or **Gandhi Brigade** (09/42): Col. Inayat Kiani

3rd Guerrilla Regiment or **Azad Brigade** (02./43): Col. Gulzara Singh /44 Col Shan Nawaz Khan

4th Guerrilla Regiment or **Nehru Brigade** (/44): LCol. Gurubaksh Singh Dhillion (surrendered; 11/46, tried for treason, but released) 08/25/45 dissolved.

5th Guerrilla Regiment or **2nd Infantry Regiment** Maj. R. W. Rodrigues /4? Col. Perm Kumar Sahgal (surrendered; 11/46, tried for treason, but released) 08/25/45 dissolved.
A.   **Deputy Commander, 5th Guerrilla Regiment**: Maj. Gurubaksh Singh Dhillion (Commanding Officer, 4th Guerrilla Regiment) /44

The Rani of Jhansi Regiment: Capt. Dr. Lakshimi Swaminathan [+ Minister-in-Charge of Woman's Organization]

-

EMPIRE of VIETNAM

VIETNAM

(Japanese Puppet State)

Empire of Vietnam Government (03/09/45 to 08/19/45)

[After the fall of France and the establishment of Vichy France, the French had lost practical control in French Indochina to Japan. But, Japan stayed in the background while giving Vichy French administrators nominal control. On 03/09/45, this change when Japan officially took over. To gain support of the Vietnamese people, Imperial Japan declared it would return sovereignty to Vietnam. The Empire of Vietnam was a short-lived puppet state of Imperial Japan governing the whole of Vietnam between 03/11/45 to 08/23/45.]

Emperior of Vietnam (03/09/45): Emperior BAO ĐAI [+ from 02/13/26, King of Annam] 08/19/45 dissolved.

Prime Minister (03/09/45): PHAM QUYNH 04/07/45 TRÂN TRONG KIM 08/19/45 dissolved.
- A. **Foreign Minister** (03/09/45): TRÂN VAN CHUONG 08/19/45 dissolved.
- B. **Justice Minister** (03/09/45): TRINH DINH THAO 08/19/45 dissolved.
- C. **Education Minister** (03/09/45): HOANG XUAN HAN 08/19/45 dissolved.
- D. **Youth Minister** (03/09/45): PHAN ANH 08/19/45 dissolved.
- E. **Economy Minister** (03/09/45): HO TA KHANH 08/19/45 dissolved.
- F. **Interior Minister** (03/09/45): unknown? 08/19/45 dissolved.
- G. **Supply Minister** (03/09/45): unknown? 08/19/45 dissolved.
- H. **Council of Nam Bo**:
  - 1. **President, Council of Nam Bo**: /45 TRÂN VAN AN 08/19/45 dissolved.
  - 2. **Deputy President, Council of Nam Bo**: /45 KHA VANG CAN 08/19/45 dissolved.

French Indochina

[For this section also see Volume VI - Italy & France]

Governor-General, French Indochina: (Capital: Saigon, Indochina): 09/36 JOSEPH-JULES BRÉVIÉ [French] (03/26/43, Vichy France Minister for Colonies [Overseas France]) 08/23/39 Gen. [Retired '39] Georges-Albert-Julien Catroux [French] (acting; replaced) 06/27/40 VA Jean d'Decoux [French] [FN] (ousted by the Japanese; arrested and tried after the war for collaboration with the Japanese, but not convicted) 03/09/45 Japanese Governor Generals 08/15/45 vacant 09/23/45 redesignated **High Commissioner, French Indochina** - see **High Commissioner, French Indochina**.

A. **Commander-in-Chief, Troops in French Indochina [Commandant Supérieur de Troupes du Groupe l'Indochine]** (HQ: Saigon, Indochina): /38 LG Maurice-Paul-Auguste Martin [French] (retired) /40 LG Eugène Mordant [French] (retired; /44, Head, Military Resistance Indochina & Delegate-General, Provisional Government, Indochina) /44 MG Camille-Ange-Gabriel Sabattier [French]

B. *Areas of French Indochina*:
   1. **Tonkin {part of Vietnam today}** (Capital: Hanoi): **French Resident-Superior**: /37 MG Yves-Charles Châtel [French] (11/20/41, Governor-General of Algeria) /40 ÉMILE-LOUIS-FRANÇOIS GRANDJEAN [French] [+ French Resident-Superior, Annam] /41 EDOUARD-ANDRÉ DELSALLE [French] /42 JEAN-MAURICE-NORBERT HAELEWYN [French] (French Resident-Superior of Annam) /44 CAMILLE AUPELLE [French] 03/45 see **Japanese Resident** 08/15/45 **French Commissioner**: 08/18/45 PIERRE MESSMER [French] (acting) 08/22/45 JEAN-ROGER SAINTENY [French].
   2. **Annam {part of Vietnam today}** (Capital: Hué): **French Resident-Superior**: MAURICE-FERNAND GRAFFEUIL [French] /40 ÉMILE-LOUIS-FRANÇOIS GRANDJEAN [French] [+ to /41, French Resident-Superior, Tonkin] /44 JEAN-MAURICE-NORBERT HAELEWYN [French] 03/45 see **Japanese Resident** 08/15/45 under the **French Commissioner of Tonkin**.
   3. **Cochin Chine {part of Vietnam today}** (Capital: Saigon): **French Governor**: /39 RENÉ VEBER [French] (/42, Governor, French Guyana) /40 HENRI-GEORGES RIVOAL [French] /42 ERNEST-THIMOTHÉE HOEFFEL [French] 03/45 see **Japanese Governor** 08/15/45 **Imperial Delegate**: NGUYEN VAN SAM [Vietnamese]

4.   **Laos** (Capital: Vientiane): **French Resident-Superior**: EUGÈNE-HENRI-ROGER EUTROPE [French] 04/38 ANDRÈ TOUZET [French] 11/40 ADRIEN-ANTHONY-MAURICE ROQUES [French] 12/41 LOUIS-ANTOINE-MARIE BRASEY [French] 04/05/45 **Japanese Resident in Vientiane**: 03/45 MASANORI SAKO [Japanese] 08/45 and **Japanese Supreme Counselor in Luang Prabang**: 04/05/45 see **Japanese Supreme Counselor in Luang Prabang** 08/22/45 **French Commissioner**: 08/25/45 HANS IMFELD [French].

5.   **Cambodia [Cambodge]** (Capital: Phnom Penh): **French Resident-Superior**: 12/12/36 LÉON-EMMANUEL THIBAUDEAU [French] 12/29/41 JEAN de LENS [French] 03/02/43 GEORGES-ARMAND-LÉON GAUTHIER [French] 11/44 ANDRÉ-JOSEPH BERJOAN [French] 03/09/45 **Japanese Supreme Advisor**: see **Japanese Superior Advisor** 08/45 **French Resident-Superior**: 08/45 ANDRÉ-JOSEPH BERJOAN [French].

   A.   **Commanding General, Cambodia**: /40 BG Yves-Marie-Jacques-Guillaume de Boisboissel [French] (Deputy Commander, Military District XIX) /41

C.   **Military-Governor, Hanoi**: 07/40 BG Camille-Ange-Gabriel Sabattier [French] (Commanding General, Cochinchine Brigade, Indochina) 12/08/41

Japanese Occupation in Indochina

Head, Japanese Delegation to French Indochina: /40 MG Raishiro Sumida [Japanese] [see Volume IV - Japan] (Commanding General, 39th Division) /41 disbanded.

Japanese Resident in Annam (03/45): YOKOYAMA MASAYUKI [Japanese] [see Volume VI - Italy & France] 08/15/45.

Japanese Resident in Tonkin (03/45): NISHIMURA KUMAO [Japanese] [see Volume VI - Italy & France] 08/15/45.

Japanese Governor in Cochin Chine (03/45, under direct Japanese control): MINODA FUJIO [Japanese] [see Volume VI - Italy & France] 08/15/45.

Army Group Command

Southern Army (11/06/41, Southern Operations, excluding China) FM Count Hisaichi Terauchi [Japanese] [see Volume IV - Japan] (retired; 06/12/46, died of cerebral hemorrhage) 11/30/45 surrendered.

Corps Command

Japanese Military Commanders in Indochina (09/07/40): **{Japanese} Indochina Expeditionary Army** 09/07/40 MG Takuma Nishimura [Japanese] [+ Commanding General, Imperial Guards Division & Commanding General, 21st Independent Mixed Brigade] [see Volume IV - Japan] 07/05/41 disbanded and replaced by **{Japanese} Fifteenth Army** 07/05/41 LG Shojiro Iida [Japanese] [see Volume IV - Japan] [Japanese Fifteenth Army sent to Burma] /41 unknown? 11/10/42 replaced by **{Japanese} Indochina Garrison Army** 11/10/42 LG Viscount Kazumoto Machijiri [Japanese] [see Volume IV - Japan] (replaced) 11/22/44 LG Yuitsu Tsuchihashi [Japanese] [see Volume IV - Japan] (Commanding General, Thirty-Eighth Army) 12/11/44 redesignated **{Japanese} Thirty-Eighth Army** 12/11/44 LG Yuitsu Tsuchihashi [Japanese] [see Volume IV - Japan] 08/15/45.

Allied Occupation Force in Indochina

Commander, Allied (Chinese) Occupation Force for Indochina (09/09/45; above the 16th parallel): Gen. Lu Han [Chinese] [see Volume VIII - China] 03/06/46

Chairman of the Allied Control Commission & Commander, Allied Land Forces, French Indochina [ALFFIC] (09/06/45; below 16th parallel): Gen. Sir Douglas David Gracey [British] [see Volume II - The British Commonwealth & Volume III - The United States] 01/28/46.

French High Commissioners, French Indochina (Starting 09/23/45)

High Commissioner, French Indochina 09/23/45 JEAN-MARIE-ARSÈNE CÉDILE [French] [see Volume VI - Italy & France] (acting) 10/05/45 LG Philippe-François-Marie-Jacques Leclerc de Hauteclocque, Count of Hauteclocque [French] [+ Commanding General, Far East Expeditionary Corps] [see Volume VI - Italy & France] (acting) 10/31/45 VA Georges-Louis-Marie Thierry d'Argenlieu [French] [FN] [see Volume VI - Italy & France].

Democratic Republic of Vietnam (proclaimed 09/02/45)

President, Indochinese Communist Party (10/30; officially dissolved by the French 11/11/45, but continued in secret to 05/51): HO CHI MINH [NGUYEN AI QUOC] [+ 08/25/45 to 08/29/45, Chairman, Committee of Liberation of the Vietnamese People; + 08/29/45 to 03/02/46, Chairman, Provisional Government; + 09/02/45, Prime Minister, Provisional Government; + 03/02/46, President, Provisional Government].

First Secretary, Indochinese Communist Party (05/41): TRUONG CHINH.

Chairman, Committee of Liberation of the Vietnamese People ["Viet Minh"] (08/25/45): HO CHI MINH [NGUYEN AI QUOC] [+ President, Indochinese Communist Party] (Chairman, Provisional Government) 08/29/45 dissolved.

Chairman, Provisional Government (08/29/45): HO CHI MINH [NGUYEN AI QUOC] [+ President, Indochinese Communist Party; + 09/02/45, Prime Minister, Provisional Government] (President, Provisional Government) 03/02/46 dissolved.

President, Provisional Government (03/02/46): HO CHI MINH [NGUYEN AI QUOC] [+ President, Indochinese Communist Party; + 09/02/45, Prime Minister, Provisional Government].

Prime Minister, Provisional Government (09/02/45): HO CHI MINH [NGUYEN AI QUOC] [+ President, Indochinese Communist Party; + 03/02/46, President, Provisional Government]

KINGDOM of CAMBODIA

(Japanese Puppet State)

Kingdom of Cambodia Government (03/09/45 to 08/15/45)

[After the fall of France and the establishment of Vichy France, the French had lost practical control in French Indochina to Japan. But, Japan stayed in the background while giving Vichy French administrators nominal control. On 03/09/45, this change when Japan officially took over. To gain support of the Cambodian people, Imperial Japan dissolved the French colonial rule and pressured Cambodia to declare its independence within the Greater East Asia Co-Prosperity Sphere. Four days later King Sihanouk declared Kampuchea [Cambodia] independent. The Kingdom of Cambodia was a short-lived puppet state of Imperial Japan governing between 03/09/45 to 08/15/45.]

King of Cambodia: 08/09/27 King SISOWATH MONIVONG (died) 04/24/41 King NORODOM SIHANOUK [grandson of King Sisowath].

Prime Minister (03/18/45): King NORODOM SIHANOUK [+ King of Cambodia] 08/14/45 SON NGOC THANH 10/16/45 Prince SISOVATH MONIRETH 12/15/46

A. **Foreign Minister** (03/18/45): unknown? 05/45 SON NGOC THANH (Prime Minister) 08/14/45

French Indochina
[For this section also see Volume VI - Italy & France]

Governor-General, French Indochina: (Capital: Saigon, Indochina): 09/36 JOSEPH-JULES BRÉVIÉ [French] (03/26/43, Vichy France Minister for Colonies [Overseas France]) 08/23/39 Gen. [Retired '39] Georges-Albert-Julien Catroux [French] (acting; replaced) 06/27/40 VA Jean d'Decoux [French] [FN] (ousted by the Japanese; arrested and tried after the war for collaboration with the Japanese, but not convicted) 03/09/45 Japanese Governor Generals 08/15/45 vacant 09/23/45 redesignated **High Commissioner, French Indochina** - see **High Commissioner, French Indochina**.

A. **Commander-in-Chief, Troops in French Indochina [Commandant Supérieur de Troupes du Groupe l'Indochine]** (HQ: Saigon, Indochina): /38 LG Maurice-Paul-Auguste Martin [French] (retired) /40 LG Eugène Mordant [French] (retired; /44, Head, Military Resistance Indochina & Delegate-General, Provisional Government, Indochina) /44 MG Camille-Ange-Gabriel Sabattier [French]

B. ***Areas of French Indochina***:
1. **Tonkin {part of Vietnam today}** (Capital: Hanoi): **French Resident-Superior**: /37 MG Yves-Charles Châtel [French] (11/20/41, Governor-General of Algeria) /40 ÉMILE-LOUIS-FRANÇOIS GRANDJEAN [French] [+ French Resident-Superior, Annam] /41 EDOUARD-ANDRÉ DELSALLE [French] /42 JEAN-MAURICE-NORBERT HAELEWYN [French] (French Resident-Superior of Annam) /44 CAMILLE AUPELLE [French] 03/45 see **Japanese Resident** 08/15/45 **French Commissioner**: 08/18/45 PIERRE MESSMER [French] (acting) 08/22/45 JEAN-ROGER SAINTENY [French].
2. **Annam {part of Vietnam today}** (Capital: Hué): **French Resident-Superior**: MAURICE-FERNAND GRAFFEUIL [French] /40 ÉMILE-LOUIS-FRANÇOIS GRANDJEAN [French] [+ to /41, French Resident-Superior, Tonkin] /44 JEAN-MAURICE-NORBERT HAELEWYN [French] 03/45 see **Japanese Resident** 08/15/45 under the **French Commissioner of Tonkin**.
3. **Cochin Chine {part of Vietnam today}** (Capital: Saigon): **French Governor**: /39 RENÉ VEBER [French] (/42, Governor, French Guyana) /40 HENRI-GEORGES RIVOAL [French] /42 ERNEST-THIMOTHÉE HOEFFEL [French] 03/45 see **Japanese Governor** 08/15/45 **Imperial Delegate**: NGUYEN VAN SAM [Vietnamese]

4. **Laos** (Capital: Vientiane): **French Resident-Superior**: EUGÈNE-HENRI-ROGER EUTROPE [French] 04/38 ANDRÈ TOUZET [French] 11/40 ADRIEN-ANTHONY-MAURICE ROQUES [French] 12/41 LOUIS-ANTOINE-MARIE BRASEY [French] 04/05/45 **Japanese Resident in Vientiane**: 03/45 MASANORI SAKO [Japanese] 08/45 and **Japanese Supreme Counselor in Luang Prabang**: 04/05/45 see **Japanese Supreme Counselor in Luang Prabang** 08/22/45 **French Commissioner**: 08/25/45 HANS IMFELD [French].

5. **Cambodia [Cambodge]** (Capital: Phnom Penh): **French Resident-Superior**: 12/12/36 LÉON-EMMANUEL THIBAUDEAU [French] 12/29/41 JEAN de LENS [French] 03/02/43 GEORGES-ARMAND-LÉON GAUTHIER [French] 11/44 ANDRÉ-JOSEPH BERJOAN [French] 03/09/45 **Japanese Supreme Advisor**: 03/14/45 see **Japanese Supreme Advisor** 08/45 **French Resident-Superior**: 08/45 ANDRÉ-JOSEPH BERJOAN [French].

    A. **Commanding General, Cambodia**: /40 BG Yves-Marie-Jacques-Guillaume de Boisboissel [French] (Deputy Commander, Military District XIX) /41

C. **Military-Governor, Hanoi**: 07/40 BG Camille-Ange-Gabriel Sabattier [French] (Commanding General, Cochinchine Brigade, Indochina) 12/08/41

Japanese Occupation in Indochina

Head, Japanese Delegation to French Indochina: /40 MG Raishiro Sumida [Japanese] [see Volume IV - Japan] (Commanding General, 39th Division) /41 disbanded.

Japanese Supreme Advisor: 03/14/45 KUBO [Japanese] [see Volume Vi - Italy & France] 08/15/45.

Army Group Command

Southern Army (11/06/41, Southern Operations, excluding China) FM Count Hisaichi Terauchi [Japanese] [see Volume IV - Japan] (retired; 06/12/46, died of cerebral hemorrhage) 11/30/45 surrendered.

Corps Command

Japanese Military Commanders in Indochina (09/07/40): **{Japanese} Indochina Expeditionary Army** 09/07/40 MG Takuma Nishimura [Japanese] [+ Commanding General, Imperial Guards Division & Commanding General, 21st Independent Mixed Brigade] [see Volume IV - Japan] 07/05/41 disbanded and replaced by **{Japanese} Fifteenth Army** 07/05/41 LG Shojiro Iida [Japanese] [see Volume IV - Japan] [Japanese Fifteenth Army sent to Burma] /41 unknown? 11/10/42 replaced by **{Japanese} Indochina Garrison Army** 11/10/42 LG Viscount Kazumoto Machijiri [Japanese] [see Volume IV - Japan] (replaced) 11/22/44 LG Yuitsu Tsuchihashi [Japanese] [see Volume IV - Japan] (Commanding General, Thirty-Eighth Army) 12/11/44 redesignated **{Japanese} Thirty-Eighth Army** 12/11/44 LG Yuitsu Tsuchihashi [Japanese] [see Volume IV - Japan] 08/15/45.

Allied Occupation Force in Indochina

Commander, Allied (Chinese) Occupation Force for Indochina (09/09/45; above the 16th parallel): Gen. Lu Han [Chinese] [see Volume VIII - China] 03/06/46

Chairman of the Allied Control Commission & Commander, Allied Land Forces, French Indochina [ALFFIC] (09/06/45; below 16th parallel): Gen. Sir Douglas David Gracey [British] [see Volume II - The British Commonwealth & Volume III - The United States] 01/28/46.

French Commissioners, Cambodia (Starting 10/15/45)

French Commissioner, Cambodia: 10/15/45 HUARD [French] [see Volume VI - Italy & France].

KINGDOM of LUANG PHRA BANG
[LAOS]

(Japanese Puppet State)

[After the fall of France and the establishment of Vichy France, the French had lost practical control in French Indochina to Japan. But, Japan stayed in the background while giving Vichy French administrators nominal control. On 03/09/45, this change when Japan officially took over. To gain support of the Laoian people, Imperial Japan dissolved the French colonial rule and pressured Luang Phta Bang to declare its independence within the Greater East Asia Co-Prosperity Sphere. Four days later King Sihanouk declared Kampuchea [Cambodia] independent. The Kingdom of Cambodia was a short-lived puppet state of Imperial Japan governing between 03/09/45 to 08/15/45.]

Governments Located in Present Day Laos Prior to 1945

Kingdom of Luang Phra Bang (1707; officially formed in 1353 as **Lan Xang Hom Khao**; 1707 renamed **Luang Phra Bang**): 03/26/1904 King SISAVANG VONG [+ 09/15/45, King of Laos] 09/15/45 United Kingdom of Laos proclaimed 05/15/46 King SISAVANG VONG [+ 09/15/45, King of Laos].

Wiang Chhan [Viang Chan] (French colony since 10/17/1887; under the control of the French Resident-Superior; 08/21/41, incorporated into the **Kingdom of Luang Phra Bang**): see **French Resident-Superior.**

Principality of Champasak [Nakhon Champasak] (1791; 11/22/04, principality under French Protectorate; 09/15/45, incorporated into united **Kingdom of Laos**; 08/27/46, principality extinguished): 11/22/1904 Prince BUA LAPHAN 11/45 Prince BOUN OUM 08/26/46 principality extinguished.

Xiang Khuang (10/03/1893, made a French colonial possession; under the control of the French Resident-Superior; 08/21/41, incorporated into the **Kingdom of Luang Phra Bang**): see **French Resident-Superior.**

Kingdom of Luang Phra Bang (Laos) Government (03/09/45 to 08/15/45)

King of Luang Phra Bang (Laos) (1707; officially formed in 1353 as **Lan Xang Hom Khao**; 1707 renamed **Luang Phra Bang**): 03/26/1904 King SISAVANG VONG (King of Laos) 09/15/45 United Kingdom of Laos proclaimed 05/15/46 King SISAVANG VONG [+ 09/15/45, King of Laos].

Prime Minister (08/21/41): Prince PHETSARATH RATTANAVONGGA (Head of State, Kingdom of Laos) 10/10/45 dissolved.

Kingdom of Laos Government (proclaimed 09/15/45)

King of Laos (09/15/45): King SISAVANG VONG 10/20/45 see **Head of State, Kingdom of Laos** 04/23/46 King SISAVANG VONG [+ King of Luang Phra Bang].

Head of State, Kingdom of Laos (10/20/45): Prince PHETSARATH RATTANAVONGGA (11/28/46, in exile in Bangkok Thailand) 04/23/46 King SISAVANG VONG becomes the head of state again - see **King of Laos**.

Prime Minister, Kingdom of Laos (09/15/45): Prince PHETSARATH RATTANAVONGGA (Head of State, Kingdom of Laos) 10/20/45 Prince PHAYA KHAMMAO [+ Chairman of Provisional Government of Laos] 04/23/46 Prince KINDAVONG.

French Indochina

[For this section also see Volume VI - Italy & France]

Governor-General, French Indochina: (Capital: Saigon, Indochina): 09/36 JOSEPH-JULES BRÉVIÉ [French] (03/26/43, Vichy France Minister for Colonies [Overseas France]) 08/23/39 Gen. [Retired '39] Georges-Albert-Julien Catroux [French] (acting; replaced) 06/27/40 VA Jean d'Decoux [French] [FN] (ousted by the Japanese; arrested and tried after the war for collaboration with the Japanese, but not convicted) 03/09/45 Japanese Governor Generals 08/15/45 vacant 09/23/45 redesignated **High Commissioner, French Indochina** - see **High Commissioner, French Indochina**.

A. **Commander-in-Chief, Troops in French Indochina [Commandant Supérieur de Troupes du Groupe l'Indochine]** (HQ: Saigon, Indochina): /38 LG Maurice-Paul-Auguste Martin [French] (retired) /40 LG Eugène Mordant [French] (retired; /44, Head, Military Resistance Indochina & Delegate-General, Provisional Government, Indochina) /44 MG Camille-Ange-Gabriel Sabattier [French]

B. ***Areas of French Indochina***:

   1. **Tonkin {part of Vietnam today}** (Capital: Hanoi): **French Resident-Superior**: /37 MG Yves-Charles Châtel [French] (11/20/41, Governor-General of Algeria) /40 ÉMILE-LOUIS-FRANÇOIS GRANDJEAN [French] [+ French Resident-Superior, Annam] /41 EDOUARD-ANDRÉ DELSALLE [French] /42 JEAN-MAURICE-NORBERT HAELEWYN [French] (French Resident-Superior of Annam) /44 CAMILLE AUPELLE [French] 03/45 see **Japanese Resident** 08/15/45 **French Commissioner**: 08/18/45 PIERRE MESSMER [French] (acting) 08/22/45 JEAN-ROGER SAINTENY [French]·

   2. **Annam {part of Vietnam today}** (Capital: Hué): **French Resident-Superior**: MAURICE-FERNAND GRAFFEUIL [French] /40 ÉMILE-LOUIS-FRANÇOIS GRANDJEAN [French] [+ to /41, French Resident-Superior, Tonkin] /44 JEAN-MAURICE-NORBERT HAELEWYN [French] 03/45 see **Japanese Resident** 08/15/45 under the **French Commissioner of Tonkin**.

   3. **Cochin Chine {part of Vietnam today}** (Capital: Saigon): **French Governor**: /39 RENÉ VEBER [French] (/42, Governor, French Guyana) /40 HENRI-GEORGES RIVOAL [French] /42 ERNEST-THIMOTHÉE HOEFFEL [French] 03/45 see **Japanese Governor** 08/15/45 **Imperial Delegate**: NGUYEN VAN SAM [Vietnamese]

   4. **Laos** (Capital: Vientiane): **French Resident-Superior**: EUGÈNE-HENRI-

ROGER EUTROPE [French] 04/38 ANDRÈ TOUZET [French] 11/40 ADRIEN-ANTHONY-MAURICE ROQUES [French] 12/41 LOUIS-ANTOINE-MARIE BRASEY [French] 04/05/45 **Japanese Resident in Vientiane**: 03/45 MASANORI SAKO [Japanese] 08/45 and **Japanese Supreme Counselor in Luang Prabang**: 04/05/45 see **Japanese Supreme Counselor in Luang Prabang** 08/22/45 **French Commissioner**: 08/25/45 HANS IMFELD [French].

5. **Cambodia [Cambodge]** (Capital: Phnom Penh): **French Resident-Superior**: 12/12/36 LÉON-EMMANUEL THIBAUDEAU [French] 12/29/41 JEAN de LENS [French] 03/02/43 GEORGES-ARMAND-LÉON GAUTHIER [French] 11/44 ANDRÉ-JOSEPH BERJOAN [French] 03/09/45 **Japanese Supreme Advisor**: 03/14/45 see **Japanese Supreme Advisor** 08/45 **French Resident-Superior**: 08/45 ANDRÉ-JOSEPH BERJOAN [French].

    A. **Commanding General, Cambodia**: /40 BG Yves-Marie-Jacques-Guillaume de Boisboissel [French] (Deputy Commander, Military District XIX) /41

C. **Military-Governor, Hanoi**: 07/40 BG Camille-Ange-Gabriel Sabattier [French] (Commanding General, Cochinchine Brigade, Indochina) 12/08/41

Japanese Occupation in Indochina

Head, Japanese Delegation to French Indochina: /40 MG Raishiro Sumida [Japanese] [see Volume IV - Japan] (Commanding General, 39th Division) /41 disbanded.

Japanese Resident in Vientiane: 03/45 SAKO MASANORI [Japanese] [see Volume VI - Italy & France] 08/15/45.

Japanese Supreme Counselor in Luang Prabang: 03/14/45 ISHIBASHI [Japanese] [see Volume VI - Italy & France] 08/15/45.

Army Group Command

Southern Army (11/06/41, Southern Operations, excluding China) FM Count Hisaichi Terauchi [Japanese] [see Volume IV - Japan] (retired; 06/12/46, died of cerebral hemorrhage) 11/30/45 surrendered.

Corps Command

Japanese Military Commanders in Indochina (09/07/40): **{Japanese} Indochina Expeditionary Army** 09/07/40 MG Takuma Nishimura [Japanese] [+ Commanding General, Imperial Guards Division & Commanding General, 21st Independent Mixed Brigade] [see Volume IV - Japan] 07/05/41 disbanded and replaced by **{Japanese} Fifteenth Army** 07/05/41 LG Shojiro Iida [Japanese] [see Volume IV - Japan] [Japanese Fifteenth Army sent to Burma] /41 unknown? 11/10/42 replaced by **{Japanese} Indochina Garrison Army** 11/10/42 LG Viscount Kazumoto Machijiri [Japanese] [see Volume IV - Japan] (replaced) 11/22/44 LG Yuitsu Tsuchihashi [Japanese] [see Volume IV - Japan] (Commanding General, Thirty-Eighth Army) 12/11/44 redesignated **{Japanese} Thirty-Eighth Army** 12/11/44 LG Yuitsu Tsuchihashi [Japanese] [see Volume IV - Japan] 08/15/45.

Allied Occupation Force in Indochina

Commander, Allied (Chinese) Occupation Force for Indochina (09/09/45; above the 16th parallel): Gen. Lu Han [Chinese] [see Volume VIII - China] 03/06/46

A.   **Commanding General, Chinese (Nationalist) 93rd Division**: 09/23/45 MG Lu Kuo-chuan [Chinese] [see Volume VIII - China].

Chairman of the Allied Control Commission & Commander, Allied Land Forces, French Indochina [ALFFIC] (09/06/45; below 16th parallel): Gen. Sir Douglas David Gracey [British] [see Volume II - The British Commonwealth & Volume III - The United States] 01/28/46.

French Commissioners, Laos (Starting 03/17/46)

French Commissioner, Laos: 10/15/45 HANS IMFELD [French] [see Volume VI - Italy & France].

BIBLIOGRAPHY
BOOKS USED IN THIS SERIES

Abbott, Peter, et. al., *Germany's Eastern Front Allies 1941-45*. Men-at-Arms Series, #131. London: Osprey Publishing Ltd, 1982.

Adair, Paul. *Hitler's Greatest Defeat.* London: Arms and Armour, 1994.

Adam, Henry et al. *Italy at War.* Times-Life Books, World War II Series, Vol. 33. Chicago: Times-Life Books, 1982.

Alexander, Bevin. *How Hitler Could Have Won World War II.* New York: Crown Publishers, 2000.

Allen, Peter. *One More River: The Rhine Crossings of 1945.* New York: Charles Scribner's Sons, 1980.

Ambrose, Stephen E. *The Supreme Commander: The War Years of General Dwight D, Eisenhower.* Garden City, New York: Doubleday & Comp. Inc., 1969.

------. *D-Day June 6, 1944: The Climactic Battle of World War II.* New York. A Touchtone Book, Published by Simon & Schuster, 1994.

Anders, Wladyslaw. *Hitler's Defeat in Russia.* Chicago, Regnery, 1953.

------. *Russian Volunteers in Hitler's Army.* Bayside, New York: Axis Europa, 1998.

Argyle, Christopher. *Chronology of World War II: The Day by Day Illustrated Record 1939-45.* London: Marshall Cavendish, 1980.

Auerbach, William. *Last of the Panzers: German Tanks 1944-45.* Tank Illustrated #9. London: Arms & Armour Press, 1984.

The Australian Army at War: 1939-1944. London: His Majesty's Stationary Office, 1944.

Axworthy, Mark et. al., *The Romanian Army of World War 2.* Men-at-Arms Series, #246. London: Osprey Publishing Ltd, 1991.

------, et. al. *Third Axis Fourth Ally: Rumanian Armed Forces in the European War, 1941-1945.* London: Arms and Armour, 1995.

Bailey, Ronald H. et. al. *The Home Front: U.S.A.* Times-Life Books, World War II Series, Vol. 8. Chicago: Times-Life Books, 1978.

------. et al.*Partisans and Guerrillas.* Time-Life Books, World War II Series, Vol. 12. Chicago: Times-Life Books, 1978.

------ et. al. *The Air War in Europe.* Times-Life Books, World War II Series, Vol. 16. Chicago: Times-Life Books, 1979

------ et. al. *Prisoners of War.* Times-Life Books, World War II Series, Vol. 30. Chicago: Times-Life Books, 1981.

Bailey, Thomas A. And Paul B. Ryan. *Hitler vs. Roosevelt: The Undeclared Naval War.* New York: The Free Press, 1979.

Balin, George. *Afrika Corps.* Tank Illustrated #17. London: Arms & Armour Press, 1985.

Banyard, Peter. *The Rise of the Dictators 1919-1939.* New York: Aladdin Books, 1986.

Barker, A. J. *Pearl Harbor.* Ballantine's Illustrated History of World War II, Battle Book No. 10. New York: Ballantine Books, 1969.

Barnett, Correlli. *The Desert Generals.* Bloomington, Indiana: Indiana University Press, 1960.

------ (Edited by). *Hitler's Generals.* New York: Grove Weidenfeld, 1989.

Bekker, Cajus. *Hitler's Naval War.* New York: Zebra Books, Kensington Publishing Corp., 1977.

Benford, Timothy B., *The World War II Quiz & Fact Book*. New York: Berkley Books,1984.

Bethell, Nicholas et. al. *Russia Besieged.* Times-Life Books, World War II Series, Vol. 6. Chicago: Times-Life Books, 1977.

Beyevor, Antony. *Stalingrad: The Fateful Siege: 1942-1943.* New York: Viking, 1998.

Bekker, Cajus. *Hitler's Naval War.* New York: Kensington Publishing Corp., 1971.

Bethell, Nicholas et. al. *Russia Besieged.* Times-Life Books, World War II Series, Vol. 6. Chicago: Times-Life Books, 1977.

Bidwell, Shelford. *The Chindit War: Stilwell, Wingate and the Campaign in Burma: 1944.* New York: Macmillan Publishing Co., Inc., 1979.

Bishop, Chris. *Order of Battle: German Infantry in WWII.* London: Amber Books, 2009.

------. *Order of Battle: German Panzers in WWII.* London: Amber Books, 2009.

Bishop, Edward. *Their Finest Hour: The Story of the Battle of Britain 1940.* New York: Ballantine Books, 1968

Blumenson, Martin. *Sicily: Whose Victory?.* Ballantine's Illustrated History of World War II, Campaign Book No. 3. New York: Ballantine Books, 1968.

------. *Eisenhower.* Ballantine's Illustrated History of the Violent Century, War Leader Book No. 9. New York: Ballantine Books, 1972.

Blumenson, Martin et al. *Liberation.* Times-Life Books, World War II Series, Vol. 14. Chicago: Times-Life Books, 1978.

Boatner, III, Mark M. *The Biographical Dictionary of World War II.* Novato, CA: Presidio, 1996.

Botting, Douglas et. al. *The Second Front.* Times-Life Books, World War II Series, Vol. 13. Chicago: Times-Life Books, 1978.

------ et al. *The Aftermath: Europe.* Times-Life Books, World War II Series, Vol. 38. Chicago: Times-Life Books, 1983.

Bowman, Martin W. *USAAF Handbook 1939-1945.* Mechanicsburg, Pennsylvania: Stackpole Books, 1997.

Bradley, Omar N. *A Soldier's Story.* New York: Henry Holt, 1951.

Bradley, Omar N. and Clay Blair. *A General's Life: An Autobiography.* New York: Simon & Schuster1983.

Breuer, William B. *Operation Dragoon: The Allied Invasion of the South of France.* Novato, California: Presidio, 1987.

Britt-Smith, Richard. *Hitler's Generals.* San Rafael: Presidio Press, 1976.

Carell, Paul. *The Foxes of the Desert.* New York: E. P. Dutton, 1960.

------ *Hitler Moves East, 1941-43.* Boston: Little, Brown and Company, 1965 (republished by Bantam Books, New York: 1971.)

------. *Invasion: They're Coming.* New York: E. P. Dutton, . (republished by Bantam Books, New York: 1973.)

------. *Stalingrad: Defeat of the German 6th Army.* Atglen, Pennsylvania: Schiffer, 1993.

Calvert, Michael. *Slim.* Ballantine's Illustrated History of the Violent Century, War Leader Book No. 12. New York: Ballantine Books, 1973.

Chant, Christopher, ed. *Hitler's Generals.* New York: Chartwell Books, Inc., 1979.

Chapman, Guy. *Why France Fell: The Defeat of the French Army in 1940.* New York: Rinehart and Winston, 1968.

Chuikov, Vasili. *Battle for Stalingrad.* New York: Holt, Rinehart and Winston, 1964.

Churchill, Winston (Forwarded by). *D-Day, Operation Overlord.* London: Salamander Books Limited, 1993.

Clark, Alan. *Barbarossa: The Russian-German Conflict, 1941-45.* New York: William Morrow and Company, 1965.

Clark, Mark W. *Calculated Risk.* New York: Harper & Brothers Publishing, 1950.

Cole, Hugh M. *The Ardennes: The Battle of the Bulge.* United States Army in World War II: European Theater of Operations, Office of the Chief of Military History, United States Department of Army. Washington D. C.: United States Government Printing Office, 1965.

Collier, Basil. *The War in the Far East 1941-1945. A Military History.* New York: William Morrow & Company, Inc., 1969.

Collier, Richard et al. *The War in the Desert.* Times-Life Books, World War II Series, Vol. 7. Chicago: Times-Life Books, 1977.

Cooper, Matthew. *The German Army: 1933-1945.* Briarcliff Manor, N.Y.: Stein and Day/Publishers, 1978.

------ & James Lucas. *Panzer: The Armoured Forces of the Third Reich.* New York: St. Martin's Press, 1978.

Cormack, Andrew, et. al., *Germany's Eastern Front Allies 1941-45.* Men-at-Arms Series, #225. London: Osprey Publishing Ltd, 1990.

Costello, John. *The Pacific War 1941-1945.* New York: Quill 1982.

Cowley, Robert (Edited by). *The Collected What If?* New York: G. P. Putnam's, 1999.

Craig, William. *The Fall of Japan.* New York: Dell Publishing Group, 1967.

Creswell, Capt. John, R.N. *Generals and Admirals. The Story of Amphibious Command.* London: Longmans, Green and Company, 1952.

Cross, Robin. *Citadel: The Battle of Kursk.* London: Michael O'Mara Books Ltd., 1993

Davis, Franklin M., Jr. et. al. *Across the Rhine.* Times-Life Books, World War II Series, Vol. 22. Chicago: Times-Life Books, 1980.

Deighton, Len. *Fighter.* New York: Ballantine Books, 1977.

D'Este, Carlo. *Bitter Victory: The Battle for Sicily, 1943.* New York: Harper Perennial, 1991.

Dollinger, Hans. *The Decline and Fall of Nazi Germany and Imperial Japan.* New York: Bonanza Books, 1967.

Downing, David. *The Devil's Virtuosos: German Generals at War 1940-5.* New York: St. Martin's Press, 1977.

Duffy, Christopher. *Red Storm on the Reich.* New York: Atheneum, 1991.

Dupuy, Trevor N. *A Genius for War: The German Army and General Staff, 1807-1945.*

Editors of Time-Life Books et al. *Japan at War.* Times-Life Books, World War II Series, Vol. 26. Chicago: Times-Life Books, 1980.

------ et al. *The Aftermath: Asia.* Times-Life Books, World War II Series, Vol. 39. Chicago: Times-Life Books, 1983.

----- et al. *Absolute Victory: America's Greatest Generation and Their World War II Triumph.* New York: Time Inc. Home Entertainment, 2005

Edwards, Roger. *German Airborne Troops, 1939-45.* New York: Doubleday and Company, 1974.

Eisenhower, David. *Eisenhower at War 1943-1945.* New York: Vintage Books, 1987.

Eisenhower, Dwight D. *Crusade in Europe.* New York: Avon, 1968.

Elliott, MG J. G. *Unfading Honour: The Story of the Indian Army 1939-1945.* New York: A. S. Barnes and Co., Inc., 1965.

Ellis, John. *The World War II Databook.* London: Aurum Press Ltd, 1993.

Ellis, L. E. *Victory in the West. Volume I, The Battle of Normandy.* London: Her Majesty's

Stationery Office, 1962.

------, *Victory in the West. Volume II, The Defeat of Germany*. London: Her Majesty's Stationery Office, 1968.

Elson, Robert et. al. *Prelude to War*. Times-Life Books, World War II Series, Vol. 1. Chicago: Times-Life Books, 1979.

Elting, John R. et. al. *Battles for Scandinavia*. Times-Life Books, World War II Series, Vol. 28. Chicago: Times-Life Books, 1981.

Erickson, John. *The Road to Stalingrad*. Harper and Row, 1975.

------. *The Road to Berlin*. New York: Harper and Row, 1983.

Essame, MG H. *Normandy Bridgehead*. Ballantine's Illustrated History of World War II, Campaign Book No. 10. New York: Ballantine Books, 1970.

Ethell, Jeffrey. *U. S. Army Air Forces, World War II*. Warbirds Illustrated #38. London: Arms & Armour Press, 1986.

Faber, Harold. *Luftwaffe: A History*. Chicago: Times Books, 1977.

Falk, Stanley. *Liberation of the Philippines*. Ballantine's Illustrated History of World War II, Campaign Book No. 10. New York: Ballantine Books, 1971.

Farago, Ladislas (Edited by). *The Last Days of Patton*. New York: Berkley Books, 1982.

Fisher, Ernest F., Jr. *Cassino to the Alps*. United States Army in World War II: Mediterranean Theater of Operations, Office of the Chief of Military History, United States Department of Army. Washington D. C.: United States Government Printing Office, 1977.

Fodor, Denis J. et al. *The Neutrals*. Times-Life Books, World War II Series, Vol. 35. Chicago: Times-Life Books, 1982.

Forty, George. *Patton's Third War at War*. London: Arms and Armour Press, 1976.

Frank, Benis M. *Okinawa: Touchstone to Victory*. Ballantine's Illustrated History of World War II, Battle Book No. 12. New York: Ballantine Books, 1969.

Frankland, Noble. *Bomber Offensive: The Devastation of Europe*. Ballantine's Illustrated History of World War II, Campaign Book No. 7. New York: Ballantine Books, 1970.

Fuller, Richard. *Shōkan, Hirohito's Samurai, Leaders of the Japanese Armed Forces, 1926-1945*. London: Arms and Armour Press, 1992.

Gailey, Harry A. *The War in the Pacific: From Pearl Harbor to Tokyo Bay*. Novato, California: Presidio, 1995.

Gavin, James M. *On to Berlin*. New York: Viking, 1978.

German Army Order of Battle, October 1942. Military Intelligence Service. Lancer Militaria. Mt. Ida, Arkansas. (First published by Military Intelligence Service, 1942.)

German Order of Battle 1944: The Directory, Prepared by Allied Intelligence, of Regiments, Formations and Units of the German Armed Forces. Greenhill Books, London and Stackpole Books, Pennsylvania, 1994. (First published by Her Majesty's Stationery Office, 1944.)

Gilbert, Alton Keith. *A Born Leader: The Life of Admiral John Sidney McCann, Pacific Carrier Commander*. Philadelphia: Casemate, 2006.

Gilbert, Martin. *The Second World War: A Complete History*. New York: Henry Holt and Company, 1989.

Goerlitz, Walter. *Paulus and Stalingrad*. New York: Citadel, 1963.

Goolrick, William K. and Ogden Tanner et al. *The Battle of the Bulge*. Times-Life Books, World War II Series, Vol. 18. Chicago: Times-Life Books, 1979.

Goralski, Robert. *World War II Almanac, 1931-1945*. New York: G. P. Putnam's Sons,

1981.

Gow, Ian. *Okinawa 1945: Gateway to Japan.* Garden City, New York: Doubleday & Company, Inc. 1985.

Granatstein, J. L. *The Generals: The Canadian Army's Senior Commanders in the Second World War.* Toronto: Stoddart Publishing, 1993.

Green, William & Gordon Swanborough. *Flying Colors.* Carrollton, Texas: Salamander Books Ltd. And Pilot Press Ltd., 1981.

Grigg, John. *1943: The Victory That Never Was.* New York: Zebra Books, 1980.

Guderian, Heinz. *Panzer Leader.* New York: Ballantine Books, 1957.

Hamilton, Nigel. *Master of the Battlefield: Monty's War Years 1942-1944.* New York: McGraw-Hill Book Company, 1983.

------. *Monty: Final Years of the Field-Marshal 1944-1976.* New York: McGarw-Hill Book Company, 1987.

Hart, B. H. Liddell. *History of the Second World War.* 2 Vols. New York: G. P. Putnam's Sons, 1972.

------. *The German Generals Talk.* New York: Quill, 1979.

Haskew, Michael E., *Encyclopedia of the Elite Forces in the Second World War.* London: Amber Books, 2007.

Hastings, Max. *Overlord: D-Day & the Battle for Normandy.* New York: Simon and Schuster, 1964.

Haupt, Werner. *Assault on Moscow, 1941: The Offensive, the Battle, the Retreat.* Atglen, Pennsylvania: Schiffer, 1996.

------. *Army Group Center: The Wehrmacht in Russia.* Atglen, Pennsylvania: Schiffer, 1997.

------. *Army Group North: The Wehrmacht in Russia.* Atglen, Pennsylvania: Schiffer, 1997.

------. *Army Group South: The Wehrmacht in Russia.* Atglen, Pennsylvania: Schiffer, 1998.

------. *Elite German Divisions in World War II.* Atglen, Pennsylvania: Schiffer Publishing Ltd., 2001.

Heckmann, Wolf. *Rommel's War in Africa.* Garden City, New York: Doubleday & Comp. Inc. 1981.

Herzstern, Robert Edwin et al. *The Nazis.* Times-Life Books, World War II Series, Vol. 21. Chicago: Times-Life Books, 1980.

Hibbert, Christopher. *Anzio: The Bid for Rome.* New York: Ballantine Books, 1970.

Higgins, Trumbull. *Hitler and Russia: 1941-1946.* New York: Columbia Univ. Press, 1973.

Hoyt, Edwin P. *199 Days: The Battle: The Battle for Stalingrad.* New York: Doherty, 1993.

------. *Yamamoto: The Man Who Planned the Attack on Pearl Harbor.* Guilford, Connecticut: The Lyons Press, 2001.

Humble, Richard. *United States Fleet Carriers of World War II.* Dorset, United Kingdom: Blandford Press, 1984.

Irving, David. *The Trail of the Fox: The Search for the True Field Marshal Rommel.* New York: E. P. Dutton, 1979.

Jackson, Robert. *Churchill's Moat: The Channel War 1939-1945.* Shrewsbury, United Kingdom: Airlife Publishing Ltd., 1995.

------. *The Royal Navy in World War II.* Annapolis, Maryland: Naval Institute Press, 1997.

Jackson, W. G. F. *The Battle for North Africa.* New York: Mason/Charter, 1975.

Jeffers, H. Paul. *Taking Command.* New York: New American Library, 2009.

Jones, James. *WWII.* New York: Ballantine Books, 1975.

Jordan, David. *Wolfpack.* New York: Barnes & Noble Books, 2002.

Jukes, Geoffrey. *Stalingrad: The Turning Point*. Ballantine's Illustrated History of World War II, Battle Book No. 3. New York: Ballantine Books, 1968.

Keegan, John. *Waffen-SS: The Asphalt Soldiers*. Ballantine's Illustrated History of World War II. New York: Ballantine Books, 1970.

------ (General editor). *The Rand McNally Encyclopedia of World War II*. Chicago: Rand McNally and Company, 1977.

------, *Who Was Who in World War II*. New York: Thomas Y. Crowell Publishers, 1978.

------ (Edited by). *Churchill's Generals*. New York: Quill & William Morrow Publishing, 1991.

Kemp, Anthony. *The Maginot Line: Myth & Reality*. New York: Military Heritage Press, 1988.

Koburger, Charles W. Jr., *The Cyrano Fleet, Franch and Its Navy, 1940-1942*. New York: Praeger, 1989.

Kursietis, Andris J. *The Hungarian Army and Its Military Leadership in World War II*. Bayside, New York: Axis Europa Books & Magazines, 1996.

Lanning, Lt. Col. (Ret.) Michael Lee. *The Military 100*. Secaucus, New Jersey: A Citadel Press Book, 1996.

Lash, Joseph P. *Roosevelt and Churchill 1939-1945*. New York: W. W. Norton & Company, Inc.,1976.

Lewin, Ronald. *Rommel as a Military Commander*. New York: Ballantine Books, 1970.

-------, *Montgomery as a Military Commander*. New York: Stein and day Publishers, 1971.

Lodge, Brett. *Lavarack: Rival General*. St. Leonards, Australia: Allen & Unwin, 1998.

Lord, Walter. *Incredible Victory: The Battle of Midway*. Short Hill, New Jersey: Burford Books, 1967.

Lucas, James. *Panzer Army Africa*. San Rafael, California: Presidio Press, 1977.

------. *War on the Eastern Front, 1941-1945: The German Soldier in Russia*. New York: Stein and Day Publishers, 1980.

------. *Storming Eagles: German Airborne Forces in World War Two*. London: Arms & Armour Press, 1988.

------ (General Editor). *Command: A Historical Dictionary of Military Leaders*. New York: Military Press, 1988.

------. *Hitler's Mountain Troops*. London: Arms & Armour Press, 1992.

------. *Battle Group!: German Kampfgruppen Action of World War Two*. London, Arms & Armour, 1993.

------. *Hitler's Enforcers: Leaders of the German War Machine 1939-1945*. London: Arms & Armour Press, 1996

------, *German Army Handbook 1939-1945*. Bridgend, London: Sutton Publishing Limited, 1998.

------. *Hitler's Commanders: German Bravery in the Field, 1939-1945*. London: Cassell & Company, 2000.

Luck, Hans von. *Panzer Commander*. New York: A Dell Book, Bantan Doubleday Dell Publishing Group, 1989

Lunde, Henrik O., *Finland's War of Choice*. Philadelphia: Casemate Publishing, 2011.

Lyall, Gavin (Edited by). *The War in the Air: The Royal Air Force in World War II*. New York: William Morrow & Company, Inc., 1968.

MacDonald, Charles B. *A Time for Trumpets: The Untold Story of the Battle of the Bulge*. New York: Bantam Books, 1984.

MacIntyre, Donald. *The Naval War Against Hitler*. New York: Charles Scribner's Sons,

1971.

Macksey, Maj. K. J. *Panzer Division: The Mailed Fist.* Ballantine's Illustrated History of World War II, Weapons Book No. 2. New York: Ballantine Books, 1968.

------. *Afrika Korps.* Ballantine's Illustrated History of the Violent Century, Campaign Book No. 1. New York: Ballantine Books, 1968.

Macksey, Kenneth. *Guderian: Creator of the Blitzkrieg.* New York: Stein and Day Publishers, 1975.

------, *Guderian Panzer General.* London: Lionel Leventhal Limited, 1975.

------. *Military Errors of World War Two.* London: Arms & Armour, 1987.

------ (Edited by). *Hitler's Options: Alternate Decisions of World War II.* London: Greenhill Books, 1995.

Madej, W. Victor. *German Army Order of Battle 1939-1945.* New Martinsville, West Virginia: Game Marketing Comp., 1978.

------. *German Army Order of Battle 1939-1945: Volume I.* Allentown, Pennsylvania: Game Marketing Company., 1981.

------. *German Army Oder of Battle 1939-1945 Supplement.* Allentown, Pennsylvania: Game Marketing Company, 1981.

------, *Southeastern Europe Axis Armed Forces Order of Battle.* Allentown, Pennsylvania: Game Publishing Company, 19832.

------, *Red Army Order of Battle 1941 - 1943.* Allentown, Pennsylvania: Game Publishing Company, 1983.

------. *German Army Order of Battle: The Replacement Army, 1939-1945.* Allentown, Pennsylvania: Game Publishing Company, 1984.

------. *German Army Order of Battle: Field Army and Officer Corps 1939-1945.* Allentown, Pennsylvania: Game Publishing Company, 1985.

------. *Italian Army Order of Battle: 1940-1944.* Allentown, Pennsylvania: Game Publishing Company, 1987.

Mallmann Showell, Jak P. *The German Navy in World War Two.* Naval Institute Press. Annapolis, Maryland, 1979.

Malony, C. J. C. *The Mediterranean and the Middle East. Vol. 5. The Campaign in Sicily (1943) and the Campaign in Italy (3 Sept 1943 - 31 March 1944).* London. Her Majesty's Stationery Office, 1973.

------. *The Mediterranean and the Middle East. Vol. 6. Victory in the Mediterranean Part I (1 Apr - 4 Jun 1944).* London: Her Majesty's Stationery Office, 1984.

Manstein, Erich von. *Lost Victories.* Chicago: Henry Regnery, 1958.

March, Cyril, ed. *The Rise and Fall of the German Air Force, 1933-1945.* New York: St. Martin's, 1983.

Marston, Daniel. *The Pacific War Companion: From Pearl Harbor to Hiroshima.* Oxford, United Kingdom. Osprey Publishing, 2005.

Martienssen, Anthony. *Hitler and his Admirals.* New York: E. P. Dutton & Co., Inc., 1949.

Masson, Phillipe. *De Gaulle.* Ballantine's Illustrated History of the Violent Century, War Leader Book No. 7. New York: Ballantine Books, 1972.

Matanle, Ivor. *World War II.* Godalming, Surrey, England: Colour Library Books, Ltd., 1989.

Maurer, Maurer. (Edited by). *Air Force Combat Units of World War II.* Edison, New Jersey: Chartwell Books, 1994.

Mayer, S. L. (Edited by). *The Rise and Fall of Imperial Japan 1894-1945.* New York: Military Press, 1976.

Mayer, Sydney L. *MacArthur.* Ballantine's Illustrated History of the Violent Century, War Leader Book No. 2. New York: Ballantine Books, 1971.

McCombs, Don and Worth, Fred L. *World War II: Super Facts.* New York: Warner Books, 1983.

McKee, Alexander. *The Race for the Rhine Bridges.* New York: Stein and Day Publishers, 1971.

McNab, Chris. *Order of Battle: German Kriegsmarine in WWII.* London: Amber Books, 2009.

------. *Order of Battle: German Luftwaffe in WWII.* London: Amber Books, 2009.

Mellenthin, MG F. W. von. *Panzer Battles.* Norman: University of Oklahoma Press, 1956. (Republished by Ballantine Books, New York: 1971.)

------. *German Generals of World War II.* Norman: University of Oklahoma Press, 1977.

Miller, Russell et. al. *The Resistance.* Times-Life Books, World War II Series, Vol. 17. Chicago: Times-Life Books, 1979.

------. *The Commandos.* Times-Life Books, World War II Series, Vol. 31. Chicago: Times-Life Books, 1981.

Mitcham, Samuel W., Jr. *Rommel's Last Battle: The Desert Fox and the Normandy Campaign.* Briarcliff Manor, New York: Stein and Day Publishers, 1983.

------. *Hitler's Legions: The German Army Order of Battle, World War II.* Briarcliff Manor, New York: Stein and Day Publishers, 1985.

------. *Men of the Luftwaffe.* Novato, California: Presidio Press, 1988.

------. *Triumphant Fix.* New York: Jove Books 1990.

------. *The Men of Barbarossa, Commanders of the German Invasion of Russia, 1941.* Philadelphia: Casemate Publishing, 2009.

Mitcham, Samuel W., Jr. and Gene Mueller. *Hitler's Commanders.* Scarborough House. Lanham, Maryland, 1992.

Mitcham, Samuel W., Jr. and Friedrich von Stauffenberg. *The Battle of Sicily.* New York: Orion Books, 1991.

Morison, Samuel Eliot. *The History of the United States Naval Operations in World War II. 14 vols.* Boston: Little, Brown, 1947-62.

------. *The Two-Ocean War.* New York: Ballantine Books, 1963.

Moser, Don et. al. *Blitzkrieg.* Times-Life Books, World War II Series, Vol. 9. Chicago: Times-Life Books, 1978.

Mosley, Leonard. *The Reich Marshal: A Biography of Hermann Goering.* New York: Dell Publishing Co., Inc., 1974.

------ et. al. *The Battle of Britain.* Times-Life Books, World War II Series, Vol. 3. Chicago: Times-Life Books, 1977.

Moulton, J. L. *Battle for Antwerp.* New York: Hippocrene Books, Inc., 1978.

Mungo, MG Melvin. *Manstein, Hitler's Greatest General.* New York: Thomas Dunne Books, St. Martin's Press, 2010.

Murphy, Audie. *To Hell and Back.* New York: Bantam, 1979.

Natkiel, Richard. *Atlas of World War II.* New York: The Military Press, 1985.

Nafziger, George F. *German Order of Battle, World War II, Volume 1, Panzer, Panzer Grenadier, Light and Cavalry Divisions.* Privately Published, 1994.

------. *German Order of Battle, World War II, Volume 2, The Waffen SS, Luftwaffe, Fallschirmjager, Naval and Mountain Divisions.* Privately Published, 1994.

------. *German Order of Battle, World War II, Volume 3, German Artillery: Independent*

Battalions, Railroad, Coastal Flak, and Sturmgeschutz. Privately Published, 1994.

------. *German Order of Battle, World War II, Volume 4, German Infantry Divisions*. Privately Published, 1994.

------. *German Order of Battle, World War II, Volume 5, German Infantry Divisions Nos 300-999, Named Divisions, and Corps Detachments*. Privately Published, 1994.

------. *German Order of Battle, World War II, Volume 6, German Security, Static/Garrison, Jager, Light, Reserve and Replacement and Training Divisions*. Privately Published, 1994.

------. *Bulgarian Order of Battle, World War II, An Organizational History of the Bulgarian Army in World War II*. Pisgah, Ohio: Privately Published, 1995.

------. *French Order of Battle, World War II, 1939-1945, á la Gloire, de Ínfanterie Française*. Pisgah, Ohio: Privately Published, 1995.

------. *German Order of Battle, World War II, Foreigners in Field Gra, The Cossack, Russian, Croatian, and Italian Soldiers in the Wehrmacht*. Pisgah, Ohio: Privately Published, 1995.

------. *Rumanian Order of Battle, World War II, An Organizational History of the Rumanian Army in World War II*. Pisgah, Ohio: Privately Published, 1995

------. *Italian Order of Battle, World War II, Volume 1, An Organizational History of the Itlian Army in World War II: Armored, Motorized, Alpini & Cavalry Divisions*. Pisgah, Ohio: Privately Published, 1996.

------. *Italian Order of Battle, World War II, Volume 2, An Organizational History of the Itlian Army in World War II: The Infantry Divisions*. Pisgah, Ohio: Privately Published, 1996.

------. *Italian Order of Battle, World War II, Volume 3, An Organizational History of the Itlian Army in World War II: Black Shirt, Mountain, Assault & Landing Divisions, Corps Troops and 1944 Liberation Army*. Pisgah, Ohio: Privately Published, 1996.

------. *The Afrika Korps, An Organizational History, 1941-1943*. Privately Published, 1997.

Niehorster, Leo W. G. *The Royal Hungarian Army, 1920-1945. Volume I Organization and History*. New York: Axis Europa Books, 1998.

Packard, Jerrold M., *Neither Friend Nor Foe, The European Neutrals in World War II*. New York: Charles Scribner's Sons, 1992.

Paine, Lauran. *German Military Intelligence in World War II: The Abwehr*. New York: Military Heritage Press, 1984.

Parrish, Thomas (Edited by). *Simon and Schuster Encyclopedia of World War II*. New York: Simon and Schuster, 1978.

Payne, Robert. *The Life and Death of Adolf Hitler*. New York: Praeger Publishers, 1973.

Patton, George S., Jr. *War As I Knew It*. Boston: Houghton Mifflin, 1947.

Perret, Geoffrey. *There's a War to be Won: The United States Army in World War II*. New York: Ballantine Books, 1981.

------. *Winged Victory: The Army Air Forces in World War II*. New York: Random House, 1993.

Perrett, Bryan. *A History of Blitzkrieg*. New York: Stein and Day Publishers, 1983. (Republished by Jove Books, New York: 1989.)

Persons, Benjamin S. *Relieved of Command*. Manhattan, Kansas: Sunflower University Press, 1997

Pfannes, Charles E. And Victor A. Salamone. *The Great Commanders of World War II. Volume I: The Germans*. New York: Zebra Books, Kensington Publishing Company,

1980.

------. *The Great Commanders of World War II. Volume I: The Germans.* New York: Zebra Books, Kensington Publishing Company, 1981.

------. *The Great Commanders of World War II. Volume III: The Americans.* New York: Zebra Books, Kensington Publishing Company, 1981.

------. *The Great Admirals of World War II. Volume I: The Americans.* New York: Zebra Books, Kensington Publishing Company, 1983.

Piekalkiewicz, Janusz. *The Air War 1939-1945.* Dorset, United Kingdom: Blandford Press, 1985.

Pitt, Barrie et al. *The Battle of the Atlantic.* Times-Life Books, World War II Series, Vol. 5. Chicago: Times-Life Books, 1977.

Playfair, I. S. O. *The Mediterranean and the Middle East. Vol. 1. The Early Success Against Italy (to May 1941).* London: His Majesty's Stationery Office, 1954.

------. *The Mediterranean and the Middle East. Vol. 2. The Germans Come to the Help of their Ally (1941).* London: His Majesty's Stationery Office, 1956.

------. *The Mediterranean and the Middle East. Vol. 3. British Fortunes Reach Their Lowest Ebb (9/41-9/42).* London: His Majesty's Stationery Office, 1960.

------ and C. J. C. Malony. *The Mediterranean and the Middle East. Vol. 4. The Destruction of the Axis Forces in Africa.* London: His Majesty's Stationery Office, 1966.

Poirier, Robert G. & Albert Z. Connor. *The Red Army Order of Battle in the Great Patriotic War.* Novato, CA: Presidio Press, 1985.

Porten, Edward P. von der. *The German Navy in World War II.* New York: Ballantine Books, 1969.

Powell, Geoffrey. *The Devil's Birthday: The Bridges to Arnhem 1944.* New York Franklin Watts, 1984.

Prange, Gordon W. With Donald M. Goldstein and Katherine V. Dillon. *Pearl Harbor: The Verdict of History.* New York: McGrew-Hill Book Company, 1986.

Preston, Anthony (Foreword by). *Jane's Fighting Ships of World War II.* London: The Random House Group Ltd, 2001.

Preston, Paul. *The Spanish Civil War: An Illustrated Chronicle 1936-39.* New York: Groves Press, Inc., 1986.

Price, Dr. Alfred. *The Luftwaffe Data Book.* London: Greenhill Books, 1997.

Quarrie, Bruce. *Hitler's Samurai: The Waffen-SS in Action.* Wellingborough, England: Patrick Stephens, Third Printing, 1986.

Ready, J. Lee, *World War Two, Nation by Nation.* London: Arms and Armour Press, 1995.

Reynolds, Clark G. *Famous American Admirals.* New York: Van Nostrand Reinhold Company, 1978.

Rich, Norman. *Hitler's War Aims.* New York: W. W. Norman & Company, Inc., 1973.

Rigge, Simon et al. *War in the Outposts.* Times-Life Books, World War II Series, Vol. 24. Chicago: Times-Life Books, 1980.

Rikmenspoel, Marc J. *Waffen-SS: The Encyclopedia.* Garden City, New York: The Military Book Club, 2002.

Rommel, Erwin. *The Rommel Papers.* New York: Harcourt Brace Jovanovich, 1953. (Edited by B. H. Liddell Hart.)

------. *Rommel and his Art of War.* London: Greenhill Books, 2003

Rooney, D. D. *Stilwell.* Ballantine's Illustrated History of the Violent Century, War Leader

Book No. 4. New York: Ballantine Books, 1971.

Roskill, B. W. *The War at Sea 1939-45. Vol. 1. The Defensive.* London: Her Majesty's Stationery Office, 1954.

------. *The War at Sea 1939-45. Vol. 2. The Period of Balance.* London: Her Majesty's Stationery Office, 1956.

------. *The War at Sea 1939-45. Vol. 3. The Offensive Part 1.* London: Her Majesty's Stationery Office, 1960.

------. *The War at Sea 1939-45. Vol. 4. The Offensive Part 2.* London: Her Majesty's Stationery Office, 1963.

Rottman, Gordon L. *World War II Pacific Island Guide: A Geo-Military Study.* Westport, Connecticut: Greenwood Press, 2002.

Ruffner, Kevin Conley, et. al., *Luftwaffe Field Divisions 1941-45.* Men-at-Arms Series, #229. London: Osprey Publishing Ltd, 1990.

Ruge, Friedrich. *Der Geefrieg. The German Navy's Story 1939-1945.* United States Naval Institute. Annapolis, Maryland, 1957.

------, *Rommel in Normandy.* San Rafael, Calif.: Presidio Press, 1979.

Russell, Francis et al. *The Secret War.* Times-Life Books, World War II Series, Vol. 29. Chicago: Times-Life Books, 1981.

Rutherford, Ward. *Blitzkrieg 1940.* New York: G. P. Putnam's Sons, 1980.

Ryan, Cornelius. *The Longest Day.* New York: Simon and Schuster, 1959.

------. *The Last Battle.* New York: Simon and Schuster, 1966.

------. *A Bridge Too Far.* New York: Simon and Schuster, 1974.

Salisbury, Harrison E. *The 900 Days: The Siege of Leningrad.* New York: Avon, 1969.

Schmidt, H. W. *With Rommel in the Desert.* London: Harrap, 1951.

Seaton, Albert. *The Battle for Moscow.* New York: Stein and Day, 1971.

------. *Russo-German War, 1941-45.* New York: Praeger, 1976.

------. *The Fall of Fortress Europe, 1943-1945.* London: Batsford, 1981.

Sharp, Charles C. *Soviet Order of Battle, World War II, Volume 1, "The Deadly Beginning" - Soviet Tank, Mechanized, Motorized Division and Tank Brigades of 1940 - 1942.* Published by George F. Nafziger, 1995.

------. *Soviet Order of Battle, World War II, Volume 1I, "School of Battle" - Soviet Tank Corps and Tank Brigades January 1942 to 1945.* Published by George F. Nafziger, 1995.

------. *Soviet Order of Battle, World War II, Volume 1II, "Red Storm" - Soviet Mechanized Corps and Guards Armored Units 1942 to 1945.* Published by George F. Nafziger, 1995.

------. *Soviet Order of Battle, World War II, Volume 1V, "Red Guards" - Soviet Guards Rifle and Airborne Units 1941 to 1945.* Published by George F. Nafziger, 1995.

------. *Soviet Order of Battle, World War II, Volume V, "Red Sabers" - Soviet Cavalry Corps, Divisions, and Brigades 1941 to 1945.* Published by George F. Nafziger, 1995.

------. *Soviet Order of Battle, World War II, Volume V1, "Red Thunder" - Soviet Artillery Corps, Divisions, and Brigades 1941 to 1945.* Published by George F. Nafziger, 1995.

------. *Soviet Order of Battle, World War II, Volume VI1, "Red Death" - Soviet Mountain, Naval, NKVD, and Allied Divisions and Brigades 1941 to 1945.* Published by George F. Nafziger, 1995.

------. *Soviet Order of Battle, World War II, Volume VII1, "Red Legions" - Soviet Rifle*

Divisions Formed Before June 1941. Published by George F. Nafziger, 1995.

------, *Soviet Order of Battle, World War II, Volume V1X, "Red Tide" - Soviet Rifle Divisions Formed June to December 1941.* Published by George F. Nafziger, 1996.

------, *Soviet Order of Battle, World War II, Volume X, "Red Swarm" - Soviet Rifle Divisions Formed From 1942 to 1945.* Published by George F. Nafziger, 1996.

------, *Soviet Order of Battle, World War II, Volume X1, "Red Volunteers" - Soviet Militia Units, Rifle and s 1941 - 1945.* Published by George F. Nafziger, 1996.

Sharp, Lee. *The French Army 1939-1940, Organisation: Order of Battle : Operational History, Volume 1.* Milton Keyes, Great Britain: The Military Press, 2002.

------, *The French Army 1939-1940, Organisation: Order of Battle : Operational History, Volume 1I.* Milton Keyes, Great Britain: The Military Press, 2001.

------, *The French Army 1939-1940, Organisation: Order of Battle : Operational History, Volume 1II.* Milton Keyes, Great Britain: The Military Press, 2003.

Shaw, Jonn et. al. *Red Army Resurgent.* Times-Life Books, World War II Series, Vol. 20. Chicago: Times-Life Books, 1979.

Shirer, William L. *The Rise and Fall of the Third Reich.* New York: Simon and Schuster, 1960.

Showalter, Dennis, *Patton and Rommel. Men of War in the Twentieth Century.* New York: The Berkley Publishing Group, 2005.

Shtemenho, S. M., *The Soviet General Staff at War /1941-1945/.* Moscow: Progress Publishers, 1970, Second Printing, 1975.

Shukman, Harold (Edited by). *Stalin's Generals.* New York: Weidenfeld and Nicolson, 1993.

Simons, Gerald et. al. *Victory in Europe.* Times-Life Books, World War II Series, Vol. 36. Chicago: Times-Life Books, 1982

Slaughterhouse: The Encyclopedia of the Eastern Front. The Military Book Club. Garden City, New York, 2002.

Smurthwaite, David. *The Pacific War Atlas 1941-1945.* London: Mirabel Books Ltd., 1995.

Snyder, Dr. Louis L. *Encyclopedia of the Third Reich.* London: Robert Hale, McGraw-Hill, Inc., 1976.

Sokolov, Marshal Sergei (Foreword by). *Battles Hitler Lost.* New York: Jove Books, The Berkley Publishing Group, 1988.

Spector, Ronald H. *Eagle Against the Sun. The American War with Japan.* New York: The Free Press, 1985.

Stanton, Shelby L. *World War II Order of Battle.* New York: Galahad Books, 1991.

Stein, George. *The Waffen-SS.* New York: Cornell University Press, 1966.

Steinberg, Rafael et. al. *Island Fighting.* Times-Life Books, World War II Series, Vol. 10. Chicago: Times-Life Books, 1978.

----- et. al. *Return to the Philippines.* Times-Life Books, World War II Series, Vol. 15. Chicago: Times-Life Books, 1980.

Stolfi, R. H. S. *Hitler's Panzers East: World War II Reinterpreted.* Norman, Oklahoma: University of Oklahoma Press, 1992.

Strategy and Tactics of the Great Commanders of World War II and Their Battles. Greenwich, Conn.: Dorset Press, 1990.

Strawson, John. *The Itatian Campaign.* London: Secker & Warburg, 1987.

Sulzberger, C. L. *The American Heritage Picture History of World War II.* New York: Crown Publishers, 1966.

Sutherland, Jon, and Diane Canwell. *Vichy Air Forces at War.* Barnsley, United Kingdom: Pen & Sword Aviation, 2011.

Taylor, James and Shaw, Warren. *The Third Reich Almanac.* New York: World Almanac, 1987.

Thompson, R. W. *D-Day: Spearhead of Invasion.* Ballantine's Illustrated History of the the Violent Century, Battle Book No. 1. New York: Ballantine Books, 1968.

Toland, John. *The Last 100 Days.* New York: Random House, 1965.

------. *The Rising Sun: The Decline and Fall of the Japanese Empire 1936-1945 (2 Volumes).* New York: Random House, 1970.

------. *Adolf Hitler.* New York: Ballantine Books, 1977. (Originally published by Random House, New York: 1976.)

Tsouras, Peter G. (Edited by). *Panzers on the Eastern Front: General Erhard Raus and his Panzer Divisions in Russia, 1941-1945.* London: Lionel Leventhal Limited, 2002.

------ (Edited by). *Hitler Triumphant: Alternate Decisions of World War II.* London: Greenhill Books, 2006.

U. S. War Department. *Handbook on Japanese Military Forces.* London: Greenhill Books, 1991. (New Introduction by David Isby & Afterword by Jeffrey Ethell).

Wallace, Robert et. al. *The Italian Campaign.* Times-Life Books, World War II Series, Vol. 11. Chicago: Times-Life Books, 1978.

Warlimont, Gen. Walter. *Inside Hitler's Headquarters 1939-45.* Novato, California: Presidio Press, 1962.

Wernick, Robert et. al. *Blitzkrieg.* Times-Life Books, World War II Series, Vol. 2. Chicago: Times-Life Books, 1977.

West Point Military History Series. *The Second World War: Military Campaign Atlas.* Wayne, New Jersey: Avery Publishing Group Inc., 1989 (series editor Thomas E. Griess.)

------. *The Second World War: Asia & the Pacific.* Wayne, New Jersey: Avery Publishing Group Inc., 1989 (series editor Thomas E. Griess.)

------. *The Second World War: Europe & the Mediterranean.* Wayne, New Jersey: Avery Publishing Group Inc., 1989 (series editor Thomas E. Griess.)

Wheeler, Keith et. al. *The Road to Tokyo.* Times-Life Books, World War II Series, Vol. 19. Chicago: Times-Life Books, 1979.

------ et al. *War Under the Pacific.* Times-Life Books, World War II Series, Vol. 23. Chicago: Times-Life Books, 1981.

------ et al. *Bombers Over Japan.* Times-Life Books, World War II Series, Vol. 34. Chicago: Times-Life Books, 1982.

------ et al. *The Fall of Japan.* Times-Life Books, World War II Series, Vol. 37. Chicago: Times-Life Books, 1983.

Whipple, A. B. C. et. al. *The Mediterranean.* Times-Life Books, World War II Series, Vol. 27. Chicago: Times-Life Books, 1981.

White, David Fairbank. *Bitter Ocean: The Battle of the Atlantic 1939-1`945.* New York: Simon & Schuster, 2006.

Whiting, Charles. *Patton.* Ballantine's Illustrated History of World War II, War Leader Book No. 1. New York: Ballantine Books, 1970.

------. *Bradley.* Ballantine's Illustrated History of the Violent Century, War Leader Book No. 5. New York: Ballantine Books, 1971.

------. *West Wall: The Battle for Hitler's Siegfried Line.* Staplehurst, England:

Spellmount1999.

Whiting, Charles et al. *The Home Front: Germany.* Times-Life Books, World War II Series, Vol. 32. Chicago: Times-Life Books, 1982.

Williams, John. *France: Summer 1940.* Ballantine's Illustrated History of World War II, Campaign Book No. 6. New York: Ballantine Books, 1969.

Wistrich, Robert. *Who's Who in Nazi Germany.* New York: MacMillan Publishing Company, 1982.

World War II Surrender Documents. *Germany Surrenders 1945.* Washington, D. C.: The National Archives, 1976.

World War II Surrender Documents. *Japan Surrenders 1945.* Washington, D. C.: The National Archives, 1976.

Wykes, Alan. *The Siege of Leningrad.* Ballantine's Illustrated History of World War II, Battle Book No. 5. New York: Ballantine Books, 1968.

Young, Desmond. *Rommel: The Desert Fox.* New York: Harper and Row, Publisher, 1965.

Zoology, Steven J. Et al. *Operation Barbatossa,* Tank Illustrated #16. London: Arms & Armour Press, 1985.

Zaloga, Steven & Victor Madej. *The Polish Campaign 1939.* New York: Hippocrene Books, Inc, 1991.

Zinh, Arthur et. al. *The Rising Sun.* Times-Life Books, World War II Series, Vol. 4. Chicago: Times-Life Books, 1977.

Ziemke, Earl F. et. al. *The Soviet Juggernaut.* Times-Life Books, World War II Series, Vol. 25. Chicago: Times-Life Books, 1980.

INTERNET SITES

Ammentorp, Steen, The Generals of WWII , - www.generals.dk.

Barrass, M. B., The Royal Air Force, - www.rafweb.org/menu.htm.

Battleships of World War II, - www.voodoo.cz/battleships/

Clancey, Patrick, The Official Chronology of the U.S. Navy in World War II; transcribed and formatted for HTML by, - www.ibiblio.org/hyperwar/USN/USN-Chron/USN-Chron-1939.html.

D'Adamo, Cristiano, Francesco Cestra, Marc De Angelis, Pierluigi Malvezzi, Robert Maulini, Vince O'Hara, Andrea Piccinotti, Ammiraglio Attilio Ranieri, Achille Rastelli, Comandante Salvatore Romano, Alberto Rosselli, Sebastiano Tringali, and Francesco Mattesini, Regia Marina Italiana, - www.regiamarina.net.

Kuznetsov, V., About Admiral of the Fleet of the Soviet Union N. G. Kuznetsov, - admiral.centro.ru/start_e.htm.

Liddell Hart Center, King's College London, - www.kd.ac.uk?lhcma/search/ocsearch.html.

Naval War In The Pacific 1941-1945, pacific.valka.cz/personel.

Niehorster, Dr. Leo, World War II Armed Forces, - niehorster.orbat.com.

Nishida, Hiroshi, Imperial Japanese Navy, - homepage2.nifty.com/nishidah/e/ .

Senior Officers, November 1, 1940, - www.geocities.com/scs028a/seniorofficers1940.html?200515.

Smith, Gordon (edited by), NAVAL-HISTORY.NET - www.naval-history.net/index.htm.

Swigart, Soren & Axel Schudak, The World at War: From Versailles to the Cold War. worldatwar.net.

Tully, Anthony P., Jon Parshall, Allyn D. Nevitt, Robert Hackett with Sander Kingsepp, Imperial Japanese Navy Page, - www.combined fleet.com.

United States Air Force, - www.af.mil/bios.

United States Marine Corps, History and Museums Division, - hqinet001.hqmc.usmc.mil/HD/Historical/Whos_Who.

Wendel, Marcus, Axis History Factbook, - www.axishistory.com.

WW2-Cruisers - www.world-war.co.uk

Book Index

CAF - Croatian Air Force
CN - Croatian Navy
FN - French Navy
RTN - Royal Thailand Navy

RRAF - Royal Romanian Air Force
RRN - Royal Romanian Navy
BN - Bulgarian Navy
RTAF - Royal Thailand Air Force

FinN - Finnish Navy
FinAF - Finnish Air Force
GAF - German Air Force
HN - Hungarian Navy

Bulgaria Index

Burma Index

Cambodia Index

China Index

Croatia Index

Czechoslavakia Index

Finland Index

France Index

Germany Index

RICHTHOFEN, HERBERT Baron von, 187
Schliepper, MG Franz, 221
Schröder GdFk Ludwig von [GAF], 290
WÖRMANN, Dr. ERNST, 382

Hungary Index

India [Azad Hind] Index

Italy Index

Japan Index

Sonobe, LG Waichiro [Ichiro], 382
SUGIHARA, CHIUNE, 354
Sugiyama, Gen. Hajime, 372, 381
Sumida, MG Raishiro, 422, 432, 441
Tada, Gen. Hayao, 381
Tanaka, LG Shizuichi, 407
Tani, LG Hisao, 382
Terauchi, FM Count Hisaichi, 381 (2), 398, 407,
     422, 432, 441
Tsuchihashi, LG Yuitsu, 422 (2), 432 (2), 441 (2)
Uchiyama, LG Eitaro, 382
Ueda, Gen. Kenkichi, 356, 372
Umezu, Gen. Yoshijiro, 356 (2), 372 (2)
Ushiroku, LG Jun, 381, 382
Yamada, Gen. Otozō, 356, 372, 381
Yamashita, LG Tomoyoki "Tiger of Malaya", 356,
     372, 407
YAMAUCHI, TOYONORI, 369
Yamawaki, LG Masataka, 372

Laos Index

BOUN OUM, Prince, 437
BUA LAPHAN, Prince, 437
KINDAVONG, Prince, 438
PHAYA KHAMMAO, Prince, 438
PHETSARATH RATTANAVONGGA, Prince, 438
     (3)
SISAVANG VONG, King, 437 (2), 438 (5)

Manchukuo [Manchuria] Index

Chang Wen-tao, Gen., 358
Chi Hsing, Gen., 357
Chŭ Kudō, LG, 353
DING JIANXIU, 354
KANG-DE [AISINGIORO PU-YI], Emperor, 353,
     361
Li Chi-chun, MG, 359
LI SHAOGENG, 354
LÜ RONGHUAN, 354
Oda Takeshi, Gen., 357
RUAN ZHENDUO, 354
Xi Qia [Hsi Hsia; Xi Xia], LG, 354 (3)
XIE JIESHI, 354 (3)
Yu Cheng-shen, Gen., 358
Yu Chih-shan, Gen., 357
YU ZHISHAN, 354
YUAN JINKAI, 354
ZANG SHIYI [TSANG SHIH-YI], 353, 354
Zhang Haipeng [Chang Hai-peng], Gen., 355, 358
     (4)
Zhang Jinghui [Chang Ching-hui], Gen., 354 (2)
ZHANG YANQING, 354
Zheng Xiaoxu [Chang Hsiao-hisn], 354

Mengjiang [Inner Mongolia] Index

Bai Fengxiang, MG, 373
D E W A N G   [T H E   W A N G   o r
     DEMCHUGDONGRUB], Prince, 369 (2),
     370 (2), 371 (2), 373,

Philippines Index

AQUINO y QUIAMBAO, BENIGNO SIMEON Sr.,
     403, 405 (3)
BARTOLOMÉ VARGAS y CELIS, JORGE, 403,
     405
OSMEÑA, SERGIO, 403
QUEZON ANTONIO y MOLINA, MANUEL LUIS,
     403
PACIANO LAUREL y GARCIA, JOSÉ, 404, 405
     (2)
ROXAS y ACUÑA, MANUEL, 403
SANTOS, JOSÉ ABAD, 403, 404
YULO, JOSÉ, 403, 404, 405
ZULUETA, JOSÉ, 403

Romania Index

Aldea, MG Aurel, 8, 14
Alecu, Col. Nicolae, 44
Alexiu, MG Paul, 22, 43, 46
ALIMĂNIŞTEANU, DUMITRU, 9
Alinescu, BG Barbu, 18, 40, 70
ANDRE, PETRE, 9
ANGHELESCU, CONSTANTIN, 8
Anton, BG Constantin St., 18
Antonescu, MG Ilie, 15, 17, 18, 32, 59, 61, 66
Antonescu, Mar. Ion Victor, 7 (2), 9, 10 (3), 11, 14,
     20, 79
ANTONESCU, MIHAI, 7, 8, 9
Antonescu, BG Petre, 11, 23 (2), 37, 478
Apostolescu, BG Constantin,
Arbore, MG Ioan, 10, 22, 70 (2)
Argeşanu, MG Gheorghe, 7 (2), 10, 25, 80
ARGETOIANU, CONSTANTIN, 7, 9, 12 (2)
Arhip, MG Ioan, 14, 15, 25, 39 (2), 45, 65
Atanasescu, MG Constantin, 18
Atanasiu, Gen. Vasile, 18, 22, 25, 26, 79
AVERESCU, ALEXANDRU, 8
Avramescu, Gen. Gheorghe, 15, 23 (2), 26, 27,
     29, 43, 79
Badescu, BG Constantin, 39, 44 (2), 68 (2)
Bagulescu, MG Gheorghe, 9 (3), 17 (2)
Balaban, BG Stefan, 32, 41, 49, 64, 68, 70
Balan, BG Grigore, 54 (3), 71

GIGURTU, ION, 7, 9, 12
GLATZ, ALEXANDRA, 10
Glogojanu, MG Ion, 43, 53
GOGA, OCTAVIAN, 7
Grigorescu, BG Traian, 44
GROZA, PETRU, 7
HOHENZOLLERN-SIGMARINGEN, King CAROL
    II, 7
HOHENZOLLERN-SIGMARINGEN, King MIHAI
    [MICHAEL] I, 7
Hrisafi, BG Nicolae, 41
Iacobici, LG Iosif, 10, 11, 14, 23 (2), 79
IAMANDI, VICTOR, 9 (2), 10
Ilasievici, Gen, Constantin, 7, 10, 20, 23, 79
Ilcuş, LG Ioan, 10, 23, 28, 79
Iliescu, BG Manole, 44
Iliescu, MG Victor Traian, 9, 12, 40
Ioaniţiu, MG Alexandru, 14, 16
Ioanovici, MG Romulus, 41, 44, 54
Ionaşcu, MG Costin, 18, 25, 42, 43, 64, 72
Ionescu, BG Emilian [RRAF], 7, 34
Ionescu, MG Gheorghe Ştefan, 14 (2)
Ionescu, LG Teodor, 25, 39, 79
Ionescu-Sinaia, MG Gheorghe, 14, 23, 30, 31, 33
    (2), 38, 44
IONESCU-SIŞEŞTI, GHEORGHE, 12
Iordachescu, MG Constantin, 39, 43, 54, 57
IORGA, NICOLAE, 8
Iucal, BG Ioan, 17, 43 (2), 49, 68
Jienescu, Col. Gheorghe [RRAF], 11, 19
JINGA, VICTOR, 12
Juganaru, BG Enache, 16, 23, 27, 54, 64, 68
Korne, BG Radu, 37, 54, 59, 61, 62 (2)
Lăcătuşcu, MG Mihail, 15, 28 (2), 29, 31, 47 (3)
Lascăr, MG Mihail, 41, 51, 54
LEON, GHEORGHE N., 9
Leonida, BG Paul, 14, 16, 69
Leoveanu, LG Emanoil, 15, 16, 26, 27 (2), 28, 31,
    49, 53, 79
Leventi, LG Gheorghe, 22, 27, 41, 79
Liteanu, MG Gheorghe, 8
Macici, LG Nicolae, 22, 25, 79
Magereanu, BG Nicolae, 52
MĂGUREANU, MIHAIL, 8
Mainescu, MG Vasile, 10, 15 (2), 31, 59 (2), 61
Manafu, MG Marin, 30, 31 (2), 32 (2), 42, 59
MANIU, IULIU, 7
MANOILESCU, MIHAIL, 9
Manoliu, BG Constantin, 10, 13
Manoliu, MG Gheorghe, 32, 54, 55 (2)
Marcell, Col. Béla, 105
Marcellariu, RA Horia [RRN], 36
Mardari, MG Socrat, 7, 14 (3)
Marinescu, BG Gabriel, 8 (3)
Marinescu, MG Gheorghe D., 33 (4), 70
Marinescu, BG Gheorghe Gh., 37, 41, 46, 54 (2),
    65

Marinescu, MG Nicolae M., 12 (3), 16
Marinescu, Col. Nivolae, 64
Mazareanu, Col. Ion, 66
Mazareanu, BG Sotir, 40, 49 (2), 55 (3)
Mazarini, MG Nicolae, 14, 40
MICESCU, ESTRATE, 9
Mihaescu, MG Ioan, 14, 16, 18, 22 (2), 31, 32, 38
    (2), 40, 49
Mihail, Gen. Gheorghe, 7, 10, 14 (2), 18, 79
Mitrănescu, LG Florea, 27, 28 (2), 47, 79
Mociulschi, MG Leonard, 29, 54, 55 (2)
Momiceanu, BG Scarlat, 45, 54, 65, 68 (2), 70
Mosiu, BG Gheorge, 17, 28, 33 (2), 42, 47, 69
Mosteoru, MG Grigore, 33, 45, 47, 68
Moţaş, LG Dumitru, 20, 79
Munteanu, BG Gheorghe, 16, 59 (2), 60, 61 (2)
Mustata, Col. Ion, 64
Nasta, BG Alexandru, 28, 31, 38, 40, 49 (2), 55,
    58, 66, 72
NEAGU, ALEXANDRU, 9
Nedelea, BG Savu, 42, 44
Neferu, Col. Dumitru, 61
Negulescu, LG Ion, 10, 30, 79
NETTA, GHERON, 9
Nicolau, MG Grigore, 10, 15, 27, 38, 40, 42 (2)
Nicolau, Col. Ion, 33
Nicolescu, Col. Alexandru, 66, 67
Nicolescu-Cociu, MG Radu, 28, 37, 44, 48 (2), 55
Nicolici, BG Alexandru, 41, 64, 69
Niculescu, LG Constantin, 7, 27, 31, 79
Niculescu, BG Gheorghe, 15 (2), 17 (2), 43 (2), 62
NICULESCU-BUZEŞTI, GRIGORE, 9
NIŢESCU, VOICU, 12
Opriş, BG Ştefan, 38 (2), 64
Orasanu, BG Alexandru, 42
Orezeanu, MG Teodor Constantin, 16
OTTESCU, NICOLAE, 8
Palangeanu, BG Emil, 12, 18
Palangeanu, MG Nicolae, 31, 71
Panaitiu, MG Constantin, 38, 42 (2), 43 (2)
Pantazi, LG Constantin, 10 (2), 79
Papadopol, MG Constantin, 46, 68
Paraschiv, MG Dobre, 22 (2)
Paraschivescu, BG Emil, 38, 46, 68
Partenie, MG Ilie, 27, 29
Pascu, BG Vasile, 16, 38, 46, 55, 70, 72
Patageanu, MG Nicolae, 31
PENESCU, NICOLAE, 8
Petculescu, BG Atanasie, 26, 27, 46, 47 (2), 70
Petrescu, BG Dumitru, 40, 64
Petrescu, BG Nicolae T., 15, 38, 50, 70 (2), 71
PETRESCU-COMNEN, NICOLAE, 9 (2)
Petrovicescu, MG Constantin, 8
Pleniceanu, BG J., 43
Poenaru, BG Alexandru, 17, 41, 45, 69
POP, TRAIAN, 8
Popescu, BG Constantin, 37

Serbia Index

Slovakia Index

Thailand [Siam] Index

Union of Soviet Socialist Republic Index

United Kingdom Index

United States Index

Vietnam Index